Peter Norton's®
Guide to Access® 2000 Programming

Peter Norton
Virginia Andersen

D1400709

SAMS

201 West 103rd Street, Indianapolis, Indiana 46290

Associate Publisher
Michael Stephens

Executive Editor
Rosemarie Graham

Acquisitions Editor
Angela Kozlowski

Development Editor
Gus Miklos

Managing Editor
Charlotte Clapp

Project Editor
George E. Nedeff

Copy Editor
Bart Reed

Indexer
Joy Dean Lee

Proofreader
Cynthia Fields

Technical Editors
Dallas G. Releford
Mark Duvall

Team Coordinator
Carol Ackerman

Media Developer
John Warriner

Interior Design
Gary Adair

Cover Design
Aren Howell

Copy Writer
Eric Borgert

Layout Technicians
Susan Geiselman
Mark Walchle

Overview

Contents

Acknowledgments

No one ever writes a book alone. I have been so very fortunate to have the help of many talented and patient people to whom I owe a sincere debt of thanks.

First, it has been a real pleasure to work with the talented and highly competent editorial staff at Macmillan. They have all been so professional and efficient throughout the complex process of getting a computer book on the bookshelf. It has been a real pleasure to work with Gus Miklos and George Nedeff, my development and production editors. They are quick in response and always very helpful. Many thanks also go to Bart Reed, the copy editor who once again so carefully worked out the bugs in my manuscript. I was very fortunate to be assigned two most competent technical editors, Dallas Releford and Mark Duvall, who helped to verify the conversion of VBA code to Visual Basic.

Being mostly left-brain, I owe a definite debt of gratitude to the Macmillan art department for their handsome artistic contributions to the first edition of this book. All the logos carry over well to version 2000.

I would also like to thank Matt Wagner, my agent at Waterside Productions, who found this very special opportunity for me.

I still very much appreciate the expertise Don Kiely applied to the chapter about publishing on the Web in the first edition as well as to Michael Groh, who took time out from his busy life as Editor of the *Access-Visual Basic Advisor* publication to write the first edition chapters about working in a multiuser environment. Not only were the chapters well-written and informative, but they were easily converted to Access 2000.

My friend Pat Starr was the inspiration for the Pat's Pets application. She and her daughter Barbara were very helpful in gathering the material for the pet store inventory database. Mary Sue and Merv, both experienced in real estate, were the ready and willing source for the Elgin Enterprises information.

More thanks again to my patient husband, Jack, who has not only been tolerant of my hours at the computer every day but who also helped by acquiring and entering much of the data you see in the databases in this book. He even rode his bicycle around our town snapping pictures of properties for the real estate application. Thanks, Jack!

The ultimate thanks should go to the late Dr. Grace Hopper, who told me in 1948 that there would be a future for women in "high-speed digital computers." She was right.

About the Authors

Computer software entrepreneur and writer **Peter Norton** established his technical expertise and accessible style from the earliest days of the PC. His *Norton Utilities* was the first product of its kind, giving early computer owners control over their hardware and protection against myriad problems. His flagship titles, *Peter Norton's DOS Guide* and *Peter Norton's Inside the PC* (Sams Publishing), have provided the same insight and education to computer users worldwide for nearly two decades. Peter's books, like his many software products, are among the best selling and most respected in the history of personal computing.

Peter Norton's former column in *PC Week* was among the highest regarded in that magazine's history. His expanding series of computer books continues to bring superior education to users, always in Peter's trademark style, which is never condescending nor pedantic. From their earliest days, changing the "black box" into a "glass box," Peter's books, like his software, remain among the most powerful tools available to beginners and experienced users, alike.

In 1990, Peter sold his software development business to Symantec Corporation, allowing him to devote more time to his family, civic affairs, philanthropy, and art collecting. He lives with his wife, Eileen, and two children in Santa Monica, California.

Virginia Andersen has written or significantly contributed to dozens of books about computer-based applications, including Microsoft's Access 95, 97, and now 2000, Word 95, 97, and 2000, and Office 95 and 97, Borland's dBASE and Paradox, Corel's WordPerfect, and Lotus 1-2-3. She has also written textbooks and instructor's manuals as well as thousands of computer-related definitions for a scientific dictionary. Virginia is certified as a Microsoft Access 97 MOUS expert.

She has taught courses in computer science, information management, and mathematics at the University of Southern California graduate school and other universities for over 15 years. She concurrently spent over 25 years applying computers to such projects as mapping the surface of the moon for the Apollo landing site, estimating the reliability of the Apollo parachute system, and detecting submarines with computerized undersea surveillance tools.

Her years of practical experience made good use of her Bachelor's degree in mathematics from Stanford University and her two Master's degrees from the University of Southern California—one in computer science and the other in systems management.

She lives in Southern California with her husband, Jack, three computers, 49 rose bushes, and two cats.

Tell Us What You Think!

As the reader of this book, *you* are our most important critic and commentator. We value your opinion and want to know what we're doing right, what we could do better, what areas you'd like to see us publish in, and any other words of wisdom you're willing to pass our way.

As an Associate Publisher for Sams, I welcome your comments. You can fax, email, or write me directly to let me know what you did or didn't like about this book—as well as what we can do to make our books stronger.

Please note that I cannot help you with technical problems related to the topic of this book, and that due to the high volume of mail I receive, I might not be able to reply to every message.

When you write, please be sure to include this book's title and author as well as your name and phone or fax number. I will carefully review your comments and share them with the author and editors who worked on the book.

Fax: 317-581-4770

Email: mstephens@mcp.com

Mail: Michael Stephens
         Associate Publisher
         Sams Publishing
         201 West 103rd Street
         Indianapolis, IN 46290 USA

Introduction

During my years teaching computer science and information management for the University of Southern California, I was continually amazed at the variety of ways my students applied relational database and spreadsheet tools to practical problems. They proved to me that a database is not some inert pile of data to be shoveled clumsily about, but instead a sensitive information source that can be carefully manipulated to suit almost any requirement. I have always wanted to show my readers that Access, my personal favorite among database management systems, can be used not only for traditional information storage and retrieval, but for real-time decision making, as well.

As the lines between Microsoft programs disappear, Access can take advantage of its Office 2000 companions' new features as well as its own. I hope that as you work with this book to program Access applications, you'll see what I saw—Access 2000 truly is the information management tool for the next century.

Finishing a book and seeing it on the shelf of the local bookstore, though highly gratifying, is not the end of the story. During my years as a university instructor, I found that the student critiques submitted at the end of each term were a rich source of ideas for improving the course material and the approach to the subject. If you have any comments or suggestions about this book, either the text or the material on the accompanying CD, please contact me at VandersenZ@aol.com.

Conventions Used in This Book

Note: Notes tell you interesting facts or important points that relate to the surrounding text. Notes can even help you keep out of trouble.

Technical Note: Technical details provide background information or explanations for how Access works. The Technical icon can help you learn more about the reasons why.

Tip: Tips tell you new ways of doing things that you might not have thought about before. Tip boxes also provide an alternative way of doing something that you might like better than the first approach.

Warning: The Warning icon alerts you to potential hazards that can cause serious problems with your application, with data, or with your hardware or network system. Be sure you understand a warning thoroughly before you carry out the instructions that follow it.

Peter's Principle

The Peter's Principle sets off text that will help you with some basic tenets you'll find useful as you work with Access and databases. You'll also find some interesting facts and experiences that will enrich your knowledge and maybe make you smile.

ANALYSIS

The Analysis icon indicates text that explains the meaning of code segments or describes the behind-the-scenes actions that have occurred.

ARCHITECTURE

Knowing how something works or how it's structured gives you a broader understanding of the details you work with in your programs. The Architecture icon denotes the internal structure of the Access model or of hardware components in a network environment.

COMPATIBILITY

Whenever you upgrade from one version of an application such as Access or use Access with other software components, you must know whether the components are compatible. The Compatibility icon clues you in to tips, techniques, and notes the will make you aware of these issues.

DEVELOPMENT

Watch for the Development icon to show you points you should keep in mind while developing your database. Many of these cases are ways to avoid problems later or to create a better overall system.

LOOKING AHEAD

These sections point to cross references to future sections where you'll gain a better understanding of the current topic or to future chapters where you'll see how the smaller pieces work together to form a smooth-flowing bigger picture.

NETWORKING

Because of the importance of sharing information from a database, you'll often find Access working across a network or on the Internet. The Networking icon points to problems, tips, and explanations related to networking issues.

PERFORMANCE

With the large size of many databases and the traffic in network connections, performance is an important factor for all database users. The Performance icon shows you problems or points you should consider regarding performance and ways to make your system work more quickly.

TROUBLESHOOTING

Finding problems or knowing in advance what might cause a problem is an important way to avoid programmer frustration. The Troubleshooting icon points to clues to finding problems or tells how to avoid future problems.

PART I

Getting Your Bearings

Why Program Access?

As the premiere database management system, Microsoft Access is used by millions all over the world. If it's so good at storing and retrieving information, why would anyone want to go to the trouble of programming an application created by Access? Although Access, with all its wizards and other versatile tools, can produce an amazingly complete and detailed finished application, it cannot provide all necessary capabilities and services to all users without some help.

By design, Access is meant to provide the most universally useful database features, which it does with remarkable thoroughness. However, each user or organization is bound to have special needs and processes that require enhancing the Access database tables, forms, reports, data access pages, and queries. As a bonus, programming Access can create a foolproof user interface and significant error-trapping procedures that can ensure vital database validity. Here are some examples of tasks you can perform with Access:

- Suppose your database is quite large and you need to make the same change to a lot of records at once. With Visual Basic procedures in an Access application, you can run through the entire recordset very efficiently in one operation rather than change the values one by one in a form.

- Suppose you're operating a mail-order book business and need to add state tax to the orders within your own state. You would need to look at the value in the State field of each customer's address. You can create an Access program that can do this for you. It can also add the tax if the customer is in your home state or omit it, if not.

- The validity of your database is very important. You can add procedures that catch errors in data entry and display meaningful messages to the user. If the error is not significant, you can display a reminder to return to and complete the data entry at a later time. You can even add a procedure that doesn't allow the user to move on until the error is corrected.

- Suppose you want to extract certain records, such as those for customers from a particular state, but each time you run the program you want to see the list of customers from a different state. Using Visual Basic code in Access, you can add a prompt to enter the desired value when you run the program.

These are only a few examples of how you can benefit by programming Access.

Access as a Front-End Development Tool

Back in the old days, if a noncomputer person wanted a system to manage an important database, he or she had to hire an expensive programmer/consultant. With the advent of tools such as Access and Excel, someone with little programming expertise, but a clear picture of the requirements, can create a sophisticated application in a short amount of time. Access replaces the high-priced programmer who sat between the end user and the computer.

Technical Note: A Short History Lesson

The growth of computer hardware and software has evolved through several generations since the early 1950s, when Honeywell introduced the first truly electronic computers. The transition from one generation to the next was clearly defined in the early years. For example, the step from vacuum tubes to transistors and then the next step to integrated circuits were quite distinct and dramatic.

Programming technology was no less evolutionary. In the first generation, programmers were forced to write instructions in machine code consisting solely of numbers. At least they were permitted to use decimal numbers rather than the binary code the computer understands. The second generation opened up the world of assembly languages, which were different for each model of computer. Numeric machine code had been replaced by three-letter codes that were a little easier for humans to keep track of.

In the early 1950s, the third generation of programming languages was born. Thanks to the late Dr. Grace Hopper, the concept of a language translator made programming possible in plain language. FORTRAN (FORmula TRANslation), COBOL (COmmon Business Oriented Language), BASIC (Beginners All-purpose Symbolic Instruction Code), and many others became quite popular in the 1950s and 1960s. The compilers and interpreters translated the high-level code into binary for machine consumption.

The early BASIC, developed at Dartmouth College in the early 1960s for instructional use, was a conversational procedural language. That is, each instruction the student entered was immediately interpreted and executed. The object-oriented Visual Basic of today is quite different. Programs written in VB are first compiled into machine language and then executed as a package.

The fourth-generation languages, often referred to as *4GLs*, brought forth many front-end applications that served as intermediaries between the user and the program generator. Access is an example of a fourth-generation language. It creates code in the background to carry out what you tell it, interactively, to do. The code that's produced is *event driven*; that is, nothing will happen while the program is running unless something else happens first—the user clicks a button, presses a key, moves the mouse pointer, or takes some other action.

continues

The fifth generation is a bit fuzzier. It includes expert and knowledge-based systems, artificial intelligence, and language-translation machines. Many expert systems, such as programs for medical diagnosis and oil exploration, were quite successful because their scope was extremely limited.

Much research has been poured into creating computers and programs that can think and reason as well as humans. In 1981, Japan announced its plan to capture and store all human knowledge by developing the fifth generation of computers. These intelligent supercomputers would be able to learn, reason, and make decisions. They also would be able to converse with humans in natural languages and understand pictures. Their natural language capabilities would even accurately translate idiomatic phrases into other languages. Naysayers and skeptics had a good time making jokes about trying to translate English to Russian and back. One such joke had the computer translate the saying "out of sight, out of mind" to Russian and back. When returned to English, it became "an invisible maniac."

It seems unlikely that anyone will ever be able to store all human knowledge into one machine, as the Japanese planned, and expect it to be able to reason using that body of knowledge. But, who knows?

As versatile as Access is, building a well-suited, totally responsive and integrated application for a specific use still requires some customization through additional programming. Access employs three programming languages to enable you to add the fine-tuning to an application. The Structured Query Language (SQL) is the language Access uses behind the scenes in queries that can extract, manipulate, and relate data from one or more tables. Macros consist of lists of actions that execute in response to an event such as a button click or when data in a form changes. Visual Basic code is a highly flexible and comprehensive language you can use to develop complete user-interactive applications. Each of these language components is discussed in detail in later chapters. In addition, other universal languages such as Hypertext Markup Language (HTML) and Visual Basic Scripting can be used with Access applications.

Creating End-User Applications

End user is a term often used to describe someone who has the need to use the computer for database management or other intricate efforts but lacks the time or training to learn all the nuances and complexities of the system. Therefore, a *developer*, the one who does have the time and training, creates a system that is simple on the outside but quite complex on the inside.

An end-user application provides smooth movement through all the computerized activities of the supported organization and responds quickly and appropriately to user actions. The developer also attempts to program responses to all foreseeable error conditions, whether caused by the user, invalid data, or the system itself.

Displaying Information

Message boxes, such as the one shown in Figure 1.1, are an important part of any application. Although the message in the figure is just for fun, message boxes provide relevant and helpful information about current activity or explain the reason for an error condition. In cases in which the user tries to delete a record or a value, a message might ask him or her to confirm the deletion. Message boxes do not require input from the user, only that the box be closed before proceeding.

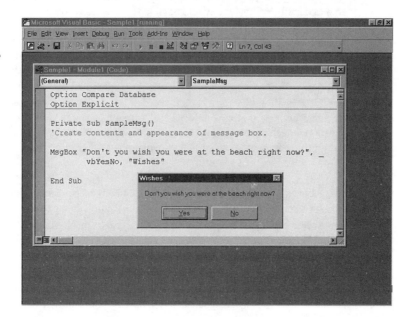

A message box might contain up to three command buttons with various labels such as OK, Cancel, and Retry. Message boxes can display a choice of icons that indicate the type of message, such as information or warning, and also have a custom caption in the title bar.

Responding to User Actions and Input

Access provides many special tools called *wizards* that ask you for information about what you want to build and create the complete package behind the scenes using the specifications you enter. One of them is the Access Command Button Wizard, which attaches actions to a command button's OnClick event property. This results in a procedure that's executed when the user clicks the button. An example is a command button on a form that closes the form and returns to the previous window.

Another important aspect of user interaction is requesting information from the user (for example, a query that extracts records meeting a certain condition, such as customers whose addresses are in California). The procedure displays a dialog box and asks the user to enter the state code, which is then used as the selection criterion in the query.

Dialog boxes differ from message boxes in that they require a user response. Dialog boxes ask questions, offer options, and acquire additional information. You're certainly familiar with Access's dialog boxes, and now you'll get a chance to create your own with Access programming.

Trapping Errors

In addition to the data validation rules you specify in the table definition, you can create procedures that alert the user to data errors such as conflicts between two values. For example, the user checks the Paid check box on a customer form and then enters a value in the Amount Due field. The procedure could test the value in the Paid field (Yes or No) and, if Yes, set the GotFocus property of the Amount Due text box to No. This would prevent the user from even reaching the Amount Due field. The procedure also could set the Amount Due to zero when the Paid field is checked.

The user cannot always interpret the cryptic error messages that Access displays. In trying to make the application foolproof, it helps to intercept these error messages and substitute a more helpful message. Access assigns a code number to each type of trappable error, which your procedure can decode to select a more appropriate custom message. For example, user errors on data entry such as entering data in one field that is not compatible with data entered in another field can cause form errors. Forms have an OnError event property to which you can attach the substitute message procedure.

Frustrating system and runtime errors are less predictable, but just as disabling for the user. With programming, you can create error-handling procedures to help solve the problem that caused the error, or at least give the user some information about why the error occurred and how to respond to it.

Peter's Principle: Building Error Traps

You and your users will be a lot happier if you get in the habit of building error traps throughout your application. As you create the application, make mental notes about all the places in the system where the user or the system could possibly make an error. Then add code that executes in the event of an error, even if it's just to stop the procedure and display an error message to the puzzled user. You'll notice when you examine wizard-created procedures that they abound in error-contingency plans.

Returning Results of Calculations and Comparisons

With the Access Expression Builder, you can specify some rather complex expressions as the source of the data for a text box via the text box's Control Source property. Using a function is a shortcut to creating the expression. Many commonly-used functions are included with Access, such as financial functions that compute interest rates or payment amounts. Other functions return mathematical values such as average, standard deviation, or trigonometric value. You can create your own functions using macros or Visual Basic code that will return any type of value you need. After you've built the function, you can refer to it by name from other forms and reports in the database.

Most functions also will accept arguments in place of actual values, so they can be used to calculate the result based on a value specified by the user. For example, suppose you've built a function to compute the annual income from a bond after the user has entered the annual rate. The annual rate is the argument of the function. When the user enters a rate, the function calculates the resulting income.

Following Conditional Branching and Loops

Conditional branching and looping procedures are a very important part of programming an application. Figure 1.2 illustrates three popular branching techniques. *Conditional branching* refers to determining the next course of action based on the outcome of a comparison. For example, if the Balance Due field contains a positive value greater than zero, go to the procedure that prints invoices; if not, go on to the next step in the regular path.

Another case of conditional branching is accomplished with the Select Case statement. When you have a list of several alternatives, the Select Case statement specifies which action to take with each of the different values. For example, salesmen have a graduated scale of commission depending on their sales volume. Each sales volume interval has its own Case statement to compute the amount of commission. When computing the amount of commission a salesman has earned, the procedure reads the total sales and jumps to the matching Case statement.

Looping procedures enable you to perform a series of operations on an entire recordset. For example, to update the current inventory in a retail store, you process the transaction against the master list, one record at a time. Items sold are subtracted from the number in stock, and items received are added. After the loop is begun, it continues until the end of the recordset is reached, updating where necessary and skipping the records with no matching transactions.

Sharing Data with Other Applications and the Web

The boundaries between Microsoft Office 2000 applications have dimmed almost to the point of being invisible. For example, Access can easily import charts and graphs from Excel, and Word can use an Access database as a data source for creating form letters with mail merge.

FIGURE 1.2

Three popular branching techniques.

If . . . Then . . . Else Conditional Branching

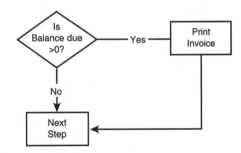

With Case Conditional Branching

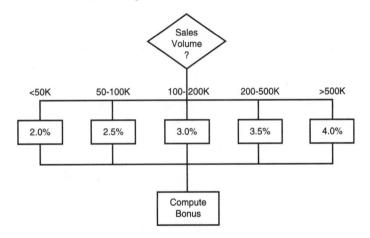

Looping

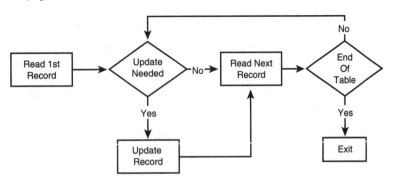

New features enable you to send a database via email as well as to create hyperlinks that you can click to jump to another location. The destination might be in another file in your system or as far away as the World Wide Web.

LOOKING AHEAD

Chapter 17, "Linking with Other Office Applications," describes exchanging data with other Microsoft applications. Chapter 18, "Working in a Multiuser Environment," discusses sharing and controlling databases in a workgroup settings. Chapter 20, "Posting Your Database on the Web," gives more information about HTML and publishing dynamic Access data on the Web.

Understanding the Access Programming Languages

Access speaks three programming languages fluently: Structured Query Language (SQL), macros, and Visual Basic (VB). SQL is the language Access uses behind the scenes in query design. Macros are lists of actions that are to be followed when the user clicks a button or some other specific event occurs.

Visual Basic is a much more comprehensive and complex language that can be used to do almost anything while the application is running. It consists of objects, collections, events, methods, procedures, statements, and properties.

LOOKING AHEAD

Chapter 9, "Writing Visual Basic Procedures," presents more details about Visual Basic program structure and syntax. Appendix A, "What's New in Programming Access 2000?," highlights the new programming and application development features and capabilities that appear in Access 2000.

Structured Query Language (SQL)

The queries you create in the Access Design View grid are implemented in SQL code. While you're building a query, you can look at the SQL code any time by switching to SQL view. To switch the view, select it from the View menu or click the View toolbar button and then choose SQL View from the pull-down menu.

Figure 1.3 shows a relatively simple select query in the Query Design window. The query concerns the decision to reorder certain products. When the In Stock amount falls below the reorder level plus 1, the product is placed on order. The query is based on two related tables: the list of products in the Products table and the supplier information in the Supplier table. The tables are linked by the Supplier ID field.

The query extracts relevant data from records matching the selection criteria but does not include any product whose category code (Cat Code) begins with 1, which is the major level code for fish-related products. Figure 1.4 shows the SQL code that was generated from the settings in the Design View grid.

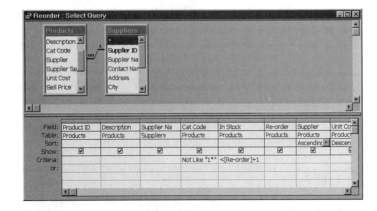

FIGURE 1.3

A select query that extracts information for reordering.

FIGURE 1.4

The SQL code generated by the query in Figure 1.3.

The complete SQL statement is as follows:

```
SELECT Products.[Product ID], Products.Description,
Suppliers.[Supplier Name], Products.[Cat Code], Products.[In Stock],
Products.[Re-order], Products.Supplier, Products.[Unit Cost],
Suppliers.[Contact Name], Suppliers.City, Suppliers.State,
Suppliers.PostalCode, Suppliers.Address, Suppliers.[Supplier ID],
Suppliers.PhoneNumber
FROM Suppliers INNER JOIN Products ON [Suppliers].
[Supplier ID]=[Products].[Supplier]
WHERE ((([Products].[Cat Code]) Not Like "1*") And
(([Products].[In Stock])<[Re-order]+1))
ORDER BY [Products].[Supplier], [Products].[Unit Cost] DESC;
```

In the first section of the SQL code, the SELECT operator lists which fields are to be included in the query result. The fields are named using both the table and field names with the dot operator between them. In the expression SELECT Products.[Product ID], the operator tells Access to look in the Products table for the Product ID field. Field names that contain a space or a dash must be enclosed in square brackets.

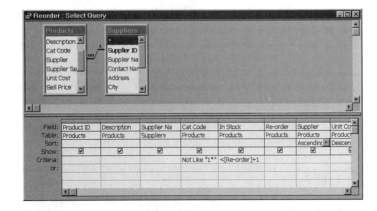
LOOKING AHEAD

See Chapter 2, "Reviewing Access Database Elements," for more information about the naming conventions used in Access.

The FROM and INNER JOIN operators specify the relationship between the two tables: Suppliers is the parent table, which has a one-to-many relationship with the Products table. The linking fields are specified by the ON operator: The Supplier ID field in the

Suppliers table is linked to the Supplier field in the Products table. In other words, you can look up supplier information for a product by finding a record in the Suppliers table that has the same supplier code as the record in the Products table.

The WHERE operator lists the selection criteria specified in the criteria row of the Design View grid. This shows that the answer table should include records for all the products that need to be reordered (except fish products).

The final operator, ORDER BY, specifies the sort order: in ascending order by supplier and, secondarily, in descending order of unit cost.

LOOKING AHEAD   Chapter 7, "Programming with SQL," takes a closer look at the SQL language, its uses, and its components.

Macro Coding

Unlike macros found in other applications, Access macros are not merely recordings of keystrokes. An Access macro consists of a list of actions that are carried out, step-by-step, in response to an event. For example, a macro can run when the user presses a command button, when a form closes, or when a text box control in a form gets focus. A macro also can execute when a specific condition occurs. Such a conditional macro might display a message box when data entered into a field has a certain value.

Macros are created in a special macro grid in the Macro Builder window. To begin a new macro, use one of the following methods:

- Choose New in the Macros page of the Database window.
- Click Build (…) next to one of the properties on the property sheet and then choose Macro Builder in the Choose Builder dialog box.

If you start a macro from the Macro Builder, you're asked to name the macro before proceeding. The macro grid displays at least two columns with two optional columns available, as needed (see Figure 1.5). The default columns are Action and Comment. To add the Macro Name and Condition columns, choose Macro Names or Conditions from the View menu.

To enter the action that's to take place when the macro runs, choose from the Action pull-down menu. ApplyFilter, Beep, CancelEvent, GoToPage, Maximize, and ShowAllRecords are just a few of the more than 50 macro actions in the list. Many of the actions have additional arguments that can be specified in a pane that opens below the grid when an action is selected.

Figure 1.6 shows three windows: a form with a macro attached to the Type text box, the Macro Builder window, and the result of running the macro. The active window (the message box in the upper-right corner) is displayed when the word *Dog* is entered in the Type field of the MacroEx form shown in the upper-left window and Tab is pressed to move on. The macro condition tells Access to carry out the specified action if the value "Dog" is entered in the Type field. The large bottom window shows the macro code in the macro design window. The macro is named DogMacro, and the action is the command MsgBox, which displays a message box. The action arguments below the grid pane specify the text of the message box and whether to beep when the message appears.

FIGURE 1.5

The macro grid can consist of up to four columns.

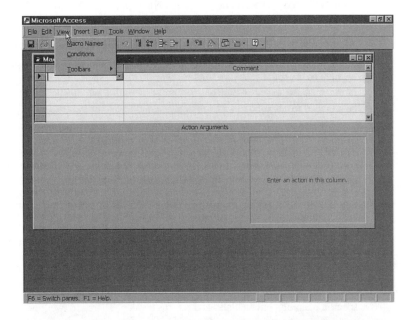

FIGURE 1.6

A macro that displays a message box.

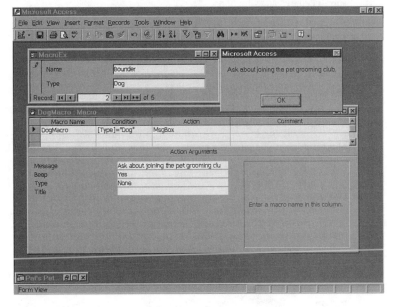

The last two lines in the Action Arguments pane, Type and Title, specify what kind of icon you want displayed in the message box and enable you to add a custom title, respectively. You can choose to display no icon or the Critical, Warning?, Warning!, or Information icon. The default for Type is None, and the default for Title is Microsoft Access.

After you've built the macro, you attach it to the event property of the button, text box, or other control. To attach a macro, set the event property the macro is meant to respond to, such as OnUpdate, OnClick, or OnGotFocus, to the macro. The names of all the macros in the database appear in the control's property pull-down menu. Conditional macros can be attached to a text box in a form and respond to one or more specific values.

Macros are useful for straightforward responses to events, but they do have some limitations. For example, you cannot use a macro to set up error handling or to loop through a recordset to process transactions. A macro does not return a value; therefore, it cannot be used to retrieve user input or to return a calculated value or the result of a comparison.

LOOKING AHEAD See Chapter 8, "Creating Menus," for more information about creating and running macros in Access.

Visual Basic (VB)

Everything you can do with macros you can do with Visual Basic (and a whole lot more). VB code takes the form of a *procedure*, which is a block of code that performs a specific operation or calculates and returns a value. There are two kinds of procedures: subprocedures and functions.

Subprocedures carry out one or more operations but do not return any values, whereas *functions* not only carry out the operations but also return values. Access provides many event procedure examples in the VB Help topics that you can copy and paste into a control event property. Then you can make changes in the code to fit your application, such as changing variable names. You can also use the Access Code Builder to create your own custom procedures that will perform any actions you want.

The following is a pair of simple subprocedures that move focus between the two pages of a form when you click the command buttons named Page1 and Page2:

```
Private Sub Page1_Click()
      Me.GoToPage1
End Sub
Private Sub Page2_Click()
      Me.GoToPage2
End Sub
```

Note: The Me keyword in the procedure is a shortcut for implicitly referring to the currently active object, whether it's a form, subform, report, or subreport. You can leave off the form or report name completely and Access will infer that you mean the current object. Using the Me keyword eliminates any doubt or ambiguity about the object to which you're referring.

The GoToPage method moves the focus to the specified page in the current form. You learn more about methods and their syntax in Chapter 9.

Access provides many built-in functions for all types of operations: Math, Text, Error Handling, Program Flow, Database, and several other categories. You can view the list of built-in functions in the Expression Builder dialog box (see Figure 1.7). Functions return values to the program: character strings, numeric values, and true/false values. For example, the function IsNull() is often used to find out whether a field has a value. IsNull() returns True if the field is empty or False if it has a value.

FIGURE 1.7

Access provides many built-in functions.

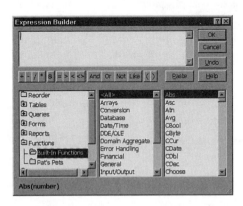

Custom functions can be created in the Expression Builder dialog box or in the Code Builder window. The following custom function displays the initials extracted from the first and last names in a form:

```
Private Function Initials() As String
' Display initials.
        Initials = Left(FirstName, 1) & Left(LastName, 1)
End Function
```

The Initials function uses the built-in Left() function to extract the first character of each name. The & symbol concatenates the two letters to form the returned value, Initials. After building and naming the function, you can use it as the control source property instead of the whole expression by entering =Initials() in the property sheet.

Macros can be converted into VB functions very easily. Select the macro in the database window and choose Tools|Macro. Then choose Convert Macros to Visual Basic. Figure 1.8 shows the macro DogMacro converted to a VB function. Notice the underline "continuation character" that can be used when a long VB statement does not fit on the screen. Access ignores the character and treats the multiple lines as a single statement.

This has been a very brief introduction to VB procedures. The remaining chapters go into much more detail about how to construct and use subprocedures and functions. Chapter 9 is devoted to programming and debugging VB procedures.

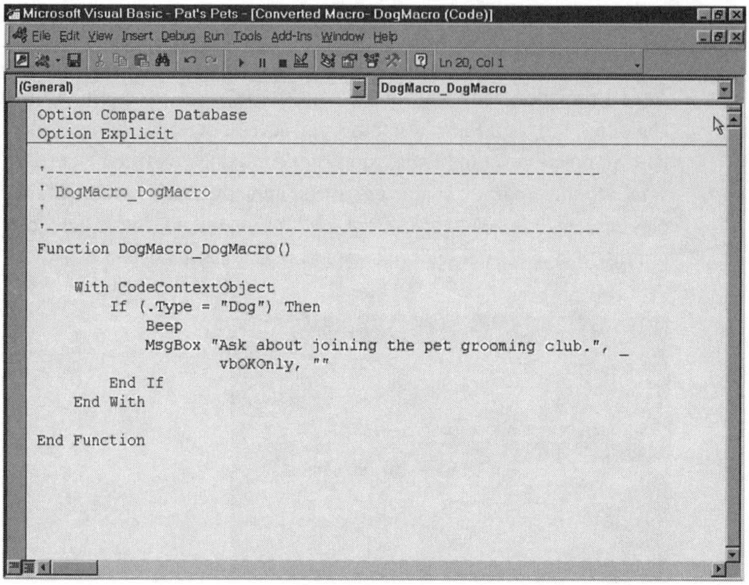

FIGURE 1.8
DogMacro *converted to a Visual Basic function.*

```
Microsoft Visual Basic - Pat's Pets - [Converted Macro- DogMacro (Code)]
File  Edit  View  Insert  Debug  Run  Tools  Add-Ins  Window  Help
                                                              Ln 20, Col 1
(General)                              DogMacro_DogMacro

   Option Compare Database
   Option Explicit


   '-------------------------------------------------------------
   ' DogMacro_DogMacro
   '
   '-------------------------------------------------------------
   Function DogMacro_DogMacro()

       With CodeContextObject
           If (.Type = "Dog") Then
               Beep
               MsgBox "Ask about joining the pet grooming club.", _
                      vbOKOnly, ""
           End If
       End With

   End Function
```

Deciding Which Language to Use

Each of Access's programming languages has special capabilities as well as some common functionality. For example, a query constructed in the Design View grid is coded in SQL but could just as well be programmed as an object in VB. As shown earlier, a macro easily can be converted to a VB procedure.

Queries are the primary means of viewing, changing, and analyzing data from one or more tables in a database. The three major types of queries are select, action, and SQL. *Select queries* retrieve information, calculate totals, and build crosstabs but do not change the data in the tables. *Action queries* affect data in tables. Both select and action queries can be used as control sources in form, report, and data access page designs. There are four types of action queries:

- The *make-table query* creates a new table from data already existing in one or more tables.

- The *delete query* deletes entire records from one or more tables based on the selection criteria.

- The *append query* adds complete records or only specific fields to one or more tables.

- The *update query* changes data in existing tables based on information in the Design View grid.

SQL queries accomplish more complex tasks and are coded using SQL statements rather than created in the query Design View grid. These include the following types:

- The *union query* combines corresponding fields from one or more tables or queries into a single field. For example, you have retail pet supply stores in several shopping centers around town and want to combine the sales data from all of them into one table.

- The *pass-through query* works directly with tables in an ODBC (Open Database Connectivity) database by dealing with the server rather than linking to the tables from Access.

- The *data-definition query* makes changes to a table definition, such as creating and deleting tables, adding fields, and creating indexes.

- The *subquery* builds a SELECT statement within an existing select or action query. The subquery selects a subset of the records already extracted by the main query.

If you want to perform any of these tasks for working with tables, you must use the SQL language. The first three are built into the SQL view of the query window. A subquery is built by entering the SQL SELECT statement in the Criteria row of the Design View grid.

LOOKING AHEAD

Chapter 8 covers SQL and building SQL queries in more detail.

The choice between macros and Visual Basic code depends on what you want to do. Macros can perform simple tasks such as previewing a report and hiding a toolbar. Also, macros are easy to build. In the Macro Builder window, you're coached in creating the syntax and the argument definition. Some tasks can be done only with a macro (for example, performing some startup action when the database first opens or assigning an action to a keystroke or a key combination).

Programming in VB has many advantages, and for some tasks, you must use VB instead of a macro. Here are some examples:

- One advantage is that VB procedures are contained within the form or report definition, whereas macros are separate objects, listed in the Macros tab of the database window. If you move or copy a form or report to another database, the VB procedures automatically move with it, but not the macros. They must be moved or copied separately.

- If none of the built-in functions do exactly what you want, you can build custom function procedures with VB. Custom functions can also take the place of complicated expressions wherever they're used. Once created, custom functions are available from the Expression Builder.

- Macros process an entire set of records at once, giving you no opportunity to control individual transactions. By using VB procedures, you can step through the records and process them one at a time, varying the action depending on the values encountered.

- The arguments set for a macro cannot be changed while the macro is running. While a VB procedure is running, you can pass arguments to it or specify variables as the arguments.

- As mentioned earlier, a VB procedure can detect an error, intercept the error message, and replace it with a more meaningful message to the user.

- VB is extremely flexible when creating and manipulating database object definitions. You can change properties as well as add and delete controls.

In summary, the choice between building queries using the Design View grid and coding in SQL depends on the type of query you want to build. The line between the two techniques is clear. On the other hand, it's not so clear whether to use a macro or VB to carry out actions. Macros are simple to create and easy to use, but there are many advantages to using VB almost exclusively.

COMPATIBILITY

Access 2000 has migrated from the Visual Basic for Applications (VBA) language used in Access 97 to the more standard Visual Basic. While modules created with Access 97 are successfully converted to VB, many of the objects, properties, and methods have been replaced by new language elements. For purposes of backward compatibility, most of these replaced elements have been hidden rather than removed. By default, they do not appear in the Object Browser lists, but you can view them by setting one of the Object Browser options. Appendix B, "Converting from Earlier Versions of Access," contains more information about conversion considerations and potential problems.

LOOKING AHEAD

Chapter 8 discusses macros and how to create them, and Chapter 9 takes a look at Visual Basic procedures and how to write and edit the code. Chapter 10, "Debugging Visual Basic Procedures," discusses debugging VB subprocedures and functions as well as handling errors.

How Do the Wizards Fit In?

The talented wizards provided by Access give you an additional step up toward creating custom databases. Access, itself, is an application front-end development environment, and with the added expertise of the wizards, database development becomes quick and easy.

LOOKING AHEAD

The wizards all create VB code in the background that you can edit and augment in order to complete or add fine-tuning to the database. Chapter 4, "Creating an Application with a Wizard," shows how to create a new database beginning with one of the Database Wizard's templates. Chapter 5, "Examining and Modifying the Wizard's Code," examines the code generated by the wizard and makes some changes that modify the objects in the database.

Summary

This chapter presented an introduction to the world of programming in Access. It described the role Access plays in application development. The three Access programming languages were compared and their usage discussed.

The next chapter, "Reviewing Access Database Elements," examines the Access database objects and clearly defines the terminology that Access uses. If you're already an expert in using Access, you might want to skip the next chapter and go directly to Chapter 3, "Touring the World of Object-Oriented Programming," which discusses object-oriented, event-driven programming concepts, strategies, and advantages.

Reviewing Access Database Elements

The purpose of this chapter is to review all the elements that make up the Access database environment. This chapter defines the major objects included in a database and examines the smaller components that play a part in tables, forms, reports, and data access pages. In addition, you learn what makes each element look and behave the way you want.

If you're well acquainted with Access and its elements, you might want to skim over this chapter and proceed to Chapter 3, "Touring the World of Object-Oriented Programming," which addresses the characteristics of object-oriented programming and how they tie in with your Access application.

Objects and Collections

The catchall term *object* refers to an element of an application. In fact, the application itself is an object that contains all the other objects, such as tables, queries, forms, report, data access pages, macros, and modules. In Access, objects form a hierarchy beginning with the application in a program or library and ending with the detailed controls, properties, and Web options that make up forms, reports, and data access pages. Figure 2.1 illustrates the Access object hierarchy.

Applying property settings and methods to the top-level Application object applies them to the entire application, which sets and retrieves all the options specified in the Options dialog box. For example, checking the Show Status bar and Startup dialog box properties in the View tab of the Options dialog box, as shown in Figure 2.2, applies to the current application. You can also apply methods and properties to an application to change the default menu bar to a customized one, set the active object upon startup, and automatically save all files when quitting the application.

Most applications include several forms, reports, data access pages, modules, and references. When one or more forms are open, the group is called a *Forms collection*. For example, you may be looking through a Products list in a form and at the same time have the Suppliers information form open for lookup. These two forms belong to the Forms collection. Other forms in the application that are not active are not part of the Forms collection.

FIGURE 2.1
The Access object hierarchy.

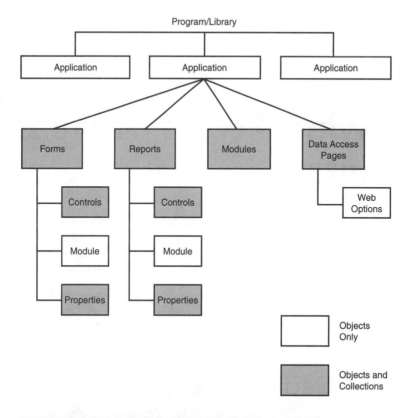

FIGURE 2.1
The Access object hierarchy.

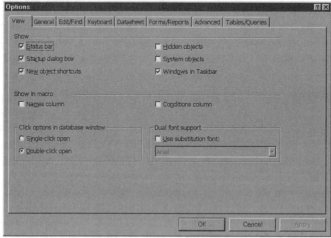

FIGURE 2.2
You can set application properties and methods in the Options dialog box.

Similarly, sets of open reports, data access pages, and modules are members of their corresponding collections. The objects in these collections are all of the same type. That is, they're all forms, all reports, all data access pages, or all modules.

An Access database may also include a References collection containing a set of references to another application's or project's type library. When you set a reference object, you can use the objects supplied by that application in your Visual Basic code. The References collection is the group of currently active references.

Data access pages are new to Access 2000. They're Web pages with a connection to an Access database. The Data Access Pages collection represents the set of open data access pages.

> **Tip:** Collections come in handy in Visual Basic because you can refer to a member of a collection not only by name but also by its index within the collection. Forms are indexed based on the order in which they were opened, beginning with zero. For example, the first form opened is indexed as Forms(0), where Forms is the name of the collection and (0) indicates that it was the first form opened and is still open. The next forms are indexed as Forms(1), Forms(2), and so on. If you close the first form, Forms(0), the others move up in the index: Forms(1) now becomes Forms(0), and so on. Indexes in a reports collection behave the same way.

Access Objects

Several other Access objects are associated with a specific application. For example, the *Screen object* refers to whatever form, report, or control currently has focus. For example, while you're modifying a report design, the Report Design window becomes the Screen object. You cannot open a form by referring to the Screen object, but you can refer to it to find out which object is active.

The DoCmd object of an application lets you run most of the Access actions from a Visual Basic procedure. For example, when you click the Save toolbar button or choose File|Save, Access carries out the Save action. In a VB procedure, adding the Save method to the DoCmd object creates the statement DoCmd.Save, which does the same thing as the Access Save action. Similarly, the FindNext action that executes when you click the Find Next button in the Find and Replace dialog box can be converted to the Visual Basic statement DoCmd.FindNext. A few of the Access actions, such as AddMenu and StopMacro, are not covered by DoCmd methods.

> **Note:** The terms *action* and *method* can get confusing. An *action* is a command in a macro or by itself that responds to a menu selection or button click. A *method* is a procedure that applies to an object. The Save action saves a specified Access object or the current one. The Save method carries out the Save action in VBA and applies to the DoCmd object.

The *Assistant object* represents the Office Assistant with any options you've set for the application.

The *Command Bars object* contains the set of command bars and command bar controls used in the application. Some command bars may be the default whereas others may have been customized.

The *Default Web Page object* contains the global attributes used when you save a data access page as a Web page. The options also apply when you open a Web page. Any Web options you've set for a specific page override the application-level options contained in the Default Web Page object.

Control Objects

At the lowest level, the *Control objects* are contained in and are subordinate to Form and Report objects. Controls include all the design elements you use to create forms and reports, such as text boxes, buttons, and labels. A Control object can also be contained within or attached to another control.

Bound controls are linked directly to a field in a table, query, or other element of the database. *Unbound controls* are used to display information not related to any database element. *Calculated controls* are text boxes that display the results of a calculation. The control source for a calculated control is a formula or expression using data from the underlying table or query or another control. Calculated controls can be bound or unbound.

An example of a calculated control is a text box that contains the total cost of an order by multiplying the number of items by their unit cost. The calculated control, Extended Cost, would have the following expression in its Control Source property box, where Qty and Unit Cost are both fields in the underlying table or query:

```
=[Qty]*[Unit Cost]
```

Table 2.1 describes the different types of Access controls you can use in form and report designs.

Table 2.1 Types of Access Controls

Control	Description
Label	Displays descriptive text such as titles and field captions. This control is unbound.
Text Box	Displays data from a table or query. This control is usually bound.
Option Group	Displays a set of mutually exclusive alternatives, one of which must be selected. Consists of a frame containing other controls such as toggle buttons, check boxes, option buttons, and labels in its collection.

Control	Description
Toggle Button	Displays a Yes or No value from a table or query (bound) or accepts user input (unbound).
Option Button	Same as Toggle Button.
Check Box	Same as Toggle Button.
Combo Box	Displays a pull-down list of valid field values (bound) or stores a value for use by another control (unbound).
List Box	Displays a list of valid field values (bound) or stores a value for use by another control (unbound).
Command Button	Starts a set of actions stored in a macro or event procedure.
Image	Displays a picture or other image created in a different application that's either linked or inserted.
Unbound Object Frame	Contains a bitmap, picture or other object created by another source.
Bound Object Frame	Contains an OLE object or other field from the underlying table.
Page Break	Creates a multiple-page form.
Tab	Displays information on separate form pages but as a single set.
Subform	A subordinate form containing data related to the data in the main or primary form.
Subreport	A subordinate report containing data related to the data in the main report.
Line	Displays a horizontal or vertical line.
Rectangle	Displays a box.
Hyperlink	Displays a label that, when clicked, jumps to a file, another location, or an HTML page on the Web or on an intranet.
ActiveX	Displays a custom control. *ActiveX control* is the new term for *OLE control*.

Most of the controls listed in Table 2.1 are also available to data access page designs. The Control toolbox used when creating a data access page contains additional controls, such as Scrolling Text and Hotspot Image, that are appropriate to Web pages.

Access provides more controls than are shown on the toolbox. If you click the More Controls button on the toolbox, you'll see a list of additional controls available, including ActiveX controls (see Figure 2.3). Note that your list might be different from the list shown in the figure.

FIGURE 2.3

The list of additional controls.

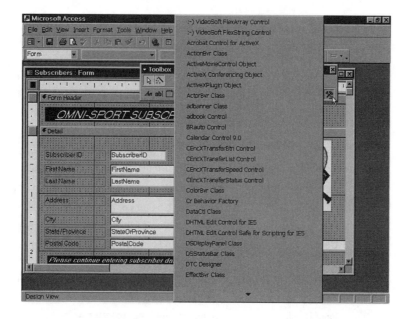

Controls Collection

Unlike Forms, Reports, and Data Access Pages collections, whose members are all the same type, a Controls collection is composed of varying types of objects: buttons, text boxes, labels, lines, rectangles, and any other element of the design. A Controls collection belongs to and is a member of the Form, Report, Data Access Page, or Control object that contains the controls.

> **Note:** You can use the Visual Basic Count property to determine how many forms or reports are open or how many controls a form or report contains. Count comes in handy when setting the tab order. You can also use it to loop through the controls in a form or report and perform an operation on each one. You'll learn more about this and other VB properties in Chapter 9, "Writing Visual Basic Procedures."

A Control object contained within another control becomes a member of the Controls collection for that control. For example, the controls within an option group belong to the option group's Controls collection. Similarly, a Label control that's attached to a Text Box control is a member of the Controls collection for that text box.

The Tab control of a multiple-tab form has a special type of Controls collection, called a *Pages collection*, that contains the Page objects that make up the tab set. Each Page control, in turn, has a Controls collection made up of all the controls on the page.

As with a Forms or Reports collection, the items in a Controls collection can be referenced by name or by index number.

Using Access Control Identifiers

Being sticklers for precision, computers demand unambiguous identifiers when you refer to controls. When you create formulas and other expressions using the Expression Builder, you'll notice that each control is identified not only by name but also by the name of the object that contains it. For example, if you use the FirstName field from the Subscribers table in a formula, the Expression Builder displays the name as

```
[Subscribers]![FirstName]
```

The exclamation point operator separating the object names indicates that the item that follows, FirstName, is a user-assigned name.

If Access has defined the item that follows, the separator you use is the dot (.) operator. For example, in the statement

```
SubscriberID.DefaultValue = Forms!Subscribers!SubscriberID
```

DefaultValue is an Access property, so it's preceded by a dot operator. Subscribers is the user-assigned name of the form and SubscriberID is the user-assigned name for the referenced field, so they're both preceded by the ! operator, often referred to as the *bang operator*.

COMPATIBILITY

The bang (!) operator was not available in Access versions 1.*x* and 2, so you might have to change some of the dot (.) operators in these versions to bang operators in order to establish a compatible reference to an object you've named. All subsequent versions of Access use the dot/bang convention.

> **Tip:** Instead of typing the whole explicit object reference to a control on an open form or report, you can use the Me keyword. The Me keyword implicitly refers to the current form or report Controls collection and is faster than using the full reference. For example, Me!FirstName refers to the Text Box control named FirstName in the active form or report. If the control name contains a space, it must be enclosed in brackets—for example, Me![First Name].

Properties

Every object in Access has a specific list of attributes, called *properties*, that can be set to make the object look and behave just the way you want. The major database objects, tables, queries, forms, reports, data access pages, and macros have the same set of general properties. Every control in a form, report, or data access page design also has a set of properties that determine the characteristics of the control as well as the appearance of any text or values it might contain.

Database Object Properties

To see the properties of one of the database objects, select the object name in the database window, without opening the object, and click the Properties button. You can also right-click the object name and choose Properties from the shortcut menu. Figure 2.4 shows the property window for the DogMacro macro written in Chapter 1, "Why Program Access?"

FIGURE 2.4
The properties of DogMacro.

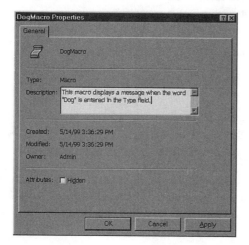

The Properties button is not usually available if the object is open in a view other than Design view. Clicking the Properties button when a form, report, or data access page is open in Design view opens the property sheet for the currently selected section or control in the design rather than the properties of the host object itself.

The properties of a query are a little different. With the query open in Design view, clicking the Properties button displays the Query Properties sheet if the insertion point is in the upper pane in the query design grid (see Figure 2.5). With the insertion point in the lower pane, clicking the Properties button opens the Field Properties sheet with two tabs, General and Lookup, as shown in Figure 2.6. If the query is open in SQL view, the Query Properties sheet lists fewer properties.

> **Technical Note:** Although it seems logical to think of a table or query and the fields in it as Access objects, they really aren't. Any object that has anything to do with the data itself is actually a DAO (Data Access Object) object. These include table and query definitions, recordsets, indexes, and relationships between tables. Recordset objects are used to work with data at the record level. Fields are contained in and subordinate to Recordset objects.
>
> DAO objects are also grouped in collections similar to Access collections. A table definition contains a Fields collection and an Indexes collection, a query

definition contains a Fields collection and a Parameters collection, and a record-set contains a Fields collection. You'll learn more about DAO objects in Chapter 3.

FIGURE 2.5
The properties of a query object.

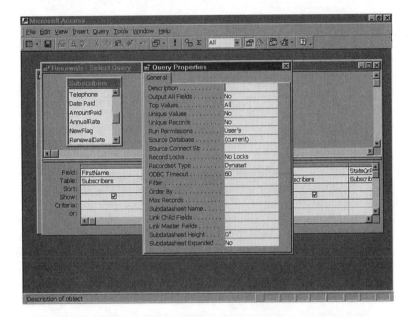

FIGURE 2.6
The field properties of a query object.

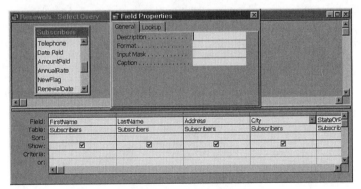

Control Properties

Each type of control has its own set of properties that can be viewed in one of the five tabs of the property sheet. Figure 2.7 shows the property sheet for a Text Box control. Many of the properties offer a pull-down list of valid settings for that control. Many other properties, such as the Control Source and Event properties, offer the assistance of the Code Builder, the Expression Builder, or the Macro Builder when you click the Build button (...) at the right of the property box. Still others, such as Caption and Status Bar Text, must be typed in manually.

FIGURE 2.7
The property sheet for a Text Box control.

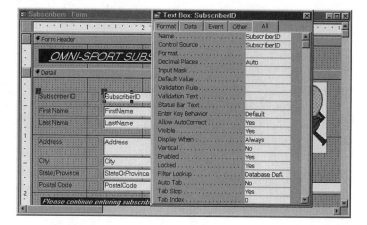

For convenience, the property sheet segregates the properties into four tabs: Format, Data, Event, and Other. To see all the properties for the selected control, open the fifth tab: All. Table 2.2 describes and shows examples of the four types of control properties.

Table 2.2 Types of Control Properties

Type	Description	Examples
Format	Change a control's appearance	Date/Time format, Number of decimal places, Color and size, and Font style and weight
Data	Specify the source of the data and what you're allowed to do with it	Control Source Input Mask, Validation Rule, and Text Default Value
Event	Specify how a control is to react when the event occurs	Before/After Update, On Got/Lost Focus, On Click, and On Exit
Other	Set properties that do not fit into other categories	Name, Tab Stop (Yes or No), Control Tip, Text Help, and Context ID

Tip: If you've entered a property setting that's too long to view completely in the property box, you can open a Zoom box that will show it all. Right-click the property box and choose Zoom from the shortcut.

Referencing Objects by Property

There may be times when you want to refer to an object by its state rather than by its name. For example, you might want to work with the open form or the control that currently has focus. To do this during a procedure, you can refer to the object by the relevant property. Some properties relate to the attributes of the object itself, such as Active or Previous, whereas others refer to an object related in some way. For example, the Parent property of a control refers to the form or report that contains it or a control or section that contains other controls.

Referencing properties can relate to a Screen object such as a control in an open report or form, to a form or report, or to a specific control. Table 2.3 describes the properties that can be used to reference Access objects.

Table 2.3 Properties Used to Refer to Objects

Property	Reference	Applies To
ActiveControl	The control that has focus on the screen	Screen object, form, or report
ActiveDataAccess Page	The data access page that has focus	Data access page
ActiveDatasheet	The datasheet that has focus on the screen	Screen object
ActiveForm	The form that has focus or contains a subform or control with focus	Screen object
ActiveReport	The report that has focus or contains a subreport or control with focus	Screen object
Form	The form itself or the form corresponding to a Subform control	Form or Subform control
Me	The form, report, or class module where VB is currently running	Form or report
Module	The module associated with a form or report	Form or report module
Parent	The form or report that contains the control	Control
PreviousControl	The control that had focus just before the current one	Screen object

continues

Table 2.3 Continued

Property	Reference	Applies To
RecordsetClone	The recordset specified as the basis of a form	Form
Report	The report itself or the report corresponding to a Subreport control	Report or Subreport control
Section	The section of a form or report or the section that contains the control	Section or control

Events and Event Procedures and Methods

An *event* is an occurrence that involves a particular object. For example, a specific key press, a mouse click, a change in data, a control getting or losing focus, a form opening, and a report closing are all events. Events usually are the result of some user action but can also be caused by a procedure or by the system itself. Access lists many events as object properties, and many more are available through Visual Basic.

In an event-driven application such as Access, when an event occurs, some kind of action takes place. The response to the event is often to run an event procedure or a macro. An *event procedure* is a named sequence of VB code statements that automatically executes in response to the occurrence of an event. A macro, as you learned in Chapter 1 is a list of actions written in the Access macro language that is carried out in sequence. You can also write your own custom VB procedure as a response to an event.

Methods, on the other hand, are procedures that an object or control can perform. An example is the DropDown method, which executes when you click the drop-down arrow next to a combo box to display the list of values.

Events and Event Procedures

Responding to events is the way to make all the objects in the database work smoothly together. For example, when data changes, it can trigger matching changes elsewhere in the database. Also, clicking a command button can change the object on the screen or add a new record.

Events are properties of Access objects and controls. Each type of object has a specific list of event properties. Figure 2.8 shows a partial list of the events associated with a Form object.

FIGURE 2.8

A partial list of event properties belonging to a Form object.

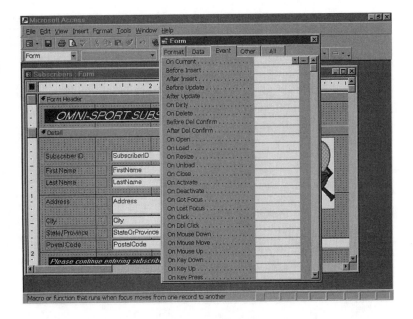

DEVELOPMENT

To define the appropriate response to an event, you can specify a macro that you've already written and stored in the database or create an event procedure. To attach a macro to an event, select the macro name from the Event Property pull-down menu. If you want to attach an event procedure to the event, you have two choices: call on one of the control wizards when adding the control to the design or enter the procedure statements yourself.

The control wizards can create event procedures for most standard operations such as closing a form, adding a new record, printing a report, and so on. When you use a wizard to add a control to a form, report, or data access page design, the wizard generates the VB code required to execute the event procedure.

If your event procedure requires custom processes, you can use the Code Builder. To open the Code Builder, click the Build (...) button next to the event property and choose Code Builder from the Choose Builder dialog box. The Visual Basic Editor window opens with the first and last statements of the procedure already in place. Event procedures all begin with the `Private` (or `Public`) `Sub` statement and end with the `End Sub` statement. All the procedure statements belong between those two.

Figure 2.9 shows a form with two buttons: one added with the help of the Command Button Wizard and the other manually added and defined. The upper button, Bye Bye, closes the form when it is clicked. The first procedure in the module window is the one the wizard created to do just that.

FIGURE 2.9
Two button-click event procedures.

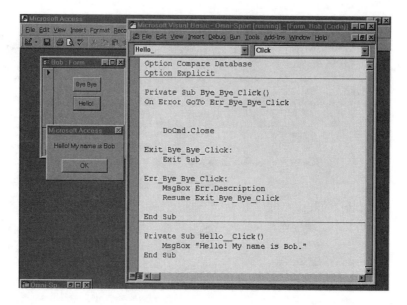

Wizards always try to consider the possibility of an error occurring so that the application won't stall out if one pops up. The first statement created by the wizard, `On Error GoTo Err_Bye_Bye_Click`, branches to an error routine later in the procedure if an error occurs. The next statement, `DoCmd.Close`, closes the form. The `Exit` statement simply tells Access to go from there to the end of the procedure and skip the error routine.

LOOKING AHEAD

Chapter 10, "Debugging Visual Basic Procedures," contains more information about writing procedures with error contingency and trapping features.

The lower button, Hello!, wasn't added with the help of the wizard but by invoking the Code Builder to add the event procedure. The Code Builder displays a template containing the `Private Sub` and `End Sub` lines between which you enter the procedure statements. Notice the two boxes at the top of the Visual Basic Editor window that contain `Hello_` and `Click`. `Hello_`, on the left, is the name of the object. If you click the pull-down arrow next to `Hello_`, you'll see a list of all the objects in the current form. If you want to create an event procedure for another object in the form, simply choose the object from the pull-down list.

In the top-right box you can see that `Click` is the name of the event procedure. If you click that pull-down arrow, you'll see all the procedures that apply to the currently displayed object. Again, you can select a different procedure and add another event response to the object.

Methods

Each object or collection in Access has a specific set of methods it can perform. Form and Report objects have eight methods they can perform, whereas a Control object has only five. Data Access Page objects have only one method.

Here are some form method examples:

- The `GoToPage` method moves focus to the first control on the specified page in the current form.
- The `Refresh` method updates all the records in the underlying record source with the changes that were made in the form.
- The `SetFocus` method moves focus to the specified form or control or the specified field on the active datasheet.

LOOKING AHEAD Chapter 9 describes in more detail the use of methods in programming Access applications.

Macros and Modules

Macros and modules are both major Access database objects that determine how the application functions. In Chapter 1 you saw how to create a macro using the Macro Builder, and earlier in this chapter you were introduced to the event procedures that are stored in modules. *Modules* are collections of procedures that relate to the entire application or to a specific form or report.

The similarity between macros and modules lies in the fact that both determine how the application responds to events. Their principal difference is a matter of complexity and versatility. Macros are lists of actions taken one at a time. A macro can contain some conditional statements (for example, the `DogMacro` in Chapter 1 displayed a message box only if the Type field value was `Dog`). If you want to use complicated branching and looping, this must be done in a procedure.

Macros

Macros can help you accomplish many useful tasks in an application. Here are a few examples:

- Set more powerful and flexible record or field validation rules for a control or for the field in the underlying table to which the control is bound.
- Display a customized error message for different types of data entry errors, such as a prompt to enter a zip code if the Address field is filled in.
- Synchronize records on related forms so that information from the same record appears in all the forms at the same time.

- Move between pages, records, and controls in a form by assigning specific key combinations to these actions. For example, press Shift+P to go back one page in a form and press Ctrl+P to move forward.
- Create custom menu bars and shortcut menus.
- Set control, form, or report properties absolutely or conditionally. For example, if a payment is long overdue, you can display the value in red in the form.
- Add a conditional page break to a report that forces a new page only if a certain condition is met.
- Print a report from a form.

LOOKING AHEAD

These are only a few of the things you can accomplish with a macro. All of these tasks can also be done via procedures. Chapter 8, "Creating Macros," demonstrates in more detail the process of creating and running macros.

Modules

A *module* is a collection of statements, declarations, and procedures stored together in a database. Access includes two types of modules: class and standard. Class modules are divided into form modules and report modules. A form or report module contains all the procedures—event procedures, functions and subprocedures—that are called from a particular form or report.

COMPATIBILITY

In Access 95, a class module was not available to any form or report other than the one with which it was associated. In Access 97 and Access 2000, you can create a special class module that can exist on its own without belonging on a specific form or report. It's listed in the Modules page of the database window along with the standard modules and can be used as a template to define custom objects.

Standard modules, previously called *global modules*, contain procedures not directly associated with a specific report or form. You can run a procedure in the standard module from anywhere in the database. The standard module is a convenient place to store frequently used procedures—for example, a function that tests to see whether a specific control is active and returns a Yes or No value.

If you want to see the code in a class module associated with a form or report, you don't need to open the form or report. Select the object name in the database window and click the Code button on the toolbar. Figure 2.10 shows the class module for the Subscribers form that's created later in Chapter 4, "Creating an Application with a Wizard."

To view the code in one of the standard modules, select the module name in the Modules page of the database window and click Design. You can also open the Visual Basic Editor window by clicking the Code toolbar button. Figure 2.11 shows the function IsLoaded(), which is the only procedure in this standard module. The IsLoaded() function tests to see whether a specified object is open, either in Form or Datasheet view, and returns the value Yes or No.

FIGURE 2.10

Click the Code button to see the procedures stored in a class module.

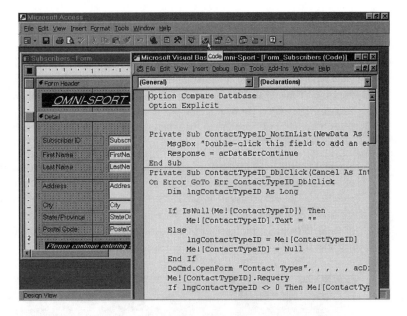

FIGURE 2.11

The contents of the Global Code module.

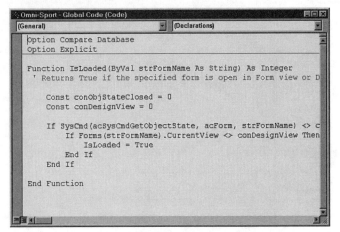

This function code might look like Greek to you now, but soon you'll find reading a procedure as easy as reading the sports page.

LOOKING AHEAD

Refer to Chapter 9 for more information about standard and class modules and how to understand, create, and use them.

Using the Object Browser

The Access 2000 Object Browser is really a tool for developers of Visual Basic code, but it's a good place to review the Access objects discussed in this chapter. The Object Browser is only available from the VB Editor window. To open the Object Browser, click the Object Browser toolbar button in the module window or choose View|Object Browser. The Object Browser dialog box displays information about all the objects, properties, methods, and constants in the selected project or library that can be used in VB procedures.

Figure 2.12 shows the Object Browser displaying the classes of Access objects, with the object AcFindMatch highlighted in the left column. In the right column, you can see the members of the AcFindMatch object. Perhaps you recognize the members of the class as the Match options in the Find and Replace dialog box, where you tell Access what part of the field to search for the Find What text—Any Part of Field, Whole Field, and Start of Field.

FIGURE 2.12
The Object Browser displays classes of objects and their members.

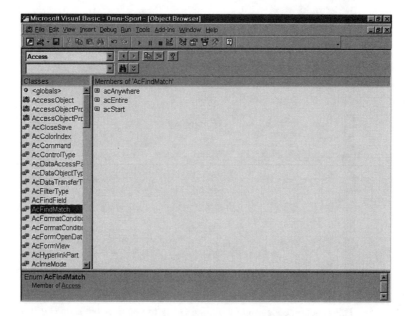

Tip: The Object Browser not only displays the names of the object classes and their members, but you can use it to paste code into a module. You simply select the method or property and copy it to the Clipboard; then you switch to the module window and paste the code in the module.

The icons preceding the class and member names indicate the types of objects. For example, the first three items in the Classes list are object classes and the rest are enumerated constants. The members of the AcFindMatch class are all values.

Figure 2.13 shows the Object Browser scrolled further down the Classes list, which now shows object class icons and a module icon. The ComboBox class is selected, showing both property and event procedure members, as you can tell from the accompanying icons.

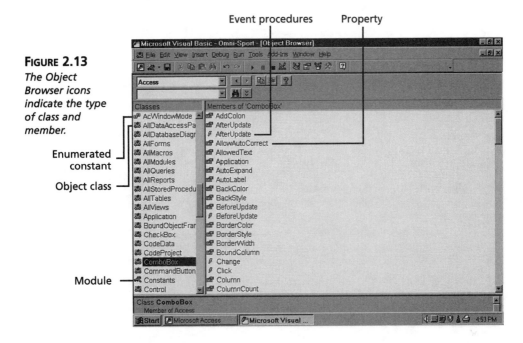

FIGURE 2.13
The Object Browser icons indicate the type of class and member.

LOOKING AHEAD There's a lot more you can do with the Object Browser, as you'll see in Chapter 9 where you'll find more information about using the Object Browser to help you write VB code.

Summary

This chapter has reviewed and examined the elements that make up an Access application and illustrated them in the object hierarchy. It has also briefly described how to build object identifiers. Object properties were also discussed. As a lead-in to the following chapters, the subjects of event procedures and modules were introduced.

Chapter 3, "Touring the World of Object-Oriented Programming," follows with a more detailed picture of object-oriented, event-driven programming and how it contrasts with old-fashioned procedural programming. It also discusses the elements that make up the Visual Basic objects and the accepted naming conventions used in VB. In addition, Chapter 3 describes the DAO (Data Access Objects) and ADO (ActiveX Data Object) features available to Access.

Touring the World of Object-Oriented Programming

This chapter takes a closer look at the elements that are essential to object-oriented, event-driven programming. Without getting into the details of code generation, this chapter discusses properties and methods in more detail and introduces the concepts of variables and constants. It also discusses how information flows to and from functions and procedures. The elements that control the flow of database processing are also introduced.

Comparing with Procedural Languages

In procedural languages such as Fortran and COBOL, the application drives the process. The program statements determine what happens next. With event-driven languages, events control what happens next. If no events occur, nothing happens.

A program written in a procedural language begins executing at the beginning of the program and, with the bit in its teeth, runs to the end along a defined path. It might call functions and subroutines along the way or branch to a different path, but only because the program was written to behave this way.

With an event-driven program, a user action or some other system event runs the job. The user is holding the reins and the code responds. Because you don't know what the user will do next, your application must be prepared for anything. It's important to account for all possible forms of user action and even make provisions for errors or exceptional events.

How Do Object-Oriented Languages Work?

In the Visual Basic object-oriented language, there are three essential pieces: objects, events, and methods. *Objects*, as discussed in Chapter 2, "Reviewing Access Database

Elements," are all the elements that make up an application: tables and forms and their controls, reports, queries, data access pages, and so on. When something happens to an object, it's called an *event*. The object responds to the event by performing some kind of action, composed of one or more *methods*.

Not all objects are met with all events, nor can all objects perform all methods. Here are some examples of events:

- Field data changes.
- A mouse button is clicked.
- The user presses a key.
- An object gets or loses focus.
- A form opens, closes, or is resized (that is, maximized, minimized, or restored).
- A report is formatted or printed.
- A runtime error occurs.

Each type of object has a specific set of properties that determines its appearance and how it responds to a given event. The properties that rule an object's response to events are called *event properties*. When you want to specify how the object reacts, you set its event property to a macro or a procedure that contains the desired actions. Table 3.1 lists a few of the nearly 50 events that can occur. It also shows corresponding event properties and the objects to which they apply.

Table 3.1 Examples of Events and Event Properties

Event	Event Property	Apply to Objects
GotFocus	OnGotFocus	Forms and form controls
Activate	OnActivate	Forms and reports
Change	OnChange	Combo boxes, tabs, and text boxes
NotInList	OnNotInList	Combo boxes
Print	OnPrint	Report sections
Updated	OnUpdated	ActiveX controls and bound and unbound object frame controls

The final piece of the puzzle is the *method*. Each object has a set of methods that can be applied to it. A method is an action such as GoToRecord, ApplyFilter, and OpenForm. Such actions are specified in the object's event property settings. If you do not choose an event property for the object, it responds with a built-in behavior defined for each type of object. For example, when a text box gets focus and you have not specified its OnGetFocus event property, the built-in method changes the text box color.

If you have set the object's event property to a macro or an event procedure, Access first processes the built-in behavior and then executes your macro or procedure. For example, suppose you click a command button that moves the focus to the second page of a form. The button briefly changes to appear pressed in (the built-in behavior) and then quickly runs the macro to move to the next page in the form.

Getting Familiar with the Fundamental Elements

Objects are the fundamental building blocks in an Access application. That catchall term includes everything from the most sophisticated form or report to the tiniest command button or check box. In Chapter 2 you examined many of the Access objects, how to refer to them, and how they behave. This chapter focuses more on the elements that directly relate to the VB programming language, such as the variables, constants, arguments used by procedures, and the elements that control the program flow.

In an application, objects are tied together with macros and procedures that determine the value or status of an object and pass the information along to another object.

LOOKING AHEAD Although this chapter discusses in detail the major elements used in database application development, the art of putting it all together in meaningful program code is examined more closely in Chapter 5, "Examining and Modifying the Wizard's Code." In that chapter, you'll analyze the procedures and modules that the Database Wizard creates in Chapter 4, "Creating an Application with a Wizard."

Variables

Variables are named locations in memory used to store values temporarily. Variables are used in a program to perform calculations and manipulate table data. They're similar to fields but exist only in VB, not in a recordset. Variables must be declared before they can be used in a procedure. Declaring a variable can be as simple as giving it a name. You can be more thorough by also telling Access what kind of data you're planning to use in the variable—numeric, string, and so on.

The *scope* of a variable refers to who has access to it. This depends on where and how you declare the variable. The variable might be limited to the procedure that contains the declaration, to several procedures throughout a specific module, or to the entire application. The *lifetime* of a variable refers to how long the variable has a value. A variable gains a value when it's declared. It takes on the default value for that data type, if you don't supply a specific value. When a variable loses scope, it ceases to exist.

Variables should have unique names to avoid any conflicts, at least within their own scope. They are also a specified data type. The value of a variable can change over its lifetime, but the name remains the same.

Declaring Variables

You have two ways to declare variables: implicit and explicit. To implicitly declare a variable, all that's required is to use the variable name in a procedure. When you implicitly declare a variable, you're essentially throwing it out there, for better or for worse. For example, the following statements declare the variable MyName implicitly in a procedure:

```
MyName = "Bob"
MsgBox MyName
```

Figure 3.1 shows the results of running this short procedure.

FIGURE 3.1
Declaring a variable implicitly.

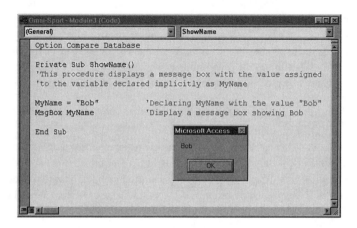

DEVELOPMENT There are risks with implicitly declaring variables. For example, if you misspell an implicitly declared variable later in the procedure when referring to it, Access thinks it's just another variable and you might get some surprising results.

> **Peter's Principle:** Add Lots of Comments
>
> Be generous with comments in all the procedures you write. Even if it's crystal clear to you at the time, weeks later you'll waste precious time trying to figure out what exactly the procedure is supposed to do. Here's an example of adding a comment to a line:
>
> ```
> MyName = "Bob"        'Sets MyName variable to the value "Bob".
> ```
>
> Comments are preceded by an apostrophe ('). Access ignores this mark and all text that follows it. You can place a comment on a line by itself or inline with a statement. In either case, precede the comment with an apostrophe.

Explicitly declaring variables means naming them and specifying their data type ahead of the first program statement. When you declare the variables explicitly, Access can spot a misspelled variable later in the procedure because it's not one of the ones you declared.

You can declare variables in a procedure or a module. The location and syntax of the declaration determines the scope of the variable. The most common way to declare a variable is with the Dim statement.

The *scope* of a variable refers to its availability for use by other procedures. When you declare a variable, you are specifying the scope. Declaring the variable at the procedure level with the Dim statement makes the variable available throughout the procedure and any procedures that are called by the host procedure. A variable declared outside a procedure is considered module-level and is available to all procedures in the module. If you add Private to the variable declaration, the variable is available only to the procedures in the host module. Adding Public to the declaration makes the variable available to all procedures in the application or project.

The *lifetime* of a variable is also an important concept. The lifetime refers to the period of time in which the variable has a value. The value may change during the lifetime but it still has a value. All variables are initialized with a default value when the are declared in a procedure. The default value depends on the data type. For example, numeric variables begin as 0, strings begin as zero-length strings, and Variant variables are initialized as Empty. Variables lose their values only when the procedure in which they were declared ends.

> **Technical Note:** The term Dim does not mean that the declaration appears in a subdued color. Dim is left over from earlier programming languages, where it was an abbreviated form of the Dimension statement. In those days, compilers read only the first five or six characters of a command anyway, so it was okay to abbreviate. One requirement of those early programs was to tell the computer how much memory would be needed to run the program. The Dimension statement, which appeared at the beginning of the program, specified any variables, such as vectors or arrays, that were not part of the data set but would require space.

Figure 3.2 illustrates declaring the MyName variable explicitly. Notice that Access gives you some help with the declaration. When you begin typing the data type, a list of relevant objects shows up. Automatically displaying this member list is one of the coding options available in the Module tab of the Options dialog box. If you don't want to see the member list when you begin typing, clear the option in the Options dialog box. You can choose to continue typing, press Esc to remove the list, or take one of the following actions to choose the appropriate name from the list:

- Press Tab to enter the highlighted item and remain on the same code line. Double-clicking the item also enters it into the statement.
- Press the spacebar to enter the item followed by a space so that you can continue with the declaration.
- Press Enter to enter the item and move to the next line in the procedure.

FIGURE 3.2
Declaring
strMyName *explicit-*
ly as a string
variable.

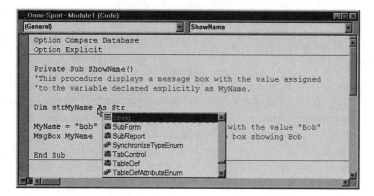

In the figure, you also see that the variable name is preceded by the str tag, which iden-tifies it as a string data type. This is a good practice that improves the code readability.

LOOKING AHEAD

A complete description of the data types that can be used in Access appears in the sec-tion, "Types of Data Variables," later in this chapter.

When you declare a variable in a procedure with Dim, that variable is available only with-in the procedure. Its scope is local and its lifetime is over when the procedure ends. You can also declare a variable in a procedure using Static instead of Dim. The scope of a Static variable is still within the procedure where it's declared, but the variable retains its value between calls to that procedure. The next time the same procedure is run, the value of the variable is the same as when the procedure was closed. A Static declaration is handy for computing running totals, for example.

When a variable is declared with the Dim statement in the declarations section of a mod-ule instead of in a procedure, it's available to any procedure in the module. This is useful when several procedures need access to the same information, perhaps passing values back and forth.

You can also declare a variable as Public in any procedure or module. A Public variable is available to the entire application. A Public variable is useful, for example, for making your company's CEO's name available throughout your application.

DEVELOPMENT

> **Tip:** Except in special circumstances, it's best to use explicitly defined private declarations at the procedure level. This saves memory because the space the variable occupies is released as soon as the variable disappears. In addition, you don't run the risk of using the same variable name twice for two different and conflicting purposes.

TROUBLESHOOTING

When you first start a new module, Access automatically enters the first two lines (see Figure 3.3). The Option Compare statement determines the sort order to be used in the module. The second statement, Option Explicit, requires that you explicitly declare all the variables you intend to use. If the module includes the Option Explicit statement, implicitly declared variables are not permitted. Figure 3.4 shows the compilation error that appears if Access encounters a variable you have not explicitly defined. The undefined variable is also highlighted.

FIGURE 3.3

Access includes a statement in a new module that requires all variables be declared explicitly.

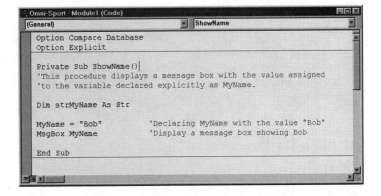

FIGURE 3.4

Access displays a compile error when it doesn't recognize a variable.

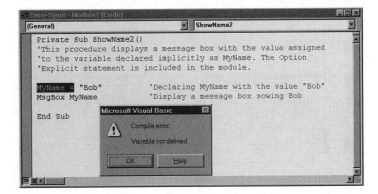

When you choose OK in the error message dialog box, Access points to the name of the procedure containing the error, making it easy for you to find and correct the problem.

LOOKING AHEAD

Chapter 10, "Debugging Visual Basic Procedures," contains more information about error messages and how to respond to them. It also describes many debugging techniques such as setting breakpoints and stepping through program code one statement at a time.

The alternative to declaring variables explicitly is to delete the default Option Explicit statement and declare variables implicitly as you refer to them. Both the Option Explicit and the Option Compare statements apply to the entire module and all the procedures and functions in it.

> **Note:** The `Option Compare` statement determines how Access compares character strings in your module. Your choices are `Database`, `Binary`, and `Text`. The default option is `Database`, which uses whatever sort order you've specified for your database. `Option Compare Database` is used only in Access applications. `Option Compare Binary` uses a sort order based on the internally stored binary values in which all uppercase letters come first, followed by lowercase letters. If the `Option Compare` statement is not used at all, the default comparison method is `Binary`. The third option is `Text`, which is case insensitive and based on your local language. Use the default `Option Compare Database` except in special cases such as in a module that uses a bookmark and must be case sensitive. In this situation, use the `Binary` option, which is case sensitive. You can use different `Option Compare` statements in modules within the same database.

Using a Declared Variable

After you've declared a variable and given it a value in the procedure, you can assign that value to an object in your application. Figure 3.5 shows a procedure that runs when `MyForm` is activated. It first declares `strFavCD` as a string variable and then gives it the value "Placido Domingo." The next statement changes the `MyForm` caption property from the default (Form) to that value. Notice that the form in the background shows *Placido Domingo* in the title bar.

FIGURE 3.5
Changing the form caption to a variable.

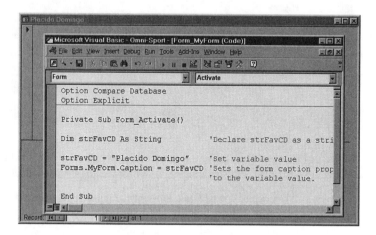

This procedure is included in the `Form_MyForm` class module and is available only to this form.

Naming Variables

DEVELOPMENT

When you declare a variable, you must give it a name. The name you assign can be very helpful when you try to maintain the program weeks after you've written it. In addition to the naming rules imposed by Access, certain naming conventions have been developed by programmers over the years to make their jobs easier. Variable base names are mixed case, using upper- and lowercase letters to help readability. For example, the name MyFirstJob is easier to read than myfirstjob. The optional tags preceding the variable base name can indicate the type of variable. strMyFirstJob indicates it's a string variable.

LOOKING AHEAD

The section "Naming Conventions," later in this chapter, presents more details about the popular Leszynski Naming Conventions (LNC).

Types of Data Variables

Variables come in the same data types as fields, except they're classified as VB data types instead of DAO data types. Table 3.2 lists the VB variable data types and gives an example of each. Notice that each example of a variable name in the table is preceded by a tag indicating its type.

Table 3.2   Variable Data Types

Data Type	Description	Example
Byte	One-byte unsigned integer	bytNewValue
Integer	Two-byte signed integer	intAltitude
Long	Four-byte signed integer	lngPopulation
Single	Four-byte floating-point number	sglWeight
Double	Eight-byte floating-point number	dblNatlDebt
Currency	Eight-byte number with fixed decimal	curFebSales
String	String of characters	strGreeting
Variant	Most kinds of data; 16 bytes plus one additional byte for each character in a string	varAnyVal
Boolean	Two bytes (True or False)	blnGiveUp
Date	Eight-byte date/time value	dtmMyBirthday
Object	Four-byte address referring to any object	objEntryForm
Decimal	12-byte subtype of Variant data type	varDecVal

PERFORMANCE

The Variant data type can store all kinds of data: strings, numbers, dates and times, or one of its special values—Null or Empty. Variants are easy to use but require more memory space than other types of data. If you don't specify a data type when you declare your variables, Access uses Variant by default.

The Variant value Empty indicates that a variable has not yet been assigned a value. Empty is replaced by a value as soon as one is assigned, even if it's 0. Null indicates that a variable intentionally contains no valid value. You can use these special Variant values to test for Null and empty fields in an error-trapping procedure. The Error value in a Variant is used to indicate that an error has occurred during the execution of a procedure. When a Variant value is set to Nothing, all system and memory resources are released.

Look in Chapter 10 for information about how to detect and intercept errors.

Arrays

Arrays are finite groups of variables of all the same type and with a common name. Each element of the array is identified by a unique index number. Arrays are very useful for looping through a recordset and storing field values in the array items from a number of records. The code is simpler and has fewer statements.

Arrays are declared just like other variables, depending on the scope you want them to enjoy. If you want them to be accessible to all the procedures in the module, declare them in the declarations section of the module or declare them as Public in the procedure. For a local array, declare it with a Dim or Static statement in the procedure.

The only difference between arrays and other variables is that an array has an index. When you declare an ordinary (fixed-size) array, you include upper and lower bounds that specify the maximum number of items you expect the array to handle. The following statements are examples of declaring arrays:

```
Dim intCountCD(25) As Integer    'Declares 25 elements, indexed 0 through 24.

Dim strSingers(15) As String     'Declares 15 elements, indexed 0 through 14.
```

To give you an idea of how arrays can be useful, suppose you run a mail-order business that specializes in CDs and you want to keep a current catalog of the most popular singers and titles.

The following statements give an example of using an array in a procedure. You've sorted the CDs by date of release, with the newest ones first, and you want the names of the performers of the latest 15 recordings. The following statements first declare a 15-item array for storing the singers' names. Then they loop through the recordset and copy the Singer values from the first 15 records. The DoCmd.GoToRecord.acNext method is a recordset method.

```
Dim intI As Integer
Dim strSinger(1 To 15) As String
For intI = 1 To 15    'Initializes the index.
        DoCmd.GoToRecord.acNext    'Moves to next record
        strSinger(intI) = me!Singer
Next intI    'Increments the index and loops.
```

You can also declare multidimensional arrays with a declaration such as the following:

```
Dim int3D(5, 1 To 10, 5 To 8)
```

This declaration specifies a three-dimensional array with one dimension indexed from 0 to 5, the second from 1 to 10, and the third from 5 to 8. Int3D(4,8,6) is an element of this array.

> **Warning:** Be careful when you're estimating the size of your array, especially with multidimensional arrays. Declaring an array reserves memory for the entire array, whether you fill it up or not. Remember also that if your array contains a Variant data type variable, even more memory is used for each item.

Objects and Object Variables

Between the wizards and the design windows, you might be able to create and modify all the forms and reports you'll ever need, but it's important to know that you can do the same thing within a procedure. VB statements can create, modify, or delete any object at runtime. An example was shown earlier in Figure 3.5, where the procedure changed the form's caption when the form was activated at runtime.

Recall that Access groups objects into collections: a Forms collection, a Reports collection, and so on. When you refer to an object in VB, you use the collection identifier to help specify the object. Table 3.3 shows three ways to refer to an object in a procedure. In the Syntax column, the items that appear in italic are placeholders for information you enter. See Chapter 9, "Writing Visual Basic Procedures," for more information about VB language syntax.

Table 3.3   How to Refer to an Object in a Procedure

Syntax	Example	Comment
identifier!objectname	Forms!MyForm	If the name contains a space or punctuation, enclose in square brackets.
identifier("objectname")	Forms("MyForm")	If the object name is a variable name instead of a literal, do not use quotation marks.
identifier(index)	Forms(2)	Used to move through the open objects in a collection.

The first example in the table uses the ! operator, which signifies that what follows is a user-named object. If the form name were My Form (with a space between My and Form), the object name would be Forms![My Form] with My Form enclosed in braces.

The second example uses quotation marks within parentheses to designate the object name. Once again, to refer to My Form, the object name would be Forms("My Form"). If the object is a declared variable, you do not use the quotation marks.

The third example in this table refers to a form by using its position in the collection as an index. Forms(2) refers to the form that was opened third, with respect to the still-active forms. The first form opened would be Forms(0).

An object variable is used to refer to a specific object. The variable can be used later in the procedure in place of the full name of the object itself. The difference between declaring a data variable and an object variable is that the data variable actually stores the value in a location in memory. The object variable stores only a pointer to the physical object in the database.

> **Note:** You can use several object variables to refer to the same object. If the object changes, every object variable that refers to it will reflect the change. For example, if you change the prices of some of the CDs in your catalog, all the object variables that refer to those CDs will also show the changes because they point to the changed value.

To establish the connection between an object variable and the object, use the Set statement. For example, the following statements open the CDs table in the current database, Music:

```
Dim dbsMusic As Database
Dim rstCDs As Recordset

Set dbsMusic = CurrentDb()
Set rstCDs = dbsMusic.OpenRecordSet("CDs")
```

The two Dim statements declare the object variables as Database and Recordset, respectively. The first Set statement assigns the object variable name dbsMusic to the open Music database. The dbs tag indicates that the variable refers to a database object. The next Set statement defines the rstCDs object variable as the CDs table in the dbsMusic object. The rst tag indicates the referenced object is a recordset.

Set statements can appear anywhere in a procedure or module, but the Dim and Static declaration statements must precede any action statements.

The Set statement comes with two keywords: New and Nothing. The New keyword actually creates a new instance of an existing class object, such as a form. An *instance* is a temporary copy of an open object. By using instances of a form, you can view several copies of the same form at once on the screen.

For example, the following statements create a new instance of the form CDs. The new instance will have all the same controls and properties as the original:

```
Dim frmNew As Form_CDs
Set frmNew = New Form_CDs
```

The new instance is hidden at first. To see both forms onscreen, add the following statement:

```
frmNew.Visible = True
```

When you're finished with an instance of an object, it's a good idea to remove it and release the memory and other system resources. To remove the instance, disassociate it from the object variable with the following statement:

```
Set frmNew = Nothing
```

Constants

Constants are named values that, once set, do not change during the execution of the module or procedure in which they're declared. Using constants makes your code much easier to read and maintain because the constant names can give you a clue as to what they represent. You set or change the value in only one place: the declaration. A constant can represent a numeric or string value, or it can refer to another constant. An expression containing a combination of arithmetic or logical operators can also be named as a constant.

Constants are defined by either the system or the user. After the constant is defined, you can use it anywhere within its scope, and its value remains the same. *Constant scoping* is discussed later in this section.

Access supports two kinds of constants: symbolic and intrinsic. *Symbolic constants*, also called *user-defined constants*, are defined in a module or procedure using the Const statement and keep their value during execution of the module or procedure. Access, VB, ADO, and DAO provide the *intrinsic* or *system-defined constants* that can be used anywhere in all modules. Intrinsic constants are listed and available in the Object Browser window when you click "<globals>" in the corresponding library.

Symbolic Constants

Symbolic constants represent values that you intend to use repeatedly in a module, such as a fixed interest rate or the title of your favorite CD. After you've given the variable a meaningful name and declared the value, you can use the name in place of the value anywhere in your module. Because you declare it only once, to make a change in the value, you need to change only the declaration of the value. For example, if the interest rate (or your favorite CD) changes, you only need to change the value of the constant where it's declared rather than everywhere it occurs in the code.

To declare a symbolic constant, use the Const statement in the declarations section at the beginning of the module or procedure. The following examples show statements declaring a numeric and string constant, respectively:

```
Const conIntRate = .075
Const conFavCD = "Placido Domingo"
```

The three-letter tag con in the constant names also improves the readability by clearly indicating that when the constant appears later in the code, it's indeed a symbolic constant. You need only look at the declarations section of the procedure or module to find out the value. This is just one example of the adopted naming conventions that help you decipher code.

> **Tip:** You cannot change the value of a constant during a procedure—it remains the same until you change the value in the declaration. Also, be careful not to assign a name to your constant that's the same as one of the intrinsic constants. None of the intrinsic constants begin with con, so if you stick to this convention, you'll be safe.

Scoping Symbolic Constants

The scope of a symbolic constant depends on where you've declared it. Similar to variables, if you declare a constant in a procedure, it's available only within that procedure. Declaring a constant in the declarations section of a module makes it available throughout the module. Constants declared in a module are considered Private unless specifically declared Public. Public constants are available to any module in the entire application.

> **Tip:** Keeping all your user-defined constants private is a good idea. Declaring constants as Public might cause a conflict with other constants of the same name in another module. It's also a good idea to explicitly declare constants in a module as Private to avoid any doubt.

Intrinsic Constants

In addition to the constants that Access provides, you can use any of the constants from the ADO, DAO, and VB libraries available in the Object Browser dialog box. This gives you access to hundreds of constants. You also can add references to other object libraries if that's not enough. Intrinsic constants are always available.

> **Tip:** To find out which constants are related to a certain object classes and their members, open the Object Browser and scroll down the lists of constants that are available in the object libraries. You can also open the Help topic for the specific function, event, method, or property to see the associated intrinsic constants.

LOOKING AHEAD
Chapter 17, "Linking with Other Office Applications," discusses adding references to other application libraries and using their objects in VB code.

Many intrinsic constants are directly related to a particular function, event, method, or property. For example, the `acLeftButton` constant is an Access constant used as a bit mask in event procedures for the `MouseDown`, `MouseUp`, and `MouseMove` events to determine whether the left mouse button was involved in the event. The constant is automatically declared by Access and set to `True` or `False`, depending on whether the event occurred.

DEVELOPMENT

COMPATIBILITY

The names of the intrinsic constants have two-letter prefixes that indicate from which library they come. Access object constants begin with `Ac`, DAO constants with `Db`, and those from the VB library begin with `Vb`. The member constants begin with the same prefix in lowercase. Table 3.4 describes the categories of intrinsic constants and gives some examples.

Table 3.4 Categories of Intrinsic Constants

Category	Example	Description
Action	acGoTo	Used with the GoToRecord method.
	acAnywhere	Used with the FindRecord method.
	acFormEdit	Used with the OpenForm method.
Event procedure	acLeftButton	Used with the MouseDown, MouseUp, and MouseMove events.
	acApplyFilter	Used with the ApplyFilter event.
	acDeleteOK	Used with the AfterDelConfirm event.
DAO	dbEditInProgress	The Edit method has been invoked.
	dbSecNoAccess	A permissions property. User is not permitted access.
	dbOpenTable	Opens a table-type recordset.
Keycode	vbKey[keyname]	Used in event procedures for the KeyUp and KeyDown events.
Security	acSec[permission]	Assigns permissions to objects using VBA.
	dbSec[permission]	Sets permission properties of objects.
RunCommand method	acCmdInsertRows	Same as supplying the InsertRows value for the action in a macro.
	acCmdAutoFormat	Same as supplying the AutoFormat value for the RunCommand action in a macro.

continues

Table 3.4   Continued

Category	Example	Description
Miscellaneous	acLBGetValue	Used with a function to fill a list box or combo box.
	acEffectChisel	Specifies the state of the SpecialEffect property.
VarType function	vbNull	Returns 1 if the variable has no valid value.
	vbCurrency	Returns 6 if the variable is of the currency data type.
	vbDate	Returns 7 if the variable is a date.

COMPATIBILITY

In future versions of Access, the values returned by some of the intrinsic constants might change, but the names will not. Therefore, it's wise to use the constant name in your code instead of the value it returns. To find the value of the constant, look it up in the Object Browser. Figure 3.6 shows the Object Browser window with the highlighted vbCurrency constant, which is a member of the VbVarType class. You can see the value of the constant in the lower panel of the window.

FIGURE 3.6

Finding the value of an intrinsic constant with the Object Browser.

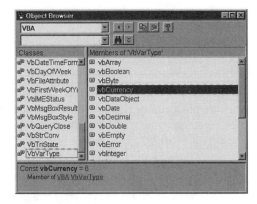

Arguments

Arguments are bits of information that a procedure or method uses during execution. Arguments can be required or optional. You pass them to the procedure by naming them in the procedure definition right after the name of the procedure. For example, the following statement defines the ArgProc procedure as requiring three arguments:

```
Private Sub ArgProc(strArg1 As String, intArg2 As Integer, dtmArg3 As Date)
```

The first argument, strArg1, is declared as a string variable, the second as an integer, and the third as a date. When you call this procedure, you can supply the actual argument values in two different ways: by position or by name.

To supply the argument by position, place the values in the same order as in the procedure definition, separated by a comma and a space:

```
ArgProc "Bob", 15, #5/5/00#
```

The string variable is enclosed in quotation marks, and the date is enclosed in date delimiter characters (#). To pass the arguments to the procedure by name, you don't need to follow the order in the procedure definition because you're specifically identifying each argument. The name of the argument is followed by the colon/equal sign pair (:=), and the arguments are separated by commas. Here's an example:

```
ArgProc dtmArg3:=#5/5/00#, strArg1:="Bob", intArg2:=15
```

Some arguments are optional and must be labeled as such in the procedure definition:

```
OptArgProc(strArg1 As String, intArg2 As Integer, Optional dtmArg3 As Date)
```

DEVELOPMENT

When the procedure is called, you can omit the optional arguments. If the optional arguments are in the middle of the argument list, you must still use commas to separate the arguments even if you don't include the optional ones. For that reason, it helps to list all the optional arguments last in the list. You can set a default value for an optional argument. For example, the following sets the default value of dtmArg3 to 5/5/00:

```
OptArgProc(strArg1 As String, intArg2 As Integer, Optional dtmArg3
➥As Date = #5/5/00#)
```

When you pass arguments to a function procedure, you do not need to enclose them in parentheses unless the function returns a value. For example, the first statement in the following list returns Yes or No from the MsgBox() function, and the second statement only displays a message and does not return a value:

```
strAnswer = MsgBox("Are you here on business?", 4, "Question 1")

MsgBox "Well done!", 0
```

Figure 3.7 shows an example of a custom procedure that uses a built-in VBA function to compute the monthly payment on a $100,000 loan with a 7.5% annual percentage rate and a 30-year duration. The complete code appears in Listing 3.1.

Listing 3.1 Calculating a Payment Amount

```
Sub GetPmt()

Dim Fmt As String, varLoanVal As Variant, varFuture As Variant
Dim varAPR As Variant, varTotPmts As Variant, Payment As Variant
```

continues

Listing 3.1   Continued

```
varLoanVal = 100000          'Loan amount $100,000
varFuture = 0                'Loan paid off at end of period.
varAPR = 0.075               'Interest rate 7.5%.
varTotPmts = 360             'Monthly payments for 30 years.
Fmt = "$###,###,##0.00"      'Define payment format.

'The arguments are passed to the Pmt() function.

Payment = Pmt(varAPR / 12, varTotPmts, -varLoanVal, varFuture)
MsgBox "Your payments will be: " & Format(Payment, Fmt) _
    & " per month."

End Sub
```

FIGURE 3.7
A procedure using arguments to compute monthly payments.

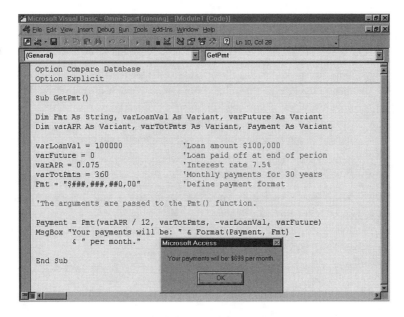

The Dim statements declare the Fmt variable as a string and all the rest as Variants because they're numbers to be used in the calculation. Numbers that are not intended for calculations, such as zip codes, can be declared as string variables. Then four of the variables are explicitly evaluated in the next four statements.

The Fmt variable defines the format for the monthly payment amount displayed in the message box. The next statement invokes the built-in function Pmt() and passes the variable arguments to it in the proper order, separated by commas. The last statement displays a message box with the results of the calculation. This procedure would be more useful if it displayed an input box requesting the loan information from the user; however, this is a simpler example.

Arguments usually are passed by reference to a variable, but you can also pass them by value by using the ByVal keyword in the procedure declaration. In Figure 3.8, the procedure GetOct passes a value to a function named Octal to find the octal equivalent to a decimal number. The function Octal is defined as receiving the argument as an integer value and uses the built-in function Oct() to return the octal equivalent. The procedure code appears in Listing 3.2.

FIGURE 3.8

A procedure calls a function that expects an argument by value.

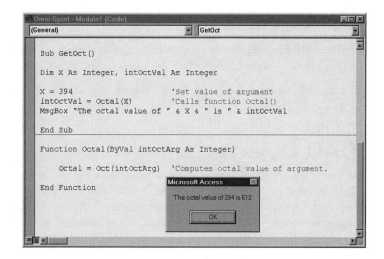

Listing 3.2   Passing Arguments by Value

```
Private Sub GetOct()

Dim X As Integer, intOctVal As Integer

X = 394                     'Set value of argument.
intOctVal = Octal(X)        'Calls function Octal()
MsgBox "The octal value of " & X & " is " & intOctVal

End Sub

Function Octal(ByVal intOctArg As Integer)

    Octal = Oct(intOctArg)    'Computes octal value of argument.

End Function
```

PERFORMANCE

Note: Passing arguments by value can slow down the execution of the procedure. When you pass an argument by reference, you're really giving the procedure a pointer to the argument, which takes up only four bytes of space for any data type. Passing an argument by value copies the value, which can require up to 16 bytes. This takes longer to pass and uses up more memory.

Some methods, such as the `SelectObject` VB method, require arguments before they can execute the corresponding action. The only argument the `SelectObject` method requires is *objecttype*, which must be one of the intrinsic constants: `acDataAccessPage`, `acDiagram`, `acForm`, `acMacro`, `acModule`, `acQuery`, `acReport`, `acServerView`, `acStoredProcedure`, or `acTable`. Two optional arguments are the specific object name and whether to select the object in the database window or an object that's already open. For example, the statement

```
DoCmd.SelectObject acForm, "Switchboard", True
```

runs the `SelectObject` action to open a form named Switchboard in the database window. `acForm` is the intrinsic constant for the Access form object.

LOOKING AHEAD In Chapter 5 you'll see many examples of including arguments when calling procedures and methods. The `DoCmd.SelectObject` statement is one of them.

DAO Objects

In 1993, Microsoft Corporation introduced its Jet DBEngine and Data Access Objects (DAOs), which greatly enhanced Visual Basic 3.0 as a database application tool. Jet became the primary means of connecting to and maintaining data in desktop databases. In contrast with Access objects that are static, such as forms and reports, DAO objects are all related to the underlying data and are dynamic.

Figure 3.9 illustrates the DAO object hierarchy for Microsoft Jet workspaces. All the objects in the tree also form collections. For example, you might have more than one database in your workspace and probably more than one table definition in your database. To go even higher in the tree, there may be a Workspaces collection on a network served by the same DBEngine.

Many of the DAO objects are familiar to Access users, but a few might be new. Table 3.5 describes the DAO objects.

Table 3.5   The DAO Objects

Object	Description
Container	An object that groups types of document objects together (for example, information about saved databases, tables and queries, or relationships)
Database	The currently open database
Field	A field in a table or query definition, recordset, relation, or index
Index	An index defined for a table
Parameter	A parameter supplied to a parameter query
QueryDef	A saved query in a database

Object	Description
Recordset	A set of records in a table or a set extracted by a query
Relation	A relationship defined between two table or query fields
TableDef	A saved structure of a base table in a database or a linked table

FIGURE 3.9
The DAO object hierarchy for Microsoft Jet workspaces.

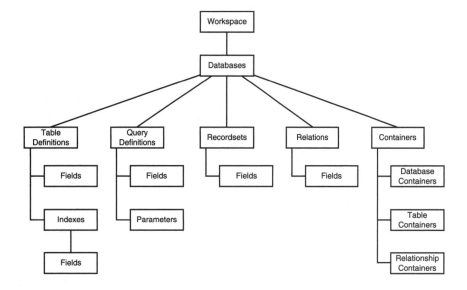

All the DAO objects in Table 3.5 can be referred to by declaring object variables. For example, the following statements declare database and query variables and then assign the current database to the variable dbs. The third statement begins to define a new query, and the last statement specifies the name for the new query:

```
Dim dbs As Database, qry As Query

Set dbs = CurrentDB()

Set qry = dbs.CreateQueryDef()

qry.Name = "Calif"
```

Next, you would add some SQL statements in VB code that define the query and open a form with the new query as the record source. The form would display only those records that meet the criteria in the SQL SELECT statement.

Each DAO object has a corresponding set of properties, methods, events, and functions:

- There are nearly 100 DAO object properties, including FieldSize, DefaultType, KeepLocal, OrdinalPosition, SourceTable, and Required.

- DAO objects can use over 50 methods, including CreateField, CreateQueryDef, CreateRelation, FindPrevious, and MoveNext.
- There are 12 data events that involve DAO objects, including AfterUpdate, BeforeInsert, Current, Delete, and NotInList.
- Eleven functions, all dealing with field values, can be used with DAO objects. These include Avg(), Count(), First(), Last(), Max(), Min(), StDev(), StDevP(), Sum(), Var(), and VarP().

After you begin working in VBA code, the distinction between Access objects and DAO objects will begin to blur and you'll view them both simply as members of the Access programming family.

COMPATIBILITY

Several objects, methods, properties, and statements have been deleted from Visual Basic 4.0, but they're still supported in the interest of backward compatibility. For example, the terms *dynaset* and *snapshot* are no longer used, so all the CreateDynaset and CreateSnapshot methods have been replaced by the OpenRecordset method. Refer to the DAO Reference Help for more details about obsolete features.

ADO Objects

The ADO (ActiveX Data Object) programming model is similar to the DAO model, except it's designed to gain access to and update a wide variety of data sources. ADO is a consistent application programming interface that forms a bridge between the application and the OLE database. When you use ADO, you're connected to the data source, where you can execute commands to retrieve, store, or update data. ADO also detects errors and guards against errors.

The ADO programming model consists of objects, methods, properties, and events. Figure 3.10 illustrates the ADO object hierarchy. Instead of the workspace used with DAO, the ADO model defines a connection as the major component.

Table 3.6 lists and describes the ADO objects.

Table 3.6 The ADO Objects

Object	Description
Connection	The object that provides the environment necessary for exchanging data with the data source. The connection can be made directly or through an intermediary such as the Microsoft Internet Information Server (IIS).
Command	The command sent across the connection that manipulates the data source. A command can add, delete, or update data in the data source. It can also retrieve record data in a table.
Error	Errors such as failing to establish a connection, execute a command, or perform an operation can occur at any time. One error can give rise to one or more Error objects.

Object	Description
Parameter	An optional variable part of a command that you can provide when you issue the command. This is useful when you're executing commands that operate like functions.
Field	A column in a recordset. Each field has a name, data type, and value.
Recordset	The local storage of data returned from a query of the data source. You can view and modify the data stored in the recordset.
Property	Every ADO object possesses a set of properties that describe the object or control its behavior. Built-in properties are always available. Dynamic properties are added by the underlying data provider and last only while the provider is active.

FIGURE 3.10
The ADO object hierarchy.

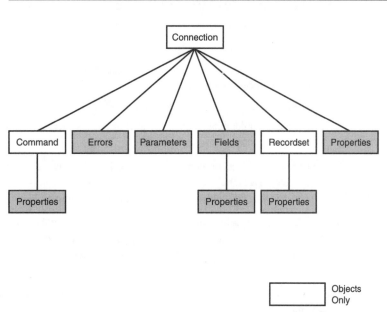

Events are also part of the ADO model but are not explicitly included. They are instead represented as calls to event handlers that are available for examination before the operation starts so that you can modify the parameters, cancel the procedure, or run the procedure.

ADO objects have a set of associated properties, methods, and events:

- Over 50 built-in ADO properties, including Bookmark, DataSource, EditMode, and MaxRecords. In addition, six dynamic properties are available, including Name, UniqueTable, and Resynch.

- ADO objects can make use of nearly 40 methods, including `Append`, `BeginTrans`, `CommitTrans`, `Find`, and `Save`.
- There are 20 events that apply to ADO connections or recordsets, including `BeginTransComplete`, `ConnectComplete`, `FetchComplete`, and `WillChangeField`.

> **Tip:** If your connection is not direct but through an intermediary, you can use the Remote Data Server (RDS) model, which provides a three-tiered connection system. See the Help topic for more information about the RDS programming model.

Naming Conventions

Access imposes certain rules for naming variables and constants:

- All names must begin with a letter.
- The name can contain only letters, numbers, and the underscore character. Punctuation and spaces are not allowed.
- The name can contain up to 255 characters.
- The name cannot contain any keywords or other words reserved by Visual Basic, such as `IF`, `LOOP`, `CLOSE`, `OR`, and `MOD`.

COMPATIBILITY

In addition to these rules, programmers over the years have gradually accepted a naming convention that makes their code easier to decipher months later. Such standard terminology also makes the code understandable to another programmer.

You saw an example earlier when a constant was named using the `con` prefix (which is actually a tag, as you'll see later). Many intrinsic constants also have tags that indicate their host library. Tags are in all lowercase letters, and the names are written with mixed case.

The naming conventions outlined here are included in the Leszynski Naming Conventions (LNC) and have been in use for Visual Basic development since 1995. The following is the general structure of the LNC, where *BaseName* is the name of the object unadorned by add-ons:

```
[prefix][tag]BaseName[qualifier][suffix]
```

The base name is the only part of the name that can contain multiple uppercase letters. The tag helps to characterize the base name and identify the class of object. The prefix is an identifier before the tag that narrows the tag character. The prefix can indicate the scope or another characteristic of the variable.

The qualifier is an add-on to the base name that describes how the object appears in context. For example, `intAttendMax` is the maximum value in the `Attend` set of values. The suffix adds more detailed information about the object to discriminate between two members of the set that might appear identical without the qualifier. Suffixes are often separated from the base name by an underscore for better visibility.

The most useful element of the naming conventions is the tag. Table 3.7 gives some examples of tags used with Visual Basic and Access objects.

Table 3.7   Examples of Using Tags with Visual Basic and Access Objects

Object	Tag
Button	btn
Collection	col
Combo box	cbo
Control	ctl
Database	dbs
Font	fnt
Form	frm
Image	img
Label	lbl
Menu	mnu
Menu item	mni
Recordset	rst
Report	rpt
Submenu	msub
Toolbar	tbr

Data variables have their own set of tags, depending on the type of variable. Examples of tags used for different data types were shown earlier in Table 3.2, which provides a list of variable data types.

For more information about the hundreds of other examples of LNC, see "Leszynski Naming Conventions for Microsoft Access, Version 95.1 for Access 1.x, 2.x, 7.x," published by Kwery Corporation, 1995.

Controlling the Program Flow

The last remaining major elements in event-driven programs are those that control the program flow. In addition to those statements that call a sub or function procedure, there are four major areas of flow control: exiting or pausing the program, branching to another part of the program, looping through the program code, and making decisions about what to do next.

With the End, Exit, and Stop keywords, you can quit running the program altogether, only leave the procedure and return to the previous procedure, or suspend processing while you do something else. Another keyword, DoEvents, yields the application so the operating system can attend to other events. Branching to another part of the program can be conditional, unconditional, or temporary.

The decision-making statements don't actually branch to another location in the program; instead, they choose which set of statements to execute. The If…Then…Else statement executes a series of statements if the condition is met and a second set of statements if not. When there's an expression that has several different values, you can use the Select Case statement, which executes a specific set of statements corresponding to the value of the expression.

Looping enables you to repeat a series of program statements a specific number of times or until a certain condition is met. One type of loop repeats the code while or until the condition is True. Another type executes the code a specific number of times. The third type repeats the set of statements for each object in the specified collection, such as all records in the recordset or all forms in the Forms collection.

Table 3.8 lists and briefly describes the keywords used in statements and functions to control program flow.

Table 3.8 Flow-Control Keywords

Keyword	Description
Actions That Exit or Pause	
Exit	Exits a block of code such as Do…Loop and For…Next or a sub, function, or property procedure. Does not define the end of the code structure but only branches to the end of the block.
End	Ends a procedure or block of code. Closes files and releases variables.
Stop	Suspends execution; closes nothing.
DoEvents	A function that turns execution over to the operating system for processing other events.
Actions That Branch to Another Set of Statements	
Call	Branches to a sub or function procedure or a DLL library procedure.
GoTo	Branches unconditionally to the specified line number or label within the procedure.
GoSub…Return	Branches to a subroutine within the procedure and returns at the end of the subroutine.
On Error	Branches to an error-processing routine if an error occurs.

Keyword	Description
Actions That Branch to Another Set of Statements	
On…GoSub	Branches to one of a list of destinations, depending on the value of an expression, and then returns to the next statement after On…GoSub.
On…GoTo	Same as On…GoSub, except it does not return to the next statement when finished.
Actions That Loop Through Code	
Do…Loop	Repeats the set of statements while the condition is True or until it becomes True.
For…Next	Repeats the set of statements a specified number of times.
For Each…Next	Repeats the set of statements for each object in the specified collection or array.
Resume	Resumes execution of a procedure after completing an error-handling routine.
While…Wend	Repeats the set of statements as long as the specified condition remains True.
With	Executes a set of statements on a single user-defined object.
Actions That Make Decisions	
Choose	A function that selects and returns a value from a list of choices based on the index that specifies its position in the list.
If…Then…Else	Executes a sequence of statements if the specified condition is True and another set if False.
Select Case	Executes one of several alternative sets of statements, depending on the value of the specified expression.
Switch	A function that examines a list of expressions and returns a value or expression related to the first expression in the list that is True.

Each of the flow-control statements has a definite syntax that must be followed. For example, the On…GoSub syntax is as follows:

```
On expression GoSub destinationlist
```

Here, *expression* is numeric and evaluates (or is rounded) to an integer between 0 and 255. Also, *destinationlist* is a list of line numbers or labels, each of which corresponds to a value resulting from the expression.

The following is the Do…Loop syntax:

```
Do [{While|Until} condition]       'Sets up condition for loop.
                                   'You must use While or Until.
```

```
    [statements]                  'Do while (or until) condition is met.
    [Exit Do]                     'Jumps to next statement after Loop.
    [statements]                  'Repeated while/until condition is met.
Loop                              'Ends loop.
```

The following is the If…Then…Else syntax:

```
If [conditions] Then [ifstatements] [Else elsestatements] End If
```

Here, at least one condition is required, and the If statements are executed if *conditions* evaluates to True. Otherwise, the optional Else statements are executed. The block of code must end with an End If line.

You'll see many examples of how to control program flow in the remaining chapters of this book. Refer to the Visual Basic Reference Help for specific information about each of the statements and functions.

Summary

This chapter has presented quite a lot of detail about object-oriented, event-driven programming and the elements that are behind the process. You were introduced to variables and constants, how to declare and use them, and what types are available.

One of the uses for variables is to pass them to a procedure or method as an argument to be used during execution.

DAO objects present the dynamic side of database management by addressing all the features of an Access database that are concerned with the data itself: the recordsets, queries, relations, and so on. In addition, the ADO programming model offers a means to access and modify data from sources in other applications.

Finally, the elements of an event-driven program must include ways to conditionally change the flow of processing. VBA includes strategies for branching to a different course or to one of a set of different courses as well as looping until a specified condition exists.

LOOKING AHEAD

Chapter 4, "Creating an Application with a Wizard," shows how to create a new database, and Chapter 5, "Examining and Modifying the Wizard's Code," puts much of this chapter's information to use.

PART II

Let Your Wizard Do the Coding

4

Creating an Application with a Wizard

When you first started learning Access, you probably used many of its clever wizards. There are wizards hovering in the Access background waiting to help you to create forms, reports, custom controls, and links to other applications or the Web (to name just a few). Each of these wizards creates program code behind the scenes to carry out the selections you make in the wizard dialog boxes.

LOOKING AHEAD In this chapter, you'll create a database to maintain a list of subscribers to the monthly *Omni-Sport* magazine. It's a simple database that consists of a single table, a data entry and review form, a query, and some reports and mailing labels. Chapter 5, "Examining and Modifying the Wizard's Code," explores the program code built during this development process.

Welcome to the *Omni-Sport* Subscriber Database

The main purpose of the *Omni-Sport* magazine's database is to maintain current information about the magazine subscribers: their names, addresses, and payment data. It's important to know when each subscription is due for renewal so that timely notices can be sent. Promotional material is also sent periodically to subscribers.

The first and most important effort in designing any new database is to determine what the user wants out of it. Once that has been specified, at least in broad terms, you can define what must go into the database in order to produce the desired output.

After specifying both the output and the input, you can set about distributing the data among related tables. In this example, however, the database is limited to one table for simplicity. In real life, the database would be more efficient if the data were divided among two or more tables, linked by the Subscriber key field.

DEVELOPMENT

The completed database is contained in the \Source\Databases directory on the CD-ROM that accompanies this book. However, if you choose to follow the steps in this chapter to modify the Database Wizard's creation, you can import just the table data from the CD-ROM into the new database after you define the table structure. The subscriber records are contained in the Copy of Subscribers table in the Objects to Copy database. After populating the database, proceed with modifying the form and report designs.

> **Peter's Principle:** Creating a Database from Gathered Data
>
> Anyone who finds a need for a database no doubt has already accumulated a lot of information. The trick in developing a database for existing data is to mold existing tools to match the requirements rather than the other way around. This makes it a lot easier for the users to transition to the new system if it looks somewhat familiar. This and other exercises in this book will help you see what tools are available in Access and how you can use them to build a suitable database application. The cases studied in this book represent four different uses for databases—from simple data storage and retrieval to an online decision-support system. Some of the techniques presented might be of use to you during your own database development.

Describing the *Omni-Sport* Output

In addition to the up-to-date list of current subscribers, *Omni-Sport* management requires a method of creating renewal notices to send to people whose subscriptions are near or past expiration. Other types of useful printed output may include the following:

- Summaries of popular areas of subscriber interest
- Mailing labels for all or some part of the list
- Form letters announcing special offers
- Financial analyses to develop editorial strategies

Assembling *Omni-Sport* Input

In addition to the complete subscriber list with names and addresses, *Omni-Sport* might decide it needs additional information about its customers. For example, it might want to send gifts to first-time subscribers or give a discount to those who pay for more than one year. In that case, the table must include a flag for first-time subscribers and specify the amount paid. If *Omni-Sport* offers a special rate when a subscriber buys more than one year of the magazine, the database should reflect that.

If *Omni-Sport* sends personal questionnaires to new subscribers to glean information about their households (income bracket, age group, number of adults, children, and primary sports interests, for example), you need to store this information as well. Not all subscribers will respond, of course, but you still need to make room to store what information does come in. Enough readers will respond to the questionnaire to lend a measure of statistical significance to the survey.

The questionnaire responses can be used by the editorial staff in selecting articles about the most popular topics or by the peripheral sales staff (videos, tickets, and memorabilia, for example) in sending promotional material to those who have expressed interest in a particular sport or activity.

Defining the Database Objects

As mentioned earlier, the *Omni-Sport* database contains a single table, Subscribers, that holds all the subscriber information. The Database Wizard creates most of the fields needed in the *Omni-Sport* database, but there still are many changes to be made.

The database must contain at least one data-entry form. The form built by the wizard for data entry shows two pages. The first page contains the address information, and the second contains a collection of miscellaneous data. This arrangement will work nicely for *Omni-Sport*. After removing some of the fields from the second page, you'll have room for the additional subscriber information submitted in response to the questionnaire.

The database must provide a means to print the subscriber list. A complete list is helpful for periodic error checking and looking up information in response to reader questions.

In order to determine which subscribers need to be reminded to renew, a query should be included in the design. The query will accept the user's input about the time frame to look for—for example, any subscription that expires within 90 days from today. You might even want to send increasingly urgent letters as the expiration date approaches. Other queries can extract and summarize sales and interest data for review by management and the editorial staff.

Using the Database Wizard

When you start the Database Wizard, you have a choice of several predesigned databases from which to choose. The one you want to build might not exactly match any of the wizard's suggestions, but you can pick one that's close to meeting your requirements and modify the finished product.

No set of wizards will produce exactly the application you want, but they can give you a real head start in the process. After the wizard has finished performing its magic, you can modify the design by deleting unnecessary objects, changing the table structure, and modifying the form and report designs to match. You can even dig into the Visual Basic code and the macros to make changes in how the application responds to certain events.

Selecting the Application Type

When you first start Access, one of the choices in the opening screen is Create a New Database Using Access Database Wizards, Pages, and Projects, as shown in Figure 4.1. When you click the Access Database Wizards, Pages, and Projects option, the New dialog box opens with the Databases tab active, as shown in Figure 4.2. If you're already running Access, you can start a new database by clicking the New button or choosing File|New. The General tab of the New dialog box appears this time, offering a choice of Database, Data Access Page, Project (Existing Database), or Project (New Database). Choose the Databases tab to see the 10 different database templates.

FIGURE 4.1
The opening Access screen.

FIGURE 4.2
The Databases tab contains 10 pre-designed database templates.

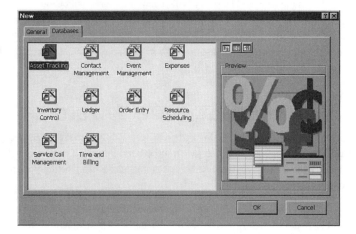

Tip: If you don't see the Microsoft Access opening dialog box shown in Figure 4.1 when you start Access, the Startup Dialog Box option might not be checked. Open an existing database and choose Tools|Options and then check Startup Dialog Box in the Show group on the View tab. (You must have some database open to have the Options dialog box available.) The next time you start Access, the opening screen will appear.

The New dialog box has buttons, similar to those in the Open dialog box, that change the view of the items in the tab: Large Icons (the default), List, and Details. In addition to the filename, the Details option shows the size, type, and date of the last modification. If a preview of the selected template is available, it appears in the Preview box.

Most of the templates are rather complex for the simple Subscriber application, but the Contact Management template can easily be modified for use by *Omni-Sport*.

After you select a template, the File New Database dialog box appears. Here, you can enter a name for the new database and tell Access where to store it. The default filename for a new database using the Address Book template is ContactManagement1, and the default folder is My Documents (unless you've changed this option). Keeping related files together in a folder where you can find them again is always a good idea. In spite of the advanced searching capability of Access, it's a lot easier if you already know where you have stored your important files.

Follow these steps to begin creating the *Omni-Sport* Subscriber database:

1. Choose the Contact Management template and click OK. The File New Database dialog box appears.

2. Type the name **Omni-Sport** in the File Name text box.

3. Choose the folder in which you want to store the database and then click Create.

After a few moments, the Database Wizard introductory screen appears showing what information the new database will contain (see Figure 4.3). The database window shows behind this dialog box. You'll probably eventually want to store more than just the subscriber address information, but to keep it simple, *Omni-Sport* will use only the Contact Information elements. Click Next to move to the next dialog box for the opportunity to include additional fields in the tables.

When you look over the general types of information the new database will store, you can begin to compare that with what you need in your database. Within the topics displayed, the specific data items are distributed in several tables, each of which has many fields. The next step is to choose from the lists of tables and fields the Database Wizard has to offer.

FIGURE 4.3
The Database Wizard shows what information will be stored in the new database.

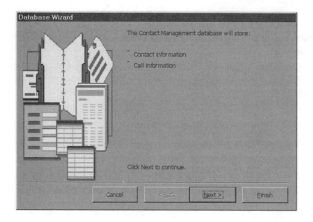

Choosing the Fields

Figure 4.4 shows the second wizard dialog box, in which you can choose the fields to add to tables in the database. The dialog box is divided into two areas: On the left is a list of the tables that will be included in the database, and on the right is a list of the fields in the selected table. In this example, there are three tables: Contact Information, Call Information, and a lookup table called Contact Types. Other examples can have as many as five or more related tables.

FIGURE 4.4
Choose the fields you want to add to the database.

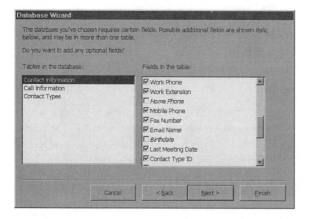

Most of the fields in the tables of the Contact Management database template are required, and they appear in regular font and are checked in the list. There are, however, several optional fields that you can add to your design. These appear in italic and are not checked. The figure shows Home Phone and Birthdate as optional fields that can be added to the Contact Information table. If you try to clear any of the checked fields (not italic), Access will inform you that the field is required and cannot be removed. The field may be required because it links the table to another or because it is part of an index or primary key.

The Subscribers table should include information about the subscription renewal date and the list of sports interests that were checked in a recent poll of readers. The optional fields in the displayed list closest to these are Birthdate, which you can change to Date Paid, and Contact's Interests, which you can change to Sports Interests. You can change their names and control sources after the wizard is finished.

To continue with the *Omni-Sport* Subscribers database, follow these steps:

1. Scroll down the list of fields and check the Birthdate and Contact's Interests fields.
2. Click Next.

The next two dialog boxes offer 10 different screen display styles and six report styles. As you select different styles, a sample appears in the left pane. After the report style dialog box closes, the wizard asks for a title for the new database. Figure 4.5 shows this dialog box as it first appears. You also have the option to include a picture in the header of all the reports that the wizard builds. This is handy for including a company logo on printed reports.

Note: If you design a report on your own later, you'll have to add the picture yourself; the Database Wizard will have no part in the report design.

FIGURE 4.5
The Database Wizard asks if you want a special title for your new database.

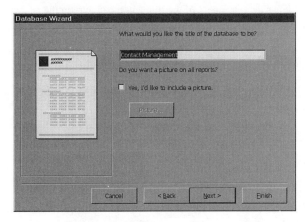

Follow these steps to continue with the *Omni-Sport* database design:

1. Choose Next, accepting the default style selections, until you reach the dialog box requesting a title for the database.
2. Type **Omni-Sport** in the text box.

3. Click the check box labeled Yes, I'd like to include a picture. Then, click the Picture command button.

4. Use the Insert Picture dialog box to locate the picture you want to use. (Figure 4.6 shows a list of pictures from the Images folder on your CD-ROM.)

FIGURE 4.6

Use the Insert Picture dialog box to locate and add a picture to all the reports in your new database.

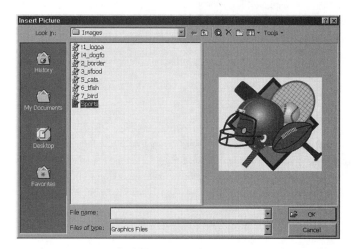

5. Select the picture filename, in this case "Sports," and click OK to return to the Database Wizard dialog box, which now looks like Figure 4.7. The preview at the left shows the placement of the title and the picture in the header of a sample report.

FIGURE 4.7

The Database Wizard dialog box with the new database name and a picture.

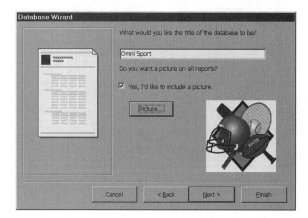

6. Click Next to move to the last dialog box. Then, choose Finish to close the dialog box and start the database.

After a few moments, the Main Switchboard appears with a list of available actions (see Figure 4.8). A *switchboard* is the user's primary point of entry into an application. It displays a list of actions the user may take next to work with the information. Clicking an option triggers an event procedure or a function that opens a form, previews a report, or carries out some other action. The Database Wizard makes a switchboard for you, but you'll see in Chapter 14, "Adding Real-time Features," how easy it is to make one yourself.

The first option in the new switchboard, Enter/View Contacts, opens the data-entry form shown in Figure 4.9. Notice that this is a two-page form with additional contact information on page 2, accessed by clicking the "2" button. The two optional fields you added are on the second page of the form. To return to the Main Switchboard, close the form window or choose Window|Main Switchboard.

FIGURE 4.8

The first option in the Main Switchboard takes you to the Contacts data-entry form.

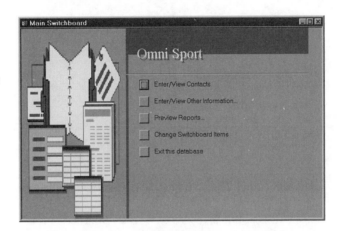

FIGURE 4.9

The first page of the form shows the fields for the contact's name, address, and phone numbers.

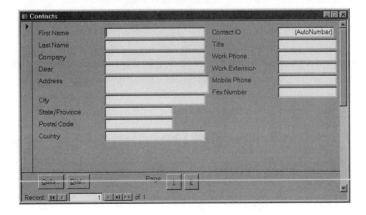

This form will require some revision to make it suitable for the *Omni-Sport* database. For example, the Company, Dear, and several of the phone number fields are unnecessary. Other fields would be more appropriate with different names. Several more fields need to be added to store the personal questionnaire information.

The second option on the Main Switchboard opens the Reports Switchboard (see Figure 4.10). This switchboard lists the reports that the wizard has prepared. One of these reports, the Weekly Call Summary Report, is completely irrelevant for this application and can be deleted from the database. You can create other reports that are useful to *Omni-Sport* using the Report Wizard and add them as items to this switchboard. The final option on the Report Switchboard returns the user to the Main Switchboard.

FIGURE 4.10
The Reports Switchboard offers a choice of report previews.

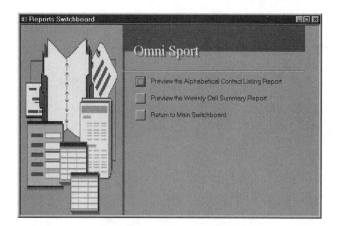

The Change Switchboard Items option on the Main Switchboard comes in very handy for customizing both the Main and the Reports Switchboards later in this chapter. This option activates the Switchboard Manager, which is used to change any item on any switchboard in the current database. You can edit the text of the switchboard caption that appears in its title bar or any item on the switchboard. You also can add new options and delete existing ones. When you add a new item to a switchboard, you must also specify the command Access is to execute when the item is clicked. You'll learn more about this in the section, "Changing the Switchboards," later in this chapter.

Modifying the Database Design

The first step in customizing this new database is to modify the underlying table by deleting the unwanted items from the table and then adding the other fields the application needs. In addition, you need to add any default values and data validation specifications as well as lookup tables and input masks, where appropriate. There's no data in the table yet, so Access won't object to deleting fields from the table structure.

> **Tip:** The Name AutoCorrect feature, new with Access 2000, automatically repairs any naming errors that occur because of name changes. The option is available in the General tab of the Options dialog box (Tools|Options). When this option is selected, if you change a field name in the table structure, the name is automatically changed everywhere the field was used as a control source in an object's design. The name of the Text Box control in the design itself is not changed, only its Control Source property. You need to update the control's Name property if you plan to refer to it in Visual Basic code. The control's label must also be updated with the new field name.

Next, remove the unwanted items from the form and report designs. Finally, customize the switchboard captions and individual items to reflect the needs of the *Omni-Sport* application.

Restructuring the Contact Management Database

To begin the restructuring of the newly created database, close the switchboard form and resize the database window. Because you're going to remove some fields from the Contacts table that may be involved in a relationship, open the Relationships window and delete the relationships among the three tables.

Next, return to the database window and delete the Calls and Contact Types tables as well as all forms except Contacts and Switchboard.

Before you begin to change the table structure, rename the table in the database view. Right-click the Contacts table name and choose Rename from the shortcut menu. Type **Subscribers** in place of "Contacts" and then press Enter.

Figure 4.11 shows the AutoForm-Columnar form created from the Contacts table, with all the fields, as it was when the Database Wizard finished. Compare this with Figure 4.12, which shows how the Contacts table must be modified for use by *Omni-Sport* for its application.

First delete the unwanted fields from the Subscribers table structure. Then modify the remaining fields and add new fields as described in Table 4.1 and the paragraphs that follow.

FIGURE 4.11
*The AutoForm
showing the
Contacts table
fields.*

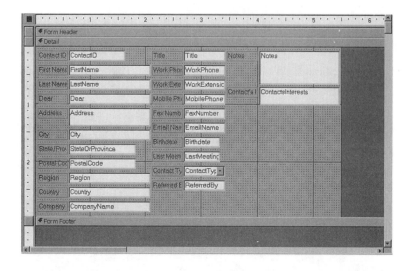

FIGURE 4.12
*The AutoForm
showing fields
changed for the
Omni-Sport
Subscribers table.*

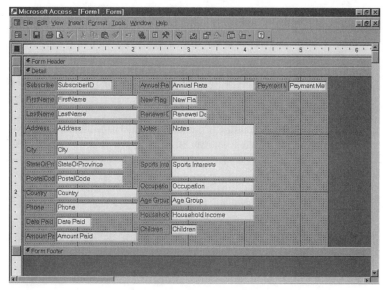

Table 4.1 Subscribers Table Structure

Field	Type	Req'd	New (N) or Renamed (R)	Comments
SubscriberID	AutoNum	X	R	Key field
FirstName	Text			
LastName	Text			Indexed (Duplicates OK)

Field	Type	Req'd	New (N) or Renamed (R)	Comments
Address	Text	X		
City	Text	X		Indexed (Duplicates OK)
StateOrProv	Text	X		
PostalCode	Text	X		Indexed (Duplicates OK)
Country	Text	X		Default: USA
Phone	Text		R	
Date Paid	Date/Time	X	R	Default: current date
Amount Paid	Currency		N	Indexed (Duplicates OK)
Annual Rate	Currency		N	Default: $29.00
New Flag	Yes/No		N	Default: No
Renewal Date	Date/Time		N	
Notes	Memo			
Sports Interests	Text		R	
Occupation	Text		N	
Age Group	Text		N	Lookup table
Household Income	Text		N	Lookup table
Children	Yes/No		N	
Payment Method	Text		N	Lookup table

Four of the fields also have input masks included as field properties in the table definition that help with data entry. The first three were added by the wizard and the fourth is new:

- *PostalCode input mask:* 00000\-9999. This requires digits only and displays the value with a dash—for example, 92118-2450.

- *Phone input mask:* !\(999") "000\-0000. This requires digits but fills the field from left to right (that's what ! means) and includes parentheses, a space, and a dash—for example, (818) 555-3648. The backward slash (\) indicates that what follows is a literal rather than a special character. The quotation marks specify a closing parenthesis and that a space be inserted between the third 9 and the first 0.

- *Date Paid input mask:* 99/99/00;0. This displays a date in the short format—for example, 10/25/01. The 0 in the second part means to store the literal characters (the slashes) with the value entered. Unless you expect to have a wide range of year dates, you can leave it as two-digit year. If you are dealing with historical dates between 1900 and 1929, you would have to use four digits in the input mask to get the correct date: 99/99/0000;0.

- *Renewal Date input mask:* 99/99/00;0. This is the same as the Date Paid mask.

Input Masks for Y2K

The Office 2000 Y2K Compliance complicates the date input mask setting. Using the built-in 99/99/00 mask, you can enter only two digits representing the year. Values between 00 and 29 are automatically assumed to belong in the 2000's while values 30 and over are assumed to be in 1900's. The year values are stored as four digits even if you entered only two.

If you try this out for yourself, set the Format property for the Date/Time field to Long Date so you can view the resulting year value.

If you are not satisfied with the automatic century assignment, you can change the input mask to 99/99/0000 or 99/99/9999. In the first case, the user is required to enter all four year digits. In the second case (all 9's), the user can enter two digits or all four. If only two digits are entered, the Y2K feature takes over. Entering all four overrides the Y2K feature and stores the entered value.

Another option, 99/99/9900, doesn't work well. You must enter two spaces before you can enter the two-digit year value.

Two new logical fields are added: New Flag and Children. Each has a default value of No. In addition, there are three lookup fields containing lists of values that can be selected during data entry. Table 4.2 shows these fields and their respective value lists.

Table 4.2   Subscribers Table Lookup Values

Field	Values	
Payment Method	Cash	
	Check	
	Credit Card	
Age Group	A	<20 Years
	B	20–30 Years
	C	30–40 Years
	D	40–50 Years
	E	50–60 Years
	F	>60 Years

Field	Values	
Household Income	1	<$15,000
	2	$15,000–$25,000
	3	$25,000–$40,000
	4	$40,000–$65,000
	5	>$65,000

To create these lookup fields, choose Lookup Wizard from the Data Type pull-down menu in the table design window. When you create a two-column list, such as those for Age Group and Household Income, you should store the value in the first column in the field, using the second column only as an explanation of the codes in the first column.

Importing the Subscribers Data

Now that all the necessary changes have been made to the Subscribers table structure, you can enter data. You can either enter your own data or import the subscriber records from the CD-ROM that accompanies this book. You can import table data directly from the *Omni-Sport* database in the Databases folder. Access can import both the table definition and the data or only the definition. In this case, only the data is imported as a separate table and then the records are appended to the empty Subscribers table.

> **Warning:** Because your Subscribers table contains no records, you do not risk losing data by pasting, which can overwrite existing data. If you have already entered records, you should use an Append query to add the new records to the table without writing over the old ones.

Use the following steps to get the record data from the Subscribers table of the *Omni-Sport* database on the CD-ROM:

1. Open the new *Omni-Sport* database window and show the Tables page.

2. Choose File|Get External Data|Import.

3. In the Import dialog box, locate the *Omni-Sport* database in the Databases folder on the CD-ROM (\Source\Databases).

4. Select the *Omni-Sport* database and click Import.

5. In the Import Objects dialog box, select Subscribers on the Tables tab and click OK (see Figure 4.13). You return to the original database window where the new table is named *Subscribers1*. Access is careful not to overwrite a file with the same name by adding a suffix that uniquely identifies it.

FIGURE 4.13
The Import Objects dialog box.

6. To copy the records from the Subscribers1 table to the original Subscribers table, right-click Subscribers1 and choose Copy from the shortcut menu.

7. Right-click in an empty area of the Tables page and click Paste to open the Paste dialog box. Type **Subscribers** in the Table Name text box and choose Append Data to Existing Table. Click OK.

8. Open the Subscribers table to view the imported records.

The record data is still in the Subscribers1 table in your database. You can either delete the table or keep it as a backup copy of the Subscribers table.

With the Subscribers table filled, it's time to move on and modify the rest of the database objects the Database Wizard created.

Modifying the Data-Entry Form

After you make all the desired changes to the table structure and add records to the table, the next step is to look at the data-entry form design. It should contain all the fields in the table, arranged in a logical and uncluttered manner. Figures 4.14 and 4.15 show pages 1 and 2 of the original form design that the Database Wizard created for entering and reviewing the contacts' data. There are many changes to be made in the design, including adding and deleting fields, changing field names to match the changes in the table, rearranging the controls in the form, adding a title and a picture, deleting and adding command buttons, and changing several control properties. Stay in the design view to make these changes.

Changing Fields and Field Layout

All the fields that were removed from the table structure are now bound Text Box controls whose control sources Access doesn't recognize. They should be removed from the form design. If you switch to form view, those fields will display "#name?," indicating a missing control source. To delete a control or label, select it and press the Delete button.

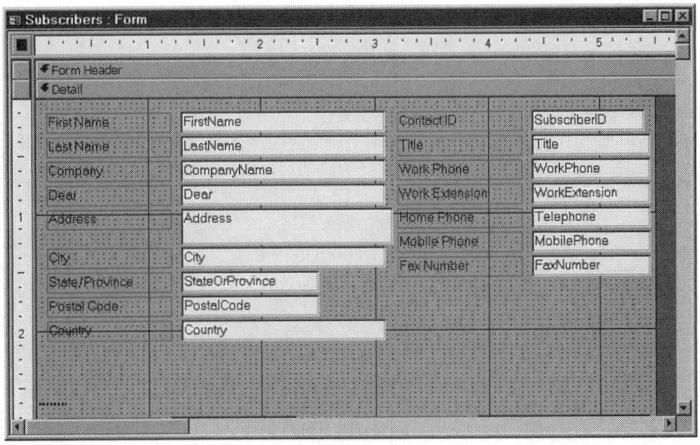

FIGURE 4.14
Page 1 of the Subscribers form design.

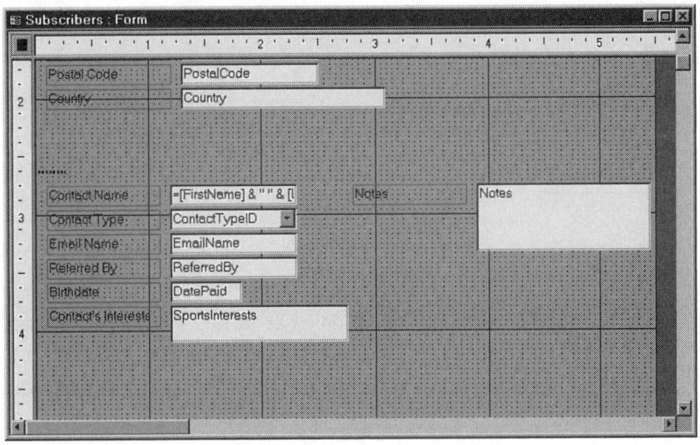

FIGURE 4.15
Page 2 of the Subscribers form design.

If the Name AutoCorrect feature is in effect, you don't have to change the Control Source properties for the renamed fields. You do need to change the attached label and the control Name property. To change a label, double-click the label, type in the new text, and then press Enter. To change the text box name, edit the Name property.

> **Tip:** If you want to delete several controls at once, hold down the Shift key as you select the controls. This selects them as a group. Then press the Delete button to delete them all.

Table 4.3 describes the changes to make in the form's Text Box and Label controls.

Table 4.3 Changes in Text Box and Label Controls

Control Name	Action
Company	Delete text box and label
Dear	Delete text box and label
ContactID	Change label to *Subscriber ID*
Title	Delete text box and label
WorkPhone	Delete text box and label
WorkExtension	Delete text box and label
HomePhone	Change label to *Phone*
MobilePhone	Delete text box and label
FaxNumber	Delete text box and label
ContactName	Delete text box and label
ContactType	Delete text box and label
EmailName	Delete text box and label
ReferredBy	Delete text box and label
Birthdate	Change label to *Date Paid*
Contact's Interests	Change label to *Sports Interests*

Next, add the nine new fields that were not included in the Contacts table: Amount Paid, Annual Rate, New Flag, Renewal Date, Occupation, Age Group, Household Income, Children, and Payment Method. Refer to Table 4.1 for details of the new fields. Reposition and resize the new fields to resemble the design shown in Figures 4.16 and 4.17. Added features—titles and other text, a picture, a rectangle, and a new button—will be added later.

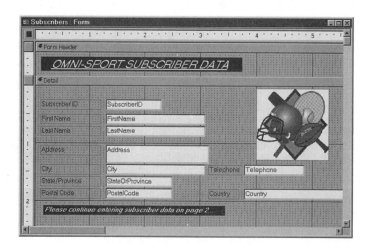

FIGURE 4.16
Page 1 of the new Subscribers data-entry and viewing form design.

FIGURE 4.17
*Page 2 of the new
Subscribers data-
entry and viewing
form design.*

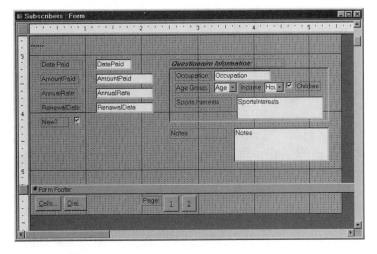

FIGURE 4.17
*Page 2 of the new
Subscribers data-
entry and viewing
form design.*

Changing the Tab Order

The *tab order* is the sequence of controls that receive focus as the user presses the Tab key. When you create a form, the tab order is automatically set to the order in which you placed the controls on the form design. When data is entered, the focus might not move through the fields in a logical progression. You can change the tab order to any sequence you want: logically from left to right and top to bottom or some other pattern. Also, you might want to skip some fields altogether.

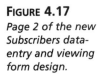

You can prevent the user from being able to reach a field by removing it from the tab order, either conditionally when an event occurs or completely. For example, when the Renewal Date is specified as a calculated field and filled in by an expression, the user should not be able to reach the field by pressing Tab to change the value. To keep a control from ever receiving focus, change its Tab Stop property in the Other tab of the text box property sheet to No.

With the form open in the design view, choose View|Tab Order. The Tab Order dialog box, shown in Figure 4.18, displays a list of tab stops in the currently selected section (Detail, in this case). The control names have been changed to match the new field names. The controls appear in the list in the same order in which they receive focus in the form when the Tab key is pressed repeatedly.

> **Note:** The names that first appear in the Tab Order list are the names that were current when the form was created. If you've changed the names in the table after the form was created, they're not changed in the form. They do, however, refer to the same controls in the same order. Keeping the old name can be confusing. It's better to change the control names to match the new field names.

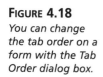

To move a tab stop to another position, select the control name and then release the mouse button. Position the mouse pointer on the small row selector square at the left end of the selected item until the pointer appears as an up-left pointing arrow. You now can click and drag the line to a new position. To move several rows at once, click and drag over them to select them and then reposition them as a group.

If you want focus to move through the form only from left to right and top to bottom, choose Auto Order in the Tab Order dialog box. The list is automatically rearranged to reflect the physical layout of the controls in the form design.

Customizing the Form's Appearance

Next, add a title on page 1 of the form and change its font and color properties as you like. Then, add an instruction to the user to continue entering data on page 2 of the form. If you want, locate the same picture added by the Database Wizard and place it in the upper-right corner of page 1.

On page 2, it would be convenient to group the personal questionnaire information in one place on the form. Perform the following steps to add a Rectangle control that frames these fields:

1. Click the Rectangle tool on the toolbar and draw a rectangle around the group of fields. The fields may seem to disappear.

2. With the rectangle selected, choose Format|Send to Back. The fields should now reappear.

3. Open the property sheet and change the rectangle's Special Effect property to Sunken and press Enter.

The form design now should look like the finished product, as shown in Figures 4.16 and 4.17, except for the buttons in the form footer.

Changing Buttons in the Form

Because there's no need to telephone the subscribers on a regular basis or to review the Weekly Calls Summary report, remove the Calls and Dial buttons from the form footer.

Simply select the button and press Delete. Keep the page 1 and 2 buttons, which switch form pages.

There are two ways to return to the main switchboard from the form view: Close the form or choose the switchboard name from the Window menu (which leaves the form open). It would be convenient to have a button on the form footer that closes the form and returns to the main switchboard automatically. To add this button, call on the Command Button Wizard:

1. In the design view, make sure the Control Wizards button is activated on the toolbox and click the Command Button tool. Then click in the form where you want the button. The first Command Button Wizard dialog box shows a list of action categories and a list of actions in the selected category.

2. Choose Form Operations in the Categories list and then Close Form in the Actions list (see Figure 4.19).

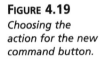

FIGURE 4.19

Choosing the action for the new command button.

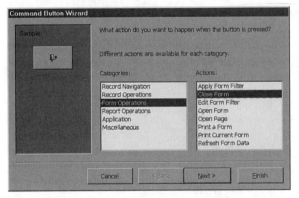

3. Click Next. The wizard now offers a choice between a picture or text on the button. Choose Text and type **Return to Switchboard**.

4. Click Next and name the button **Go To Switchboard** (or something else more meaningful than the default name) and then click Finish.

> **Note:** If you've changed the Display FormPage startup option from Switchboard to (none), the form will simply close without displaying the *Omni-Sport* Switchboard when you click the new Return to Switchboard button in the form view.

Now is the time to test the new form by switching to form view. Figures 4.20 and 4.21 show pages 1 and 2 of the new form with data from the first subscriber record.

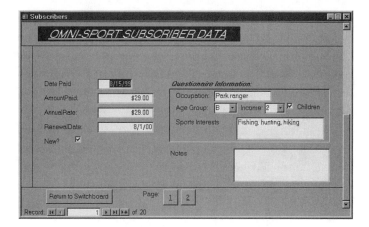

FIGURE 4.20
*Page 1 of the new
form showing
record data.*

FIGURE 4.21
*Page 2 of the
new form.*

Customizing Reports

The Database Wizard provided two report designs in the Contact Management database, neither of which is appropriate for the *Omni-Sport* application. Many of the fields in the Contacts table are different from the fields in the Subscribers table, as you saw while modifying the form design. It's easier to delete the reports created by the Database Wizard and use the Report Wizard and start fresh to create a new report.

Figure 4.22 shows a preview of a simple AutoReport-Columnar report, based on the Subscribers table, named *Subscribers of Omni-Sport*. After creating the report with the Report Wizard, you can add the company logo image and other visual features to the design.

FIGURE 4.22

A preview of the new Subscribers of Omni-Sport report.

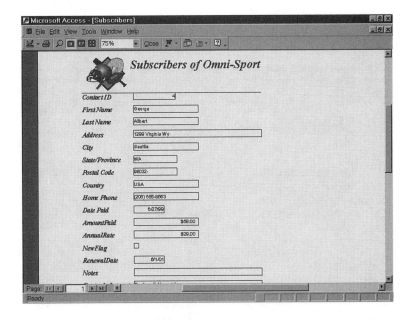

Note: If you'd been able to use one of the reports created by the Database Wizard for the Contacts Management database, you would see that the Database Wizard included the picture that was inserted in one of the dialog boxes. When you create a new report after the wizard is finished, you must insert the picture manually.

Creating Mailing Labels

Because the *Omni-Sport* business depends heavily on mailing magazines and other information to its subscribers, a mailing label report design would be very useful. You can easily create such a report using the Label Wizard:

1. Click New in the Report page and choose Label Wizard from the New Report dialog box.

2. Choose the Subscribers table as the basis for the report and then choose OK. In the next two dialog boxes, the Wizard offers lists of commercially available label stock and choices in label size, font, and color.

3. Choose Next until the Label Wizard displays a list of available fields and a Prototype label panel, where you construct the label layout.

4. Select each of the name and address fields in turn and click the right arrow. Be sure to add a space between entries and start a new line where necessary. Figure

4.23 shows the Label Wizard dialog box after the fields have been placed in the prototype label.

FIGURE 4.23

The prototype label shows all the name and address fields.

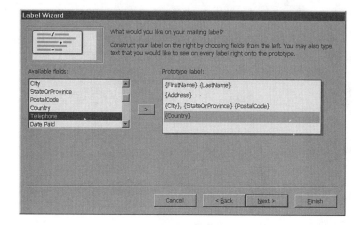

5. In the next dialog box, the Wizard offers the option of sorting the labels by one of the fields. Choose PostalCode and then click Next.

6. In the final dialog box, enter **Subscriber Labels - All** as the name for the report. Then click Finish. Figure 4.24 shows the preview of the new labels, sorted by postal code.

FIGURE 4.24

A preview of the new mailing labels, sorted by postal code.

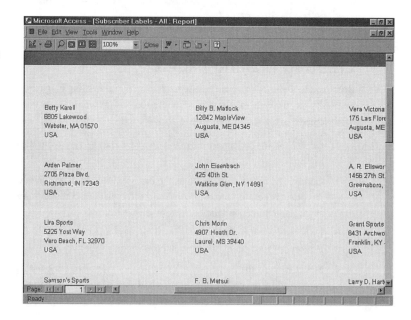

Another report that could be quite useful to the *Omni-Sport* user is a mailing label report that prints labels only for the subscribers who need to be reminded to renew their subscriptions. The easiest way to build this report is to copy the one that prints all the labels and then change the record source to a query that extracts the records for which the renewal date is close at hand.

First, create a query based on the Subscribers table, adding only the fields that make up the address plus the Renewal Date field. Then add an expression to the query design that limits the records to those with a renewal date of less than 90 days away. Type **<Date()+90** in the criteria line below RenewalDate. Of course, the records that are extracted by the query depend on the current system date as compared with the dates entered in the table.

After the query is complete, make a copy of the Subscriber Labels - All report design and save it as Labels - Renewals:

1. Right-click Subscriber Labels - All in the Report window and choose Copy from the shortcut menu.

2. Click Paste and then type **Subscriber Labels - Renewals** in the Paste Report As dialog box. Then click OK.

3. Open the new label report in design view and change its Record Source property to the query Renewals.

4. Close the design window.

It would help the *Omni-Sport* subscription staff keep track of the renewal correspondence by also printing a list of the subscribers who are reminded to renew. Figure 4.25 shows an example of a simple report created by the Report Wizard using the Renewals query as the record source. An unbound control was added to the report footer showing the total number of records in the list.

Changing the Switchboards

The last job you need to do to convert the Contact Management database for use at *Omni-Sport* is to modify the user interface. The user deals mainly with the switchboards that the Database Wizard created. You use the Switchboard Manager to change the captions in the title bars of the switchboards as well as the items listed as actions.

To change the switchboards, return to the Main Switchboard and choose Change Switchboard Items from the list. If you're in the database window, open the Switchboard form in form view and then choose Change Switchboard Items. The Switchboard Manager dialog box shows the names of all the switchboards in the database and indicates which is the default. The default switchboard is the one the appears at startup if the Display Form/Page option is set to Switchboard in the Startup dialog box (Tools|Startup).

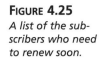

FIGURE 4.25
*A list of the sub-
scribers who need
to renew soon.*

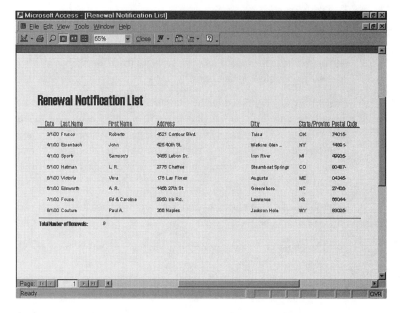

Note: The Database Wizard has provided this convenient way to reach the Switchboard Manager. When you create your own database without the help of the wizard, you can call up the Switchboard Manager by choosing Tools|Database Utilities and then clicking Switchboard Manager.

With the Switchboard Manager, you can create new switchboards, edit or delete existing ones, or change the default. Here's how to change the text in the Main Switchboard:

Tip: In the Edit Switchboard Page dialog box, you can tell which items in the list are actually subordinate switchboards by the ellipses following the text.

1. Select Main Switchboard in the list and then choose Edit. The Edit Switchboard Page dialog box appears (see Figure 4.26).

2. Change the switchboard name to **Omni-Sport Switchboard**. Next, select the Enter/View Contacts item, click Edit, and then change Contacts to **Subscribers** in the Edit Switchboard Item dialog box (see Figure 4.27).

3. The command that's executed when this item is clicked is Open Form in Edit Mode. The Command pull-down menu contains several other appropriate commands from which to choose.

4. Select Subscribers from the Form pull-down menu and click OK.

FIGURE 4.26

You modify a switchboard in the Edit Switchboard Page dialog box.

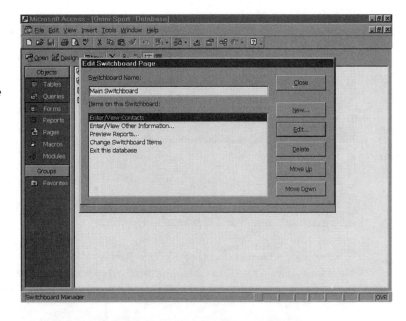

FIGURE 4.27

Change the text and resulting action in the Edit Switchboard Item dialog box.

In the Edit Switchboard Page dialog box, select the Enter/View Other Information item and click Delete. Then select the Preview Reports switchboard and click Edit to make changes in the list of report previews. Two reports are deleted and three are added. Here's how to modify the *Omni-Sport* Reports Switchboard:

1. In the Switchboard Manager dialog box, select the Reports Switchboard and then click Edit.

2. Change the name to **Omni-Sport Reports Switchboard** and then delete the both Preview items.

3. Choose New and type **Subscriber Labels - All** as the text. Select Open Report from the Command pull-down menu and select Subscriber Labels - All from the Report pull-down menu. Then click OK.

4. Repeat step 3 to add previews of the Subscriber Labels - Renewals report and the Renewal Notification List report.

Figure 4.28 shows the Edit Switchboard Page dialog box with the list of items it now includes in the *Omni-Sport* Reports switchboard. Notice that the new items appear at the bottom of the list. It's preferable to have the exit option—Return to Main Switchboard—last in the list. To move an item in the list, select the item and click the Move Up or Move Down button until the item is in the desired position.

FIGURE 4.28
The Edit Switchboard Page dialog box shows the new items at the bottom of the list.

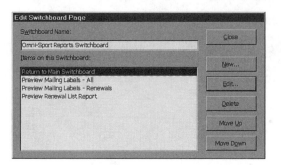

In the *Omni-Sport* Reports Switchboard, select Return to Main Switchboard and click Move Down three times. Then click Close twice. When you return to the main switchboard, test the new items to see if they perform the correct operations. Figure 4.29 shows the modified *Omni-Sport* Reports Switchboard.

FIGURE 4.29
The modified Omni-Sport switchboard.

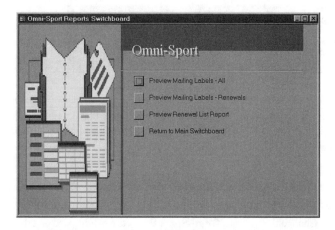

LOOKING AHEAD

Some applications greet the user with a special screen called a *splash screen*. This screen appears for only a few seconds before launching into the main switchboard. The splash screen contains no command buttons or other input controls; it just serves as a greeting upon opening the database. Chapter 5, "Examining and Modifying the Wizard's Code," delves into the program code that can accomplish such a display.

Summary

This chapter has demonstrated the use of the Database Wizard to get a start on creating a new database. After selecting from the wizard's palette of choices, you modified many of the database objects to reflect the needs of the *Omni-Sport* organization.

Not only did this chapter show how to change the table structure, but it also showed how to carry the changes over into the form, report, and switchboard designs.

The next chapter continues with the *Omni-Sport* database by examining the code that resulted from the wizard's work as well as from the changes made in this chapter. It also shows you how to make changes in the VB code to modify object properties and to control events.

Examining and Modifying the Wizard's Code

This chapter examines the database objects and code generated by the Database Wizard in Chapter 4, "Creating an Application with a Wizard." Much of the Visual Basic syntax is explained in the context of the application. After a review of the class modules, you'll make some changes that add functionality and alter the behavior and appearance of some of the controls.

Inspecting the Wizard's Creation

The Database Wizard built all the necessary components for the *Omni-Sport* database. Now it's time to open up the curtains and see what the wizard has created for you.

The *Omni-Sport* Database Objects

When you open the database, the *Omni-Sport* main switchboard appears on the screen. To see the objects the wizard built into the database, click the Database Window toolbar button. Other ways to restore the database window include choosing Window|Omni-Sport: Database or clicking the Resize button in the minimized database window at the bottom of the screen.

Tables

In the Tables page of the database window, you'll see that there are two tables in the database: the Subscribers table, which contains all the subscriber records, and a second table named Switchboard Items. The wizard created the Switchboard Items table to hold the information about all the items on all the switchboards you specified for the database. Figure 5.1 shows the Switchboard Items table in datasheet view.

The first field, SwitchboardID, identifies the individual switchboards. In this table, the main *Omni-Sport* Switchboard is named *1*, and the *Omni-Sport* Report switchboard is named *3*.

FIGURE 5.1

*The Switchboard
Items table.*

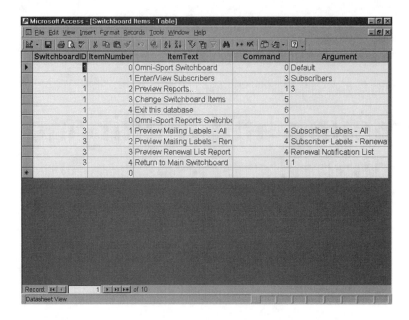

SwitchboardID	ItemNumber	ItemText	Command	Argument
1	0	Omni-Sport Switchboard	0	Default
1	1	Enter/View Subscribers	3	Subscribers
1	2	Preview Reports...	1	3
1	3	Change Switchboard Items	5	
1	4	Exit this database	6	
3	0	Omni-Sport Reports Switchbc	0	
3	1	Preview Mailing Labels - All	4	Subscriber Labels - All
3	2	Preview Mailing Labels - Ren	4	Subscriber Labels - Renewa
3	3	Preview Renewal List Report	4	Renewal Notification List
3	4	Return to Main Switchboard	1	1
	0			

ItemNumber, the second field, refers to the switchboard's caption and to each of the items on the switchboard. The items are numbered sequentially within the switchboard, with the caption numbered 0. For example, both switchboards have four items numbered 1 to 4. Each switchboard is limited to eight items by the Switchboard Manager, but you can add more manually, if necessary, later. ItemText is just that—the text that accompanies the item button on the screen.

The last two fields, Command and Argument, are used when the corresponding option is selected. The Command value determines which of nine predefined commands to execute. The Argument specifies the name of the form, report, or page to open, if any. In addition, the Argument value for the main switchboard indicates that it's the default switchboard design—the one that appears at startup if you set the Display Form/Page startup option to Switchboard.

The Command and Argument values are passed to the event procedure, the HandleButtonClick() function, that's attached to the On Click event properties of all the switchboard items and their labels. The function is called when you choose one of the switchboard options. The values in the Command and Arguments fields are passed to the function as arguments. The function uses the passed Command value in a Select Case statement to execute the correct response to the button click.

For example, if you click the first item in the main switchboard, Enter/View Subscribers, the command identified as 3 (OpenForm) is executed with the Subscribers argument, telling Access to open the form named Subscribers.

If you look at ItemNumber 2 for the main switchboard, you see that the command is 1 (GoToSwitchboard). This time the argument is 3, which is the identifier for the Preview Reports switchboard. Therefore, when this item is chosen, the version of the switchboard form that represents the Preview Reports switchboard appears.

Forms

On the Forms page of the database window are two forms: the Subscribers form that was modified in Chapter 4 from the wizard's original template and the Switchboard form. The fact that there's only one switchboard form when the application includes two switchboards might seem strange. But if you look carefully at the two switchboards, you'll see that they're the same design with different items. The Switchboard Items table contains all the items from both switchboards so that when a form opens, the switchboard number (1 or 3) determines which items to display.

Reports

The Reports page shows the three new reports used for printing labels and a list of subscribers whose subscriptions are due for renewal. These were created in Chapter 4.

Queries and Data Access Pages

The Queries page shows the query used to extract records for renewal reminders. No data access pages were created for the *Omni-Sport* database.

Macros and Modules

The Macros page is empty, but the Modules page shows a module named Global Code that contains any procedures the wizard wanted to make available to the entire application. In the "Viewing Database Code" section of this chapter, you'll see the code in this module as well as the code in the class modules for the two forms in the database.

Changing the Startup Options

The wizard designed this database for the end user so that the main switchboard always appears when the database is opened. You might not want to see this, especially if you intend to make changes to the database elements instead of run the application. As the startup options stand, it takes extra steps to remove the switchboard and restore the database window as the initial window.

> **Tip:** The easiest way to bypass the opening switchboard and all other startup options is to hold down the Shift key while you open the database.

One of the startup options available in the Startup dialog box is to display a custom form or data access page when the database opens (see Figure 5.2). To open the Startup dialog box, choose Tools|Startup. In the *Omni-Sport* database, the Display Form/Page option is

set to Switchboard, which means that when you start the database, the form specified as
the default switchboard in the Switchboard Items table appears. To change the startup so
that you open the database and view only the database window instead, click the down
arrow in the Display Form/Page box and choose (None). This change affects only this
database and will take effect the next time you open it.

FIGURE 5.2

*The Startup dialog
box.*

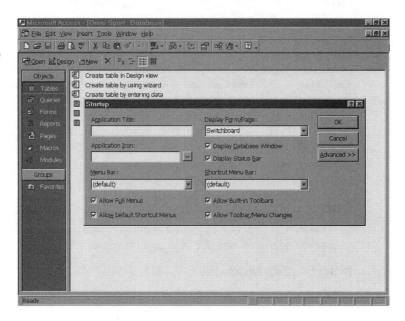

Table 5.1 describes the options in the Startup dialog box.

Table 5.1   The Startup Dialog Box Options

Option	Description
Application Title	You can enter a custom title to display in the title bar instead of the default, "Microsoft Access."
Application Icon	You can insert a custom icon to display in the title bar instead of the Microsoft Access key icon. Enter the filename.
Menu Bar	You can choose a custom menu bar to use as the default.
Allow Full Menus	Enables the user to have access to all menu commands. You can clear this option to hide menus that give the user access to design windows.

Option	Description
Allow Default Shortcut Menus	Allows access to all default shortcut menu options. You can clear this option to disable all shortcut menus.
Display Form/Page	Specifies the form or page to display upon startup.
Display Database Window	Displays the database window upon startup (minimized if a switchboard is displayed at startup).
Display Status Bar	Displays the status bar upon startup.
Shortcut Menu Bar	You can choose to display a custom shortcut menu as the default.
Allow Built-in Toolbars	Displays and permits use of the default toolbars.
Allow Toolbar/Menu Changes	You can clear this option to lock toolbars and menus. Clearing this option disables the Close button on toolbars, the right mouse button click on a toolbar, and the Tools|Customize menu command.

TROUBLESHOOTING

Note: By clicking the Advanced button, you can choose an additional startup option that deals with developing and debugging Visual Basic code. The Use Access Special Keys option lets you press special key combinations to view the database window, display the Immediate window during debugging, toggle between custom and built-in menu bars, or suspend execution and display the current module in the module window.

Any changes you make in the Startup dialog box will take place the next time you open the database.

Viewing Database Code

Access offers you several ways to get to the module window to view VB code. Without first opening the form, report, or module, you can select the name in the database window and click the Code button on the toolbar (see Figure 5.3). Access opens the object in design view and then displays the corresponding class module in the module window. If you want to view the code in one of the module objects, select the module in the Modules page and then click Design or the Code button.

If a form or report is already open in design view, you can still click the Code button to see the underlying code in the module window.

Code button

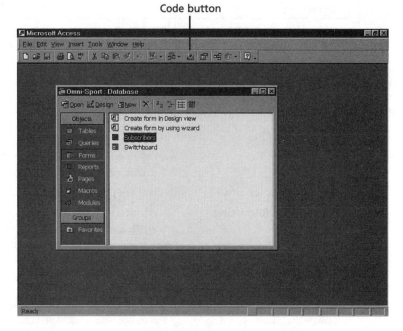

Open the module window by clicking the Code button.

The Global Code Module

The Global Code module contains a single function, IsLoaded(), created for *Omni-Sport* by the Database Wizard. IsLoaded() is a general-purpose function that sets an object's IsLoaded property to True or False, depending on the current view, and returns the value. In this case, it checks to make sure a form is open in any view but the design view before setting the property to True. Excluding access to the design view is a precaution that prevents the user from making unauthorized changes in the design. The full listing of the Global Code module is shown in Listing 5.1.

DEVELOPMENT

Listing 5.1   The Global Code Module

```
Option Compare Database
Option Explicit

Function IsLoaded(ByVal strFormName As String) As Integer
  ' Returns True if the specified form is open in Form view or Datasheet view

  Const conObjStateClosed = 0
  Const conDesignView = 0

  If SysCmd(acSysCmdGetObjectState, acForm, strFormName) <>
➥conObjStateClosed Then
```

```
    If Forms(strFormName).CurrentView <> conDesignView Then
        IsLoaded = True
    End If
  End If

End Function
```

ANALYSIS

The first Option statement sets the sort order to the same as that used in the database. The second statement requires that all variables be explicitly declared. Both these statements are added by default.

The Function statement names the function IsLoaded() and declares the return value as an integer variable. The ByVal keyword indicates that the argument strFormName will be passed by value. strFormName is also explicitly declared as a string variable.

The comment that follows the function statement describes the purpose of the function: to return a True value if the form named by the calling procedure is open in either form or datasheet view, but not in design view. This is done in the If...Then statements after two constants are declared and set to zero. The constants are then used to compare and evaluate the results of the If...Then statements.

This procedure is a good example of nested If...Then statements. Nesting If...Then statements is a way to test for a combination of conditions. Here, the first test is to see whether the form is open. If it is, the inner If...Then condition tests the type of view. The compound condition might be worded, "If the form is open but not in form view, then...."

The first If...Then statement uses the SysCmd function to test the value of the form's object state:

```
If SysCmd(acSysCmdGetObjectState, acForm, strFormName) <>
➥conObjStateClosed Then
```

The arguments in the SysCmd() function first specify the action (GetObjectState) and then the object type (acForm) followed by the object name, which is passed by value to the argument strFormName. The object name is the one selected in the Form tab of the database window. The <> symbol means *not equal*. The value of the constant conObjStateClosed is 0. So the expression in effect reads, "If the current state of the form is not closed, then..."

The ObjectState is a property of the form and has a value of 0 if the form is closed, 1 if open, 2 if new, and 3 if changed but not saved (also called *dirty*). Therefore, with the comparison operator <>, this condition is asking if the ObjectState of the form is not equal to 0 (that is, not closed). If the form is not closed, the function goes on to the next statement, where it tests for the view. If the form is closed, the condition is not met and the function ends.

The second If…Then statement uses the CurrentView property of the form to see whether it's in the design view. The values of the CurrentView property are 0 for design view, 1 for form view, and 2 for datasheet view. The condition

```
Forms.(strFormName).CurrentView <> conDesignView
```

uses the standard Forms collection identifier with the form name value that was passed to the function to compare the CurrentView property with the conDesignView constant, which was set to 0. If the CurrentView property equals 0, the form is in design view and the function ends. If the CurrentView property is any other value, the IsLoaded property is set to True. The function ends and control is returned to the calling procedure.

This is a fairly simple block of code, but you can see that even a simple function can involve many intricate details. The class modules for the Switchboard and Subscribers forms are much more complicated but still can be interpreted with patience.

The Switchboard Form Class Module

The Switchboard form class module created by the Database Wizard consists of four procedures:

- Subprocedure Form_Open minimizes the database window and opens the switchboard page that's marked as the default.
- Subprocedure Form_Current updates the form caption and calls the procedure that fills in the list of options.
- Subprocedure FillOptions adds the options to the switchboard. The list of options depends on which form is to be displayed. Both switchboards use the same form design with different options, as defined by the Switchboard Items table.
- Function procedure HandleButtonClick() responds to a button click that selects a switchboard option.

Each of these procedures is described in the next sections.

LOOKING AHEAD

For more explanation about the statements in this and later modules, see Chapter 9, "Writing Visual Basic Procedures."

Initializing the Switchboard Form

When the database first opens, the options selected in the Startup dialog box take effect. In this database, the Display Database Window option is selected so that the database window opens first. The Display Form/Page option is set to the default Switchboard form so that after the database window is opened and minimized, the Switchboard page appears.

The Form_Open procedure is specified in the form property sheet as the event procedure for the switchboard form's On Open event property. When you click the Code button with the Switchboard form selected in the database window, the module window opens showing the procedure code (see Figure 5.4). The two boxes above the code pane show the name of the current object (Form) and the procedure (Open). The full listing of the Form_Open procedure is shown in Listing 5.2.

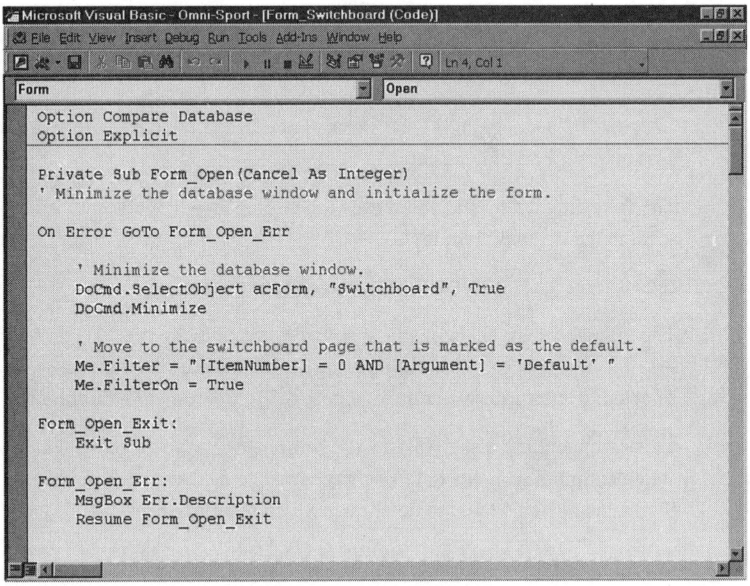

FIGURE 5.4

The Form_Open *procedure is the event procedure attached to the* On Open *event.*

Listing 5.2   The Sub Form_Open Procedure

```
Private Sub Form_Open(Cancel As Integer)
' Minimize the database window and initialize the form.

On Error GoTo Form_Open_Err

  ' Minimize the database window.
  DoCmd.SelectObject acForm, "Switchboard", True
  DoCmd.Minimize

  ' Move to the switchboard page that is marked as the default.
  Me.Filter = "[ItemNumber] = 0 AND [Argument] = 'Default' "
  Me.FilterOn = True

Form_Open_Exit:
  Exit Sub

Form_Open_Err:
  MsgBox Err.Description
  Resume Form_Open_Exit

End Sub
```

Notice that all the procedures the wizard has created include an `On Error` statement that branches to an error-handling routine. In this procedure, `On Error` sends control to the `Form_Open_Err` line, which displays the error message and then passes control to the `Form_Open_Exit` line. `Form_Open_Exit:` and `Form_Open_Err:` are line labels used as branch destinations for the `GoTo` and `Resume` commands. The error-handling routine is always placed after the exit routine so that it will be executed only if an error occurs and control branches to it.

Chapter 10, "Debugging Visual Basic Procedures," contains information about adding custom error-handling features to your procedures.

The following `DoCmd` statement uses the `SelectObject` method to select the Switchboard form in the database window:

```
DoCmd.SelectObject acForm, "Switchboard", True
```

The arguments are `acForm`, which specifies the object type, `"Switchboard"`, which names the object, and `True`, which indicates that the object in the database window is to be selected. If the form were already open, the last argument would be `False`.

This command merely highlights the form name in the database window. The next `DoCmd` statement minimizes the database window. The next two statements use the values in the Switchboard Items table to determine which form to open:

```
Me.Filter = "[ItemNumber] = 0 AND [Argument] = 'Default' "
  Me.FilterOn = True
```

`Me.Filter` sets the filter property to the switchboard form that's specified as the default. ItemNumber and Argument are fields in the Switchboard Items table. An item with a value of `0` is a switchboard, and one with `Default` as the Argument value is the main switchboard. The second statement activates the filter. The switchboard is not yet displayed—the caption and options must be specified first.

Updating the Switchboard Caption

The `Form_Current` procedure is called when the form becomes current; it's specified as the event procedure for the form's `On Current` event property. If no caption has been specified in the Switchboard Items table, the title bar remains blank. The complete procedure is shown in Listing 5.3.

Listing 5.3 The `Sub Form_Current` Procedure

```
Private Sub Form_Current()
' Update the caption and fill in the list of options.

  Me.Caption = Nz(Me![ItemText], "")
  FillOptions

End Sub
```

ANALYSIS

Computers can behave irrationally when things are not completely defined. For example, when a computer encounters a blank where it expects a value, it doesn't know what to do unless you tell it how to respond.

The Nz() function is used to do just that. The first argument in the function is the name of the field value to return, and the second argument is what to return if the field is blank. If the value is Null, the Nz() function can return a zero, a zero-length string, or some other value, such as N/A or Unknown.

Here, the Nz() function sets the Caption property of the current form (Me) to the ItemText value in the Switchboard Items table. If the ItemText value is blank (Null), the function sets the caption to a zero-length string (""), and no text will appear in the switchboard title bar.

The last statement, FillOptions, branches to the FillOptions subprocedure to add the options to the switchboard.

Filling in the Switchboard Options

Because the same form design is used for both switchboards in this database, each time you open a switchboard, the items need to be refreshed. The FillOptions procedure is called from the Form_Current procedure after the caption has been determined.

This is a rather complex procedure that uses a SQL statement to build a query that retrieves the items that go with the open switchboard. All of this happens before the switchboard finally appears on the screen. A complete listing of the FillOptions procedure is shown in Listing 5.4.

Listing 5.4   The Sub FillOptions Procedure

```
Private Sub FillOptions()
' Fill in the options for this switchboard page.

  ' The number of buttons on the form.
  Const conNumButtons = 8

  Dim con As Object
  Dim rs As Object
  Dim stSQL As String
  Dim intOption As Integer

  ' Set the focus to the first button on the form,
  ' and then hide all of the buttons on the form
  ' but the first. You can't hide the field with the focus.
  Me![Option1].SetFocus
  For intOption = 2 To conNumButtons
    Me("Option" & intOption).Visible = False
    Me("OptionLabel" & intOption).Visible = False
```

continues

Listing 5.4 Continued

```
Next intOption

' Open the table of Switchboard Items, and find
' the first item for this Switchboard Page.
Set con = Application.CurrentProject.Connection
stSQL = "SELECT * FROM [Switchboard Items]"
stSQL = stSQL & " WHERE [ItemNumber] > 0 AND "
➡ & "[SwitchboardID]=" & Me![SwitchboardID]
stSQL = stSQL & " ORDER BY [ItemNumber];"
Set rs = CreateObject("ADODB.Recordset")
rs.Open stSQL, con,1      '1 = adOpenKeyset

' If there are no options for this Switchboard Page,
' display a message. Otherwise, fill the page with the items.
If (rs.EOF) Then
  Me![OptionLabel1].Caption = "There are no items for
  ➡this switchboard page"
Else
  While (Not (rs.EOF))
    Me("Option" & rs![ItemNumber]).Visible = True
    Me("OptionLabel" & rs![ItemNumber]).Visible = True
    Me("OptionLabel" & rs![ItemNumber]).Caption = rst![ItemText]
    rs.MoveNext
  Wend
End If

' Close the recordset and the database.
rs.Close
Set rs = Nothing
Set con = Nothing

End Sub
```

ANALYSIS

The first declaration sets the constant conNumButtons, which establishes the maximum number of buttons on a switchboard equal to 8. Next, four variables are declared for later use: two ADO objects representing a database and a recordset, a string of SQL code, and an integer. The recordset variable, rs, represents the records from the Switchboard Items table that belong to the form that's opening—the results of running the SQL query. The integer serves as an index for the list of switchboard items.

After the Declarations section, the procedure concentrates on the switchboard options with this code fragment:

```
Me![Option1].SetFocus
  For intOption = 2 To conNumButtons
    Me("Option" & intOption).Visible = False
    Me("OptionLabel" & intOption).Visible = False
  Next intOption
```

Me![Option1].SetFocus moves focus to the first button on the form. The For…Next loop runs through the remaining options and their labels, from number 2 to number 8, hiding them by setting their Visible properties to False, one by one.

The next block of code sets the database variable, con, to the newly opened database (*Omni-Sport* in this case), creates a SQL statement to extract the options and their labels from the Switchboard Items table that apply to the current switchboard page, and then creates a new recordset out of the results of the query:

```
Set con = Application.CurrentProject.Connection
  stSQL = "SELECT * FROM [Switchboard Items]"
  stSQL = strSQL & " WHERE [ItemNumber] > 0 AND
➥[SwitchboardID]=" & Me![SwitchboardID]
  stSQL = strSQL & " ORDER BY [ItemNumber];"
  Set rs = CreateObject(ADODB.Recordset")
  rs.Open stSQL, con, 1        '1 = adOpenKeyset
```

It takes three statements to build the SQL code only because the screen is not wide enough for you to see the whole thing on one line. The three strings are concatenated together as they are constructed to form the complete SQL statement. The first line, SELECT * FROM [Switchboard Items], selects all the fields in the Switchboard Items table. The second line imposes the selection criteria and adds it to the first string with the & character. The criteria finds records whose ItemNumber value is greater than 0 (not a switchboard, itself) and whose SwitchboardID value is the same as the current form. The third line sorts the options by ItemNumber values.

The Set rs statement creates the new recordset object as an ADO database recordset. The final statement uses the Open method to open the recordset, specifying the source as the stSQL statement and the active connection, con, as the current database. The final argument in the Open method, 1, is the value of the adOpenKeyset constant. Refer to the Visual Basic Open Method (ADO Recordset) Help topic for more specific information about the Open method and its arguments.

LOOKING AHEAD

For more information about creating SQL statements, turn to Chapter 7, "Programming with SQL."

The next code segment actually places the items in the switchboard form after checking to make sure there's at least one item for the form:

```
If (rs.EOF) Then
    Me![OptionLabel1].Caption = "There are no items for
    ➥this switchboard page"
  Else
    While (Not (rs.EOF))
      Me("Option" & rs![ItemNumber]).Visible = True
      Me("OptionLabel" & rs![ItemNumber]).Visible = True
      Me("OptionLabel" & rs![ItemNumber]).Caption = rs![ItemText]
      rs.MoveNext
    Wend
  End If
```

If the query has not found any records, the recordset will already be at the end of file (EOF), and rs.EOF will have a value of True. The If…Then statement displays a message to that effect and branches to End If.

If there are options in the recordset, the While…Wend loop in the Else structure proceeds to add each item button and label to the switchboard form and then displays the switchboard caption in the title bar. The While…Wend loop continues until it reaches the end of the item list created by the query.

The final statements in the FillOptions procedure close the recordset created by the query, clear the rs and con variables, and then close the database.

Responding to Switchboard Selections

The HandleButtonClick() function is the most complex Switchboard form event procedure. It's specified as the event procedure for the On Click event property of every button on every switchboard form. The identity of the button that has been clicked must be passed to the function so that it can choose the appropriate action. The function uses the Select Case structure to recognize which button was clicked and to select the action.

LOOKING AHEAD Chapter 6, "How to Get Help with Access Programming," contains information about how to get help with macros, SQL, and VB programming.

Listing 5.5 shows the complete HandleButtonClick() function.

Listing 5.5   The HandleButtonClick() Function

```
Private Function HandleButtonClick(intBtn As Integer)
' This function is called when a button is clicked.
' intBtn indicates which button was clicked.

  ' Constants for the commands that can be executed.
  Const conCmdGotoSwitchboard = 1
  Const conCmdOpenFormAdd = 2
  Const conCmdOpenFormBrowse = 3
  Const conCmdOpenReport = 4
  Const conCmdCustomizeSwitchboard = 5
  Const conCmdExitApplication = 6
  Const conCmdRunMacro = 7
  Const conCmdRunCode = 8
  Const conCmdOpenPage = 9

  ' An error that is special cased.
  Const conErrDoCmdCancelled = 2501

  Dim con As Object
  Dim rs As Object
  Dim stSQL As String

On Error GoTo HandleButtonClick_Err
```

```
' Find the item in the Switchboard Items table
 ' that corresponds to the button that was clicked.
 Set con = Application.CurrentProject.Connection
 Set rs = CreateObject("ADODB.Recordset")
 stSql = "SELECT * FROM [Switchboard Items] "
 stSql = stSql & "WHERE [SwitchboardID]=" & Me![SwitchboardID] &
➥" AND [ItemNumber]=" & intBtn
 rs.Open stSql, con, 1  ' 1 = adOpenKeyset

 ' If no item matches, report the error and exit the function.
 If (rs.EOF) Then
   MsgBox "There was an error reading the Switchboard Items table."
   rs.Close
   Set rs = Nothing
   Set con = Nothing
   Exit Function
 End If

 Select Case rs![Command]

   ' Go to another switchboard.
   Case conCmdGotoSwitchboard
     Me.Filter = "[ItemNumber] = 0 AND [SwitchboardID]="
     ➥ & rs![Argument]

   ' Open a form in Add mode.
   Case conCmdOpenFormAdd
     DoCmd.OpenForm rs![Argument], , , , acAdd

   ' Open a form.
   Case conCmdOpenFormBrowse
     DoCmd.OpenForm rs![Argument]

   ' Open a report.
   Case conCmdOpenReport
     DoCmd.OpenReport rs![Argument], acPreview

   ' Customize the Switchboard.
   Case conCmdCustomizeSwitchboard
     ' Handle the case where the Switchboard Manager
     ' is not installed (e.g. Minimal Install).
     On Error Resume Next
     Application.Run "ACWZMAIN.sbm_Entry"
     If (Err <> 0) Then MsgBox "Command not available."
     On Error GoTo 0
     ' Update the form.
     Me.Filter = "[ItemNumber] = 0 AND [Argument] = 'Default' "
     Me.Caption = Nz(Me![ItemText], "")
     FillOptions
```

continues

Listing 5.5   Continued

```
      ' Exit the application.
      Case conCmdExitApplication
         CloseCurrentDatabase

      ' Run a macro.
      Case conCmdRunMacro
         DoCmd.RunMacro rs![Argument]

      ' Run code.
      Case conCmdRunCode
         Application.Run rs![Argument]

      ' Open a Data Access Page
      Case conCmdOpenPage
         DoCmd.OpenDataAccessPage rs![Argument]

      ' Any other command is unrecognized.
      Case Else
         MsgBox "Unknown option."

   End Select


   ' Close the recordset and the database.
   rs.Close

HandleButtonClick_Exit:
   On Error Resume Next
   Set rs = Nothing
   Set con = Nothing
   Exit Function

HandleButtonClick_Err:
   ' If the action was cancelled by the user for
   ' some reason, don't display an error message.
   ' Instead, resume on the next line.
   If (Err = conErrDoCmdCancelled) Then
      Resume Next
   Else
      MsgBox "There was an error executing the command.", vbCritical
      Resume HandleButtonClick_Exit
   End If

End Function
```

ANALYSIS

At the beginning of this function, nine constants are declared as numbers (from 1 to 9). These are general-purpose constants that represent the set of commands that can be executed when a button is clicked. If you take a look at the Switchboard Items table, you'll see that four of them are not used in the *Omni-Sport* switchboards. None of the switchboard items in this application opens a form to add new records (command 2), runs a macro (command 7), runs code (command 8), or opens a data access page (command 9).

The next statement declares a specific error message to be displayed if the user cancels the application for some reason. Then, two variables, con and rs, are declared as objects. A string SQL statement, stSQL, is also declared.

The On Error statement contains a GoTo command that branches to the HandleButtonClick_Err line to resume processing or display an error message and quit the function. The error routine appears at the end of the function after the Exit Function statement.

The first block of code following the declarations section looks for the option in the Switchboard Items list that matches the button that was clicked:

```
Set con = Application.CurrentProject.Connection
Set rs = CreateObject("ADODB.Recordset")
stSql = "SELECT * FROM [Switchboard Items] "
stSql = stSql & "WHERE [SwitchboardID]=" & Me![SwitchboardID] &
➥" AND [ItemNumber]=" & intBtn
rs.Open stSql, con, 1   ' 1 = adOpenKeyset

' If no item matches, report the error and exit the function.
If (rs.EOF) Then
  MsgBox "There was an error reading the Switchboard Items table."
  rs.Close
  Set rs = Nothing
  Set con = Nothing
  Exit Function
End If
```

These statements are similar to those in the FillOptions subprocedure. The first two statements set the con variable to the current database and the rs variable to a new ADO database recordset. The stSQL statement defines the one record to be included in the new recordset as the item in the switchboard table that corresponds to the button that was clicked.

If there's no match in the switchboard items list, the recordset is empty. An error message is displayed, and the recordset is closed; then the variables are cleared and the function exits.

DEVELOPMENT

This function presents a good example of the Select Case technique of executing alternative code segments. The case structure is used when a procedure must decide among several mutually exclusive courses of action. If…Then statements are used when there are only two ways to go. Nested If…Then statements can handle one or two additional decision points, but when there are more than that, the Select Case approach is much more efficient. The following sample code illustrates the principle behind the Select Case structure:

```
Select Case X        'Base path on value of X
  Case 1         'If X = 1, do this:
    · - - - - - -
    · - - - - - -
    · - - - - - -
    go to end
  Case 2         'If X = 2, do this:
    · - - - - - -
    · - - - - - -
    · - - - - - -
    go to end
  Case 3         'If X = 3, do this:
    · - - - - - -
    · - - - - - -
    · - - - - - -
    go to end
  Case Else      'If X not equal to 1, 2, or, 3
    · - - - - - - 'do this:
    · - - - - - -
End Select
```

The next block of HandleButtonClick code contains the Select Case statements that
execute the commands associated with the buttons. Most of the Case statements require
the value from the Argument field in the Switchboard Items table to be passed to the
command. The only one that doesn't need an argument is the command to close the
application.

```
Select Case rs![Command]

    ' Go to another switchboard.
    Case conCmdGotoSwitchboard
      Me.Filter = "[ItemNumber] = 0 AND [SwitchboardID]="
      ➥ & rs![Argument]

    ' Open a form in Add mode.
    Case conCmdOpenFormAdd
      DoCmd.OpenForm rs![Argument], , , , acAdd

    ' Open a form.
    Case conCmdOpenFormBrowse
      DoCmd.OpenForm rs![Argument]

    ' Open a report.
    Case conCmdOpenReport
      DoCmd.OpenReport rs![Argument], acPreview

    ' Customize the Switchboard.
    Case conCmdCustomizeSwitchboard
      ' Handle the case where the Switchboard Manager
      ' is not installed (e.g. Minimal Install).
      On Error Resume Next
```

```
        Application.Run "ACWZMAIN.sbm_Entry"
        If (Err <> 0) Then MsgBox "Command not available."
        On Error GoTo 0
        ' Update the form.
        Me.Filter = "[ItemNumber] = 0 AND [Argument] = 'Default' "
        Me.Caption = Nz(Me![ItemText], "")
        FillOptions

    ' Exit the application.
    Case conCmdExitApplication
        CloseCurrentDatabase

    ' Run a macro.
    Case conCmdRunMacro
        DoCmd.RunMacro rs![Argument]

    ' Run code.
    Case conCmdRunCode
        Application.Run rs![Argument]

    'Open a Data Access Page
    Case conOpenDataAccessPage
        DoCmd.OpenDataAccessPage rs![Argument]

    ' Any other command is unrecognized.
    Case Else
        MsgBox "Unknown option."

End Select
```

The first Case segment executes an option that displays another switchboard form. It sets
the destination switchboard with the Filter property of the current form. The filter specifies an ItemNumber value of 0 (a switchboard), so it considers only the switchboard
forms. It also sets the SwitchboardID to the value found in the item's Argument field. For
example, look at the third line in the Switchboard Items table, which is item 2 on the
main switchboard. The Command value is 1 (GoToSwitchboard), and the Argument value
is 3, the switchboard ID for the Preview Reports switchboard.

The second Case command opens a form for adding new records using the acAdd constant. The argument passed to the OpenForm method specifies which form to open. The
form appears with a blank record on the screen. The third command opens the form for
browsing and displays the first record in the recordset. The fourth command opens a
report preview. The argument passed to the OpenReport method is the name of the report.

The fifth command takes you to the Switchboard Manager, if it's installed. If it's not
installed, a runtime error occurs when the Application.Run command is reached. The On
Error Resume Next statement that precedes this tells Access to skip the statement that
caused the error and move to the next command after it.

If the Switchboard Manager is not installed, the `Application.Run` command will cause an error, so execution moves to the `If...Then` statement that evaluates the error number. If the error number is not `0` (that is, a runtime error did in fact occur), the error message is displayed. Then `On Error GoTo 0` disables the error handler. The last three statements in this `Case` block open the switchboard form, update the caption, and call the `FillOptions` procedure to implement the changes made with the Switchboard Manager, if any.

The next four `Case` blocks close the current database, run the specified macro, run the specified application, and open the data access page specified as the argument for the switchboard item.

The `Case Else` code block is the catchall for any alternatives that are not considered in the earlier `Case` statements. This displays an error message saying that Access doesn't recognize the option selected.

The last code segments are part of the `Exit` subroutine. They close the recordset and the database, clear the declared variables, and exit the function. Following the `Exit` subroutine, the `HandleButtonClick_Err` subroutine displays an error message only if the error was a runtime error and was not caused by the user canceling the execution.

> **Tip:** If you look at the property sheets for the buttons and their labels, you'll see that both controls have an event procedure attached to the `On Click` event property. This means that you don't have to click squarely on the button—you can click anywhere in the item label and the same event will occur. This is a standard convenience for the user.

The Subscribers Form Class Module

When you click the Code button to see the class module for the Subscribers form, you'll see that procedures that apply to the buttons you removed from the Contacts form are still there. The Calls and Dial buttons were deleted, but their `On Click` event procedures remain. There are also two subprocedures that refer to the Contact Type ID combo box. All four of these procedures can safely be deleted from the module by selecting the text in the module window and pressing Delete.

After you delete the unwanted procedures, the remaining Subscribers form class module is much simpler than the Switchboard module. It consists of three event procedures that correspond to the three command buttons on the form: Return to Switchboard, Page 1, and Page 2 (see Figure 5.5). These procedures were developed by the wizards and are straightforward. The complete Subscribers form class module is shown in Listing 5.6.

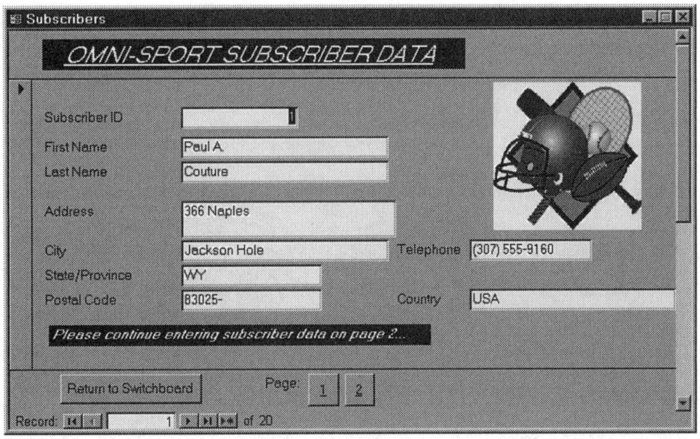

Figure 5.5

Command buttons in the Subscribers form footer.

Listing 5.6   The Subscribers Form Class Module

```
Option Compare Database
Option Explicit

Private Sub Page1_Click()
  Me.GoToPage 1
End Sub

Private Sub Page2_Click()
  Me.GoToPage 2
End Sub

Private Sub Go_To_Switchboard_Click()
On Error GoTo Err_Go_To_Switchboard_Click

  DoCmd.Close

Exit_Go_To_Switchboard_Click:
  Exit Sub

Err_Go_To_Switchboard_Click:
  MsgBox Err.Description
  Resume Exit_Go_To_Switchboard_Click

End Sub
```

The first two procedures, Page1_Click and Page2_Click, are the event procedures that execute when you click the 1 and 2 buttons in the form footer. These were included in the database template and contain no error-handling routines.

The third procedure, Go_To_Switchboard, closes the form when the Return to Switchboard button is clicked. This procedure was created by the Command Button

Wizard and contains an error handler. Notice that the procedure name reflects the name you entered for the command button when you were creating it with the Command Button Wizard. If you had not entered a custom name, the procedure name would be simply Command*n*_Click.

> **Tip:** The Return to Switchboard button returns you to the main switchboard only if you've opened the form by choosing Enter/Review Subscribers from the main switchboard. If you opened the form from the Forms page of the database window, you'll return to the database window instead.

Maximizing the Main Switchboard

If you want the opening switchboard to fill the screen when the database opens, you can add a command to the Switchboard form class module. In the first procedure, Form_Open, add the command DoCmd.Maximize just before the Form_Open_Exit line.

Modifying the Subscribers Form

Although the Database Wizard did an admirable job creating the *Omni-Sport* database, there are still some fine touches yet to add and other things to change. For example, it would be easier to enter new subscribers records if the form had a combo box for the payment method. This way, the user could simply choose from the pull-down list instead of typing the data.

The form doesn't really need scrollbars, so they can be removed. Also, the Return to Switchboard command button lacks an accelerator key. Finally, the Page 2 command button would be more informative with a ScreenTip.

An added convenience would be to automatically calculate the new renewal date after an Amount Paid value has been entered.

In the next sections, these changes are made to the Subscribers form—some from the property sheet and others with VB code.

Changing a Text Box to a Combo Box

To change a control type in a form, you first select the control in the design view and then choose Format|Change To. You also can right-click the control and select Change To in the shortcut menu. Figure 5.6 shows the Change To options available for a text box control. You can change a text box to a label, list box, or combo box.

When you change a text box to either a list box or combo box, you must specify the value list from which the user can choose. After selecting Combo Box as the new control type, open the property sheet for the control and add the following property settings:

- Choose Value List as the row source type.
- Type **"Check";"Cash";"Credit Card"** in the Row Source property line (see Figure 5.7).

FIGURE 5.6

Changing a text box control to a combo box.

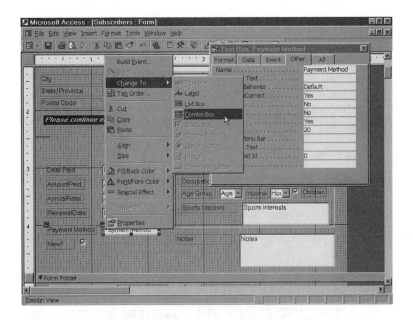

FIGURE 5.7

Adding a value list as a row source.

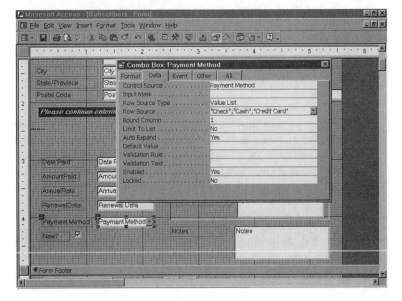

Each of the values is enclosed in quotation marks, and they're separated by semicolons. The pull-down list in the Row Source property displays a list of all the tables and queries in the database. Figure 5.8 shows the form with the new combo box.

The Limit To List property is set to No by default, which allows the user to enter a value not specified in the list. If you don't want any other values in the Payment Method field, set this property to Yes.

FIGURE 5.8
The Subscribers form with the new combo box.

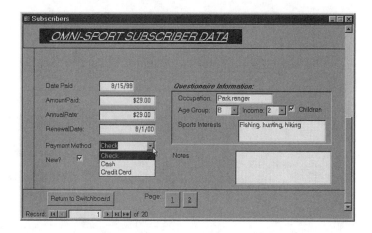

Changing Form and Control Properties with Visual Basic

You already know how to change form and control properties using the property sheet. For example, to add a ScreenTip to a command button, enter the text of the tip in the Control Tip property. Instead of using the property sheets to change simple properties, let's take a look at how to do the same thing with a Visual Basic procedure.

The form and control property changes are easily done with a single VB event procedure that executes when the form is opened. To create the Form_Open() subprocedure, click the Build button next to the On Open event property and choose Code Builder from the Choose Builder dialog box. The existing Subscribers form class module opens in the module window with the beginnings of the new procedure, named Form_Open.

> **Tip:** While you're entering code in the module window, you can switch back and forth between the form design view and the module window by clicking the View Microsoft Access toolbar button (the rightmost button on the Visual Basic Standard toolbar). This is very useful for checking control names and properties.

To remove the scrollbars from the form, change the `ScrollBars` property to `0`, which is the value for the Neither option, by typing **Me.Scrollbars = 0**. Me refers to the current object (which is the form), and `Scrollbars` is a property of the form.

Next, change the caption of the Return to Switchboard button to identify the letter *R* as the accelerator key by placing an ampersand (&) symbol in front of it. Type the following command:

```
Me![Go To Switchboard].Caption = "&Return to Switchboard"
```

Notice that the name of the button is not the same as the caption. If in doubt, you can look at the `Name` property for the button. If they don't match, you'll get an error message.

The last change is to add a ScreenTip to the Page 2 command button. Type the following command:

```
Me![Page2].ControlTipText = "Click to enter data on page 2."
```

The exclamation point following `Me` in this command means that what follows is a user-named object, not an Access-named object. `ControlTipText` is a property of the command button.

The procedure looks like this after these commands are added:

```
Private Sub Form_Open(Cancel As Integer)

'Remove scrollbars add an accelerator key to the
'Return to Switchboard button and add a ControlTip
'to the Page2 button.

  Me.ScrollBars = 0
  Me![Go To Switchboard].Caption = "&Return to Switchboard"
  Me![Page2].ControlTipText =
➥ "Click to enter data on page 2."

End Sub
```

Figure 5.9 shows the Subscribers form with a ScreenTip and the new accelerator key—the underlined *R*.

> **Tip:** When you're building VB procedures, remember to add plenty of comments reminding you of what each segment of code is intended to do. You won't be sorry.

Updating a Field Value

To automatically update the Renewal Date field, create a procedure that calculates the new date after the Amount Paid field is updated. This requires some date arithmetic as well as computing the number of months that have been paid for. The event procedure is attached to the `AfterUpdate` event of the Amount Paid text box control so that it changes the renewal date only if an amount has been entered in the Amount Paid field.

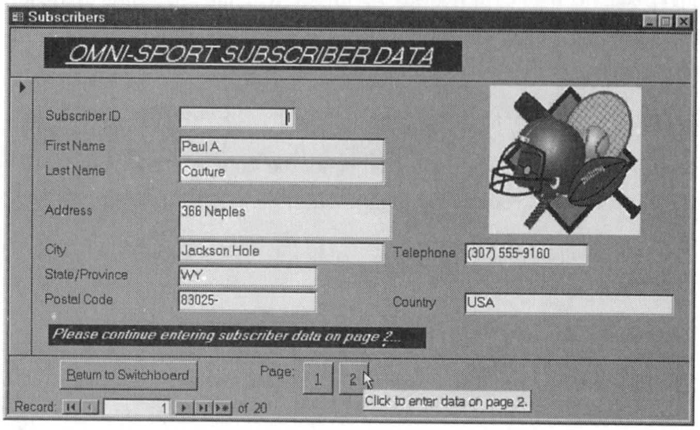

FIGURE 5.9
*The modified
Subscribers form.*

To create this procedure, select the Amount Paid text box and open the Code Builder from the `AfterUpdate` event property. First, declare two variables as variant data types: `varMonths`, which will contain the number of paid months, and `varResult`, which represents the value in the Renewal Date field. Type the declaration statement **`Dim varMonths As Variant, varResult As Variant`**.

> **Tip:** If you don't specify a data type in the `Dim` statement, Access automatically assumes a Variant type, but it's always a good idea to be completely explicit in Visual Basic code.

DEVELOPMENT

TROUBLESHOOTING

A problem can occur when you enter new subscriber information because the Renewal Date field is empty, which Access looks at as null. Therefore, the procedure must make provisions for a `Null` value using the `Nz()` function, which specifies a value to use if the field is null. For simplicity, set the value to today's date if Renewal Date is blank with the following statement:

```
dtmResult = Nz(RenewalDate, Date)
```

Then, when the amount paid is entered, the renewal date is advanced by the number of months paid for.

Next, compute the number of months by dividing the amount paid by the annual rate and multiplying by 12:

```
varMonths = AmountPaid / AnnualRate * 12
```

Be sure the Annual Rate field contains a value; otherwise, you'll get an error message about trying to divide by 0. You can set the default value in the table structure or in the form design to be sure there is one.

Finally, compute the renewal date by adding the number of paid months to the value already in the Renewal Date field:

```
RenewalDate = DateSerial(Year(varResult), Month(varResult) + varMonths, 1)
```

This statement uses the DateSerial function to compute the new date. The arguments are year, month, and day, and the function returns a date variable. In this example, the year argument is extracted from the RenewalDate value. The month argument is also obtained from the Renewal Date field but with the bytMonths value added to it. The day argument is specified as 1, the first day of the month. Therefore, if a subscriber has a renewal date of February 12, 2000 and has paid for 18 months of magazines, his new renewal date would be July 1, 2002.

LOOKING AHEAD

If you want to see how to step through code to test it as you write it, turn to Chapter 10.

The complete procedure is shown in Listing 5.7. Note that an underscore character at the end of a line indicates a continuation of the statement on the next line.

Listing 5.7   Adding a Calculated Field

```
Private Sub AmountPaid_AfterUpdate()
'Update the Renewal Date field after entering payment amount.

  Dim varMonths As Variant, varResult As Variant

'Set Renewal Date to today if Renewal Date is blank.
  varResult = Nz(RenewalDate, Date)

  varMonths = [AmountPaid] / [AnnualRate] * 12

  RenewalDate = DateSerial(Year(varResult), Month(varResult) + _
    varMonths, 1)

End Sub
```

Note: When a field is calculated from the value entered into another field, it can be a good idea to keep the user from having access to the calculated field. To do this, change the Tab Stop property to No. If you want the user to be able to override the automatic calculation, keep the Tab Stop property as Yes.

Adding a New Report

To find out which subscribers enjoy a particular sport, you can construct a query to extract the records with *baseball*, for example, somewhere in the Sports Interests field. After creating a new report based on the selection query, the report can be added to the Preview Reports switchboard with the help of the Switchboard Manager.

Figure 5.10 shows a new query that retrieves all the fields in the Subscribers table but selects only those records with *baseball* or *basketball* in the Sports Interests field. Notice that the Show check box is cleared in the Sports Interests column used as the criterion so that you don't have two instances of the field in the query result. Figure 5.11 shows a simple tabular report based on the query.

FIGURE 5.10
The query that selects baseball and basketball fans.

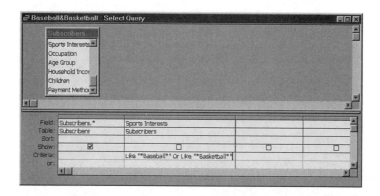

FIGURE 5.11
The Baseball and Basketball Fans report.

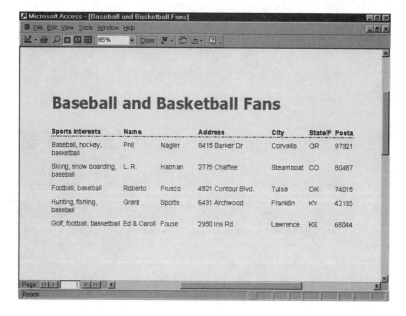

To add this new report to the Preview Reports switchboard, open the Switchboard Manager by choosing from the main switchboard items. Then follow these steps:

1. Select the *Omni-Sport* Reports Switchboard in the Switchboard Manager dialog box and click Edit.

2. Click New in the Edit Switchboard Page dialog box.

3. In the Edit Switchboard Item dialog box, enter **Preview Baseball/Basketball Fans** as the text.

> **Warning:** If you try to use the ampersand (&) character in a switchboard item caption, it will turn out as a short underline character. The & symbol is a reserved character in Access.

4. Select Open Report as the command. Select the Baseball and Basketball Fans report and then click OK.

5. In the Edit Switchboard Page dialog box, click Move Up once to place the new item above the Return to Main Switchboard item. Then click Close twice to return to the main switchboard.

Figure 5.12 shows the *Omni-Sport* Reports Switchboard with the new report listed as one of the items.

Figure 5.12
The new report item in the Omni-Sport Reports Switchboard.

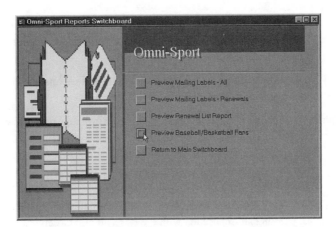

If you look at the Switchboard Items table after adding the new item, you can see the new item 4 for the Preview Reports switchboard that previews the new report. The last item, Return to Main Switchboard, has moved to item 5 in the list because the new item was moved up in the Edit Switchboard Page dialog box.

The new report seems limited in its scope. It would be more useful if the user were able to enter the sport to look for. To do this, the command attached to the switchboard item would have to be either Run Macro (7) or Run Code (8) instead of Open Report.

The procedure would use an InputBox() function, like this:

```
stSport = InputBox("Please enter a sport.", "Get Sport Fans")
```

This displays the input box shown in Figure 5.13. The function specifies the message to instruct the user and the title of the box. It returns the name of the sport entered by the user.

FIGURE 5.13

The user enters the sport of interest.

Next, a SQL statement uses this value to create a query that selects records from the Subscribers table that contain the word somewhere in the Sports Interests field. Finally, the report based on the query is opened for preview.

You could even design the input box to accept two or three sports and then create the query to look for all of them.

Another way to enable the user to enter a sport of interest is to base the report on a parameter query that prompts for one or more sport names.

Summary

This chapter has explored the tables, forms, and reports the Database Wizard created in Chapter 4, "Creating an Application with a Wizard." It also closely examined the Visual Basic modules that enable the database to function smoothly as well as how to change the database startup options.

After interpreting the code in the form class modules, changes were made to alter the form's appearance and the behavior of some of the controls. Changes were also made to the switchboards that act as the user interface.

In the next chapter, "How to Get Help with Access Programming," you'll see the many ways you can receive help from Access and Visual Basic while you're building databases.

How to Get Help with Access Programming

Access is a very helpful mentor. It offers help, both online and as a lookup tool. If you get into trouble, you can click a button, and a context-sensitive message appears with useful guidance and explanations. If you have a specific question, you can contact the omniscient Office Assistant. Help can be close at hand, even via the World Wide Web. The completely redesigned Help feature in Office 2000 is much more versatile than previous versions.

You probably have sought help while learning to use Access, but this chapter goes a little beyond the usual help features. In addition to covering how to look up special terms and access reference lists, this chapter teaches you how to get help while creating macros, SQL code, and Visual Basic procedures. You'll also get a glimpse of how to create your own customized help tools such as ScreenTips, status bar messages, and help topics.

Asking What's This?

The What's This? button is very helpful for finding out about specific menu and shortcut menu commands, toolbar buttons, and almost any other screen item. This feature is available through the Help menu and in many dialog boxes. To use the What's This? feature, choose Help|What's This?. When you do, the mouse pointer turns into a question mark pointer. Next, click the item you have doubts about, and Access will display a ScreenTip. To remove the tip, click anywhere else on the screen or press Esc. Figure 6.1 shows the What's This? tip for the Code toolbar button. The tip not only explains the button, but it also tells you that the Code command is available from the View menu.

Most dialog boxes also have a What's This? button in the upper-right corner (the button with a question mark icon at the right end of the standard toolbar) that you can use to learn about the options in the box. Click the button and then click the option. Figure 6.2 shows the tip for the Perform Name AutoCorrect option in the General tab of the Options dialog box. When checked, this option repairs naming errors caused by field name changes.

FIGURE 6.1

Viewing the What's This? tip for the Code button.

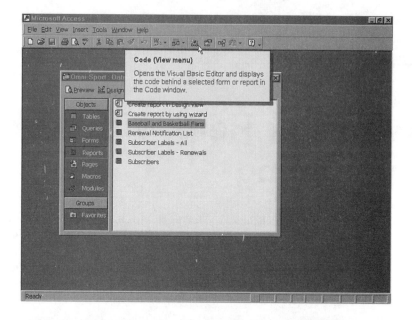

FIGURE 6.2

Viewing the What's This? tip for the Perform Name AutoCorrect option.

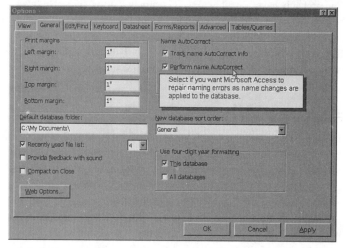

Finding and Printing Help Topics

The Office Assistant was a new feature in Microsoft Office 97. The Office Assistant is an animated multimedia character that answers questions, offers tips for more efficient processing, and provides help with specific Access activities. It displays tips and options in a balloon when asked or when an error occurs.

When you choose Help|Microsoft Access Help, the Office Assistant appears with a list of topics it thinks may be relevant to what you're doing at the moment. The list of topics will vary. If one of the topics matches your question, select the option, and the Help window opens displaying the Help topic. Figure 6.3 shows a Help topic accessed from the Office Assistant while working in the report design window. The first option in the list was selected.

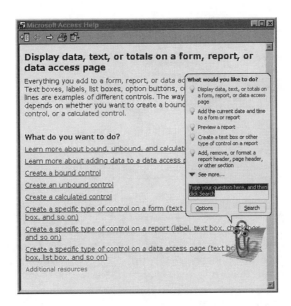

FIGURE 6.3
Choosing a Help topic from the Office Assistant's list.

If none of the Assistant's first suggestions quite match your question, click See more... to display additional topics. The final suggestion in the list is often None of the Above, Look for More Help on the Web. See the section "Getting Help from the Web," later in this chapter, for more information about getting remote help and technical assistance.

If a word in the Help topic appears in a different color without underlining, you can click it to see the definition of the word or phrase. If the text appears in a different color but with underlining, it's a hyperlink that jumps to another Help topic. The two horizontal arrows in the header of the Help window move you forward and back among Help pages you've accessed.

Another way to get help with a specific problem is to type a question in the Office Assistant text box and then click Search or simply press Enter. Figure 6.4 shows the result of asking the Office Assistant "What is a macro?" pressing Enter, and then selecting the first topic in the list: Macros: What They Are and How They Work.

FIGURE 6.4
*Getting help with
a specific
question.*

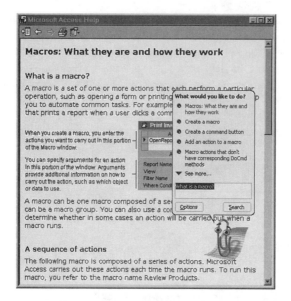

Tip: You can move the Assistant around on the screen by clicking and dragging the character. If the Assistant's balloon gets in the way of the text you want to see in the Help window, click the character, and the balloon disappears. To restore the list of topics in the balloon, click the character again. If you want to hide the Assistant completely, right-click the character and choose Hide from the shortcut menu.

To print the currently displayed topic from the Help window, click the Print button or choose Print from the Options button pull-down menu. This opens the Print dialog box, where you can select your print options.

Navigating in the Help Window

The Help window consists of two panes: the Topic pane, which displays the text of Help topics, and the Navigation pane, which enables you to search for yourself. You can expand the Help window to see the three tabs in the Navigation pane: Contents, Answer Wizard, and Index. Click the Show button (the leftmost button) in the Help window header or click the Options button down arrow and choose Show Tabs from the pull-down menu. When the Navigation pane is visible, *Show* changes to *Hide* so that you can repeat the process to remove the Navigation pane from view.

The other Options button commands include the following:

- Forward, Back, and Home navigate among Help topics already accessed.
- Stop ceases the current operation.

- Refresh redisplays the topic to reflect changes and deletions.

- Internet Options opens a dialog box where you can customize your connection and other Web-related options.

- Print opens the Print dialog box.

Figure 6.5 shows the Contents tab of the Help window, which lists all the major topic categories.

FIGURE 6.5

The three Help window tabs in the Navigation pane.

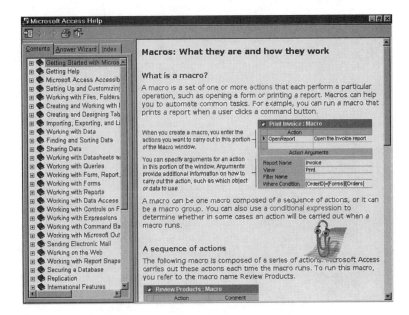

To expand a major topic and view an individual topic, click the expand symbol (+) next to the closed book. Many of the major topics, in turn, have subtopics that can be further expanded until you reach the list of individual topics symbolized by the question mark in place of an open or closed book. Figure 6.6 shows the Visual Basic Language Reference topic and the Functions subtopic both expanded. The Functions subtopic includes alphabetized groupings of functions from which to choose. Notice that if the title of a topic exceeds the width of the Navigation pane, a ScreenTip shows the entire title when you rest the mouse pointer on the topic. You can also drag the dividing line between the two panes of the Help window to adjust the widths to your needs.

You can use the Answer Wizard to get a list of topics that may answer a specific question. Type the question in the What Would You Like To box and click Search. Figure 6.7 shows a list of topics that may answer your question about when the OnGotFocus event occurs. The first topic in the list is displayed in the Help window. To see another topic, select it from the list. If your question is too vague, the Answer Wizard will ask to rephrase it. Also, if the list of topics is very long and far afield from the answer you're looking for, you may need to be more specific with the question.

FIGURE 6.6

Expanding topic groups until you reach the topic you want.

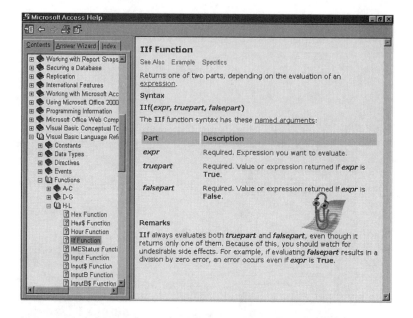

FIGURE 6.7

Asking the Answer Wizard a specific question.

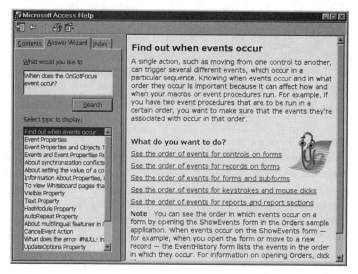

In the Index tab of the Help dialog box, you can type a keyword that reflects the topic for which you want help in the Type Keywords box. As you type, the list of keywords in the Or Choose Keywords box below scrolls down to a matching keyword or as near as it can get. If you find a matching keyword, double-click it. If there's no matching keyword, click Search. Both methods display a list of related topics in the bottom box and return the keyword list to the top. The number of topics is also displayed. Figure 6.8 shows the

Index tab after searching for topics related to the OnGotFocus event. The first topic in the list of 14 topics found is displayed in the Topic pane.

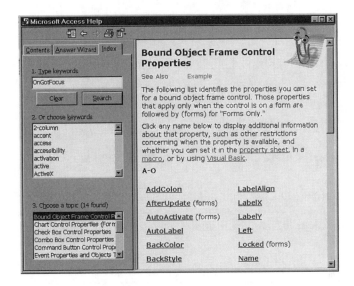

FIGURE 6.8
Looking up
OnGotFocus *in the*
Index tab of the
Help window.

Hiding and Showing the Assistant

If the Assistant is showing, it automatically recognizes trouble and offers tips for solving or avoiding problems. If the Assistant is hidden, you can show it by doing one of the following:

- Click the Help button on the toolbar
- Choose Help|Microsoft Access Help
- Choose Help|Show the Office Assistant
- Press F1 (if that option is selected for the Office Assistant)

It's also available from many dialog boxes. To remove the Assistant from the screen, choose Help|Hide the Office Assistant or right-click the character and choose Hide from the shortcut menu.

Modifying the Office Assistant

When you click Options in the Assistant balloon, the Office Assistant dialog box opens showing two tabs: Options and Gallery. The Options tab, shown in Figure 6.9, contains many settings related to the way the Assistant responds and the tips it displays. The first option, Use the Office Assistant, determines whether the Office Assistant is available to answer questions. If you clear this option, you can still get help through the Help menu command. The figure shows the default settings. Table 6.1 describes the Office Assistant options.

FIGURE 6.9
Use the Options tab to set the Office Assistant options.

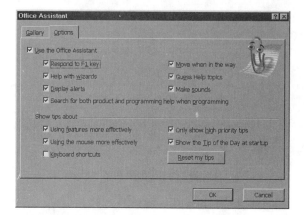

Warning: Be careful about making changes to the Office Assistant. The Assistant is shared with all the Office programs in your system, and any change you make will affect them as well.

Table 6.1   The Office Assistant Options

Option	Description
Assistant Capabilities	
Respond to F1 key	Shows the Assistant when F1 is pressed, except in property sheets and other places where the Assistant is not used.
Help with wizards	Makes the Assistant available to wizards. Most wizards use the Assistant.
Display alerts	Shows program and system messages in the Office Assistant balloon. Clear this option to see the messages in a normal dialog box.
Search for both product and programming help when programming	Adds programming Help topics to search when you're working with Visual Basic.
Move when in the way	Moves the Assistant out of the way of dialog boxes and automatically shrinks it when it has not been used for five minutes.
Guess Help topics	Shows Help topics based on what was happening when you asked for help.
Make sounds	Allows the Assistant to play sounds such as a cat purring, a robot squeaking, a volcano erupting, or a ball bouncing.

Option	Description
	Show Tips About
Using features more effectively	Suggests new features or better ways to use existing features.
Using the mouse more effectively	Shows tips on using the mouse.
Keyboard shortcuts	Shows tips about accelerator keys.
Only show high priority tips	Shows only important tips such as shortcuts or time-savers.
Show the Tip of the Day at startup	Shows a tip when Access starts.
Reset my tips	Allows tips to be repeated.

The Respond to F1 Key option usually opens the Office Assistant when you press F1. If you want to go directly to the Help dialog box when you press F1 without using the Assistant, clear that option.

> **Note:** The topics that the Office Assistant searches for depend on the window you have active. When you're in the module window, the Assistant looks for only programming topics plus provides help with actions and properties. In any other window, the Assistant searches for only product topics. To include product topics in the search while you're in the module window, check the Office Assistant option labeled Search for Both Product and Programming Help when Programming.

The Tip of the Day at Startup option can be either helpful or a nuisance. One tip advises the viewer that he or she could get hurt if he or she runs with scissors. Figure 6.10 shows a Tip of the Day displaying upon Access startup.

When you become tired of the Office Assistant character you're using, you can change it within the Gallery tab of the Office Assistant dialog box. To preview the characters, click Next or Back. You have a choice of eight characters, ranging from a bouncing rubber ball to Albert Einstein. Some of the animation is fascinating. For example, a fiery volcano erupts in the Mother Nature assistant when an error occurs. The default Clippit paper clip assistant is an amusing cartoon character with blinking eyes and a variety of body contortions. Figure 6.11 shows the Links character in the Gallery tab of the Office Assistant dialog box. To change the character, you must use the installation disk.

FIGURE 6.10

The Office Assistant displays a Tip of the Day at startup.

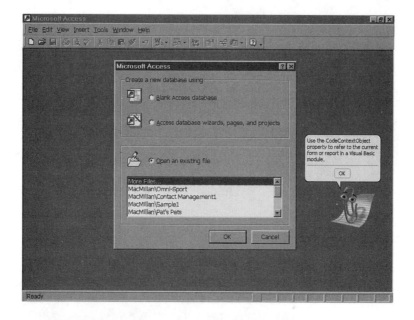

FIGURE 6.11

You can change the Office Assistant character in the Gallery tab.

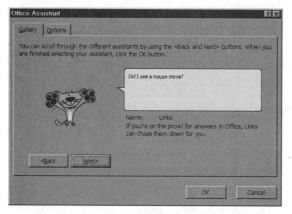

Tip: You can customize the Office Assistant, its balloon, and all the items in the balloon by programming. The Assistant is an object, itself, with objects, properties, and methods of its own that can be modified using Visual Basic. Once again, however, be aware that any changes you make to the Office Assistant apply to all Office users in your installation.

Getting Help with Macros and SQL

When you're working in the Macro Builder window, help is available directly from the Help window or through the Office Assistant. If you select an action in the Action column and press F1, the Microsoft Access Visual Basic Reference Help topic for that action opens automatically, whether the Assistant is set to respond to the F1 key or not. Figure 6.12 shows the Help topic that opens when you press F1 with the mouse pointer on the OpenForm action in the macro window.

FIGURE 6.12
Getting help while creating a macro.

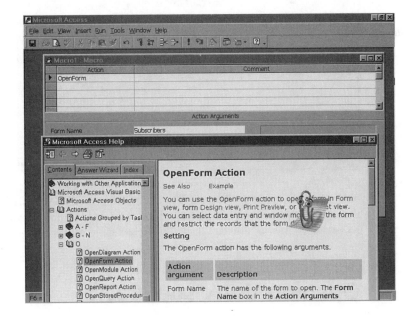

When the Assistant is set to respond to the F1 key, if you select any other part of the macro window and press F1, the Office Assistant offers to run a macro or answer a question. If you have cleared the Assistant's F1 key response option, pressing F1 displays either a ScreenTip explaining the column that contains the insertion point or a relevant Help topic. What's displayed depends on the position of the mouse pointer: If it is in a row that already contains an action, the column explanation is displayed; otherwise, the Help window opens.

Clicking the Office Assistant character always displays the balloon offering to run a macro or answer a question.

Choosing Help|What's This? and then clicking in the macro design window displays the Microsoft Access Reference Help topic for the selected action or an explanation of the column (if no action is selected).

When you're building a query, either in SQL or design view, you can use the Office Assistant to look for help. Pressing F1 in either view opens the Assistant with several Help topic options (see Figure 6.13). If the Assistant is not set to respond to the F1 key, the Help window opens showing the default topic, Ways to Get Assistance While You Work.

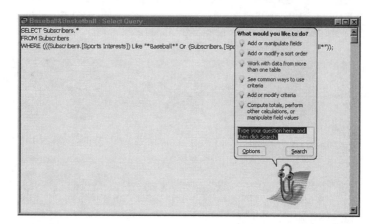

Figure 6.13
The Office Assistant offers help during query design.

Asking for help with Help|What's This? while you're in the SQL view displays a definition of the SQL view regardless of the location of the insertion point. If you're in the query design view, you can use What's This? to ask for an explanation of any of the items on the screen.

Opening the Visual Basic Reference Help

The Access 2000 Contents tab contains three major Help topics that can be expanded to show a wide variety of Visual Basic information:

- Visual Basic Conceptual Topics opens nearly 50 individual topics such as Calling Sub and Function Procedures, Looping Through Code, and Understanding Visual Basic Syntax.

- Visual Basic Language Reference lists 14 subtopics, such as Constants, which expands in turn to show topics referring to different types of intrinsic Visual Basic constants. The Methods subtopic expands to show a list of topics covering all the Visual Basic methods.

- Microsoft Office Visual Basic Reference contains two individual topics and five subtopics—Conceptual Information, Events, Methods, Objects and Collections, and Properties.

Note: Visual Basic Programming Help is not installed, by default, but is installed upon first use.

To get help with VB topics, use the Help Contents tab to reach one of the major topics. From there, you can open other subtopics to find information about VB code syntax, actions, constants, events, functions, and many other subjects. To print information about any of these subjects, select the topic and click Print. Topics such as actions, events, and functions have so many subtopics that they're often grouped in alphabetic order (refer to Figure 6.12).

After you open a Help topic for a particular VB term, the window offers several ways to see more information. Figure 6.14 shows the Click Event Help topic. When you click one of the hyperlinks in the top part of the window, Access displays additional informa-tion. For example, the See Also hyperlink opens a dialog box with a list of related topics and where they're located. (The See Also option is not available in the Help topic shown in Figure 6.14.) To display the new topic, click Display. To return to the Help window, choose Cancel.

Figure 6.14

Click a jump word to see more information.

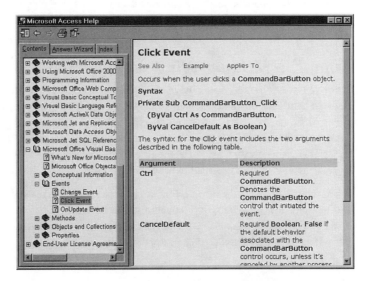

When you click the Example hyperlink, the Help window shows a sample procedure demonstrating the use of the event (see Figure 6.15). If one of the examples resembles a procedure you can use in your application, you can copy it to the Clipboard and then paste it into your procedure, where you can make changes to variable names, for exam-ple, as needed.

FIGURE 6.15
Click Example to see sample code.

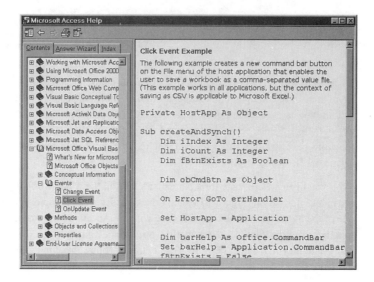

The Applies To hyperlink opens a dialog box displaying a list of objects to which the event applies. For example, the `Click` event applies to the `CommandBarButton` object, whose Help topic is located in the Microsoft Office Visual Basic Reference major topic.

From the Module Window

While you're writing VB code in the module window, you can get help with a particular keyword by placing the mouse pointer on the word and pressing F1 or by asking the Office Assistant. Pressing F1 takes you directly to the Help topic window for the selected constant, method, property, function, statement, or object. When you click the Assistant, it displays a balloon with a list of Help topics related to the current activity. You also can type a topic in the Office Assistant balloon and ask it to search for the information.

TROUBLESHOOTING

When an error occurs in the module window, such as a `Select Case` statement with no `End Select` statement, a message box appears describing the type of error (see Figure 6.16). The box has two buttons: OK and Help. Choose Help to open the Microsoft Visual Basic Help topic related to the error.

DEVELOPMENT

> **Tip:** While you're writing a VB procedure, keeping the Help window active so you can switch back and forth between Help and your application saves time. To switch between the two, press Alt+Tab or click in the Windows taskbar. If you want to copy code from the examples in the language reference Help topics, keep both windows open onscreen and move from one to the other as you copy and paste.

FIGURE 6.16
An error message appears when a compile error occurs.

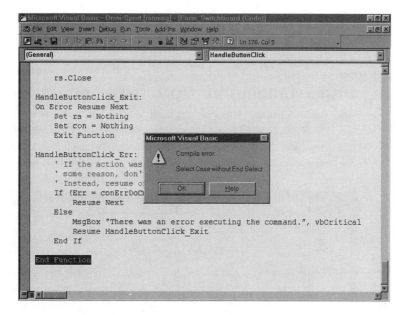

From the Object Browser

The Object Browser window has a Help button (with a fat question mark icon) that you can click to get information about a selected class, method, event, or property. In Figure 6.17, the IsLoaded property of an AccessObject class is selected. Clicking the Help button displays the Help topic IsLoaded Property in the Properties subtopic of the Microsoft Access Visual Basic Help group.

FIGURE 6.17
Click Help to display the Help topic for the selected property.

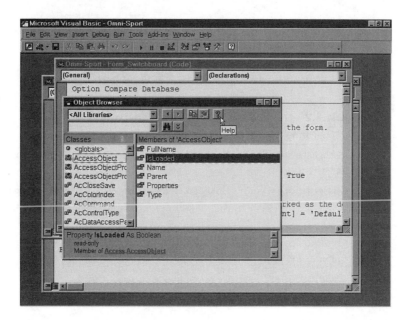

You also can press F1 to see the same Help topic for the selected keyword.

LOOKING AHEAD   See Chapter 10, "Debugging Visual Basic Procedures," for more information about using the Object Browser.

Understanding VB Document Conventions

After you've found the Help topic you want, you need to be able to interpret the information. Visual Basic uses standard typographic conventions in its documentation. Figure 6.18 shows part of the Do...Loop Statement Help topic, which includes many of the conventions.

FIGURE 6.18

The Do...Loop *Statement Help topic uses typographic conventions.*

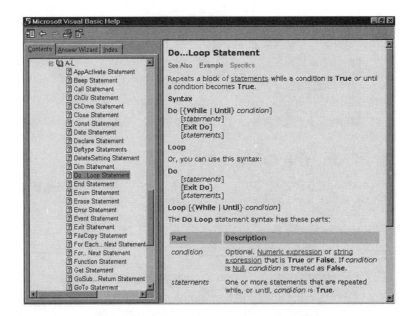

Table 6.2 describes the conventions used in Visual Basic documentation.

Table 6.2   Visual Basic Typographic Conventions

Convention	Description	Examples
Language-specific keywords	Bold with initial caps	**Do, Loop, Exit Do, True**
User entries	Bold and all lowercase	**exit, setup** (If bold, you can use positional or named-argument syntax.)
Placeholders for information you supply	Italic and all lowercase	*statements, condition*

Convention	Description	Examples
Placeholders for arguments	Bold, italic, and lowercase	*filename*, *pathname* (Use positional or named argument syntax.)
Optional items	Enclosed in square brackets	[`Exit Do`], [`statements`]
Mandatory choice	Enclosed in brackets and separated by a vertical bar	{`While¦Until`}
Key names	Small capitals	ESC, ENTER, TAB
Key combinations	Plus sign between key names	ALT+TAB, CTRL+P

Getting Help from the Web

If none of the items in the Office Assistant list appear to answer your question, click None of the Above, Look for More Help on the Web (this appears at the bottom of the list of topics in the Office Assistant balloon). Figure 6.19 shows the Help window that can connect you to the Microsoft Web site. If you click the Search Tips hyperlink, you'll get suggestions on how to rephrase your question or how to use keywords to narrow your search. If you still can't find the information you want, you can enter more details about your question in the box at the bottom of the window and send it to the Microsoft Web site. You're automatically connected to the Microsoft Office Update Web site to search for help there. Microsoft can use your feedback to improve future versions of Help. You must have Microsoft Internet Explorer operational in order to access the help available on the Web.

Tip: You can also access the Microsoft Office Web sites by choosing Help|Office on the Web. From the Update Web site, you can download free product enhancements and reach technical resources such as the Microsoft Software Library, which contains free binary files and the Microsoft Knowledge Base, which, in turn, includes product information for Office support engineers and customers.

LOOKING AHEAD

Browsing the Internet is a complex subject in itself—entire books are devoted to the subject. This topic is covered only briefly in this book. Chapter 20, "Posting Your Database to the Web," addresses the subject of creating dynamic data access pages and publishing on the Web.

FIGURE 6.19
Help is also available on the Web.

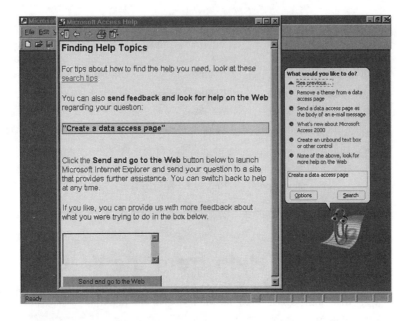

Creating Your Own Help

Although the Access Help features are very comprehensive and versatile, they nevertheless are self-centered. They answer questions about using Access, creating macros, writing VB code, and other related topics, but nothing about your application. A complete application should include customized help for its special features.

Many help tools are very easy to create, whereas others are more complex. *ScreenTips*, the general term for those messages that appear when you rest your mouse pointer on a toolbar button, menu option, or control, are easy to add and very effective. Status bar messages are also useful and easy to create, but users often do not refer to the status bar for help.

Creating your own help topics that will respond to the What's This? feature or the F1 key are more complex and require access to the Windows Help Compiler or to the compiler that's part of the Microsoft Help Workshop.

Adding ScreenTips and Status Bar Messages

ScreenTips include ControlTips and ToolTips. A *ControlTip* displays text when you rest the mouse pointer on a control in a form or report. A *ToolTip* is associated with a specific button or combo box on a toolbar, either built in or custom.

Shortcut key text displays the shortcut key combination you specify for a built-in toolbar button or menu option. If a shortcut key combination has been assigned to a toolbar button, it's displayed with the ToolTip. A shortcut key combination for a menu command appears to the right of the command in the menu.

ControlTip text is one of the properties of a control in a form. To add text you want to display, open the form in design view, select the control, and open the property sheet. Next, type the text in the ControlTip Text property box. You can enter up to 255 characters. It's not necessary to enclose the text in quotation marks.

You add ToolTips and shortcut key text by customizing the command bar—either a toolbar or a menu bar. Both aids are command properties that you reach by choosing View|Toolbars|Customize. In the Customize dialog box, select the toolbar or menu to which you want to add the tip or shortcut key so that it shows on the screen. With the Customize dialog box remaining open, right-click the button or menu command and choose Properties from the shortcut menu (see Figure 6.20).

FIGURE 6.20
Use the shortcut menu to change a toolbar button.

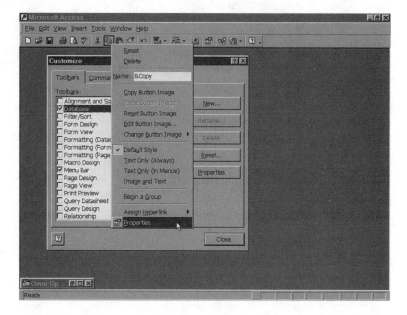

Figure 6.21 shows the Database Control Properties dialog box for the Copy button on the Database toolbar. Enter the shortcut key combination in the Shortcut Text property box. Then you can type the ScreenTip text in the ScreenTip Property box. If you don't specify a custom ScreenTip, the button's caption is displayed.

For the ScreenTip to appear, close the Properties dialog box and click the Options tab of the Customize dialog box and set the Show ScreenTips On Toolbars option. If you want the shortcut key text to appear in the ScreenTip as well, choose the Show Shortcut Keys In Screen Tips option. Entering the shortcut key text does not automatically assign the action to the keys; you still must create an AutoKeys macro.

FIGURE 6.21
Add a ToolTip or shortcut key to a button or menu command.

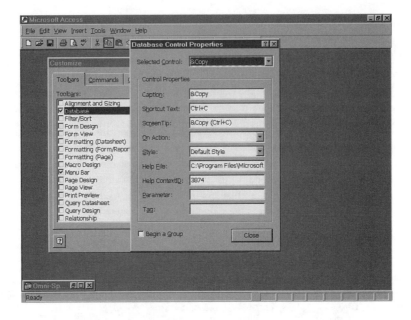

LOOKING AHEAD Read Chapter 8, "Creating Menus," for more information about customizing command bars and assigning AutoKeys.

Status bar text also applies to controls in a form and is one of the control's properties. Open the form or report in design view, select the control, and type the text you want to see in the Status Bar Text property box. Again, you can enter up to 255 characters, but you'll only see what will fit in the bar, which depends on the font and the size of the window.

Creating Custom Help Topics

Access provides context-sensitive Help topics that you can bring up by pressing F1 or by choosing What's This? from the Help menu. You can create your own Help topics that will also respond to those user actions.

Using a word processing program or a text editor, create the Help source file and save it in Rich Text Format (RTF). You can have as many topics as you want in the source file, numbered consecutively. Then, compile the Help file using the Windows Help Compiler. Be sure to save the Help file in the same folder with your application, where it's readily available.

> **Note:** The Windows Help Compiler program is included in the Microsoft Office 2000 Developer's Edition, Microsoft Visual Basic for Applications, Microsoft Visual C++, and Microsoft Windows Software Development Kit (SDK). A Help-authoring kit is also available from Microsoft.

To relate the Help topics with a form or report, open the form or report property sheet and type the filename in the Help File property box (on the Other tab). Next, enter the number of the topic that applies to the whole form or report in the Help Context ID property box. If you want a Help topic displayed when you select a specific control and press F1, enter the Help Context ID information in the control's property sheet, using the number for the topic that refers expressly to that control.

What's This? tips appear when you choose What's This? from the Help menu (or press Shift+F1) and then click a toolbar button or menu command. You can attach your own Help topics to these command items the same way as adding ScreenTips. With the Customize dialog box open, show the toolbar and right-click the button you want to add the Help topic to. Then choose Properties from the shortcut menu and enter the Help path and name in the Help File box and the context ID in the Help Context ID box. Notice in Figure 6.21 (shown earlier) that the Copy toolbar button includes the Help Context ID #3874 from

```
...\Program Files\Microsoft Office\Office\1033\actip9.hlp
```

Help features are extremely important when developing end-user applications. The type of custom help you provide depends on the experience of the ultimate users and the business they are in. Office and Access provide such a wide variety of flexible help tools, you are limited only by your imagination.

Summary

This chapter has given you several avenues to follow to get help with writing macros, SQL code, and VB procedures. You also saw how to use the Office Assistant to help with developing an application. Access also provides a variety of ways to help you create customized help for your application end users.

LOOKING AHEAD

In the next chapter, "Programming with SQL," you'll begin programming in earnest with SQL code. Using SQL, you can create select queries as well as several types of action queries, such as delete, update, append, and make-table.

PART III

Diving Into Syntax

Programming with SQL

Queries are the primary means of retrieving information from a database. With a query, you can select specific information and display it sorted by field values and even add summaries to the presentation. Queries are often used as the basis for forms and reports. Other queries can create new tables, append data to existing tables, delete records, and find duplicate records. Access queries are implemented in Structured Query Language (SQL) statements that you can review and edit.

This chapter reviews the types of queries and when you would use them. It also examines the SQL statements that operate behind the scenes and how to write your own SQL instructions. Other sections describe how to run SQL statements within VB code. The examples in this and the next chapter are drawn from the Clayview City College database that is included in the Source\Databases folder on the CD-ROM that accompanies this book. The Clayview City College database begins to show the power of relational data-bases by distributing data to multiple related tables, such as Students, Classes, Departments, and Instructors. From the examples shown in the Clayview City College database, you can understand the many ways to extract specific data from the database in a variety of ways.

Types of Queries

When you build a query in the query design view, Access is working in the background writing equivalent SQL statements. To view the SQL code, choose View|SQL View or choose SQL View from the View pull-down menu. You can use either the SQL code or the query definition as the record source for a form or report. Using the query definition is a little faster because it's already compiled, whereas the SQL code must be compiled every time it's referenced.

Access offers several types of queries, from select queries that retrieve specific informa-tion to make-table queries that actually create new database objects.

Select Queries

The first type of query you'll learn about is the simple *select query*. The select query can retrieve information from one or more tables and often is used as the record source for a form or report. You can also run a query on a query instead of a table, thereby creating a *subquery*—a query within a query.

Figure 7.1 shows a query created for the Clayview City College database to serve as the record source of a report analyzing the students' grade point averages. It retrieves student information including name, class, number of units, grade, and major. The GPA Report computes the grade point average of each student based on the retrieved information. Figure 7.2 shows the query in datasheet view.

FIGURE 7.1
A select query in the query design grid.

Class ID	Units	Grade	Student ID	First Name	Last Name	Major	GdPts
1	3	C	4	Brandon	Reese	Political Science	2
1	3	A	2	John	Smith	Marketing	4
1	3	B	3	Margaret	Jones	Medicine	3
1	3	A	1	Nancy	Drew	MIS	4
1	3	B	6	Robert	Ryan	English	3
2	3	A	1	Nancy	Drew	MIS	4
2	3	B	4	Brandon	Reese	Political Science	3
2	3	B	5	Deborah	Rutter	Computer Science	3
2	3	B+	6	Robert	Ryan	English	3
2	3	A	7	Mathew	Peterson	Computer Science	4
3	3	A	2	John	Smith	Marketing	4
3	3	A	4	Brandon	Reese	Political Science	4
3	3	A	6	Robert	Ryan	English	4
3	3	A	1	Nancy	Drew	MIS	4
3	3	A	5	Deborah	Rutter	Computer Science	4
4	4	A	1	Nancy	Drew	MIS	4
4	4	B	2	John	Smith	Marketing	3
5	5	C	2	John	Smith	Marketing	2
2	3	B	3	Margaret	Jones	Medicine	3
4	4	B	3	Margaret	Jones	Medicine	3
5	5	A	3	Margaret	Jones	Medicine	4

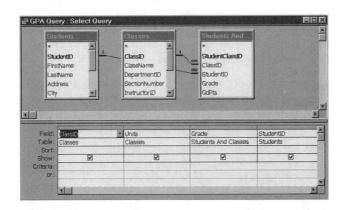

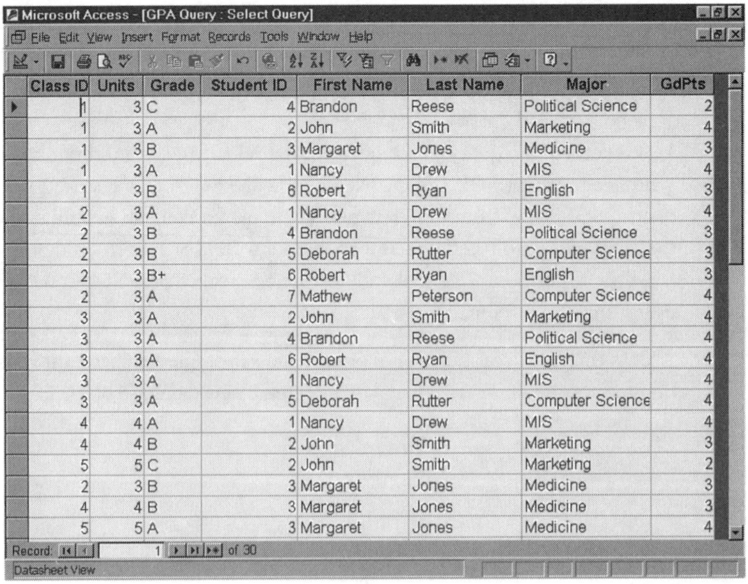

FIGURE 7.2
The select query in datasheet view.

The SQL code demonstrates the use of statements containing keywords that define the query design (see Figure 7.3). The elements of the SQL structure are discussed in the section, "Dissecting SQL Statements," later in this chapter.

FIGURE 7.3
The select query in SQL view.

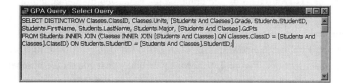

```
GPA Query : Select Query
SELECT DISTINCTROW Classes.ClassID, Classes.Units, [Students And Classes].Grade, Students.StudentID,
Students.FirstName, Students.LastName, Students.Major, [Students And Classes].GdPts
FROM Students INNER JOIN (Classes INNER JOIN [Students And Classes] ON Classes.ClassID = [Students And
Classes].ClassID) ON Students.StudentID = [Students And Classes].StudentID;
```

PERFORMANCE

If you've set the record source for a form or report to a SQL statement, you can speed up processing by using the equivalent query instead. Save the SQL statement as a query and then set the Record Source property to the name of the query.

Crosstab Queries

A *crosstab query* is a type of select query that helps analyze the effects of one type of information on another. It forms a two-dimensional matrix with one field as the row values and the other as the column values with the information associated with the row-column pairs as the intersecting values. For example, a crosstab query could show you the grade point averages for each student for each semester. The student names would appear in the rows, and the semesters would appear in the column headings, with the GPAs in the body of the matrix. The Crosstab Wizard is very helpful when you're creating a crosstab query.

Parameter Queries

A *parameter query* is a special type of select query that bases its selection of records on input from the user. A parameter query displays a dialog box prompting for information such as a student's name, a class number, or a date interval for sales transactions. You also can create a custom dialog box to receive the criteria for selecting records to include. Such queries can be used as the record source for reports and forms that can require varying criteria.

The SQL statements for a parameter query are the same as those for a select query, except for a leading PARAMETERS declaration that specifies all the parameters requested when the query is run.

> **Note:** If you've designed a form or report based on a query and you remove a field from the underlying query, Access expects you to enter the missing value. The query is treated like a parameter query, and a parameter dialog box is displayed. With the Name AutoCorrect option checked, renaming a field no longer causes this problem.

Summary Queries

In some queries, it might be useful to include total or summary information, such as the number of students in each class or the students' overall grade point averages. Such summary queries group records and compute the requested mathematical or statistical function. To add a summary to a query, choose View|Totals. Access adds the words *Group By* in the Total row of every field in the grid. To summarize the contents of one of the fields, click the Total down arrow and select from the list. Table 7.1 describes your choices of aggregate functions. Figure 7.4 shows a new query that counts the number of students in each class. The equivalent SQL code is shown in Figure 7.5.

FIGURE 7.4
A query that counts the number of students in each class.

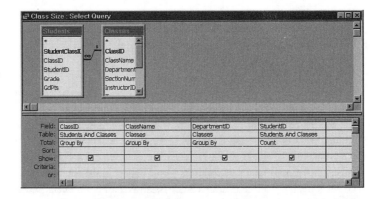

FIGURE 7.5
The summary query in SQL view.

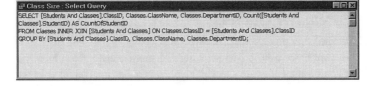

Table 7.1 Summary Query Aggregate Functions

Function	Description
Avg	Computes the average of values in a field.
Count	Counts the number of values in a field. Does not include Null values.
First	Returns the field value from the first record in the result set.
Last	Returns the field value from the last record in the result set.
Max	Returns the highest value in a field.
Min	Returns the lowest value in a field.
StDev	Computes the standard deviation of values in a field.
Sum	Computes the total of values in a field.
Var	Computes the variance of values in a field.

The First and Last functions are handy for showing the range of values in a field.

Each of these functions has an equivalent SQL aggregate function. Three additional options appear on the Totals list:

- GROUP BY, the default option, defines the groups to perform calculations with.
- EXPRESSION creates a calculated field using one of the aggregate functions in the expression.
- WHERE specifies the criteria for a field that you're not using for grouping. You can hide the field in the result set by clearing the Show check box.

> **Note:** Aggregate queries do not include records with null values in the specified field. The Count function will not include them in the total and they will not be included in any other calculation. To count the null values, use the asterisk (*) wildcard with the Count function: Count(*). To make sure the records with null values are included in other aggregate functions, you can search for the Null values and change them to 0.

PERFORMANCE

When you're grouping records by the values of a joined field in a summary query, be sure to specify GROUP BY for the field on the same side of the relationship as the field you're summarizing. Access performs the aggregate function first and then joins only the necessary fields. If you group by the field in the other table, Access joins all records first and then computes the aggregate value, which can slow down processing.

Action Queries

Action queries affect the data in tables. Using Action queries, you can make changes to several records at once (such as updating a field, deleting whole records, and adding new records) or make an entirely new table from fields in one or more existing tables.

You can create action queries in the query design window, and each one has an equivalent SQL statement that includes all the operators and clauses necessary to define the operation.

Update Queries

The *update query* changes the values in a field based on specific criteria. For example, suppose you want to increase the price of certain types of items in the store by 5 percent. The query would multiply the price field value in the records for that type of merchandise by 1.05. You can change several fields at once with the same update query, and you can also use the update query to update records in more than one table.

> **Warning:** Be careful with action queries. You cannot use Undo to reverse them. Luckily, Access displays a warning box before carrying out the action query and gives you a chance to change your mind. To be safe, always create a backup copy of the table before running an action query.

Append Queries

The *append query* adds one or more records to the end of one or more existing tables. An append query can be very useful for transferring records to an archive when the information is no longer active but is worth saving. For example, at the end of each semester, student grades for each class can be appended to the existing student record archive.

Delete Queries

A *delete query* empties part or all of a table. It removes entire records rather than a single field value. If you completely empty a table, the structure, indexes, properties, and field attributes remain. You can delete records based on specified criteria, such as students who have dropped a course. If you just want to delete a field value, use the update query and set the value to Null.

> **Tip:** Because the action queries are irreversible, run a select query using the criteria you would use in the delete query. This way, you can see the list of records that will be deleted and make sure you really want to remove them.

If you want to delete records on the one side of a one-to-many relationship, use the *cascade delete* option. This removes all the orphan records when the parent is deleted. For example, if you delete a specific chemistry class from the Classes table, all the records in the Students And Classes table that contain that ClassID value will also be deleted.

Make-Table Queries

The *make-table query* creates a new table from fields in one or more existing tables. This type of query is useful for creating archive tables that contain all the information for a specific period of time, such as student records for the entire school year. Make-table queries are also used to create backup tables or tables to be exported to another database.

Figure 7.6 shows a make-table query that creates a table with records for all the students with "A" in the Grade field. The new table includes fields from both the Students and the Students And Classes tables. In order to have a student name appear only once in the list, add the aggregate clause Count in the Total line of the ClassID field. The resulting table, Honor Roll, contains seven student records, representing all the students with at least one grade of A (see Figure 7.7). The CountOfClassID field shows the number of classes in which that student earned an A.

FIGURE 7.6

The make-table query in SQL view.

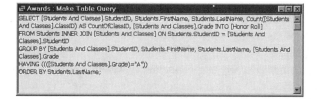

```
Awards : Make Table Query
SELECT [Students And Classes].StudentID, Students.FirstName, Students.LastName, Count([Students
And Classes].ClassID) AS CountOfClassID, [Students And Classes].Grade INTO [Honor Roll]
FROM Students INNER JOIN [Students And Classes] ON Students.StudentID = [Students And
Classes].StudentID
GROUP BY [Students And Classes].StudentID, Students.FirstName, Students.LastName, [Students And
Classes].Grade
HAVING ((([Students And Classes].Grade)="A"))
ORDER BY Students.LastName;
```

FIGURE 7.7

The Honor Roll table created by the make-table query.

	StudentID	FirstName	LastName	CountOfClassI	Grade
▶	1	Nancy	Drew	3	A
	2	John	Smith	2	A
	3	Margaret	Jones	1	A
	4	Brandon	Reese	1	A
	5	Deborah	Rutter	2	A
	6	Robert	Ryan	1	A
	7	Mathew	Peterson	2	A
*					

Record: 1 of 7

As more student grades are reported to the dean's office, their records can be added to the Honor Roll using the append query. Figure 7.8 shows the append query that can be used to add the new outstanding students to the list.

FIGURE 7.8

The append query that adds records of A students to the Honor Roll table.

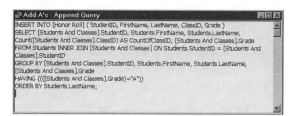

```
Add A's : Append Query
INSERT INTO [Honor Roll] ( StudentID, FirstName, LastName, ClassID, Grade )
SELECT [Students And Classes].StudentID, Students.FirstName, Students.LastName,
Count([Students And Classes].ClassID) AS CountOfClassID, [Students And Classes].Grade
FROM Students INNER JOIN [Students And Classes] ON Students.StudentID = [Students And
Classes].StudentID
GROUP BY [Students And Classes].StudentID, Students.FirstName, Students.LastName,
[Students And Classes].Grade
HAVING ((([Students And Classes].Grade)="A"))
ORDER BY Students.LastName;
```

> **Tip:** If you plan to include a lot of queries in your database, creating a table with the names and descriptions of all the saved queries will help you keep track of them. It's all too easy to forget which query did what when you have a lot of them cryptically named.

SQL Queries

When you're operating in a client/server environment, you can use SQL queries to communicate with the back-end SQL server. The front end—the client—is where you sit, and the database is handled by the server at the back end. All SQL queries must be constructed in SQL code and can be run from a macro or embedded in a Visual Basic procedure.

Here are some examples of SQL queries:

- A *union query* that combines fields from one or more tables or queries into a single field or column in a third table.
- A *pass-through query* that works directly with the ODBC databases (for example, the Microsoft FoxPro), using commands in that server's vocabulary.
- A *data-definition query* that creates, deletes, or changes tables in the current database and also creates indexes.
- A *subquery* that places a SQL SELECT statement within another select or action query. Used in the Criteria row of the query design grid.

PERFORMANCE

When working with a front-end/back-end application, try to avoid queries that can only be processed by the local client computer. The Jet database engine works faster if it stays on the external database server. Some of the query operations that the Jet database engine must perform locally include the following:

- JOIN operations using a query with the DISTINCT predicate of a GROUP BY clause.
- Multiple-level GROUP BY arguments and totals.
- Statements with TOP *n* or TOP *n* PERCENT predicates.
- Any user-defined functions or any operators or functions not supported by the server. Some servers also do not support the LIKE operator used with Text and Memo fields.

Union Queries

A *union query* is useful for compiling information from more than one table or query into a new table. For example, Clayview City College is interested in keeping track of its alumni as well as getting new graduates involved in alumni activities. A table that combines names from both the student and alumni lists with their home cities would be useful for periodic mailings.

Use the following process to create a SQL union query:

1. Click New in the Queries page of the database window and choose Design View in the New Query dialog box. Then click OK.
2. In the query design view, close the Show Table dialog box without adding any tables to the design.
3. Choose Query|SQL Specific|Union.
4. Enter the SQL SELECT statements, the first one alone and the second following the UNION operation. Each SELECT statement must return the same number of fields and in a matching order. The corresponding fields must be of compatible data types, except that a number field can correspond with a text field.

   For example, the following SQL statement combines the first and last name fields from both the Alumni and Students tables and then sorts the results by city:

```
SELECT [FirstName],[LastName],[City]
FROM [Alumni]
UNION SELECT [FirstName],[LastName],[City]
FROM [Students]
ORDER BY [City];
```

Pass-Through Queries

A pass-through query works directly with the Access tables on an ODBC database server, such as the Microsoft FoxPro, without having to link to the tables. You can use a pass-through query to run stored procedures that update records or return specific records. A pass-through query could be used to update the grade point averages of the students at the end of the semester.

To create a pass-through query, open the query design view without adding any tables and choose Query|SQL Specific|Pass-Through. In the Query Properties sheet, set the connection information for the database to which you want to connect (see Figure 7.9). Either type in the information or click Build in the ODBC Connect Str property. If you don't specify a connection string, Access uses the default setting, "ODBC;". With the default setting, you're prompted for connection information each time you run the pass-through query.

Figure 7.9

Set the properties for a pass-through query.

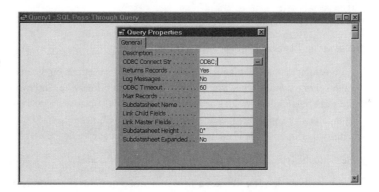

The Returns Records property allows Access to accept returned records from the query. If you don't expect records from the query, set the property to No. In addition to records, the query can return messages from the server. In that case, set the Log Messages property to Yes, and Access will create a table that contains all the returned messages. The table name is the username followed by a hyphen (-) and a sequential record number beginning with 00. For example, ADMIN-00, ADMIN-01, and so on.

The ODBC Timeout property sets the number of seconds to wait before triggering a Timeout error when running a query on an ODBC data source. The Max Records property sets the maximum number of records to return by a query running on an ODBC data source.

Data-Definition Queries

You can use a *data-definition query* to create a new table, change or delete an existing table in the current database, or create a new index. After choosing Query|SQL Specific|Data-Definition in the query design window, type the desired SQL statement. You have a choice of four data-definition statements to use in the query:

- CREATE TABLE creates a new table.
- ALTER TABLE adds a new field or constraint to the existing table or drops a field or constraint.
- DROP removes a table from a database or an index from a table.
- CREATE INDEX builds an index for one or more fields in an existing table.

When you use CREATE TABLE, you name the table, list the fields together with their data types, and include the primary key field. This is directly analogous to using the table design view to create a new table. You can also add indexes by using the CONSTRAINT clause. The following SQL statement is an example of a data-definition query that creates a table named Alumni:

```
CREATE TABLE Alumni
([AlumID] integer,
[LastName] text,
[FirstName] string,
      'additional fields here
CONSTRAINT [Index1] PRIMARY KEY ([AlumID]))
```

A constraint is much like an index. It places some restrictions on the table and the field values. For example, when you assign a field as the primary key, no two records can have the same value in that field. The preceding CONSTRAINT clause assigns the AlumID field as an index and specifies it as the primary key. You also can use the CONSTRAINT clause with two or more fields if necessary to achieve a unique value.

Here are the types of constraints you can impose on a table:

- PRIMARY KEY. Designates a field or a group of fields as the primary key. All primary key values must be unique and not null. Only one primary key can be designated for a table.
- UNIQUE. Specifies a field as a unique key. Also, the same value cannot occur in two records.
- NOT NULL. Restricts the specified field to non-null values.
- FOREIGN KEY. Designates a field from a related table as the primary key for this table.

The new Create Table query appears in the Query page of the database window with a Design icon.

The ALTER TABLE statement enables you to add a new field to a table with the ADD COLUMN clause or drop a field from the table with the DROP COLUMN clause. In addition, you can add or drop indexes with the CONSTRAINT clause. You cannot add or delete more than one field or index at a time with the ALTER TABLE statement.

Here are some examples of using the ALTER TABLE statement:

```
ALTER TABLE Alumni ADD COLUMN Spouse TEXT(30)
```

The preceding line adds the 30-character spouse name to the Alumni table. The next line removes the Sports field from the Roster table:

```
ALTER TABLE Roster DROP COLUMN Sports
```

The following line insists that the City field in the Alumni table not be blank:

```
ALTER TABLE Alumni ADD CONSTRAINT City NOT NULL
```

The DROP statement deletes an existing table, procedure, or view from a database or an existing index from a table. To delete a table, all you need to do is specify the table with the TABLE clause. To delete an index, use the INDEX clause and include the name of the index and its table. To delete a procedure or view, use the PROCEDURE or VIEW clause with the name of the object.

The CREATE INDEX statement creates a new index for a table. For example, the following line creates an index named Mailing for the Alumni table using the last name then first name:

```
CREATE INDEX Mailing ON Alumni ([LastName], [FirstName])
```

Figure 7.10 shows the new Alumni table structure with the indexes created by the data-definition query.

FIGURE 7.10

The new Alumni table structure with indexes added by the data-definition query.

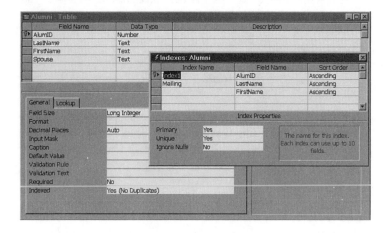

The statement also has several keywords, such as UNIQUE, PRIMARY, ASC, DESC, DISALLOW NULL, and IGNORE NULL, that further specify the new index.

Subqueries

You can use a subquery instead of an expression to define selection criteria for a field in the main query or define a new field to be added to the main query. Access runs the subquery first and then runs the main query on the results of the subquery. The combination returns records from the main query that meet the restrictions placed on the records that have already passed the subquery criteria. Placing a subquery in the main query design saves the trouble of storing two query definitions.

You can add the subquery SELECT statement to the main query in the design view or embed the statement in the SQL code. To define criteria for a field while in design view, type the SELECT SQL statement in the Criteria cell of the field. To define a new field for the query, type the SELECT statement in the Field cell of an empty column. The SELECT statement must be enclosed in parentheses. Access automatically precedes the statement with Expr$n$, where n is the index of the expression (1 if this is the only expression in the query).

In SQL, a subquery is a SELECT statement nested inside another SELECT statement or a SELECT INTO, INSERT INTO, DELETE, or UPDATE statement. The subquery SELECT statement follows the WHERE or HAVING clause of the main query.

The subquery uses the SELECT…FROM…WHERE or HAVING syntax to define the criteria. In addition, you have a choice of predicates: ANY, ALL, or SOME. ANY and SOME both retrieve records in the main query that meet the requirements of any records retrieved by the subquery. ALL is more restrictive in that it retrieves records from the main query only if they satisfy the comparison with all the records returned by the subquery.

The following SQL query uses a subquery to extract the records of students from the Students table who have received a grade of C, as stored in the Students And Classes table:

```
SELECT * FROM Students
WHERE StudentID IN
(SELECT StudentID FROM [Students And Classes]
WHERE Grade = "C")
```

PERFORMANCE

To improve query performance, avoid using calculated fields in a subquery. This can slow down getting results from the top-level query. If you need an expression to receive the desired output, consider placing the expression in a control on the form or report instead of in the query used as the record source.

Types of Table Joins

Many of the SQL statements you've seen so far have clauses referring to *joins*. Now is a good time to review joins and the way related tables are linked.

You can use inner, right-outer, and left-outer joins in any FROM clause in a SQL statement. The type you use depends on what you want the query to select. An inner join operation is the most common type. It includes records from two tables only if the values in the common fields match. Records with different values in the common fields are not included. Right- and left-outer joins are used to include all the records from one table, even if there are no matching records from the second table.

Inner Joins

When you add a table to a query design, Access automatically sets the join as an inner join, but you can change it to a right- or left-outer join with the Relationships feature. Click the Relationships toolbar button or choose Tools|Relationships to display all the related tables in the current database. Then, select a relationship line and choose Relationships|Edit Relationship. You can also right-click the relationship line and choose Edit Relationship from the shortcut menu. Click Join Type and choose the join you want from the Join Properties dialog box (see Figure 7.11).

FIGURE 7.11
Choose the type of join in the Join Properties dialog box.

TECHNICAL NOTE

In Figure 7.11, the first option is an inner join, the second is a left-outer join, and the third is a right-outer join. The relationship between the Students and Students And Classes tables is implemented by two inner joins. If you look at the SQL view of a query linking these two tables, you'll see the INNER JOIN clauses in the SQL statement:

```
INNER JOIN (Students INNER JOIN [Students And Classes] ON
Students.StudentID = [Students And Classes].StudentID) ON
Classes.ClassID = [Students And Classes].ClassID
```

ANALYSIS

This statement nests INNER JOIN clauses. The first links the Students table with the Students And Classes table by student ID. The second links the Classes table with the Students And Classes table by class ID.

You can nest all types of joins within an INNER JOIN, but you cannot nest an INNER JOIN within either a RIGHT JOIN or LEFT JOIN.

The comparison operator doesn't always need to be equal (=). You can specify that the fields compare in other ways, such as less than (<), greater than (>), less than or equal to (<=), greater than or equal to (>=), or not equal (<>). You can also link several ON clauses within a JOIN clause, combining them with the AND or OR keywords.

Left and Right Joins

Right- and left-outer join operations refer to the sequence of listing the tables in the JOIN clause. Here's the general syntax, where *table1* is the left table and *table2* is the right:

```
FROM table1 [LEFT¦RIGHT] JOIN table2 ON table1.field = table2.field2
```

The right join operation includes all the records from *table2* and only those from *table1* when the common fields match. The left join returns all the records from *table1* and only those of *table2* when they match. For example, the following statement would retrieve all the records from the Students And Classes table but only those from the Cumulative Class Percentiles table that have matching StudentIDfields:

```
FROM [Cumulative Class Percentiles] RIGHT JOIN [Students And Classes]
ON [Cumulative Class Percentiles].StudentID =
[Students And Classes].StudentID
```

Self Joins

Suppose the Students And Classes table includes a field named TA (teaching assistant) that contains the StudentID value for the student assigned to the class. You could create a self join that joins two copies of the table and replace the student ID with the student's name in one copy.

To create a self join, two copies of the same table are included in the query. The second copy is given an alias. The join combines records from the same table when the joined fields contain the same value. The SQL statement for a self join looks like any other select query with the original table and its copy. For example, if you create a self join in a query using the Students table, the first instance is named *Students* and the second is named *Students_1*. Access automatically adds "_1" to form an alias.

Dissecting SQL Statements

To see the SQL statements behind a query in the design view, choose View|SQL View or click the View button and select SQL view. If you're working on a report in the design view, you can look at the SQL statements by right-clicking the report RecordSource property and choosing Zoom from the shortcut menu. Clicking Build in the RecordSource property opens the design grid. Figure 7.12 shows the query design for the SQL statement that's the record source for the Class Results Summary report. Notice that the title bar indicates that the design represents a SQL statement instead of a query definition. Scroll right in the design grid to see the other columns.

The next section looks carefully at some examples of various types of queries and the elements contained in their SQL statements. Not all features and options are examined in this chapter. For a complete description of each element of a query SQL syntax, refer to the Microsoft SQL Jet Reference in the Help Contents window.

FIGURE 7.12
The query design view for a SQL statement.

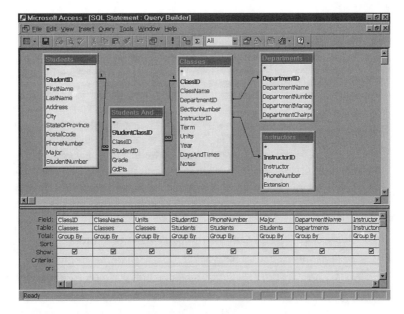

Inspecting a Select Query Statement

The SQL code for this simple select query might look forbidding, but a close look reveals order and consistency in its construction.

Listing 7.1 shows the SQL statement used as the record source for the Class Results Summary report.

Listing 7.1   The SQL Statement Record Source for the Class Results Summary Report

```
SELECT DISTINCTROW Classes.ClassID, Classes.ClassName,
Classes.Units, Students.StudentID, Students.PhoneNumber,
Students.Major, Departments.DepartmentName,
Instructors.Instructor,
[LastName] & ", " & [FirstName] AS [Student Name],
[Students And Classes].GdPts, [Students And Classes].Grade,
Classes.DaysAndTimes
FROM Students INNER JOIN ((Instructors RIGHT JOIN
(Departments RIGHT JOIN Classes
ON Departments.DepartmentID = Classes.DepartmentID)
ON InstructorsInstructorID = Classes.InstructorID)
INNER JOIN [Students And Classes]
ON Classes.ClassID = [Students And Classes].ClassID)
ON Students.StudentID = [Students And Classes].StudentID
GROUP BY Classes.ClassID, Classes.ClassName, Classes.Units,
```

continues

Listing 7.1   Continued

```
Students.StudentID, Students.PhoneNumber, Students.Major,
Departments.DepartmentName, Instructors.Instructor,
[LastName] & ", " & [FirstName], [Students And Classes].GdPts,
[Students And Classes].Grade, Classes.DaysAndTimes;
```

Several SQL keywords appear in this rather complicated statement, beginning with SELECT, which instructs the Jet DBEngine to return information as a set of records. The SELECT statement has many parts and keywords. The first word following SELECT is the predicate DISTINCTROW. The predicate restricts the number of records returned. If a predicate is not used, all the records are returned. Table 7.2 describes alternative predicate settings.

Table 7.2   SELECT Statement Predicate Alternatives

Predicate	Description
ALL	Selects all the records that meet the conditions in the SQL statement. ALL is assumed if no predicate is specified.
DISTINCT	Selects only records whose values in the fields listed in the SELECT statement are unique. The combination of all the selected fields must be unique. For example, if two students have the same last name, only one of the student records would be selected.
DISTINCTROW	Omits duplicate records whose fields are identical, rather than just one of the selected fields. Without DISTINCTROW, the query returns any multiple rows with the same values in the selected fields.
TOP*n*[PERCENT]	Returns the specified number or percent of records from the top or bottom of an ordered list.

The next eight elements of the SQL statement define the fields to be included in the query result: Classes.ClassID, Classes.ClassName, Classes.Units, and so on. The next clause,

```
[LastName] & ", " & [FirstName] AS [Student Name]
```

concatenates the student's last name and first name with a comma and space between the names and identifies the entire name as Student Name. It will appear in the report as Student Name. Three more fields are specified—two from the Students And Classes table and one from the Classes table.

The FROM statement contains three nested join statements—one INNER JOIN statement and two RIGHT JOIN statements. Refer to the query design in Figure 7.12 to follow the logic. The first phrase

```
FROM Students INNER JOIN
```

starts the linking procedure, which is completed with the last line:

```
ON Students.StudentID = [Students And Classes].StudentID
```

Together these two lines establish an inner join between the Students table and the Students And Classes table by matching the StudentID field. The inner join retrieves only the records from each table that have matching values in the common field. Between these two lines, other joins are specified.

Beginning with the following line, the SQL statement begins to define the relationship lines in the query definition. First the Departments table is connected to the Classes table with a right join by matching the DepartmentID fields. Then the Classes table is joined to the Instructors table by matching the InstructorID fields, again with a right join:

```
((Instructors RIGHT JOIN
```

It might look like something is missing, but Classes is implied as the table to join with the Instructors table after it's used in the Departments join phrase.

Next, the Students And Classes table is joined to the Classes table by the ClassID field with the following statement:

```
INNER JOIN [Students And Classes] ON Classes.ClassID =
[Students And Classes].ClassID
```

The final SQL statement specifies the grouping of the records for the report. Records are grouped first by information from the Classes table and then by student information. All fields in the SELECT field list must be included in the GROUP BY list, even if it doesn't make much sense. The fields in the list appear in the same order as in the query design grid.

Inspecting a Parameter Query Statement

To create a parameter query, type a prompt in the Criteria cell of the field whose value you want the user to enter. For example, to retrieve information about students in a specific class, type **[Enter ClassID]** in the Criteria row of the ClassID field. Clear the Show check box in the StudentID (Students And Classes) column to prevent two copies of the student name appearing in the query result. Listing 7.2 shows the resulting SQL code.

Listing 7.2   A Parameter Query

```
SELECT DISTINCTROW Students.StudentID, Students.FirstName,
Students.LastName, [Students And Classes].ClassID,
[Students And Classes].Grade
FROM Students INNER JOIN [Students And Classes] ON Students.StudentID =
[Students And Classes].StudentID
WHERE (([Students And Classes].ClassID)=[Enter ClassID]);
```

Notice that in the WHERE clause, the ClassID value in the Students And Classes table must equal the value entered as the parameter variable, [Enter ClassID], to be included in the query result. Figure 7.13 shows the results of running this query and entering "4" into the Enter Parameter Value dialog box.

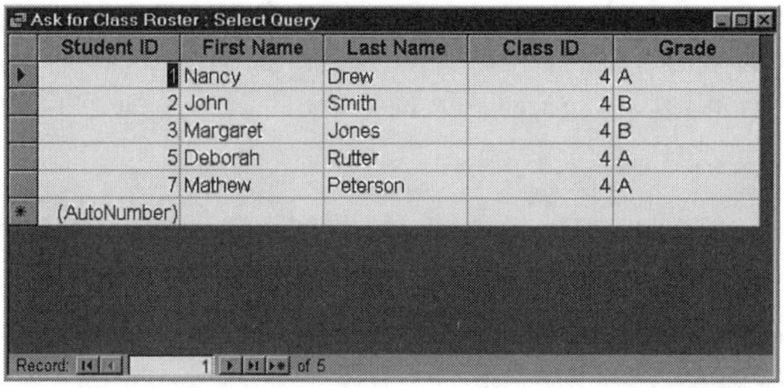

FIGURE 7.13

Class roster for class number 4.

	Student ID	First Name	Last Name	Class ID	Grade
▶	1	Nancy	Drew	4	A
	2	John	Smith	4	B
	3	Margaret	Jones	4	B
	5	Deborah	Rutter	4	A
	7	Mathew	Peterson	4	A
*	(AutoNumber)				

Inspecting Action Query Statements

Many of the same keywords and operators used in select queries are also used in action queries.

The following example of a make-table SQL query creates a new table named Alumni. The query in Listing 7.3 represents the entries you would make in the table design window, complete with field name and data type definitions and an index designated as the primary key.

Listing 7.3   A Make-Table SQL Query

```
CREATE TABLE Alumni
([AlumID] integer,
[LastName] text,
[FirstName] text,
[Address] text,
[City] text,
[State] text,
[Zip] text,
[Country] text,
```

```
[LastContribDate] date,
CONSTRAINT [Index1] PRIMARY KEY ([AlumID]))
```

The code in Listing 7.4 is the SQL statement that represents the append query, Add A's, which adds new student records for every student who has received an A grade in a class. The records are added to the Honor Roll table.

Listing 7.4   An Append Query

```
INSERT INTO [Honor Roll] ( StudentID, FirstName, LastName, ClassID, Grade )
SELECT [Students And Classes].StudentID, Students.FirstName,
Students.LastName, Count([Students And Classes].ClassID) AS CountOfClassID,
[Students And Classes].Grade
FROM Students INNER JOIN [Students And Classes] ON Students.StudentID =
[Students And Classes].StudentID
GROUP BY [Students And Classes].StudentID, Students.FirstName,
Students.LastName, [Students And Classes].Grade
HAVING (((([Students And Classes].Grade)="A"))
ORDER BY Students.LastName;
```

ANALYSIS

The first line, INSERT INTO, establishes the action query as an append query and specifies the target table as Honor Roll. Next, the statement lists the names of the fields to include.

The FROM and GROUP BY clauses are the same as for select queries. The HAVING clause is similar to WHERE. After the records are grouped with GROUP BY, HAVING determines which records are displayed. This query displays records whose Grade value is "A," ordered by the student's last name, and counts the number of students with A grades.

Inspecting a SQL Query Statement

Listing 7.5 is an example of a SQL union query that combines names and addresses from two unrelated tables into a single table.

Listing 7.5   A Union Query

```
SELECT [FirstName],[LastName] AS [Alumni/LastName],[City]
FROM [Alumni]
WHERE [Country] = "USA"
UNION SELECT [FirstName],[LastName],[City]
FROM [Students]
WHERE [Country] = "USA"
ORDER BY [City];
```

ANALYSYIS

The first SELECT clause in Listing 7.5 retrieves the first and last names and the city from the Alumni table. It also renames the last name as Alumni/LastName to distinguish alumni from students. The records are limited to alumni residing in the United States.

The UNION SELECT clause retrieves corresponding student information, again limiting the records to students who live in the United States. Finally, the ORDER BY clause sorts the records by city to make it easier for the two factions to communicate.

If you want to include duplicate records in the union, use UNION ALL instead of UNION.

Writing SQL Statements

The easiest way to write a SQL statement is to start with a query design in the Design View grid and then switch to SQL view for any necessary changes. The keywords and parentheses are already placed in their proper positions. An additional advantage is that you minimize the risk of misspelling an Access object and causing an error that must be tracked down.

When the statement is created, you can use the SQL code as the record source for a report or form by pasting it into the RecordSource property. To do so, select all or part of the code in the SQL view and press Ctrl+C, which copies the selection to the Clipboard. Next, place the insertion point in the RecordSource property of the form or report and press Ctrl+V. The SQL code now appears in the property sheet. To see it all, right-click the code and choose Zoom from the shortcut menu.

DEVELOPMENT

PERFORMANCE

An alternative to pasting the SQL code in the property sheet is to save the query definition and use the query name instead of the SQL statement as the record source. This strategy has two advantages: The query definition is saved and available for use by other forms and reports, and the processing runs a little faster because the query has already been compiled. A SQL statement must be recompiled each time it is referenced.

When you use a wizard to create a report or form, it fills in the SQL statement for you and uses it as the RecordSource property. If you want to save the query for use in another form or report, click Build in the property sheet to open the query design view. Then, name and save the query definition.

If you haven't already created the query to be used as the record source, click Build in the RecordSource property to open the query design view. Use the Design View grid to create the query. When you save the query, the name appears in the RecordSource property.

> **Note:** You can create most queries in the query design view. The exception is the SQL-specific query that communicates with the back-end server. They must be created using SQL statements.

To see the SQL code of a query already specified in the RecordSource property, click Build to open the query design window and switch to SQL view.

Running SQL Statements

Select queries are run when you open the form or report that uses them as the record source. You can, of course, run a query from the Queries page of the database window. You can also run action and data-definition queries by using the RunSQL action in a macro or from within a Visual Basic procedure.

Using a Macro

Action queries that append, delete, or update records in a table and save the results in a new table can be run from a macro if the SQL statement does not exceed 256 characters. If it does, you must use a Visual Basic procedure, which can handle up to 32,768 characters. Figure 7.14 shows a macro that runs a short SQL statement to create a new table for listing the best text books for Clayview City College.

FIGURE 7.14

The MakeBest *macro creates a new table.*

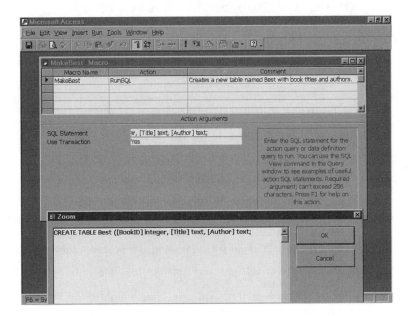

You can also use a macro to run a data-definition query.

> **Tip:** The RunSQL action does not run a select or crosstab query. To run one of those from a macro, use the OpenQuery action and set the View argument to open the query in datasheet view. The FindA macro shown in Figure 7.15 opens the Count A select query in datasheet view, effectively running the query.

FIGURE 7.15
The FindA *macro*
opens the Count A
query in
datasheet view.

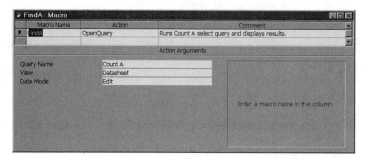

If you want to run a select query or a crosstab query from a macro, use the OpenQuery
action and set the View argument to Datasheet.

Using a Visual Basic Procedure

To run an action or data-definition query from within a VB procedure, use the DoCmd
object with the RunSQL method. The entire SQL statement must be enclosed in quotation
marks and declared as a string variable. The following VB code runs the make-table
query shown earlier that creates the Alumni table:

```
DoCmd.RunSQL "CREATE TABLE Alumni ([AlumID] integer, [LastName] text," & _
"[FirstName] text, [Address] text,[City] text, [State] text, "& _
"[Zip] text, [Country] text, [LastContribDate] date," & _
"CONSTRAINT [Index1] PRIMARY KEY ([AlumID]));"
```

TROUBLESHOOTING   Be careful to use correct SQL structure and keywords because VBA does not check for
errors in SQL syntax.

You can also create a query definition within a VB procedure using the DAO 3.6
CreateQueryDef method. For example, the following code fragment creates a select
query that returns records from the Classes table for all classes from the fall term. The
query is named Fall Semester and is saved in the current database.

```
Dim dbs As Object, qdf As Object, strSQL As String
Set dbs = CurrentDb
strSQL = "SELECT * FROM Classes WHERE Term = "Fall";
Set qdf = dbs.CreateQueryDef("Fall Semester", strSQL)
```

> **Tip:** If you're inserting an action query into a VB procedure, the user will see a
> warning box asking for confirmation before running the query. To avoid this
> confusion for the user, turn off the Warning feature just before the query and
> then turn it back on in the next statement after the query.

DEVELOPMENT   Placing queries within Visual Basic procedures also gives you the opportunity to control
program flow and pass parameters to the query. Procedures run a little slower with
embedded SQL query strings than procedures that refer to queries already constructed

and compiled. However, if you need the flexibility, you can sacrifice some of the processing speed.

Looking Ahead

For more information on using macros in your application, see Chapter 8, "Creating Macros." Chapter 9, "Writing Visual Basic Procedures," contains more information on the DoCmd object and its uses.

Performance

Technical Note: Optimization Techniques for SQL

When databases become very large and expressions in queries become complex, database management must be as efficient as possible. The Microsoft Jet database engine automatically assesses the query specifications and determines the most efficient method of executing the query. The strategy depends on the size of the table and the index as well as a concept called the *Rushmore technology*.

Rushmore is used to optimize certain types of complex expressions in the criteria row of the Design View grid or in a SQL statement. Simple expressions can be optimized if they include an indexed field and one of the standard comparison operators, such as <, >, =, Between, and so on. The field can have its own index or it can be the first field in a multiple-field index.

A small table can be queried easily by reading the table records. However, if the table contains quite a lot of information—many large records—it's more efficient to work with indexes. If the indexes are, themselves, large, reading the data might be just as efficient as compounding the index values.

When you create an index for a table, you're actually creating a small table with a field for each field in the index plus a pointer to the record it represents. An index table has as many records as the base table, but each record is much smaller. The Rushmore technology works only with the indexes, without reading the table records directly. The concept uses indexes to process the WHERE and JOIN clauses in a SQL statement. It looks at all the indexes and applies the criteria to the specified index and tags the index entries that meet the criteria. After scanning all the indexes, it compares tags and combines the results with AND or OR operators, depending on the criteria.

Rushmore can optimize a complex expression by combining two simple, optimizable expressions with the OR or AND operator. If one or both of the simple expressions is not optimizable, Rushmore is not used. Rushmore queries also work with Microsoft FoxPro and dBASE tables but not with ODBC data sources.

Even more time is saved when the query returns a count based on a field contained in the index Rushmore doesn't bother with the records—it just counts the items in the indexes.

Another technique used by the Jet database engine is a process that displays the first few records retrieved by the query while completing the query process in the background.

continues

The Jet engine also uses *multithreading* to process queries involving multiple-index searches. It reads through one index on the first thread and retrieves entries that match the criteria. These retrievals are simultaneously passed to another thread for further matching and retrieval. This process is called *read ahead and write behind* and is a form of parallel processing.

Summary

This chapter has examined the types of queries you can use to retrieve information from Access tables. It has also demonstrated how to use SQL to define queries that feed report and form designs. The process of running a SQL statement with a macro or from a VBA procedure was also discussed.

The next chapter, "Creating Macros," discusses creating and using macros for several purposes. It also examines events, which objects they apply to, and when they occur. You'll also learn how to attach a macro to an event property to carry out a specific task.

Creating Macros

Macros are easy-to-build, easy-to-use collections of actions that can make your application run smoothly. A simple macro can consist of a single action that causes the system to beep when you click a button. A more complex macro can contain multiple actions that open a form and automatically update fields in the form.

Chapter 1, "Why Program Access?", briefly discusses macros as one of the Access programming languages. This chapter looks into programming with macros in more detail and shows you how to use them in an application. It also describes when it's better to use a Visual Basic procedure instead of a macro and how to convert macros to Visual Basic event procedures.

What Can Macros Do?

Each macro action performs a specific operation, such as setting a value, opening a form, or closing a dialog box. Any task you perform repeatedly is a candidate for a macro. The macro runs in response to an event, such as a button click or a field update. Each action in the macro is carried out in sequence. To run a macro, you refer to it by name, often attaching it to the appropriate event property of a form, control, or report.

Macros are easy to create and can be used to perform quite a variety of operations, including the following:

- Opening a report for preview or printing
- Synchronizing data in two or more forms
- Navigating among controls, records, and form pages
- Setting object properties, often based on another value
- Validating newly entered data or displaying a message
- Performing alternative actions depending on conditions
- Performing actions at startup
- And almost anything else you can think of

Macros work like robots. They perform a series of actions, one at a time, until they run out of actions. The exception is when you've added a macro condition such as IsNull() that tests for a blank value. If the condition returns True, the action is carried out; if not, the macro skips to the next action. By skillfully arranging the macro actions, you can create an If...Then...Else program flow.

After the macro is completed and checked out, you can attach it by name to an event property so that it's executed when the event occurs.

Individual related macros can be grouped into a macro group for easier handling. For example, you could group all the macros that are attached to the command buttons in a form.

When an event occurs, Access automatically responds with a built-in behavior that varies by object. For example, when you click a button, it appears pressed in; when you enter new data, it's automatically checked for the correct data type. When you attach a macro or event procedure to an object's event property, the built-in response occurs first and then the macro or event procedure is executed.

| DEVELOPMENT |

The most significant thing a macro cannot do is trap errors. For that, you must use a VB event procedure and attach it to the object's OnError event property.

Touring the Macro Design Window

To start a new macro, click New in the Macros page of the database window or choose Insert|Macro. You can also click the down arrow next to the New Object button and choose Macro from the drop-down list.

The macro design window, shown in Figure 8.1, has two parts: the upper pane, which contains the action and comment columns, and the lower pane, in which you specify any action arguments that apply to the selected action. The number and type of arguments depends on the action you've added. The lower pane also displays a box with instructions about the currently selected part of the macro window. In Figure 8.1, the insertion point is in the Action column, so the instruction is "Enter an action in this column."

The macro design window has six new buttons on the toolbar, with six corresponding menu items. The Macro Names and Conditions buttons show or hide the corresponding columns in the macro design. The View menu also has those commands.

The Insert Rows button inserts a blank row above the selected row. You can also choose Insert|Rows to add one or more blank rows and Edit|Delete Rows to delete selected rows. If you select more than one row and click Insert Rows, Access inserts the same number of rows as are selected. The Delete Rows button deletes one or more selected macro rows. You can click the Undo button to reverse both inserting and deleting rows.

The Run button (the one with the large exclamation point icon) runs the macro, and the Single Step button runs the macro one action at a time. These two options are also found on the Run menu.

FIGURE 8.1

*An empty macro
design window.*

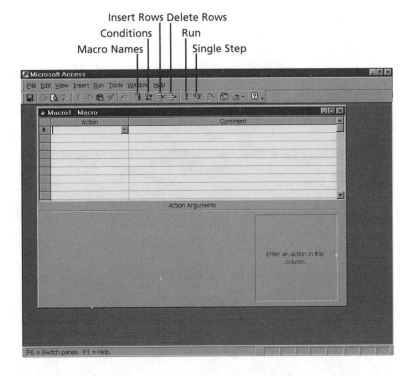

Insert Rows Delete Rows
Conditions   Run
Macro Names   Single Step

Tip: If you expect to be using the Macro Name and Condition columns with most of the macros you create, you can set two options, Names column and Conditions column in the Show in macro group in the View tab of the Options dialog box, that will always show them by default.

When you begin to add an action to the macro, the lower pane displays the action argument list. Figure 8.2 shows a new macro named GoStudents with a single action, OpenForm. The design window now has four columns, with the addition of the Macro Name and Condition columns.

After you add the OpenForm action to the macro, the arguments for the action appear in the Action Arguments pane. They include the name of the form, the view you want to see, any filter name or Where condition you want to impose, the data mode, and the window mode. You can often select these arguments from a pull-down menu. For example, with the OpenForm action, the Form Name argument displays a drop-down list of all the forms in the current database. From the View argument list, you can choose Form, Design, Print Preview, or Datasheet, as the instruction box describes.

Enter an expression or the name of a saved query in the Filter Name argument. In the Where Condition line, you can click Build to get help from the Expression Builder to create the correct expression. The Data Mode argument lets you decide whether to allow the user to edit or enter data or to keep the form "read-only." The last argument for this action, Window Mode, lets you select from Normal, Hidden, Icon, and Dialog. The Normal setting displays the form the way it's specified in the form properties. Hidden hides the form, and Icon displays the form minimized. The Dialog setting sets the form's Modal and Pop-Up properties both to Yes, which makes the form act like a dialog box.

Other actions have a different group of arguments, and some have none.

FIGURE 8.2

Adding an
`OpenForm` *action to the macro.*

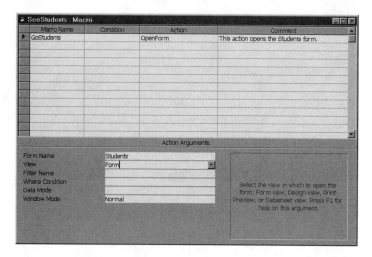

Looking at the Macro Structure

The only required elements in a macro are the actions and perhaps some of the corresponding action arguments. Many of the arguments are optional, such as the Filter Name and Where Condition arguments for the `OpenForm` action. Other arguments, such as Window Mode, assume default values, which you can change as desired. Normal is the default setting for the Window Mode argument of the `OpenForm` action.

Access provides over 50 actions that you can use in macros. Table 8.1, in the section "Setting Actions and Arguments," lists the macro actions. They fall into several categories, such as working with data in forms and reports, executing other commands and applications, transferring objects and data among applications, manipulating Access objects, and other miscellaneous tasks (such as beeping and displaying information on the screen).

Action arguments provide more specific information about how you want Access to carry out the action (for example, the form name, record number, or filter condition).

You use the Condition column to set conditions under which the macro action is to run. For example, if a student's grade is *A*, then display a message box with a congratulatory message. This condition is not to be confused with the Where condition in the Action Arguments pane, which is used to filter the records that are to appear in the form or report.

Creating and Debugging Macros

To begin creating a new macro, choose New in the Macros page of the database window or choose Macro from the Insert menu. The macro design window opens. Here, you can add the actions and arguments that will accomplish the objective of the macro. The ample use of comments in building a macro will help you later in interpreting what it's supposed to do and when.

Tip: Preceding the macro names with the prefix *mac* helps to differentiate macros from other objects in the database.

Setting Actions and Arguments

The Action column contains a pull-down menu from which you can select the action you want the macro to execute (see Figure 8.3). Another way to enter the action is to type the first few characters of the action. Access completes that action name as you type; when it reaches the action you want, press Enter. The Action Arguments pane then shows the arguments for that action.

FIGURE 8.3
Choose an action from the pull-down menu.

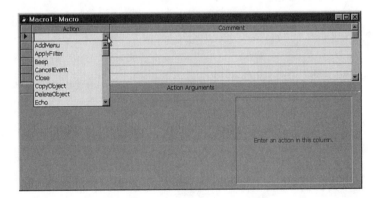

Enter the action argument for each action or use the pull-down menu. If the action requires the name of a form or other database object, the pull-down menu in the Action Argument pane displays the names of all the objects of that type in the current database. Be sure to begin setting arguments from the top of the argument list in the Action Arguments pane, because a setting in one of the arguments might change the choices in a later argument.

Adding a Where condition limits the records that appear in a form or report. You can use the Expression Builder to help with the condition expression, or you can type it directly in the argument line. Figure 8.4 shows an OpenForm action that includes a Where condition argument that will show only records whose ClassID value matches that in the active Students form. Here's the complete Where condition in the macro:

```
[ClassID]=[Forms]![Students]![ClassID]
```

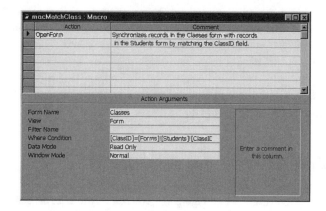

FIGURE 8.4
Adding a Where condition to the macro.

The form is opened as read-only, and the user will not be able to add or edit any of the records. This technique is often used to synchronize the records between a main form and a lookup form.

Table 8.1 lists the actions you can add to a macro, grouped by general purpose. Some of the actions fall into more than one group.

Table 8.1 Macro Actions

Purpose	Actions
Limit data in form or report	ApplyFilter
Navigate through data	FindNext, FindRecord, GoToControl, GoToPage, and GoToRecord
Execute a command	RunCommand
Exit Access	Quit
Run a query, a procedure, another macro, SQL code, or another application	OpenQuery, RunCode, RunMacro, RunSQL, and RunApp
Stop execution without exiting Access	CancelEvent, Quit, StopAllMacros, and StopMacro
Export an Access object to other applications	OutputTo and SendObject

Purpose	Actions
Exchange data with other data formats	`TransferDatabase`, `TransferSpreadsheet`, and `TransferText`
Manipulate Access objects	`Close`, `CopyObject`, `DeleteObject`, `OpenDataAccessPage`, `OpenDiagram`, `OpenForm`, `OpenModule`, `OpenQuery`, `OpenReport`, `OpenStoredProcedure`, `OpenTable`, `OpenView`, `Rename`, `Save`, and `SelectObject`
Print an Access object	`OpenForm`, `OpenQuery`, `OpenReport` (setting the view to Print Preview), and `PrintOut`
Resize or move a window	`Maximize`, `Minimize`, `MoveSize`, and `Restore`
Specify the value of a field, control, or object property	`SetValue`
Update data or the screen	`RepaintObject`, `Requery`, `ShowAllRecords`
Create a custom or global menu bar or shortcut menu	`AddMenu`
Specify the state of an item on a custom or global menu bar (enabled or disabled; checked or unchecked)	`SetMenuItem`
Show an item or information on the screen	`Echo`, `HourGlass`, `MsgBox`, and `SetWarnings`
Generate keystrokes	`SendKeys`
Show or hide a built-in or custom toolbar	`ShowToolbar`
Sound a beep	`Beep`

Creating a Macro Group

COMPATIBILITY

When you have several macros that are used with the same form or related in some other way, keeping track of them is easier if they're in a macro group. In earlier versions of Access, such groups were called *macro libraries*. To create a macro group, choose New in the Macros tab of the database window and open the Macro Names column in the design window. As you create the macros for the group, give each one a name and add the desired actions. Leaving a blank line between the individual macros in the group is not necessary but it does make it easier to read the list.

One of the easiest ways to add a macro action that involves a database object is to drag the object from the database window to the Action column of the macro design. Access automatically adds the appropriate arguments, which you can change or add to, as you want.

With this method, you can create several macros at once by having both the database window and the macro design window open at the same time. Figure 8.5 shows a switchboard for the Clayview City College that gives the user a list of forms he or she can open. The switchboard shows five items: four to enter or view data and one to return to the main switchboard.

FIGURE 8.5
A switchboard for opening forms.

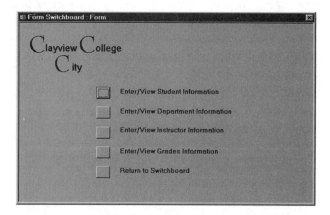

To create the macros that open the forms listed in the Clayview City College switchboard, follow these steps:

1. With the database window open, click the Macros page and choose New to open the macro design window.

2. Choose Window|Tile Vertically to show both windows on the screen.

3. Click the Forms page in the database window and then click and drag the Students form name to the Action column of the first row. The form name is automatically entered into the Action Arguments pane.

4. Repeat Step 3 for the other forms named in the switchboard items: Classes, Departments, Instructors, and Grades, leaving a blank line between each one.

5. Click the Macro Names button to add that column and enter a name for each macro, using the mac tag preceding each macro to identify the object as a macro.

6. Finally, add the last macro, the Close action, which responds to the Return to Switchboard item.

Figure 8.6 shows the results with the action OpenForm automatically entered and the last form name, Grades, in the argument list.

FIGURE 8.6
Dragging an object from the database window builds a macro.

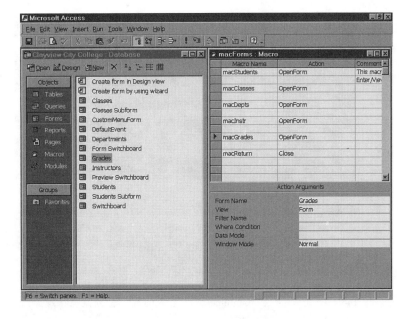

Notice that the macro group has a different name than any of the macros in the group. When you refer to a macro in the group, use the group name as well as the macro name. For example, to attach the `macClasses` macro to the `OnClick` event property of a button, use `macForms.macClasses`.

The same technique can be used to create the macro group for the Preview Switchboard items that preview various reports.

Assigning AutoKeys

Instead of assigning an action or set of actions to a macro name, you can use a specific key combination, such as Ctrl+F3, by creating macros in an `AutoKeys` macro group. Each key combination can trigger a list of actions or simply execute the `RunMacro` action with the name of an existing macro.

To assign a key combination to a macro action, use the key combination as the macro name, using the key name syntax. For example, the caret symbol (^) represents the Ctrl key and the plus sign (+) represents the Shift key. Key names such as F7, Insert, and Delete are enclosed in curly brackets ({}).

Figure 8.7 shows an example of an `AutoKeys` macro group with a single macro that runs when you press Ctrl+L. You can add as many macros to the `AutoKeys` group as you need.

FIGURE 8.7

An AutoKeys *key combination that displays a message box.*

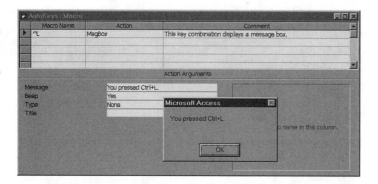

> **Warning:** Access uses certain key combinations for special operations, such as Ctrl+C for Copy and Ctrl+V for Paste. If you assign different actions to any of these key combinations, your actions will replace the ones Access specified. You might get some surprising results.

Table 8.2 lists the key combinations that are available as AutoKeys key combinations and shows examples of the syntax.

Table 8.2   Available AutoKeys Key Combinations

Key Combination	Examples
Ctrl+*any letter or number*	^F or ^9
Any function key by itself	{F7}
Ctrl+*any function key*	^{F3}
Shift+*any function key*	+{F6}
Insert	{INSERT}
Ctrl+Insert	^{INSERT}
Shift+Insert	+{INSERT}
Delete	{DELETE} or {DEL}
Ctrl+Delete	^{DELETE} or ^{DEL}
Shift+Delete	+{DELETE} or +{DEL}

You can run a macro named as a key combination by selecting it in the Macros tab of the database window and choosing Run. To run the macro by pressing the keys, you must save it in the AutoKeys macro group.

The macro AutoKeys feature is analogous to the SendKeys statement in Visual Basic.

Debugging a Macro

If an error occurs while you're running a macro as a whole rather than step-by-step, an error message appears, and it's up to you to find which action caused the error. The easiest way to debug the macro is to change to Single Step mode and run the macro one action at a time. With Single Step, the macro executes the actions, one at a time. That way, you can pinpoint the action causing the trouble.

To start Single Step, in the macro design window, choose Run|Single Step (or click the Single Step button) and then choose Run. The Macro Single Step dialog box appears, displaying the specifics of the first action (see Figure 8.8). You can see the row selector pointing to the macStudents macro in the macro design window in the background. The dialog box displays the macro name, the current value of the condition, and the action name and its arguments. If you haven't specified a condition for the action, it automatically evaluates to True.

FIGURE 8.8

The Macro Single Step dialog box provides information about the current action.

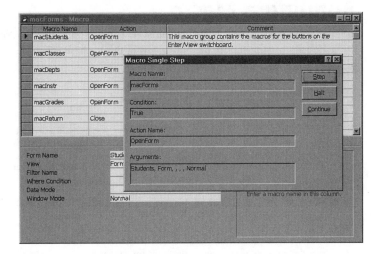

The Macro Single Step dialog box has three options:

- *Step*. Executes this action and displays the next action in the macro
- *Halt*. Stops the macro and closes the dialog box
- *Continue*. Turns off the Single Step mode and runs the rest of the macro in normal mode

If an error occurs in one step, the appropriate Access error message appears. Choosing OK to close the error message opens the Action Failed dialog box, which displays the action that caused the error together with its arguments. This dialog box is similar to the Macro Single Step dialog box, but it has only one option: Halt. You must close the dialog box and correct the error in the action before you can run the macro again.

Note: You can stop the execution of a macro and change to Single Step at any time by pressing Ctrl+Break.

The Single Step mode remains in effect until you cancel it. To discontinue Single Step execution, click the Single Step button again or choose Run|Single Step to clear the option.

Warning: You can copy, move, or delete a macro just like any other object. However, when you rename a macro, Access does not update the macro name in the property sheet. You must remember to change all references to the macro to the new name.

Running a Macro

You must save a macro before you can run it. After doing so, you have several ways to run it: directly from the macro design window or the database window, from another macro or procedure, or in response to an event.

Here are the ways you can run a macro:

- From the macro design window, click Run on the toolbar or choose Run|Run. If the macro refers to a field or other object in a form that's not open, it will not run from the macro design window or the database window.

- From the database window, select the macro name and choose Run or right-click the macro name and choose Run from the shortcut menu.

- From another macro, use the RunMacro action and enter the macro name in the Action Argument list.

- From a VB procedure, use the DoCmd object and the RunMacro method (for example, DoCmd.RunMacro "macForms.macClasses").

- In response to an event, attach the macro to the object's corresponding event property.

Note: If you try to run a group macro from the macro design window or the database window, only the first macro in the group executes.

Attaching a Macro to an Event Property

After you've created the macro that contains the desired response for a specific event, such as a button click or a text box update, you can attach the macro to the event property of the control. To do this, open the property sheet for the control and click the Events tab. Then, choose the macro name from the pull-down menu in the desired event property.

DEVELOPMENT

If you haven't created the macro yet, click the Build button in the event property and choose Macro Builder from the Choose Builder dialog box. Then, name and create the macro. The new macro is automatically attached to that event and is also stored in the database, where it's available for use with other events.

To attach a macro to the same property of more than one object, select all the objects and then select the macro name from the pull-down menu in the event property sheet. Figure 8.9 illustrates attaching the macForms.macGrades macro to the OnClick property of both a button and its label in the Forms switchboard. Notice that the property sheet indicates a multiple selection, and only the events common to all selected objects are listed. When you view the switchboard, clicking either the button or the label opens the Grades form.

FIGURE 8.9
Attaching a macro
to two objects.

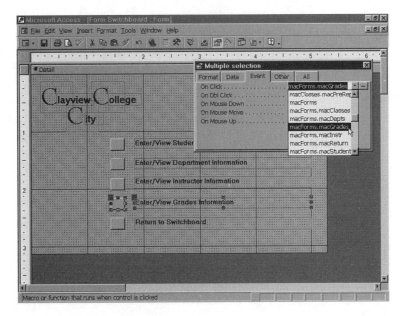

Forms, form sections and controls, reports, and report sections all have events associated with their object types. For example, a toggle button can respond to a click event, whereas a report section can respond to a format event. Table 8.3 lists the events, describes when they occur in relation to other events for the same objects, and shows the types of objects to which they apply. To find out which specific control types the event applies to, look at the Help topic.

Table 8.3   Events and the Objects to Which They Apply

Event	When It Occurs	Applies To
Activate	When the object becomes the active window.	Forms and reports
AfterDelConfirm	After the user confirms deletions and when records are deleted or the user cancels the deletion.	Forms
AfterInsert	After a new record is created.	Forms
AfterUpdate	After a record or form control is updated with modified data.	Forms and form controls
ApplyFilter	When the user applies or removes a filter.	Forms
BeforeDelConfirm	Between the user performing a delete action and Access asking for confirmation of the deletion.	Forms
BeforeInsert	After the user types the first character of the record but before the record is added.	Forms
BeforeUpdate	Before data in a record or form control is updated. Also when a control or record loses focus or the user chooses Record|Save Record.	Forms and form controls
Change	When the contents of a text box or combo box are changed. Also when the user changes a character or a control Text property.	Form controls
Click	When the user presses and releases the left mouse button.	Forms and form controls
Close	When a form or report is closed and removed from the screen.	Forms and reports
Current	When the focus moves to a record or a form is refreshed or requeried.	Forms
DblClick	When the user presses and releases the left mouse button twice.	Forms, form sections, and form controls
Deactivate	When a different window replaces the form or report as the active window.	Forms and reports

Event	When It Occurs	Applies To
Delete	When the user performs a delete action but before the record is deleted.	Forms
Dirty	When data has been changed but not yet saved.	Forms
Enter	Before a control receives focus from a control on the same form, or as the first control on a newly opened form receives focus.	Form controls
Error	A runtime error occurs. Includes Jet DBEngine but not VB errors.	Forms and reports
Exit	Before a control loses focus to another control on the same form.	Form controls
Filter	When the user chooses Filter By Form or Advanced Filter/Sort to create a new filter or to modify an existing filter.	Forms
Format	Access assigns data to a report section before formatting the section for preview or print.	Report sections
GotFocus	When a form or control receives focus. A form receives focus only if it contains no controls or all controls are disabled.	Forms and form controls
KeyDown	When the User presses a key while a form or control has focus.	Forms and form controls
KeyPress	When the user presses and releases a key or key combination that matches an ANSI character code. Only while the form or control has focus.	Forms and form controls
KeyUp	When the user releases a pressed key while the form or control has focus.	Forms and form controls
Load	When the form is opened and records are displayed.	Forms
LostFocus	When the form or control loses focus.	Forms and form controls

continues

Table 8.3 Continued

Event	When It Occurs	Applies To
MouseDown	When the user presses a mouse button while the pointer is on a form or control.	Forms, form sections, and form controls
MouseMove	When the user moves the mouse pointer over a form, form section, or control.	Forms, form sections, and form controls
MouseUp	When the user releases a pressed mouse button over a form or control.	Forms, form sections, and form controls
NoData	After an empty report is formatted for printing, before printing.	Reports
NotInList	When a value entered in combo box is not in the combo box list.	Combo box controls on a form
Open (form)	When a form is opened but before the first record is displayed.	Forms
Open (report)	When a report is opened but before previewing or printing.	Reports
Page	After a report page is formatted for printing, before printing.	Reports
Print	After a report section is formatted for printing, before printing.	Report sections
Resize	When a form size changes or a form is first opened and expanded to its previously saved size.	Forms
Retreat	On returning to a previous report section for multiple formatting passes.	Report sections
Timer	At regular intervals set by the form's TimeInterval property.	Forms
Unload	After the form is closed but before it's removed from the screen.	Forms
Updated	When an OLE object's data has been changed by the source application.	ActiveX, bound and unbound object frames

Note: When you look up specific events in the Help topics, you'll find that some of the events, such as After Update and Before Update, that apply to check boxes, option buttons, and toggle buttons, do not apply if the control is part of an option group. The event then applies only to the group as a whole.

Sequence of Events

In order for your macro or event procedure to perform the operations you want when you want them to, it's important to understand the sequence of events. You need to know to which of the control event properties to attach a macro in order to accomplish the desired outcome. Many events occur when you're moving from one record to another for entering and editing data in a form. Even moving the mouse pointer around on the screen triggers events.

The following sections show some sequences of events that occur under specific circumstances. Many more scenarios can play out as you work in an application, but these will give you an idea of the way events trigger.

Events for Forms and Controls

When a form is first opened, the following events occur:

```
Open↓
  Load↓
    Resize↓
      Activate↓
        Current
```

If the form has no active control when it opens, the GotFocus event for the form triggers after Activate but before Current. If there's an active control, it gets focus.

The Current event can be used to set a property such as the caption or the size of the form or report when it first opens. For example, the SetValue macro in Figure 8.10 sets the caption of the Classes form to the value found in the Class field. The Item argument identifies the form property, Caption, and the Expression argument sets the new value to be the same as the Class Name field. You can use the Expression Builder to create the expression or enter it yourself. The important thing to remember is not to use an equal sign in the Expression argument.

Attaching the macCaption macro to the OnCurrent property of the form causes the caption to change as you move through the records. Figure 8.11 shows the form with the new event property setting. Instead of the default form caption in the title bar, the form now shows the name of the currently displayed class: Relational Database Design.

FIGURE 8.10

A macro that changes the Classes form caption to the value of the Class Name field.

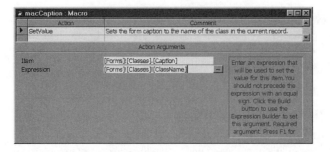

FIGURE 8.11

The form caption is the class name.

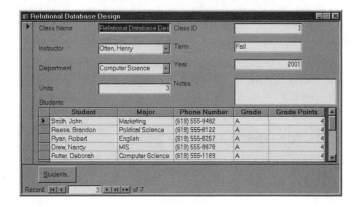

You can also use the Current event to show or hide custom menus and toolbars.

When the form closes, the following events occur:

```
Unload↓
  Deactivate↓
  Close
```

If the form has no active control when it closes, the LostFocus event for the form is triggered between Unload and Deactivate. If there was an active control, the Exit and LostFocus events for the control occur when the form closes, before the Unload event.

When you open a form and move between controls on that form, the first series of events opens the form and moves to the first control (C1):

```
Open↓
  Load↓
  Resize↓
    Activate↓
      Current↓
        Enter(C1)↓
        GotFocus(C1)
```

As you move from control to control on the form, the Exit and LostFocus events occur for the control you're leaving (C1) and Enter and GotFocus events occur for the control that you're moving to (C2). You can attach a macro to any of the control properties associated with these events.

```
Exit(C1)↓
  LostFocus(C1)↓
    Enter(C2)↓
      GotFocus(C2)
```

The OnGotFocus and OnEnter properties are often used to execute an action when you move to a field or other control. Figure 8.12 shows the results of a macro that triggers when the insertion point enters an empty Grade field in the Classes subform. The macro is attached to the OnGotFocus property of the Grade field and to the OnLostFocus property of the Telephone field, which precedes the Grade field in the tab order. When you move out of the Grade field without entering a value, the message "Enter a grade A to F. You may add + or –" appears in the status bar.

FIGURE 8.12

The OnGotFocus *event property displays a message in the status bar.*

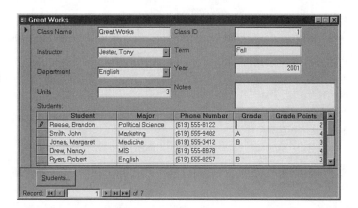

The macro tests for a blank Grade field and, if blank (Null), carries out the SetValue action, which displays the message in the status bar. The Expression Builder was used to designate the status bar text property as the Item argument (see Figure 8.13). The Expression argument is the text to be displayed, enclosed in quotation marks. Figure 8.14 shows the completed macCaption macro.

FIGURE 8.13

The Expression Builder helps with complex expressions.

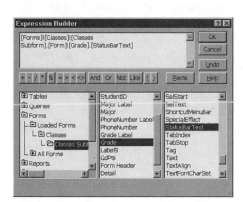

FIGURE 8.14
The completed macCaption *macro.*

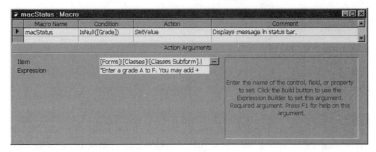

LOOKING AHEAD

Another macro is developed in the section "Controlling the Flow with Macro Conditions," later in this chapter, that updates the GdPts field with the value corresponding to the grade that's entered. This requires a more complex action condition that's equivalent to a Select Case statement in Visual Basic code. This macro is attached to the AfterUpdate event for the Grade field.

If you switch to another form, the last active control remains active on the first form. When you return to the first form, you're right back where you left off.

When you save a new record by choosing Records|SaveRecord, the following events occur:

```
BeforeInsert (form)
  BeforeUpdate(C2)↓
   AfterUpdate(C2)↓
     BeforeUpdate(form)↓
      AfterUpdate(form)↓
       AfterInsert(form)
```

When you delete a record, Access displays a dialog box asking for confirmation of the deletion with the following events:

```
Delete↓
 BeforeDelConfirm↓
  (display deletion confirmation dialog box)↓
   AfterDelConfirm
```

The BeforeDelConfirm event places the record in a buffer, and then Access displays a confirmation dialog box. If you cancel the BeforeDelConfirm event, the dialog box is not displayed and the AfterDelConfirm event does not occur. The AfterDelConfirm event occurs after the Deletion Confirm dialog box is displayed and returns the response to the confirmation.

You can attach a macro or procedure to the OnDelete event property of a control that will prevent a record from being deleted or specify that the record can only be deleted under special circumstances.

Note: If you select multiple records and choose Delete, the Delete event occurs for every one of the records first. Then it triggers the BeforeDelConfirm event.

Events for Keystrokes and Mouse Clicks

A *keyboard event* occurs when you press a key or send keystrokes while a form or control has focus. A *mouse event* occurs when you use the mouse buttons while the pointer is on a form, section, or control. A mouse event can also occur when you move the mouse pointer over part of a form, section, or control.

Pressing and releasing a key causes the following events to occur:

```
KeyDown↓
 KeyPress↓
  KeyUp
```

If the keystroke changes the value in a text box, the Change event occurs once for every key you press before reaching KeyUp.

Note: A change in the value of a calculated control or the selection of a value from a combo box does not trigger a Change event.

Updating data in one text box and then clicking a second text box triggers the update and exit events before passing focus to the second control. The sequence looks like this (the KeyDown/KeyPress/KeyUp loop repeats for each key pressed):

```
KeyDown↓
 KeyPress↓
  KeyUp↓
   BeforeUpdate(C1)↓
    AfterUpdate(C1)↓
     Exit(C1)↓
      LostFocus(C1)↓
       Enter(C2)↓
        GotFocus(C2)↓
         KeyDown(C2)↓
          KeyPress(C2)↓
           KeyUp(C2)
```

If the keystroke you press while in the first control moves focus to another control instead of entering a character, the KeyDown event applies to the first control and the KeyPress and KeyUp events apply to the second.

Note: If you enter a value in a combo box that's not in the list of values and you've set the LimitToList property for the control to Yes, you'll get an error

continues

message. Actually, the NotInList event occurs, which triggers an error event to which you can attach a macro or event procedure to its OnError property, to display a custom message:

```
KeyDown↓
 KeyPress↓
  Change↓
   KeyUp↓
    NotInList↓
     Error
```

To add a new record, move to the blank record and begin by entering a single character in the first control in the record. The following sequence of events occurs:

```
Current(new record)↓
 Enter(C1)↓
  GotFocus(C1)↓
   KeyDown(C1)↓
    KeyPress(C1)↓
     BeforeInsert(new record)↓
      Change(C1)↓
       KeyUp(C1)
```

Then, click another text box in the same record (no longer new) and enter text:

```
BeforeUpdate(C1)↓
AfterUpdate(C1)↓
 Exit(C1)↓
  LostFocus(C1)↓
   Enter(C2)↓
    GotFocus(C2)↓
     MouseDown(C2)↓
      MouseUp(C2)↓
       Click(C2)↓
        KeyDown(C2)↓
         KeyPress(C2)↓
          Change(C2)↓
           KeyUp(C2)
```

In the preceding sequence, you can see that clicking a mouse button also triggers the MouseDown/MouseUp/Click sequence of events. You've already seen how to attach macros to the OnClick property of command buttons.

Using the mouse to move from one control to another causes the following sequence of events:

```
Exit(C1)↓
 LostFocus(C1)↓
  Enter(C2)↓
   GotFocus(C2)↓
    MouseDown(C2)↓
     MouseUp(C2)↓
      Click(C2)
```

Double-clicking the mouse button causes both Click and DoubleClick events to occur. The MouseMove event, which is independent of the other mouse events, occurs whenever you move the mouse pointer over a control, form, or section. This event can be used to display ScreenTips when the pointer pauses on a button on a form.

Events for Reports and Report Sections

Reports and report sections have fewer event properties than forms and controls. When you open a report to preview or print it and then close it or make another window the active window, the following events occur:

```
Open↓
 Activate↓
  Close↓
   Deactivate
```

The Format and Print events happen to report sections after the report is activated:

```
Open(report)↓
 Activate(report)↓
  Format(section)↓
   Print(section)↓
    Close(report)↓
     Deactivate(report)
```

Default Events

More than three-quarters of the macros used in an application are attached to objects' default events. Default events are not triggered automatically; they simply are the events most often associated with a particular object. For example, the Click event is the most common event associated with toggle and command buttons, and Open is the most common event for reports. Not all objects have default events.

Table 8.4 lists the default events and their associated objects.

Table 8.4   Default Events for Access Objects

Default Event	Objects
Click	Form detail section and the following controls: check box, command button, image, label, option button, rectangle, and toggle button
BeforeUpdate	Combo box, list box, option group, and text box
Updated	Chart and bound and unbound object frames
Enter	Subform
Load	Form
Open	Report
Format	Report section

Access provides a shortcut for creating a macro or event procedure that responds to the default event. First, right-click the control and choose Build Event from the shortcut menu. Then choose Macro Builder in the Choose Builder dialog box to open the macro design window. The macro you create here will automatically be attached to the default event property of the control. This saves you the step of attaching it yourself.

To see how this works, follow these steps:

1. Create a new blank form based on the Classes table and add two of the text box controls, such as Class Name and Instructor ID, to the form.

2. Right-click the Class Name text box control and choose Build Event from the shortcut menu.

3. Choose Macro Builder from the Choose Builder dialog box and name the macro DefaultEvent.

4. In the blank macro design window, choose MsgBox in the Action column and enter a message such as **This is a default event for a text box** (see Figure 8.15). Then close the macro window. Unlike the status bar text, you do not enclose the message text in quotation marks unless you want them to appear in the message.

FIGURE 8.15

Building a macro to be attached to the default event property.

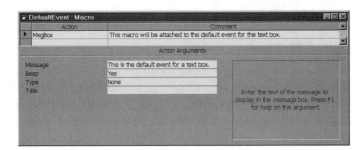

5. Open the property sheet for the text box control and look at the event properties. The new macro, DefaultEvent, is attached to the BeforeUpdate event property for the text box (see Figure 8.16).

FIGURE 8.16

The new macro attached to the BeforeUpdate event property.

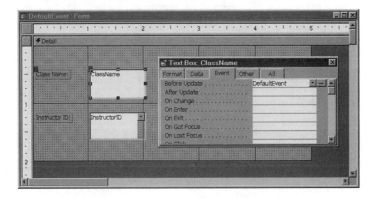

When you open the DefaultEvent form, enter a value in the Class Name field and then press Tab. The BeforeUpdate event occurs, which displays the message from the macro definition. Figure 8.17 shows the form after a class name has been entered and Tab was pressed to move to the Instructor ID text box control.

FIGURE 8.17

A message appears after the class name is entered before the record is updated.

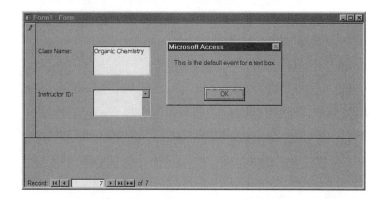

Controlling the Flow with Macro Conditions

PERFORMANCE

By listing macro actions with conditions, you can control the flow of operations in an application. In some cases, you might want to carry out the action only if the condition returns True. If the condition is not True, the macro stops or moves on to the next action, if there is one. You can even construct actions and conditions to mimic If...Then...Else and Select Case situations.

Figure 8.18 shows a straightforward macro that uses the MsgBox() function to request confirmation before deleting an Instructor record from the table. The DeleteConfirm macro that cancels the event is attached to the OnDelete form event property and is triggered when you choose Edit|Delete Record. The figure also shows a record in the Instructors form and the message box that asks for confirmation.

FIGURE 8.18

The DeleteConfirm macro asks for confirmation before deleting an Instructors record.

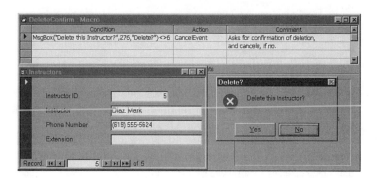

The complex action condition uses the MsgBox() function to display a special message box. The first argument in the function is the actual message, the second specifies the box type, and the third is the box caption. The number, 276, determines what you'll see in the box and is the total of the values that represent the display elements: button type Yes/No (4 points), icon style Stop sign (16 points), and the second button (No) as the default (256 points).

The condition returns the value of the button selected: Yes = 6, No = 7. Therefore, the condition allows the action (CancelEvent) to take place if the value of the selected button is not 6, which means the user does not really intend to delete the record. If it returns 6 (Yes), the deletion is intentional and the Delete event takes place. Table 8.5 lists the MsgBox() box type elements and their values.

Table 8.5 MsgBox() Function Arguments

Box Type Element	Value
OK button	0
OK and Cancel buttons	1
Abort, Retry and Ignore buttons	2
Yes, No and Cancel buttons	3
Yes and No buttons	4
Retry and Cancel buttons	5
No icon	0
Stop sign icon (Critical Message)	16
? Question mark icon (Warning Query)	32
! Exclamation mark icon (Warning Message)	48
I Information icon (Information Message)	64
First button default	0
Second button default	256
Third button default	512
Fourth button default	768

The MsgBox() function returns a value depending on which button was selected: OK = 1, Cancel = 2, Abort = 3, Retry = 4, Ignore = 5, Yes = 6, and No = 7.

You can also use macros to validate data beyond what's specified in the table definition. For example, the Grades macro group shown in Figure 8.19 contains a macro with two conditions. One makes sure the Grade field is not blank by displaying a message box with a prompt to enter a grade if the user leaves it empty. The other appears if the user enters a letter grade other than a letter between A and F. Both conditions are placed in the same AddGrade macro because they apply to the same event—BeforeUpdate.

FIGURE 8.19

The Grades *macro group validates entered grade values.*

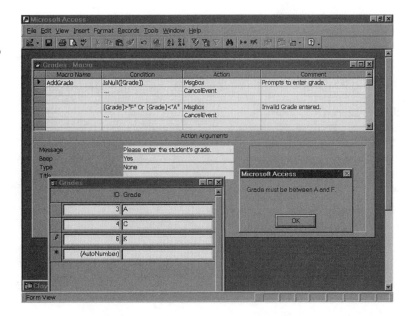

The figure shows the macro, the Grades form with an invalid entry, and the message box with the error message.

> **Tip:** If you want to be even more precise, you could add another criterion to the macro Condition precluding a grade of E. The Condition expression would read [Grade]>"F" OR [Grade]<"A" OR [Grade]="E". Then you may want to change the message to "You have entered an invalid grade."

The AddGrade macro demonstrates the use of ellipses to extend the condition beyond one action. The IsNull([Grade]) condition applies to both the MsgBox action on the first line and the CancelEvent action on the second line. The argument pane shows the message that displays if the grade is left blank. If the first condition returns False, Access skips to the next action that does not have an ellipsis in the Condition column.

The second condition that tests for a valid grade also extends to the CancelEvent action on the next line. CancelEvent stops the BeforeUpdate event and leaves the insertion point in the Grade text box.

The SetGdPts macro in Figure 8.20 is an example of using a macro to perform a Select Case statement. It includes a series of conditions that, one by one, determine what value to place in the GdPts field. If the grade entered is *A*, 4 is entered automatically in the GdPts field when the Grade text box control loses focus. The comparison LIKE "A*" uses the * wildcard to allow for A+ and A– grades. The default value of the GdPts field is set to 0 in the table definition; therefore, if none of the conditions in the macro is met, the field reverts to 0, the implied Case Else clause.

FIGURE 8.20
The SetGdPts
macro fills in the
GdPts value
depending on the
grade entered.

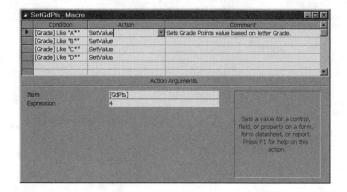

The SetGdPts macro is attached to the Grade OnLostFocus event property. After the grade is entered and the focus moves to another control, the GdPts field value is set.

Creating an AutoExec Macro

If there's one particular action or series of actions you want to execute whenever you open the database, you can create a special macro named AutoExec. You can use it to do such things as open a switchboard form, request a password, or ask the user to enter his or her name.

A database can contain only one AutoExec macro. When Access starts a database, it looks for a macro named AutoExec and, if it finds one, executes the macro. You can set many of the same options in this macro that appear in the Startup dialog box.

DEVELOPMENT

> **Warning:** The AutoExec runs after the startup options are applied, so if you include a conflicting action in the AutoExec macro, it will override the startup options. For example, you've set the Display Form setting in the Startup dialog box to Main Switchboard and then you include an OpenForm action in the AutoExec macro that opens the Students form. When you start the database, the Main Switchboard opens briefly and then gives way to the Students form.

To bypass the AutoExec macro, press Shift when you open the database. This also bypasses the other options set in the Startup dialog box.

Note: The database object has an AllowByPassKey property that you can create and set to keep the user from using Shift to bypass the startup settings and the AutoExec macro. This property is useful when you deliver an application to an end user who should not be allowed to change the way the application starts. When set to True (-1), the property enables the user to use Shift to bypass both the startup settings and the AutoExec macro. When set to False (0), the Shift key doesn't bypass anything. The setting takes effect the next time the database is opened.

Be sure to keep this property set to True until all the bugs are out of your application.

Creating Menus and Toolbars from Macros

Using the AddMenu macro action, you can create custom menus and shortcut menus for a particular database object or all Access windows. The AddMenu action has three arguments: the menu name, the menu macro name, and optional status bar text. The menu name is the command name that appears in the main menu bar at the top of the window. The menu macro name is the name of the macro group that contains the macros for the menu commands you want to see in the menu drop-down list.

Figure 8.21 shows a form with a custom menu bar containing two menus: Forms and Reports. The commands in the menus are taken from macro groups that contain the responses to buttons on the Forms and Preview Switchboards. Notice that the custom menu replaces the default Access menu because it's attached to the MenuBar property of the form. The figure also shows the CCC Main Menu macro that produced the menu commands.

Each menu on the menu bar requires a separate AddMenu action. The text you type in the Comment column for the action appears in the status bar when you choose the menu command.

To create a line between two menu items in the custom menu, enter a hyphen in the macro name column between the two macros you want to separate. To add an accelerator key to a menu item, type & just before the letter in the macro name. To create a submenu for any of the menu items, add an AddMenu action to the macro and name another menu macro.

After you create the menu macro, attach it to the MenuBar or ShortcutMenuBar property of a form, form control, or report. A customized shortcut menu replaces the built-in shortcut menu for form, form control, and report objects.

FIGURE 8.21

A custom menu bar with two menus.

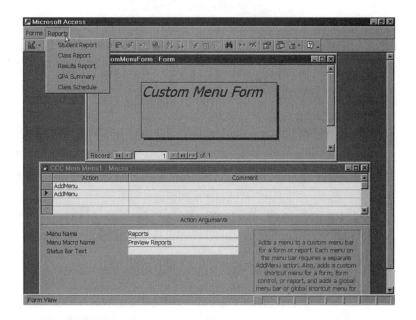

LOOKING AHEAD

Although you can still create custom menus with AddMenu macros, Microsoft recommends that you use the Customize dialog box instead. To open it, choose View|Toolbars|Customize or choose Customize from the toolbar shortcut menu. See Chapter 11, "Creating an Application from an Existing Database," for more information about creating your own customized menus, shortcut menus, and toolbars without using macros. With Customize, you can even add original icons to a custom menu or toolbar item.

COMPATIBILITY

Custom toolbars created with Access 97 are compatible with Access 2000. Custom menu bars and shortcut menus created with the Access 95 Menu Builder are interpreted as Access 2000–style menu bars and shortcut menus when you open a converted database, but they're not actually converted. Until they're converted, you cannot use the Customize dialog box to make changes in them.

A quick way to convert a menu or shortcut menu is to use the Tools menu. Select the menu macro in the database window and choose Tools|Create Menu From Macro (or Toolbar or Shortcut Menu). The new menu appears immediately at the top of the window above the built-in main menu. A new toolbar appears in the lower-right corner of the window. You can drag both around on the screen wherever you want them to appear, and you can even dock the new toolbar. A new shortcut menu does not appear until you open the Customize dialog box and check Shortcut Menus.

To remove a built-in toolbar from the screen, right-click any toolbar or menu bar and clear the check mark next to the name. If the toolbar is not docked, simply click the Close button.

If a custom command bar is assigned as a property of a form or report (Menu Bar, Toolbar, or Shortcut Menu), it automatically appears when you open the form or report. When you close the form or report, the command bar disappears from the screen. If, however, you check the command bar name in the Customize dialog box to display it, it remains on the screen until you clear the check box in the Customize dialog box. The command bar name is not available in the list displayed by right-clicking a toolbar.

Looking Up Macros

If you want to see the names of all the macros in the current database, choose File|Database Properties and then click the Contents tab. All the database objects are listed in the Contents box, beginning with the tables. Scroll down the list until you come to the Macros section of the list. Figure 8.22 shows some of the macros in the Clayview City College database.

FIGURE 8.22

The Contents tab shows a list of all the current database objects.

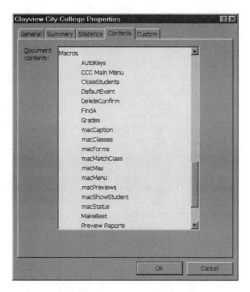

To keep a record of the specifications of a macro, you can print the description. Select the macro name and then click the Print toolbar button or use File|Print. This opens the Print Macro Definition dialog box, which gives you the option of including any or all three of features of the macro definition: Properties, Actions and Arguments, and Permissions by User and Group. After making your selections, choose OK, and the macro definition prints. Figure 8.23 shows the first page of the definition of the macForms macro group.

Figure 8.23

The printed macForms *macro group definition.*

Actions

Name	Condition	Action	Argument	Value
macStudents				
		OpenForm	Form Name:	Students
			View:	Form
			Filter Name:	
			Where Condition:	
			Data Mode:	-1
			Window Mode:	Normal

This macro group contains the macros for the buttons on the Enter/View switchboard.

Name	Condition	Action	Argument	Value
macClasses				
		OpenForm	Form Name:	Classes
			View:	Form
			Filter Name:	
			Where Condition:	
			Data Mode:	-1
			Window Mode:	Normal
macDepts				
		OpenForm	Form Name:	Departments
			View:	Form
			Filter Name:	
			Where Condition:	
			Data Mode:	-1
			Window Mode:	Normal
macInstr				
		OpenForm	Form Name:	Departments
			View:	Form
			Filter Name:	
			Where Condition:	
			Data Mode:	-1
			Window Mode:	Normal
macGrades				
		OpenForm	Form Name:	Grades
			View:	Form
			Filter Name:	
			Where Condition:	
			Data Mode:	-1
			Window Mode:	Normal
macReturn				
		Close	Object Type:	
			Object Name:	
			Save:	Prompt

Converting Macros to VBA Code

Many activities in an application can easily be carried out using macros. Others, such as error trapping, transaction processing, and passing arguments to a procedure while it's running, require Visual Basic procedures. You can convert any macro or all macros for a form or report to VB procedures. Some programmers feel more comfortable with all operations carried out by procedures.

To convert a single macro to a procedure, select the macro name in the database window and choose Tools|Macro|Convert Macros to Visual Basic. (You cannot convert a macro that's open in the design window.) The Convert Macro dialog box opens with two options, both selected by default:

- Add error handling to generated functions
- Include macro comments

The first option includes OnError statements that branch to error-handling routines in the procedure. The second option adds all the comments you placed in the macro design as comments in the VB code. Choose Convert to complete the conversion. Access displays a message when the conversion is complete. Figure 8.24 shows the macMatchClass macro in the macro design window.

FIGURE 8.24
The original macMatchClass *macro in the macro design window.*

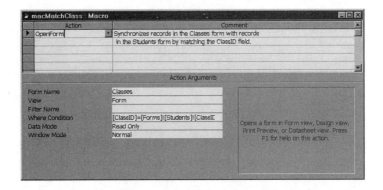

Figure 8.25 shows the Visual Basic function resulting from converting the macro. The text of the macro comments are added to the function as comments preceded by apostrophes. An error-handling routine has also been added in accordance with the selections made in the Convert Macro dialog box.

Another method of converting a macro to Visual Basic is to select the macro name in the database window and choose File|Save As to open the Save As dialog box. Then, you choose Module in the As box. The same Convert Macro dialog box offers the options of adding error-handing and including the comments. The conversion produces the same procedure as using the Tools menu.

FIGURE 8.25

The macro converted to a Visual Basic function.

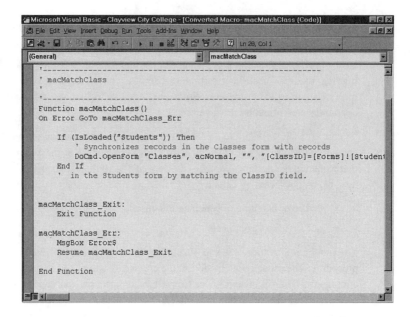

```
' ---------------------------------------------------------------
' macMatchClass
'
' ---------------------------------------------------------------
Function macMatchClass ()
On Error GoTo macMatchClass_Err

    If (IsLoaded("Students")) Then
        ' Synchronizes records in the Classes form with records
        DoCmd.OpenForm "Classes", acNormal, "", "[ClassID]=[Forms]![Student
    End If
    ' in the Students form by matching the ClassID field.


macMatchClass_Exit:
    Exit Function

macMatchClass_Err:
    MsgBox Error$
    Resume macMatchClass_Exit

End Function
```

You can also convert all the macros associated with a form in one operation. First, open the form in design view and then choose Tools|Macro|Convert Form's Macros to Visual Basic. The Convert Macros dialog box opens as before. Choose Convert, and Access converts all the macros for that form into functions and procedures in the class module for the form. You can do the same with all macros associated with a report.

Summary

In this chapter, you've seen some of the operations you can perform with macros. Macros are easy to create and attach to events that affect the database objects. There are more than 50 actions you can execute under the control of a macro. The chapter also introduced the importance of understanding the sequence of events so that you attach a macro to the correct event property.

Macros can also be used to carry out conditional branching and even act as Select Case constructs. You've also seen how to build custom menus and toolbars from special macros. In the final section, you learned how to convert macros to VB procedures. The next chapter, "Writing Visual Basic Procedures," discusses VB procedures and how to use the Microsoft Visual Basic Editor.

Writing Visual Basic Procedures

In Chapter 5, "Examining and Modifying the Wizard's Code," you had a chance to examine the code that the Database Wizard created while building the *Omni-Sport* database. In this chapter, you'll create your own Visual Basic code to further customize the database forms, reports, and switchboards.

In addition to showing you how to use the Visual Basic Editor module window to enter and modify Visual Basic code, this chapter demonstrates the flexibility of VB procedures. It also discusses other convenient tools, such as the Properties Window, the Project Explorer, and the Object Browser, all of which provide assistance while creating code.

Planning Ahead

> **Peter's Principle:** As with any endeavor, especially in the computer realm, it's best to plan ahead and try to anticipate how the user will interact with the system and how the system should respond. In planning a Visual Basic program, divide the process into small increments, each with a specific purpose. Then, create a procedure or function for each one separately. Splitting the program into short, single-purpose tasks makes debugging and maintenance much easier. Adding frequent comments also helps you interpret the code later on.

DEVELOPMENT

Another good practice is to use consistent names for variables and objects, such as *rst* for recordset objects and *dbs* for database objects. Following a standard naming convention also makes it easier for another programmer to maintain and upgrade the code.

Generalizing where possible saves time and space. You can write a procedure that can be used in more than one instance or by more than one object. For example, the IsLoaded() function in the Global Module of the *Omni-Sport* database is a global function and is accessible to any form in the database. The code needn't be repeated in each form in the database that uses the function.

Another good policy is to create object-specific class modules with the code for a certain form or report. These modules are stored with the form or report and are accessible only to the host object. Keeping procedures in class modules also helps to prevent conflicts among procedures that use the same variable names.

After you've determined what your application should contain and how it should respond to all the expected events, you can start to build the application using the Access wizards. They give you a good starting point to begin customizing the database.

Which Language Should You Use?

Although macros and SQL statements are easy to create and use in an application, there are certain times when you should or must use Visual Basic. For example, to make an application more comfortable for the user, you can intercept the cryptic error messages that are popular with database management systems and replace them with diagnostic messages that are more informative. You can even add some advice about getting out of the problem. You can do this only with Visual Basic programming.

Macros can run with arguments you've supplied, but if you want to be able to change their values during execution, you must write a Visual Basic procedure.

Access provides many built-in, intrinsic functions, such as `Date()` and `Pmt()`, that return values when you supply the arguments. Intrinsic functions are available to both macros and VB procedures. If you want to create your own custom functions, you must do so with a VB function procedure. Visual Basic procedures can also create and modify objects just like a wizard. You can change the appearance and behavior of form controls and other objects with procedures.

Using Visual Basic also optimizes application performance because the compiled VB code runs faster than a macro that carries out the same operation.

How Does Visual Basic Work?

Visual Basic is an object-oriented, event-driven programming language, which means it responds to events as they happen to the objects in the database. *Events* are actions recognized by a form, a form control, or a report. Using VB code, you can make the object respond to the event any way you want.

You've already seen many examples of procedures and functions that respond to events, such as a form that opens when you click a command button or a calculated field that's updated when you enter data in another field. Events are not always user initiated—the system can generate events as well. For example, you can create a procedure that sets options when the application starts up.

Technical Note: Before continuing, a review of Visual Basic terms is in order. Table 9.1 defines a few of the more commonly used programming terms.

Table 9.1 Common Visual Basic Programming Terms

Term	Definition
Module	A collection of declarations, procedures, and functions stored as a named unit.
Class module	A collection of procedures and functions existing independently or in association with a form or report.
Standard module	A module whose procedures are available to the application as a whole.
Procedure	A self-contained series of statements that execute as a whole to perform a single task.
Subprocedure	A type of procedure that performs a specific operation.
Function	A procedure that returns a specific value that can be used in an expression.
Event procedure	A procedure that automatically executes in response to a specific event.
Method	A procedure that operates on a specific type of object. Similar to a statement or function.
Statement	A complete unit consisting of one line of code that expresses an operation, declaration, or definition.
Constant	A representation of a value that doesn't change during execution. Either supplied by Access or defined by the user.
Variable	A named location in storage that can be modified during execution.
Action	The basic unit of a macro that defines what operation is executed. Can be run from a VB procedure.
Property	A named attribute of an object, field, or control that defines the object's characteristics and behavior.
Keyword	A reserved word that has a special meaning in the Visual Basic language.
Argument	A constant, variable, or expression that supplies information to an action, event, method, property, or procedure. Also called a *parameter*.

Touring the Visual Basic Editor Window

Visual Basic code is written, edited, and displayed in the Visual Basic Editor module window. Figure 9.1 shows the module window with a function that creates a full name from the first and last names in the Subscribers table from the *Omni-Sport* database. Table 9.2 describes each of the new toolbar buttons. Rest the mouse pointer on the button to see the ToolTip with the name of the button. You can open the module window for a class module associated with a form or report whether or not the object is open. To see the code for a class module, perform one of the following actions:

- Select the form or report name in the database window and click the Code toolbar button or choose View|Code.

- In the form or report design view, click Code on the toolbar or choose View|Code.

- Click Build in an event property for an object in the report or form design and then select Code Builder in the Choose Builder dialog box and click OK.

- Select the module name in the database window, choose Design in the database window, click Code on the toolbar, or choose View|Code.

FIGURE 9.1
Visual Basic code displays in the module window.

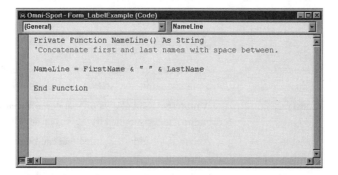

Note: If you open the class module for a form or report from the database window, the form or report design view opens first. When you close the module window, the design view remains open.

If no procedures exist for the object you've selected, Access starts one for you. Only the two Option statements, Option Compare Database and Option Explicit, appear in the module window, ready for you to create the new procedure.

The module window has several new toolbar buttons and menu items specifically related to writing and debugging VB code. Equivalent commands are available from the View, Insert, and Run menus. The new toolbar buttons are explained in Table 9.2.

Table 9.2 The Module Window Standard Toolbar Buttons

Button	Description
View Microsoft Access	Keeps the module window open and displays the active Access window.
Insert Module	Inserts a new module, class module, or procedure into the current module. Choosing Procedure opens the Add Procedure dialog box, where you enter the name, type, and scope for the new procedure.
Run Sub/User Form	Runs the procedure containing the insertion point, runs the active user form, or runs a macro if neither is active. If the procedure is in a class module, the form or report must be open in design view. This button becomes a Continue button when you're in break mode.
Break	Stops code execution and switches to break mode.
Reset	Stops all code running, clears all variables, and resets the project.
Design Mode	Toggles design mode on and off. When you're in design mode, no code from the project is running and events will not execute.
Project Explorer	Displays the Project Explorer to display a list of currently open projects and their contents.
Properties Window	Displays the Properties window, where you can see the current property settings of the selected object.
Object Browser	Opens the Object Browser window, which displays lists of libraries, classes, methods, properties, events, and constants you can use in code. It also shows the modules and procedures already defined for the project.

Note: To view a single procedure instead of all the procedures in a module, use the two small buttons in the bottom-left corner of the window. The left one changes to Procedure View and the right one to Module View.

Three additional toolbars that contain buttons for commonly used menu items are available in the module window:

- The Debug toolbar contains buttons that enable you to step through code one statement at a time, view intermediate results, display the current value of a selected expression, and other useful debug activities.

- The Edit toolbar contains buttons that help create accurate code. You can also use the Edit toolbar buttons to add comment blocks and to toggle and move among bookmarks in the code. See the section "Declare Variables and Set Values" for details of the Edit toolbar commands.

- The UserForm toolbar contains buttons that are useful for designing and working with User Forms, such as Bring To Front and Send To Back, Group and Ungroup, Align, Center, Make Same Size, and Zoom.

LOOKING AHEAD

See Chapter 10, "Debugging Visual Basic Procedures," for more information about the Debug toolbar. The UserForm toolbar is discussed in Chapter 16, "Customizing Input and Output."

To navigate among procedures in a module, press Ctrl+PgUp to move to the previous procedure and Ctrl+PgDn to move to the next procedure. You can also use the Object and Procedure boxes in the module window to move to a specific procedure. These boxes appear just beneath the toolbar. Click the Object box arrow and select the object whose procedure you want to see in the Object box. Then click the Procedure arrow to select from the list of events that apply to the selected object. Any event that has a related event procedure appears in bold in the list. Figure 9.2 shows the module window listing all the events for the Go To Switchboard button. The `Click` event is bold, indicating that an event procedure exists for this button.

FIGURE 9.2

Choose from the Procedure box to move to a specific procedure.

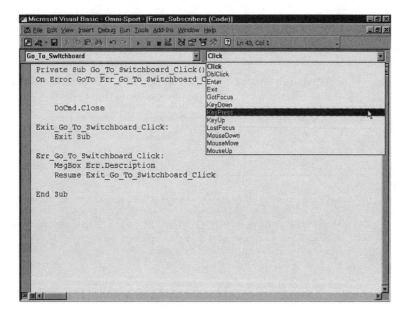

Select the event from the list to see the event procedure or select an event that is not bold to start a new event procedure for that event.

Setting Visual Basic Environment Options

To change some of the features of the module window, choose Tools|Options (see Figure 9.3).

FIGURE 9.3

Setting Visual Basic Editor options.

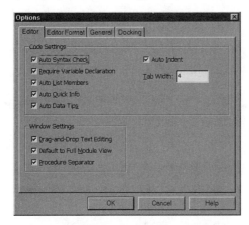

The Options dialog box contains four tabs:

- The Editor tab contains options that apply to the behavior of the editor.
- The Editor Format tab options determine the appearance of the Editor window (for example, color and font).
- The General tab contains miscellaneous options that apply to grid settings, error trapping, and compilation.
- The Docking tab options control the position of the VB windows.

Table 9.3 describes each of the options found on the Editor tab of the Options dialog box. All the options are checked by default.

Table 9.3   Visual Basic Editor Options

Option	Description
Auto Syntax Check	Checks for syntax errors as you type.
Require Variable Declaration	Automatically includes Option Explicit in the Declarations section of every new module in the database, including class modules.
Auto List Members	Displays a list of valid choices as you type a statement.

continues

Table 9.3   Continued

Option	Description
Auto Quick Info	Displays syntax information when you type a procedure or method name. The current element you're entering appears in bold in the syntax statement.
Auto Data Tips	Shows the current value of a variable when you pause the mouse pointer on the variable name. You must be in break mode to see it.
Auto Indent	Automatically indents a line of code to match the previous line.
Tab Width	Sets the default width of the indent when you press Tab. The default is 4.
Drag-and-Drop Text Editing	When selected, this option enables you to drag and drop text as an alternative to cutting and pasting.
Default to Full Module View	Shows all the procedures in the module as the default view. Clear this option to change the default view to show a single procedure.
Procedure Separator	Draws a line across the screen between procedures in the module view.

Tip: If Auto List Members is checked, Access helps you complete statements as you type by displaying a list of relevant objects, properties, and methods that are appropriate to the statement you're typing. If you don't want this assistance, clear the option in the Editor tab of the Options dialog box.

The Editor Format tab contains additional options that set the appearance of the code text (see Figure 9.4):

- The Code Colors options lists the items that can be customized, establishes the colors of the foreground and background for the selected type of text, and the color of the margin indicator.

- Font and Size options determine the appearance of the text.

- The Margin Indicator Bar is a bar displayed at the left of the code pane that contains pointers to code used as break points or to statements containing errors.

The Code Colors options can be applied to normal, selection, syntax error, comment, keyword, identifier, and several other types of text. You can specify the foreground, background, and indicator colors. Each of these pull-down menus displays a palette of colors from which to choose.

FIGURE 9.4
Setting Visual Basic Editor Format options.

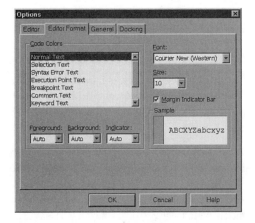

The General tab of the Options dialog box contains miscellaneous options in four groups (see Figure 9.5):

FIGURE 9.5
Setting Visual Basic Editor General options.

- Form Grid Settings applies to UserForm objects that are part of an application user interface. Options include displaying a grid on a form and specifying in points the height and width of the grid cells. With Align Controls to Grid checked, the outer edges of controls are automatically aligned to the closest grid lines.

- Show ToolTips displays ToolTips for the toolbar buttons.

- Collapse Proj. Hides Windows applies only to Access projects and automatically closes the project, UserForm, object, or module windows when a project is collapsed in the Project Explorer.

- Edit and Continue/Notify Before State Loss displays a message informing you that the action you've requested will reset all module-level variables in the running project.

- The Selected Error Trapping options determine whether to enter break mode when any error occurs, regardless of error handlers or the location of the code (class or standard module), enter break mode only upon encountering an unhandled error in a class module, or enter break mode on any other unhandled error.

- Compile options include Compile On Demand, in which a project compiles before it starts or when needed, and Background Compile, which uses idle time to complete compilation in the background. Compile On Demand must be set if you want to check Background Compile.

The options available on the Docking tab of the Options dialog box specify which windows in the Visual Basic Environment can be anchored to an adjacent dockable window in the module window. The windows include Immediate, Locals, Watch, Project Explorer, Properties, and Object Browser. The first three of these windows are used during debugging and are discussed in Chapter 10, "Debugging Visual Basic Procedures."

Browsing the Project Explorer Window

The Project Explorer displays a hierarchical list of the current projects and their class objects and modules (see Figure 9.6). The three buttons in the Project Explorer change the display in the window to display code or objects or to toggle the folders. The class objects refer to the forms and reports that contain class modules. If the form or report has no class module, it will not appear in the Project Explorer list.

FIGURE 9.6
The Project Explorer shows a list of current projects and their objects.

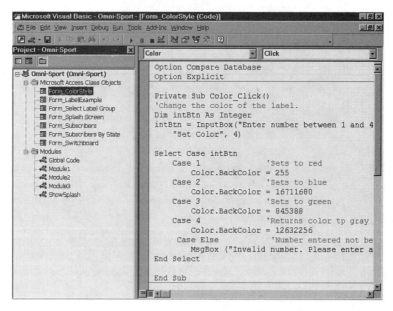

To display the Project Explorer windows, click the Project Explorer toolbar button or choose View|Project Explorer. The command is also available from the shortcut menu. The *Omni-Sport* project and both its folders are expanded to show all the items in the project. Click the minus sign (-) to collapse the lists.

To see the code for one of the forms or modules, select the item and click View Code. To return to the Access window and look at the object form or report in design view, click View Object. The View Object button is dimmed if you select a module instead of a form or report. With the Toggle Folders button pressed in, the objects are listed in separate folders. Clicking the Toggle Folders button lists all the items without specifying folders.

The Project Explorer shortcut menu also offers View Code and View Object commands along with other commands, such as viewing the current project properties, inserting a module or class module, importing or exporting a file, and printing the current project code.

Types of Visual Basic Modules

DEVELOPMENT

Modules are containers for code segments and can contain declarations, event procedures, subprocedures, and functions. VB also includes three types of modules: standard, class, and independent class modules. *Standard modules* are separate objects in the database that store code you want to use anywhere in the application. Standard module names appear on the Modules page of the database window.

When you create a new form or report that contains code, Access creates a *class module* for it and includes it in the design. When you add an event procedure to the form or report, Access adds it to the class module. If you copy the form or report to another database, the class module is copied along with it. Deleting a form or report also deletes its class module.

You can also create class modules, independent of any form or report, that appear with the standard modules on the Modules page of the database window. An independent class module can be used to build a custom object on the same level as forms and reports.

The Modules collection contains all open modules in the application—class or standard, compiled or not.

Types of Procedures and Their Elements

VB has two kinds of procedures: subprocedures and functions. A *subprocedure* performs an operation but does not return a value to the application. Because it does not return a value, it cannot be used in an expression. *Functions*, on the other hand, return a value and therefore can be used in an expression. Access provides many built-in functions, and you can also create your own custom functions.

Procedures contain declarations, statements, and expressions. *Declarations* explicitly establish the data type of variables and constants that appear in the procedure or module. The Declarations section must appear at the beginning of the procedure. A *statement* expresses a specific operation, declaration, or definition. Statements are usually placed singly on one line of the procedure. You can combine two or more statements on a single line by separating them with a colon (:). For example, the following statement puts three statements on one line:

```
intA = 1: intB = 2: intC = 3
```

Note: The disadvantage of placing more than one command on a line comes during debugging when you try to set a breakpoint. Although you can step through the code, one statement at a time, a breakpoint is attached to the whole line rather than one of the statements on the line.

If a statement is long, it can be continued on the next line by using the line continuation pair: a space followed by an underscore. For example, the statement that evaluates an expression and sets `LabelAddress` to that value runs to three lines:

```
'The first two lines end with a space and an underscore.
LabelAddress = NameLine & strLineFeed & _
    Address & strLineFeed & City & ", " _
    StateOrProvince & " " & PostalCode
```

Expressions, such as the preceding one, set the value of the object on the left of the equal sign to the value derived from the terms on the right.

Use the standard Access naming rules when you name procedures, constants, variables, and arguments in VB:

- The first character must be a letter.
- The name can contain letters, numbers, and the underscore character but no other punctuation.
- The name can contain no more than 255 characters.
- Do not use any keywords that Visual Basic uses as part of the programming language, such as `If` and `Loop`.

Subprocedures

A *subprocedure* is a set of one or more distinct operations. You use a subprocedure to automate tasks that you perform repeatedly. A subprocedure can even be assigned to a menu item so that you can run it from the menu.

Subprocedures are also useful for operations you might want to run under different circumstances, such as when a button on a form is clicked and when a certain control gets focus. The event properties of both controls would call the same procedure. The procedure code doesn't need to be repeated in each event procedure.

Event procedures are by far the most common subprocedures that you'll find in an application. They're actually subprocedures that have been assigned as the responses to events that happen to objects. A subprocedure that's not used as a response to an event is referred to as a *general procedure*.

> **Warning:** Be sure you've settled on the names of the controls you're going to attach event procedures to before you create the procedures. However, if you do change the control's name after writing the procedure, remember to change the name of the procedure, as well. If Access does not associate the procedure with the event property of a control, the procedure becomes a general procedure.

The subprocedure statement specifies the procedure name, arguments, and code statements and has the following syntax:

```
[Private|Public][Static]Sub name [(arglist)]
    [statements]
    [Exit Sub]
    [statements]
End Sub
```

ANALYSIS

In this standard syntactic definition, the words in bold are keywords and must be typed exactly as shown. The words in italic are user-provided names. Any element in square brackets ([ ]) is optional. Keywords separated by a vertical line (|) indicate a mutually exclusive option. For example, you can use Public or Private, but not both. If an argument list is included, the list must be enclosed in parentheses, and the arguments must be separated by commas. All these elements are described in the section "Procedure Elements," because they're shared by functions.

> **Note:** Two or more keywords separated by vertical lines but enclosed in braces ({}) indicate a mandatory entry. You must choose one of the keywords or the default option will automatically be used. An example is the Option Compare statement, which includes {Binary | Text | Database} in its syntax. One of them must be used with Option Compare. Database is the default keyword.

The Sub keyword declares the procedure by name. Everything between the Sub and End Sub lines are executed when you run the procedure.

Functions

A *function procedure* derives a value and returns it to the project. The returned value has the same name as the function and can be used in an expression elsewhere, such as in a calculated field in a form or in a Select Case branching operation. You can even assign the function as a control property setting. For example, the NameLine function builds a full name from the FirstName and LastName field values. The value returned by the function is a string variable named NameLine that can be used by another procedure in the module:

```
Private Function NameLine() As String
'Concatenate first and last names with space between.
    NameLine = FirstName & " " & LastName
End Function
```

The Function statement has the following syntax:

```
[Private|Public][Static]Function name [(arglist)][As type]
    [statements]
    [name = expression]
    [Exit Function]
    [statements]
    [name = expression]
End Function
```

ANALYSIS

The value the function returns is the value assigned by the expression to the name of the function. If the function does not assign a value to its name, the function returns one of the following default values:

- 0 for numeric functions
- A zero-length string ("") for string functions
- Empty for Variant functions

To use the value returned by the function, place the function name on the right side of an expression in another procedure.

Procedure Elements

Both types of procedures share most of the same syntactic elements. Table 9.4 describes their use and limitations.

Table 9.4 Procedure Elements

Element	Description
Public	Makes the procedure available to all other procedures in all other modules in the project. (Optional.)
Private	Limits the procedure to other procedures in this module. (Optional.)
Static	Preserves the value of local variables between procedure calls. Has no effect on variables used by this procedure but created in another procedure. (Optional.)
name	The name of a sub or function. (Required.)

Element	Description
arglist	The list of variables passed to the procedure when it is called. Names in this list are separated by commas. (Optional.)
As *type*	Indicates the data type of the value returned by a function: Boolean, Byte, Currency, Decimal, Date, Double, Integer, Long, Object, Single, String, or Variant. If you don't specify a data type, Access uses Variant. (Optional.)
statements	A group of statements to be carried out in the procedure. (Optional.)
Exit Sub(Function)	Exits from the procedure before the normal End statement. Processing resumes at the statement following the statement that called the procedure. The procedure may contain more than one Exit statement.
expression	A return value from a function. (Optional.)

ANALYSIS

The argument list also has a required structure and syntax that applies to both types of procedures:

[Optional][ByVal][ByRef][ParamArray]*varname*[()][**As** *type*] [=*defaultvalue*]

Table 9.5 describes the argument list elements.

Table 9.5   Argument List Elements

Element	Description
Optional	The argument is not required. (Optional.)
ByVal	The value of the argument is passed. (Optional.)
ByRef	The argument is passed by referring to the address of another variable. (Optional.)
ParamArray	Indicates the argument in the list is an array of Variant elements. This enables you to pass a varying number of Variant arguments. This element must be the final argument in the list. (Optional.)
varname	The name representing the argument used in the procedure. If the argument is an array, the dimensions of the array must follow, enclosed in parentheses. (Required.)
type	Same as in a procedure statement. (Optional.)
=*defaultvalue*	Any constant or constant expression to be used as the default value for an optional argument. (Optional.)

Declaring Variables and Constants

You use declaration statements, usually the Dim statement, to define variables for the procedure or module. To declare constants and set their values, use the Const statement. Where and how you declare variables and constants defines their scope and lifetime. Declarations are placed at the top of a procedure to define procedure-level variables and constants. To have them available to all procedures in the module, place the declarations at the top of the module, right after the two Option statements and before the Sub or Function statement.

If you don't specify a data type in the declaration, the Variant type is assumed. Refer to Chapter 3, "Touring the World of Object-Oriented Programming," for a complete discussion of VB data types and declarations, as well as how to reference objects in code statements.

You can use the Public, Private, and Static keywords in declaration statements to set the scope of the variables and constants the same way as in Sub and Function statements.

What Can You Do with a Procedure?

The principal use for procedures in Access is to define a response to an event and accomplish the purpose of the application. If the application is designed properly, each procedure performs a separate operation, such as validating newly entered data, opening a form, displaying a report for preview, or evaluating an expression and branching to the next procedure.

This section contains a sampling of some of the things you can do with procedures.

Enter Data

Listing 9.1 is an example of a function that responds to data input. If the user has entered a value between 00000 and 99999 in the first five characters of the PostalCode field, "USA" is automatically entered into the Country field and the cursor moves to the first field on the second page. The event is AfterUpdate, and it occurs when the cursor leaves the PostalCode field. If you look at the event property sheet for the PostalCode text box control in the Subscribers form, you'll see [Event Procedure], indicating a subprocedure is attached to this event property.

> **Note:** The input mask for the PostalCode field is 00000\-9999 which includes a dash and the optional additional four characters so you must use the Left substring function to test for only the first five characters.

Listing 9.1   A Function That Responds to Data Input

```
Private Sub PostalCode_AfterUpdate()
'Fill in the Country field if the PostalCode is between 00000 and 99999.
    If Left(PostalCode,5) > "00000" And Left(PostalCode,5) < "99999" Then
        Country = "USA"
        GoToPage 2                      'Moves focus to the second page.
        DatePaid.SetFocus               'At the first control.
    End If
End Sub
```

ANALYSIS

The `GoToPage` action moves focus to the first control on the second page of the form. Without this action, the form moves up on the screen to expose the DatePaid field without displaying the complete second page. The `DatePaid.SetFocus` statement is not really necessary because the `GoToPage` moves the cursor to the first control on the page automatically. No declaration statements are necessary for this procedure because it contains only field names from the database and no variables.

Ask the User a Question

Using the `MsgBox()` function is a good way to impart information to the user. You can also use this function to get quick input from the user, especially if there are only two or three options from which to choose. The button responses are coded so that you can interpret the response and perform other operations depending on the response.

Figure 9.7 shows a message box that asks the user a question to which the response is Yes or No. The 36 argument in the function statement is the sum of the values corresponding to the choices for the appearance of the box: 4, which specifies the Yes and No buttons, and 32, which means to display the question mark icon. If the user clicks Yes, the function returns 6, whereas No returns 7. The message box caption, Reader Poll, is also specified by the `MsgBox()` function.

FIGURE 9.7

The `MsgBox()` *function can ask simple questions.*

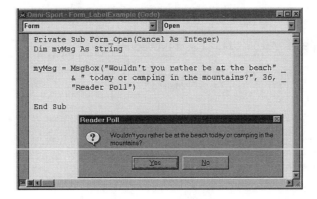

Set Startup Properties

Listing 9.2 is an example of a way to set custom startup properties instead of using the Tools|Startup dialog box.

Listing 9.2   Setting Custom Startup Properties

```
Sub Getgoing()
'Change startup properties for a database.
Dim dbs As Object
    Set dbs = CurrentDB
    dbs.StartupForm = "Subscribers"
    dbs.StartupShowDBWindow = False
    dbs.StartupShowStatusBar = True
    dbs.StartupMenuBar = "MyOwnMenu"
    dbs.AllowBuiltinToolbars = False
    dbs.AllowBreakIntoCode = False
    dbs.AllowByPassKey = True
End Sub
```

ANALYSIS   In this procedure, the database is set to the current database and the Subscribers form is set as the startup form rather than the database window. The status bar is displayed. Other properties display a custom menu bar named MyOwnMenu, hide the built-in toolbars, prevent the user from viewing code following a runtime error, and allow the user to skip the startup options by pressing the bypass key (Shift) as the database opens.

Trap Errors and Validate Data

When a wizard creates an event procedure for a control, it always adds an error contingency plan. Usually, it just branches to the end of the procedure and lets Access display whatever message it feels is appropriate. However, you can insert your own messages in place of the default messages. For example, Listing 9.3 was generated by the Button Wizard for the Return To Switchboard button in the Subscribers form.

Listing 9.3   An On Click Event Procedure

```
Private Sub Return_To_Switchboard_Click()
On Error GoTo Err_Return_To_Switchboard_Click
    DoCmd.Close
Exit_Return_To_Switchboard_Click:
    Exit Sub
Err_Return_To_Switchboard_Click:
    MsgBox Err.Description
    Resume Exit_Return_To_Switchboard_Click
End Sub
```

The On Error statement branches to the statement labeled Err_Return_To_
Switchboard_Click, which displays the Err.Description value in a message box and
then branches back to the Exit_Return_To_Switchboard line. Any line that ends with a
colon (:) is a line label rather than a statement. It marks the destination for the GoTo
statement. This structure is standard for error handling. If you want to show a different
message based on the type of error, you can change the MsgBox statement—perhaps after
testing for the code number of the error that occurred.

If, for example, you want to make sure the user has entered a Postal Code after entering
an address, you can use an If…Then…Else structure in a procedure attached to the form's
BeforeUpdate event to test for the missing values.

Filter Records for a Report

It's not as easy for the user to filter information in a report preview as it is in a form. To
filter records for a report, you usually base the report on a select query. If you want the
user to be able to decide how to filter the report in real time just before previewing it,
you can use an InputBox() function to acquire the criteria from the user.

For example, suppose you want the user to be able to preview information about subscribers from a certain state. An InputBox() function can ask for the state value and add
the response to a filter argument for the OpenReport method. The only real trick is to
include quotation marks around the two-character state abbreviation that the user enters.
This requires embedding the quotation marks within the criteria string so that the criteria
becomes [StateOrProvince] = "CA".

You can use either single or double quotation marks to embed a string within a string. In
this example, double quotation marks are used to concatenate the string variable,
stFilter. Listing 9.4 shows a Click event procedure that's attached to the On Click
event property of the By State button on the Subscribers By State form. Figure 9.8 shows
the GetFacts form with a single command button and the By State event procedure.

Listing 9.4   Creating a Filter from User Input

```
Private Sub By_State_Click()
On Error GoTo Err_By_State_Click

    Dim stDocName As String
    Dim stFilter As String
    Dim stState As String
    stState = InputBox("Enter two-character abbreviation for state.", _
        "Subscriber Preview", "WY")
    stFilter = "[StateOrProvince] = """ _
        & stState & """"
    stDocName = "Subscribers"
    DoCmd.OpenReport stDocName, acPreview, , stFilter
```

continues

Listing 9.4 Continued

```
Exit_By_State_Click:
    Exit Sub
Err_By_State_Click:
    MsgBox Err.Description
    Resume Exit_By_State_Click
End Sub
```

Figure 9.8
*The user can filter
records for a
report preview.*

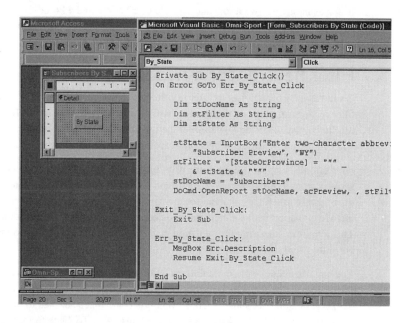

Analysis

The InputBox function includes three arguments. The first is the text that appears in the box, the second is the title of the dialog box, and the third is the optional default value to show in the text box. In this example, WY is specified as the default value in the InputBox() function.

> **Tip:** Using double quotation marks (") instead of single quotation marks (') lets you include apostrophes in the string, which would not be allowed if you used single quotation marks.

Create Mailing Labels

The two functions shown in Listing 9.5 build a label report from the database field values. If either the LastName or the Address field is blank, no label is created in the report.

The first function creates the name line for the label. Writing this as a separate function enables you to use the function for other purposes within the form class module. The second function uses the results of the NameLine function in an expression that builds the rest of the label. The two characters, Chr(13) and Chr(10), are the ASCII character codes for carriage return and line feed. Used together, they place the next characters on the next line, just as though the user had pressed Enter.

Listing 9.5   Creating Mailing Labels

```
Private Function NameLine() As String
'Concatenate first and last names with space between.
    NameLine = FirstName & " " & LastName
End Function

Private Function LabelAddress() As String
'Build mailing label address from Subscribers fields.
Dim stLineFeed As String
'Set stLineFeed to the carriage return and line feed ASCII code.
stLineFeed = Chr(13) & Chr(10)
'Check for blank LastName or Address.
If IsNull(LastName) Or IsNull(Address) Then
    LabelAddress = ""
Else
    LabelAddress = NameLine & stLineFeed & _
        Address & stLineFeed & City & ", " & _
        StateOrProvince & " " & PostalCode
End If
End Function
```

Figure 9.9 shows the LabelExample form in form view. NameLine is an unbound text box whose value is set to the Subscriber's full name by the NameLine function shown in Listing 9.5. LabelAddress is another unbound text box that gets its value from the LabelAddress function.

FIGURE 9.9
Results of the
NameLine *and*
LabelAddress
functions.

The procedure containing these functions is attached to the form's OnOpen event property.

Change Form Control Properties

The ColorStyle form contains two label controls that have procedures attached to their Click events (see Figure 9.10). Both of the procedures use the InputBox() function to display a box requesting user input. The message asks the user to enter a number between 1 and 4. Each number causes a change in background color for one of the labels and font style for the other. Figure 9.11 shows the color label changed to green and the style label changed to italic.

FIGURE 9.10

The ColorStyle form can change label control properties.

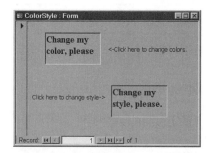

FIGURE 9.11

Changing properties in the ColorStyle form.

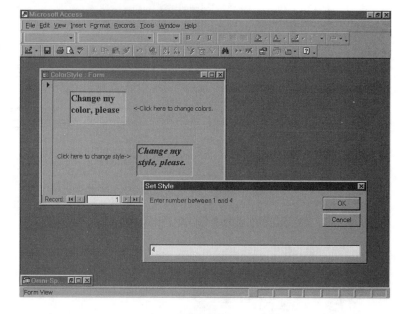

Listing 9.6 shows the two procedures that change the properties of the label controls based on user entry in the input box.

Listing 9.6 Changing Label Color and Style Properties

```
Private Sub Color_Click()
'Change the color of the label.
Dim intBtn As Integer
intBtn = InputBox("Enter number between 1 and 4", _
    "Set Color", 4)
Select Case intBtn
    Case 1               'Sets to red
        Color.BackColor = 255
    Case 2               'Sets to blue
        Color.BackColor = 16711680
    Case 3               'Sets to green
        Color.BackColor = 845388
    Case 4               'Returns color to gray
        Color.BackColor = 12632256
    Case Else                'Number entered not between 1 & 4
        MsgBox ("Invalid number. Please enter again.")
End Select
End Sub

Private Sub Style_Click()
'Change font size, italic or bold.
Dim intBtn As Integer
intBtn = InputBox("Enter number between 1 and 4", _
    "Set Style", 4)
Select Case intBtn
    Case 1               'Sets font size to 8 pts
        Style.FontSize = 8
    Case 2               'Sets to italic
        Style.FontItalic = True
    Case 3               'Sets to bold
        Style.FontBold = True
    Case 4               'Resets original style
        Style.FontSize = 14
        Style.FontItalic = False
        Style.FontBold = False
    Case Else            'Number entered not between 1 & 4
        MsgBox ("Invalid number. Please enter again.")
    End Select
End Sub
```

ANALYSIS

These procedures are good examples of how to refer to Access objects in VB code. After the label controls are added, they're named Color and Style, respectively. The default names, Text1 or whatever, could have been used as references, but it's easier to see what the procedures do if the controls have more relevant names. For example, Style.FontSize refers to the Style label control, and FontSize is the property to set. Both InputBox() functions specify 4 as the default value.

If the user enters a number not within the accepted range, a `Case Else` statement displays a message box requesting a number between 1 and 4. Control returns to the ColorStyle form when the user clicks OK.

Set Properties in the Properties Window

You can open the Properties window to view the design-time properties for selected objects. The window lists the current settings in alphabetic order or arranged in property sheet categories. Figure 9.12 shows the Properties window for the Color label control on the ColorStyle form. Notice the `BackColor` property is set to the default color—gray.

FIGURE 9.12

Setting properties in the Properties window.

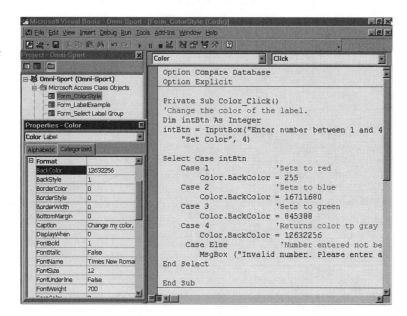

To open the Properties window, click the Properties button or choose View|Properties. Choose the object from the drop-down list at the top of the window. If the Project Explorer is open, you can also choose the object from its list. If you want to change a property, select the property in the left column and enter a new value in the right column. Properties that have a predefined set of valid settings display a list from which to choose.

To try this out, change the `BackColor` property to 255 (red) and then click the View Microsoft Access toolbar button. If the Project Explorer window is open, click the Show Object button. You'll see that the Color label is now red.

Add an Item to a Combo Box

The `NotInList` event property of a combo box control enables you to create an event procedure that will allow the user to add a new item to the list for the current session. There's a combo box in the Subscribers form that lists three types of payment methods:

Cash, Check, and Credit Card. You might want to include advertisers in your subscription list and send free copies to them. Because entering a payment method that implies money changing hands could confuse the bookkeeping department, you need to be able to add another value to the list.

> **Tip:** You must have the combo box's `LimitToList` property set to Yes to trigger the `NotInList` event.

The first time the user enters an advertiser and specifies that the subscription is complimentary, the event `NotInList` is triggered. For this event, you can create the event procedure shown in Listing 9.7, which adds Complimentary to the combo box list. To enter this code, select Subscribers in the form page of the database window and click Code. In the module window, choose `Payment_Method` from the object list and `NotInList` from the procedure list.

Listing 9.7 Adding to a Combo Box List

```
Private Sub PaymentMethod_NotInList(NewData As String, Response As Integer)
'Allows user to add a new item to the list.
    Dim ctl As Control
    'Set the control object to the combo box.
    Set ctl = Me!PaymentMethod
    'Ask user to confirm they want to add the new value.

    If MsgBox("Do you want to add the value to the list?", vbOKCancel) _
          = vbOK Then
        'Set Response argument to show a value is to be added.
        Response = acDataErrAdded
        'Add string to value list in row source.
        ctl.RowSource = ctl.RowSource & ";" & NewData
    Else
        'If user chose Cancel, undo change and suppress error msg.
        Response = acDataErrContinue
        ctl.Undo
    End If
End Sub
```

Figure 9.13 shows the result of attempting to move from the Payment Method text box to another control after entering a value that's not in the value list for the combo box.

> **Note:** The `Response` argument indicates how the event is to be handled. The argument is set to one of three intrinsic values, depending on the user's response to the `MsgBox()`. In the preceding procedure, if the user responds with
>
> *continues*

OK, the Response argument is set to the constant acDataErrAdded, which adds the entry and updates the combo box list. If the user chooses Cancel, the Response argument is set to acDataErrContinue and the combo box is not changed. The third constant for Response is the default, acDataErrDisplay, which displays the default error message. In this case, the user is not allowed to add a new value to the combo box list.

Figure 9.13

The NotInList *event displays a message box.*

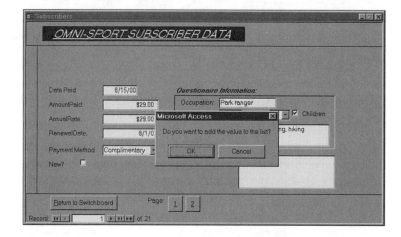

This procedure adds the new item to the value list in the Row Source property. If you click the combo box list for the next record without closing the form, you'll see that value in the drop-down list (see Figure 9.14). The Complimentary value does appear in the Subscribers record after the record is saved.

Figure 9.14

The new item appears in the combo box list for the next record.

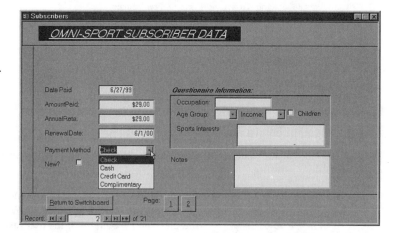

DEVELOPMENT

Tip: The *Omni-Sport* Subscribers table in this chapter uses the Lookup property in the table structure to specify the items in the combo box list. The NotInList() function cannot add to this list. Any value you add in the Subscribers form is temporarily approved and added to the displayed list but not to the list of values stored in the Lookup property.

If you look at the list of values in the Row Source property, you can see that *Complimentary* is added to the list but not enclosed in quotation marks. When you close the form and open it again, the new value is no longer displayed in the combo box and is removed from the row source value list. You must add values to the table definition or to the Row Source property in the property sheet, enclosed in quotation marks. The Row Source property shows the values from the lookup table.

If, however, the combo box references a separate table as the source of the list of values, the Row Source property shows the name of the lookup table. The NotInList event procedure can be used to add new values to this table.

Use DoCmd to Run a Macro

Many applications greet the user with a welcoming screen that displays for a short time and then gives way to the main switchboard. Figure 9.15 shows a splash screen for the *Omni-Sport* application. The form includes only the magazine logo and a brief message. It's unrelated to any table data.

FIGURE 9.15
The Omni-Sport *splash screen.*

The macro group, SplashScreen, has two macros: Splash, which opens and maximizes the splash screen, and GoSwitchboard, which closes the temporary screen and opens the main switchboard. A new independent procedure, ShowSplash, uses the DoCmd object to run the Splash macro (see Figure 9.16).

FIGURE 9.16
The DoCmd *object
runs the*
SplashScreen.
Splash *macro.*

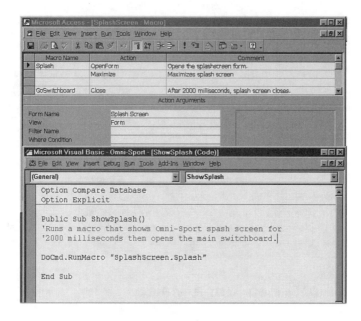

To make the screen temporary, set the form's Timer Interval property to the number of milliseconds you want the splash screen to remain onscreen. If you want it to appear for only two seconds, set the property to 2000. Then you must tell Access what you want it to do when the time runs out. In this case, the macro SplashScreen.GoSwitchboard runs when the time is up (see Figure 9.17). Notice the status bar text that explains the On Timer event property.

FIGURE 9.17
*Changing the
Splash Screen
form timing
properties.*

To run the procedure, select ShowSplash in the module window and choose Run.

> **Tip:** If your VB module window is maximized, the splash screen is hidden behind it. To see the results of the procedure and the macro, resize the module window and drag it out of the way.

> **Note:** To include this welcoming screen in the application, change the startup options to show it at startup instead of the Switchboard form. The timer properties will still be in effect. You could even add a check box in the temporary screen that gives the user the choice of preventing the screen from appearing again at startup. When checked, the check box's Click event procedure will change the startup option to go directly to the main switchboard.

Creating a Procedure

DEVELOPMENT

Creating a new procedure involves a series of steps. First, if the procedure responds to an event such as a button click, use the appropriate wizard to get started. Then, declare all the necessary variables and constants. The body of the procedure contains the response to the event or other operations. The last section cleans up afterward by closing objects, restoring values, and adding error-handling statements, if necessary.

After planning the procedure, open the Access module window and type the VB code. The module window contains many helpful tools and menu items to enable you to create bug-free code. In an earlier tour of the module window, you saw the toolbar buttons and the object and procedure boxes. You also learned how to set the module options by choosing Tools|Options, and became acquainted with the Project Explorer and the Properties window. You'll now see how some of these options can help when you're entering code.

Design the Form

The procedure created in this section is an event procedure to be attached to a command button. The form shown in Figure 9.18 is designed to be opened when the user selects Preview Mailing Labels - All from the Preview Switchboard. The form offers the choice of previewing labels for one of three geographic regions or labels for all the subscribers. The procedure uses the value returned by the option group to set the filter for the report.

In order for the form to act like a pop-up window, some of the form properties need to be changed. In the form's property sheet, change the following properties:

- Type **Select Label Group** in the Caption property.
- Set Scrollbars to Neither.
- Set RecordSelectors to No.

- Set Navigation Buttons to No.
- Set AutoCenter to Yes.
- Set Border Style to Dialog.

FIGURE 9.18
*The Select Label
Group form offers
four choices.*

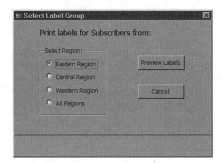

Declare Variables and Set Values

It's always easier to start an event procedure for a Command Button control with the help
of the Command Button Wizard. Figure 9.19 shows the module window with the procedure created by the wizard. The procedure specifies which report to open and in what
view. It also includes the default error-handling statements. Now comes the job of completing the procedure by adding a filter based on the value returned by the Region option
group.

FIGURE 9.19
The Click *proce-
dure created by
the Button
Wizard.*

```
Private Sub PreviewLabels_Click()
On Error GoTo Err_PreviewLabels_Click

    Dim stDocName As String

    stDocName = "Subscriber Labels - All"
    DoCmd.OpenReport stDocName, acPreview

Exit_PreviewLabels_Click:
    Exit Sub

Err_PreviewLabels_Click:
    MsgBox Err.Description
    Resume Exit_PreviewLabels_Click

End Sub
```

First, add a comment at the start of the procedure that describes its purpose. Then declare
the string variable stFilter in the Declarations section. As you type Dim stFilter As
Str, the Auto List displays an alphabetical list of valid choices to fill out the declaration
(see Figure 9.20). To choose from the list, perform one of the following actions:

- Press Tab to accept the highlighted name and remain on the same line with no trailing space.

- Press the spacebar to accept the highlighted name, add a space, and remain on the same line.

- Press Enter to accept the highlighted name and move to the next line in the procedure.

FIGURE 9.20
The Auto List shows valid choices as you type.

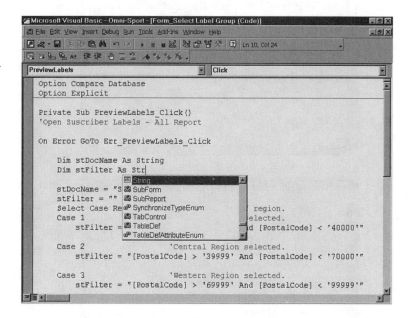

One of the options in the option group is All Regions, which previews all the labels, regardless of region. When this option is chosen, there will be no filter; therefore, set the `stFilter` variable to a zero-length string before running the case. Add the following line below the line that sets the `stDocName` to the report name:

```
stFilter = ""
```

You can see the added line in the code behind the AutoList in Figure 9.20.

Many of the options from the Editor tab of the Options dialog box are also available from the module window shortcut menu. If you've turned any of the coding options off, use the shortcut menu for temporary help. Figure 9.21 shows the module window shortcut menu. Here's a list of the options:

- List Properties/Methods displays a list of all the properties and methods in the current database, beginning with the property or method closest to the current word in the procedure (see Figure 9.22). You can tell `stDocName` is a property by the icon next to it.

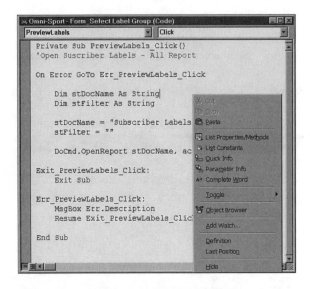

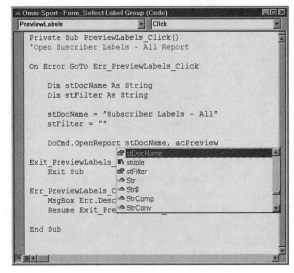

- List Constants is available only if the insertion point is in an enumerated constant. For example, with the insertion point in the word `acPreview`, the list shows three other view constants: `acViewDesign`, `acViewNormal`, and `acViewPreview`.
- Quick Info displays information about the current object, such as name, type, scope, and value. For example, with the insertion point in `Region` in the `Select Case` line, Quick Info displays `Region As OptionGroup`.

- Parameter Info displays syntax information for the statement that contains the insertion point. The current argument appears in bold in the syntax (see Figure 9.23).

FIGURE 9.23
*The Parameter
Info option dis-
plays syntax infor-
mation for the
current statement.*

FIGURE 9.23
*The Parameter
Info option dis-
plays syntax infor-
mation for the
current statement.*

```
Omni-Sport - Form_Select Label Group (Code)
PreviewLabels          ▼  │ Click                ▼
Private Sub PreviewLabels_Click()
'Open Suscriber Labels - All Report

On Error GoTo Err_PreviewLabels_Click

    Dim stDocName As String
    Dim stFilter As String

    stDocName = "Subscriber Labels - All"
    stFilter = ""

    DoCmd.OpenReport stDocName, acPreview
        OpenReport(ReportName, [View As AcView = acViewNormal],
Exit_Previ [FilterName], [WhereCondition])
    Exit Sub

Err_PreviewLabels_Click:
    MsgBox Err.Description
    Resume Exit_PreviewLabels_Click

End Sub
```

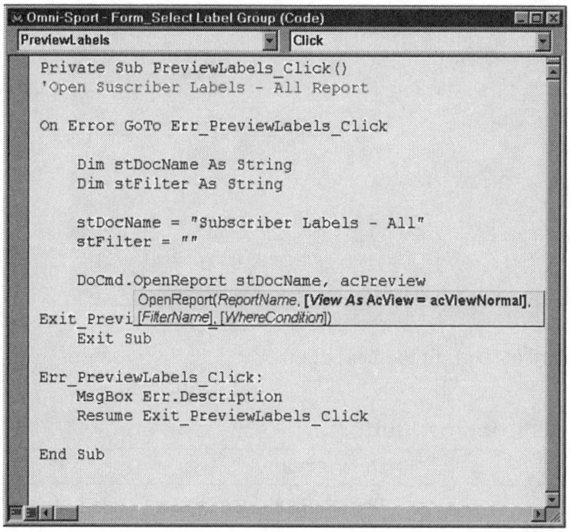

- Complete Word finishes the word you have begun if it's unambiguous; otherwise, it displays a list of words beginning with the characters you've entered.

Tip: The Editor tab of the Options dialog box shows an Auto Quick Info coding option which, when selected, displays syntax information as you type. This is analogous to the Parameter Info selection in the shortcut menu rather than the Quick Info option. Maybe this will be made more consistent in later versions of Access, but for now don't let it confuse you.

LOOKING AHEAD

You use the other options in the shortcut menu when you're debugging a procedure. See Chapter 10, "Debugging Visual Basic Procedures," for more information about these items.

All these shortcut menu items are also available from the Edit menu and the Edit toolbar. The Edit toolbar includes buttons for the five options just described in addition to some special module text-editing features (see Figure 9.24). Table 9.6 describes the buttons on the Edit toolbar.

```
Omni-Sport - Form_Select Label Group (Code)
(General)                          (Declarations)
Option Compare Database
Option Explicit

Private Sub PreviewLabels_Click()
'Open Suscriber Labels - All Report

On Error GoTo Err_PreviewLabels_Click

    Dim stDocName As String
    Dim stFilter As String

    stDocName = "Subscriber Labels - All"
    stFilter = ""
    Select Case Region          'User's choice of region.
    Case 1                      'Eastern Region selected.
        stFilter = "[PostalCode] > '00000' And [PostalCode]
```

Table 9.6 describes the Edit toolbar buttons.

Table 9.6   Edit Toolbar Buttons

Button	Description
Indent	Shifts all selected lines of code to the next tab stop
Outdent	Shifts all selected lines of code to the previous tab stop
Toggle Breakpoint	Sets or removes a breakpoint at the current line
Comment Block	Adds the comment character (') at the beginning of each line in the selected block of code
Uncomment Block	Removes the comment character (') from the beginning of each line in the selected block of code
Toggle Bookmark	Sets or removes a bookmark at the active line of code
Next Bookmark	Moves to the next bookmark in the bookmark stack
Previous Bookmark	Moves to the previous bookmark in the bookmark stack
Clear All Bookmarks	Removes all bookmarks from the stack

Add the Case Structure to Create the Filter String

A case structure based on Region as the test expression can use the value returned by the Region option group as the differentiating value. Option buttons in a group return default or specified values, depending on how you define the controls. In this case, the default sequential integers are accepted so that the buttons return the values 1 through 4. The regions are roughly divided by postal code, so that the filter specifies a range of postal code values, as follows:

- Between 00000 and 40000—Eastern region.
- Between 39999 and 70000—Central region.
- Between 69999 and 99999—Western region.

The final option, All Regions, leaves the filter as the zero-length string. Type the following statements immediately below the On Error GoTo statement, omitting the final quotation mark, and then press Enter:

```
Select Case Region          'User's choice of region
   Case 1                   'Eastern Region selected.
        stFilter = "Left([PostalCode],5) > '00000' And
            Left([PostalCode],5) < '40000'
```

If you forget the closing quotation mark, Access automatically adds it when you press Enter. That's one of the syntax errors that Access fixes for you. Continue with the next statements, which set the other filters for the Central and Western regions. Listing 9.8 shows the complete listing for the Select Label Group form class module. The listing includes the procedure the Command Button Wizard created for the OnClick event for the Cancel button on the form. Be sure to add plenty of comments as you enter the code statements.

Listing 9.8 The Select Label Group Class Module

```
Option Compare Database
Option Explicit

Private Sub PreviewLabels_Click()
'Open Subcriber Labels - All Report

On Error GoTo Err_PreviewLabels_Click

    Dim stDocName As String
    Dim stFilter As String

    stDocName = "Subscriber Labels - All"
    stFilter = ""
    Select Case Region       'User's choice of region.
    Case 1                   'Eastern Region selected.
       stFilter = "Left([PostalCode],5) > '00000' And
           Left([PostalCode],5) < '40000'"

    Case 2                   'Central Region selected.
       stFilter = "Left([PostalCode],5) > '39999' And
           Left([PostalCode],5) < '70000'"

    Case 3                   'Western Region selected.
       stFilter = "Left([PostalCode],5) > '69999' And
           Left([PostalCode],5) < '99999'"
```

continues

Listing 9.8   Continued

```
    End Select

    DoCmd.OpenReport stDocName, acPreview, , stFilter
    DoCmd.Close acForm, "Select Label Group"

Exit_PreviewLabels_Click:
    Exit Sub

Err_PreviewLabels_Click:
    MsgBox Err.Description
    Resume Exit_PreviewLabels_Click

End Sub

Private Sub Cancel_Click()
On Error GoTo Err_Cancel_Click

    DoCmd.Close

Exit_Cancel_Click:
    Exit Sub

Err_Cancel_Click:
    MsgBox Err.Description
    Resume Exit_Cancel_Click

End Sub
```

> **Note:** If you want to create a new procedure for one of the objects in the form
> without relying on a wizard, you can use the object pull-down menu at the top
> left of the module window to see a list of all the objects in the current form or
> report. To start a new event procedure for one of these controls, select the con-
> trol from the object pull-down menu. Then use the pull-down menu on the
> right, which lists all the events that apply to that object. The procedures already
> created in the module appear in bold in the list. Select the event procedure you
> want to create and type the code statements. If you select an existing proce-
> dure, it opens in the window so you can make changes.

Change the Switchboard

Now that you have a form that offers a selection of label previews and a procedure that
responds to the Preview Labels button, you need to insert the capability into the application. Because it applies to reports, you should place the access to the report on the
Preview Reports Switchboard. You can either add a new option or change an existing
option.

To divert the Preview Switchboard item to a different object (a form, in this case, instead of a report), all you need to do is change the Switchboard table. The table also determines the switchboard item text and caption. You can also use the Switchboard Manager, if you prefer, by choosing Tools|Database Utilities|Switchboard Manager.

Open the Switchboard table in datasheet view and make the following changes:

- Change the ItemText for item 3 on switchboard 3 to Preview Labels By Region.
- Change the command on the same line to 3 (OpenForm).
- Change the argument to Select Label Group.

Close the table and try out the new option. Figure 9.25 shows the new dialog box in which you select the labels you want to preview.

FIGURE 9.25
Making a selection in the Preview Switchboard opens the new form.

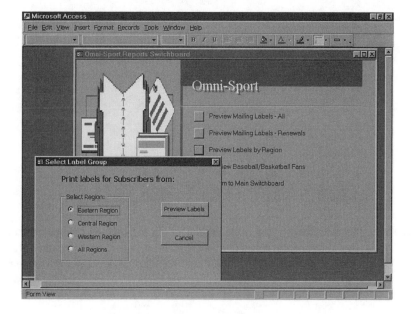

The Object Browser

The Object Browser is a useful tool for looking up objects available to Access and seeing which methods and properties can be used with each object. The information includes definitions of objects and their properties, methods, events, and constants as well as their related functions and statements. When you find the item you want, you can copy and paste it into the procedure. As procedures become more complicated, the Object Browser can ensure correct spelling and pairing up of objects with their methods and properties.

You must be in the module window to use the Object Browser. To open the Object Browser, click the Object Browser button or choose View|Object Browser. The Definition option in the module shortcut menu also opens the Object Browser window and displays the definition of the current term.

When you open the Object Browser window, you have a choice of projects and libraries, including the current database, *Omni-Sport* (see Figure 9.26). Each library has a slightly different collection of objects and associated members. The left pane of the window shows the list of all the object classes in the currently referenced libraries, whereas the right pane shows a list of members of the selected object class. The lower pane displays the definition of the currently selected class and member.

FIGURE 9.26
The Object Browser offers a choice of libraries.

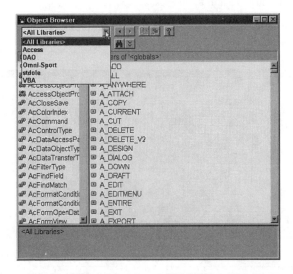

DEVELOPMENT

To add another library to the Project/Library list, right-click in the Object Browser window and choose References from the shortcut menu. Then check the libraries you want in the References dialog box and click OK. You can also click Browse to add other references in the system to the current project. Another way to open the References dialog box is to choose Tools|References.

The Classes list displays all the available classes in the library or project that's selected in the Project/Libraries box. If you've written code for a class, the class name appears in bold. The first item in the Classes list is always <globals>, which is a list of all the globally accessible members.

The Members list displays all the elements of the class selected in the Classes pane. Members of a class of objects include all the methods, properties, events, and constants that belong to that class and also include related functions and statements. Items that have code associated with them appear in bold. The icons preceding the names in the lists indicate the type of class and member. For example, Figure 9.26 shows enumerated constants on the left and members constants on the right.

Figure 9.27 shows the class Report as a member of the Access library and some of the members of the Report class.

FIGURE 9.27

*The icons indicate
the type of object
and member.*

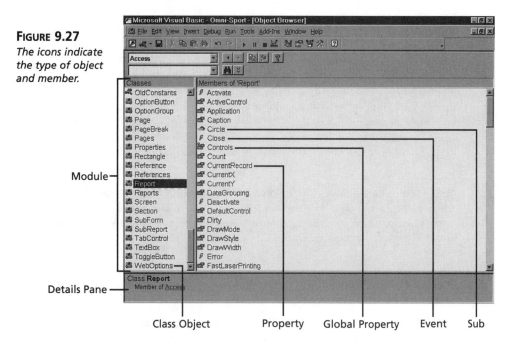

Module

Details Pane

Class Object   Property   Global Property   Event   Sub

In addition to lists of all the elements of a library or project, the Object Browser has many helpful features:

- The <globals> item that appears at the top of the class list displays a list of all the members in the selected library that can be accessed globally.

- The Go Back and Go Forward buttons navigate through the items you've previously selected.

- The Copy To Clipboard button copies a selected object to the Clipboard from which you can paste it into your own procedure.

- View Definition button opens the module window and displays the user-defined sub or function procedure. For example, choose *Omni-Sport* from the Project/Library list, select Form_Select Label Group from the Class list and Preview_Labels_Click from the Members list, and then click View Definition. The procedure code appears in the module window.

- To find a class or member in the current library, type the name in the Search Text box and then click Search. After the search is completed, click the Show Search Results button to open the results pane.

- If you need help with a specific object, method, property, or event, select it and click the Help button or press F1. The Help topic for that item opens. When you close the Help window, you return to the Object Browser.

The Object Browser window can remain open while you're writing a procedure, and you can continue to reference it by switching back and forth between windows.

Run a Visual Basic Procedure

To check out a new procedure, you must be able to run it. You can run an event procedure by causing the event to occur. Any procedure that does not take arguments can be run from the module window by choosing Run|Run Sub/User Form (or you can click Run Sub/User Form on the toolbar) with the cursor anywhere in the procedure. If the procedure does take arguments, the underlying object must be open in design view. General procedures stored in the Modules tab of the database window can be run from the module window.

TROUBLESHOOTING

> **Tip:** If your procedure stops before execution is completed and the Run|Run Sub/User Form option is dimmed, you might need to switch the underlying form to design view. The procedure will not run from the module window if the form is in form view.

You can also call a procedure from another procedure or run it from a macro by using the RunCode action.

Functions cannot be run like sub and general procedures from the module window. To check out a function procedure, use it in an expression in another procedure and run that procedure to see if the function gives the right return value. You can also test a function from the Debug window, as described later in Chapter 10, "Debugging Visual Basic Procedures."

Summary

In this chapter, you became acquainted with the module window and saw how to change some of the coding and window options. Many of the options offer automatic help during code generation. This chapter also discussed the types of modules and procedures and their syntax.

Many procedures were developed, demonstrating the wide variety of operations that can be accomplished with Visual Basic procedures. Examples included displaying a message to the user, filtering records for a report, and creating a temporary welcoming screen.

Finally, the chapter briefly approached the subject of running VB procedures, which is resumed in Chapter 10, "Debugging Visual Basic Procedures," where you explore the debugging process.

Debugging Visual Basic Procedures

In Visual Basic, a subprocedure is supposed to perform some operation, and a function is supposed to return a value. When the operation is not what you intended or the returned value is not what you expected, the debugging process begins. This chapter discusses the many tools Access provides to help you track down and correct errors in your Visual Basic code.

With these tools, you can monitor variables and properties while code is running, move slowly through code execution, and suspend execution at specified locations in the procedure.

Types of Bugs and How to Avoid Them

According to the *Academic Press Dictionary of Science and Technology*, a bug is "an error in either the mechanics or the logic of a computer program." In an Access application, you can encounter three major types of bugs. First, *compile errors* are the result of an incorrect statement. For example, a variable is misspelled, the End If is missing from an If...Then...Else structure, or some required punctuation is missing. Access automatically displays an error message when a compile error occurs, unless you've cleared the Auto Syntax Check option in the Module Options dialog box.

Runtime errors occur when the program tries to execute an impossible operation, such as dividing by zero, passing an invalid argument, or writing to a floppy disk that's not in place. You can expect runtime errors when you're developing new procedures, especially if they're complex. This is one more reason to keep procedures short and limited to a single operation.

Errors in *logic* cause a procedure to produce the wrong answer or not do what is expected. Procedures containing logic errors might compile and run correctly, but still give incorrect results. An example is if you base a case structure on the value returned from a message box and use the wrong button code. You can spot logic errors by stepping through the code one statement at a time and analyzing the results of each step.

VBA provides the tools you need to find all three types. With these debugging aids, you can execute your code one line at a time, watch the results of each step, and trace through a list of nested procedure calls.

Peter's Principle: Prevention Is Still the Best Medicine

Instead of chasing bugs after you write the procedures, it's better to avoid them, if possible. You've heard this before, but it's still good advice. Break up the program into single-purpose sub and function procedures and be generous with comments. Explicitly declare all variables to help prevent misspelled variable names, which can cause compile errors. Using a naming convention that gives information about a variable, such as its data type and what it stands for, can help prevent errors caused by misunderstanding the purpose of the variable. For example, the variable `strFilter` cannot be mistaken for anything but a string expression to be used as a filter for a recordset.

The trick to successful debugging is to zero in on the statement where the error occurs by processing the code a piece at a time in the debug window. When you find where the program goes astray, you can work backward and locate the cause of the problem. Using the debug window, you can also insert different values in variables and properties to see the effects on the outcome.

Dealing with Compile Errors

DEVELOPMENT

If the Auto Syntax Check option is in force, many errors are caught as you type. Syntax errors, such as failing to end a statement with the proper characters or placing two operators together with no expression between them, are noticed when you press Enter to move to the next line of code. Access automatically corrects some simple omissions, such as leaving out the closing quotation mark. If you don't want to be interrupted with syntax error alerts as you type, clear the Auto Syntax Check option in the Editor tab of the Options dialog box. Syntax will be checked later during compilation.

When a syntax error occurs, Access displays an error message that explains the type of error. Figure 10.1 shows the result of leaving a trailing quotation mark at the end of the statement. The offending statement is shown in red in the module window, and the mistake is highlighted in dark blue. Click OK to close the message box and correct the error or click Help to display the relevant Help topic.

During the compilation process, Access reads the entire procedure and tries to reconcile all the pieces. Does every `If...Then...Else` structure have an `End If` to match? Does every `Select Case` have an `End Select`? Is every variable declared? To compile the procedures in a module, choose Debug|Compile. When compilation errors occur, Access displays error messages, and you can correct the code in the module window.

More complex errors require the assistance of the debugging tools, which can help you track down and correct elusive bugs. Before proceeding any further with correcting Visual Basic code, take a look at the debugging tools that Access provides.

FIGURE 10.1

The message box explains the compile error.

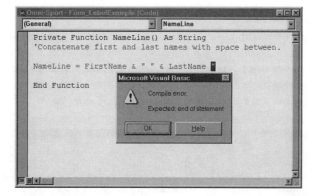

Understanding the Visual Basic Editor Debug Tools

Several tools are available from the Visual Basic Editor window that display code results and values of expressions and even change values during execution suspension. The *Debug toolbar* has several new buttons that can suspend code execution, step through code one statement at a time, and display intermediate results in special windows.

In addition to the Debug toolbar, the Visual Basic Editor window provides three debug windows that can help you find and correct errors in your code. Each window is capable of supporting your efforts in a slightly different way:

- The *Immediate window* is a flexible scratchpad that you can use to view the results of a line of code or the value of a field, control, property, or expression. You can even assign a new value to a variable, field, column, or property and check out the results immediately.

- The *Locals window* automatically displays the name, current value, and the type of all the variables and objects in the current procedure. The information is updated whenever there's a break in execution. You can also use the Locals window to enter a new value and see the change it causes.

- You can specify certain values to watch by entering the expressions in the *Watch window.* The expression can be a variable, a property, a function call, or any other valid expression. You can also ask for an instant watch to see the value of an expression not specified as a watch expression. When you run the code, the value of the expression shows in the Watch window. You can edit or delete a watch expression in the Watch window.

To see the results of a line of code in one of these windows, you must first suspend execution. The easiest way to suspend code execution is to set a breakpoint at one or more lines in the code. See the section "Setting and Clearing Breakpoints," later in this chapter.

Using the Debug Toolbar

The Debug toolbar is always available in the Visual Basic Editor window. To show it, right-click in the Standard toolbar and check Debug in the list of available toolbars. Figure 10.2 shows the Editor window with both the Standard and Debug toolbars. The first four buttons on the Debug toolbar operate the same as the same buttons on the Standard toolbar. Table 10.1 describes the remaining buttons on the Debug toolbar.

FIGURE 10.2

The Debug toolbar.

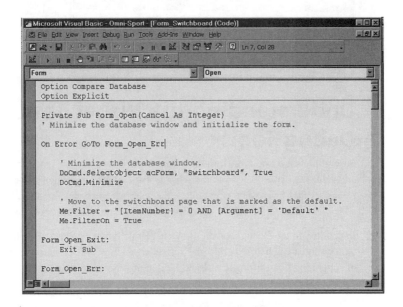

Table 10.1   Debug Toolbar Buttons

Button	Description
Toggle Breakpoint	Sets or removes the breakpoint at the current code line.
Step Into	Begins executing code one statement at a time.
Step Over	Executes each procedure as if it were one statement. Steps across a procedure instead of into it.
Step Out	Executes all remaining statements as a single statement and exits to the statement following the one that initially called the procedure.
Locals Window	Displays the Locals window.
Immediate Window	Displays the Immediate window.
Watch Window	Displays the Watch window.
Quick Watch	Opens the Quick Watch dialog box, showing the current value of the selected expression.
Call Stack	Displays the Calls dialog box, showing the list of procedures that have been started but are not completed.

Setting and Clearing Breakpoints

Some of the debugging tasks require suspension of execution before they display values. The easiest way to pause execution at a specific line of code is to set a breakpoint at that line. A *breakpoint* is a statement that you have marked as a stopping place for VB.

A breakpoint suspends execution before processing the breakpoint statement and leaves the procedure still running, but just in an idle state. Everything stands still; the variables and properties keep the same values. When a breakpoint line is reached, execution is suspended, and you can take a look in one of the debug windows to see the current expression values. If the error has not yet occurred, it might be caused by the breakpoint line itself, which is the next one to be executed. When you reach a breakpoint, you can continue stepping through the code until you find the problem.

> **Tip:** You can set only executable statements as breakpoints, not declarations or definitions.

Setting a breakpoint couldn't be easier. Simply click in the indicator margin next to the line you want to mark as the breakpoint—that is, the next statement to be executed. You can also place the insertion point in the line and click the Toggle Breakpoint button on the Debug toolbar or choose Debug|Toggle Breakpoint. You can have as many breakpoints in a procedure as you want.

When you set a breakpoint at a line of code, the line is displayed in the breakpoint color defined in the Editor Format tab of the Options dialog box. When execution reaches a breakpoint, the color changes again and an arrow appears in the margin indicator bar, identifying it as the next statement to be executed. Figure 10.3 shows two breakpoints set at the `Color_Click` event procedure in the ColorStyle form class module, with execution stopped at the first breakpoint.

To set these breakpoints and run the code to the first one, do the following:

1. Select the ColorStyle form name in the database window and click Code.
2. In the VB Editor window, place the insertion point in the `Select Case` line and click Toggle Breakpoint.
3. Repeat step 2 to set a breakpoint at the `End Select` line.
4. Click the View Microsoft Access button on the Standard toolbar to return to the Access window and switch to form view, which initiates the class module.
5. In form view, click the Color label, which initiates the `Color_Click` event procedure, and then enter **2** in the input box and click OK. You automatically return to the VB Editor window.

When you click the Color label in the `ColorStyle` form, you initiate the `Color_Click` event procedure, which displays the input box. After you respond to the request for a number, the procedure stops at the Select Case statement, which begins to evaluate the number you entered. If you click Continue, the procedure continues and changes the color of the label, corresponding to the number you entered. Return to the Access window to see the result.

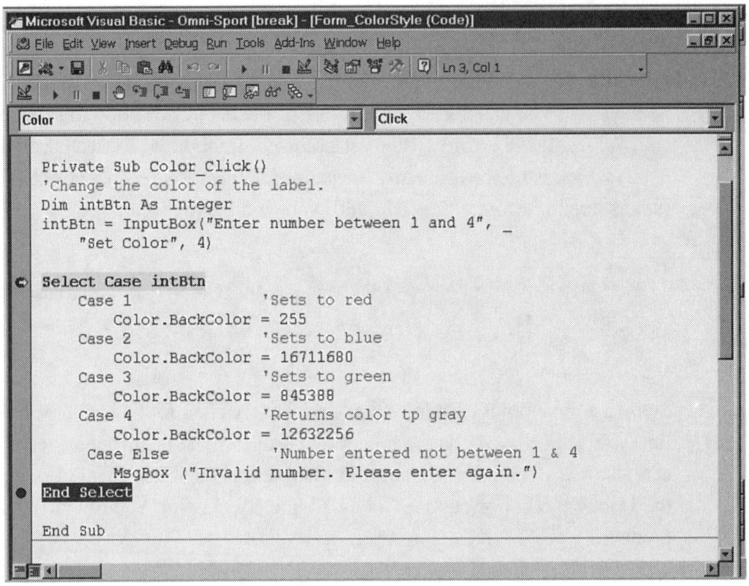

FIGURE 10.3

Breakpoints set in the Color_Click *event procedure.*

After you've paused execution at a breakpoint, choose Run|Continue or click the Continue button on the Standard toolbar to proceed.

> **Warning:** Be careful about setting breakpoints in event procedures, especially mouse and key event procedures. For example, if you stop execution in a Mouse Down procedure and then resume, Access thinks the mouse button is still down. You must press the mouse button down before the Mouse Up event occurs, but pressing the mouse button down executes the Mouse Down event procedure again. Mouse_Up might never occur. It's safer to use the Debug.Print statement in the code to test for the values in such event procedures.

When you decide to stop running the procedure, you can use End or Reset. Clicking End on the toolbar or in an error dialog box stops code execution and leaves the module-level variables with their current values. End is also available on the Run menu. If you want to restore the module-level variables to their original values, click Reset on the toolbar or choose Run|Reset.

> **Tip:** If you set a breakpoint at a line that contains multiple statements separated by colons (:), the code is suspended at the first statement in the line, regardless of the location of the insertion point in the line when you set the breakpoint.

Breakpoints are automatically removed when you close the module; however, to remove them while the module is still open, reverse the process: place the insertion point in the statement and click the Toggle Breakpoint button, choose Debug|Toggle Breakpoint, or click the breakpoint indicator in the margin. To clear all breakpoints in the current application, choose Debug|Clear All Breakpoints.

When you save your code, the breakpoints are not saved with it. You must reset them the next time you open the procedure for debugging.

DEVELOPMENT

Another way to suspend code execution is to insert a Stop statement in the procedure just before the line where you want to stop. A Stop statement works like a breakpoint, except it stays in the code until you remove it. Breakpoints need to be reset when you start the procedures again, but Stop keeps the stopping point throughout a long debug process. The only problem is remembering to remove all the Stop statements when debugging is over. You can also press Ctrl+Break to stop execution. This last method is helpful if you realize you've accidentally programmed an infinite loop that will never stop repeating.

> **Tip:** One way clever programmers remind themselves to remove these debug stopping points from large programs is to add a Debug.Print statement just before each stop. The statement can display a message in the Immediate window explaining that the stop is intentional and should be removed after the program is checked out.

Working in the Immediate Window

You can do a lot in the Immediate window. The Immediate window can display the results of a single line of code, including values of controls, fields, and properties or the result of an expression. You can also use the Immediate window to assign new values to variables, fields, columns, or properties and run the procedure with the new values. To use the Immediate window during code execution, suspend execution at that point by clicking Stop and then click Immediate Window on the Debug toolbar.

Typing a question mark means "Print" to the Immediate window. When you type an expression preceded by ? and then press Enter, the value of the expression is displayed in the Immediate window.

Figure 10.4 shows the Immediate window while the Switchboard form is opening in form view. The first lines of code in the Form_Open event procedure remove the scrollbars, set a custom caption in the title bar, and create a ToolTip for the Page 2 button. The first line of code has been executed, and the second line is highlighted, indicating that it will be executed next. After you type the **?Me.ScrollBars** line in the Immediate window and press Enter, the value of the ScrollBars property is displayed in the Immediate window.

Figure 10.4

Viewing the value of the form's ScrollBars *property.*

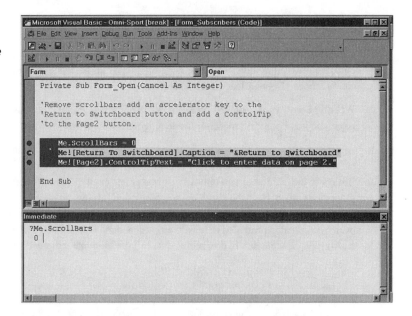

Click Continue in either toolbar to proceed to execute the next statement. If you type **?** followed by the name of the other properties in the Immediate window, you can see the new settings. Figure 10.5 shows the Immediate window with the results of executing all three statements specified as breakpoints. A breakpoint was added to the End Sub statement to keep the module window open after executing the other three breakpoints.

> **Tip:** You can open the Immediate window at any time without first opening the module window by pressing Ctrl+G. This works if you've checked the Use Access Special Keys option in the Startup dialog box. Choose Tools|Startup and then click the Advanced button.

You saw earlier that typing **?** (which is the shorthand for Print) followed by a property displays the property's value in the debug window. Another way to show the value in the Immediate window is to add the statement Debug.Print Me.ScrollBars to the code. When the code stops running at the breakpoint, you can view the value in the Immediate window by pressing Ctrl+G.

FIGURE 10.5
The Immediate window shows the values at breakpoints.

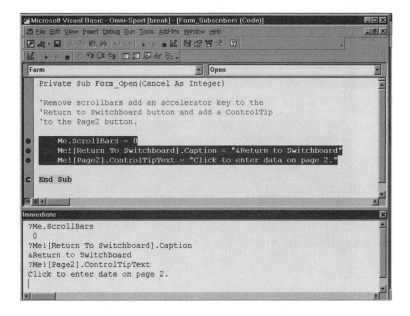

What you ask for in the Immediate window doesn't need to be part of the form or report associated with the current module—it can be any type of expression, as long as it does not refer to an object it doesn't have access to.

For example, you can use the WeekDay() function to find out what day of the week your birthday falls on in 2001. Open any procedure in the module window and click the Immediate Window button on the Debug toolbar or press Ctrl+G to open the Immediate window. Next, type the following, using the # delimiters for the date value:

```
MyDate = #January 15, 2001#
?WeekDay(MyDate)
```

Now press Enter. The Immediate window in Figure 10.6 shows that the date falls on a Monday (day number 2).

The Immediate window also lets you evaluate more complicated expressions, such as calculating the number of days between two dates or the price to charge for a product given the cost and the markup percentage. Figure 10.7 shows the Immediate window with the results of two such expressions. You can see two identical results below the ?WeekDay(MyDate) expression. This occurs when you place the insertion point in the expression again and press Enter. The result of the DateSerial() function shows that the year 2000 is a leap year containing 366 days.

> **Tip:** When you want to repeat a line in the Immediate window, you don't need to retype it. Simply place the insertion point anywhere in the line and press Enter. The line will execute with the latest values.

FIGURE 10.6

Showing the day of the week.

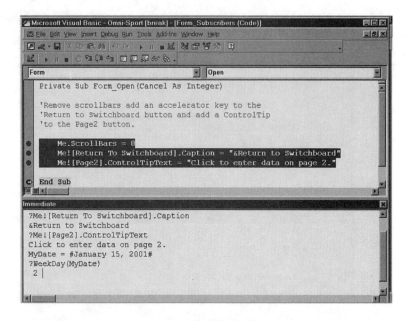

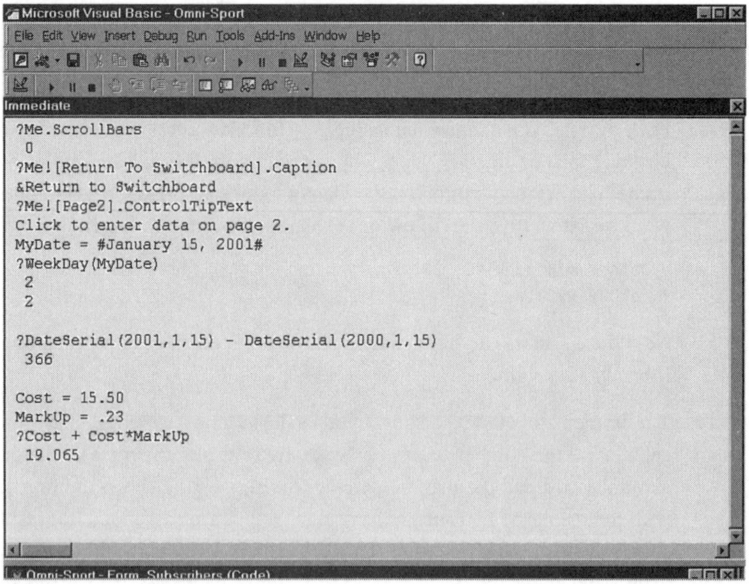

FIGURE 10.7

Evaluating other expressions in the Immediate window.

To run a subprocedure from the Immediate window, type the name and the arguments and then press Enter. For example, typing **MySub arg1, arg2, arg3** would run the subprocedure MySub.

When you run a sub, you do not use ? or Print, because subs do not return values. The procedure simply runs; then you need to examine the objects it worked on to see if it executed properly.

To execute or test a function, you use ? or Print to display the returned value. For example, you can test the IsLoaded() function in the Global Module of the *Omni-Sport* database using the following steps:

1. Open the Subscribers form in form view and then press Ctrl+G to display the Immediate window within the VB Editor window.

2. In the Immediate window, type **stFormName = "Subscribers"** and then press Enter.

3. On the second line, type **?IsLoaded(stFormName)** and press Enter. The pane shows -1 (True), indicating that the form is loaded.

4. Type **stFormName = "ColorStyle"** and press Enter. Then repeat the line from step 3 and press Enter. This time the returned value is 0 (False) because the ColorStyle form is not loaded. Figure 10.8 shows the Immediate window with the results of the IsLoaded() function test.

FIGURE 10.8
Testing a function in the Immediate window.

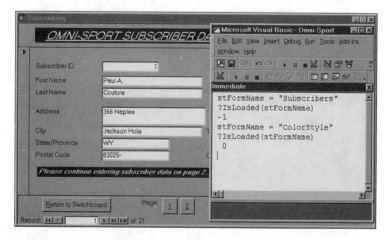

When a procedure has suspended execution, you can assign or change the values of variables and properties in the Immediate window and then continue execution. You'll learn more about this in the section "Controlling Execution."

The Immediate window retains all the entries as you work in the debug window; the list can become quite lengthy. You can delete lines as you go along by selecting them and pressing Delete. If you keep them, you can navigate through the list using the standard mouse, arrow keys, or the Home, End, and PgUp/PgDn keys. Ctrl+PgUp moves up one screen of lines and Ctrl+PgDn moves down one screen. The number of lines depends on the height of the window.

Working in the Locals Window

The Locals window displays a list of all the objects and variables used by the current procedure. The list shows the expression, current value, and type. The first item in the list indicates the current module: the module name for a standard module or the variable Me for a class module.

The values in the list are updated every time execution is suspended. The execution mode changes from run to break when you're stepping through code or when a breakpoint is encountered. In break mode, you can change the value of a variable in the list and continue execution.

ANALYSIS

The Locals window shows the list of variables encountered in the Style_Click event procedure in the ColorStyle form class module (see Figure 10.9). Two breakpoints are set in the procedure so that execution will pause, and you can view the variables the code uses. The value of the intBtn variable, shown in the Locals window, is still 0 because the number has not yet been entered in the InputBox function. You can drag the column dividers in the Locals window to adjust the column widths.

FIGURE 10.9

Viewing the values of the objects and variables in the Locals window.

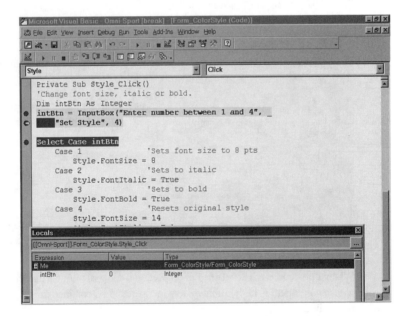

The first expression in the list is the system-defined variable Me, which is an object reference to the current object—the ColorStyle form. The second is the locally declared variable intBtn, which has not yet been set to a value. When you enter a number in the input box and move to the next line of code, the value changes. You can also change the value of the intBtn variable by entering the new value in the Locals window.

The plus sign to the left of the Me reference indicates that it can be expanded to show an alphabetized list of all the data members and properties in the form with their current values and type (see Figure 10.10). If the current module is a standard module rather than a class module, the list begins with the name of the current module instead of Me.

FIGURE 10.10

Expanding the Me variable shows all the data members and properties.

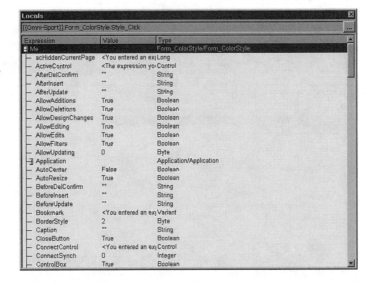

Working in the Watch Window

The principal difference between the Locals window and the Watch window is that all the variables and expressions are listed in the Locals window, but only those you set watches for are displayed in the Watch window. Also, values in the Locals window are updated only when code is suspended, whereas values in the Watch window change while code is running. You can use either window to change the value of a variable or expression in place during a break. The Locals window empties when the procedure ends. The Watch window retains the watches you've added until you delete them.

As in the Locals window, you can change the value of an expression or variable in place in the Watch window. You can also drag the column dividers to adjust the column widths.

> **Tip:** Limiting the number of watches you set can help speed up the code execution. Each watch requires processing time to update as the values change.

The Watch window list is similar to the Locals list, except that the Watch list also includes the context of the expression, usually the name of the procedure in which it originates. The Watch window can be more efficient during debugging because it updates only those expressions and variables you're interested in.

You use the Watch window to keep an eye on the value of specific variables and expressions during code execution. Figure 10.11 shows the module window with the `Select Case intBtn` line highlighted, indicating that it's the next statement to be executed. Watches have been set for the `intBtn` integer variable and two of the Style label properties: `FontItalic` and `FontSize`.

FIGURE 10.11
The Watch window shows the `intBtn` value is 2.

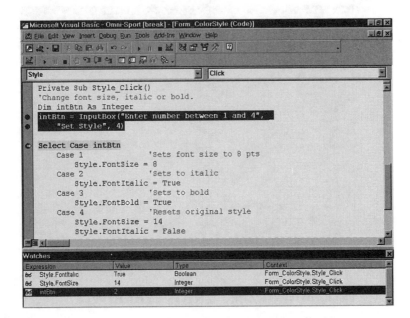

The Watch window shows that the value of the `intBtn` variable has been set to 2, the value returned by the `InputBox` function. The `Style.FontItalic` and `Style.FontSize` properties still have their default values of `True` and 14, respectively. These may change depending on the value entered in the `InputBox` function, which is implemented by the case structure.

When you add a watch to the list, you can set the expression to any variable, property, function call, or other expression in the module. You can also ask Access to stop execution when the expression changes value or reaches a certain value or when a loop has iterated a specific number of times. You'll learn more about specifying and adding watches in the section "Watching Results."

Controlling Execution

TROUBLESHOOTING

Because errors are often embedded deep in the code, you can't always locate them after the procedure ends, whether it ends prematurely or normally. It's very helpful to be able to step through code and execute only the parts that are still causing errors. You've already seen how to set breakpoints where you want the code to stop after running part of a procedure. Access gives you several other ways to control code execution while your code is displayed in the module window:

- Stepping through code one statement at a time
- Skipping over called procedures
- Skipping to the statement that contains the cursor
- Exiting the code and resetting the variables and expressions to their original values
- Moving to a specified statement when code stops

Stepping Through Code

Before you can begin to step through code, you need to suspend execution by clicking Break or choosing Run|Break. You can also halt execution by switching to design time by choosing Run|Reset *projectname* or clicking Reset.

To enter the step mode of code execution, click the Step Into toolbar button or choose Debug|Step Into; then click Continue or choose Run|Continue. The first line of the current procedure is highlighted in yellow and an arrow in the left indicator margin points to the line as the next one to be executed. When you click Continue again, that statement is executed and the indicator moves to the next line. As you step through your code, the Locals window displays the values of the expressions and variables encountered. You can use the Immediate window to examine the current value of specific variables.

Figure 10.12 shows the ColorStyle form's `Color_Click` event procedure in the module window running in step mode. When the `intBtn` input box was displayed, the value 2 was entered. The Locals window shows the `intBtn` expression with the entered value. The `?intBtn` statement in the Immediate window responds with the same value.

FIGURE 10.12
Stepping through the `Color_Click` event procedure.

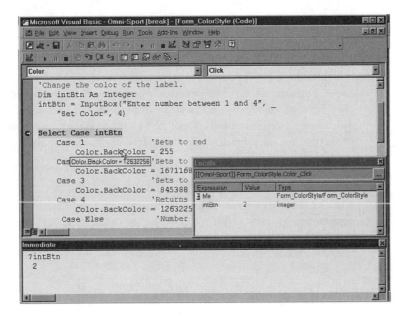

When the mouse pointer rests on the Color.BackColor property, the Auto Data Tip option displays the current value of the property. It still has the default color setting, 12632256, because the case statements have not yet evaluated the intBtn expression and applied the property changes.

At this point, you can change the value of the intBtn expression by typing **intBtn = 3** in the Immediate window and pressing Enter. Figure 10.13 shows the results: The Locals window value has changed to 3, and the Auto Data Tip displays intBtn = 3 when the mouse pointer pauses over the expression in the Select Case statement.

Figure 10.13
Changing the value of an expression during a step through.

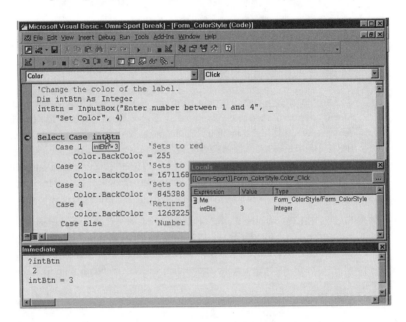

You could also change the intBtn value by selecting the line in the Locals window and typing a new value.

Stepping through the rest of the procedure moves to Case 1 and then to Case 2. When Case 3 is executed, it finds a match with intBtn and executes the statement that follows, which changes the background color of the Colors box in the form to green. Clicking the Continue button skips directly to the End Select line and then to End Sub.

Figure 10.14 shows the Debug menu with the step-through options as well as options for setting breakpoints and adding expressions to the Watch window.

When a procedure calls another procedure, Step Into moves into the called procedure and steps through it line by line. If you know that the called procedure is already bug free, use Step Over to run the whole procedure as a unit and return to the next statement in the calling procedure.

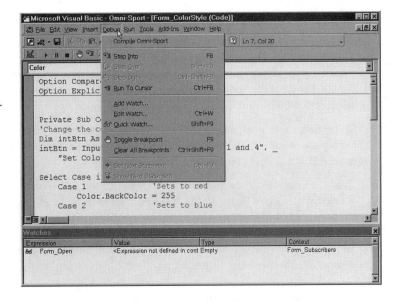

FIGURE 10.14

The Debug menu with options for stepping through code and adding watch expressions.

For example, suppose you're stepping through Proc A and reach a statement that calls Proc B. You don't want to step through Proc B, so you click Step Over. Proc B runs, and it's when finished, the next statement in Proc A is highlighted and ready to execute.

If you want to run the rest of the current called procedure and return quickly to the next line in the procedure that called it, use Step Out. If this procedure was not called by another, it runs to the end. If the current procedure calls others, they too are run before returning to the calling procedure.

When you want to skip over part of a procedure that's already checked out, you can use the Run To Cursor option. Place the cursor in the statement where you want processing to stop and then choose Debug|Run To Cursor or right-click and choose Run To Cursor from the shortcut menu.

Two other options are available on the Debug menu that let you skip over parts of the code or even back up and run a segment again: Set Next Statement and Show Next Statement. Place the insertion point in the statement you want to run next and choose Debug|Set Next Statement. The yellow highlight and indicator move to the line containing the cursor. The Show Next Statement option moves to the statement that will be executed after the current one. These two options are not available unless the execution was stopped by a breakpoint or a `Stop` statement. These two options are also available in the module window shortcut menu.

> **Tip:** If fixing a bug requires moving a block of code from one place to another in a procedure, select the statements and press Ctrl+X, which places the code on the Clipboard. Then, move to where you want the code and press Ctrl+V to paste it in place.

Watching Results

Instead of showing the changing values of all the variables and expressions in the Locals window, the Watch window is a more efficient tool for monitoring just the expressions of interest. By specifying one or more expressions to watch, their values are continuously displayed in the Watch window. Another alternative is Quick Watch, which gives you a snapshot of the current value of a single selected expression.

Setting a watch on an expression involves three specifications: what expression to monitor, when to monitor it, and how Access is to respond to the expression. All these are set in the Add Watch dialog box.

To add an expression to the Watch window, choose Debug|Add Watch to open the Add Watch dialog box (see Figure 10.15). If the insertion point is already in an expression in the module window, the expression appears in the dialog box; otherwise, you can type the expression in the Add Watch dialog box. You can watch a variable, property, function call, or any other valid expression. Add Watch is also available on the module window shortcut menu when code is suspended.

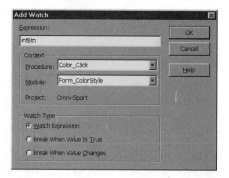

FIGURE 10.15

Adding an expression to the Watch window.

The Context entries in the Add Watch dialog box define the range over which to monitor the expression. By default, the context is the procedure and module in which the expression occurs. Setting the scope as narrow as possible is more efficient than setting the context to all procedures and modules in the current project. The Procedure pull-down menu lists all the procedures in the current module as well as <All Procedures>, and the Module pull-down menu lists all the modules in the current database and <All Modules>.

The Watch Type option group gives you a choice of how to react to the expression. The first option, Watch Expression, is the default, which displays the value in the Watch window continuously while code is running. If you want to pause execution when the watch expression evaluates to True, choose Break When Value Is True. The third option, Break When Value Changes, suspends execution when the watch expression value changes.

> **Tip:** If you want to add another watch expression to the list in the Watch window, select it in the module window and drag it to the Watch pane. This quickly adds the watch expression using the default context and watch type options.

ANALYSIS

Figure 10.16 shows the Watch window with the variable intBtn as the watch expression in three watch types, each indicated by a different icon. The first is the default watch expression, the second is Break When Value Is True, and the third is Break When Value Changes. The code has executed to the point where 2 was entered in the input box that requested the variable to be used in the Select Case structure. The Immediate window shows the entered value. Then the statement intBtn = 3 was entered in the Immediate window, which updated the value in the Watch window.

FIGURE 10.16
Watching the
intBtn *variable.*

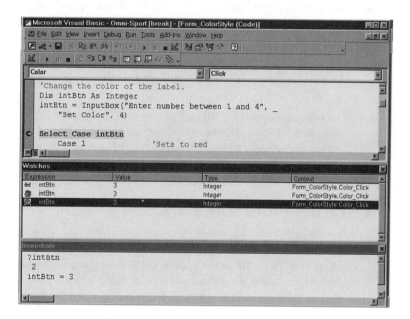

To edit a watch expression, select the expression in the Watch window list and choose Debug|Edit Watch or choose Edit Watch from the Watch window shortcut menu. The Edit Watch dialog box is the same as the Add Watch dialog box, except that it also has a Delete button. Change the watch type of context and then choose OK. To delete the watch expression, choose Delete in the Edit Watch dialog box or right-click the watch line and choose Delete Watch from the shortcut menu.

If you just want a temporary look at an expression, use the Quick Watch feature. Suspend execution and select the expression whose value you want to see. After selecting the variable or expression in the module window, choose Debug|Quick Watch or click the Quick

Watch toolbar button on the Debug toolbar. The Quick Watch dialog box opens, showing the context and current value of the watch expression (see Figure 10.17). If you want to add the expression to the Watch window now, choose Add in the Quick Watch dialog box.

FIGURE 10.17
Quick Watch gives you a snapshot of the expression.

If the procedure that contains the expression is not running, the Context and Expression boxes show the proper entries, but the Value box shows <Out of context>.

Access provides many shortcut keys to maneuver around the module and debug windows to accomplish debugging tasks. If you've checked the Show Shortcut Keys in ScreenTips option in the Options tab of the Customize dialog box, you can see the shortcut keys you can use in place of most of the menu commands in the module window.

> **Warning:** If you've assigned a set of actions to one of the reserved key combinations, this will replace the default actions, and you might get some unexpected results when you try to use them during debugging. Try always to use a key combination that Access hasn't reserved for special purpose.

Tracing Procedure Calls

ARCHITECTURE

When the module contains several procedures, some of which call upon others to perform subordinate operations, the calling procedure and all those it has called are active at the same time. To see the currently active nested procedures, use the Call Stack feature. *Stack* is a term used in programming to indicate a first-in-first-out list in which the top item in the list is the most recently added item and the first to be removed from the list.

The Call Stack dialog box helps to trace how an application runs through a series of procedures. To see the list of procedure calls, suspend code execution and perform one of the following actions:

- Click the Call Stack toolbar button on the Debug toolbar.
- Choose View|Call Stack.
- Click Build (...) in bar at the top of the Locals window.

The switchboard form created for the *Omni-Sport* project is a good example of procedures calling others. After the form opens, the Current event occurs, which invokes the Form_Current event procedure. This procedure calls the FillOptions procedure to add the options to the switchboard.

Figure 10.18 shows the Call Stack dialog box after the *Omni-Sport* Switchboard form class module is suspended by setting a breakpoint at the statement that removes the options label from all but the first option in the switchboard. It shows the names of the database, module, and procedures. The first procedure to execute is the Form_Switchboard.Form_Open event procedure, followed by some non-Basic code and the Form_Current event procedure. The procedure that's interrupted is the Switchboard.FillOptions subprocedure. The non-Basic code contains the instructions that set the filter during the Form_Open procedure.

FIGURE 10.18

Using Call Stack to see nested procedure calls.

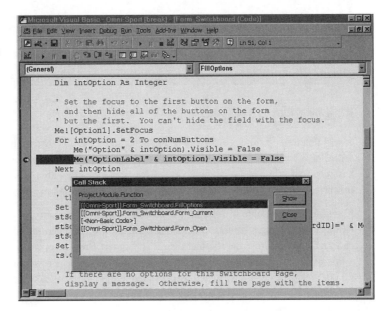

If you want to see the statement that called one of the procedures in the list, select the procedure below the current procedure in the list in the Call Stack dialog box and choose Show. The module window shows the calling procedure, Form_Current, with an indicator pointing to the calling statement, FillOptions, in the Form_Current event procedure (see Figure 10.19).

If you choose Show with the current procedure selected in the Call Stack dialog box, the statement that was current when the code was suspended is highlighted in the module window.

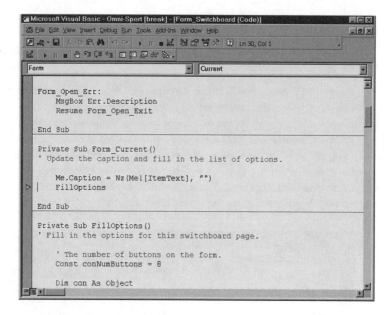

```
Form_Open_Err:
    MsgBox Err.Description
    Resume Form_Open_Exit

End Sub

Private Sub Form_Current()
' Update the caption and fill in the list of options.

    Me.Caption = Nz(Me![ItemText], "")
    FillOptions

End Sub

Private Sub FillOptions()
' Fill in the options for this switchboard page.

    ' The number of buttons on the form.
    Const conNumButtons = 8

    Dim con As Object
```

Getting Help

In addition to the help offered by the Help menu and the Office Assistant, the error message dialog boxes often include a button that opens a Help topic to explain the error that has occurred. While in the module window, you can get help with a specific method, function, property, object, or statement by clicking the keyword and pressing F1.

If you're having trouble with a specific VB object, method, property, or constant, the Object Browser might be able to help. Click the keyword and choose View|Definition or choose Definition from the shortcut menu. The Object Browser opens, showing the definition of the selected keyword. Figure 10.20 shows the Object Browser with the definition of the acForm constant, which was selected in the module window. Notice that the Auto Data Tips option also displays a ScreenTip with the current value of the object.

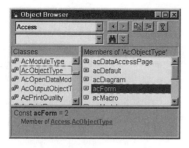

To open the Object Browser for general use, click the Object Browser toolbar button, choose View|Object Browser, or choose Object Browser from the module window shortcut menu.

Sometimes it's necessary to backtrack through the sequence of breakpoints and other stopping places in the database modules. The Last Position option on the module window shortcut menu moves to the last statement where the cursor stopped in any module and procedure in the current database. If the module was closed, it's reopened and the cursor appears at the line that stopped the code execution. Repeatedly choosing Last Position retraces your steps through the entire session in the module window.

Handling Runtime Errors

Runtime errors are errors that Access can detect only when running the application. They can happen during the debug phase of development or after the application has reached the hands of the end user. Runtime errors occur in macros as well, but you can't trap errors in macros because macro errors do not have key code numbers like Visual Basic runtime errors. This is another good reason to use VB procedures in an application.

Error handling is a process of anticipating errors and adding code that will execute when an error occurs. This may be no more than displaying the default VB message and branching to an Exit or End statement, or it might identify specific errors by code number and display custom messages. The Access wizards always include error handling in their event procedures.

During Debugging

DEVELOPMENT

Runtime errors that occur during debugging are not as much a concern as those that appear after the application has been completed. The error message is usually clear enough for a developer to understand. Such errors happen when you have misspelled a field name or referenced a nonexisting property. If you've misspelled a variable, the error is caught during compilation. Figure 10.21 shows an example of a runtime error occurring as a result of misspelling the TryMe command button name in the Form_Load event procedure for the RunTimeBug form.

FIGURE 10.21

A runtime error during debugging.

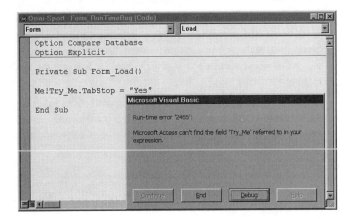

The error message box offers the choices of Continue, End, Debug, and Help:

- Continue is available if the error message is only a warning and the error does not preclude further execution.

- Choosing Debug returns to the module window with the faulty statement highlighted in yellow.

- Choosing End stops code execution and the module window remains active (if that's where you ran the procedure). If you choose End and close the form, the runtime error message reoccurs the next time you try to load the same form.

- Many runtime error messages also include a Help button that can take you to the relevant Help topic. The Help button is dimmed in Figure 10.21 because there is no Help topic related to the TryMe command button.

After you correct the error, you might have to reset the code before you run it again.

> **Note:** While you're in the debug phase, make sure you've checked the Use Access Special Keys option in the Startup dialog box. This enables you to press Ctrl+Break to stop execution and to look at the VB code after a runtime error has occurred. This option also enables the Ctrl+G key combination that displays the Immediate window. This option is in the Advanced expansion of the Startup dialog box.

You can set the error-trapping options for handling runtime errors in your VB code. These settings determine how to enter the break mode when an error occurs in the procedure. The error-trapping options are also available on the General tab of the Visual Basic Editor Options dialog box. You have three choices (see Figure 10.22):

- *Break on All Errors* does just what it says—it breaks on all handled and unhandled errors in all modules: class and standard. The module that contains the error appears in the debug window with the offending line highlighted.

- *Break in Class Module* is useful for debugging class modules. This option breaks on all unhandled errors in both class and standard modules. The project enters break mode at the line of code that caused the error. If the error is in a class module, the module becomes active in the debug window and the line with the error is highlighted.

- *Break on Unhandled Errors* breaks on unhandled errors in a standard module. If the unhandled error is in a class module, VB breaks on the line that called the class module containing the error rather than on the line in the class module that contains the error.

FIGURE 10.22

Set error-trapping options in the General tab of the VB Editor Options dialog box.

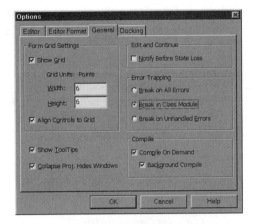

Sometimes it's necessary to simulate a runtime error to check out the error-handling code. The Raise method of the Err object can be used to simulate any VB or user-defined error. For example, the following line of code would generate the error caused by a type mismatch:

```
Err.Raise Number:=13     'Simulates "Type mismatch" run-time error.
```

The method also takes optional named arguments that specify the object or application that generated the error, an expression describing the error, a path to where help for the error can be found, and the Help topic related to the reason for the error rather than the error message.

> **Note:** The Visual Basic errors are numbered from 0 to 65535. Numbers in the range 0 to 512 are reserved for system errors. You can assign a number in the range 513 to 65535 to define a custom error and add 513 to generate the error number. For example, use vbObjectError + 513 as the number argument in the Raise method.

For the User

The messages that appear when runtime errors occur might be clear to the developer, but the user might be confused by some of the messages. Replacing them with more meaningful messages and appropriate courses of action often helps the application run more smoothly in its intended environment. You obviously cannot foresee all possible errors, but you can anticipate a few likely ones and provide for them. Unexpected errors can also route to general-purpose error-handling code.

Errors in VB, ADO, and DAO are objects in themselves and have properties just like any other object. The VB Err object holds information about one error at a time. Two of the properties of interest to error handlers are the error number and description. You can use these properties to determine what kind of error has occurred.

An error involving an ADO or DAO operation results in the creation of an Error object and an Errors collection. Error objects also have number and description properties. The number and description properties of the first Error object in the Errors collection should match the number and description of the VB Err object.

Error handling is a four-step process:

1. When an error occurs, route processing to the error handler.
2. Find out what kind of error occurred.
3. Branch to the appropriate error-handling operation.
4. Resume or exit the procedure.

Routing After an Error

DEVELOPMENT

The On Error statement enables error-handling code and specifies the location of the routine. You can also use On Error to disable error handling during debugging. You can place the On Error statement anywhere in the procedure, but you should insert it before any statement that could cause an error. The statement syntax is as follows:

```
On Error GoTo label
```

> **Note:** The error-handling code marked by a line label or number is not a separate function or subprocedure. It's a block of code within a procedure.

The label argument is required and can be a line label such as ErrHandler: or a line number. The line must be in the current procedure; otherwise, you'll get a compile error. When an error occurs, execution branches to the line that marks the beginning of the error handler. For example, the following statements branch to the ErrHandler: line:

```
Sub Procedure PossibleError()
'Enable error handler.
On Error GoTo ErrHandler
'Code that may cause a run-time error.
.
.
.
ErrHandler:
'Code to handle errors.
.
.
.
End Sub
```

The two other versions of the `On Error` statement disable error handling or ignore the error entirely:

- `On Error GoTo 0` disables error handling, which is helpful during development because code execution suspends at the statement that caused the error instead of branching to the error handler. That way, you can pinpoint the culprit. `On Error GoTo 0` also clears the number and description properties of the `Err` object the same as the `Clear` method.
- `On Error Resume Next` ignores the line that caused the error and executes the statement following the one that caused the error. This can be helpful if you want to check the properties of the error object and respond to the error right in the code.

At the end of the error-handling routine, the optional `Resume` statement sends execution back to the main part of the procedure. Use `Resume` if you want to specify where to continue execution. You have three choices with the `Resume` statement:

- `Resume` or `Resume 0`. Branches back to the statement that caused the error.
- `Resume Next`. Branches back to the statement following the line that caused the error. Use this form of the `Resume` statement when you want to resume execution without repeating the erroneous line.
- `Resume label`. Branches to a specific line in the procedure to continue execution.

`Resume` and `Resume 0` are handy when the user responds incorrectly to a request for information, such as entering a table or query name. The error handler can display instructions to reenter the value and then branch back to the statement that requested the entry in the first place.

`Resume Next` is used when the error handler can correct the error and continue with the procedure instead of repeating the statement that caused the error.

`Resume label` is used when you want to branch to another location in the procedure (often to an `Exit Sub` or `Exit Function` routine).

Identifying and Dealing with the Error

It's the job of the error-handling code to find out what error occurred and to execute the code specified for that error. Several language elements are used in error identification, including the `Err` VB object, the ADO and DAO `Error` object and Errors collection, the `AccessError` method, and the `Error` event. The elements you use depend on what kind of errors you expect to occur in the procedure. You might need to use different elements in different parts of an application.

After a VB error occurs, the `Err` object contains the error code number, which you can examine to find out which error occurred. Only a few of the hundreds of VB errors can be expected to occur as a result of user interaction or a system situation. Determine which are most likely to occur and include code to intercept them. The rest can be treated as a group in the error-handler code and can fall back on the default error messages.

The following code demonstrates how to use the Err object to respond to a Disk Not Ready error (VB error number 71). First, declare a constant and set it to the anticipated error number; then test for that number in the error-handling code. If that's the error that occurred, a custom message is displayed in a message box. Then, execution is returned with the Resume statement to the line that caused the error, where the user again has the opportunity to save the file to disk. If a different error occurred, the Else statement displays a message with the error number and description. Then, Resume Next branches to the statement that follows the one that caused the error. Here's the code:

```
Sub Procedure PossibleError()
'Declare constant as an anticipated error.
Const conDiskUnready As Integer = 71
'Enable error handler.
On Error GoTo ErrHandler
'Code that may cause a run-time error.
    .
    .
    .
Exit_PossibleError:
    Exit Sub
    .
    .
ErrHandler:
'Check Err object property.
    If Err = conDiskUnready Then
        MsgBox "Be sure a disk is in the drive and the door closed."
        Resume
    Else
'Display error number and description.
        MsgBox "Error number " & Err.Number & ": " & Err.Description
        Resume Next
    End If
End Sub
```

You can also use a Select Case structure to branch to different error-handling code by first declaring a series of constants as specific error numbers. Then, use the constant names as case expressions.

ADO and DAO errors that happen while dealing with data access objects, such as table and query definitions, often occur in a group forming a collection. When such an error occurs, the VB Err object contains the number and description of the first error. The same error recognition and trapping routine that relies on the Err properties can be used here.

You can also use the Error event to trap errors that occur in form or report class modules by attaching an event procedure to the object's On Error property. The Error event procedure requires the DataErr argument, which is the integer number of the error that occurred. The VB `Err` object does not contain the error number after the `Error` event occurs. Therefore, you need to use the value of the `DataErr` argument with the `AccessError` method to find out the error number and description.

The `Error` statement and `Error` function are maintained for backward compatibility with earlier versions of Access. When writing new code, use the `Err` and `Error` objects, the `AccessError` function, and the `Error` event instead.

Exiting the Procedure

Any procedure that contains an error-handling routine should also have an `Exit` routine that exits the procedure before reaching the error handler if no error occurs. Placing the `Exit` routine before the error-handling routine does not upset the procedure flow and guarantees that the error-handling routine will not be executed unless an error occurs. If an error occurs, the error handler can branch to the `Exit` routine upon completion to end execution.

The structure of a typical procedure that includes error handling looks like this:

```
Sub Procedure PossibleError()
'Enable error handler.
On Error GoTo ErrHandler
.       'Code that may cause a run-time error.
.
.
Exit_PossibleError:
    Exit Sub
ErrHandler:
'Code to handle errors.
.
.
Resume Exit_PossibleError
End Sub
```

Runtime Errors in Nested Procedures

In an application that includes nested procedures, an error can occur in any one of them. If the procedure containing the error has no error-handling routine, VB looks back up the call list for the nearest error handler. When it finds one, the error is passed to that error handler for processing. If no handler exists in any of the procedures, execution stops and the default error message is displayed.

When the procedure can't handle the error that occurred, you can use the `Raise` method to regenerate the error and look back through the calls list for a procedure that can. First, save the error number as an integer variable, such as `intErr`, and clear the `Err` number property with `Err.Clear`. Then, regenerate the runtime error with the following statement:

```
Err.Raise Number:=intErr.
```

Conditional Compilation

Conditional compilation is a method of including or excluding blocks of code in the final product. For example, suppose an application contains debugging procedures that you don't want to remove and yet don't want to include in the delivered application. A conditional compilation could skip the debugging code and compile the rest. Perhaps you're preparing an application for delivery to another country that uses different date and currency formats or even a different language. You could write two separate procedures for each operation that displays these values and compile one or the other, selectively.

First, declare the conditional compiler constant, #Const, in the module that contains the blocks of code; then embed the code segments in the conditional compilation directive. The directive looks much like the normal If...Then...Else structure, except that each statement is preceded by a pound sign (#). A subprocedure that contains debugging routines can be conditionally compiled with the following directive:

```
Sub condComp()
#Const conDebug = True
#If conDebug Then
.               'code with debug statements
.
.
.
#Else
.               'normal code
.
.
.
#End If
```

The first expression must evaluate to True or False. Additional If statements can be nested within the first when there are more than two conditions to consider. The compiler compiles the blocks of code based on the value of the declared #Const constant. The code excluded by the conditional compilation is omitted from the executable file.

> **Note:** Unlike the usual If...Then...Else structure, which you can combine on one line of code separated by colons, conditional compilation directives must all appear on separate lines.

Visual Basic defines certain compiler constants for use with the #If...Then...#Else structure on either 16-bit or 32-bit platforms. Each constant evaluates to True or False, depending on the development environment. For example, the constant Vba6 is True if the environment is VBA, version 6.0; otherwise, it's False. Win32 evaluates to True if the environment is 32-bit Windows and False if not. Mac is True if the environment is Macintosh and False if not.

Summary

This chapter has been devoted to finding and trapping errors during code generation, compilation, debugging, and execution. It examined the three debug windows and the ways each one can help you create error-free VB code. The features include monitoring and changing the values of variables and expressions in the Immediate, Locals, and Watch windows. In addition, you can control execution during debugging by stepping through code and setting breakpoints to suspend execution at critical points so that you can examining intermediate results.

A later section in this chapter addressed the problem of trapping runtime errors in an application so that error messages can be more informative to the user. Finally, the chapter discussed the process of conditionally compiling code to exclude segments from the final product.

| **LOOKING AHEAD** | The next chapter, "Creating an Application from an Existing Database," introduces you to a retail pet store application created in Access that includes all the data and processes required for day-to-day operation of the store, inventory management, and even some long-range strategic planning for expansion and improvement of customer services. |

PART IV

Developing a Multiple-Table Application

Creating an Application from an Existing Database

This chapter examines the current information-management system in place at Pat's Pets, a suburban retail pet supply store, as well as preparing it for upgrading to a more sophisticated and automatic system. The current system is predominantly manual, with only a single table maintained in an outdated local computer. The importance of involving the user in design decisions is emphasized in this chapter.

The first part of this chapter focuses on the development aspects of database applications. Even if development is not your responsibility, it's essential that you have a clear picture of how development and programming work together to optimize the usefulness of the application. This is especially true when you're converting from a manual database management system to an advanced technology such as Access.

Analyzing the Existing System

ANALYSIS

The first thing to consider when you're designing a new database system is all the ways the user wants to use the information and to describe all the products of the system. Determine what kinds of reports can be used and how the information should be filtered, grouped, and summarized. The user interface, usually a data-entry and viewing form, must be carefully thought out with the end user in mind. A beginning user needs more help in the form of ScreenTips, Help messages, and error trapping. A more advanced user might not need a very sophisticated environment but still requires a smooth-running data management system.

DEVELOPMENT

Rarely does a developer get the opportunity to start from scratch to design an information-management system. The organization usually has a semiautomated system in place and wants to upgrade. Human nature puts limits on the amount of change a user will tolerate. Users are reluctant to accept drastic changes in their method of operating. It's essential to take the existing procedures into consideration when you're designing a new system so that it can evolve smoothly. Unless the current operation is completely at odds with a more automated system, it's best to try to absorb at least the general procedures into the new system.

This chapter, together with the next three chapters, focuses on Pat's Pets, a suburban retail store in Southern California that deals in supplies as well as food and services for dogs, cats, fish, birds, and small animals. The customer base is growing rapidly, and the product lines are also expanding to the point where the current data-handling system is inadequate.

The manager/owner of Pat's Pets feels that her business would improve if the store's information-management system were more automated. Fewer mistakes in product ordering and pricing would be made, better customer relations could be maintained, and less time would be spent digging through files in search of a specific piece of information. In addition, if historical sales data were organized and stored, she could examine trends in seasonal sales and product popularity. Expansion possibilities into the surrounding growing community could also be tested against the historical data.

Current Operations

In the current system at Pat's Pets, the only table that's maintained is the inventory list of products. This is updated weekly from the sales receipts, at which time the manager reads the printed list to find products whose stock levels have reached a point where they should be reordered. All sales figures are accumulated at the cash register.

The Products table includes the following information (see Figure 11.1):

FIGURE 11.1
The Pat's Pets Products list.

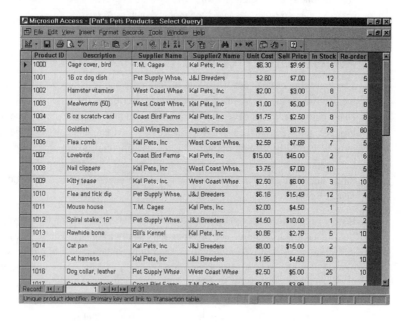

Product ID	Description	Supplier Name	Supplier2 Name	Unit Cost	Sell Price	In Stock	Re-order
1000	Cage cover, bird	T.M. Cages	Kal Pets, Inc	$6.30	$9.95	6	4
1001	16 oz dog dish	Pet Supply Whse.	J&J Breeders	$2.60	$7.00	12	5
1002	Hamster vitamins	West Coast Whse.	Kal Pets, Inc	$2.00	$3.00	8	5
1003	Mealworms (50)	West Coast Whse.	Kal Pets, Inc	$1.00	$5.00	10	8
1004	6 oz scratch-card	Coast Bird Farms	Kal Pets, Inc	$1.75	$2.50	8	8
1005	Goldfish	Gull Wing Ranch	Aquatic Foods	$0.30	$0.75	79	60
1006	Flea comb	Kal Pets, Inc	West Coast Whse.	$2.59	$7.69	7	5
1007	Lovebirds	Coast Bird Farms	Kal Pets, Inc	$15.00	$45.00	2	6
1008	Nail clippers	Kal Pets, Inc	West Coast Whse.	$3.75	$7.00	10	5
1009	Kitty tease	Kal Pets, Inc	West Coast Whse.	$2.50	$6.00	3	10
1010	Flea and tick dip	Pet Supply Whse.	J&J Breeders	$6.16	$15.49	12	4
1011	Mouse house	T.M. Cages	Kal Pets, Inc	$2.00	$4.50	1	2
1012	Spiral stake, 16"	Pet Supply Whse.	J&J Breeders	$4.50	$10.00	1	2
1013	Rawhide bone	Bill's Kennel	Kal Pets, Inc	$0.86	$2.79	5	10
1014	Cat pan	Kal Pets, Inc	J&J Breeders	$8.00	$15.00	2	4
1015	Cat harness	Kal Pets, Inc	J&J Breeders	$1.95	$4.50	20	10
1016	Dog collar, leather	Pet Supply Whse.	West Coast Whse.	$2.50	$5.00	25	10
1017	Canary bead/hook	Coast Bird Farms	T.M. Cages	$2.00	$3.98	2	4

Record: 1 of 31

Unique product identifier. Primary key and link to Transaction table.

Note: Although Figure 11.1 shows the product information as an Access table, the store data is not actually managed yet by a modern database management system like Access. It appears in Access in the figure merely to show you the data that we will be working with.

- *Product ID*. The store's unique number for this product.
- *Description*. A text field that describes the product.
- *Main Supplier Name*. A text field that shows the name of the principal supplier of the product.
- *Supplier2 Name*. A text field that shows the name of the backup supplier of the product.
- *Unit Cost*. A currency field showing the cost of the item, not including shipping and handling. This is updated only when the supplier changes prices.
- *Sell Price*. A currency field containing the current selling price of the product. This is updated when the cost is changed or when a promotional sale is planned.
- *In Stock*. A number field that shows the actual count of items in stock. It must be updated regularly.
- *Re-order*. A number field that shows the level at which the product should be reordered. This amount can change depending on demand.

On a daily or weekly basis, store clerks update the Products inventory list by subtracting items that were sold or damaged in the store during the period. At the same time, shipping invoices showing items received are used to add quantities to the In Stock field. Any new products are added to the list, and products that have been dropped are removed. The inventory list provides a relatively current status of the store but keeps no records of past performance of individual products or product categories.

Quarterly, or more often if necessary, the inventory list is compared with the actual quantity of each item in the store, either on display or in the storage area.

Periodically, the store manager reviews the products list, notes products that have fallen below the desired restocking level, and makes a note to place an order for the products. If several orders are to be placed with the same supplier, she might look for other products whose in-stock level is close to the reorder level. Ordering these at the same time might save shipping costs. Orders are prepared manually either on the supplier's or the Pat's Pets order form. The addresses and telephone numbers of the suppliers are kept in a card file.

All data is now maintained in the single Products table while displayed in datasheet view. Currently, there are no data-validation criteria to help prevent errors from entering the database, other than not allowing duplicate Product ID values.

Investigating Improvements

To provide complete sales and inventory management, additional tables must be defined and related to one another. For example, a transactions table that keeps track of all the transactions as they occur should be added. This table will become the focal point of the new system and will be related to the products table by the unique product identifier. If the new system includes automated point-of-sale registers linked to the inventory control system, the transaction data would not need to be manually entered. In the Pat's Pets example, this is not the case.

In addition to the transactions table, a supplier table could contain the name, address, telephone numbers, and a personal contact name for each of the suppliers. The supplier table would relate to the product table with a unique supplier ID. A separate table containing the definition of the product category would eliminate the need to repeat the full category term in every product and transaction record.

A new table containing customer information would be nearly standalone, except for the category of products the customers are interested in. Additional tables could be included to manage employee information, but such data will not be included in this case study.

The heart of any application is the user interface, which must be easy to use and as nearly foolproof as possible. Many of the users are employees who have little or no experience with computer systems. The system must be so simple to use that the training period will be brief. The data entry form that's central to this inventory control application is the transactions log, which is updated every day. The form must be armed with data-validation features in the background and clearly marked interactive tools, informative messages, and custom Help in the foreground.

Figure 11.2 shows a typical data entry form. The five fields within the rectangle at the top of the form are entered by the user. Much of the other information on the form is acquired from related tables. The form can be used for sales, purchases, and shrinkage. Shrinkage is the reduction of stock level for reasons other than sales—for example, breakage or theft.

Lookup forms are also essential to a good application. What good is it to store data if you can't get it back as useful information? Some helpful lookup forms could display all the products from a particular supplier, all customers who have dogs or raise tropical fish, or all the stocked items in a specific product category. Figure 11.3 shows a lookup form that lists all the products currently acquired from one supplier. This form is actually a form with a subform.

The physical inventory process would go much faster if the product list included the item's display location in the store and in storage. The list could then be sorted by location, printed, and carried around the store to verify the current inventory level.

Instead of scrolling through the products table and comparing the quantity in stock with the reorder level, a query could extract the records for items that need to be reordered. If this is vital to the store's operation, a prompt can be displayed at startup showing how many items need to be reordered and offering to go directly to the order form. In the order form, after the user enters the product identifier, the supplier information can be filled in automatically and a list of the other products from the same supplier can be displayed for adding to the order list, as desired.

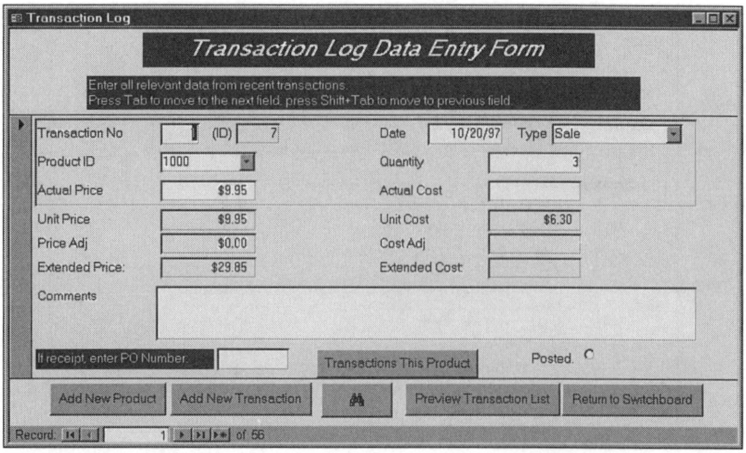

FIGURE 11.2
The Transactions Log Data Entry form.

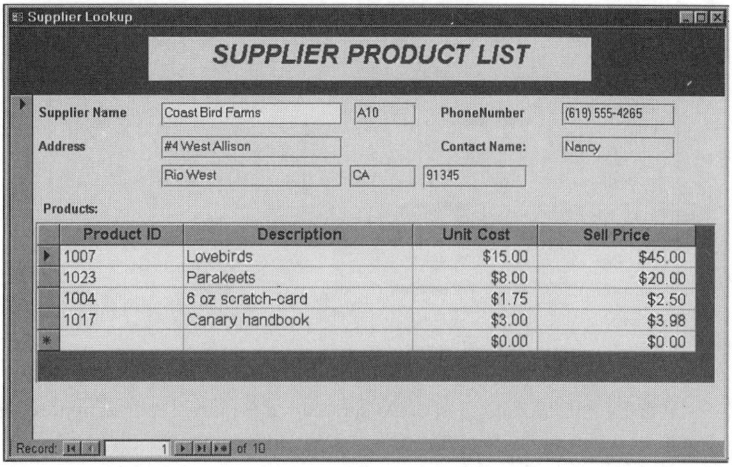

FIGURE 11.3
A lookup form showing products from one supplier.

The variety of reports that can be printed from an application is limited only by the user's imagination. Many useful reports can be designed with information from one or more tables. For example, a report could be designed to be a catalog with each major category of products beginning on a new page. The products may be further arranged in columns by subcategory, such as pet, pet food, and pet supplies. A catalog listing without the cost data can be kept at the sales counter where customers can look up items of interest.

Another useful report would be a supplier list that relates products to their suppliers (see Figure 11.4). This information would also be online in a form, but the printed report is also helpful. A report listing the products that need to be ordered, complete with the supplier name and telephone number, could also be printed for reference when orders are placed.

FIGURE 11.4

A report listing suppliers and their products.

SUPPLIER PRODUCT LIST

Supplier Name	Coast Bird Farms	A10	*PhoneNumber*	(619) 555-4265
Address	#4 West Allison			
	Rio West	CA	91345	

Products:

	Description	*Unit Cost*
1004	6 oz scratch-card	$1.75
1007	Lovebirds	$15.00
1017	Canary handbook	$3.00
1023	Parakeets	$8.00

Supplier Name	Gull Wing Ranch	A12	*PhoneNumber*	(619) 555-8356
Address	615 De Hesa Rd			
	Corona Mar	CA	91228	

Products:

	Description	*Unit Cost*
1005	Goldfish	$0.30
1026	Feeder guppies	$0.20

Supplier Name	T.M. Cages	B15	*PhoneNumber*	(619) 555-1178
Address	1400 Lemon Ave			
	Del Mesa	CA	91228	

Products:

	Description	*Unit Cost*
1000	Cage cover, bird	$6.30
1011	Mouse house	$2.00
1022	Wild bird feeder	$3.00
1024	Rabbit cage	$10.00

A helpful historical report could summarize the purchasing activities over a period of time, organized by supplier. The report could summarize the purchases from each supplier, keep a subtotal, and provide a grand total at the end of the report. Figure 11.5 shows the first page of a Transactions by Supplier report.

Similar summarizing reports can be designed to monitor sales activity. A report that includes charts and graphs can be very helpful in analyzing the store's performance. Figure 11.6 shows a chart that can be created from Access data using the Microsoft Chart applet from within Access.

FIGURE 11.5

A report summarizing purchases from each supplier.

Transactions by Supplier

Supplier Name	Date	Description	Quantity	Unit Cost	Extended Cost
Aquatic Foods					
	10/27/97	Live ghost shrimp	10	$7.00	$70.00
	10/27/97	Brine shrimp	10	$2.00	$20.00
				Total This Supplier:	**$20.00**
				SubTotal So Far:	**$90.00**
Bill's Kennel					
	10/20/97	Small dog biscuit (50#)	1	$10.20	$10.20
	10/20/97	Rawhide bone	3	$0.86	$2.58
	10/21/97	Rawhide bone	4	$0.86	$3.44
	10/21/97	Small dog biscuit (50#)	1	$1.30	$1.30
	10/23/97	Rawhide bone	3	$0.86	$2.58
	10/26/97	Rawhide bone	2	$0.86	$1.72
	10/27/97	Rawhide bone	3	$0.86	$2.58
				Total This Supplier:	**$22.58**
				SubTotal So Far:	**$114.40**
Coast Bird Farms					
	10/20/97	Lovebirds	2	$15.00	$30.00
	10/21/97	Parakeets	1	$8.00	$8.00
	10/22/97	Lovebirds	2	$15.00	$30.00
	10/24/97	Lovebirds	2	$15.00	$30.00
				Total This Supplier:	**$52.58**
				SubTotal So Far:	**$212.40**
Gull Wing Ranch					
	10/23/97	Goldfish	20	$0.30	$6.00
				Total This Supplier:	**$58.58**
				SubTotal So Far:	**$218.40**
Kal Pets, Inc					
	10/20/97	Flea comb	3	$15.00	$45.00
	10/20/97	Nail clippers	3	$3.75	$11.25
	10/22/97	Cat harness	2	$1.95	$3.90

Sunday, March 23, 1997   Page 1 of 3

FIGURE 11.6

Sales performance for Pat's Pets, summarized in a bar chart.

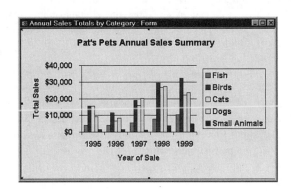

Here are some other reports that would be useful to Pat's Pets:

- A current price list in alphabetical order or grouped by category or by main supplier
- A list of products grouped by major category (for example, birds, cats, and dogs)
- A list of customers grouped by pets of interest
- A summary of transactions, including calculated profits
- Form letters reminding customers of dog grooming services due
- Form letters and mailing labels for sales promotions

Enhancements to be considered for later implementations include tracking cost fluctuations over time that might prompt price changes. Adding a second vendor for some of the products would allow you to compare their performance and cost strategies. Seasonal product performance is also a valid analysis to add to the design. As the application design matures, additional ideas for improvement can come forward. It's important to freeze the design at some point and proceed with development, saving the new ideas for the next phase.

The Application Development Process

DEVELOPMENT

The application development process consists of seven distinct phases that begin after you determine the informational and operational needs of the user. It's important to realize that although these steps appear to be sequential, the design process is actually iterative. You often return to a previous step and make changes as the goals of the application become more distinct. Users invariably expand their expectations when they begin to realize the power and flexibility that's available to them with an Access application.

The first step is an analysis of the data requirements and how the elements relate to one another. In this step, data is grouped into separate tables by subject and frequency of use, and the links among the tables are defined.

The second step involves actually creating the table definitions and defining indexes, key fields, required fields, and data validation rules. If any of the fields can be linked to a lookup table, these are also defined. After completing the table definitions, you add enough data to be able to test the application thoroughly. These two steps are covered in this chapter.

The principal user interface in a database management system is a form used for entering and viewing the data that's the basis for the application. At Pat's Pets, the basic data is the product inventory and sales activity. Of secondary interest is supplier and customer information. The third step in application development is the design of the main data entry form. The fields in the form must be carefully arranged in a logical order and with meaningful labels to help prevent entry errors.

In the fourth step, macros, event procedures, and functions are added to the form design so that it will perform appropriately to user actions.

LOOKING AHEAD

Chapter 12, "Customizing Data Entry," demonstrates steps 3 and 4 with the development of the Pat's Pets application.

Additional forms and reports are added to the application in the fifth stage of development. These can include lookup forms to retrieve selected information, filtered and sorted in useful ways. You can design reports to filter, sort, group, and summarize information in any number of ways.

LOOKING AHEAD

Chapter 13, "Customizing the Reports," teaches you how to create additional forms and a variety of reports for Pat's Pets, including sales summaries with charts and graphs.

The sixth step adds features that connect all the pieces together into a smoothly functioning operation, such as command buttons, customized menus and toolbars, and pop-up forms for user input.

The seventh and final step creates a starting place, such as a main switchboard, that gives the user the opportunity to decide what to do next. Subordinate switchboards are also added as necessary (for example, to choose one from a list of reports to open for preview).

LOOKING AHEAD

In Chapter 14, "Adding Real-Time Features," you finish the Pat's Pets application by adding switchboards, error trapping, and some management-decision features.

Designing the Pat's Pets Database

In most cases, the bulk of the necessary data is available in the current system, and the main task is to rearrange it into related tables to reduce the redundancy of data and improve processing efficiency. If the current system is inadequate—really inadequate, not just unable to keep up with the volume—you must give some extra thought to procedures for collecting the necessary data. For example, if you want to build a mailing list for sending out promotional material, you can offer free dog or cat treats to customers as an incentive to sign up.

The Pat's Pets current system does not accumulate transaction data. It concentrates on the more static physical inventory that's affected by the flow of products in and out of the store. What's really needed here is a way to measure this flow to be able to track progress and extract information that can be used in making business decisions.

Defining and Relating Tables

"The data that is used together stays together" should be the motto of the database developer. Items of data used for the same purpose should be stored in the same table unless there will be a lot of repetition. If that's the case, you should separate the repeated data into another, related table and add a field that links the two tables. The frequency of use is also a factor in data distribution. Store seldom-used data out of the way in a separate table.

In the new Pat's Pets database design, the transaction data is in one table, the product data in another, and the supplier data in a third. Customer data is stored in a fourth table.

Access requires a key field in every table to ensure that each record is unique. In the Pat's Pets database, you can assign a unique product code to each product in the store and a unique identifier to each supplier and each customer.

The transactions table poses a slightly different problem. Neither the product code nor the date can guarantee a unique record. You might sell more than one of a given item in one day, and you certainly hope to make more than one sale per day. You might also receive a shipment of a product the same day you sell some of the same items. Even combining the values in both the date and product code fields fails to create a unique value. Unless you want to maintain your own transaction record numbers, you can use Access to create a special field that will always contain a unique value. The transaction record number field has no other use than to create a unique record.

Because the tables in a relational database are related by common fields, you must define these fields. They must contain the same kind of data (number, text, date, and so on), and they must be the same length. They need not have the same name because part of the database design is specifying which fields you want to use to join the two tables.

For Pat's Pets, the product and supplier tables are related by the supplier's name. This can cause problems with long names that are easily misspelled. Computers are perfectionists and often disregard what you mean in favor of what you actually enter. Using a short code for each supplier is not only easier to remember, but it also saves space. The Supplier table can correlate the code with the supplier's full name and other information.

If the Transactions table is to be used to update the current inventory in the Products table, these two tables must be related as well. Once again, you could use the full name of the product, but a code would be more efficient both in time and space. The product code serves a dual purpose by also having a unique value that can make sure there are no duplicate records in the database. The Category table, which is used for looking up category codes, stores the category names and code numbers. Figure 11.7 shows how the four tables are related by common fields.

The Relationships window in Figure 11.8 shows the types of relationships that exist between the four tables. The Category table is related to the Products table by the Cat Code field with a one-to-one relationship. A one-to-one relationship is typical of lookup tables.

FIGURE **11.7**
The Pat's Pets database includes four related tables.

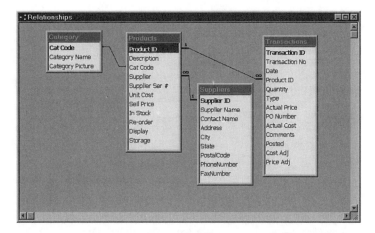

The Products table is related to the Transactions table by Product ID in a one-to-many relationship, indicating that a single product could be involved in many transactions. The Suppliers table is related to the Products table by the Supplier ID field with a one-to-many relationship, indicating that a supplier can offer more than one product for sale.

Peter's Principle: Creating a Many-to-Many Relationship

In a many-to-many relationship, a record in one table (call it Table A) can have several matching records in another table (Table B), and vice versa. Neither table is considered the parent because the linking field is not the primary key in either table. The only way you can create such a relationship is by creating a third table, called a *junction table*. This new table has a primary key that's actually a combination of at least the primary keys from Tables A and B. The junction table then acts as the bridge between Tables A and B when you build two one-to-many relationships among them. You can add other fields to the junction table like any other table.

Figure 11.8 shows a junction table linking two tables in the Order Entry database template. Because several products could be included in a single order and several orders could include the same product, this represents a many-to-many relationship. To solve the relationship problem, the junction table, Order Details, was created with a primary key that combines the foreign keys from the Products table (ProductID) and the Orders table (OrderID). Two one-to-many relationships then link the Products and Orders tables to the Order Details table.

Tables 11.1, 11.2, and 11.3 describe the structure of each of the three principal tables in the Pat's Pets database.

FIGURE 11.8
Creating a junction table for a many-to-many relationship.

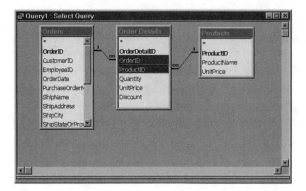

Table 11.1 Transactions Table Structure

Field Name	Data Type	Description
Transaction ID	AutoNumber	The primary key field (provided by Access).
Transaction No	Number	The user-entered transaction number.
Date	Date/Time	The date of the transaction.
Product ID	Text	The linking field to the Products table.
Quantity	Number	The number of items sold or purchased.
Type	Text	This field has three valid values: Sale, Purchase, and Shrinkage.
Actual Price	Currency	The selling price.
PO Number	Number	The Purchase Order number.
Actual Cost	Currency	The purchase cost.
Comments	Memo	Additional information about the transaction.
Posted	Yes/No	A check box that's automatically checked when the Products table is updated with the transaction.
Cost Adjustment	Currency	A calculated field containing the difference between the Unit Cost in the Products table and the Actual Cost.
Price Adjustment	Currency	A calculated field containing the difference between the Unit Price in the Products table and the Actual Price.

Field properties, validation rules, default values, and secondary indexes for the Transactions table are discussed in the next section of this chapter.

Table 11.2 Products Table Structure

Field Name	Data Type	Description
Product ID	Text	The unique product identifier. This is the primary key, linked to the Transactions table.
Description	Text	The item description.
Cat Code	Text	The product category; one of a list of valid values.
Supplier	Text	A short field containing a supplier code. Used to relate to the Suppliers table.
Supplier Ser #	Text	The Supplier item number for the product.
Unit Cost	Currency	The cost of the item, not including shipping and handling.
Sell Price	Currency	The normal retail price.
In Stock	Number	The quantity in stock. May be negative if back ordered.
Re-order	Number	The lower limit of the stock level, below which the item should be reordered.
Display	Text	The code for the display location in store.
Storage	Text	The code for the storage location.

Additional information about the Products table appears in the next section of this chapter.

Table 11.3 Suppliers Table Structure

Field Name	Data Type	Description
Supplier ID	Text	The unique supplier identifier. This is the primary key field, linked to the Products table.
Supplier Name	Text	The supplier's company name.
Contact Name	Text	The person to contact at the supplier.
Address	Text	The supplier's street address.
City	Text	The supplier's city.
State	Text	The supplier's state.
PostalCode	Text	The supplier's postal code.
PhoneNumber	Text	The supplier's voice phone number.
FaxNumber	Text	The supplier's fax phone number.

You may want to add a Comments field to the Suppliers table to keep track of delivery schedules and estimates of lead time. If you can know the lead time, you will know when you need to place orders to receive them before you run out of the product.

The Category table shown in Figure 11.7 is a lookup table that contains details of each category, such as the name and a picture. The Category table is linked to the Products table with a one-to-one relationship by the Cat Code.

One additional table is part of the Pat's Pets application: the Customer table, which contains customer names, addresses, and a memo field with comments about the types of purchases made and services used at the store. The Customer table is unrelated to the other tables in the application. The purpose of the Customer table is to maintain a mailing list of clients and their interest in pets.

Defining Field Properties

Each table already has a unique key field that ensures no two records will be identical. Other field properties can be anticipated at this stage of application development. For example, considering how the data can be filtered and sorted will lead to adding indexes. Filtering and sorting records works much faster if the records are indexed on the fields of interest.

It's also not too early to define data validation rules for fields and records. Field validation rules ensure that the field contains proper values, whereas record validation tests for conflicts between field values in the same record.

Indexes and Sort Orders

One of the most important features of Access is that once the data is placed into a database, you can retrieve the data in many different ways and turn it into information. You can sort and filter, group and summarize the data to present information in ways that are highly useful to the users. For example, in Pat's Pets, the manager could learn about current sales trends and stock products accordingly.

To summarize the coverage Pat's Pets provides in all types of pet supplies, sort the products by category code. To isolate the products for a specific type of pet, filter the records by category code. To analyze sales, sort the transactions first by type—sales as opposed to purchases or shrinkage—and then by product or product category. To make mailing quicker, sort both the suppliers and customers by postal code. To target dog owners for a special mailing, filter the customer records by the major category code for dog-related items.

Many other possibilities can be imagined, and indexes can be added at any time, even after the tables are populated. For the Pat's Pets application, the following indexes seem appropriate at this time:

- Products table by Cat Code and an index combining values from the Supplier field with the Category field.
- Suppliers and Customer tables by Postal Code.
- Transactions table by Product ID and Supplier ID.

All the added indexes allow duplicate values in the indexed fields. Figure 11.9 shows the indexes that have been defined for the Products table, and Figure 11.10 shows the indexes for the Transactions table.

FIGURE 11.9
The Products table indexes.

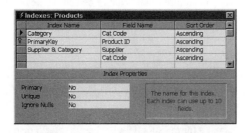

FIGURE 11.10
The Transactions table indexes.

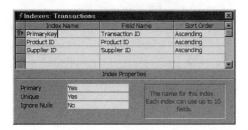

The indexes appear in alphabetical order in the Indexes dialog box, and the primary key field shows the key icon. The primary key index also has the Primary and Unique properties set to Yes. None of the indexes will ignore null values unless you specify this.

Default Values and Data Validation Rules

One of the most crucial aspects of maintaining a database is to prevent errors from creeping in. It's easier to prevent errors than to find them and correct them after they're hidden in the forest of data. Access provides several ways to make sure the data you enter is valid and error-free.

One way is to specify the field as required. Access will not let you save a record without an entry in a required field. Other validation rules, for example, insist that a value fall within a given range of values or that a value may never be negative.

The following rules are appropriate for the Pat's Pets application:

- The Product ID field in the Transactions table must match a value in the Products table.
- The Re-order field quantity in the Products table must be between 1 and 100, with a default value of 0.
- The Date field in the Transactions table has a default value of the current date.

- The Supplier field in the Transactions table has a blank default value because the supplier's name should appear only when the transaction is a purchase.
- The Sell Price field value in the Products table must be greater than the Unit Cost field value (a record validation rule) and cannot be zero (a field validation rule).

More requirements will no doubt turn up as the application develops.

Data Formats

Display formats can make the user's job much easier. You can impart additional information by customizing the appearance of field values. The following field format properties are suggested for the Pat's Pets database:

- Using the format @;"Unk" for the suppliers FaxNumber field displays the number, if any; otherwise, it displays Unk, for *unknown*.
- Using > as the format for the Suppliers ID field in both the Suppliers and Products tables converts all letters to uppercase to conform to the customary ID code.
- Using the format 0;!0![Red];"Out";"N/A" for the In Stock field in the Products table will display at least one digit if the value is greater than zero. If the value is negative, the product is back-ordered and the value is displayed in red and enclosed in exclamation marks. If it's zero, the word *Out* is displayed, and if blank, *N/A* is displayed.
- The Posted Yes/No field is displayed as a check box rather than a text field containing the word Yes or No.

Adding Lookup Tables

Access provides three ways to link a field to a list of valid values: by entering the values in the field definition, by listing the values as the row source in the property sheet of the Text Box control, or by naming a separate table or query as the row source for the field values.

The advantage of using a separate table or query for the list of values is that the user can add values to the list by responding to the NotInList() function. Because you want the user to be able to add new product categories as the store expands, use the Category table as the lookup row source for the Cat Code field.

You might not want the user to be able to add to the list of valid transaction types, however, in which case you should enter the values in the field property pane of the table definition or in the property sheet in the form design.

Populating the Database

COMPATIBILITY

If the existing Products table was stored in an earlier version of Access or another database system such as dBASE or Paradox, it could easily be converted to Access 2000 without having to reenter all the data. The other tables must be filled in manually. At this stage of application development, add only enough data to be able to test the system thoroughly. For example, include enough data to produce a report with two pages. This way you check out headers and other elements on a page other than the first page. Also, be sure to have enough items to test filters and sort routines as well as summaries and calculated fields. Filling up the database at this time is unnecessary and wastes development time.

If a table has only a few fields, the easiest way to enter data is in datasheet view. A table with too many fields to fit onscreen can be viewed in form view by creating an AutoForm object, which will show all the fields for one record at once onscreen. You don't need to save the form—just create it again the next time you need to enter more data.

User Interaction

At this point, development slips quietly into programming. After you've defined all the pieces of the application (development), it's time to decide how they will work together in response to user actions (programming). It's important to step through all possible scenarios and try to anticipate the user's actions. The user has one entry point into the application, which is usually a main switchboard showing a list of major activities from which to choose. Each of these items leads to further defined subactivities, until the user reaches a specific operation or goal.

The most common activities in a database application are data entry and editing and data retrieval. Data entry and editing is usually done in forms, which can be helpful if they're properly designed to take into account the user's actions. Command buttons can give the user options for further action, and validity checks can help prevent entry errors.

ScreenTips, Help options, and status bar messages can provide guidance to new users, as necessary. In addition, pop-up forms can be displayed on demand that will show additional information about items in the current form. For example, the user could place the cursor in the Supplier field and press a key combination that would run a macro that displays a pop-up dialog box with the supplier's name and other information.

Data retrieval usually involves a report based on one or more tables or queries and requires little or no user interaction, once selected. Some reports can ask for user input to set a specific filter or other parameter. If the application includes sensitive information, security measures can be added that limit access to certain data.

You can create customized command bars to use in place of the default menu bar, toolbar, and shortcut menus. The items would be specifically related to the application, with selected general-purpose options such as Print and Save.

The remaining sections step you through scenarios in which the user enters new data, edits existing data, and previews a report. The processes of posting and archiving transactions are also described.

The Transactions Data Entry/Edit Scenario

Most of the data activity occurs with the Transactions table. The transactions are intend-ed to be entered daily. Changes to the Products table other than in-stock quantities are not as frequent, although new products are added and prices are changed now and then. New suppliers are also added to the suppliers list, and changes in telephone numbers and contact personnel also occur.

In this scenario, the user has some recent transactions to enter into the Transactions table. When the Pat's Pets application starts up, a main switchboard appears. One of the options is Enter/Edit Transactions. Other options on the main switchboard can include the following:

- *Enter/Edit Other Data*. Opens up a second switchboard with options for the other tables in the database

- *Preview Reports*. Opens up another switchboard with a list of the available reports, including customer mailing labels and supplier order forms

- *Post and Archive Transactions*. Enables the user to update the Products table with recent transactions and remove completed transactions from the table

- *Exit the Database*. Closes the database and returns to the Access window

If the user selects Enter/Edit Transaction Data, the Transaction Log form opens, showing the first record in the table (refer to Figure 11.2 for a sample form). In the form, the fol-lowing actions are taken:

1. To add new records, click Add New Transaction or click the New Record button in the navigation bar. To edit an existing record, use the navigation buttons to locate the record. The records are ordered by the Transaction ID value that Access assigns, which is not displayed in the form. They're not ordered by the Transaction No field. If this creates a problem, the table can be sorted by transaction number before the form opens.

2. Enter the transaction number. The Transaction No field does not contain unique values. Together, the Transaction No and Product ID fields form a unique combi-nation.

3. Press Tab to move to the next field, Date, which is by default the current system date. Change it if necessary and press Tab to move to the Type field.

4. Enter the transaction type here. It must be one of three values: Sale, Purchase, or Shrinkage. A combo box is appropriate for this text box control (with no added items allowed).

5. Move to the Product ID and enter the value. When this text box control loses focus, the Unit Price and Unit Cost fields are filled in with values from the Products table for that item.

What happens next depends on the type of transaction being entered. If the transaction type is *shrinkage*, the Unit Price should be set to $0 because no revenue was received. The price and cost fields should not be in the tab order in the form because they're automatically filled in. If the transaction type is *purchase*, focus moves to the PO Number field and then to the Supplier field.

The Posted field is not available to the user. It's for information only and is automatically checked when the transaction is posted to the Products table in a separate operation. The Posted field is also tested when the user wants to archive transactions to the history file. Records for which this field is unchecked are not ready for archiving, no matter what the date of the transaction may be.

To finish entering the transaction record data, take the following actions:

1. Enter any comments in the Comments field, such as the reason for the shrinkage—shoplifting, rain damage, or chewed by mice.

2. The Extended Price and Extended Cost fields are automatically calculated with the values from the Products table after the Product ID number is entered. They're not in the tab order for the user.

3. The buttons in the form footer let the user choose what to do next: add another transaction, print the list, or return to the switchboard.

The only trouble the user could get into with this form is entering an invalid Product ID number. When this happens, Access displays a message that the value must match the join key. You can trap the error and replace the message with something more helpful to the user. Even though the Cost and Price fields are not in the tab order, the users can click in the fields and change the data if they want. Any changes made in a record in this form are also made to the Products table.

The users should not be allowed to delete any records from the Transactions table because they represent past events. However, errors might have been made that need correcting, in which case allowing deletion only with a password may be an alternative.

Entering or Editing Product Data

To reach the Products form for data entry and editing, the user selects Enter/Edit Other Data from the main switchboard. A second switchboard gives the user the option of opening a form for each of the other tables in the database: Products, Suppliers, and Customers. Choosing Products opens a form, such as the one shown in Figure 11.11, and the following actions can be taken:

- To add a new product, click the Add New Product command button or click the new record navigation button. To edit an existing record, use the navigation buttons to locate the record.

- Enter a unique Product ID value followed by the product description. Because the categories are stored in a lookup table, click the combo box arrow and choose from the list. The list shows the name of the category as well as the code. The code is the value that's stored in the record.

- Enter the Supplier ID code and the supplier's serial number for the new product. If the Supplier ID value is not in the Suppliers table, Access will display an error message that you should intercept and replace with a more understandable message.

- The rest of the form should not present any problems for the user. The command buttons in the form footer give the user a choice of the next operation—print the list of products or close the form and return to the main switchboard.

FIGURE 11.11
A Products data entry form.

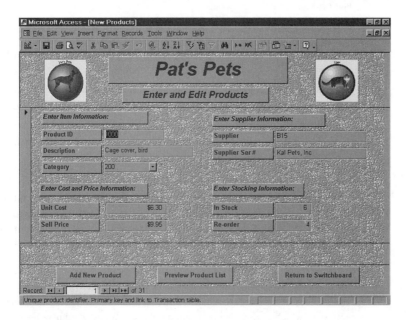

The Suppliers table is quite straightforward, with little or no error checking required, except for the unique ID value. The Customer table requires no error checking or data validation.

Previewing Reports

A preview switchboard lists the reports that have been designed for the Pat's Pets application. Many of the reports can accept a user-specified filter. For example, for a report that lists all the products related to small animals, the user would enter the major category code. Other reports require a specified time period, such as quarter or year.

One of the reports will print mailing labels for customers. This report can be filtered to include only those customers with specific pet interests.

If no records meet the criteria set by the user, a message is displayed indicating there's no information for this selection. This is preferable to displaying a blank page.

From the preview window, the user can print the report or close the window. When printing is completed, the main switchboard returns to the screen.

Posting Transactions

The Pat's Pets manager posts the day's transactions to the Products table at the close of business or at some other regular interval. Transaction posting is an item on the main switchboard. Little user interaction is required once the transaction-posting operation begins. You might want to give the user the choice of posting all unposted transactions or only those that occurred on a certain date or during a particular time period. If no date is chosen, all transactions are posted.

If you want, you can place a command button on the Transactions Log form that will post transactions after data entry is complete.

The posting module performs the following tasks:

- It filters out the transaction records that show the Posted field as unchecked.
- It creates an update query that updates the In Stock field in the Products table, subtracting the quantities listed as sales and shrinkage transactions and adding quantities listed as purchase transactions.
- After each In Stock quantity is updated, the Transactions record Posted field is checked.
- When all the transactions have been posted, a message is displayed to the user, indicating the number of records updated.

After the operation is complete, the main switchboard returns to the screen.

This set of procedures must be carefully tested to ensure that each transaction is posted only once. The user should have no trouble with this operation.

Archiving Transactions

Posting and archiving transactions are separate activities. Keeping recent transactions in a current table is a handy reference, but the Transactions table could become infinitely large if it's not purged from time to time. Saving historic transaction information can be quite useful in analyzing marketing and sales trends. Archiving can be done periodically, monthly, or quarterly, depending on the level of activity.

When the user chooses to archive transactions, an input box is displayed asking for the time period of the transactions to remove from the active table. This can be expressed as a range of dates or a single cutoff date—for example, "Archive all transactions that occurred before November 1, 1997." Only those records with the Posted field checked will be transferred to the archive table, even if the date falls within the selected range.

The archiving module performs the following tasks:

- It extracts any transactions whose date meets the criterion and whose Posted field is checked.

- It creates an append query that adds the records to the transaction history table.

- It displays a warning showing the number of records that are about to be added to the archive and deleted from the current table. The user can cancel the operation at this point.

- It deletes the records from the current Transactions table.

- It displays a message box showing the number of records moved from the current table and placed in the archive table.

After the user closes the message box, the main switchboard returns to the screen.

These procedures must also be checked out thoroughly to make sure no information is lost in the transfer.

Summary

Although you were not exposed to much programming is this chapter, you did get a view of what must go into the design of an application before the programming begins. Much time is wasted by beginning the implementation of an application before the design is carefully thought out and favorably approved by the intended user. The design process begins with an analysis of the existing system and interviews with the users to determine how the new application should perform.

This chapter discussed the distribution of data among related tables and how to minimize the possibility of errors in the database by the use of data validation rules. Finally, user interaction with the system was discussed, and several scenarios stepped through the most common operations.

In the next chapter, the data entry forms for the Transactions and Products tables are designed with the underlying class modules that contain event procedures and error-trapping code.

Customizing Data Entry

The data entry form is the primary interaction tool that links the user with a database. It's essential that there be a high level of understanding between man and machine if the application is to succeed. In many situations, difficulties can occur at points where two different mediums connect. For example, in a building, the line where the wall material meets the flooring or where one type of plumbing material joins with another can present interface problems.

Computer-based applications are no different. The point at which data moves from mind to machine can present interpretation difficulties. A properly designed and implemented data entry system can minimize the possibility of data errors. This chapter discusses several of the data entry vehicles in the Pat's Pets application.

Create Simple Data Entry Forms

When you need to create a relatively simple data entry tool, you can save some work by using the Form Wizard to build the basic structure and then add your own custom features. The Products and Suppliers tables lend themselves well to simple forms because there's not a lot of interaction with other tables, and neither insists on elaborate data validation. However, both have unique key fields that can cause an error if two records contain the same value. You can add a procedure to trap this error.

After the Form Wizard is finished, you can rearrange and resize the controls as well as add a title and pictures, if desired. After arranging the fields, recheck the tab order and make any necessary changes in the control properties.

Next, add command buttons to the form footer with the help of the Button Wizard, which also writes the Click event procedure code for the buttons. At this point, you can modify these procedures and add some new ones of your own. New procedures can change the form appearance upon opening, trap data errors, and calculate field values.

The forms designed in this chapter are all quite different for a reason. You can see how simpler forms may be easier to use than ones that are more cluttered. One form has explicit instructions for the user; both use the labels on the command buttons to convey their purposes.

The Pet Products Data Entry Form

The Pat's Pets Pet Products form was started by the wizard; then the controls were rearranged and resized (see Figure 12.1). A title, subtitle, and instructions for each area of data were added. Next, three command buttons were added:

- *Add New Product.* Moves to an empty record at the end of the table.

- *Preview Product List.* Opens the Product List report for preview. The Button Wizard needs a name for the target report. This report can be a simple AutoReport now, named Product List. A more useful report can be designed later and substituted for it.

DEVELOPMENT

- *Return to Switchboard.* Closes the form and brings up the switchboard (if the Pet Products form was opened via the switchboard). This button should appear on every form to give the user an escape route other than clicking the Close button.

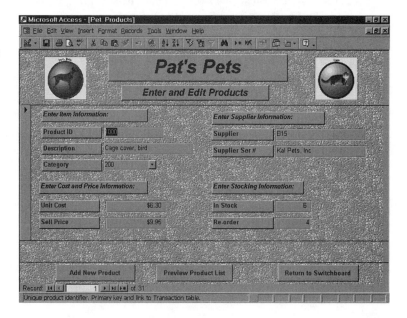

FIGURE 12.1
A data entry form for the Products table.

After the Button Wizard has helped to add the three command buttons, the Pet Products class module contains the three Click event procedures shown in Listing 12.1.

Listing 12.1 The Pet Products Form Class Module

```
Private Sub Return_to_Switchboard_Click()
On Error GoTo Err_Return_to_Switchboard_Click

    DoCmd.Close

Exit_Return_to_Switchboard_Click:
    Exit Sub

Err_Return_to_Switchboard_Click:
    MsgBox Err.Description
    Resume Exit_Return_to_Switchboard_Click

End Sub

Private Sub Add_Record_Click()
On Error GoTo Err_Add_Record_Click

    DoCmd.GoToRecord , , acNewRec

Exit_Add_Record_Click:
    Exit Sub

Err_Add_Record_Click:
    MsgBox Err.Description
    Resume Exit_Add_Record_Click

End Sub

Private Sub ProdList_Click()
On Error GoTo Err_ProdList_Click

    Dim stDocName As String

    stDocName = "Product List"
    DoCmd.OpenReport stDocName, acPreview

Exit_ProdList_Click:
    Exit Sub

Err_ProdList_Click:
    MsgBox Err.Description
    Resume Exit_ProdList_Click

End Sub
```

The wizards are notoriously close-mouthed about comments in their procedures. It's up to you to add sufficient comments for later reference.

Add a Form Startup Procedure

When a form opens, it might not be maximized, depending on the window that was open before it. Many forms are large and need to be maximized in the window in order for all the controls to be seen. An event procedure that executes when the form opens can use the Maximize method.

To add this procedure, open the module window for the Pet Products form and choose Form from the Object list and Load from the Procedure list. Figure 12.2 shows the beginnings of the new procedure. Although this procedure is simple enough not to require explanation, you should get into the habit of commenting all procedures. Just below the Private Sub line, enter the following code:

```
'Maximize the form window at startup.
DoCmd.Maximize
```

FIGURE 12.2
Starting a
Form_Load *event*
procedure.

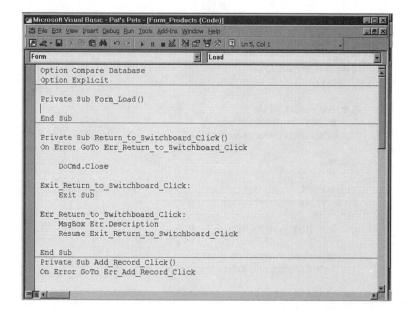

Change a Control Type

Changing a text box to a combo box, thus giving the user access to the value list, can save you time entering data as well as ensure valid values. One of the tables discussed in the previous chapter is the Category table, which can be used as a lookup table wherever the Cat Code field appears. The Pet Products form includes the Category field, which stores the category code. To change the text box to a combo box, carry out the following steps:

1. Open the Pet Products form in design view.

2. Right-click the Cat Code text box and point to Change To in the shortcut menu and then choose Combo Box. A down arrow appears in the Cat Code control, indicating it's now a combo box.

3. The category codes are not yet in the combo box list. Open the property sheet for the Cat Code control and make the following changes to the Data properties:

   Change Row Source Type to Table/query.

   Change Row Source to Category, the table with the Cat Code values.

   Change Bound Column to 1, the column in the Category table that contains the value you want stored in the Cat Code field.

   Change Limit to List to No so the user can add new categories if necessary.

4. Click the Format property sheet tab and make these changes:

   Set Column Count to 2 so you can see both the Cat Code and Category Name fields.

   Change Column Heads to No.

   Type **0.4";1.25"** in the Column Widths property to specify the width of both columns when the list is displayed.

   Type **1.65"** in the List Width property to increase the width of the pull-down list to wider than the control in the form.

5. Switch to form view and click the Category combo box (see Figure 12.3).

FIGURE 12.3
The new Category combo box.

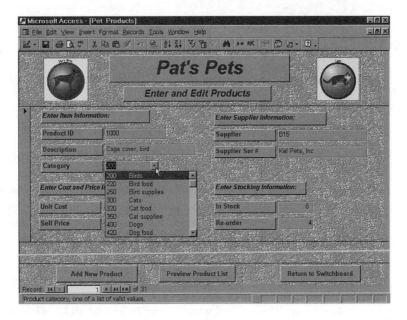

Set the Tab Order

The progress of focus through the controls in the form by pressing the Tab key is called the *tab order*. By default, the tab order is the sequence in which the controls were added to the form design. If you move controls around after the wizard has started the form design, the tab order does not automatically change to match the new positions without your help. You can set the order any way you like or use the Auto Order option, which moves the cursor from left to right and top to bottom.

You have two ways to set the tab order within a form section: by changing the Tab Index property of the control or by using the Tab Order dialog box. To use the Tab Index property, change the number in the property sheet. You can enter any number between 0 and one less than the number of controls in the section. When you enter a number already used by a control, the others are adjusted accordingly.

To use the Tab Order dialog box, choose View|Tab Order (see Figure 12.4). The dialog box shows a list of all the controls that can receive focus in each of the form sections. Even if you've set the control's Tab Stop property to No, the control still appears on the list. To move a control within the order, select it and drag it to a new position in the list. To revert to the automatic sequence, click Auto Order. To change the order of controls in another section, click the appropriate section. The Pet Products form has two controls in the header (the two images) and three in the footer (the command buttons).

FIGURE 12.4

Change the tab sequence in the Tab Order dialog box.

In the Pet Products form, the order is set in the dialog box to move the cursor down through the item information, to the supplier fields, to the cost and price fields, and finally to the stocking data. Notice that pressing Tab after filling out the Re-order field, instead of moving focus to the command buttons, causes Access to display the next record with the cursor in the first text box. If you want the user to be able to reach the buttons with the Tab key, you must place the buttons in the detail section with the text boxes and other data-related controls.

By setting the Tab Stop property to No, you can keep the user from reaching the control by pressing Tab. He or she can still reach it by clicking the mouse, but it does not automatically receive focus. The section, "Create the Transaction Log Data Entry Form," discusses the Transaction Log form and shows how to reach or skip a tab stop based on the value selected for the transaction type.

Combining the settings for the Enabled and Locked properties, you can regulate the amount of access the user has to a control. The Enabled property determines whether a control can get focus in form view. The Locked property specifies whether the data in a control can be edited in form view. You can use the two properties together with the following effects:

- *Set both to* Yes. The control is accessible and the data is displayed normally and can be copied but not changed.

- *Set* Enabled *to* Yes *and* Locked *to* No. The control is accessible and the data is displayed normally and can be copied or changed.

- *Set* Enabled *to* No *and* Locked *to* Yes. The control is inaccessible and the data is displayed normally but cannot be copied or changed.

- *Set both to* No. The control and data both are disabled and appear dimmed.

Tip: Setting the Enabled property in an AfterUpdate event procedure lets you have conditional control over the accessibility of command buttons and other controls. For example, suppose a form has a Preview Report button that opens one of a set of product reports based on a product category. Until the user chooses the category to use in the report's filter, the button should not be available. Set the Enabled property to No, and when the user selects a category from an option box or a combo box, the AfterUpdate event procedure runs and sets the Enabled property to Yes. Be sure to reset the property to No after the report is previewed. When you set Yes and No property values in VB, you use True and False.

Data Validation

DEVELOPMENT

The only data validation the Products table requires is that the Product ID field have a unique value. If you try to save a new record with a duplicate Product ID field, Access will display the following error message:

The changes you requested to the table were not successful because they would create duplicate values in the index, primary index, or relationship. Change the data in the field or fields that contain duplicate data, remove the index, or redefine the index to permit duplicate entries and try again.

Although this message may make sense to some, it's not specific about which field is in question. It would be a help to the user if you trapped this error and displayed a more definitive message. You can write a procedure to attach to the form's Error event. In order to trap the error, you need to find the error code number that Access stores in a system variable named DataErr. Look in the Help index for Trappable Microsoft Jet and

DAO Errors to see a complete list of trappable data-related errors. Access also has an extensive list of error codes that relates to Access objects. The Error event applies to both forms and reports.

The Form_Error procedure statement has the following syntax:

Private Sub Form_Error(DataErr **As Integer**, Response **As Integer**)

The words appearing in bold in a syntax statement are keywords that must be typed exactly as shown.

The DataErr argument is the error code that's returned by the Err object when an error occurs. It's passed automatically to the procedure. The Response argument determines whether an error message should be displayed.

If you set the Response argument to the intrinsic constant acDataErrContinue, the default error message is not displayed and the error is ignored. Then, it's up to you to deal with the error—for example, by displaying your own error message and focusing back on the key field. The other Response setting, acDataErrDisplay (the default), displays the Access error message.

Add the Form_Error event procedure to the Pet Products form by choosing Form from the Object list in the module window and Error from the Procedure list. Then, type the following code between the Private Sub and End Sub lines, once again starting with a comment:

```
'Trap duplicate Product ID value and display message.

Dim stMsg As String
Const conDupKey = 3022

    If DataErr = conDupKey Then
        stMsg = "You have entered a duplicate Product ID. "
        stMsg = stMsg & "Please enter a unique value."
        MsgBox stMsg
        Product_ID.SetFocus
        Response = acDataErrContinue
    End If
```

The Dim statement declares a string variable to represent your error message. Next, a constant is declared with the value 3022, which is the code number for the duplicate key field error. The If…Then statement tests the DataErr value and, if it's 3022, displays the message you stored in stMsg. The next line, Product_ID.SetFocus, returns focus to the Product ID field, where you can correct the error. The last line before End If sets the response to skip displaying the default message and continues processing. That is, it gives control back to the user to enter a unique value in the Product ID field.

Figure 12.5 shows the message caused by trying to save a record with a duplicate Product ID value.

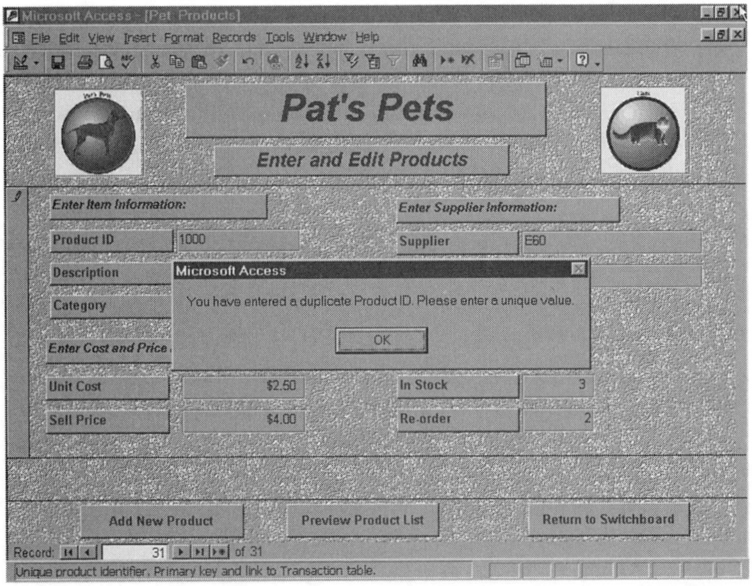

Figure 12.5
The new error-handling message.

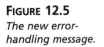

Tip: This procedure is general in nature and can be copied to other form class modules with minor changes to the field name.

The Supplier Data Entry Form

PERFORMANCE

The second form, Supplier Form, is similar to the Pet Products form. The form itself is at risk of overdoing the user instructions (see Figure 12.6). How much guidance you give in the form depends on the skill level of the prospective user. When in doubt, keep it simple. Elaborate forms also take longer to load and can be distracting.

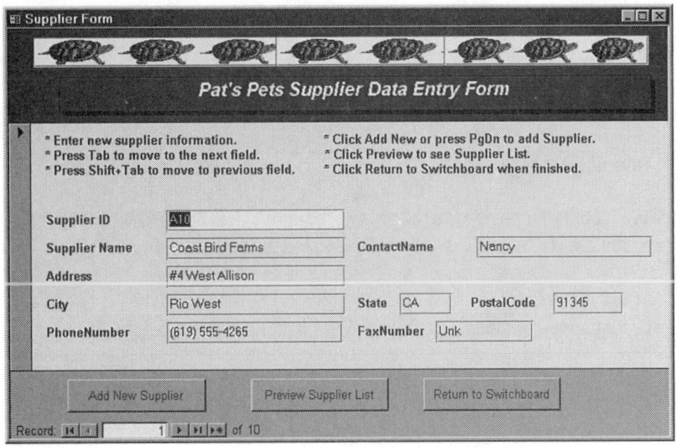

Figure 12.6
The completed Supplier Form.

Once again, the Button Wizard has helped to create the event procedures for the command buttons in the form footer. Supplier ID is the key field for the table and must not contain any duplicate values, so an `Error` event procedure is also appropriate for this form. Listing 12.2 shows the finished class module for Supplier Form with added comments. The `Form_Error` subprocedure was copied from the Pet Products module and then the message was edited.

Listing 12.2   The Supplier Form Class Module

```
Option Compare Database
Option Explicit

Sub Close_Form_Click()
'Close form and return to switchboard.
On Error GoTo Err_Close_Form_Click

    DoCmd.Close

Exit_Close_Form_Click:
    Exit Sub

Err_Close_Form_Click:
    MsgBox Err.Description
    Resume Exit_Close_Form_Click

End Sub

Private Sub AddSuppl_Click()
'Add new Supplier record.
On Error GoTo Err_AddSuppl_Click

    DoCmd.GoToRecord , , acNewRec

Exit_AddSuppl_Click:
    Exit Sub

Err_AddSuppl_Click:
    MsgBox Err.Description
    Resume Exit_AddSuppl_Click

End Sub

Private Sub Form_Error(DataErr As Integer, Response As Integer)
'Trap duplicate Supplier ID value and display message.

Dim stMsg As String
Const conDupKey = 3022

    If DataErr = conDupKey Then
        stMsg = "You have entered a duplicate Supplier ID. "
```

```
        stMsg = stMsg & "Please enter a unique value."
        MsgBox stMsg
        Supplier_ID.SetFocus
        Response = acDataErrContinue
    End If

End Sub

Private Sub Form_Load()
'Maximize the form window on startup.

DoCmd.Maximize

End Sub

Private Sub PrevSuppl_Click()
'Preview the Supplier List report.
On Error GoTo Err_PrevSuppl_Click

    Dim stDocName As String

    stDocName = "Suppliers"
    DoCmd.OpenReport stDocName, acPreview

Exit_PrevSuppl_Click:
    Exit Sub

Err_PrevSuppl_Click:
    MsgBox Err.Description
    Resume Exit_PrevSuppl_Click

End Sub
```

Note: The only trick to adding command buttons to a form is to understand the difference between the button caption and the button name. When you use the Button Wizard, you have a chance to give the button a meaningful name, which helps you to remember which button does what. This name identifies the control the event procedure belongs to and, if you inadvertently use the button caption instead, nothing happens when you click the button. On the other hand, no error occurs when a procedure in the class module refers to a control not in the form.

Create the Transaction Log Data Entry Form

The purpose of the Transaction Log Data Entry form is to acquire and store the information about transactions that have occurred during the business day. Granted, it's a bit unreasonable to expect a store manager or clerk to sit at the computer and log in every box of bird seed and every goldfish that has moved through the store during the day. This type of information would be automatically entered by a point-of-sale system at the register. However, this example can give you some useful ideas about the interactivity among related tables in an inventory control environment.

The Transaction Log form is by far the most active of the Pat's Pets database forms and requires the most attention to the details of events and responses (see Figure 12.7). Some of the data in the form comes from the Products table and is included so that it will present a complete picture at a later date. For example, the transaction shows the actual cost and price, and the Products table furnishes the cost and price that were current at the time of the transaction. After the transaction data has been accumulated over a period of time, this comprehensive information can be used in summaries and analyses.

FIGURE 12.7
The completed Transaction Log form.

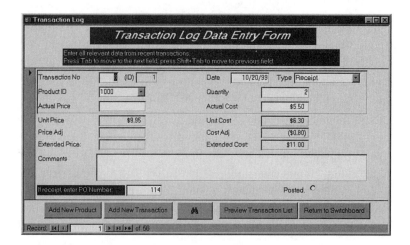

Modify the Wizard's Form

The form shown in Figure 12.8 is the result of using the Form Wizard to create a columnar form with all the fields from the Transactions table and the Unit Cost and Sell Price fields from the Products table. The style is Colorful 2. The tables are already related so that the price and cost data will correspond to the product ID.

The next step is to move the controls to a more logical sequence on the form. For example, gather the text boxes (into which the user will enter data) and place them in a rectangle at the top of the form. Then, arrange the Products fields and the calculated fields beneath the box and make them inaccessible to the user. The adjusted price and cost figures are bound to fields in the Transaction table, but the extended price and cost figures are calculated fields and are not stored. They can easily be calculated later from information that is stored.

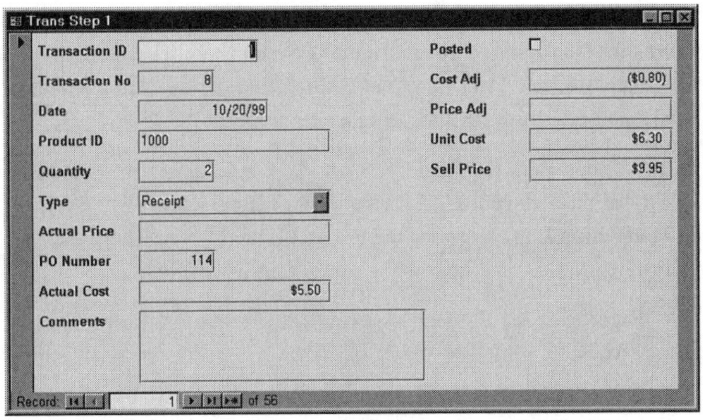

FIGURE 12.8
The form finished by the Form Wizard.

The unique key field, Transaction ID, is included and placed next to the Transaction No field for reference only. This is the AutoNumber field generated automatically by Access for each new record and is not available to the user. It actually corresponds to the line item in the transaction rather than the complete transaction.

LOOKING AHEAD The PO Number field is used only when the transaction is a receipt; therefore, it's placed at the bottom of the form. In the section "Change Text Box Appearance and Tab Order," you'll see a procedure that sets and resets the Tab Stop property of the PO Number field so that it receives focus only when the user selects Receipt as the Type value. An error is also generated if the user tries to save a record for a receipt transaction without entering a PO number. A procedure is added in the section "Add Error-Handling Procedures" to handle this error.

The Posted check box is also placed out of the way because the user never checks this box. It's automatically checked when the Transactions table is used to post recent transactions to the Products table.

LOOKING AHEAD In Chapter 14, "Adding Real-Time Features," procedures are written that post the transaction data and archive posted records to a transaction history file.

Most of the controls are much larger than they need to be for the width of the values they will contain. Resizing the controls as you rearrange them gives the form a more open look.

Change and Add Controls

Next, add the two calculated fields: Extended Price and Extended Cost. After adding the unbound Text Box controls, use the Expression Builder or simply type the expression in the Control Source data property. Type =[Quantity]*[Actual Price] as the expression for Extended Price and =[Quantity]*[Actual Cost] for the Extended Cost field. Recall that if a field name includes a space, you must enclose it in brackets, but to be consistent, Access encloses them all in brackets.

LOOKING AHEAD The adjusted price and cost values must be calculated using VB's Lost Focus event procedures for the Actual Price and Actual Cost controls. These are discussed in the section "Calculate Adjusted Price and Cost Fields" with the other procedures that the Transaction Log form requires to function properly.

During the design of the Products form, the Cat Code text box was changed to a combo box so that the user can select a value from the pull-down list. Doing the same thing in the Transaction Log form with the Product ID field would help the user select (or at least verify) the proper code. Follow the same steps as before:

1. Right-click the Product ID text box and point to Change To and choose Combo Box.

2. Open the Data property sheet for the text box and make the same changes as before. Set Row Source Type to Table/Query, Row Source to Products, and Bound Column to 1. You might not want the user to be able to add to the Product ID list, so leave the Add To List property set to No.

3. Change the Format properties by setting Column Count to 2 and removing Column Heads; then widen the columns and the list width to be able to see the full name of the products.

The Type field was already specified in the table definition as a lookup field, and the values were entered into the field property pane in the table design window.

Change Text Box Appearance and Tab Order

To distinguish quickly between text boxes that require data entry and those that just offer information, change the back colors. The wizard shows only the text box with focus in white and the others in the same color as the form background. Change the back color of all the data entry text boxes in the upper rectangle to white and the others to the same light yellow as the form. Figure 12.9 shows the modified form so far.

> **Tip:** When you look at the Format property sheet for the selected text box and click the Back Color build button to open the color palette, you'll see that the selected color is already white. This is because the control gets focus when you select it in the design, and white is the default color for text boxes with focus. Clicking the white square in the color palette will keep the text box background white even after it loses focus.

Next, add a title and some explanatory text, as necessary, to the form header as well as an instruction about the PO Number text box.

The final step in working with the controls in the design is to modify the tab order and set the Tab Stop property of all the passive text boxes to No. The Enabled property of the Posted check box should be set to No and the Locked property to Yes to keep the check box bright but unavailable. Later, when the transactions are posted to the Products table, the Posted properties are changed so that the field can be checked after the product inventory is updated.

FIGURE 12.9
The modified Transaction Log form design.

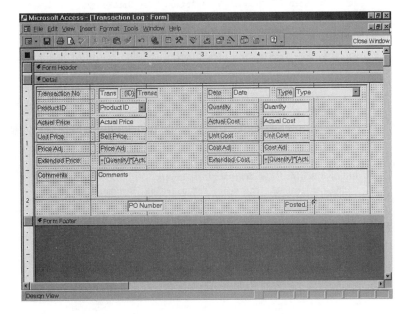

Add Command Buttons

The completed Transaction Log form shows five command buttons in the form footer that carry out the following operations when clicked:

- *Add New Product.* Moves to an empty record at the end of the table and copies the transaction number, date, and type to the new record.
- *Add New Transaction.* Moves to an empty record at the end of the table.
- *Find.* Opens the Find dialog box, where the user can enter the value for which to search. The cursor should be placed in the field to search before the button is clicked.
- *Preview Transaction List.* Opens the Transaction List report for preview.
- *Return to Switchboard.* Closes the form and returns to the switchboard (if it was open before this form opened).

All of these buttons can easily be added to the form design with the Button Wizard. The procedures generated by the wizard, with added comments, are shown in Listing 12.3 (notice that the button name as indicated in the Click procedure is the same as the caption on the button because that's the name the wizard was given for the button).

Listing 12.3   The Command Button's `OnClick` Event Procedures

```
Sub Preview_Transaction_List_Click()
'Opens Transactions report for preview.
On Error GoTo Err_Preview_Transaction_List_Click

    DoCmd.OpenReport "Transactions", acViewPreview

Exit_Preview_Transaction_List_Click:
    Exit Sub

Err_Preview_Transaction_List_Click:
    MsgBox Err.Description
    Resume Exit_Preview_Transaction_List_Click

End Sub

Private Sub Add_New_Transaction_Click()
'Adds new transaction record and disables PO Number tab stop.

On Error GoTo Err_Add_New_Transaction_Click
    DoCmd.GoToRecord , , acNewRec
    Me.PO_Number.TabStop = False
    Me.Transaction_No.SetFocus

Exit_Add_New_Transaction_Click:
    Exit Sub

Err_Add_New_Transaction_Click:
    MsgBox Err.Description
    Resume Exit_Add_New_Transaction_Click

End Sub

Private Sub Return_to_Switchboard_Click()
'Closes form and returns to switchboard.
On Error GoTo Err_Return_to_Switchboard_Click

    DoCmd.Close

Exit_Return_to_Switchboard_Click:
    Exit Sub

Err_Return_to_Switchboard_Click:
    MsgBox Err.Description
    Resume Exit_Return_to_Switchboard_Click

End Sub

Private Sub Add_New_Product_Click()
'Adds new product to current transaction.
```

```
On Error GoTo Err_Add_New_Product_Click

DoCmd.GoToRecord , , acNewRecord

Exit_Add_New_Product_Click:
    Exit Sub

Err_Add_New_Product_Click:
    MsgBox Err.Description
    Resume Exit_Add_New_Product_Click

End Sub

Private Sub Find_Record_Click()
'Opens Find dialog box.
On Error GoTo Err_Find_Record_Click

    Screen.PreviousControl.SetFocus
    DoCmd.DoMenuItem acFormBar, acEditMenu, 10, , acMenuVer70

Exit_Find_Record_Click:
    Exit Sub

Err_Find_Record_Click:
    MsgBox Err.Description
    Resume Exit_Find_Record_Click

End Sub
```

All of these procedures will do what's intended except for Add New Product. All the wizard knew was that it was to go to a new record in the form. The current transaction data must be copied from the previous record so that the user only needs to enter the product information. To do this, add the following code to the Add_New_Product_Click procedure, right after the On Error statement:

```
    Dim stTransNo As String
    Dim stType As String
    Dim dtmDate As Date

'Store previous transaction data.
    stTransNo = Me.Transaction_No
    stType = Me.Type
    dtmDate = Me.Date

'Copy transaction data to new record.
    DoCmd.GoToRecord , , acNewRec
    Me.Transaction_No = stTransNo
    Me.Type = stType
    Me.Date = dtmDate
    Me.Product_ID.SetFocus
```

The first three statements declare variables in which to store the transaction data temporarily. The next three copy the data to the variables. Then comes the DoCmd statement the wizard included, which goes to a new record in the form. The next three statements copy the transaction data to the new record. The last statement moves focus to the Product ID field because the transaction data is already filled in.

After entering the new code, compile the entire module to catch any errors in spelling or syntax.

Add Data Validation and Other Procedures

The Transaction Log form needs at least six more procedures to complete a smooth-running user interface. One procedure maximizes the form and turns off the tab stop for the PO Number text box. Another turns the PO Number tab stop back on if the transaction is a receipt. Two procedures calculate the adjusted cost and price values, and two others handle potential errors.

The first procedure in Listing 12.4, Form_Load, is similar to those for the other two forms, except for the TabStop setting. The second procedure examines the value in the Type field and sets the PO Number tab stop accordingly.

Listing 12.4 Added Transaction Log Event Procedures

```
Private Sub Form_Load()
'Maximize the form window at startup.
'Reset PO Number tab stop to false.
On Error GoTo Err_Form_Load

    DoCmd.Maximize
    Me.PO_Number.TabStop = False

Exit_Form_Load:
    Exit Sub

Err_Form_Load:
    MsgBox Err.Description
    Resume Exit_Form_Load

End Sub

Private Sub Type_AfterUpdate()
'Allow tab to PO Number field, if transaction is a receipt.
On Error GoTo Err_Type_AfterUpdate

    If Me.Type = "Receipt" Then
        Me.PO_Number.TabStop = True
    Else
        Me.PO_Number.TabStop = False
    End If
```

```
Exit_Type_AfterUpdate:
    Exit Sub

Err_Type_AfterUpdate:
    MsgBox Err.Description
    Resume Exit_Type_AfterUpdate

End Sub
```

Calculate Adjusted Price and Cost Fields

After the Actual Price and Actual Cost values are entered, Access can calculate the values to place in the Adjusted Price and Cost fields. These are bound Text Box controls that store the values in the Products table; therefore, you cannot use an expression as the control source. The two procedures in Listing 12.5 calculate the values when the ActPrice and ActCost text boxes lose focus. They also refresh the form to add the adjusted values right away and then move to the next control.

Listing 12.5   Calculating Fields from Entered Costs and Prices

```
Private Sub ActPrice_LostFocus()
'Calculates and updates Price Adjustment then moves to ActCost.
On Error GoTo Err_ActPrice_Lostfocus
    [Price Adj] = [Actual Price] - [Sell Price]
    Me.Refresh
    ActCost.SetFocus

Exit_ActPrice_LostFocus:
    Exit Sub

Err_ActPrice_Lostfocus:
    MsgBox Err.Description
    Resume Exit_ActPrice_LostFocus
End Sub

Private Sub ActCost_LostFocus()
'Computes and updates Cost Adjustment then moves to Comments.
On Error GoTo Err_ActCost_Lostfocus

    [Cost Adj] = [Actual Cost] - [Unit Cost]
    Me.Refresh
    Comments.SetFocus

Exit_ActCost_LostFocus:
    Exit Sub
```

continues

Listing 12.5   Continued

```
Err_ActCost_Lostfocus:
    MsgBox Err.Description
    Resume Exit_ActCost_LostFocus


End Sub
```

DEVELOPMENT There's a potential problem in these procedures. If the Product ID field is blank, the connection to the Sell Price and Unit Cost fields cannot be made and Jet engine error #3101 occurs: "The Microsoft Jet database engine can't find a record in the table Products with key matching field Product ID."

This is a form error that could be trapped by the Form_Error event. The problem is that this happens when the data in the form is refreshed but before you try to save the record, so any error-trapping procedure you attach to Form_Error will not be reached. You must handle the error before trying to calculate the adjusted values.

Add Error-Handling Procedures

To intercept the Jet engine error before it happens, add a procedure that runs when the Quantity text box gets focus before any value is entered. The following procedure checks for a Null value in the Product ID field and then composes an error message to display in place of the default message. After the message is displayed and the user has clicked OK, focus is returned to the Product ID field for a value to be entered. Listing 12.6 shows this error-handling procedure.

Listing 12.6   Ensuring a Transaction Has a Product ID Value

```
Private Sub Quantity_GotFocus()
'Checks to make sure Product ID has value
On Error GoTo Err_Quantity_GotFocus
Dim stMsg As String

'Display error message if Product ID field is blank.
    If IsNull(Product_ID) Then
        stMsg = "The product ID field must have a value. "
        stMsg = stMsg & "Select a value from the combo box. "
        stMsg = stMsg & "If you want to delete this record, "
        stMsg = stMsg & "select any value for the Product ID "
        stMsg = stMsg & "then choose Edit ¦ Delete Record."
        MsgBox stMsg
        Product_ID.SetFocus
        GoTo Exit_Quantity_GotFocus
    End If

Exit_Quantity_GotFocus:
    Exit Sub
```

```
Err_Quantity_GotFocus:
    MsgBox Err.Description
    Resume Exit_Quantity_GotFocus
End Sub
```

Figure 12.10 shows the message displayed when the Product ID field is blank and focus reaches the Quantity field. If you wait until focus reaches the Actual Price field, you'll get the Jet engine error message after clicking OK in the custom message.

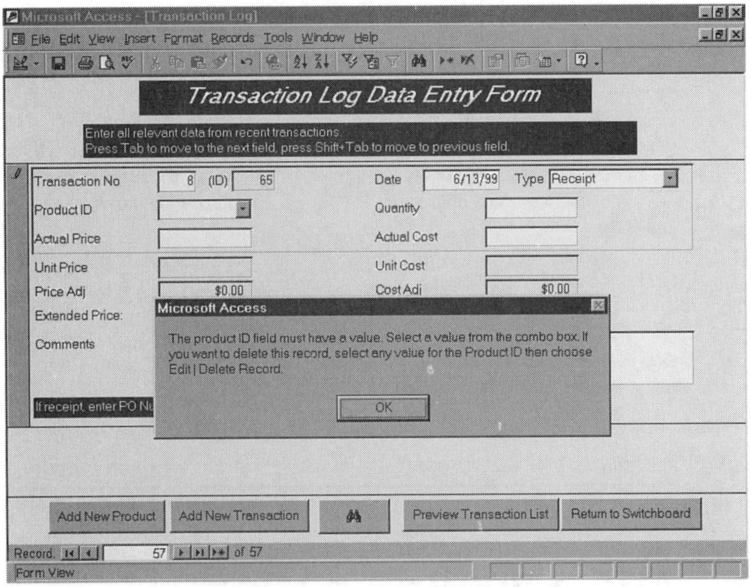

FIGURE 12.10
The adjusted price cannot be calculated without a Product ID value.

The last error handler checks for the record validation rule that says if the transaction is a receipt, there must be a PO number. A slight complication is that the PO Number field is the last tab stop on the form, so when you leave that field, focus moves to the next record but the next record is not yet committed. Unfortunately, if you add a DoCmd statement to go to the previous record, you move to the record before the one missing the PO Number.

Tip: The cure for this is to set a variable to the value of the key Transaction ID field when the PO Number control loses focus. Then, if the error occurs, set focus to the Transaction ID control and use the FindRecord method to return to that specific record. Once you've returned to the record, set focus once again to the PO Number text box, where you can enter the required value. Be sure you've entered Transaction ID as the Name property for the control in the property.

Listing 12.7 shows the event procedure that runs when the PO Number field loses focus.

Listing 12.7   Ensuring a Receipt Has a PO Number Value

```
Private Sub PO_Number_LostFocus()
'Display error message if Receipt transaction has no PO Number.
On Error GoTo Err_PO_Number_LostFocus

Dim stMsg As String, stKey As String

stMsg = "You must enter a PO Number for a Receipt transaction."
stKey = [Transaction ID]                    'Save Transaction ID value.
'Check for Receipt type and no PO Number.
If [Type] = "Receipt" And PO_Number = 0 Then
    MsgBox stMsg
    DoCmd.GoToControl "Transaction ID"   'Go to Transaction ID control.
    DoCmd.FindRecord stKey               'Move to record missing PO #.
    [PO_Number].SetFocus                 'Focus on PO Number.
End If

Exit_PO_Number_LostFocus:
    Exit Sub

Err_PO_Number_LostFocus:
    MsgBox Err.Description
    Resume Exit_PO_Number_LostFocus

End Sub
```

Add a Public Function

In Chapter 4, "Creating an Application with a Wizard," the Database Wizard built a global module containing a single function: IsLoaded(). This function is available to all the other procedures in the application. The purpose of the function, as explained in Chapter 5, "Examining and Modifying the Wizard's Code," is to test the state of a form object and return True if the form is open in form view. If the form is closed or open in design view, the function returns False.

> **Tip:** Such a function will be necessary for the Pat's Pets application when you add a pop-up form in the next section. This public function is called IsOpen(), but it contains exactly the same code. You can copy it from the *Omni-Sport* database or enter the code yourself. Click the Modules tab of the database window and click New to open the module window. The two default Option statements are already in the window, so just enter the following code:
>
> *continues*

```
Public Function IsOpen(ByVal stFormName As String) As Boolean

Const conDesignView = 0
Const conObjStateClosed = 0

IsOpen = False
If SysCmd(acSysCmdGetObjectState, acForm, stFormName) <> conObjStateClosed
➥Then
    If Forms(stFormName).CurrentView <> conDesignView Then
        IsOpen = True
    End If
End If

End Function
```

Refer to Chapter 5 for an explanation of the `SysCmd()` function.

DEVELOPMENT This is an important function because errors can occur if you try to carry out an operation that requires an open form (such as to changing the records it displays, and the form is closed). You'll call upon this function when you add a pop-up form to the Transaction Log form.

Create a Pop-Up Form

There may be times while the user is entering transactions in the Transaction Log form that he or she would like to know what other transactions have taken place lately with the same product. A pop-up form can display all these transactions without closing the Transaction Log form.

Use the Form Wizard to create a new form based on the Transactions table. Select only the Product ID, Transaction No, Date, Quantity, and Type fields. Then, on the Other tab of the property sheet, set `Pop Up` to `Yes`, which keeps the form on the screen while you're working with the other form. Switch to the Data tab and set `Allow Edits`, `Allow Deletions`, and `Allow Additions` all to `No`. Leave the `Modal` property as `No` so that you can work in other areas of the screen without having to close the form. Save the form with the name *ThisProduct*.

The new form is maximized in the window. Click and drag the window borders to resize the window so you'll be able to see all the record data but not obscure the Transaction Log form.

Next, use the Command Button Wizard to add a command button to the Transactions Log form that will display the new form as a pop-up form. Follow these steps with the wizard's dialog boxes:

1. In the first dialog box, choose Form Operations and Open Form.

2. In the second, choose ThisProduct as the form to open.

3. Next, choose the option labeled Open the Form and Find Specific Data to Display.

4. In the next dialog box, choose Product ID from both the Transaction Log and the ThisProduct field lists (see Figure 12.11).

5. In the last two dialog boxes, enter **Transactions This Product** as the button caption and **ThisProduct** as the button name.

FIGURE 12.11
Select the linking fields in the Command Button Wizard dialog box.

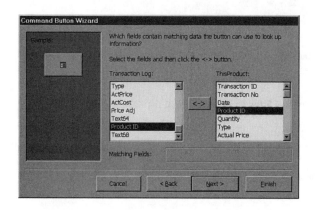

The following code is generated by the Command Button Wizard after you've made the previous selections:

```
Private Sub ThisProduct_Click()
On Error GoTo Err_ThisProduct_Click

    Dim stDocName As String
    Dim stLinkCriteria As String

    stDocName = "ThisProduct"

    stLinkCriteria = "[Product ID]=" & "'" & Me![Product ID] & "'"
    DoCmd.OpenForm stDocName, , , stLinkCriteria

Exit_ThisProduct_Click:
    Exit Sub

Err_ThisProduct_Click:
    MsgBox Err.Description
    Resume Exit_ThisProduct_Click

End Sub
```

ANALYSIS

The two declared variables, stDocName and stLinkCriteria, store the name of the pop-up form and the linking fields that connect the two forms. Then, the DoCmd statement opens the ThisProduct form with the Product ID filter that matches Product ID values.

The pop-up form stays open until the user closes it by clicking the Close button. When the user moves to a different record in the Transaction Log form, the records in the ThisProduct form still show the first products, unless he or she clicks the new button again.

Synchronize the Forms

To synchronize the two forms, add a procedure to the Transaction Log form that checks to see whether the pop-up form is open and, if it is, applies a filter that changes the records in the pop-up form to match the main form. The event procedure is attached to the GotFocus event for the Transaction Log form because when the user clicks the Next Record or another record navigation button, the form takes focus away from the ThisProduct pop-up form.

Select the Transaction Log form in the database window and click the Code toolbar button. In the module window, choose Form from the Objects list and then choose GotFocus from the Procedures list. Enter the following statements:

```
Private Sub Form_GotFocus()
'Synchronize the ThisProduct form if it is open.

Dim stProduct As String

stProduct = Product_ID
    If IsOpen("ThisProduct") Then
        Forms!ThisProduct.Filter = stProduct
        Forms!ThisProduct.FilterOn = True
    End If

End Sub
```

ANALYSIS

The procedure first stores the current Product ID value in the string variable stProduct. It then uses the new IsOpen() function to determine whether the ThisProduct form is open. If so, it sets the ThisProduct filter to the value in stProduct and sets the FilterOn property to True. If the ThisProduct form is not open, the procedure ends.

Figure 12.12 shows the ThisProduct form displaying the transaction records that involve product #1013. Notice the record navigator in the ThisProduct form shows that there are five records and that a filter is applied to the recordset.

Note: Although the record selector shows that the current record in the ThisProduct form is the same as the current record in the Transaction Log form, this does not happen automatically. The record selector was moved prior to capturing the figure.

FIGURE 12.12
The pop-up form shows the transactions for product #1013.

Close the Pop-Up with the Transaction Log

When you close the Transaction Log form, the pop-up form does not automatically close as well, so you need a procedure that closes it when the main form closes. If it's not open, it doesn't need to be closed, so the IsOpen() function is used again in this procedure to check the current state of the Form object.

Return to the module window and choose Close from the Procedures list with Form still showing in the Objects list. Then enter the following statements:

```
Private Sub Form_Close()
'Close ThisProduct popup form if still open.

    If IsOpen("ThisProduct") Then
        DoCmd.Close acForm, "ThisProduct"
    End If

End Sub
```

ANALYSIS

This simple procedure checks to see whether the ThisProduct form is open and, if so, closes it.

Switch to the Transactions Log form view and test the new synchronized pop-up form.

Create a Tabbed Form

With the Tab control, you can make multiple-tabbed forms like many of Access's own dialog boxes that have related controls grouped on each tab. The Transaction Log form would be much less cluttered if you used a tabbed form with the sales data on one page of the Tab control, the receipt data on another, and the shrinkage data on a third. It would be easier to enter all the data for one type of transaction at once and then move on to the next type.

The Tab control tool is simple to use. The first Tab control you add to a new form creates two tabs or pages. To add another tab, right-click the last page and choose Insert Page from the shortcut menu. You can add any type of control to a page of a tab control except another tab control. After creating the multitabbed form, change the page captions to indicate the contents of the page and other properties, as desired.

Start a new form for the transaction data, which will have three pages, each with one type of transaction data. To create the form, follow these steps:

1. In the Forms tab of the datasheet window, click New and then choose Design View and select Transactions as the record source. An empty form appears in the design window.

2. Open the toolbox if it's not already visible and click the Tab Control button (the one showing a raised file folders icon) and draw the control to the entire size of the new form. Figure 12.13 shows the form with two tabs, labeled *Page1* and *Page2*.

3. Add a third page by right-clicking anywhere in the form and choosing Insert Page from the shortcut menu. Access adds Page3 to the form.

4. Next, change the tab captions to **Sales**, **Receipts**, and **Shrinkage** by entering the new values in their respective Name properties on the Other tab of the property sheet.

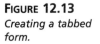

FIGURE 12.13
Creating a tabbed form.

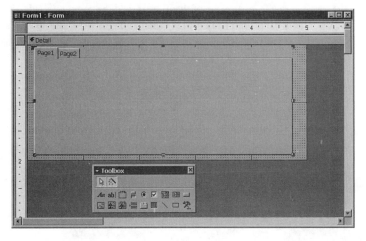

You're now ready to add the Transaction fields to the form pages. To display the field list, click the Field List toolbar button. The list of all the fields in TransQuery appear in a window to the right of the new tabbed form (see Figure 12.14). TransQuery includes all the fields from the Transactions table as well as the Sell Price and Unit Cost fields from the Products table. One by one, click and drag the field names to the tab and then resize and reposition them for appearance.

FIGURE 12.14
Drag the field names from field list to the tabbed form.

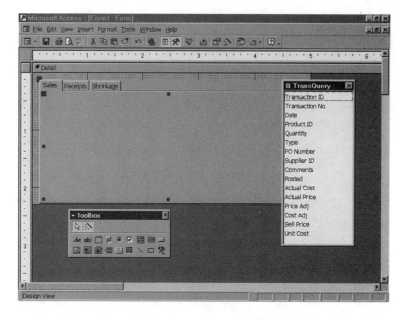

Add the common transaction fields and the price-related fields to the Sales tab and then add a command button that closes the form. Each tab should have an escape hatch so that the user can exit from any one of them. Next, add the common fields and the cost-related fields to the Receipts tab and only the common fields to the Shrinkage tab. The cost data is available in the Products table when the shrinkage transactions are posted. Figure 12.15 shows the design of the Sales tab of the TabTransForm form.

FIGURE 12.15
The finished Sales tab design.

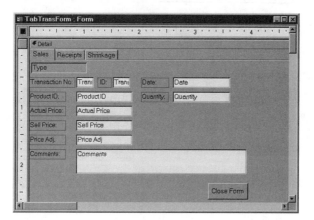

> **Note:** When you drag the same fields to the second page of the tabbed form, the label is not the field name. You must change the label of these text boxes to the field names.

The Type control at the top of the design is no longer a combo box, and the properties are deliberately set to make it unavailable for data entry. A default value is specified so that when the user adds a new record to this tab, the value is automatically set to Sale. The control is there only for confirmation when the records are viewed. Similar changes are made to the Type field on the other two tabs.

After you've laid out the form design, some procedures are required to filter the records so that only sales transactions appear in the first tab, receipts in the second, and shrinkage in the third. When the form first opens, the first tab is always the active page, so an event procedure can be attached to the form's OnLoad property that filters the records to those with "Sale" in the Type field. The following code accomplishes this:

```
Private Sub Form_Load()
'Filter records to show transactions for first page.

Dim tbc As Control
Dim stFilter As String

Set tbc = Me!TabCtl0
stFilter = "Sale"

Me.Filter = "Type = " & "'" & stFilter & "'"
Me.FilterOn = True

End Sub
```

ANALYSIS

The first statement declares the variable tbc as a control and then sets the reference to the Tab control in the current form, TabCtl0. In the Me.Filter statement, be sure to include the single quotation marks around the stFilter variable so that the filter is interpreted literally as Type = "Sale". When you need to include quotation marks in the filter, embed single quotation marks within double quotation marks. The two "'" groups on either side of and concatenated with the stFilter variable pass the quotation marks to the Filter property with the variable value.

The procedure that filters the records when the active tab changes is a little more complicated because it must set the filter depending on the current page. For this, use a Select Case structure based on the Tab control Value property. The Value property is the index number of the page in the Tab control's Pages collection. If the first page is selected, the index number is 0. If the second page is selected, the index number is 1, and so on. Once the index number is determined, you can use it in the Case structure to set the filter value. The procedure in Listing 12.8 is attached to the Tab control's OnChange property.

Listing 12.8   Segregating Transactions by Type on the Tabbed Form

```
Private Sub TabCtl0_Change()
'Filter records to show transactions for specific page.

Dim tbc As Control
Dim intPge As Integer
Dim stFilter As String

Set tbc = Me!TabCtl0
stFilter = ""

intPge = tbc.Value + 1
Select Case intPge
    Case 1
        stFilter = "Sale"
    Case 2
        stFilter = "Receipt"
    Case 3
        stFilter = "Shrinkage"
End Select
Me.Filter = "Type = " & "'" & stFilter & "'"
Me.FilterOn = True

End Sub
```

The `intPge` integer variable is calculated by adding 1 to the Tab control's `Value`; it's then used in the `Select Case` statement to add the transaction type to the filter. You cannot use 0 as a `Case` value. Figures 12.16 and 12.17 show the Receipts and Shrinkage pages of the new tabbed form. Notice that the record navigation bar shows the number of transactions of that type on the page followed by the (`Filtered`) indicator.

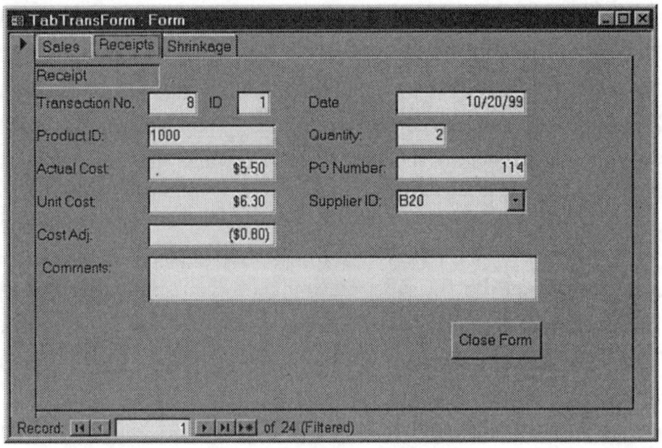

FIGURE 12.16

The Receipts page of the tabbed form.

FIGURE 12.17

The Shrinkage page of the tabbed form.

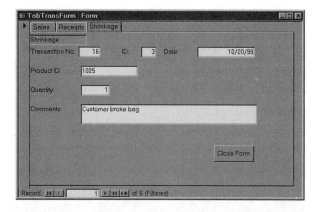

Note: If you want to delete a page from the tabbed form, right-click anywhere in the page you want to remove and then choose Delete Page from the shortcut menu. To change the page order in the Tab control, choose Page Order from the shortcut menu. Choosing Tab Order from the shortcut menu lets you change the tab order for the controls on the current page.

Three additional procedures are in the TabTransForm form class module that were created by the Command Button Wizard. These close the form when the Close Form button on any of the pages is clicked.

Add ControlTips and Other User Help

Until the user becomes accustomed to the data entry forms in the application, tips and reminders can be of help. *ControlTips* are short messages that pop up when the mouse pointer rests on a control in the form. To specify a ControlTip, enter the text in the `ControlTipText` property box. You can enter up to 255 characters in the tip, but shorter is better. Figure 12.18 shows a ControlTip that advises the user to place the cursor in the field to search before clicking the Find button.

Status bar messages are also helpful and can be attached to a control or the form itself. Again, you can enter up to 255 characters in the `StatusBarText` property box, but Access displays only as many as will fit in the status bar line. Figure 12.19 shows a message in the status bar when the Shrinkage page is active that reminds the user to enter a reason for the loss.

As discussed briefly in Chapter 6, "How to Get Help with Access Programming," you can also create compiled Help topics that display when the user presses F1 or clicks the What's This? button.

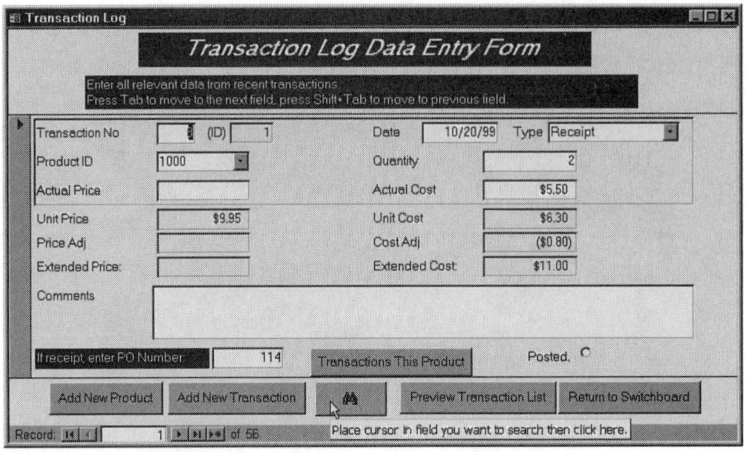

FIGURE 12.18

A ControlTip for the Find button.

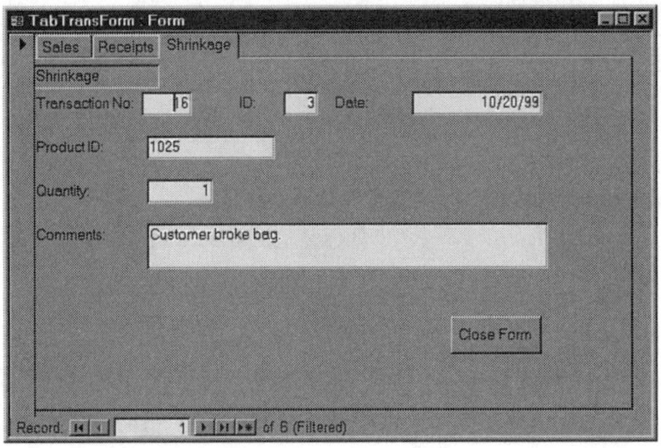

FIGURE 12.19

The status bar reminds the user to enter a reason for the loss.

Summary

This has been a rather intensive chapter, dealing with the important issues of data entry and how to prevent errors during the process. Carefully designing forms can enhance the user's understanding of the requirements of the application and can reduce the likelihood of mistakes.

Four different types of forms were designed in the chapter: two rather simple, one more complex containing fields from two tables, and the last containing multiple pages. VB code was created to add new records, preview reports, validate data, filter records, and trap errors. Where multiple forms were displayed, a procedure was written to synchronize the records in the forms.

LOOKING AHEAD

In the next chapter, "Customizing the Reports," customized reports are discussed for the Pat's Pets application—reports that sort, group, and summarize the information stored in the database.

Customizing the Reports

Preparing and printing Access reports requires far less user interaction than preparing and printing forms. However, the user still has the opportunity to make some changes in the format and other properties of a report at runtime. This chapter gives some examples of manipulating the Pat's Pets reports using custom features.

The Report Wizard

The Access 2000 Report Wizard can do just about anything you could want for a report. It can group records and provide totals, counts, and other summaries, it can sort the records based on the value in one or more fields, it can automatically shrink or grow a section based on the contents, and it can even provide a custom report style.

For most applications, the Report Wizard can create the reports you need; however, there might be some things you need that it can't do. All the report properties are set before the report opens. After that, the wizard has no jurisdiction. Any changes you want to make based on the value of the data to be included in the report are up to you. For example, if you want products whose stock levels have fallen below the restocking level to appear in bold font in the report, you must add Visual Basic code to accomplish this.

Another example is adding a filter to the report that's specified by the user at runtime. If you've already created queries that include the filters from which you want the user to select, your code will set the report record source property to the appropriate query at runtime.

Report Events

In order to be able to attach the code to the correct event, you must review which events apply to reports and report sections as well as when and in what sequence they occur. There are far fewer events for reports than for forms. They fall into two main categories: *general events*, which apply to the report as a whole, and *section events*, which apply to the report sections—the page, and group headers and footers, and the Detail section.

The general events are as follows:

- The Open event occurs when the report opens but before the report is previewed or printed. Open is the default event for report objects.
- The Close event occurs when the report is closed and removed from the screen.
- The Activate event occurs when the report receives focus and becomes the active window.
- The Deactivate event occurs when another window replaces the report window as the active window.
- The NoData event occurs when a report is being formatted for printing and the report is bound to an empty recordset.
- The Page event occurs after a report page has been formatted for printing but before printing occurs.
- The Error event occurs when a runtime error occurs in a report that has focus.

The events that apply to report sections include the following:

- The Format event occurs when Access selects the data for the section but before actually formatting it for preview or print. Format is the default event for report sections.
- The Print event occurs after formatting but before printing.
- The Retreat event occurs when Access has to back up to perform additional formatting operations with the section. Retreat applies to all sections except page headers and footers.

The Sequence of Report Events

As with forms, it's important to understand the sequence of events so that you can attach the event procedure to the right event. Generally speaking, report and report section events occur when you open a report for previewing or printing, or when you close the report.

When you open a report to print or preview it and then close it or switch to a different window, the following sequence of events occurs:

Open↓

Activate↓

Close↓

Deactivate

If you have more than one report open and you switch between them, the Deactivate event occurs for the first report, followed by the Activate event for the second report. This also occurs when you switch to another Access window. The report remains active, and the Deactivate event does not occur if you switch to a dialog box or a pop-up form or to a window in another application. The Activate event can be used to hide or display custom toolbars and other window-related features.

If the report is based on a query, the query is run after the Open event has occurred for the report. This is very useful for setting the query criteria with a macro or event procedure after the report opens but before the query is run. A macro or event procedure can also open a dialog box so that the user can specify the desired filter criteria.

The NoData event occurs after all the Format events have occurred for all the report sections and before the first Page report event occurs. NoData is used to cancel printing of a blank report. This event does not occur for a subreport if there are no records in it. You must use a different strategy to hide empty subreports. One way is to use the HasData property in a procedure to test for the empty control and then attach the procedure to the subreport section's Format or Print event.

The Sequence of Report Section Events

The report section events begin to occur after the Open and Activate report events and before the Close and Deactivate events. The sequence of events is as follows:

Open (report)↓

Activate (report)↓

Format (section)↓

Print (section)↓

Page (report)↓

Close (report)↓

Deactivate (report)

ANALYSIS

The Format event occurs with every section in the report; you can use it as a trigger for procedures that run calculations and make other runtime adjustments. In the Detail section, the Format event occurs for each record in the section. In group headers, the Format event occurs for each new group and can change data in the header as well as in the first record of the Detail section. In group footers, the Format event applies to the data in the footer and in the last record of the Detail section. With a Format event procedure, you can use the data in the current record to change properties or hide or display special text.

If you want to make changes that don't affect the page layout or format, use the Print event. The Print event occurs after all the formatting is done for the section and before it's actually printed. In the Detail section, Print occurs for each record just before Access prints it; therefore, a Print event procedure can be used to examine the data in the record before printing. In a group header, the Print event occurs for each new group, and the event has access not only to the data in the header but also the data in the first record of the Detail section. Similarly, the Print event in the group footer has access to the data in the footer as well as the data in the last record of the Detail section.

You can use the Print event to work with the data Access has ready to print. For example, you can use a macro or event procedure to calculate running totals to be printed in the page or group header or footer. If you want to change the page layout, you must use the Format event instead of Print because the page is already prepared by the time the Print event is reached. You would also use the Format event to access data in sections that you're not going to print, for example, when you don't plan to print all the pages of a report but you still want to calculate a running total of sales or receipts.

The Page event occurs after all the Format events have occurred for all the report sections and after the Print event has occurred for the current report page, but before the page is printed. If you want to change the appearance of the printed report, you can attach a macro or event procedure to the Page event. For example, using the Line or Circle methods in a procedure can add graphics to the page. You can also add pictures or other images at report printing time rather than have them embedded in the report design, where they take up disk space.

Under some circumstances, Access must return to a previous section to carry out the placement of controls and sections in the report, in which case the Retreat event occurs. For example, a group might not fit in the space left on a page if the KeepTogether property is set to Yes for either the Whole Group or With First Detail option in the Sorting and Grouping dialog box. Subforms and subreports whose CanGrow or CanShrink property is set to Yes can also affect the formatting of a previous report section. The sections on the last page of the report can also trigger the Retreat event.

After the Format event has occurred for every section on the page to determine how the controls are to be placed, the Retreat event will occur if the sections can't be printed. Access backs up to a previous section and moves it to the following page. The Retreat event occurs for every section passed over. After the Retreat events have occurred, Format occurs again to get ready to actually print the report.

> **Tip:** An event procedure that runs in response to a Retreat event can undo any changes made during the previous Format event, such as summarizing values by page or deciding whether to print a page header.

Changing Format and Properties at Runtime

The Transactions by Number report described in this section is an example of changing report and section properties at runtime. The report is designed to list the Pat's Pets transaction data grouped by transaction number.

All the transaction records in the current Transactions table are included with no filtering. The Report Wizard was used to create the basic report; then the text boxes containing information relating to the transaction number rather than the line item were moved to the group header section. A group footer was also added so that a light line could be drawn across the page to separate the groups. Figure 13.1 shows what the design looks like after some resizing and font changes.

FIGURE **13.1**

The Transactions by Number report design.

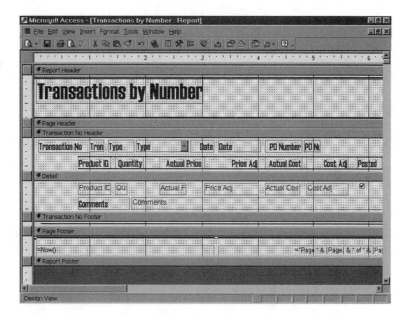

The Comments field does not have text in many of the records, and it appears as the sole control on the second line in the Detail section. An event procedure can be run when the Format event occurs for the Detail section that can test for a value in the field and, if none is found, omit the Comments label and close up the Detail section.

By default, Access leaves space for the text box value even if it's blank. The next step is to change the Detail section and the Comments control so that they will vertically close up if the text box control has no data. Setting the Can Shrink property of the text box control does not automatically set the equivalent property of the Detail section, so you must set them both.

The Can Shrink property, when set to Yes (True in VB), shrinks the section or control vertically so that no blank lines are printed. The Can Shrink property and its counterpart, Can Grow, can be set only in the control's property sheet. They do not apply to page header and footer sections.

The Can Shrink property takes care of blank Comments fields, but the label will still be printed unless you specify that it can disappear if there's no value associated with it. You can do this by attaching the code in Listing 13.1 to the Format event for the Detail section.

Listing 13.1   The `Detail_Format` Event Procedure

```
Private Sub Detail_Format(Cancel As Integer, FormatCount As Integer)
'If the Comments field is blank do not print the label.

Dim blnComments As Boolean

'Test for blank Comments field.
blnComments = Not IsNull(Comments)

'Set the visible property for the Comments label.
CommentsLabel.Visible = blnComments

End Sub
```

ANALYSIS

In this procedure, the statement

```
blnComments = Not IsNull(Comments)
```

sets the value of the Boolean variable `blnComments` to `False` if the Comments field is blank or to `True` if the field contains text. `IsNull()` returns `True` if the argument is blank, and then the `Not` keyword converts it to `False`. If there is text in the Comments field, `IsNull()` returns `False` and the `Not` keyword converts this to `True`. The last statement before `End Sub` sets the `Visible` property of the `CommentsLabel` control to the value of the Boolean variable.

> **Note:** You must know the name of the label control for the Comments text box in order to set its `Visible` property. It's not necessarily `CommandLabel`, as shown in the code. Look at the `Name` property in the Other tab of the property sheet.

Another improvement to this report is that if the transaction type is not Receipt, there is no PO number, so the PO Number label is omitted from the group header section. You don't need to set the `Can Shrink` property for the group header section to `Yes` because not printing the PO number does not change the group header height.

This event procedure is also run in response to the `Format` event, but this time when the event occurs for the group header. The code for this runtime property adjustment is similar to the code for the Comments field (see Listing 13.2).

Listing 13.2   The `Format` Event Procedure for the Group Header

```
Private Sub GroupHeader0_Format(Cancel As Integer, FormatCount As Integer)
'If the transaction is not a receipt, do not print the PO Number label.

Dim blnPONum As Boolean
```

```
'Test for blank PO Number.
blnPONum = Not IsNull(PO_Number)
PO_Number_Label.Visible = blnPONum

End Sub
```

ANALYSIS

The Not IsNull() test is run for the value in the PO Number text box and, if it's blank, the Visible property of the PO Number Label control is set accordingly.

PERFORMANCE

Images, pictures, and other graphics take up disk space if they're embedded in a report or form design. To reduce the amount of space the report requires and also to speed up loading the report, you can link the object at runtime. You can even display a pop-up box asking the user if he or she wants to include the object.

For the Transactions by Number report, the user might like to classify the printed report with the Confidential classification watermark. This can be added as a background image that's centered on the page, and it can be printed on every page of the report. The procedure in Listing 13.3 runs when the report's Open event occurs. The picture used in this example is one of the bitmaps in the Office subfolder in the Microsoft Office folder (your drive and path may be different).

Listing 13.3   The Open Event Procedure for the Transactions by Number Report

```
Private Sub Report_Open(Cancel As Integer)
'Add "Confidential" watermark before printing.

Me.Picture = "C:\Program Files\Microsoft Office\Office\Bitmaps\" & _
    "Styles\Confidential.bmp"
'Set picture properties to Clip, Linked and Center.


Me.PictureSizeMode = 0
Me.PictureType = 1
Me.PictureAlignment = 2

End Sub
```

> **Tip:** The Confidential watermark is not available in the library of bitmaps included with Office 2000. You can copy it from the report named Confidential in the Objects to Copy database on the Web site.

ANALYSIS

The last three statements before End Sub set the report properties as follows:

- PictureSizeMode to Clip (0 in VB).
- PictureType to Linked (1 in VB).
- PictureAlignment to Center (2 in VB).

Figure 13.2 shows a preview of the new Transactions by Number report. Notice that in the records that have no Comment text, the line is closed up and the group headers for sales transactions do not include a PO Number label. The Confidential watermark appears centered on the page both horizontally and vertically.

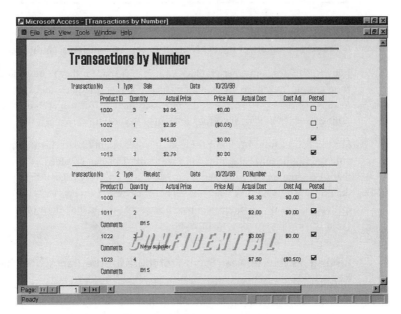

Preparing for User Input

If you have several reports that present the same basic information in different ways, you might consider using a dialog box to ask the user which report he or she would like to see. For example, three reports show transaction data in three different ways: grouped by transaction number, grouped by transaction type, and grouped by supplier with group totals and a running total. The previous section discussed the first report. This section discusses the other two as well as a user-input form for selecting which report to preview.

First, let's create the two new reports and then tie all three together with a dialog box form.

The Transactions by Type Report

Once again, let the Report Wizard start the report design by making the following choices in the wizard's dialog boxes:

1. Choose the query TransQuery as the basis for the report. This query combines data from the Transactions table and the Products table so that the unit cost and sell price are available for calculations in the report.

2. Include all the fields in the query except the transaction ID (the AutoNumber Access uses as the primary key for the Transactions table).

3. Group the records by type and sort them by transaction number.

4. Choose the Align Left 1 layout and the Soft Gray style and then name the report "Transactions by Type."

After the wizard is finished, the report layout is 21 inches wide. You'll need to resize and reposition many fields to fit them on a page, even in landscape orientation. Also, you'll need to add three unbound Text Box controls to hold the calculated fields: extended price, extended cost, and the net difference between the two. Use the Expression Builder or type the following expressions in the Control Source properties for the new text boxes:

- ExtPrice = [Quantity]*[Sell Price]
- ExtCost = [Quantity]*[Unit Cost]
- Net = [ExtPrice]-[ExtCost]

Be sure to enter the name for the first two calculated fields in their Name property boxes so you can use the names in the third expression.

The Type field would look better in the group header if the font size and style were the same as the label—Arial, 9 point, and heavy weight. The completed report design is shown in Figure 13.3.

FIGURE 13.3
The Transactions by Type report design.

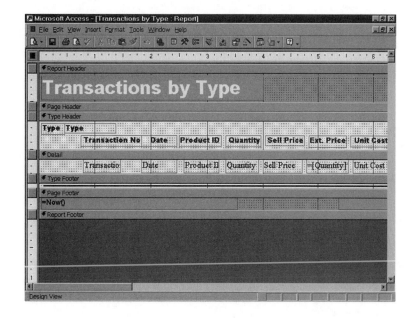

In the Transactions by Number report, some of the Text Box controls and Label controls are not printed, depending on the type of transaction. With this report, the Unit Cost and Sell Price values always appear, regardless of the transaction type, because they're from the Products table. Some VB code attached to the Detail section Format event can keep these fields from printing when they do not apply to the transaction type. For example, the Sell Price does not relate to a receipt or a shrinkage transaction.

This report needs two event procedures: one to set the Visible property of several of the Text Box controls and their labels, and a second one to restore the Visible properties to Yes after the report is printed. If not reset to Yes, the property remains No, which could affect later use of the controls.

The procedure in Listing 13.4 runs when the Format event occurs for each Detail section. It first resets all the Visible properties to Yes. This is necessary because the previous Detail section might have set some of the Visible properties to No. Then, the procedure tests the value in the Type field with a nested If...Then block.

Listing 13.4 Formatting the Report Detail Sections

```
Private Sub Detail_Format(Cancel As Integer, FormatCount As Integer)
'Select the fields to display depending on the type of transaction.
'If sale, display all fields but PO Number.
'If receipt, remove cost data.
'If shrinkage, display only cost data.
'Reset all the visible properties to True then
'change detail section display depending on type of transaction.

    Me.Unit_Cost.Visible = True
    Me.ExtCost.Visible = True
    Me.Net.Visible = True
    Me.Unit_Cost.Visible = True
    Me.ExtCost.Visible = True
    Me.Net.Visible = True
    Me.Sell_Price.Visible = True
    Me.PO_Number.Visible = True
    Me.ExtPrice.Visible = True

If Me.Type = "Receipt" Then
        Me.Unit_Cost.Visible = False
        Me.ExtCost.Visible = False
        Me.Net.Visible = False
    ElseIf [Type] = "Shrinkage" Then
        Me.Sell_Price.Visible = False
        Me.ExtPrice.Visible = False
        Me.Net.Visible = False
End If

End Sub
```

ANALYSIS

The If...Then structure tests only for Receipt and Shrinkage—if the transaction is a Sale, all the fields apply except for PO Number, which is blank anyway for a sale. The corresponding labels could also have been made invisible, but that creates a report page with large gaps. It's easier to read with the column headings left in the report.

The Report_Close procedure resets all the affected Visible properties to Yes:

```
Private Sub Report_Close()
'Reset all the visible properties to True.

    Me.Unit_Cost.Visible = True
    Me.ExtCost.Visible = True
    Me.Net.Visible = True
    Me.Unit_Cost.Visible = True
    Me.ExtCost.Visible = True
    Me.Net.Visible = True
    Me.Sell_Price.Visible = True
    Me.PO_Number.Visible = True
    Me.ExtPrice.Visible = True


End Sub
```

Figures 13.4, 13.5, and 13.6 show the three pages of the Transactions by Type report with all three types of transactions.

FIGURE 13.4

Receipt transactions.

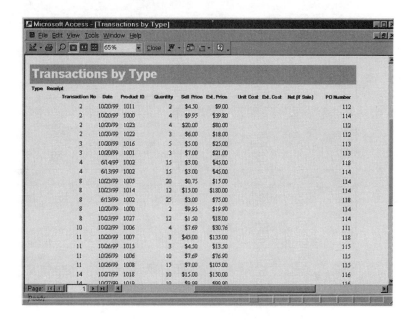

FIGURE 13.5
Sale transactions.

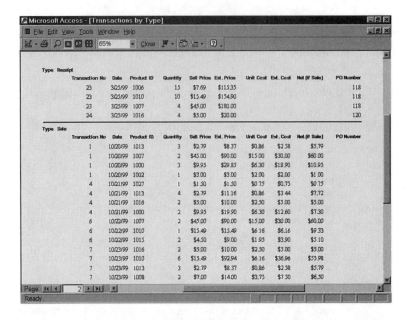

FIGURE 13.6
Shrinkage.

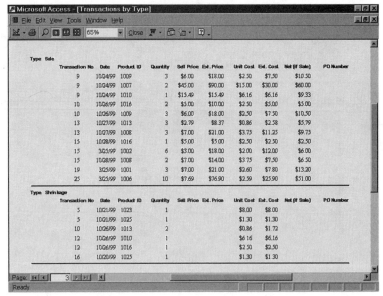

The Transactions by Supplier Report

The third transaction report groups the receipt transactions by supplier. The extended cost is calculated for each transaction and totaled for each supplier. A running total is also added to the Supplier group. A final grand total is added at the end of the report. Figure 13.7 shows a preview of the completed report, and Figure 13.8 shows the report design after the Report Wizard's product has been modified.

FIGURE 13.7

The Transactions by Supplier report preview.

Transactions by Supplier

Supplier Name	Date	Description	Quantity	Unit Cost	Extended Cost
Aquatic Foods	10/27/99	Brine shrimp	10	$4.00	$40.00
	10/27/99	Live ghost shrimp	10	$7.00	$70.00
				Total This Supplier:	**$110.00**
				SubTotal So Far:	**$110.00**
Bill's Kennel	10/22/99	Flea comb	4	$2.59	$10.36
	10/25/99	Flea and tick dip	10	$6.16	$61.60
	10/25/99	Flea comb	15	$2.59	$38.85
	10/25/99	Dog collar, leather	4	$2.50	$10.00
				Total This Supplier:	**$120.81**
				SubTotal So Far:	**$230.81**
Coast Bird Farms	10/20/99	Parakeets	4	$8.00	$32.00
	10/25/99	Lovebirds	4	$15.00	$60.00
				Total This Supplier:	**$92.00**
				SubTotal So Far:	**$322.81**
Kal Pets, Inc.	10/23/99	Cat pan	12	$8.00	$96.00
	10/23/99	Goldfish	20	$0.30	$6.00
	10/23/99	Dizzy ball toy	12	$0.75	$9.00
	10/26/99	Cat harness	3	$1.95	$5.85
	10/26/99	Nail clippers	15	$3.75	$56.25
	10/26/99	Flea comb	10	$2.59	$25.90
				Total This Supplier:	**$199.00**
				SubTotal So Far:	**$521.81**
Pet Supply Whse	10/20/99	Dog collar, leather	5	$2.50	$12.50
	10/20/99	16 oz dog dish	3	$2.60	$7.80

FIGURE 13.8

The Transactions by Supplier report design.

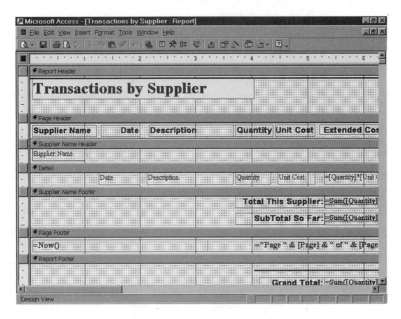

An expression is used to define both of the unbound Text Box controls, Total This Supplier and SubTotal So Far, that are placed in the group footer. The expression

```
=Sum([Quantity]*[Unit Cost])
```

can be used for both the controls. Placing the Total This Supplier in the group footer automatically totals the value for the group. The Subtotal So Far value is a running total that can be specified in the control's property sheet by setting the Running Sum property to Over All.

> **Note:** You could show a running total within the group as each line item is added to the transaction by placing the control in the Detail section. Then, you could remove the Sum operator and change the Running Sum property to Over Group. If you use this setting for the control in the group footer, it shows only the value of the last item in the group. In the footer, you must use the Sum() function.

The Transactions by Supplier report is based on an SQL statement that includes fields from three tables: Transactions, Suppliers, and Products (see Figure 13.9). An inner join is formed, linking the Transactions table to the Products table by the Product ID field. Another join links the Transactions table to the Suppliers table with the Supplier ID field. A WHERE clause limits the records to those with "Receipt" in the Type field. To see the report's SQL statement, right-click the Record Source property and choose Zoom from the shortcut menu.

FIGURE 13.9
*A SQL statement
is the record
source for the
Transactions by
Supplier report.*

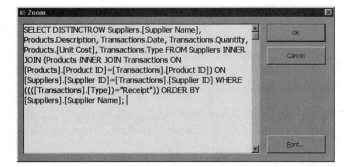

This report has no procedures in the class module. All the design work was done in the property sheet and with the SQL statement.

The User Input Form

The final piece of the scenario is the form that lets the user decide which report to pre-view. The form design contains an option group with the three reports as choices (see Figure 13.10). It has two buttons—one to preview the selected report and the other to close the form without making a selection.

FIGURE 13.10
*The Transaction
Reports user input
dialog box.*

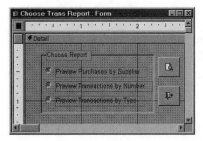

Create the form without the help of the Form Wizard and add an option group with the three options. Then, add two command buttons with the help of the Command Button Wizard: one that opens a report for preview and the other to close the form. When you tell the wizard you want to use the button to open a report, it wants to know which report. Select one of the transaction reports—you'll change this with code later.

Setting Properties

To make the form behave and look like a dialog box, change some of the form's proper-ties as follows:

- Enter **Choose Transaction Report** in the Caption property.
- Set Scrollbars to Neither.
- Set Record Selectors to No.

- Set Navigation Buttons to No.
- Set AutoCenter to Yes.
- Set Border Style to Dialog.
- Switch to the Other property tab and set Popup to Yes.
- Set Modal to Yes.

Setting the form as modal means that the user will not be able to click anywhere outside the form while it's open. Most of the dialog boxes in Access are modal and require a response from the user before moving on, even if it's only a click of the Cancel button.

Sizing the Form

To make the form the right size when it opens in the Access window, click the Resize button if the form design window is maximized. Then, drag the borders of the window to match the form itself and save the form design. Figure 13.11 shows the completed form with ControlTips added to explain the options. These are added with code in the Form_Load event procedure (this is discussed later in the chapter). You create them by typing the text in the ControlTip property box for both the control and the label.

FIGURE 13.11
The completed Choose Transaction Report form.

Next, you need to write an event procedure for the Preview command button that will select the report for preview. The Command Button Wizard has already taken care of the Close button's Click event procedure with the code shown in Listing 13.5. The DoCmd.Maximize statement has been added to maximize the window that becomes active after the form closes.

Listing 13.5   The Close_Click Event Procedure

```
Private Sub Close_Click()
On Error GoTo Err_Close_Click

    DoCmd.Close
    DoCmd.Maximize

Exit_Close_Click:
    Exit Sub
```

```
Err_Close_Click:
    MsgBox Err.Description
    Resume Exit_Close_Click

End Sub
```

ANALYSIS When the Preview command button is clicked, the OnClick procedure tests for the value returned by the option group and then opens the specified report for preview. By default, the options in a group return integer numbers beginning with 1, the value from the first selection. Therefore, if the value is 1, the Transactions by Supplier report should open for preview; if the value is 2, the Transactions by Number report should open for preview, and so on. The form also must be removed from the screen after a selection is made.

The event procedure in Listing 13.6 runs when the Preview button is clicked in the Choose Transaction Report form. You can create this procedure by modifying the code created by the Command Button Wizard, or you can write it from scratch.

Listing 13.6   The Preview Button OnClick Event Procedure

```
Private Sub PrevTransRepts_Click()
On Error GoTo Err_PrevTransRepts_Click

    Dim stDocName As String
'Use ChooseReport option group in Case structure.
    Select Case ChooseReport
        Case 1
            stDocName = "Transactions by Supplier"
        Case 2
            stDocName = "Transactions by Number"
        Case 3
            stDocName = "Transactions by Type"
    End Select
'Close dialog box and open report.
    DoCmd.Close
    DoCmd.OpenReport stDocName, acPreview

Exit_PrevTransRepts_Click:
    Exit Sub

Err_PrevTransRepts_Click:
    MsgBox Err.Description
    Resume Exit_PrevTransRepts_Click

End Sub
```

This procedure uses a Select Case block based on the value returned by the option group named ChooseReport to set the name of the report to preview. Just before the

DoCmd.OpenReport statement, the form's Visible property is set to False, removing it from the screen.

Adding ControlTips

An added touch to the form is the display of explanatory ControlTips when the mouse pointer hovers over a control or a label (refer to Figure 13.11). You can add these by typing text in the ControlTip property of the control or in code in the Form_Load event procedure. Listing 13.7 adds ControlTips to both the Option Button controls and their labels. The options and labels retain the names assigned by the Option Group wizard.

Listing 13.7   Adding ControlTips when the Form Loads

```
Private Sub Form_Load()
'Set the text of controltips for the options in the option group.
    Me.Option29.ControlTipText = "Choose to preview transactions " & _
        "grouped by Supplier with totals."
    Me.Label30.ControlTipText = "Choose to preview " & _
        "transactions grouped by Supplier with totals."
    Me.Option31.ControlTipText = "Choose to preview report of " & _
        "transactions by number."
    Me.Label32.ControlTipText = "Choose to preview " & _
        "report of transactions by number."
    Me.Option33.ControlTipText = "Choose to preview transactions " & _
        "grouped by sale, purchase and shrinkage."
    Me.Label34.ControlTipText = "Choose to preview " & _
        "transactions grouped by sale, purchase and shrinkage."

End Sub
```

DEVELOPMENT

Forms such as this one can be used as mini switchboards that branch out from a selection made on the main switchboard. For example, a main selection could be to enter or edit records, which opens a form from which the user selects the table to work with.

LOOKING AHEAD

In Chapter 14, "Adding Real-Time Features," the Pat's Pets application will be integrated with a main switchboard, the branching form created in this chapter, and other forms and dialog boxes that complete the project.

Adding Conditional Totals

In the next report design, which is a summary of the product inventory in Pat's Pets, the products are grouped by major product category, and products that must be reordered are emphasized by being printed in heavy font weight. In addition, a count of the number of items that need to be ordered is added to the group footer.

Use the Report Wizard to build the beginnings of the Summary of Product Inventory report, choosing the Products query as the record source. The Products query joins the

Category table with the Products table so that you have access to the name of the category that corresponds to the code. Group the records by the Cat Code field and sort them within the group by the Product ID field.

Next, add two Text Box controls and two Label controls to the group footer to hold the total number of products in the group and the number of products that need to be ordered. Enter names for the new unbound text boxes that resemble the field names. You can use these names in the code to set their properties. The Name property appears on the Other tab of the property sheet.

Type the expression

```
=Count([Product ID])
```

in the control source property box for the unbound text box that will show the total number of products in the category. The control source for the number of products that need to be ordered will be defined by code at runtime.

> **Tip:** If you preview the report now, you'll see that the supplier codes contain lowercase letters. The Suppliers table includes a formatting provision that converts letters to uppercase, but this is not carried over to the report design. To add this feature to the report, change the control source from Supplier to the expression =UCase([Supplier]). You must include the equal sign; otherwise, you'll get a prompt to enter the parameter value. Figure 13.12 shows the report design after these changes have been made.

FIGURE 13.12
The Summary of Product Inventory report design.

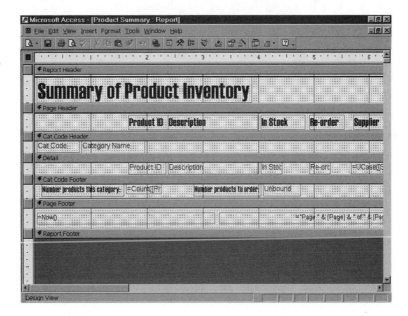

When you add a conditional count to a group, you need to initialize it to 0 every time the report opens a new group. A procedure to do this should run when the group header is formatted and ready to print so that you can use the group header OnPrint event as the trigger.

The code that changes the appearance of the In Stock and Re-order values, depending on their relative values, belongs in the Detail_Print event procedure. The calculation of the conditional count of products to reorder is also in that procedure. Listing 13.8 shows the Products Inventory report class module with both procedures.

Listing 13.8   The Products Inventory Report Class Module

```
Private Sub GroupHeader0_Print(Cancel As Integer, PrintCount As Integer)
'Reset number of products to order to 0.
ReOrdNum = 0

End Sub

Private Sub Detail_Print(Cancel As Integer, PrintCount As Integer)
'If the In-stock value is less than or equal to the Re-Order level,
'print both values in bold style.
'Define constants with normal and bold font weight values.
Const conNormal = 400
Const conBold = 800
Dim lngDiff As Long

lngDiff = [In Stock] - [Re-order]

If lngDiff < 0 Or lngDiff = 0 Then
    [In Stock].FontWeight = conBold
    [Re-order].FontWeight = conBold
Else
    [In Stock].FontWeight = conNormal
    [Re-order].FontWeight = conNormal
End If

'Add 1 to number of products to order to the group total.

If PrintCount = 1 Then
    If lngDiff < 0 Or lngDiff = 0 Then
        ReOrdNum = ReOrdNum + 1
    End If
End If

End Sub
```

ANALYSIS

Three variables are declared in the declaration section of the Detail_Print procedure: two constants that set the VB value for the Font Weight properties Normal and Bold, and a numeric integer variable that represents the difference between the In Stock value and the Re-order value. Next, the difference is calculated and then the If...Then...Else segment sets the Font Weight properties of both Text Box controls to Normal if the difference is positive or Bold if the difference is zero or negative.

Next, the ReOrdNum value is incremented if the difference between the product levels is equal to or less than zero. You would think that you could just add a statement to the If...Then block used to set the Font property to test the same expression. However, it's not that easy—PrintCount is an argument in the Detail_Print procedure. PrintCount identifies the number of times the OnPrint property for the section is evaluated. It's incremented if the section runs over to a second page, for example. Because you don't want to count any product twice, the code should increment the ReOrdNum total only if PrintCount equals 1 (that is, the first time any part of the section is printed).

Figure 13.13 shows a preview of the beginning of the Summary of Product Inventory report. You should be able to see that the Live ghost shrimp and Feeder guppies products need to be reordered. Their In Stock and Re-order values appear in bold, and the "Number products to order" value shows 2. There's also one product to order in both the Fish Supplies and Birds categories.

FIGURE 13.13
A preview of the Summary of Product Inventory report.

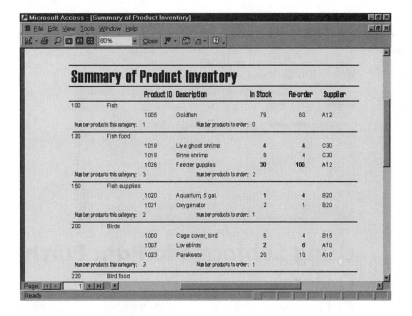

Sending a Report Snapshot

Report snapshots are new with Access 2000. A report snapshot is a special file (*.snp file extension) that contains a copy of every page of a report in high resolution with two-dimensional layout, graphics, and any other embedded objects. Once you create the snapshot file, you can electronically distribute it to others via email or the Web. The recipients can view the report in its fully formatted form and print only the pages they need. They must have the Snapshot viewer installed to be able to open the report snapshot.

Once you've created and saved a report, you can create a report snapshot from it by following these steps:

1. Select the report name in the database window and choose File|Export.

2. In the Export Report To dialog box, choose Snapshot Format in the Save As Type box.

3. Select the drive and folder where you want to save the report and enter the name. Then click Save.

When you want to send a report snapshot by email, use the Send command in the File menu or create a macro with the SendObject action. If you choose File|Send, the Snapshot view opens a new mail message with Microsoft Outlook and embeds the report snapshot as an icon (see Figure 13.14). Depending on how you've set up your messaging system, the process may be different.

FIGURE 13.14
Sending a report snapshot with an email message.

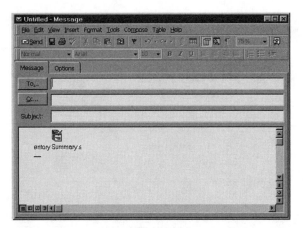

Using Subforms to Print Purchase Orders

When the inventory of a product falls below the recommended stocking level, the store manager issues purchase orders to the suppliers. Access can be of help in identifying the products that should be ordered and printing selected purchase orders. To display the products with low levels together with information about their suppliers, you can create a form with a Subform control.

The form is based on the Suppliers table, and the subform is based on the Products table. The linking fields are the Supplier ID field from the Suppliers table and the Supplier field from the Products table. In order to show only those products whose levels are low, base the subform on a query with the criterion that the In Stock quantity is less than or equal to the Re-Order level ([In Stock] < [Re-Order] + 1). The subform's Default View property should be set to Datasheet.

After placing the Text Box controls and the Subform control on the form, add three command buttons with the Command Button Wizard. One prints the current purchase order, the second prints all the orders, and the third closes the form.

Figure 13.15 shows the Reorder List form design with the Reorder subform, and Figure 13.16 shows the same form in form view.

FIGURE 13.15
The Reorder List form design.

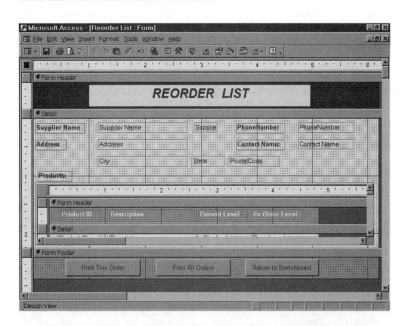

FIGURE 13.16
The completed Reorder List form.

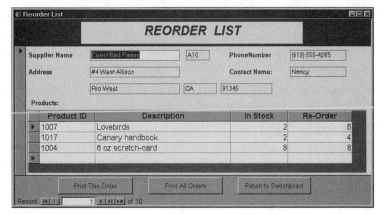

As you navigate through the supplier records, notice that some suppliers have no products in the subform. This form is meant to be used to add other products to the order lists as necessary, not to rely on the query to decide what and how much to order. For example, adding products that are approaching their reorder level to an order with other products from the same supplier can often save in shipping costs.

The event procedure that the Command Button Wizard creates prints all the records in the Order Products report by default. If you want to restrict the report to the current record, you must add a filter condition based on the Supplier Name field to the DoCmd.OpenReport statement. Copy the procedure to the PrintPO Click event procedure and add the filter. Be sure to change the references to the PrintAll Button control. With the filter, the event procedure contains the code shown in Listing 13.9.

Listing 13.9   Filtering Records Before Printing Purchase Orders

```
Private Sub Print_PO_Click()
On Error GoTo Err_Print_PO_Click

    Dim stDocName As String, stName As String
    Dim stFilter As String

    stName = [Supplier Name]
    stDocName = "Order Products"
    stFilter = "[Supplier Name] = " & "'" & stName & "'"

    DoCmd.OpenReport stDocName, acViewNormal, , stFilter

Exit_Print_PO_Click:
    Exit Sub

Err_Print_PO_Click:
    MsgBox Err.Description
    Resume Exit_Print_PO_Click

End Sub
```

The declaration statements create variables for the report name, the field to filter on, and the filter itself. The next three statements set the variable values before the DoCmd statement that prints the purchase order for the supplier currently displayed in the form view. Figure 13.17 shows the printed report for Coast Bird Farms.

The Print All Orders button's Click procedure requires no additional code statements added to the Command Button Wizard procedure.

DEVELOPMENT

The Order Products report design has some special features. To have each order print on a separate page, change the Force New Page property of the group footer to After Section. This moves to the next page after printing the data in the group footer.

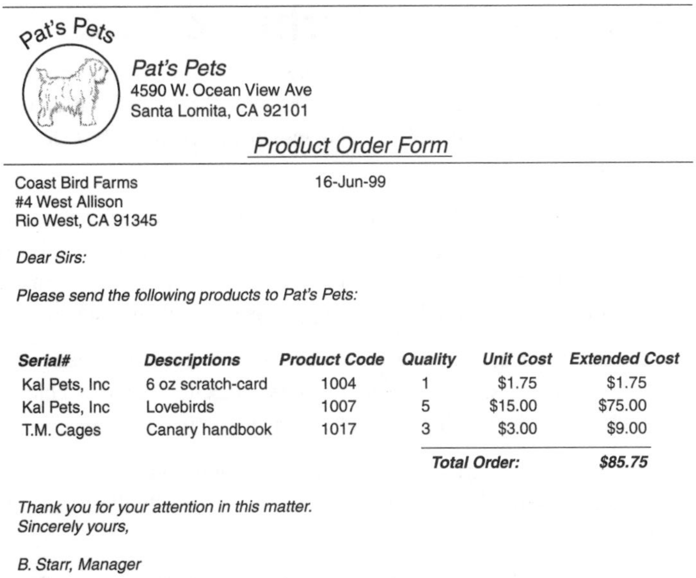

FIGURE **13.17**

A printed purchase order.

Pat's Pets
4590 W. Ocean View Ave
Santa Lomita, CA 92101

Product Order Form

Coast Bird Farms   16-Jun-99
#4 West Allison
Rio West, CA 91345

Dear Sirs:

Please send the following products to Pat's Pets:

Serial#	Descriptions	Product Code	Quality	Unit Cost	Extended Cost
Kal Pets, Inc	6 oz scratch-card	1004	1	$1.75	$1.75
Kal Pets, Inc	Lovebirds	1007	5	$15.00	$75.00
T.M. Cages	Canary handbook	1017	3	$3.00	$9.00
				Total Order:	**$85.75**

Thank you for your attention in this matter.
Sincerely yours,

B. Starr, Manager

> **Tip:** If you have any data in the page header and choose to print only the current record, the page header information will print again on a second page. To prevent this problem, place all the page header's text and controls in the group header. Figure 13.18 shows the Order Products report design with all the header information in the SupplierID group header.

FIGURE **13.18**

The Order Products report design.

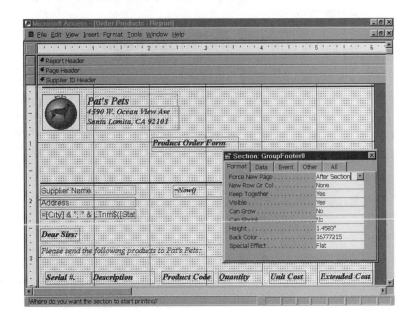

Summarizing Archived Data

Archiving information from the past helps plan for the future if the information is stored carefully and in an organized manner. The Pat's Pets store has been keeping track of sales data for several years by totaling monthly sales for each of the five major product categories.

The granularity of the data is sufficient to be able to arrange and analyze in several ways. For example, you can detect quarterly trends by grouping the monthly data in groups of three. In addition, you can analyze the growing or waning interest in a particular type of pet over the years. After all, you hardly see pot-bellied pigs anymore.

Sharp changes in the data over short periods of time can be traced to extraordinary events such as earthquakes, the invasion of a large competitor in the neighborhood, a new residential community developing nearby, or a change in management personnel.

More important for business decisions are the subtle changes that occur over time. The Access Chart Wizard is a good tool to use for graphically illustrating and comparing these trends.

LOOKING AHEAD

Another way to illustrate trends is to send the data to Excel for analysis and then import the results back to your report. Chapter 17, "Linking with Other Office Applications," includes several examples of exchanging data.

The report generated in this section is a dual-purpose report. It will print the details of the monthly sales figures for a five-year period or print only the yearly summaries. The same report design is used for both, and the required formatting changes are done at run-time by VB procedures. A pop-up form is also designed that will open either version of the report.

Create the Dual-Purpose Report

The Report Wizard is always a good place to start with a new report. The modified report design shows the records grouped by year with both the Year group header and footer (see Figure 13.19). Each detail line has two calculated fields at the right end of the section: the total amount of sales for that month and the percentage of the year's sales represented by that month. The Year group footer also contains calculated fields that total the sales for the whole year and compute the percentage of the year's sales that came from each product category.

> **Tip:** You can see in the design that the default Text*n* names are used in the Percent expressions. This is a little risky but it does save time.

Figure 13.20 shows the first page of a three-page preview of the Monthly Sales Summary report. This one has all the details for every month of the five-year period. To be able to use the same design for a report that summarizes the data and doesn't show the details, some changes need to be made to the report properties.

FIGURE 13.19
The PetSales report design.

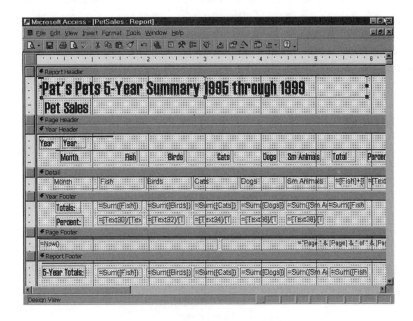

FIGURE 13.20
The first page of a preview of the Monthly Sales Summary report.

Pat's Pets 5-Year Summary 1995 through 1999
Pet Sales

Year 1995

Month	Fish	Birds	Cats	Dogs	Sm Animals	Total	Percent
Totals:	$3,900	$15,500	$15,610	$9,346	$1,311	$45,667	
Percent:	8.5%	33.9%	34.2%	20.5%	2.9%		

Year 1996

Month	Fish	Birds	Cats	Dogs	Sm Animals	Total	Percent
Totals:	$4,147	$11,478	$6,753	$8,472	$1,361	$32,211	
Percent:	12.9%	35.6%	21.0%	26.3%	4.2%		

Year 1997

Month	Fish	Birds	Cats	Dogs	Sm Animals	Total	Percent
Totals:	$5,378	$18,893	$15,758	$20,225	$1,217	$61,471	
Percent:	8.7%	30.7%	25.6%	32.9%	2.0%		

Year 1998

Month	Fish	Birds	Cats	Dogs	Sm Animals	Total	Percent
Totals:	$7,911	$29,325	$26,673	$27,383	$3,752	$95,044	
Percent:	8.3%	30.9%	28.1%	28.8%	3.9%		

Year 1999

Month	Fish	Birds	Cats	Dogs	Sm Animals	Total	Percent
Totals:	$10,307	$32,115	$22,259	$23,710	$4,791	$93,182	
Percent:	11.1%	34.5%	23.9%	25.4%	5.1%		

5-Year Tables:	$31,643	$107,311	$87,053	$89,136	$12,432	$327,575	

Determine the Differences

The first step is to make a list of how the two reports should differ. The most obvious difference is that the Detail section does not appear in the Annual Summary, only the subtotals for each year and the grand totals in the report footer. Also, it would look more professional if the column headings that refer to fields appearing only in the Detail section were removed from the Annual Summary version of the report. Finally, it's convenient to have a custom caption in the title bar for previewing reports that appear to be similar but are actually quite different.

Each section, control, and label in the report design has a name, even if it's only something like Label56. You use this name when you want to make changes. The sections are numbered, and when you want to change a section property, you refer to it by its index number, such as Section(3), which is the page header section. Table 13.1 shows the index numbers for the report sections.

Table 13.1   Report Sections and Their Index Numbers

Index	Section
0	Detail section
1	Report header
2	Report footer
3	Page header
4	Page footer
5	Group 1 header
6	Group 1 footer
7	Group 2 header
8	Group 2 footer

If you have more than two groups, their index numbers continue with 9 for the index for the Group 3 header, 10 for the Group 3 footer, and so on. To refer to the Detail section of the current report in VB code, use the following syntax:

```
Me.Section(0)
```

Create the Pop-Up Form

Before you start writing the code that will make the changes you need, create the form that will invoke the print previews. You must use the response from the pop-up form to determine which version of the report to display. The form is quite similar to the one used to choose which transaction report to preview, except it has only two options: Preview Monthly Sales and Preview Annual Sales (see Figure 13.21). The Preview button opens the report, and the value of the option selected in the option group is available to the Report_Open procedure.

FIGURE 13.21

Choose the report to preview from the pop-up form.

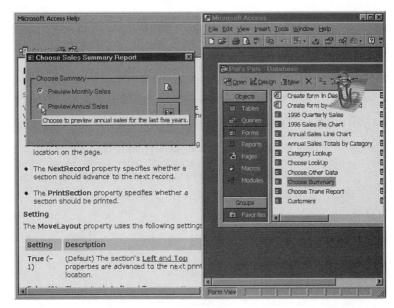

The only change you need to make in the code generated by the Form Wizard involves the Preview button's OnClick event. Because the form is a pop-up, you must close it before opening the report. Otherwise, it will stay on the screen in front of the report preview. To accomplish this, add the following statement to the event procedure:

```
Me.Visible = False
```

You make the rest of the changes after the report opens so that you make them in the report's Open event procedure.

Add to the Report's Open Event Procedure

With the report in design view, click the Code toolbar button. In the report class module, choose Report from the Objects box and Open from the Procedures box. Then, enter the code shown in Listing 13.10.

Listing 13.10   Setting Report Properties

```
Private Sub Report_Open(Cancel As Integer)
'Declare a variable for the option group value.
Dim intOpt As Integer
On Error GoTo Report_Open_Error

intOpt = Forms![Choose Summary]!ChooseSummary
    Select Case intOpt
```

continues

Listing 13.10 Continued

```
    Case 1      'Preview Monthly Sales, the first option.
       Me.Caption = "Monthly Sales Summary"
       Me.Section(0).Visible = True    'Show Detail section.
       Me.Label98.Visible = True       'Show Month column label.
       Me.Label97.Visible = True       'Show Percent column label.

    Case 2      'Preview Annual Sales, the second option.
       Me.Caption = "Annual Sales Summary"
       Me.Section(0).Visible = False   'Hide Detail section.
       Me.Label98.Visible = False      'Hide Month column label.
       Me.Label97.Visible = False      'Hide Percent column label.
    End Select

Exit Sub

Report_Open_Error:
    MsgBox Err.Description
    Exit Sub

End Sub
```

The statement

```
intOpt = Forms![Choose Summary]!ChooseSummary
```

sets the value of the integer variable to the value of the selected option in the
ChooseSummary option group in the Choose Summary form. This value is used in the
Select Case structure.

The first Case statement executes if the option group returns 1. It sets the report preview
caption to Monthly Sales Summary. Then, it sets the Detail section's and the Month and
Percent column labels' Visible properties to True. The second Case statement executes if
the option group returns 2. This changes the caption and reverses the other settings so
that the Detail section and the two column labels do not appear. If you want to get into
precise report design, you could change the length and weight of some of the lines or
change any other control properties.

After adding the procedure to the report class module, close the report design and open
the form in form view. Make a choice from the option group to see the report preview.
Figure 13.22 shows a preview of the Annual Sales Summary opened by choosing
Preview Annual Sales in the Choose Transaction Report form. Notice the caption text
that's set by the event procedure code.

> **Note:** Unless you need to change report properties at runtime, use the control
> and report property sheets. It's faster to set them in the property sheets because
> they don't need to be compiled every time the report is previewed.

FIGURE 13.22

Previewing the Annual Sales Summary report.

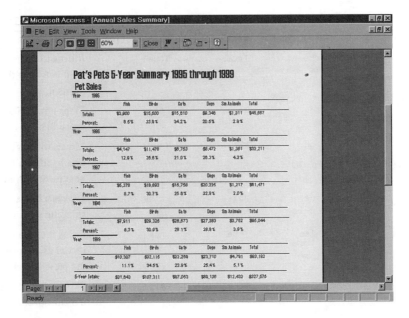

LOOKING AHEAD These reports can be greatly enhanced with charts and graphs that visually represent trends and fluctuations. In Chapter 14, "Adding Real-time Features," some charts are added to this and other reports.

Combining Report Runtime Properties

Access reports have three other runtime properties that you can combine in VB to create a template for printing the report. They change the report's layout when it's previewed, printed, or copied to a file for printing later. The MoveLayout property indicates whether to move to the next printing location on the page. The NextRecord property indicates whether a section should move to the next record. The PrintSection indicates whether to print the section.

All three of these properties are set to True by default and are reset to True before the Format event of each section. To change one of these settings, attach a macro or event procedure to the OnFormat event of the section.

These properties are used in combination with varying results, as shown in Table 13.2.

The True/False/True combination can be used when the data in a section exceeds the space allowed in the layout. This permits the data to be printed in the space that would normally be occupied by the next section. Because the NextRecord property is set to False, no record is omitted, just postponed.

Table 13.2   The Effects of Combining the Runtime Property Settings

MoveLayout	NextRecord	PrintSection	*Result*
True	True	True	Moves to the next print location; gets next the record and prints it.
True	True	False	Skips a record and leaves the space blank.
True	False	True	Moves to the next print location but doesn't advance to the next record. Prints the data.
True	False	False	Leaves a blank space without skipping a record.
False	True	True	Prints the data in the current record as an overlay on top of the previous record.
False	True	False	Skips a record without leaving a blank space.
False	False	True	Not permitted.
False	False	False	Not permitted.

Summary

Even though there's not a lot of interaction between the user and reports, there are many things that can be done behind the scenes in a report's design that can change the way it looks and behaves. This chapter has touched on a few of the ways you can program Access to customize reports.

Adding Real-Time Features

The last three chapters have provided nearly all the pieces of the Pat's Pets puzzle. All that remains is to tie everything together with a single point of user entry to the database and to add some additional Visual Basic code to handle the transaction-processing feature. This chapter completes the application by creating a switchboard with options that branch to all the capabilities required of the database.

Top-Down Versus Bottom-Up Implementation

Systems analysts are split into two schools of thought about implementing a database application: the top-down approach and the bottom-up approach.

DEVELOPMENT

With the top-down implementation process, the first piece that's developed is the user interface, a switchboard, or other tool from which the user can select what to do next. This switchboard contains all the options, but they're not linked to any form, report, or procedure at this stage. Next, the branching elements are created that give the user additional options, such as which form to open and which report to preview. Finally, the forms and reports are created, which are, in turn, linked to the choices made in the branching tools.

A top-down analysis of the Pat's Pets inventory control system yields the information management structure described in Table 14.1.

Table 14.1 A Top-Down Analysis of the Pat's Pets Application

Top Layer	Second Layer	Third Layer
Enter/Edit data	Transaction data	(none)
	Product data	
	Supplier data	
	Customer data	

continues

Table 14.1 Continued

Top Layer	Second Layer	Third Layer
Preview data	Transaction data	Summarized by supplier
		Summarized by number
		Summarized by type
	List of suppliers	
	Summary of current inventory	By product code
		By category
		By value
	Sales summaries	Monthly
		Quarterly
		Annually
Look up specific information	Product categories	
	Suppliers	
	List of shortages	Print purchase orders
Update inventory with recent transactions	(none)	(none)

Although the top-down approach is valid for analysis, it's difficult to put into practice with Access because of the wizards. When you add an option group to the switchboard, the wizard wants to know to what object the selection applies (that is, which report to open for preview or which form to open for data entry). If you haven't created these objects yet, it's difficult to use the wizards.

Starting at the Bottom

With the bottom-up approach, the implementation starts at the lowest level and works its way up, combining the elements into option groups. This method is more convenient with Access because the wizards are a big help with the option groups, command buttons, and other controls you need to make the application operate smoothly.

After defining all (or nearly all) the input and output requirements of the application, you begin by designing the forms and reports, grouped together by data or activity. Much of this has been accomplished in the previous three chapters.

Accumulating the Form and Report Objects

Each table in the database usually has a separate data entry form, but you might be able to combine two tables into one entry form. For example, to add a new category, you can add it to the combo box list while entering new products in the Products form. The Transaction Log, Supplier Form, and Products data entry forms were created in Chapter 12, "Customizing Data Entry." To round out the data entry for the retail store application, the Customers data entry form is added to the database. This can be used later for mailing promotional material or for reminding customers of upcoming events (see Figure 14.1).

FIGURE 14.1
*The new
Customers data
entry form.*

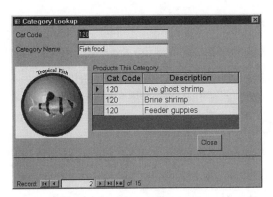

Some additional forms would be useful for looking up specific data, such as the product list grouped by category, the suppliers listed together with the products they provide to the store, and a list of the products in low supply. The Category Lookup form is composed of a form based on the Category table and a subform with data from the Products table. Records in the form and subform are linked by the Cat Code field in both the parent and child recordsets (see Figure 14.2).

FIGURE 14.2
*The Category
Lookup form.*

The Supplier Product List form was introduced in Chapter 11, "Creating an Application from an Existing Database." It shows information about each supplier in the form with a subform that contains details of their products. The Reorder List form was created in Chapter 13, "Customizing the Reports," using a similar layout as the Supplier Product List form, but using the results of a query as the record source for the subform. The query selects products whose In Stock value is less than or equal to the reorder quantity.

The product fields are also slightly different: the Supplier Product List form shows the Product ID, Description, Unit Cost, and Sell Price fields; the Reorder List form shows In Stock and Reorder field quantities instead of cost and price. It also has buttons to print one or more purchase orders using the Order Products report.

Several of the necessary reports such as the following were developed in Chapter 13:

- *Transactions by Supplier*. Groups all purchases by supplier and shows totals for the individual suppliers as well as a running total over all.

- *Transactions by Number*. Lists all transactions in the table and shows a Confidential watermark on each page. The Comment label is not printed if there's no text in the Comment field. The detail section is allowed to shrink to close up the space.

- *Transaction by Type*. Separates sales from receipts and shrinkage and lists all the details of the transaction.

- *Product Summary*. Summarizes products within their category, prints some quantities in bold if the stock levels are low, and counts the number of products in the category and the number that needs to be ordered.

- *Product List by Category*. A simple report grouped by product category with no added calculated fields.

- *Order Products*. The report used to print purchase orders from the Reorder List form. This report is not called by itself but rather through the Reorder List form.

- *Inventory Summary*. Totals the value of the products in stock in each category and provides a grand total.

- *PetSales*. The report design used for both monthly and annual sales summaries.

The only report that's missing is the Quarterly Sales Summary. A table containing sales summarized by quarter was prepared separately for this report from the same sales data as the other reports. The Quarterly Sales Summary report design resembles the monthly sales report (see Figure 14.3). A preview of the report is shown in Figure 14.4.

Building Option Pop-Up Forms

With all the lowest-level objects built, it's time to arrange them into logical groups and link them to a pop-up form showing a list of options for the user to choose from. Two of these pop-up forms were developed in Chapter 13, "Customizing the Reports," for choosing which transaction or which sales summary report to preview.

Entering new transactions is likely the most frequently performed task, so it will stand alone in the main switchboard and not require the user to take time choosing from a secondary option box. Entering data in the other database tables can be lumped together into one pop-up form. Reviewing miscellaneous reports and looking up specific information can also be conveniently grouped into separate pop-up forms.

FIGURE 14.3
The Quarterly Sales Summary report design.

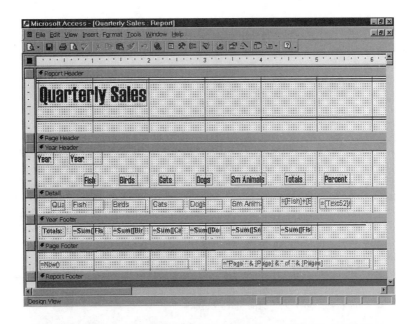

FIGURE 14.4
Preview of the Quarterly Sales Summary report.

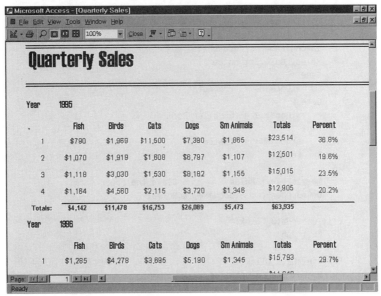

The pop-up form used to choose which table to enter data into contains three choices: Enter/Edit Products, Enter/Edit Suppliers, and Enter/Edit Customers (see Figure 14.5).

FIGURE 14.5

The Choose Other Data pop-up form.

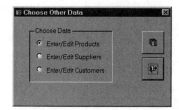

If the user requires more help in using the form, you could add "and Click Open form" to the Choose Data option group label. Use the name of the option group in the Click event procedure for the Open Form command button which is named "OtherData." When you add the command button with the help of the Command Button Wizard, you can choose only one form to open. Then you must change the code to include the options in the option group. Listing 14.1 shows the Click event procedure for the OtherData button.

Listing 14.1 The OtherData Button's Click Event Procedure

```
Private Sub OtherData_Click()
On Error GoTo Err_OtherData_Click

    Dim stDocName As String
    Dim intChoice As Integer

    intChoice = Me!ChooseData
    Select Case intChoice
    Case 1
        stDocName = "Products"
    Case 2
        stDocName = "Supplier Form"
    Case 3
        stDocName = "Customers"
    End Select

    Me.Visible = False          'Close the popup form.
    DoCmd.OpenForm stDocName, acNormal

Exit_OtherData_Click:
    Exit Sub

Err_OtherData_Click:
    MsgBox Err.Description
    Resume Exit_OtherData_Click

End Sub
```

ANALYSIS

The procedure uses both variables in the Select Case structure. The intChoice variable is set to the value of the option selected in the option group, and the stDocName variable is the name of the form to be opened. The pop-up form is a modal form and remains visible in front of the newly opened form unless you set its Visible property to False before the data entry form is opened.

Miscellaneous reports that may be of interest but are accessed less frequently can be grouped together into another pop-up form. The Preview Other Reports pop-up form includes four reports that list suppliers, current stock levels, categorized products, and the current inventory value (see Figure 14.6).

FIGURE 14.6

The Preview Other Reports pop-up form.

The event procedure for the Preview button's Click event, shown in Listing 14.2, is similar to that for the OtherData button. They both use a Select Case structure to define the string variable stDocName, with the integer variable intChoice set to the value of the selected option in the option group. Once again, the form's Visible property is set to False before the report preview is opened.

Listing 14.2 The Preview Button's Click Event Procedure

```
Private Sub Preview_Click()
On Error GoTo Err_Preview_Click

    Dim stDocName As String, intChoice As Integer
    intChoice = ChooseReport
    Select Case intChoice
        Case 1
            stDocName = "Supplier Lookup"

        Case 2
            stDocName = "Product Summary"

        Case 3
            stDocName = "Product List by Category"

        Case 4
            stDocName = "Inventory Summary"

    End Select
    Me.Visible = False
```

continues

Listing 14.2   Continued

```
    DoCmd.OpenReport stDocName, acPreview

Exit_Preview_Click:
    Exit Sub

Err_Preview_Click:
    MsgBox Err.Description
    Resume Exit_Preview_Click

End Sub
```

Three additional forms that can be used for looking up specific information are grouped together in a pop-up form (see Figure 14.7). The information they provide includes the product categories with their specific items (refer to Figure 14.1), suppliers and all their products, and suppliers with products that are in short supply. This last form (the Reorder form) is used to print the purchase orders with the Order Products report.

FIGURE 14.7
The Choose LookUp pop-up form.

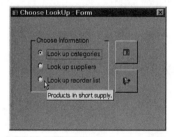

The event procedure for the Open Form button is the same as that for the Choose Other Data pop-up form, except for the names of the forms to open. All these pop-up forms also have a Close or Cancel button with the following Click event procedure that closes the form and maximizes the switchboard or other window onscreen:

```
Private Sub Cancel_Click()
On Error GoTo Err_Cancel_Click

    DoCmd.Close
    DoCmd.Maximize

Exit_Cancel_Click:
    Exit Sub

Err_Cancel_Click:
    MsgBox Err.Description
    Resume Exit_Cancel_Click

End Sub
```

Transaction Posting and Archiving Procedure

Posting transactions involves adding or subtracting the quantity of the product in the transaction to or from the in-stock quantity in the Products table. The easiest way to do this is to build a query that relates the Transactions and Products tables and filters the resulting recordset to those records whose Posted field is False. Then, working with the query results, the posting procedure can update the values and set Posted to True. Here's the Post Query SQL statement:

```
SELECT DISTINCTROW Products.[Product ID], Products.[In Stock],
Transactions.Quantity, Transactions.Type, Transactions.Posted,
Transactions.[Transaction No], Transactions.Date
FROM Products INNER JOIN Transactions ON Products.[Product ID] =
Transactions.[Product ID]
WHERE (((Transactions.Posted)=False))
ORDER BY Products.[Product ID];
```

TROUBLESHOOTING

One way to begin to write and test the code for this procedure without interfering with the actual data is to make copies of the Transactions and Products tables using different names, or to copy them to another database and work there. The trigger for the procedure can be a command button on an otherwise blank form. After you're satisfied that the procedure executes correctly, you can attach the code to an option in the switchboard.

Transaction Processing

This event procedure uses the trilogy of transaction methods: BeginTrans, CommitTrans, and Rollback. These methods are used to manage transaction processing during a session defined by a workspace object. Recall that a workspace object is a member of the Workspaces collection of the DBEngine. A workspace contains open databases, connections, groups, and users. You refer to the workspace by its name or index number. Here'are two examples:

```
DBEngine.Workspaces("MyWork")
```

and

```
DBEngine.Workspaces(0)
```

> **Technical Note:** The transactions referred to by BeginTrans and CommitTrans are the changes made to the recordset, not to be confused with the sales and receipt transactions in the pet store.

DEVELOPMENT

Using the transaction methods helps to maintain the integrity of the database by ensuring that all the changes have been completed (committed) for all the affected tables. If an error occurs during the transaction processing, the changes are undone (rolled back).

After you've committed the transactions, they cannot be rolled back. If you close the workspace object while some transactions are still pending, all the changes are automatically rolled back.

BeginTrans starts a new transaction, and CommitTrans ends the current transaction and saves all the changes to the table. Rollback ends the current transaction and restores the table to its original condition before the transactions began. Using these methods treats many data updates as a single process, which saves time and space.

Archiving Records

PERFORMANCE

A table such as the Transactions table will reach infinite proportions if it's not purged now and then. If you're not interested in the historical information, you can simply delete the old records. In this case, however, the management at Pat's Pets wants to maintain historical sales records in an effort to improve store performance. A procedure can extract transaction records that have been posted and are no longer of immediate interest and then copy them to an archive table. After safely archiving the information, the procedure can remove the same records from the Transactions table.

The archiving code is combined as a subroutine in this procedure with the posting procedure. They would normally be carried out at the same time in the store. After the transaction posting is completed, the user is asked whether he or she wants to go ahead and archive older records. If the response is Yes, the user is asked to enter a cutoff date. Two action queries are then run using SQL statements: the first is an append query that uses the INSERT INTO clause to copy the records to the archive; the second uses the DELETE clause to remove the same records from the Transactions table.

> **Note:** When constructing the Archive query, you can use Transactions* in the SQL statement to include all the fields in the table, even the AutoNumber primary key field. Access takes care of it when you archive records and makes sure that no two records have the same Transaction ID value.

The user can run the archiving procedure even if there are no records to post. After displaying a message that there are no records to post, the procedure branches to the question about archiving.

> **Tip:** It's generally faster to run an action query saved as a query than to embed the SQL statement in VB code. In this case, however, the user would be prompted twice for a cutoff date—one for the append query and one for the delete query. This could possibly result in a difference between the number of records archived and deleted which can endanger database integrity.

The Sub Post Procedure VB Code

The full procedure is included in Listing 14.3, and the paragraphs that follow explain some of its segments of code. The Post button is in an otherwise empty form for development purposes. Later the code can be attached to an item in the switchboard.

Listing 14.3 The Post Button's Click Event Procedure

```
Private Sub Post_Click()
'Automatically posts transactions and updates Products InStock
'value. Then offers to archive records before specified date.

Dim wrkDefault As Object
Dim rstPost As Object, dbsCurrent As Object
Dim rstArchive As Object
Dim intBefore As Integer, intAfter As Integer
Dim intCount As Integer, blnInTrans As Boolean
Dim varReturn As Variant, stMsg As String
Dim stSQLArchive As String, stSQLDelete As String
Dim dtmCutOff As Date, intchoice As Integer

On Error GoTo Err_Post_Click

blnInTrans = False
Set wrkDefault = DBEngine.Workspaces(0)
Set dbsCurrent = CurrentDb()
Set rstPost = dbsCurrent.OpenRecordset("Post Query")
Set rstArchive = dbsCurrent.OpenRecordset("Transaction Archive")

'Check for empty recordset and if so, display a message,
'close the recordset and exit the procedure.

If rstPost.RecordCount = 0 Then
    MsgBox ("No transactions to post")
    GoTo ArchiveTrans
End If

'Start of transaction and set blnInTrans to True.
wrkDefault.BeginTrans
blnInTrans = True
'Move to the first record.
rstPost.MoveFirst

'Set the counter to 0 and start the Do Until loop.
'Display message in status bar.
stMsg = "Posting transactions, please wait..."
varReturn = SysCmd(acSysCmdSetStatus, stMsg)
intCount = 0
```

continues

Listing 14.3   Continued

```
With rstPost

Do Until .EOF
    If ![Type] = "Receipt" Then
        .Edit
        ![In Stock] = ![In Stock] + ![Quantity]
    Else                    'The transaction is either sale or shrink.
        .Edit
        ![In Stock] = ![In Stock] - ![Quantity]
    End If
    ![Posted] = True
    .Update
    intCount = intCount + 1
    .MoveNext
Loop

'Remove message from the status bar.
varReturn = SysCmd(acSysCmdClearStatus)

If MsgBox("Save all changes?", vbQuestion + vbYesNo, _
    " Save changes") = vbYes Then
    wrkDefault.CommitTrans         'Commit the transactions.
'Display the number of transactions posted and close form.
    MsgBox (intCount & " transactions posted")
Else
    wrkDefault.Rollback            'Undo the updates.
End If

'"".Close

End With

'Subroutine to archive transactions and delete them from
'the Transactions table.

ArchiveTrans:
intchoice = MsgBox("Do you want to archive transactions now?", _
    vbYesNo + vbQuestion, "Archive?")
If intchoice = 7 Then
    GoTo Exit_Post_Click
Else
    'Count number of records in the Transaction Archive
    'and request a cutoff date.
    intBefore = rstArchive.RecordCount
    dtmCutOff = InputBox("Please enter cutoff date.", "Cutoff Date")

'Turn off the Access warning message.
DoCmd.SetWarnings False

    stSQLArchive = "INSERT INTO [Transaction Archive] " & _
```

```
            "SELECT Transactions.* FROM Transactions " & _
            "WHERE ((Transactions.Date)<= #" & dtmCutOff & "# " & _
            "AND (Transactions.Posted)=True);"
        DoCmd.RunSQL (stSQLArchive)

        stSQLDelete = "DELETE Transactions.* FROM Transactions " & _
            "WHERE ((Transactions.Date)<= #" & dtmCutOff & "# " & _
            "AND (Transactions.Posted)=True);"
        DoCmd.RunSQL (stSQLDelete)

'Compute and display number of records archived.
    rstArchive.MoveLast
    intAfter = rstArchive.RecordCount
    intCount = intAfter - intBefore
    MsgBox (intCount & " transactions were archived")

'Reset the warning message.
DoCmd.SetWarnings True
End If

Exit_Post_Click:
    Exit Sub

Err_Post_Click:
    MsgBox Err.Description
    Resume Exit_Post_Click

End Sub
```

ANALYSIS

First, the Declarations section declares the following variables, which are set in subsequent statements:

- wrkDefault is declared as the current workspace, set to DBEngine.Workspaces(0) (the first workspace in the collection).

- dbsCurrent is declared as the active database, set to CurrentDB().

- rstPost is declared as the recordset that results from the Post query.

- rstArchive is declared as the Transaction Archive recordset to which the archived records will be appended.

- intBefore is declared as an integer that stores the number of records in the Transaction Archive table before executing the archiving process.

- intAfter is declared as an integer that stores the number of records in the Transaction Archive table after appending the archived records.

- intCount is declared as an integer that's used to count the number of transactions posted or archived.

- blnInTrans is declared as a Boolean value representing the status of the transaction processing.

- varReturn is declared as the Variant value used with the SysCmd() function to display text in the status bar while the transactions are being processed.
- stMsg is declared as the message to display in the status bar during the transaction process.
- stSQLArchive is declared as the SQL statement to use for the archive action query.
- stSQLDelete is declared as the SQL statement to use for the delete action query.
- dtmCutOff is declared as the date entered by the user to be used as the criterion for both queries.
- intChoice is declared as the integer response to whether to archive records now.

Next, the If…Then segment checks for an empty recordset resulting from running the Post query. If there are no records that meet the query criteria (Posted = False), a message is displayed and control is sent to the ArchiveTrans subroutine (described later). If the recordset is not empty, the transaction begins, the transaction status is set to True, and the cursor moves to the first record in the recordset:

```
wrkDefault.BeginTrans
blnInTrans = True
rstPost.MoveFirst
```

The following two lines use the SysCmd() function to set the status bar text:

```
stMsg = "Posting transactions, please wait..."
varReturn = SysCmd(asSysCmdSetStatus, stMsg)
```

This function can also be used to display a progress meter in the status bar instead of text. There are many other intrinsic constants that you can use with the SysCmd() function to return the state of Access or one of the Access objects.

Next, the intCount counter is initialized to zero and the rstPost recordset is set as the current object with the With statement. The Do Until loop then begins processing the statements between Do Until and Loop, until the end of the rstPost file is reached:

```
With rstPost
Do Until .EOF
    If ![Type] = "Receipt" Then
        .Edit
        ![In Stock] = ![In Stock] + ![Quantity]
    Else                    'The transaction is either sale or shrinkage.
        .Edit
        ![In Stock] = ![In Stock] - ![Quantity]
    End If
    ![Posted] = True
    .Update
    intCount = intCount + 1
    .MoveNext
Loop
```

The If…Then structure first asks whether the Type field contains "Receipt." If so, the Edit method is used to copy the record to a buffer for editing. Then, the Quantity value from the Transactions record is added to the In Stock field's value from the Products table.

If the transaction is not a receipt, it's either a sale or shrinkage, both of which will decrease the In Stock field's quantity. Therefore, the Else clause subtracts the Quantity value from the In Stock value. The Edit method is used again to edit the In Stock field from the Products table.

The next three statements change the Posted value to True, use the Update method to put the updated record back in the recordset, and increment the counter. Then, the MoveNext method moves to the next record. If MoveNext moves past the last record, the EOF property changes to True and the loop stops.

The varReturn statement removes the text from the status bar, and a message box asks if the user wants to save all the changes made during the transaction processing. If the user responds Yes, the transactions are committed and another message box displays the number of transactions that were posted (see Figure 14.8). If the user responds No, the transactions are rolled back and the recordset is restored to its original condition. The rstPost recordset is then closed, and the End With statement closes the With block.

FIGURE 14.8
A message box shows the number of transactions posted.

After completing the posting, the procedure enters the ArchiveTrans subroutine and asks if the user wants to archive records now. If the response is No (value 7), the procedure ends. If Yes, the user is asked to enter the cutoff date for the action queries, and the intCount variable is set to the number of records currently in the Transaction Archive table. After the archive process, the number of records added is computed.

The first SQL statement performs an append query using the INSERT INTO statement. The query extracts records from the Transactions table whose Date field values are earlier than the date entered in the input box and appends them to a table named Transaction Archive:

```
stSQLArchive = "INSERT INTO [Transaction Archive] " & _
    "SELECT Transactions.* FROM Transactions " & _
    "WHERE ((Transactions.Date)<= #" & dtmCutOff & "# " & _
    "AND (Transactions.Posted)=True);"
DoCmd.RunSQL (stSQLArchive)
```

The second SQL statement deletes the same records from the Transactions table:

```
stSQLDelete = "DELETE Transactions.* FROM Transactions " & _
    "WHERE ((Transactions.Date)<= #" & dtmCutOff & "# " & _
    "AND (Transactions.Posted)=True);"
DoCmd.RunSQL (stSQLDelete)
```

After the SQL queries have run, the next four statements compute the number of records that were added to the archive and displays the result in a message box:

```
rstArchive.MoveLast
intAfter = rstArchive.RecordCount
intCount = intAfter - intBefore
MsgBox (intCount & " transactions were archived")
```

> **Warning:** Both these queries prompt a warning message to the user. It's important to turn these messages off before the queries begin. If you do not turn them off, the user might accept one of the operations and not the other, which results in inconsistent tables. Use DoCmd.SetWarnings False to turn them off, but be sure to turn them back on with DoCmd.SetWarnings True right after the queries are run.

After the warning messages are reset, the procedure exits.

Creating the Main Switchboard

After you've built all the necessary option pop-up forms and procedures, the next step is to create a main switchboard that serves as the single point of entry into the application. The user chooses from the list of options to accomplish an inventory task. When the task is completed, control always returns to the main switchboard.

You saw what the Switchboard Manager was able to do with the *Omni-Sport* switchboard in Chapter 4, "Creating an Application with a Wizard." You can use the same tool to create a switchboard for the Pat's Pets inventory control system now that you have all the pieces completed.

> **Tip:** If you know you're going to have to make a lot of changes to the switchboard the Switchboard Manager builds, you're better off creating the switchboard yourself from a blank form. You'll see how to do this in Chapter 16, "Customizing Input and Output."

Using the Switchboard Manager

You used the Switchboard Manager in Chapter 5, "Examining and Modifying the Wizard's Code," to make changes in the Database Wizard's switchboards by choosing the Change Switchboard Items option on the switchboard itself. Creating a new switchboard is not much different.

Most of the switchboard items you need for Pat's Pets will open one of the forms you created in Chapter 13, "Customizing the Reports," such as the form to choose which sales summary to preview. Two of the options involve running procedures: Post Transactions and Return to Access.

To start the Switchboard Manager, choose Tools|Database Utilities|Switchboard Manager. The Switchboard Manager dialog box shows a single entry: Main Switchboard (Default). After you create the switchboard, you can copy the Post_Click event procedure into the Global Module and change the name to Public Function Post, because it will not be an event procedure but rather a function called by the HandlebuttonClick() function that the Switchboard Manager wrote. More information about adding this function to the Global Module is in the section, "Finishing the Switchboard" later in this chapter.

For the Return to Access switchboard option, you can write a simple macro that closes the switchboard form. You can also have the macro maximize the database window, if you want.

To add items to the empty switchboard page, follow these steps:

1. Choose Edit to open the Edit Switchboard Page dialog box (see Figure 14.9). There are no items on the switchboard yet.

FIGURE 14.9
The Edit Switchboard Page dialog box.

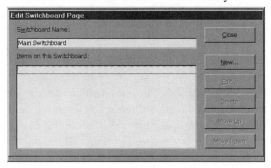

2. Click New to open the New Switchboard item dialog box, where you enter the text and the commands for each of the switchboard items.

3. Type **Enter or edit transaction data** as the text for the first item; then choose Open Form in Edit Mode from the list of nine standard commands.

4. Select Transaction Log from the list of form names in your database (see Figure 14.10). Then click OK. If you had chosen a command to preview or print a report, the list would have contained the names of all the reports in the database.

5. Repeat steps 2 through 4 to specify the items shown in Table 14.2.

6. After entering all the items, choose Close twice to return to the database window.

FIGURE 14.10
Entering an item in the Edit Switchboard Item dialog box.

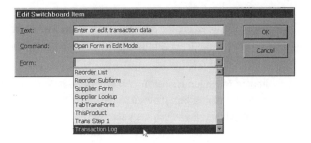

Table 14.2 Switchboard Item Specifications

Text	Command	Argument
Enter or edit transaction data	Open Form in Edit Mode	Transaction Log
Enter or edit other data	Open Form in Edit Mode	Choose Other Data
Preview transactions	Open Form in Edit Mode	Choose Trans Report
Preview other reports	Open Form in Edit Mode	Preview Other Reports
Look up information	Open Form in Edit Mode	Choose Lookup
Sales analysis	Open Form in Edit Mode	Choose Summary
Post transactions	Run Code	Post
Return to Access database	Run Code	Return_to_Access

If you look now in the Tables tab of the Pat's Pets database window, you'll see the new table named Switchboard Items that the Switchboard Manager has created, based on your input to the Switchboard Manager dialog boxes. Now move to the Forms page and open the new Switchboard form in form view (see Figure 14.11). You'll probably want to make a few changes to the appearance of the form, such as adding the store logo and adding a button that quits Access altogether.

FIGURE 14.11
The new switchboard after the Switchboard Manager is finished.

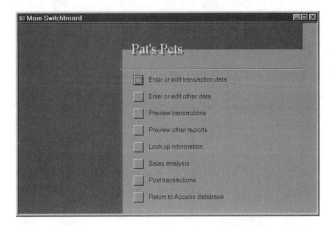

Making Changes to the Switchboard

First, increase the length of the title, which now shows only "Pat's Pets" (the name of the database), and add **Inventory Control**. Then add a label as a subtitle, if desired.

Next, add the company picture logo to the upper-left corner. Choose Insert|Picture and locate the !1_logoa.pcx file in the Images folder on the CD that accompanies this book and insert it into your form. Resize the picture to fit the space and change its Size Mode property to Stretch.

Now add a command button that quits Access by using the Command Button Wizard. Choose Application from the Categories list and Quit Application from the Actions list. Following the style set so far in this application, use the text "Quit Access" on the button. Figure 14.12 shows the completed switchboard form.

FIGURE 14.12
The Pat's Pets switchboard.

Finishing the Switchboard

The Post_Click procedure was developed as an event procedure for a button on a blank form. Copy this procedure to the Global Module and change the first line to Public Function Post(). Remember to change the On Error GoTo, Exit, and Err lines, as well to remove the Click reference. The End Sub line is automatically changed to End Function when you change the first line of code from a sub procedure to a function.

Next, create a new macro to close the form and return to the Access database window. Select Close as the action, Form as the Object Type argument and Switchboard as the Object Name argument. You can add the Maximize action to maximize the Access database window, if you like.

Return to the form view and check out each item on the switchboard. Make any necessary changes.

Tip: If you have trouble getting the item that calls the function to work, you can always create Click event procedures using the code you have and attach them to both the button and the label in the switchboard.

Customizing the Command Bar

The options represented by the buttons on the switchboard can also be made available through a custom command bar. Access 2000 has tools for creating custom menu bars and toolbars. Menu bars and toolbars are grouped together and called *command bars*. When you've started a custom menu bar, you can add your own commands to it as well as any of the hundreds of Access built-in menu commands. Access also enables you to change the properties of menu items, such as to show only icons, icons and text, or only text. You can also add ToolTip text and Help text associated with a What's This? button.

To create a custom menu bar for the Pat's Pets application, perform the following steps:

1. Right-click any toolbar or menu bar and choose Customize from the shortcut menu. You can also point to Toolbars in the View menu and click Customize. The Customize dialog box opens with three tabs: Toolbars, Commands, and Options.

2. In the Toolbars tab, click New and then enter **Pat's Pets** for the name of the menu bar; then click OK. A small menu bar appears in front of the Customize dialog box, and the new menu bar is added to the bottom of the list, as shown in Figure 14.13.

FIGURE 14.13
Starting the Pat's Pets custom menu bar.

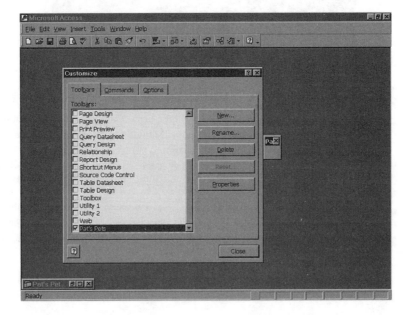

3. With the Pat's Pets menu selected, click Properties and choose Menu Bar from the Type box in the Toolbar Properties dialog box; then choose Close. Your other options for the command bar type are Toolbar and Popup.

4. Reposition the new menu bar and the Customize dialog box so you can see both at once; then open the Commands tab. Scroll down the Categories list and select New Menu.

5. Drag New Menu from the Commands list (not the Categories list) to the new menu bar and drop it in the bar. Right-click the new menu item and type the name you want in the Name box in the shortcut menu (see Figure 14.14). The first menu item is Enter Data, so type **&Enter Data** in the shortcut menu. The ampersand (&) designates the next character as the access key for the menu command.

Figure 14.14

Adding and naming a new menu item.

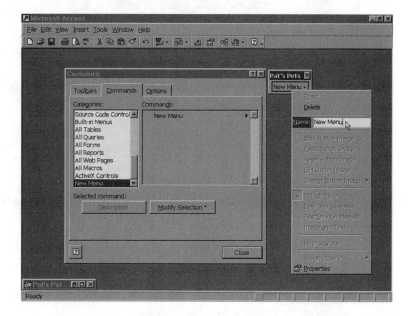

6. Repeat step 5 to add and rename the other new menu items. Then, scroll up in the Categories list and select Built-in Menus. Drag Tools from the Commands list to the end of the new menu bar.

Once you have added the menu items to the new command bar, it's time to add commands to the menu so that something happens when you click an item. You can also add submenus to a new menu item that can contain additional commands.

1. Click the Enter Data menu item and a small empty box appears just below it. This is where the menu commands will be placed.

2. The Enter Data menu item opens a variety of data entry forms, so select All Forms in the Categories list. The Commands list now shows the names of all the forms in

the Pat's Pets database. Drag and drop Transaction Log from the Commands list to the submenu box. Right-click the new item and remove the word *Log* from the name and add an ampersand (&) before the *T* to assign an access key.

3. Repeat step 2 to place the other form commands in the submenu box. Change their text from the form name to something consistent and understandable, if necessary. Figure 14.15 shows the completed Enter Data menu item.

Figure 14.15
Adding commands to a custom menu.

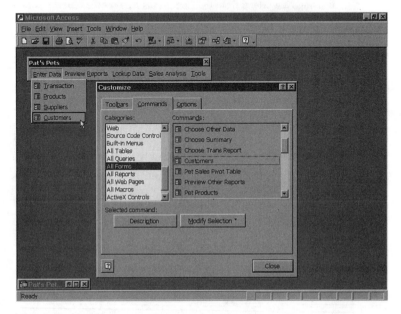

4. The Preview Reports menu presents a special case: The Transactions report has three different layouts. This calls for another New Menu item with lower-level submenu commands. Drag a New Menu item to the box below Preview Reports and name it **&Transactions**. Next, click the right-pointing arrow to add a small box to the right of the Transactions item.

5. Select the All Reports category and drag and drop the three transaction report names from the Commands list to the new box. Right-click Suppliers in the menu list and choose Begin a Group from the shortcut menu. This places a line above Suppliers, separating the rest of the reports from Transactions. Figure 14.16 shows the completed Preview Reports menu.

6. Finish adding the remaining menu commands and then drag the menu to the top of the screen to dock it.

Command bar items have many properties that you can change to create the appearance and behavior you want. The shortcut menu contains properties that can change the appearance of the menu item (see Figure 14.17). Choose Properties from the shortcut menu to open the Pat's Pets Control Properties dialog box, where you can add Help text, specify a macro or function procedure that will run when the item is selected, or specify other runtime properties (see Figure 14.18). Table 14.3 describes these properties.

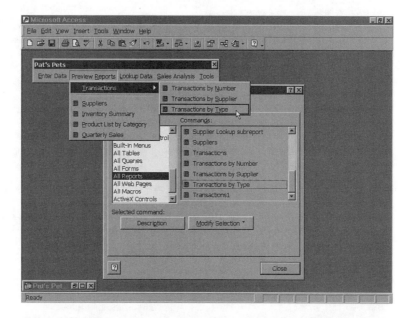

FIGURE 14.16
Creating a sub-menu.

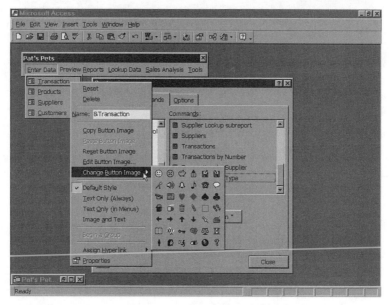

FIGURE 14.17
Select from the shortcut menu to change the menu item appearance.

FIGURE 14.18

Use the Properties dialog box to change other menu control properties.

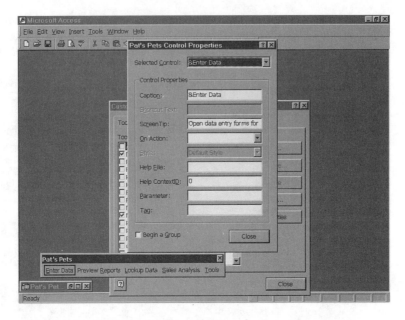

Table 14.3   Pat's Pets Menu Bar Control Properties

Property	Description
Caption	The text that appears in the menu bar.
Shortcut Text	The shortcut key or key combination that activates the menu item, such as ^K or ^F3. You can create an AutoKey macro to carry out the menu option.
ScreenTip	The text to display when the mouse pointer rests on the menu item.
On Action	The name of macro or VB function to run.
Style	Default Style, Text Only (Always), Text Only (in Menus), or Image and Text.
Help File	The path to Help file that contains the answer to the What's This? button.
Help ContextID	The identifier for the topic in the Help file.
Parameter	The parameter passed to the function named in On Action.
Tag	The string identifier that can be used later in a VB event procedure.
Begin a Group	Places a line in the menu list above the selected menu item.

If you want to delete a menu item, right-click it and choose Delete from the shortcut menu, or simply drag the menu item off the menu bar.

LOOKING AHEAD There's much more to creating and customizing menu bars and toolbars. Chapter 16, "Customizing Input and Output," contains more information about building user interfaces.

Changing Startup Options

The last step in the process of creating a welcoming switchboard is to change the startup options to display the form when the application opens. Choose Tools|Startup to open the Startup dialog box and then perform the following steps:

- Type **Pat's Pets Inventory Control System** in the Application Title box.
- Clear the Allow Built-in Toolbars check box to prevent display of the default toolbars.
- Choose Switchboard from the Display Form list and then choose Close.

Figure 14.19 shows the finished Welcome form as it appears when the Pat's Pets database opens. Notice that the Pat's Pets custom menu is displayed without the default toolbar.

FIGURE 14.19
The finished Welcome switchboard.

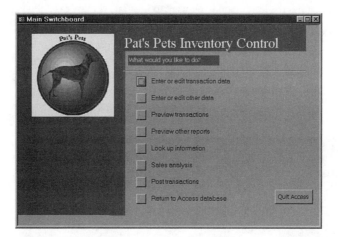

The custom menu remains onscreen until you remove it by clearing the check box in the Toolbars tab of the Customize dialog box.

Adding Charts for Visual Trend Analysis

Charts are used for two basic purposes: to track the changes that occur in one or more series of data over time and to compare relative proportions to the whole. Line charts are the most common example of the time-trend type of chart, although bar charts, column charts, and area charts can also convey the same information. Pie charts are the most common type of chart used to illustrate proportions.

The time spent planning how you want information visually represented more than pays off by resulting in the intended interpretation of the underlying data. In the Pat's Pets application, it's important to track the popularity of types of pets by comparing the sales of each category over a period of time. A simple line chart with a line for each category tracking the total sales for each year can show a major trend.

Another chart that would be useful is a bar chart showing quarterly sales in each category, one chart for each year. A pie chart can be used to illustrate the relative sales among the five categories. Pie charts have no time line, so the sales would be totaled for a single year in each chart.

Creating a Line Chart

The first chart to create in this application is the line chart tracking the sales of each category over the five-year period. Each category is represented by a separate line. To create a chart, start a new form or report, choose Chart Wizard, and then select the table or query that has the information you want to illustrate (in this case, the PetSales table).

The Chart Wizard builds a query based on the choices you make in its dialog boxes. Make the following choices in the Chart Wizard dialog boxes:

- In the first dialog box, choose the fields you want in the chart (maximum of six). Select Year and all five categories.

- Choose the line chart style in the second box (see Figure 14.20).

FIGURE 14.20
Choose the chart type from the Chart Wizard.

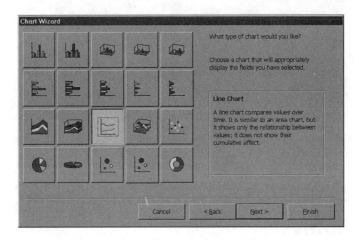

- The third dialog box, shown in Figure 14.21, helps you arrange the data in a series on the chart. First, drag and drop Year down to the X-axis at the bottom of the chart. Then, one by one drag and drop the category sales totals to the Data box on

the chart. Click the Preview Chart button in the upper-left corner of the window to
see how the chart will look as you go along.

FIGURE 14.21
*Move Year and
drag the sales
data to the chart.*

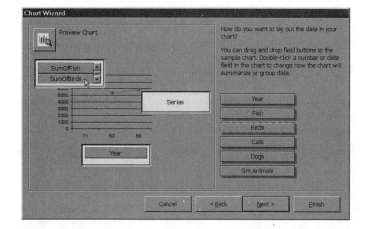

- In the last dialog box, enter **Annual Sales Line Chart** as the name for the new
  chart and then choose Finish. Don't forget to save the new form containing the
  chart.

Figure 14.22 shows how the chart looks when the Wizard is finished with it. Obviously,
it needs a little adjusting to make the legend fit in the chart, and the dollar values should
be formatted as currency. A title on the vertical axis would also help. If you want to
make changes in the data, you do that in Access, but for changes in the chart appearance,
you must use Microsoft Graph.

FIGURE 14.22
*The Chart
Wizard's product.*

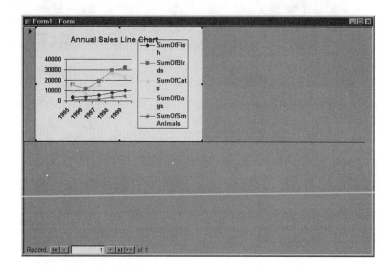

First, switch to form design view and increase the width of the chart in the form design. Then, double-click in the chart to start MS Graph in place from Access. Microsoft Graph is a stand-alone applet that you can use in place within Access. After the Chart Wizard creates the chart, you can start Graph by double-clicking anywhere in the chart object. With Graph, you can add a subtitle, change the format or scale of the axes, change to a different chart type, and make many other modifications to the chart.

The Graph window has two child windows: the Datasheet window, where you can view the underlying data, and the Chart window (see Figure 14.23). The Graph toolbar and menu bar contain all the operations you need to modify the chart. The shortcut menu also has many of the commonly used operations.

FIGURE 14.23

The Datasheet and Chart windows in MS Graph.

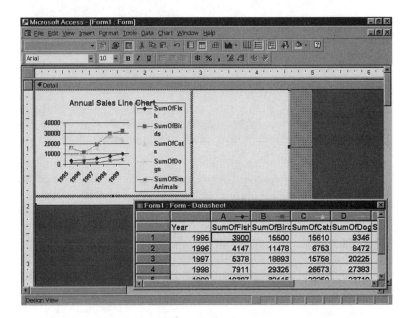

To improve the chart's appearance, perform the following steps:

1. Widen the chart so there will be enough room for the legend. Then, click and drag the legend box to the right.

2. Select the chart and resize it as necessary; then right-click the Y-axis (the dollar values) and choose Format Axis from the shortcut menu.

3. In the Format Axis dialog box, choose the Number tab and select Currency with no decimal places. Click OK.

4. Select the chart title and change it to **Pat's Pets - Annual Sales**.

5. Choose File|Exit & Return to Form1:Form. Save the form as Annual Sales Line Chart, then switch to form view (see Figure 14.24).

FIGURE 14.24

The finished line chart.

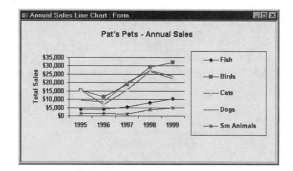

Tip: Although MS Graph says you can change the column headers in the Datasheet window to change the legend, the values do not persist when you switch to form view. The easiest way to have the legend read only the category names without the SumOf qualifier is to edit the SQL statement the Chart Wizard created as the row source. Return to the form design view and select the unbound object frame used to contain the chart. Open the property sheet and right-click in the Row Source property and then choose Zoom. Here's the SQL statement:

```
SELECT PetSales.[Year],Sum(PetSales[Fish]) AS [SumOfFish],
Sum(PetSales.[Birds]) AS [SumOfBirds],
Sum(PetSales.[Cats]) AS [SumOfCats],
Sum(PetSales.[Dogs]) AS [SumOfDogs],
Sum(PetSales.[Sm Animals]) AS [SumOfSmAnimals]
FROM [PetSales] GROUP BY [PetSales].[Year];
```

Simply remove SumOf from each of the AS clauses and then switch back to form view. If the Chart Wizard did not include the PetSales table name, you must add it to each field name to prevent a circular reference—for example, `PetSales.[Year], Sum(PetSales.[Fish])`, and so on.

You might need to return to MS Graph several times before the chart looks just the way you want it.

The line chart clearly shows a significant decline in sales of dog and cat products and a steady increase in the sales of the other three product categories. Store management may be able to speculate why this is so—perhaps the neighborhood has become more crowded and less conducive to walking dogs or more apartments are restricting the types of pets their occupants may have.

When the chart design is finished, save the form again. To insert the chart into a report, open the report in design view and use the Subform toolbar button to draw a frame for the subform. Select the name of the form that contains the chart from the Reports and Forms list displayed by the Subform/Subreport Wizard. After adding the subform, you can move it and resize it to meet your needs. Figure 14.25 shows a preview of the PetSales Annual Report with the chart added to the report footer.

Figure 14.25

The line chart is added to the PetSales Annual Report.

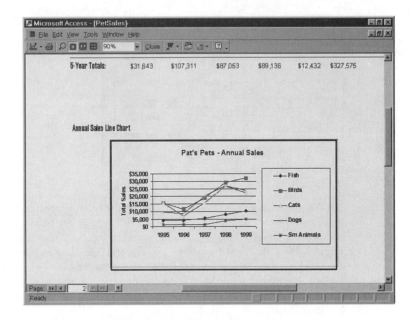

Creating a Bar Chart for One Year

Seasonal trends might be even more important for inventory management than annual sales totals. Using the Chart Wizard again, you can create a bar chart based on the Quarterly Sales table and include all the product categories. Then, in Access, you can limit the data to one year, such as 1998, which you can identify in a subtitle.

During the preparation of the chart, the Chart Wizard builds a query based on the information you've provided in the dialog boxes. It has no way of filtering the data, so you have to do the filtering in Access by changing the SQL statement that represents the Row Source property of the chart. Figure 14.26 shows the SQL statement with the HAVING filter clause added and the SumOf words edited out as before.

To make some changes in the appearance of the chart, double-click it in design view to open MS Graph. After changing the chart title, you can add a subtitle by typing in the chart. The text appears in the center of the chart, but you can drag it to a location below the title (see Figure 14.27).

FIGURE 14.26
*Change the SQL
statement to limit
the data to 1998.*

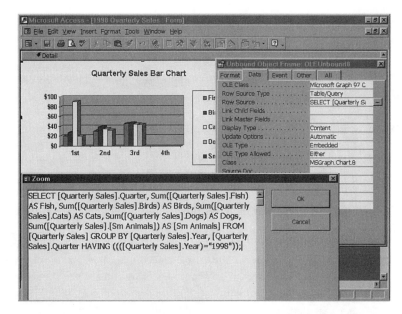

FIGURE 14.27
Adding a subtitle.

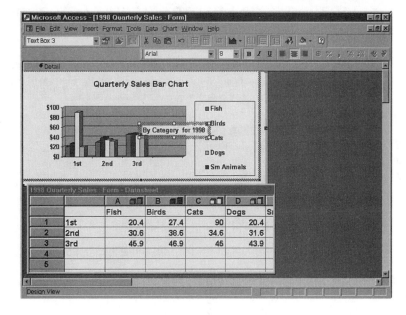

Figure 14.28 shows the finished chart in the form named 1998 Quarterly Sales Bar Chart. To create similar charts for the other years, all you need to do is change the HAVING clause of the SQL Row Source property to a different year.

FIGURE 14.28
The 1998 Quarterly Sales Bar Chart form.

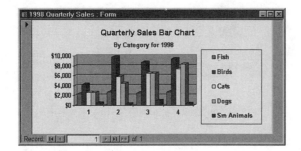

This bar chart (actually called a *"column"* chart in Access) shows a definite 2nd- and 4th-quarter rise in sales of bird-related products. Small animal products seem to have become popular during the 3rd quarter—perhaps as caged pets for classrooms at the beginning of the school year.

Creating a Pie Chart of Product Categories

Pie charts showing the proportion of sales for each category by year can be useful in allocating storage for the different products. Figure 14.29 shows a pie chart that illustrates the proportion of total sales in 1999, attributable to each product category. Cat and dog products together accounted for approximately half the total sales. Pie charts contain only a single series, so they cannot represent trends over time.

FIGURE 14.29
The 1999 Product Sales pie chart.

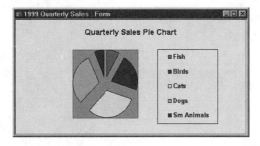

LOOKING AHEAD

There are many more things you can do with charts—more than can be covered in this chapter. In Chapter 17, "Linking with Other Office Applications," you'll see how to import spreadsheet data from Excel to use in charts.

Summary

This chapter covered a lot of material related to implementing the complete application. Links in the form of pop-up option groups were created to tie together forms and reports that relate to the same subject matter. A complete procedure for posting and archiving transaction records was also developed. All these operations were then attached to a main switchboard.

A custom menu bar was designed and set to display whenever the switchboard is in form view. Then, the startup options were changed to display the switchboard with a new application title when the Pat's Pets database opens.

The final section of this chapter briefly addressed the visual objects you can create with Access and the MS Graph applet. Such charts and graphs can help users interpret the underlying database information more quickly than poring over columns of sales figures.

PART V

Programming Access for Decision Making

Introducing a Database Decision Support System

The goal of this chapter is to show you how easily you can use an Access database application as a tool for decision making. You've already seen how Access accomplishes simple and complex data management tasks as well as how the flexible input and output capabilities can be customized to fit nearly any purpose. The decision-making environment presents new challenges to the database developer, but the Access event-driven database management system is the perfect tool for designing a valuable decision support system. Such a decision support system can easily be published on the Web where remote users may also participate.

What Is a Decision Support System?

A decision support system (DSS) is a computerized system that supports the process of making a decision. A DSS focuses on the process of making a decision rather than on the outcome of the decision or the content of the problem. For example, setting marketing budgets is a process, whereas placing specific offers on the Internet is the outcome. A DSS is more of a service than a product.

Basically, a DSS is a number cruncher and a data manipulator that processes information and presents results to the decision maker for intuitive evaluation. It's not designed around a static model—one that produces the same answer every time. Each user represents a unique problem-solving situation. One might be interested mainly in cash flow, and the next more interested in long-term appreciation.

Decisions come in roughly three major types: *structured*, *unstructured*, and *semistructured*. Structured decisions such as inventory ordering, determining the most profitable product mix, and choosing the most economical plant location are well supported by traditional computer models and data management systems. The majority of the information used in a structured decision is quantitative, and the decision model is static. Given the same input, a structured problem has the same solution every time it is solved.

Unstructured decisions are called *unstructured* either because they can't be explicitly modeled or because there's insufficient information. These decisions must be made using human intuition rather than computer support. There's little data for a computer to work with. Examples of unstructured decisions are selecting the perfect photo for a magazine cover, hiring appropriate upper-management personnel, and planning a research and development investment portfolio.

It's with the remaining type, the semistructured decision, that a DSS can become a hero. Semistructured decision making cannot rely solely on managerial judgment because there's too much information for humans to process accurately in the limited time the decision demands. Yet, you can't rely completely on the computer because there are human values and judgments to be considered as well. Here are some examples of semi-structured problems:

- Tracking the municipal bond market, where the many facts involved with yield, maturity, and the state of the market must be combined with judgment and subjective opinions. You would use the computer to search the database and make computations and then personally analyze the resulting alternatives.

- Setting market budgets for consumer products where the DSS first computes and projects anticipated trends; then your judgment takes over and superimposes external values and influences unknown to the computer.

- Analyzing the effects of different financial strategies and assumptions when planning to acquire capital for a new business.

Each of these examples combines the high-speed information processing capabilities of the computer with the human intuitive powers of the decision maker to provide a complete DSS.

> **Note:** It's interesting to note that over the years, the lines between types of problems have shifted toward structured decision making as knowledge and technology advances. Problems such as inventory management, which were once considered so complicated as to require an experienced manager with a large staff, are now routinely handled by a computer as a simple, structured problem.
>
> Another example of how knowledge redefines a problem is the five-year-old child who plays tic-tac-toe and considers it an unstructured problem—one that's uncertain and exciting, not knowing who will win. When she gains knowledge and experience with the problem, it becomes more structured and predictable.

Comparing DSS with Transaction Processing

A DSS design differs greatly from a transaction-processing system such as the inventory control system featured in the previous chapters. A DSS must be flexible, whereas transaction processing is bound by rules and procedures. If you deviate from the rules, the system fails and the data becomes corrupted. Rigid protocol and prescribed interfaces with the outside world preclude flexibility. Think of a banking system and imagine what would happen if the rules and procedures were not explicitly followed 24 hours a day, every day.

A DSS, on the other hand, must be flexible if it's to be useful. Like an event-oriented programming language, you never know what action the user will want to take next or how he'll want to arrange his priorities; the DSS must be prepared for any sequence of events and arrangement of data. Most semistructured problems can be approached from different perspectives, and the data analyzed in different logical patterns.

Solving Problems with a DSS

Getting back to decisions and the problems that demand the decisions, let's take a look at the decision makers. In an organization there are usually three levels of management with corresponding decision-making responsibilities: operational control, management control, and strategic planning (see Figure 15.1).

FIGURE 15.1
A typical organizational structure.

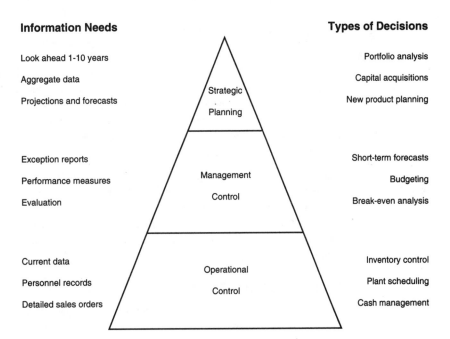

Information Needs		Types of Decisions
Look ahead 1-10 years	**Strategic Planning**	Portfolio analysis
Aggregate data		Capital acquisitions
Projections and forecasts		New product planning
Exception reports	**Management Control**	Short-term forecasts
Performance measures		Budgeting
Evaluation		Break-even analysis
Current data	**Operational Control**	Inventory control
Personnel records		Plant scheduling
Detailed sales orders		Cash management

At the operational control level, decisions are made daily that concern supervision of personnel and operations within a limited scope, such as a single department or region. At the middle level, decisions are based on information that's summarized over a period of time and across two or more departments or regions. Top-level management decisions depend on aggregated information in the form of charts and graphs that can be almost instantly assimilated for speedy decisions.

Table 15.1 describes the characteristics required of information used for decision making and how they differ between high-level strategic planning and daily operational control. The information requirements of the management control level falls in between.

Table 15.1   Information Characteristics by Decision Area

Characteristic	Strategic Control	Operational Control
Accuracy	Low	High
Level of detail	Aggregate	Detailed
Time horizon	Future	Present
Frequency of use	Infrequent	Frequent
Major source	External	Internal
Scope	Wide	Narrow
Type of info	Qualitative	Quantitative
Currency	Older	Current
Access time	Quick	Slower

In Table 15.1, there might seem to be an inconsistency between the currency and the access speed requirements. Currency relates to the age of the information. Operational managers need up-to-the-minute information in order to respond quickly to problems, whereas strategic planners prefer to look back at information after it has seasoned. They do insist, however, on immediate response to questions they might have regarding information they need to access for their decisions.

A commercial property investment search sponsored by Elgin Enterprises is used in this and the remaining chapters as an example of a DSS that can be of use to a single investor or shared with many investors, even over the Internet (see Figure 15.2). The problem can be simply stated as finding the most appropriate property in view of the client's financial status and personal preferences. The alternative decisions are the available properties listed in the database.

The Players in DSS Development

A DSS is viewed differently by the three major players in its development: the user, the developer, and the programmer. From the user's point of view, a DSS must fulfill most of the following objectives:

- Support decision making for hard or underspecified problems.
- Support decision making at all levels, providing each level with the desired degree of detail.

- Support all phases of decision making: collecting and processing raw data; devising, developing, and analyzing courses of action; recommending the course of action that best fits the user's specifications.

- Support a variety of decision-making processes that fit the decision maker's cognitive style, such as primarily factual or more intuitive.

- Above all, the DSS must be understandable and easy to use.

FIGURE 15.2

Introducing the Elgin Enterprises Investment Property Search Facility.

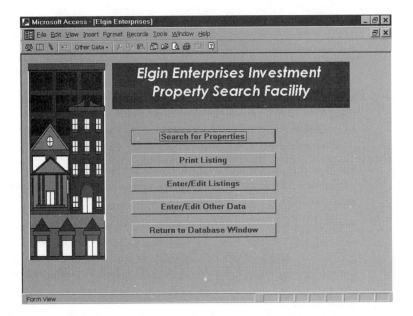

The user of the Elgin Enterprise Property Search Facility wants to be able to express his preferences in a comfortable manner and to be able to adjust them easily. The information presented by the DSS must be clear and organized in a logical manner, perhaps layered in accordance with the level of detail and interest. For example, if a property seems interesting, the client can explore additional information about it and even run some financial analyses.

DEVELOPMENT

The developer has other concerns that also fall into three categories: the dialog, data, and model subsystems. The developer is the "great explainer" who must translate the imprecise needs expressed by the decision maker into extremely precise terms for the programmer to implement. In many cases, the developer and the programmer are the same person, especially when an advanced database management system such as Access is used.

Of the three areas the developer must address, the *dialog subsystem* is the most visible and the most important. It consists of three major parts:

- *The action language.* What the user does to communicate with the DSS (click buttons, choose from menu lists, enter data, and so on).

- *The display language.* What the user sees as a result of actions taken (forms onscreen, printed reports, graphics and audio output, and so on).

- *A knowledge base.* What the user must know in order to use the DSS. This can include onscreen help and tips or a printed user's manual.

The *data subsystem* contains the information required for the decision process—often a wide variety of data from both inside and outside the organization. The higher up in the organization the decision maker is, the more information that comes from external sources. For example, the CEO of a large computer firm will be more interested in what his competitors are doing (external information) than in how his salesmen in Seattle are doing (internal information). In addition, the higher up the decision, the less detail needed for the process. Many DSSs must also include personal judgment data related to the decision process and reflect the inclination of the decision maker.

The Elgin data subsystem holds all the available information about the available properties, including a description, present value, expenses and income, and a photograph, if available.

The *models subsystem* defines the structure of the decision process. It includes equations, formulas, logical comparisons, and other building blocks for processing the information appropriately. The developer can often become mesmerized by the structure of the decision model at the expense of a simple, modular approach of taking the process one step at a time.

The Elgin model subsystem consists of a scoring algorithm that credits each property with points in proportion to the emphasis the client places on the attributes of the property, such as price, location, or cash flow. For example, if the property is in the desired price range and the client has specified the price attribute as essential, 100 points are added to the property's total score.

From the programmer's point of view, the DSS also consists of three subsystems similar to the developer's, but dealing more with the computer software. The *dialog management subsystem* focuses on the display technology and implementation of required user interaction. Figure 15.3 shows a typical dialog object that Access uses to acquire user input. The form is from the Clayview City College database described in Chapter 7, "Programming with SQL."

The *data management subsystem* handles the storage, retrieval, and validation of the information needed for the decision. The programmer creates the relational database system, extracting information from other sources as needed.

FIGURE 15.3
A typical Access dialog object.

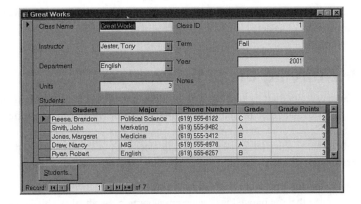

The *model management subsystem* explicitly defines the interrelationships among the variables in the decision and acts out the "What if?" scenarios. In the Elgin DSS, the model is the comparison of the values in the property database with the values selected by the client. The model consists of a series of event procedures that respond to the client's actions.

Access provides all three subsystems for the Elgin DSS. With Access, you can store all the necessary data as well as retrieve, filter, and sort it any way you want. Using VB procedures, you can generate mathematical models to manipulate the data. The input and output design capabilities provide the ideal dialog with the client.

Designing a DSS

The DSS design process is evolutionary, with the design and implementation phases nearly inseparable. There is no clear break between the two, no precise end to design—new ideas keep cropping up as users learn more about what the DSS can do for them. The decision environment might also be shifting as the problem becomes more clear. For example, the Elgin DSS might start out to be a tool for searching for residential housing and then be expanded to include all types of commercial real estate. Later, it might shift again to include real estate investment trust (REIT) funds.

The Elgin system accepts input from the potential investor in the form of a list of requirements based on property attributes such as price, cash flow, location, type of property, and gross receipt multiplier (GRM). Each attribute is ranked on a scale from "essential" to "nice to have" and "don't care," depending on the user's preferences.

The DSS model then examines all the properties listed in the database and scores them based on how well they meet the user's requirements. The results are displayed for the investor to examine the details of the listings more closely. Further economic analyses are available if desired, or the client can return to the original form and change some of the selections.

This is an example of the multi-attribute utility model in which several features of the property are considered, each one weighted according to its relative importance in the view of the decision maker.

Identifying the Right Problem

The most important facet of designing a DSS is to choose the right problem to work on. It's possible that each person involved in the DSS development has a different concept of the problem. For example, in a portfolio management system, the investment research folks want to solve the problem by hiring more high-quality analysts. They're treating the problem as an unstructured problem, solvable only with human intuition.

The computer branch of the company treats it as a structured problem to be solved by improving their automated trust accounting system. In actuality, this is a semistructured problem that can be solved by a combination of mathematical models that optimize the portfolio and the intuition of an experienced manager.

It's also important to concentrate on the problem rather than on a symptom of the problem. Sometimes it's hard to distinguish between the two. For example, the client is earning a low rate of return on a money market account, which is a symptom, not the basic problem. The problem is how to invest funds to get the best return (or the safest, if that's more important) on the capital.

The solution to the problem can also be confused with the problem itself. For example, suppose your 10-year-old car is giving you trouble, so you decide to buy a new one. You state your problem as, "How do I find the right car?" However, the problem is really how to ensure you have reliable transportation. One of the potential solutions is to buy a new car. Other solutions might be to lease a car, ride your bike to work, or take the Metro. After you decide that buying a new car is the appropriate solution to the first problem, the next problem becomes how to decide which car to buy.

At Elgin Enterprises, the major problem is matching the investor with the property that best meets his requirements and preferences. To do this, you must be able to express these factors quantitatively and find a way to match them to the stored information about the properties.

What Is the Main Objective?

When defining the main objective of a new DSS, your focus is on what the DSS is supposed to do rather than on how it will look. The dialog and results displays are designed later in the process. For example, what is the DSS intended to accomplish: optimize a portfolio strategy, pick out the best location for a new store, or identify potentially profitable investment opportunities? Keep in mind that the computer is not allowed to make the decision, only to come up with possible solutions to the problem as you've defined it.

The main objective of the Elgin Enterprises DSS is to help the client find suitable commercial real estate properties for investment. Clients can specify the factors that play a part in their particular decision styles and reflect their requirements.

What Are the Decision Factors?

After determining what the major objective of the DSS is, you must examine the factors that affect the decision. What would cause you to choose one solution over another?

The Elgin DSS will ask questions such as, "How important is location to you? Is location more important than cash flow?" Clients will be able to state their requirements both quantitatively and qualitatively. For example, one client might specify a price range between $200,000 and $300,000 and an annual cash flow of at least $15,000. At the same time, they'll tell Access that the type of property is more important than the cash flow.

After all the criteria and their relative importance has been entered, Access searches the database and accumulates a numeric score for each property based on how well it fits the client's requirements and preferences. Information about the listings that meet the selection criteria is then displayed. If the client desires, additional analyses can be run on a specified property to compute future values, return on investment, and other statistical predictions.

If none of the properties meet the client's requirements, he has the option of relaxing the requirements and rerunning the operation. This is part of the flexible feature of DSSs: the capability to trade off one factor against another. With a carefully designed dialog subsystem, the client can play "What if?" games with the information to see the outcome of different choices.

For example, the client could ask the question, "If I do this, what will it look like 10 years from now?" Using the information in the database, a projection can be run based on estimated inflation rates, property value fluctuations, or other trends.

There certainly will be subjective as well as objective decision criteria. For example, clients might prefer one location because it's close to their place of business and it will be more convenient to oversee. Or, one might prefer to invest in an apartment building in a distant area because the mother-in-law could move into it as the manager.

The decision factors must be quantifiable in some way. If they're not actually numeric values, you can assign relative values to the factors. For example, the client can assign a value of 100 to an attribute that's essential and a value of 50 to one that's only half as important.

How Can Access Help?

Access can provide all the data manipulation that's required by a DSS, including interactive dialog and flexible mathematical models. The Chart Wizard can supply visual interpretations of many of the analyses for Elgin's clients.

An added strength of Access is that it can call upon its fellow Office applications for their specific help. The financial data can be stored in Excel, where many types of charts and graphs are available. Figure 15.4 shows a 3-D column chart from the Excel array of sample charts. A column chart is useful for illustrating trends over a period of time, such as comparing the cash flow of two or three properties over a 10-year period. Figure 15.5 shows a sample exploding pie chart that can be used to show proportions of a whole, such as the relative number of properties in each region.

FIGURE 15.4
A sample 3-D col-umn chart from Excel.

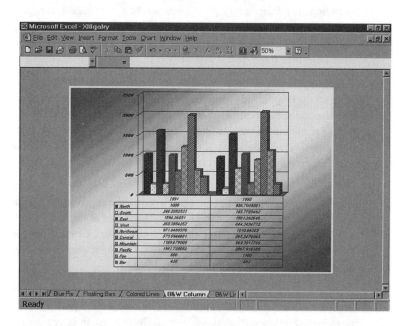

FIGURE 15.5
A sample pie chart from Excel.

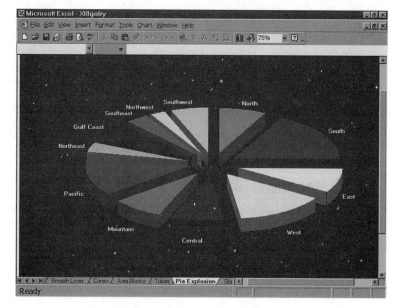

Using the new Access data access page objects, you can share and update data across the Web. Figure 15.6 shows a sample of a Web page advertising the Elgin Enterprises Investment Property Search Facility. You can post the Choice form for remote users to enter search criteria and present the results of the search in another page. See Chapter 20, "Posting Your Database to the Web," for examples of creating dynamic Web pages.

FIGURE 15.6
Create a data access page to display on the Web.

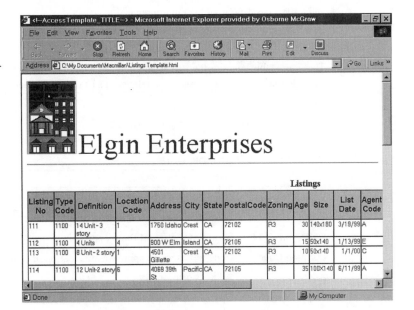

An Overview of the Elgin Enterprises Database

You already have a good idea of what the Elgin DSS is all about and what kind of decision it's intended to support. As the system develops in this chapter and the next, keep in mind that although the database is limited, it's as close to reality as possible. If loan information such as current interest rates and amount financed were included, other analyses could follow the property search. Another, more qualitative factor would be the future use of such property as buildable land.

Note: The data in the Elgin database is totally fictitious, although you'll see photographs of actual properties. The pictures were taken of local buildings to serve as sample properties only and should not be construed to be actually for sale.

The Elgin Enterprises database consists of the following four related tables:

- The Listings table contains all the relevant information about the listed properties.
- Location is a lookup table that contains descriptions of the Location Code field in the Listings table. This table has a one-to-one relationship with Listings. It includes information such as the population, average income, size in square miles, and a short description of the environment.
- Type is also a lookup table that defines the Type Code field values in the Listings table.
- The Agent table contains the names and telephone numbers for the agents referenced in the Listings table. Agents is related to Listings with a one-to-many relationship.

Table 15.2 lists the data contained in the Listings table.

Table 15.2   The Listings Table Data

Field	Data
Listing No	Unique key field entered by Elgin Enterprises
Type Code	Four-digit code indicating the type of property
Definition	Short description of the property
Location Code	Code representing approximate location of property
Address	Address of property
City	City
PostalCode	Postal code
Zoning	Specific zoning category
Age	Approximate age of the structure (if any)
Size	Approximate size of the structure (if any)
List Date	Date of most recent listing
Agent Code	Code referring to the listing agent
List Price	Currently listed price
GRM	Gross Revenue Multiplier (the ratio of list price to income)
Previous List	Previous list price (if listed before)
Taxes	Annual property tax
Expenses	Total annual expenses
Income	Total annual income
Cash Flow	Net annual income after expenses and taxes

Field	Data
Total Score	Computed score based on user's stated requirements and rankings (to be computed by the search program)
Picture	Photograph of the property (if available)

Figure 15.7 shows the data entry form for the Elgin Enterprises Listings table.

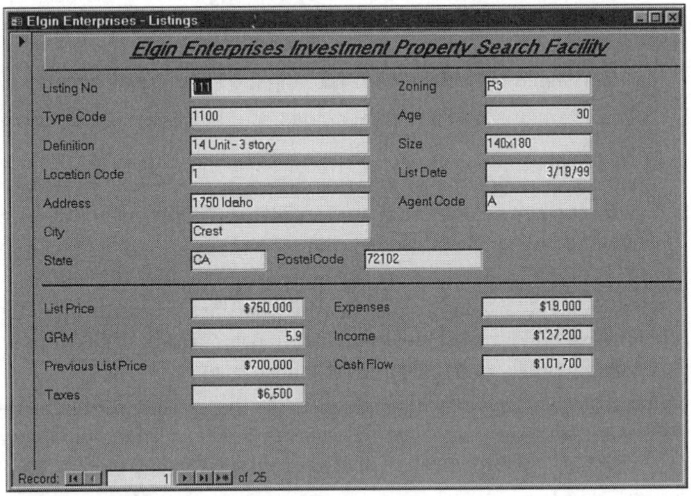

FIGURE 15.7
The Listings data entry form.

The Elgin Enterprises assistants maintain the information in the database, behind the scenes. The data is not highly volatile, so no exotic data entry operations are required.

LOOKING AHEAD

Chapter 16, "Customizing Input and Output," continues with the development of the Elgin DSS. Chapter 17, "Linking with Other Office Applications," describes how to interface and share data with the Excel and Word applications in Office 2000 to add more functionality to the DSS.

Pioneers in Decision Support Systems

Professors William A. Wallace and Frank De Balogh published a paper titled "Decision Support for Disaster Management" in the *Public Administration Review, Volume 45, Special Issue* in January 1985. In this paper, Drs. Wallace and De Balogh described several DSS models dealing with preparing for and reacting to disasters such as nuclear power plant incidents, ocean accidents that required Coast Guard search and rescue, and earthquake mitigation.

The Federal Emergency Preparedness Agency has broken down disaster management into four stages: preparedness, mitigation, emergency response, and

continues

recovery. Each stage has specific information requirements, and specific decisions are required from different levels of management at each stage.

The earthquake disaster mitigation DSS was designed at the University of Southern California Decision Support System Laboratory to help planners and other public officials make appropriate decisions to prepare for an earthquake. After an earthquake occurs, the DSS can help crews respond with mitigating actions and recover from the damage as quickly as possible.

The database contains several tables detailing building characteristics, population distribution, quake intensity, and projected costs of upgrading and retrofitting to meet the new safety standards. The information used in this prototype DSS was obtained from the City of Los Angeles Planning Department.

The system uses mathematical models to predict damage assessments by local region.

After the decision maker enters an intensity factor for the quake, the DSS computes the percentage of square footage and dollar value lost for each type and age of building. These estimates are then used to assess the potential damage an earthquake can do to existing and proposed buildings.

The model then couples the damage assessment with the estimated costs to improve buildings to new standards to compute the estimated savings that would be realized by making the improvements.

The DSS also provides summary statistics that estimate the total damage caused by an earthquake of a specific intensity, indicating the area that would be hardest hit and which types of buildings would suffer the most.

The decision maker can use this DSS to play "What if?" games by varying upgrade costs and earthquake intensity.

Summary

Although somewhat pedantic, this chapter has expanded the use of Access to the realm of decision support. Access has all the objects that a DSS requires: a dialog subsystem, a database subsystem, a model subsystem, and dynamic Web pages. All it takes to implement a DSS with Access is a little imagination and some programming skills. The next chapter completes the development of the Elgin Enterprises DSS by creating an interactive user interface and a series of procedures that operate the decision model.

Customizing Input and Output

In Chapter 15, "Introducing a Database Decision Support System," you were introduced to the Elgin Enterprises database. This chapter turns this database into a decision support system (DSS) by adding the user dialog feature, the decision model, and a means to display the results of the search for potential investment properties. You'll also design some analytical computations and summaries as additional decision-making tools.

Note: Keep in mind that the properties featured in the Elgin Enterprises database are for example only and not actual investment opportunities.

Creating the User Input Form

Clients who come to Elgin Enterprises have some idea of what kind of investment property they're looking for. They definitely have a price range in mind and might also have a preference for apartment buildings or shopping centers. There are five major categories of property attributes that can be of interest to a potential investor:

- *Location*. The area is divided into six major regions.
- *Type of property*. Includes apartments, industrial, offices, commercial, and miscellaneous.
- *Price range*.
- *Cash flow*.
- *Gross Revenue Multiplier (GRM)*. The ratio of the listed price to the annual income.

The last three categories can be broken down into intervals from which to choose. For example, prices less than $100,000, between $100,000 and $200,000, and so on. All these attributes must be displayed to the client together with a tool for ranking the perceived importance of each attribute.

This structure is an example of the multiattribute utility model mentioned in Chapter 15. The decision maker considers multiple attributes (price, location, GRM, and so on, in this case) and weights them according to their individual importance in the decision process.

Five lists of attributes is a lot of information to display in a single form onscreen, so the Elgin Enterprises developer has divided the data into a two-page tabbed form. Figure 16.1 shows the first page of the form, which includes the Location and Type selections. Beneath each option group is a list box containing the five ranking selections. After the clients choose one of the values in an attribute box, they can choose the ranking from the drop-down list. All attributes need not be selected. If an attribute is selected but no ranking is specified, it's ignored in the evaluation of the properties in the Listings table.

Figure 16.1

The Property Features tab of the Choice input form.

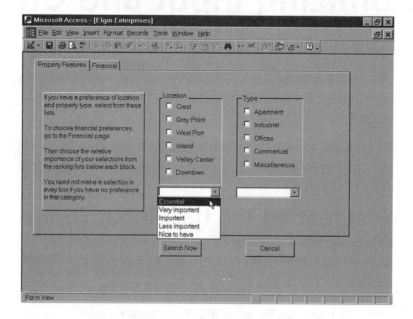

> **Note:** The Type and Location attribute lists are shown as check boxes in option groups in this example. This precludes adding more types or locations to the lists without adding them to the option groups. If you need to be able to add to these lists, change the option groups to combo boxes. Some minor changes to the VB code that interprets the choices would also be involved.

The ranking list is an unbound combo box whose row source is a two-column value list entered directly in the control property sheet. The value list equates each level of importance to a number value:

- Essential = 100
- Very important = 50
- Important = 35
- Less important = 20
- Nice to have = 10

Figure 16.2 shows the form design with one of the Row Source value lists expanded in the Zoom window. These scores are accumulated as Access evaluates each property in the Listings table with respect to the client's preferences.

FIGURE 16.2

The ranking controls are based on a value list.

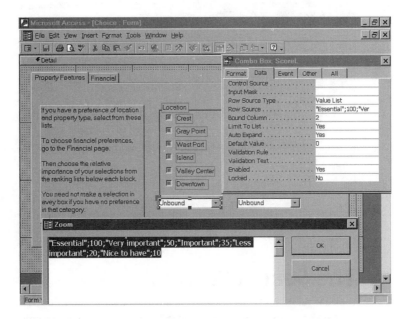

Warning: When you design a form that accepts user input such as the preference values in the Choice form, you must specify some of the form's properties. For example, if you set the Choice form's Allow Update property to No, you won't be able to make choices in the attribute lists or the value lists. Set the Allow Update property to Yes but set the Allow Deletions, Allow Additions, and Allow Filters properties all to No.

The second page of the Choice form gives the client choices in price, cash flow, and GRM ranges (see Figure 16.3). Each of these also has a ranking drop-down list for rating the relative importance of the attribute. Two buttons are placed below the Tab control so that they're available from both pages of the form. One button starts the search for properties that meet the entered criteria and the other closes the form without conducting the search.

The Choice form class module contains only four event procedures. The first two (Form_Load and Form_GotFocus) maximize the form. Attaching the Maximize method to both events guarantees that the form will be maximized no matter what has gone on in the meantime. The event procedure that runs when the Cancel button is clicked simply closes the form. The Search Now button triggers a much more complicated procedure, which is described in the next section.

FIGURE 16.3

The Financial tab of the Choice input form.

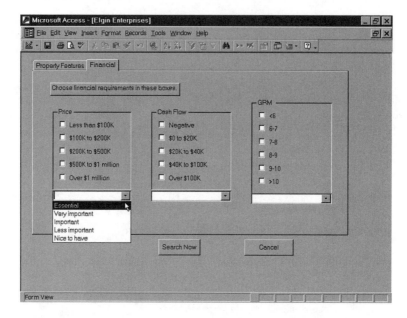

The Search Process

Once the selections have been made in the Choice form and the user clicks Search Now, the search process moves through all the listings in the Listings recordset and compares each property, attribute by attribute, with the stated preferences from the Choice form. When a property meets the desired condition, the value from the corresponding ranking list is added to the property's Total Score field. For example, if the property is of the desired type and the importance was set to Very Important, 50 is added to the property's Total Score field.

At the end of the process, the properties that have a Total Score above zero are displayed in a results form.

If the client has specified an attribute as Essential, only those properties with a Total Score field over 100 are displayed in the result. It is, of course, possible for a property to accumulate more that 100 points and still not have any of the specified "essential" attributes, but scoring high without one might actually place the property within the realm of consideration.

The Search Procedure

The Search Now button's Click event procedure contains four major routines as well as a rather extensive Declarations section. In addition to the usual database and recordset objects, integer variables are declared for each of the option group choices—intOptLoc, intOptType, and so on. Then, variables are declared for the selected value in each attribute group. The `stType` and `stLoc` attribute variables are String types. For the other three attributes that specify value ranges, you need variables for both the upper and lower values in the selected option in order to determine within which range the property falls. Finally, variables are assigned to the score value chosen for each attribute group.

ANALYSIS

The first section after the Declarations section checks to make sure at least one attribute has been selected before proceeding. An `If...Then` block tests the values returned by the option groups. If they're all zero, nothing has been selected and a message box displays, "You must select at least one category before searching." If at least one attribute has been selected, five integer variables are set to the values returned by the option groups.

The second routine uses `Select Case` structures to assign the option numbers of the selected attribute values to variables for later comparison with the values in the recordset. The preferred location attribute can use the selected value directly without the `Select Case` logic because the Location Code field in the Location table very conveniently has integer values from 1 to 6, which is the same set of integers returned by the option group selection. Of course, you can have the Option Group Wizard set any integers as the returned values for the options. Ascending integer values beginning with 1 is the default.

> **Note:** The lowest range of the Cash Flow attribute is <0, a range with only one limit. In the `Select Case`, the lower limit is set artificially to a large negative number, one that would never be exceeded. Similarly, the upper limit of the highest range is set to a very large number, $1,000,000. This magnitude of annual cash flow is not likely from the types of properties Elgin lists in the database. The highest range limit of the Price attribute is defined as $1 million to $10 million.

ANALYSIS

The third routine moves through all the records in the recordset, adding points to the property's Total Score field whenever a field value meets the stated attribute value. The number of points to add to the score is determined by the choice made in the corresponding ranking list.

The fourth and final routine displays the results of the search, displaying only those with a total score over 100, if one of the attributes was deemed Essential.

The complete listing for the Search Now command button's `Click` event, interspersed with comments, is shown in Listing 16.1.

Listing 16.1   The Search Now Button's `Click` Event Procedure

```
Private Sub Search_Click()
On Error GoTo Err_Search_Click
'Declare variables for all the attributes and scores.
```

continues

Listing 16.1 Continued

```
Dim dbsCurrent As Object, rstList As Object
Dim rstResults As Object
Dim intOptLoc As Integer, intOptType As Integer
Dim intOptPrice As Integer, intOptGRM As Integer
Dim intOptCash As Integer
Dim stType As String, stLoc As String
Dim curHiPrice As Currency, curLoPrice As Currency
Dim intHiGRM As Integer, intLoGRM As Integer
Dim curHiCash As Currency, curLoCash As Currency
Dim intScore As Integer, intScoreL As Integer
Dim intScoreT As Integer, intScoreC As Integer
Dim intScoreP As Integer, intScoreG As Integer

Set dbsCurrent = CurrentDb
Set rstList = dbsCurrent.OpenRecordset("Listings")
'Check for at least one option selection.
If LocBox = 0 And TypeBox = 0 And PriceBox = 0 And GRMBox = 0 _
        And CashBox = 0 Then
    MsgBox ("You must select at least one category before searching.")
    Me.[Property Features].SetFocus
    Me.Visible = True
End If

'Define the variables from the option group selections
intOptLoc = LocBox
intOptType = TypeBox
intOptPrice = PriceBox
intOptGRM = GRMBox
intOptCash = CashBox
```

ANALYSIS

The next code clears the stType variable and then uses Select Case to equate the returned option group value to the property type code as it appears in the Listings table:

```
'Set the selected property type.
stType = ""
Select Case intOptType
    Case 1
        stType = "1100"
    Case 2
        stType = "1200"
    Case 3
        stType = "1300"
    Case 4
        stType = "1400"
    Case 5
        stType = "1500"
End Select
```

The next statement uses the CStr() function to set the Location attribute value to the string equivalent of the integer returned by the Location option group. Then, the next three Select Case structures set the upper and lower values for the selected Price, Cash Flow, and GRM ranges attributes:

```
'Set the selected location.
stLoc = CStr(intOptLoc)

'Set the selected price range.
Select Case intOptPrice
    Case 1
        curHiPrice = 100000
        curLoPrice = 0
    Case 2
        curHiPrice = 200000
        curLoPrice = 100000
    Case 3
        curHiPrice = 500000
        curLoPrice = 200000
    Case 4
        curHiPrice = 1000000
        curLoPrice = 500000
    Case 5
        curHiPrice = 10000000
        curLoPrice = 1000000
End Select

'Set the selected cash flow range
Select Case intOptCash
    Case 1
        curHiCash = 0
        curLoCash = -100000
    Case 2
        curHiCash = 20000
        curLoCash = 0
    Case 3
        curHiCash = 40000
        curLoCash = 20000
    Case 4
        curHiCash = 60000
        curLoCash = 40000
    Case 5
        curHiCash = 100000
        curLoCash = 60000
    Case 6
        curHiCash = 1000000
        curLoCash = 100000
End Select

'Set the selected GRM range.
```

```
Select Case intOptGRM
    Case 1
        intHiGRM = 6
        intLoGRM = 0
    Case 2
        intHiGRM = 7
        intLoGRM = 6
    Case 3
        intHiGRM = 8
        intLoGRM = 7
    Case 4
        intHiGRM = 9
        intLoGRM = 8
    Case 5
        intHiGRM = 10
        intLoGRM = 9
    Case 6
        intHiGRM = 100
        intLoGRM = 10
End Select
```

ANALYSIS

Before beginning to process the recordset, integer variables set the individual attribute scores to the selections made in the corresponding ranking drop-down lists. Then, the procedure moves to the first record in the recordset to begin comparing field values with the selected attribute values.

After using the With statement to establish rstList as the local object, a Do Until EOF loop is used to move through the recordset, and If...Then statements determine whether to add the score to the Total Score field of the property. When the attribute is a range of values, the And operator is used to combine the upper and lower criteria.

You must include the .Edit method in order to be able to write the total score to the current record. Just before the end of the loop, the .Update method writes the score to the record. The .MoveNext method advances to the next record, if there is one, where the loop begins anew:

```
'Set the weight values from the Ranking lists.
intScoreT = ScoreT
intScoreL = ScoreL
intScoreP = ScoreP
intScoreG = ScoreG
intScoreC = ScoreC
'Move to the first record in the Listings table.
With rstList
    .MoveFirst

'Compute the total score for each property in the Listings table.
Do Until .EOF
    intScore = 0
    .Edit
```

```
'Get score for Location.
    If ![Location Code] = stLoc Then
        intScore = intScore + intScoreL
    End If

'Add score for Type.
    If ![Type Code] = stType Then
        intScore = intScore + intScoreT
    End If

'Add score for Price.
    If ![List Price] >= curLoPrice And _
        ![List Price] < curHiPrice Then
        intScore = intScore + intScoreP
    End If

'Add score for GRM.
    If !GRM >= intLoGRM And _
        !GRM < intHiGRM Then
        intScore = intScore + intScoreG
    End If

'Add score for Cash Flow.
    If ![Cash Flow] >= curLoCash And _
        ![Cash Flow] < curHiCash Then
        intScore = intScore + intScoreC
    End If

    ![Total Score] = intScore
    .Update
    .MoveNext
Loop
End With
```

> **Warning:** The Do Until loop does not automatically advance to the next record in the recordset. You must be sure to include the .MoveNext statement just before the Loop line; otherwise, your procedure will run forever (or at least until you press Ctrl+Alt+Del).

ANALYSIS

The last routine in the procedure prepares the results for display in the Results form. Actually, two versions of the display form are involved. One is based on a query that limits the records to those with a total score greater than or equal to 100. This version, Results100, is used if any of the attributes were deemed Essential. The other form displays all the properties that have a score above zero:

```
If intScoreL = 100 Or intScoreT = 100 Or intScoreP = 100 _
    Or intScoreG = 100 Or intScoreC = 100 Then
    Set rstResults = dbsCurrent.OpenRecordset("Results100")
    DoCmd.OpenForm "Results100", acNormal
```

```
Else
    Set rstResults = dbsCurrent.OpenRecordset("Results")
    DoCmd.OpenForm "Results", acNormal
End If

Exit_Search_Click:
    Exit Sub

Err_Search_Click:
    MsgBox Err.Description
    Resume Exit_Search_Click

End Sub
```

Displaying the Results of the Search

Once again, a tabbed form is used—this time to display the results of the property search. The property attributes are divided into three categories: information about the location and type of property, financial and environmental features, and detailed listing information. The arrangement is based on the relative importance of the information to the client. Price, type, and location were considered to be of primary interest and were placed on the first page (see Figure 16.4). The Listing Number, List Price, and Definition information appear on all three pages so that the client can easily correlate the information with the individual property.

FIGURE 16.4
The first page of the results form.

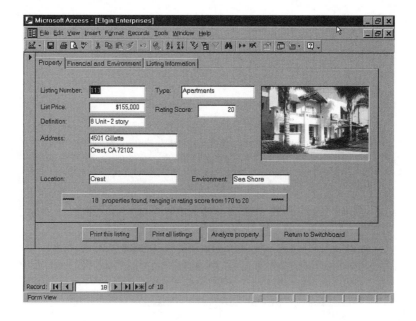

The four buttons below the Tab control are used to perform the following tasks:

- Preview the complete information in report format for the current listing
- Preview a report including all the listings found in the search
- Open the window for further analysis of the current listing
- Close the form and return to the switchboard

Note: Just a reminder that the data in the Elgin Enterprises database is fictitious, although the properties pictured in the database are real. They serve only as sample properties and should not be construed to be actually for sale.

This form design contains several special features. The first page shows a summary of the results of the search. The rectangle at the bottom of the form tells how many properties were found and the range of scores among them. Figure 16.5 shows the first page of the form in design view.

FIGURE 16.5
The design of the first page.

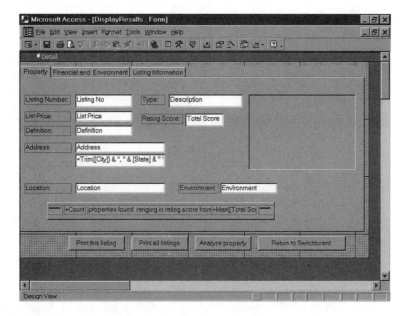

ANALYSIS The information in the rectangle concatenates two expressions with some label text in between. The first expression

```
=Count([Listing No])
```

returns the total number of properties found. After the explanatory text, the second expression

```
=Max([Total Score]) &" to "& Min([Total Score])
```

returns the highest and lowest scores in the group of properties with the word *to* in between. This summary gives the clients an idea of how restrictive or liberal their preferences are. If too few properties are found, perhaps the requirements are too limiting and the search should be rerun with more relaxed demands.

> **Tip:** In the form design, you can see the address line containing an expression concatenating the City, State, and Postal Code field values. If you see nothing in the text box but #Error when you switch to form view, there might not be anything wrong with the expression. Check for errors in the expression, and if you don't find any, delete the message and reenter the expression. The Expression Builder might be of some help, but it occasionally creates an expression that also evokes the #Error message.

If you are creating the form design, you must pay some special attention to displaying the photographs of the properties. The picture of the property appears on the first page and again on the third page of the form. The control is a bound object frame that displays the OLE object stored in the Picture field of the Listings table. Not all pictures are going to be the same size because they're cropped to show the property at its best. It's important to set the OLE object properties so that there's not an unattractive gap between the picture and the frame. You also must preserve the ratio of picture height to width. Set the following OLE object properties:

- Setting Size Mode to Zoom sizes the picture to fit the frame while preserving the scale.
- Setting Special Effect to Sunken sets off the picture in the form.
- Setting Border to Transparent removes the frame border from view.
- Setting Back Style to Transparent blends the blank frame area with the form background.

> **Note:** The photographs in the Elgin database were scanned in black and white with a rather coarse resolution to save disk space. Adding images to a database can dramatically increase its size, especially if the images are in 256 colors. If you're really short of disk space, you can display an icon representing the image instead of the whole image. To change a bound image to an icon, select the object in form view or in the datasheet, choose the appropriate object command—Photo Editor Photo Object for an Elgin photo—and then choose Convert. In the Convert dialog box, check Display as Icon. If the object is unbound, you can convert it from the form or report design window. When you want to view the image itself, double-click the icon; the OLE server is launched, and the image is displayed.

The second page of the Display Results form, shown in Figure 16.6, shows the financial and environmental information about the current listing. The only thing that needs attention on this page is the formatting of the currency Text Box controls. These fields were formatted in the table design and appear in datasheet view as currency with no decimal places, but that formatting does not carry over to a form design. You must set the format in the property sheet for these controls. Hold down the Shift key while you select all the currency fields and then open the property sheet for the multiple selection. Then change the Decimal Places format to 0 for all the fields at once.

FIGURE 16.6
The Financial and Environment page of the Results form.

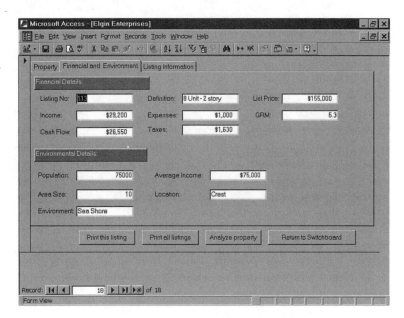

If the property seems like a potential investment, the client can move to the other pages for more details, ending up on the Listing Information page, where she can find the name and telephone number for the listing agent (see Figure 16.7). The form includes a command button that automatically dials the agent's phone number.

COMPATIBILITY

To use the AutoDialer, you need a Hayes or Hayes-compatible modem installed in your computer. To add the command button to the form, use the Command Button Wizard and choose Miscellaneous in the Categories box. Then choose AutoDialer from the Actions box. The button you see in the Display Results form uses the smaller of the two available telephone icons. To use the AutoDialer button, first select the telephone or pager number and then click the button. A dialog box opens, where you confirm the telephone number and place the call.

Another feature you can see on this page is the text that appears in the empty OLE control frame when there's no picture for the property. The text is actually a bit of text art created with Microsoft WordArt 2.0. You insert this object instead of a photo file into the

Picture field of each record that does not have a picture. If you acquire a picture later, you can simply write over the text art.

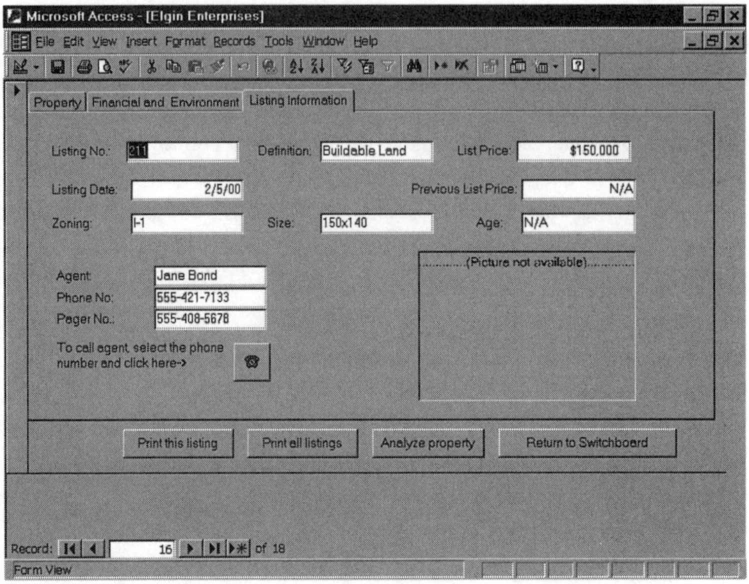

FIGURE 16.7
*The Listing
Information page
of the Results
form.*

To create and add the text art, open the table in datasheet view, place the cursor in an empty Picture field, and then follow these steps:

1. Choose Insert|Object to open the Insert Object dialog box.

2. Choose Create New and scroll down the Object Type list and select Microsoft WordArt 2.0 (see Figure 16.8).

3. Type

   ....(Picture not available).............

   in the Enter Your Text Here box and make any changes you want to the font style, size, and color; then choose OK (see Figure 16.9).

> **Tip:** Without the preceding and trailing dots, the text is expanded to the width of the bound object frame because of the Zoom Size Mode property setting for the pictures. This creates a large obtrusive message. With the dots, the line is wide enough without expanding. If you had set the Size Mode for the bound object control to Stretch, the text would be expanded both horizontally and vertically to fill the frame, which would give the message a very distorted appearance.

FIGURE 16.8

Inserting a WordArt object.

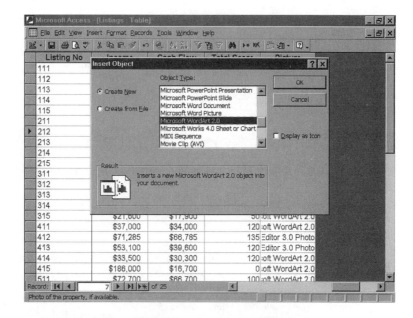

FIGURE 16.9

Entering text in the WordArt dialog box.

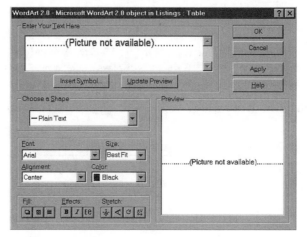

4. In the datasheet view, select the new WordArt object and click Copy; then paste it in each of the other empty Picture fields.

The Display Results Form Code

The VB code in the Display Results form class module includes the usual Maximize method when the form opens and the Close method when the Close button is clicked. Three other procedures are the Click event procedures attached to the buttons at the bottom of the form. They open reports in print preview as described in the next section, "Previewing Reports."

ANALYSIS

The first procedure was created by the Command Button Wizard when the AutoDialer button was added. It finds the selected telephone number. The nested If...Then statements test for the type and contents of the control that had focus just before the button was clicked. An IIf() function then tests the contents of the previous control and, if it's not blank, returns the value in the control, presumably the phone number. If it is blank, an empty string is returned.

> **Note:** The IIf() function (immediate If) provides a quick way to return one value if the value of an expression is True and another if it evaluates to False. The function takes three arguments: the expression to be evaluated, the True value, and the False value. The If...Then statement offers more versatile branching options, and Select Case is the most sophisticated of the three structures.

If the previous control was not one of the three types of boxes—text, list, or combo—the phone number is set to an empty string because those are the only controls that could contain a phone number. Then the following statement calls the AutoDial application and passes the phone number variable, stDialStr:

```
Application.Run "utility.wlib_AutoDial", stDialStr
```

The wizard sets two constants in the procedure to trap specific errors and resume processing without exiting. The message for the Jet 3.0 Error 91 is Object variable or With block variable not set. Error 2467 displays a similar message saying that the object variable does not exist. If any other error occurs, the procedure exits.

Listing 16.2 shows the complete listing of the Display Results form class module.

Listing 16.2   The Display Results Form Class Module

```
Private Sub Form_Load()
DoCmd.Maximize
End Sub

Private Sub Dial_Click()
On Error GoTo Err_Dial_Click

    Dim stDialStr As String
    Dim PrevCtl As Control
    Const ERR_OBJNOTEXIST = 2467
    Const ERR_OBJNOTSET = 91

    Set PrevCtl = Screen.PreviousControl

    If TypeOf PrevCtl Is TextBox Then
      stDialStr = IIf(VarType(PrevCtl) > V_NULL, PrevCtl, "")
```

```
        ElseIf TypeOf PrevCtl Is ListBox Then
          stDialStr = IIf(VarType(PrevCtl) > V_NULL, PrevCtl, "")
        ElseIf TypeOf PrevCtl Is ComboBox Then
          stDialStr = IIf(VarType(PrevCtl) > V_NULL, PrevCtl, "")
        Else
          stDialStr = ""
        End If

        Application.Run "utility.wlib_AutoDial", stDialStr

Exit_Dial_Click:
    Exit Sub

Err_Dial_Click:
    If (Err = ERR_OBJNOTEXIST) Or (Err = ERR_OBJNOTSET) Then
      Resume Next
    End If
    MsgBox Err.Description
    Resume Exit_Dial_Click

End Sub

Private Sub PrintAll_Click()
'Opens report of all listings in results of search.

DoCmd.OpenReport "All Results", acViewPreview

End Sub

Private Sub PrintThis_Click()
'Opens Print Property report for preview.
'Asks for Listing No for the property to print.

DoCmd.OpenReport "Property Listing", acViewPreview

End Sub

Private Sub Analysis_Click()
'Opens form for selecting type of financial analysis.
On Error GoTo Err_Analysis_Click

    DoCmd.OpenReport "Analysis", acViewPreview

Exit_Analysis_Click:
    Exit Sub

Err_Analysis_Click:
    MsgBox Err.Description
    Resume Exit_Analysis_Click

End Sub
```

continues

Listing 16.2   Continued

```
Private Sub Close_Click()
'Closes form and returns to the Choice form.
DoCmd.Close
End Sub
```

> **Note:** The DoCmd.Close statement closes the Display Results form and returns to
> the Choice form, where you can enter different search criteria. If you want to
> return to the main switchboard instead, add the following two statements just
> before the End Sub line:
>
> ```
> DoCmd.OpenForm "Elgin Enterprises Switchboard", acNormal
> DoCmd.Maximize
> ```

ANALYSIS

The code for the Results100 form that displays the result of a search containing an
Essential attribute is the same except for the reports that open for preview when the user
clicks to print or analyze the results. The Print All Listings button on the Results100
form opens the Results100 report, which uses the same Results100 query that the form
used as the record source. Similarly, the Analysis Results100 report is the report that
opens for preview when the user clicks the Analyze property button in the Results100
form. You could compose the SQL statements in the class modules for these forms each
time they run, but processing is quicker if the queries are already constructed.

Previewing Reports

Two reports are available from the Display Results form: One includes the information
for a single listing and the other for all the listings that were found in the search. The single listing report is based on a parameter query, and the client must enter the listing number of the desired property. This enables the report to be accessed from other points in
the application rather than only from the Display Results form. Figure 16.10 shows a
preview of the single listing report, and Figure 16.11 shows a two-page preview of the
All Results report. Each listing appears on a separate page. If the search was limited to
properties scoring 100 points or more, the Results100 report opens for preview instead of
the All Results report.

FIGURE 16.10
Previewing a single listing.

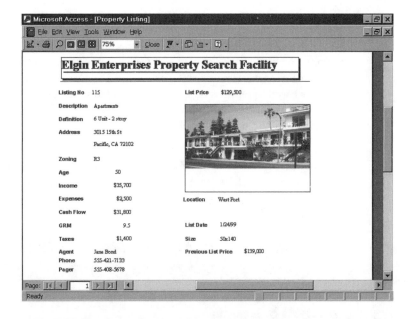

FIGURE 16.11
Previewing two pages of the All Results report.

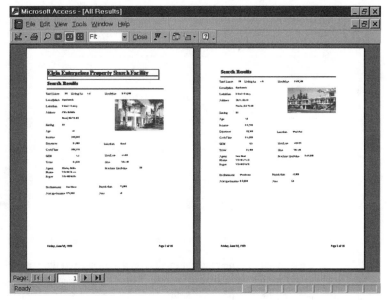

Including Computations and Trade-Offs

When clients find properties that look promising as investments, they might like to see some financial analyses of the properties. If the number of properties found during the search is small enough—less than six—comparative analyses can be performed. The results show how the properties compare with respect to such things as long-term appreciation, the annual rate of return, a 10-year projection of cash flow, and the break-even point at which the income has offset the price paid.

The Analysis command button opens a report that includes the percent annual return on the investment and the estimated breakeven point. The report is based on the same query as the form and is opened for preview with the listings ordered by total score from the highest to the lowest. Figure 16.12 shows an analysis report containing information for five properties.

FIGURE 16.12
Analyzing selected properties.

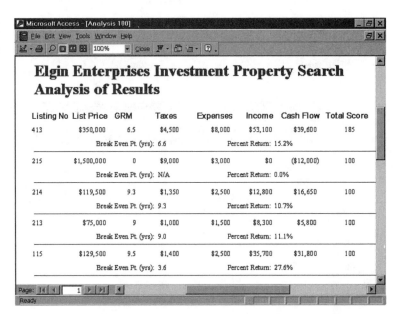

Here are the two calculated fields shown in the analysis report:

- *Break Even Pt.* The result of the list price (considered the present value) divided by the net annual income. Enter the following expression in the Control Source property of the calculated field:

  =[List Price]/[Listings.Income]

- *Percent Return.* The result of dividing the income by the list price. Enter the following expression in the Control Source property:

  =[Listings.Income]/[List Price]

DEVELOPMENT The only problem occurs when Income is 0. You get an error if you try to divide by zero. Change the expression for Break Even Point to

```
IIf([Listings.Income]=0, "N/A",[List Price]/[Listings.Income])
```

This expression uses the `IIf()` function again to define the calculated value as "N/A" if Income is 0 or the result of the division, if not. Notice in Figure 16.12 that listing #215 shows N/A as the breakeven point (because the Income is 0).

> **Tip:** If you let the Expression Builder help you with this expression, it automatically changes `[Listings.Income]` to `[Listings].[Income]`, which will cause an error message. When the Expression Builder spots a period, even within brackets, it recognizes the period as the dot operator and adds more brackets. Because Income is a user-named element, which requires the bang (!) operator, rather than an Access object, an error occurs.

You can even add charts to the report that visually compare the properties that met the search criteria. Figure 16.13 shows two charts in the Results100 report comparing the five properties on the basis of their annual percentage rates of return and total accumulated scores. The charts were created in new forms with the Chart Wizard using the results of the Results100 query, the same record source as the report. The forms were then added to the report as subforms.

FIGURE 16.13
Graphically analyzing selected properties.

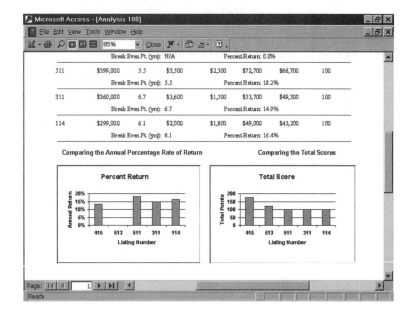

Other analyses can compare the density of listed properties in the different locations or by property type (see Figure 16.14). Such analyses can be of use to the Elgin Enterprise management in an effort to balance their inventory or concentrate on the more promising areas or types of properties.

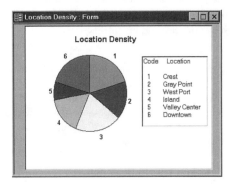

Although Access has many features you can use for numerical and statistical analysis, Excel is the Office application that specializes in these types of studies. In Chapter 17, "Linking with Other Office Applications," you'll have a chance to let Excel do the work and ship the results back to the Access reports.

Putting It All Together in an Application

Once again, the final task is to wrap up all the pieces that make up the application into a single package with one point of entry for the user. Most of the end products—the forms and reports—have been created, now you'll build the model that links them all together. Figure 16.15 shows how the objects are related and how to get from one to another.

Adding a Switchboard

The main switchboard is the customary tool for branching to the desired activity. The order of items in the switchboard should be by priority and frequency of use. Because the Elgin Enterprise application is intended primarily for the decision maker, the option to search for properties is placed at the top of the list (see Figure 16.16).

FIGURE 16.15
Model of the Elgin Enterprises decision support system.

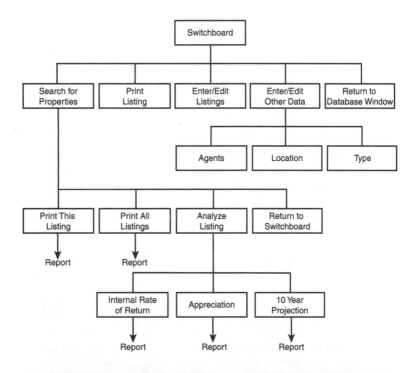

FIGURE 16.16
The Elgin Enterprises main switchboard.

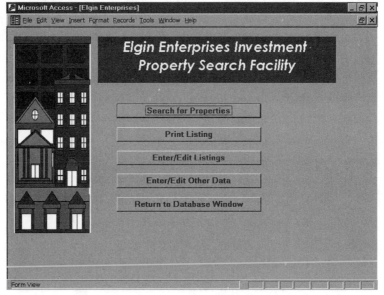

The options in the switchboard carry out the following actions:

- Search for Properties opens the Choice form for the client to begin scouting for suitable investments from the available listings.

- Print Listing is a utility operation that runs the parameter query and opens the specified listing in print preview.

- Enter/Edit Listings opens the Listings data entry form, shown in Chapter 15, "Introducing a Database Decision Support System."

- Enter/Edit Other Data opens other data entry forms. Although the Location and Type tables have data entry forms, adding records to those lists would also require adding to the attribute lists in the Search form.

- Return to Database Window closes the switchboard and returns to a maximized Access database window with the Elgin Enterprises database still current.

DEVELOPMENT

Unlike the switchboards you've seen in earlier chapters, the options in this one are simply command buttons that have been sized to contain the complete option labels.

> **Tip:** You could use traditional small command buttons with accompanying labels, but you would have to create event procedures for the labels as well as the buttons. You can select both controls and click Build to create a macro or an expression that will run when the user clicks either the button or the label. You cannot, however, create an event procedure for a multiple selection because each sub procedure is uniquely named for the control. The code for the switchboard form would have to include pairs of identical event procedures—one for the button and one for the corresponding label.

Listing 16.3 shows the event procedures associated with the Elgin Enterprises Switchboard form.

Listing 16.3 The Switchboard Form Class Module

```
Private Sub Form_GotFocus()
DoCmd.Maximize
End Sub

Private Sub Form_Load()
DoCmd.Maximize
End Sub

Private Sub Search_Click()
'Event procedure for Search button.
On Error GoTo Err_Search_Click

    Dim stDocName As String
    Dim stLinkCriteria As String
```

```
        stDocName = "Choice"
        DoCmd.OpenForm stDocName, , , stLinkCriteria

Exit_Search_Click:
    Exit Sub

Err_Search_Click:
    MsgBox Err.Description
    Resume Exit_Search_Click

End Sub

Private Sub Prop_Listing_Click()
'Event procedure for Print Listing button.
On Error GoTo Err_Prop_Listing_Click

    Dim stDocName As String

    stDocName = "Property Listing"
    DoCmd.OpenReport stDocName, acPreview

Exit_Prop_Listing_Click:
    Exit Sub

Err_Prop_Listing_Click:
    MsgBox Err.Description
    Resume Exit_Prop_Listing_Click

End Sub

Private Sub Enter_Listings_Click()
'Event procedure for Enter/Edit Listings button.
On Error GoTo Err_Enter_Listings_Click

    Dim stDocName As String
    Dim stLinkCriteria As String

    stDocName = "Listings"
    DoCmd.OpenForm stDocName, , , stLinkCriteria

Exit_Enter_Listings_Click:
    Exit Sub

Err_Enter_Listings_Click:
    MsgBox Err.Description
    Resume Exit_Enter_Listings_Click

End Sub

Private Sub Edit_Other_Click()
```

continues

Listing 16.3   Continued

```
'Event procedure for Enter/Edit Other Data button.
On Error GoTo Err_Edit_Other_Click

    Dim stDocName As String
    Dim stLinkCriteria As String

    stDocName = "Choose Data to Edit"
    DoCmd.OpenForm stDocName, , , stLinkCriteria

Exit_Edit_Other_Click:
    Exit Sub

Err_Edit_Other_Click:
    MsgBox Err.Description
    Resume Exit_Edit_Other_Click

End Sub

Private Sub Close_Click()
'Event procedure for Return to Database Window button.
On Error GoTo Err_Close_Click

    DoCmd.Close
    DoCmd.Maximize
Exit_Close_Click:
    Exit Sub

Err_Close_Click:
    MsgBox Err.Description
    Resume Exit_Close_Click

End Sub
```

If you want the switchboard form to appear when you start the application, change the startup option. Choose Tools|Startup and select Elgin Enterprises Switchboard from the Display Form/Page list.

Customizing the Command Bar

Instead of a custom menu bar, this application will have a custom toolbar with buttons. To create a custom command bar, as shown in Figure 16.17, choose View|Toolbars|Customize or right-click in a toolbar and choose Customize from the shortcut menu. Then perform the following steps:

1. In the Toolbars tab, choose New and then enter a name for the new toolbar, such as *Elgin*. A new command bar appears in the Toolbars list in the Customize dialog box.

2. With the new toolbar selected, choose Properties and make sure Toolbar is selected in the Type property box; then close the Properties dialog box. Move the Customize dialog box and the new command bar onscreen so that you can conveniently see both.

3. In the Commands tab, choose All Forms in the Categories list and Choice from the list of forms in the database. Then drag the form name from the Customize dialog box to the new command bar.

4. Choose All Reports in the Categories list and drag the Property Listing report from the Commands list to the bar.

5. Repeat step 3 to drag the Listings form to the toolbar, and then repeat step 4 to drag the All Listings report to the bar.

So far, each of the new buttons mirrors the first three options in the switchboard. Each button executes a single command—opening a form or report. The fourth switchboard option offers a choice of other data to enter or edit. To add this capability to the toolbar, you need to add a menu item with a list of the other data. Then complete the command bar by performing the following steps:

1. To add the Enter/Edit Other Data option to the bar, you must add a New Menu item by selecting New Menu in the Categories list and dragging New Menu from the Commands box.

2. Right-click New Menu and rename it *Other Data*. Then drag the three data entry forms to make them submenu items.

3. Right-click each of the new buttons and select Properties from the shortcut menu. Add appropriate ScreenTip text for each new button.

4. To change the button icon, right-click the button and point to Change Button Image in the shortcut menu. Then select from the palette of icons. If you're artistic, you can choose Edit Button Image instead and draw your own.

5. Select other categories such as File, Edit, and View and drag some of the built-in command buttons to the command bar. Figure 16.17 shows the switchboard with the custom command bar containing both custom and built-in commands.

After you add the desired buttons to the toolbar and create ToolTips for the custom buttons, the DSS development is fully functional. (I say "fully functional" here because *complete* is not an accurate term when referring to a DSS—you can always make additional improvements and changes.)

FIGURE 16.17
The Elgin switch-board with a cus-tom toolbar.

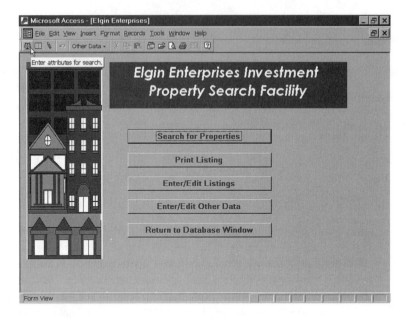

Summary

The display forms and reports created in this chapter continue the development of the Elgin Enterprises DSS. Perhaps you've acquired a feel for the extensive capabilities Access has to offer to a DSS developer. Access can literally do whatever you need in support of quantitative and qualitative decision analysis. You'll visit the Elgin database briefly in the next chapter, where it receives assistance from Excel. In Chapter 20, "Posting Your Database to the Web," the system is published as dynamic data access pages on the Web.

Linking with Other Office Applications

Like a diverse and talented office staff, each of the Microsoft Office 2000 applications has a special niche of expertise. In addition to being able to import and export data between programs, you can create live links to make the objects available for cooperative efforts.

The Automation feature of Office 2000 is the medium that makes these talents so easily available to all Office applications. Whenever necessary, Access can call upon one of its Office teammates to help out with a special task. This chapter explores Automation and sharing information among the Office applications.

Copying Objects Among Office 2000 Applications

The easiest way to exchange objects among Office applications is to copy them. You can copy Access objects from one Access database to another or to a different application.

With the new Office Clipboard, you can collect and copy up to 12 objects in it and then paste them one at a time or all at once. To copy an object to another Access database, select the object name in the database window and click Copy on the toolbar to copy the object to the Clipboard. Next, close the current database, open the database where you want to place the copy, and then click the Paste toolbar button. Then, enter a name for the newly pasted object. If you're copying a table, in the Paste As dialog box, you have a choice of pasting the table structure only, both the structure and the data, or appending the data to an existing table. Pasting an Access object copies all the object's properties, as well.

> **Note:** When you cut or copy data from an Access form or datasheet and paste it into an Excel spreadsheet, the font, alignment, and number formatting settings you've specified for the column headings and the data are preserved.

If you're pasting to a datasheet, be sure that the columns in the datasheet match the data you're adding. If you're pasting to a form and the controls in the form have the same names as the data you're copying, Access pastes the data to the matching controls. If the column names are different from the form control names or there are no column names at all, Access pastes the data in the tab order of the controls on the form.

When you paste records to another application, the field names are placed in the first row and the data follows in subsequent rows. If you copy a datasheet that has subdatasheets, Access can copy only one level at a time. When you import or link a datasheet with sub-datasheets, however, the subdatasheets are included.

After you've copied the object from one Office 2000 application to the Clipboard, you can also choose Edit|Paste Special instead of Paste to add it to a different application. The type of information you want to paste from the Clipboard varies with the source and destination applications. Table 17.1 describes the types from which you may choose in the Paste Special dialog box with each pair of applications. Both Paste and Paste Special give you in-place access to the source application from within Access to make changes in the object. If you want the object to keep up-to-date with the original information as it changes, you need to create a link instead of copying it.

Table 17.1 Paste Special Choices

Source	Destination	Paste As Types
Access	Excel	Biff5, HTML, Unicode Text, Text, and CSV
Access	Word	Formatted Text (RTF), Unformatted Text, HTML Format, and Unformatted Unicode Text
Word	Access	MS Word Document, Picture, Hyperlink, and Text
Word	Excel	MS Word Document Object, Picture (Enhanced Metafile), HTML, Unicode Text, Text, and Hyperlink
Excel	Access	MS Excel Worksheet, MS Excel Chart, Picture, Bitmap, and Text
Excel	Word	MS Excel Worksheet Object, Formatted Text (RTF), Unformatted Text, Picture, Bitmap, Picture (Enhanced Metafile), HTML Format, and Unformatted Unicode Text

In the Paste Special dialog box, you also have a choice of Paste Link, which creates a live link to the source application. This way, any changes made to the source object are reflected in the pasted object. For some objects, such as an Excel chart, a final option is to display the object as an icon. This is handy when you're working on a report and need to see it without the pasted object getting in the way.

Using the drag-and-drop method is another way to copy Access objects to other databases or other applications. You can drag a table or other object to another database if it's open in another instance of Access. To drag objects between applications, you can either have both applications visible at once and drag the object between them, as shown in Figure 17.1, or drag the object first to the Windows desktop, where it becomes a shortcut, and then open the destination application and drag the shortcut into that window. You can drag a table, query, or report from the database window to another application to make a copy of it.

FIGURE 17.1
Dragging an Access table to an Excel spreadsheet.

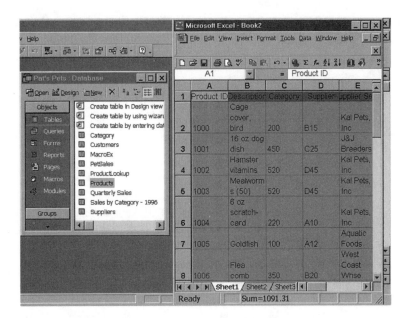

If you want to copy a range of cells from an Excel worksheet to Access, you can select and drag them to a new Access table in the datasheet view. You can also drag standard modules between Access and Excel.

Importing, Linking, and Exporting Data

Importing data into Access creates a copy of the information in a new table in a database. Importing data has no effect on the source of the data. You can make changes to your new copy, which also have no effect on the original information. Imported data is not updated when the source data is changed. For that, you must link the data to the source.

Linking, on the other hand, creates a live connection between the applications. When you create a link to external data, you can read and usually update the data without adding a copy of it to your database. This saves space in the database, but you must keep track of the location of the external data. If the original information is moved to a different folder, your database might not be able to locate it without the help of the Linked Table Manager, which is described in the next section. You can use either the application that created the data or Access to add, delete, or edit the linked data.

Before importing or linking data to Access, you must open an existing database or create a new one to use as the destination. If the datasheet has related subdatasheets, they're imported or exported as well.

Importing or Linking from Another Access Database

When you import objects from another database, you may need to import other related objects as well. For example, if you import a form that's based on a query that extracts data from related tables, you may need to import the tables as well. When you import a data access page, you import only the link to the underlying HTML file.

To import or link data from another Access database to your database, open your database and then follow these steps:

1. Click New in the Tables page of the database window.

2. In the New Table dialog box, choose Import Table or Link Table and then click OK. You can also choose File|Get External Data|Import (or Link Tables) to select the database objects for importing.

3. In the resulting Import or Link dialog box, locate the database you want to get information from and click Import or Link.

4. If you chose Import Table, the Import Objects dialog box opens with tabs for each of the database object types. You can select any of the database objects to import. If you chose Link Table, you can select only table objects, because they're the only objects that actually contain data. Click the object name to include it in the operation. If you change your mind, click it again to deselect it. You can also select or deselect all the objects in the list at once.

5. Click Options in the Import Objects dialog box to specify additional options for the import (see Figure 17.2):

   • The Import check boxes enable you to import the relationships that exist between the tables and queries you select, import the custom menus and toolbars, and include all the import/export specifications in the imported database. If, however, a custom menu or toolbar is named the same as one in the destination database, it will not be imported.

- The Import Tables options enable you to import only the table definition or both the definition and the data.

- The Import Queries options specify whether to import them as queries or as the tables that result from running the queries.

6. After completing the selections, choose Import (or Link). You're returned to the database window, where you can see the new Access objects (see Figure 17.3).

FIGURE 17.2
Selecting objects to import.

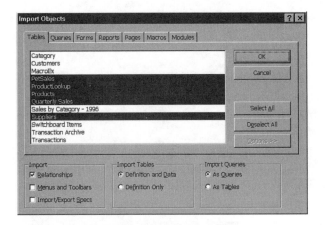

FIGURE 17.3
Tables imported and linked from another Access database.

The Category table shows an arrow next to the table icon, indicating that it's linked rather than imported. Imported Access tables look no different in the database window.

Importing objects from one Access database to another is effectively the same as copying and pasting the objects.

> **Note:** To quickly import all the objects from one database to another, choose File|Get External Data|Import. Then choose Microsoft Access in the Files of Type box. After you locate the database you want to import, choose Select All on each of the object tabs. In the Tables tab, click Options and select additional import options.

> **Tip:** The linked tables are identified in the database window with an arrow and an icon representing the origin of the data, if it's other than Access (see Figure 17.4). If you delete a table name that displays an icon, you remove the link in Access to the external database or other application, but you do not remove the table itself from the external source.

FIGURE 17.4
Tables linked from other sources show special icons.

The Agents table is linked to a dBASE table, Location to a Paradox table, More Pets to an Excel worksheet, and Text Only to an RTF text file.

> **Note:** You cannot append most imported data to an existing table in your database. The exceptions are spreadsheet data and text files. However, once the data is imported, you can run an append query in Access to add the new data to the existing tables.

Managing Linked Tables

When you link data from other sources to an Access database, the Linked Table Manager keeps track of the path to the external files. You can use the Linked Table Manager to view, refresh, or change the filename and path for the linked tables. To reach the Linked Table Manager, choose Tools|Database Utilities|Linked Table Manager. Figure 17.5

shows the files linked to the ImportDB database. Check the tables with links you want to refresh and then click OK.

Figure 17.5
The Linked Table Manager keeps track of links.

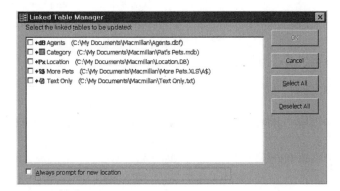

After successfully refreshing the selected table links, Access displays a confirmation message. If not successful, Access displays a dialog box in which you can specify a new link path.

> **Tip:** If you've changed the Access table name after linking, the Linked Table Manager can't refresh the link. You must delete the link and then relink the tables.

If you want to change the path to the link, select Always prompt for new location in the Linked Table Manager dialog box and then select the check box for the tables whose links you want to change. When you click OK, the Select New Location of *<tablename>* dialog box opens, where you specify the new location.

> **Note:** The Linked Table Manager doesn't actually move database or table files, it only redefines the path to the linked object. If you want them placed in a different folder, use Windows Explorer or another utility to move them and then call upon the Linked Table Manager to refresh the links.

Importing or Linking from Other Data Sources

CAPABILITY

Table 17.2 shows the other data sources from which you can import or link data. All the built-in drivers are automatically installed when you install Access 2000 and are available when you choose to import or export objects.

Table 17.2   Other Data Sources Supported by Access

Data Source	Format or Version
Access databases	1.x, 2.0, 7.0/95, 8.0/97, and 9.0/2000.
Access projects	9.0/2000.
dBASE databases	III, III+, IV, 5, and 7. *
Paradox databases	3.x, 4.x, 5.0, and 8.0. *
Excel spreadsheets	3.0, 4.0, 5.0, 7.0/95, 8.0/97, and 9.0/2000.
FoxPro	2.x and 3.0 (for importing only).
Lotus 1-2-3 spreadsheets	.wks, .wk1, .wk3, and .wk4 (when linked data is read-only).
Delimited text files	MS-DOS or Windows ANSI text format files with values separated by commas, tabs, or other specified characters. All character sets.
Fixed-width text files	MS-DOS or Windows ANSI text format files with values arranged in fields all the same width. All character sets.
HTML	1.0 (list), 2.0, 3.x (table or list).

Linking to dBASE 7 or Paradox 8.0 requires Borland Database Engine 4.x or later.

> **Tip:** If you want to import data stored in a program with a format not supported by Access, you can probably export, convert, or save it in one of the supported formats. For example, most programs—even those executing under a different operating system—can export data to a delimited or fixed-width text file, which can then be imported or linked to Access.

You can also import from or link to SQL tables and data from databases and programs that support the Open Database Connectivity (ODBC) protocol, depending on the ODBC drivers you have installed.

When you import data from Excel, you invoke the Import Spreadsheet Wizard, which gives you a choice of worksheets (if there are more than one in the selected workbook) or named ranges. The wizard then asks you to specify whether the first row in the sheet contains the names you want for the fields in the new table (see Figure 17.6). Choose Next and in the next dialog box, you can choose to store the information in a new table or in an existing table.

In the next Import Spreadsheet Wizard dialog box, you can specify information about each field, such as renaming the field and identifying the field as indexed, changing the field data type, or even leaving a field out of the import (see Figure 17.7). Select each field by clicking in the column header and make changes in its options, as necessary. The last steps with the wizard deal with setting a primary key field and naming the new table that will contain the spreadsheet data.

FIGURE 17.6
Selecting field names from a spreadsheet.

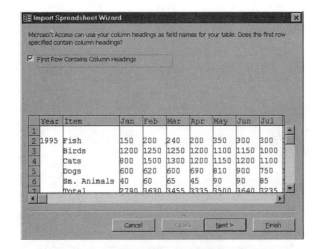

FIGURE 17.7
Specify information about each field.

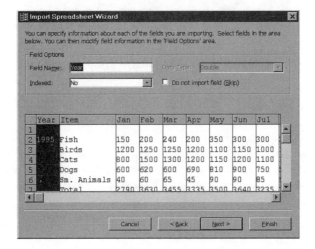

Figure 17.8 shows the table structure created when an Excel worksheet is imported into an Access database. Notice that Access has added the primary key ID field with the AutoNumber data type.

There are two other ways you can use Excel data in Access:

- You can use the Excel data in an Access report or form.
- You can convert Excel data to Access.

FIGURE 17.8
*The table struc-
ture created from
the Excel work-
sheet.*

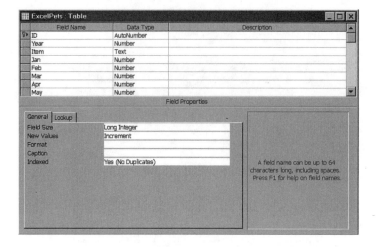

To create an Access report with Excel spreadsheet data, choose Data|Access Report in the Excel spreadsheet window to start the Access Report Wizard. After you choose whether to create the report in a new or existing database, the Access Report Wizard starts. Using the wizard, you can format the report just as any other Access report. You can also use the same process to add Excel data to an Access form.

Another option in the Excel Data menu is Convert to MS Access, which permanently converts a no-longer-used Excel spreadsheet to an existing or new Access database.

> **Note:** If you haven't installed these add-ins, Excel offers to install them for you.

When you import a table from dBASE or some other database program, the table goes right into the open database. If you link a table from dBASE, you're asked to select associated index files as well and then select a unique record identifier. This arranges the data in the source program the way you want to see it in Access.

Handling Import Errors

If errors occur while you're trying to import a text file or a spreadsheet to your database, Access creates an Import Errors table. The table contains the field names and row numbers indicating the data that caused the errors as well as descriptions of the errors. Some errors that can occur include the following:

- *Field Truncation.* The value in the text field is longer than the Field size property for the field.

- *Key Violation.* The record's primary key value already exists in the table.

- *Null in Required Field*. The field's Required property is set to Yes, which does not permit a null value.

- *Type Conversion Failure*. The value in the text of the spreadsheet field is wrong for this field.

- *Unparsable Record*. A text value contains a character reserved as a text delimiter, such as a double quotation mark (").

- *Validation Rule Failure*. The value breaks the rule set in the Validation Rule property for the field.

If Access reports that errors occurred during import, you can open the Import Errors table to find the problems. To correct the errors, you may be able to edit the data. If you're appending the text file or spreadsheet to an existing table, you may need to change the table structure to correct the errors.

After correcting the problems, import the data again.

Exporting from Access

LOOKING AHEAD

Exporting from one Access database to another is just another way of looking at importing Access objects, but exporting to other programs is a little different. A special case is exporting an Access table containing names and addresses to Word for use in a mail merge operation. You'll learn more about mail merge in the section "Mail Merge," later in this chapter.

> **Tip:** Because you can export only one object at a time, if you have several objects to export, you might want to turn things around and run the import process from the destination database instead. Open the destination database and import the objects all at once.

To export an Access object, select the name of the table or query you want to export and choose File|Export or right-click and choose the Export option from the shortcut menu. In the Export Table <*tablename*> To dialog box, choose the destination for the table or query in the Save in box; then choose the file type from the Save as type list and enter a name for the exported file. When you're finished, click Save.

> **Note:** You can export only tables from Access 2000 to earlier versions of Access. The other objects are not compatible with the previous versions. See Appendix B, "Converting from Earlier Versions of Access," for information about converting an Access 2000 database back to Access 97.

If you're exporting to Excel or to another database application, Access creates the new file using the field names as column headings. To export to Word, you must either choose a Rich Text Format (RTF) file type or export to the mail merge data source file. Table 17.3 shows the data formats to which Access can export.

Table 17.3   Access Export Data Formats

Destination	Format or Version
Access databases	2.0, 7.0/95, 8.0/97, and 9.0/2000
Access projects	9.0/2000
dBASE databases	III, III+, IV, 5, and 7 *
Paradox databases	3.x, 4.x, 5.0, and 8.0 *
Excel spreadsheets	3.0, 4.0, 5.0, 7.0/95, 8.0/97, and 9.0/2000
Visual FoxPro	3.0, 5.0, and 6.x
Lotus 1-2-3 spreadsheets	.wk1 and .wk3
Delimited text files	MS-DOS (PC-8) and Windows ANSI
Fixed-width text files	MS-DOS (PC-8) and Windows ANSI
HTML and IDC/HTX	1.1 (if a list), 2.0, and 3.x (if a table or list)

Requires Borland Database Engine 4.x or later.

> **Note:** If you export an Access table that contains names—either the table itself or one of the fields—that are not allowed in the destination database, Access edits the names. For example, if you're exporting to dBASE, which limits field names to 10 characters, the extra characters are truncated. Word limits field names to 20 characters. Many destinations also restrict the use of special characters in field names.

Creating Live Office Links

Before getting into programming live links to other Office applications through Automation, let's take a look at how you can cross into other realms using wizards and menu choices.

Access is useful as a repository for names and addresses that can be used for form letters and mailing labels. Excel, in turn, is very helpful to Access for analyzing numeric data and creating charts and graphs to illustrate trends and comparisons.

The Office Links option in the Tools menu contains three choices: Merge It with MS Word, Publish It with MS Word, and Analyze It with MS Excel. You can also reach these commands by clicking the Office Links toolbar button.

Interchanges with Word

You have three ways to exchange data with Word: Send an Access table to Word via the Mail Merge Wizard, export an Access table as an external file and specify the file type as Mail Merge, or save the datasheet, form, or report as a Rich Text Format (RTF) file. When you save the object as an RTF file, you can also automatically open it with Word and be ready to work on it immediately. In addition, from Word, you can specify an Access table or query as the data source for a mail merge operation.

Mail Merge

The cooperation between Access and Word is an example of letting the member who can best do the job do it. Although both applications can accomplish a mail merge operation alone, the most efficient way is to let the database manager handle the list of addressees and the word processor handle the main document—the form letter or other text.

This collaboration can work from either end: Word can create the main document and then call upon Access for the file to use as the data source in a Mail Merge operation, or Access can merge the table into a Word Mail Merge setup with the main document.

As an example, the Pat's Pets store has a form letter to send to customers who have recently registered with the store. The basic letter, called Main Document, has been written in Word without any of the merge fields added. The letter is contained in the New Letter.doc file in the Imports folder on the accompanying CD. When you open the Access table that contains the names and addresses of the customers, you can export it to Word and connect it with the mail merge Main Document, as follows:

1. Select the Customers table name in the Pat's Pets database window and choose Tools|Office Links|Merge It with MS Word. The Mail Merge Wizard dialog box opens (see Figure 17.9).

FIGURE 17.9
The Microsoft Word Mail Merge Wizard dialog box.

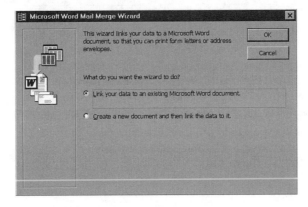

2. Choose the first option, Link your data to an existing Microsoft Word document, and then choose OK.

3. Choose New Letter in the Select Microsoft Word Document dialog box. You might need to change to the folder to which you copied the files from the Web site. Then choose Open.

4. This launches Word and displays the letter with the Mail Merge toolbar. It also launches another instance of Access to use as the live link. The Insert Merge Field drop-down list in the Mail Merge toolbar displays the fields in the Customer table of the Pat's Pets database.

5. Place the insertion point beneath the logo in the form letter and select the customers' first name, middle initial, and last name fields one at a time from the list. Be sure to add a space between the fields (see Figure 17.10).

FIGURE 17.10

Selecting fields from the Access Customer table.

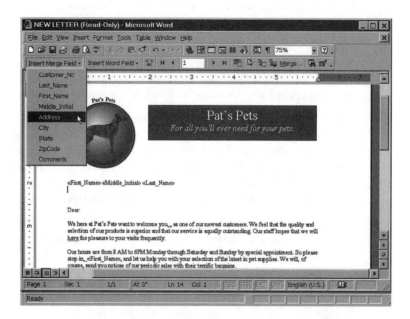

6. After placing the remaining merge fields in the letter, the Word document looks like the one shown in Figure 17.11. The Field Shading option (Tools|Options|View) has been set to Always for the figure so that you can see where all the merge fields are placed, including within the letter itself.

7. Click the Merge to New Document button on the Word Mail Merge toolbar and print the first page of the form letter (see Figure 17.12).

If you've been working in Word to create the form letter and want to select an Access table as the data source, choose Get Data in the Mail Merge Helper dialog box and select Open Data Source. Then choose Microsoft Access Databases in the Files of Type box and select the database file that contains the table or query with the names and addresses you want for the data source (see Figure 17.13). If you want to use a query as the data source, you can look at the SQL statement that defines the query by clicking the Queries tab in the Microsoft Access dialog box, selecting a query, and choosing View SQL.

FIGURE 17.11
The form letter with all the merged fields.

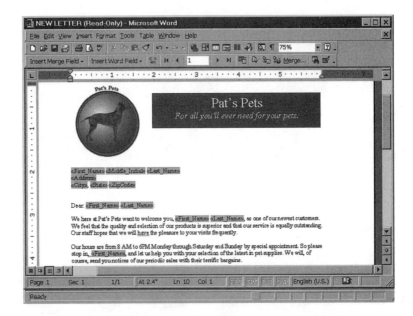

Note: When you use an Access table or query as the data source for a Word mail merge operation, the field names are used as the merge fields. If you've already completed a main document with the merge fields and the field names of the Access table or query don't match, edit the field names in either the data source or in the main document so that they do match. Word formatting rules also state that the field names can be no longer that 20 characters (additional characters are truncated). Characters other than letters, numbers, and underscores are all changed to underscores.

FIGURE 17.12
The finished print-ed form letter.

Pat's Pets

Pat's Pets
For all you'll ever need for your pets.

Phil B. Denison
820 Sunset Blvd.
Rio West, CA 91229

Dear Phil Denison:

We here at Pat's Pets want to welcome you, Phil Denison, as one of our newest customers. We feel that the quality and selection of our products is superior and that our service is equally outstanding. Our staff hopes that we will have the pleasure to your visits frequently.

Our hours are from 8 AM to 6PM Monday through Saturday and Sunday by special appointment. So please stop in, Phil, and let us help you with your selection of the latest in pet supplies. We will, of course, send you notices of our periodic sales with their terrific bargains.

Once again, let me welcome you personally to our important clientele. If there is anything we can help you with, please do not hesitate to let us know.

Sincerely yours,

Patricia Evansville

Patricia Evansville,
Manager

FIGURE 17.13
Selecting an Access table as the data source.

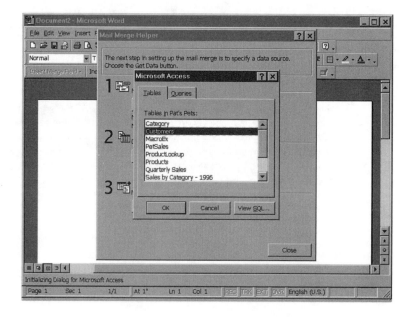

Publishing in Word

If you simply want to add some of the information from Access to a Word document, use the Publish option. You can save a table, query, form, or report by loading it in Word as an RTF file. To do this, select the object you want to save and choose Tools|Office Links|Publish It with MS Word. The output is automatically saved to the same folder as the Access application, and then Word automatically starts and opens the file. Figure 17.14 shows the Elgin Enterprises Property Listing report as published with Word.

FIGURE 17.14

An Access report published with Word.

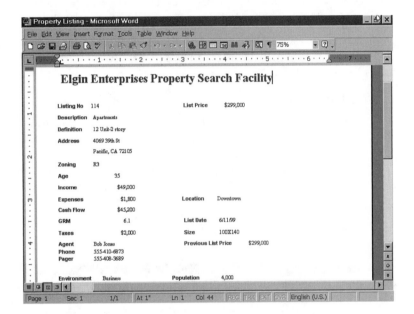

You can see in the figure that the picture of the property that was included with the Access report does not appear in the Word file. When you save a file as RTF format, only the text is saved. If you want to include other objects, they must be inserted after the file is exported to Word.

If there's a version of Word open, the file is saved to that version. If not, the file is saved to the latest version that's installed in the system. Watch the status bar for messages as the file is saved. It can take a few minutes.

If you want to save only part of an Access datasheet, select that part before choosing from the Office Links submenu of the Tools menu.

Exporting to Word

To export an Access table or query to a Word document, save the object as an RTF file and then open it from Word. Then, within Word, save the file as a document file. This creates a copy of the Access table or query and retains no connection with the original Access object.

Interchanges with Excel

You can export a table, query, form, or report to an Excel worksheet, where you can call upon Excel's analytical capabilities to process the data. If you want to create a copy in an Excel spreadsheet that will always contain current information, create a link instead. Choosing Tools|Office Links|Analyze It with Excel stores the selected Access object as an Excel file and automatically starts Excel and loads the new file.

If you just want to save a copy of the Access information in an Excel worksheet, save the Access table or query by choosing File|Export and specifying where and how you want it saved in the Export Table *<tablename>* To dialog box.

Using Office Link

The financial information in the Elgin Enterprises database offers an excellent example for linking Access with Excel. Excel can perform many more types of analyses of numeric information because that's its job. To link the Listings table from Access to a new worksheet in Excel, select Listings in the database window and choose Tools|Office Links|Analyze It with MS Excel. The status bar displays the message "Outputting object" during the process. Then, Excel launches with the new worksheet containing the Listings data (see Figure 17.15). The field names from your Access table or query become the values in the first row of the Excel spreadsheet.

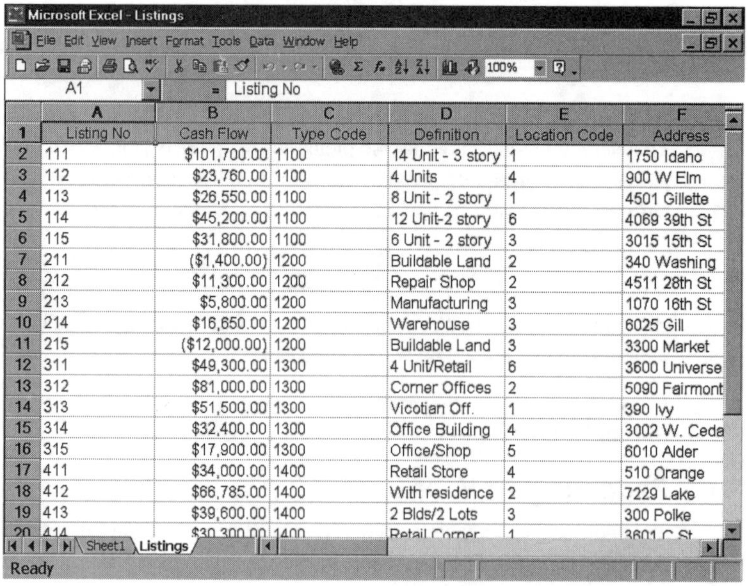

	A	B	C	D	E	F
1	Listing No	Cash Flow	Type Code	Definition	Location Code	Address
2	111	$101,700.00	1100	14 Unit - 3 story	1	1750 Idaho
3	112	$23,760.00	1100	4 Units	4	900 W Elm
4	113	$26,550.00	1100	8 Unit - 2 story	1	4501 Gillette
5	114	$45,200.00	1100	12 Unit-2 story	6	4069 39th St
6	115	$31,800.00	1100	6 Unit - 2 story	3	3015 15th St
7	211	($1,400.00)	1200	Buildable Land	2	340 Washing
8	212	$11,300.00	1200	Repair Shop	2	4511 28th St
9	213	$5,800.00	1200	Manufacturing	3	1070 16th St
10	214	$16,650.00	1200	Warehouse	3	6025 Gill
11	215	($12,000.00)	1200	Buildable Land	3	3300 Market
12	311	$49,300.00	1300	4 Unit/Retail	6	3600 Universe
13	312	$81,000.00	1300	Corner Offices	2	5090 Fairmont
14	313	$51,500.00	1300	Vicotian Off.	1	390 Ivy
15	314	$32,400.00	1300	Office Building	4	3002 W. Ceda
16	315	$17,900.00	1300	Office/Shop	5	6010 Alder
17	411	$34,000.00	1400	Retail Store	4	510 Orange
18	412	$66,785.00	1400	With residence	2	7229 Lake
19	413	$39,600.00	1400	2 Blds/2 Lots	3	300 Polke
20	414	$30,300.00	1400	Retail Corner	1	3601 C St

FIGURE 17.15
The Listings table data exported to Excel.

In Excel, you can create a range of cells containing summary information, such as the average percentage of return by property category or the average breakeven point by category. Figure 17.16 shows the Excel summaries on a separate sheet. Using the Excel Chart Wizard, you can create column charts depicting these summaries, as shown in Figure 17.17.

FIGURE 17.16
Summarizing Access data in Excel.

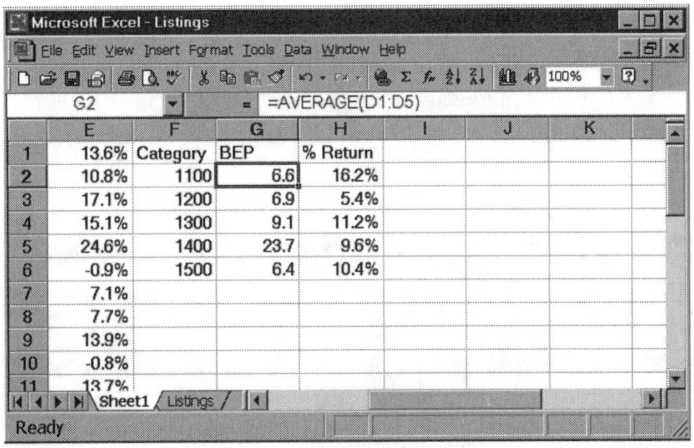

FIGURE 17.17
Adding charts to the summarized data.

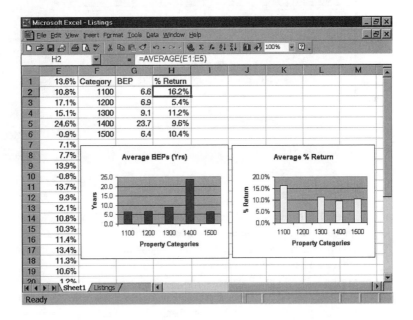

Now all that remains is to copy the charts to an Access report that will include text information about Elgin Enterprises and its investment opportunities. The easiest way is to start a new report or open an existing report and copy the charts into it one at a time.

To place the charts in an Access report, follow these steps:

1. Select one of the charts in the Excel worksheet and click Copy.

2. Switch to the Access database window and click New in the Reports tab. Then choose Design View to open a blank report design window.

3. Click Paste. The chart appears in the report design detail section.

4. Return to the Excel window, select the other chart, and then click Copy again. Both chart objects appear in the Clipboard.

5. In the Access window again, click Paste. The second chart appears below the first. Click and drag the second chart to a position beside the first one (see Figure 17.18).

FIGURE 17.18
The new Access report with two Excel charts.

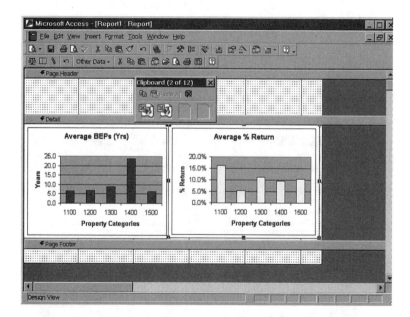

The link between Access and Excel is now complete. If you want to make a change in one of the charts, double-click the chart in the report design, and Excel, the source application, launches in place within Access. Right-click the chart and choose Chart Options from the shortcut menu to change any of the formatting options (see Figure 17.19). The chart was moved in the figure so you can see it with the Chart Options dialog box open. Additional worksheet tabs are available in the Excel space that enable you to view the supporting worksheet data. You can change the data in the worksheet, and the changes will be reflected in the chart.

To return to Access, click anywhere in the report design outside the chart.

FIGURE 17.19
Activating the link with Excel to change chart options.

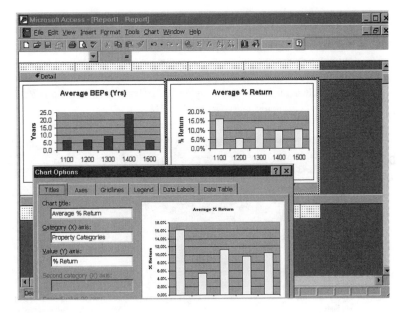

Exporting to Excel

To export a table or query to an Excel spreadsheet, select the object name in the database window and then choose File|Export. In the Export Table <*tablename*> To dialog box, choose a spreadsheet format and the spreadsheet where you want to save it in the Save In dialog box; then click Save. You can also create a new spreadsheet to save it in.

CAPABILITY

> **Warning:** If you attempt to export an Access table or query to an existing Excel spreadsheet file created in an early version of Excel, you might delete and replace the contents of the worksheet. Exporting to an Excel version 5.0 or later workbook copies the data to the next available worksheet instead. Be careful to add an empty worksheet if you're exporting to one of the earlier versions.

The only objects you can export to an Excel spreadsheet are tables and queries. You can, however, save the output of any object in an Excel spreadsheet using the same File|Export process. In the Export Table To dialog box, choose one of the newer Excel formats (Excel 5 or later) or RTF. Then, check the Save Formatted option in the Save In dialog box to preserve several formatting options, such as displaying the data in the lookup fields as well as the fonts and the field widths as they were in Access. This also saves any group levels in a report as Excel outline levels. This option slows down the process but will save you time in the long run if you need consistency.

Creating a PivotTable

A PivotTable is similar to a crosstab query except that it's interactive. It performs calculations such as sums and counts on the underlying data, depending on how you've arranged the rows and columns. Excel can use data in an Access table to create a PivotTable in an Access form. Figure 17.20 shows an example of a PivotTable summarizing Pat's Pets annual sales over the last five years.

FIGURE 17.20
A PivotTable in an Access form.

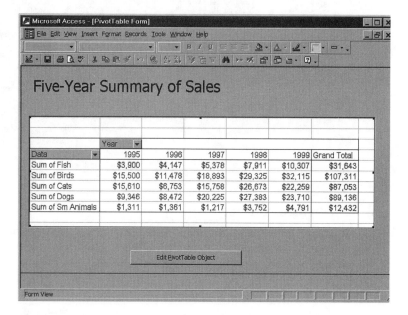

The table was created by calling up the PivotTable Wizard from Access, as follows:

1. Start a new form, choosing the PivotTable Wizard and the PetSales table. The wizard shows an explanatory dialog box followed by a dialog box in which you can choose which fields to include in the table.

2. Select Year and the five pet category fields; then choose Next. In the next PivotTable Wizard dialog box, click Layout.

3. The next PivotTable Wizard dialog box displays a diagram into which you drag the fields.

4. Drag the Year field to the Column heading position in the diagram and the product category fields to the Data block. Then choose OK (see Figure 17.21).

5. You return to the previous dialog box. Click Finish. The finished form appears in Access form view (refer to Figure 17.20).

FIGURE 17.21

Using the PivotTable Wizard.

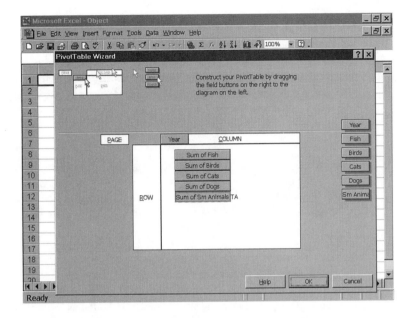

The Edit PivotTable Object button takes you back to Excel, where you can make changes to the table formatting such as formatting the sales figures as currency with no decimal points. To format the sales figures, select the range of cells that contain the sales data and choose Format|Cells. Then choose Currency on the Number tab. The form shown in Figure 17.20 has also been resized and a title has been added.

Because the data is not stored in the PivotTable, each time you use the form with the table, you must refresh the data if there have been any changes.

Introducing Automation

If you recall OLE Automation in earlier versions of Office, this version of Automation will not be a stranger. Automation is a feature of the industry-standard technology known as *Component Object Model* (COM), which its members use to expose their objects to other members of the model. For example, a database application can expose a report, form, or table as a separate, identifiable object for use by Word, Excel, or any other application that supports Automation.

If an application supports Automation, you can access its objects through VB and then manipulate the objects with methods or by setting the objects' properties. Access is an ActiveX component that supports Automation. An *ActiveX component* is defined as an application that can use objects supplied by another application or expose its own objects for use by another. Such applications were formerly known as *OLE Automation servers and controllers*.

Creating a New Automation Object

If you want to use an object from another Automation component, you must first set a reference to that application's type library. After you set the reference, you have access to all the objects in the library, together with their properties and methods. After setting a reference to a VB project in another Access database, you can also call any of the public procedures in that type library. Setting a reference to an ActiveX control enables you to add the control to an Access form.

> **Note:** You can set a reference to a type library in another Access 97 or Access 2000 database this way. However, if you want a reference to a library in a database from a previous version, you must convert the database to Access 2000 first.

To set a reference to another Automation component's applications, choose Tools|References. The References option is available only when the module window is open. You can, however, set a reference from a VB procedure. Figure 17.22 shows the References dialog box displaying a list of nearly 150 different available references. Your list may vary, depending on your system. Scroll down the list and check the object libraries for Excel 9.0, Graph 9.0, and Word 9.0 to add them to your list of available libraries.

FIGURE 17.22

Adding references to type libraries.

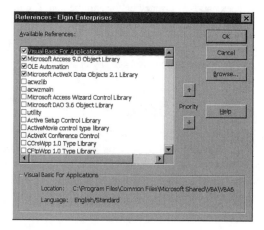

In Chapter 9, "Writing Visual Basic Procedures," you were introduced to the Object Browser, where you can select the desired type library from a list. After you've set new references with the References dialog box, their libraries appear in the Object Browser list (see Figure 17.23). When you select one of the new libraries, you can see all the objects in the Object Browser together with their methods and properties. This makes it much easier to know what's available to each object in another application with which you're not all that familiar. Drop-down lists of methods and constants as well as other related information are also displayed as you enter code relating to the applications you've referenced.

FIGURE 17.23
The new libraries appear in the Object Browser.

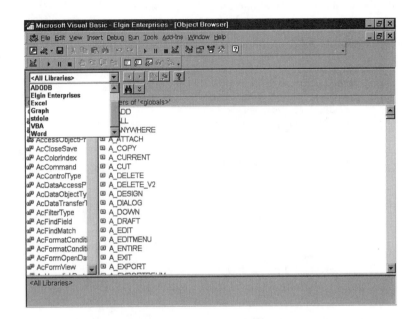

Through Automation, you can manipulate the objects in the other applications by referring to them by class. For example, a Word 9.0 document is referred to as Word.Document, and an Excel 9.0 worksheet is referred to as Excel.Worksheet.

Creating a New Application Object

From Access, you can now create a new Excel object (or other component application object) and change its properties and call its methods just as you would with an Access object. You have two ways to create a new application object: by using the New keyword in the declaration statement or by calling the CreateObject() function after declaring the application object variable. Here are examples:

```
Dim appExcel As New Excel.Application
```

or

```
Dim appExcel As Excel.Application
Set appExcel = CreateObject("Excel.Application")
```

After the object is created, you can manipulate it in VB code by using the object variable name you assigned to it.

ANALYSIS

You can also use CreateObject() to create one of the other application objects, such as a Word document or an Excel worksheet. For example, the code in Listing 17.1 creates a new Excel application that automatically starts Excel. After setting the other variables to a new workbook and worksheet, the code adds text to cell A1. Then, the worksheet is saved in the specified directory and Excel closes.

Listing 17.1   Creating a New Excel Application

```
Sub GetWorkSheet()
'Create a new Excel workbook with one worksheet.
Dim xlApp As Excel.Application
Dim xlBook As Excel.Workbook
Dim xlSheet As Excel.Worksheet

Set xlApp = CreateObject("Excel.Application")
Set xlBook = xlApp.Workbooks.Add
Set xlSheet = xlBook.Worksheets(1)

'Make the worksheet visible.
xlSheet.Application.Visible = True

'Add text to cell A1 and change the font properties.
With xlSheet.Cells(1, 1)
    .Value = "This is Cell A1"
    .Font.Size = 14
    .Font.Name = "Arial"
    .Font.Italic = True
End With

'Save the new worksheet, close Excel and clear the object variable.
xlSheet.SaveAs "C:\Test.xls"
xlSheet.Application.Quit
Set xlSheet = Nothing

End Sub
```

ANALYSIS

The preceding With…End With block of code keeps xlSheet.Cells(1, 1) active for changing several properties at once. The index for Cells must be numeric, so Cells(1, 1) refers to cell A1.

Figure 17.24 shows the new Excel worksheet with the formatted text in cell A1.

Note: In this example, declaring and setting the application, workbook, and worksheet variables binds the new object when the module is compiled. If you set only the worksheet object, the binding does not occur until the code is run. You'll get an error message if you try to run the code from the module window without first setting the application and workbook objects.

FIGURE 17.24
The new work-sheet created from an Access procedure.

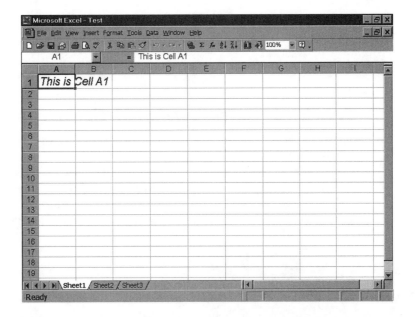

ANALYSIS

The GetObject() function accesses an ActiveX object from a file and assigns the object to an object variable you've declared. The GetObject() syntax is GetObject([*path-name*][,*class*]), where both arguments are optional. However, if you omit the *pathname* argument, you must include the *class* argument. The *class* argument uses the syntax *appname.objecttype*, where *appname* is the name of the application providing the object and *objecttype* is the type or class of the object you want to access. For example, the following line of code will create a reference to an existing Word document:

```
Set objDoc = GetObject("C:\Winword\Letters\Macmillan.doc")
```

If you already have the application running, you can also use the GetObject() function as an alternative to creating a new object by specifying the pathname as a zero-length string (""). If you omit the *pathname* argument, GetObject returns the currently active object that matches the type you declared for the object variable, if any. If an active object isn't available, an error occurs.

You can use VB procedures to work with Word documents from within Access, too. Word has its own set of objects, properties, and methods you can scan with the help of the Object Browser by choosing the Word type library. The following fragment of VB code uses the GetObject() function to open the Word document named New Letter, which can be copied from the Imports folder on the accompanying CD:

```
Sub OpenLetter()
Dim wrd As Object

Set wrd = GetObject(, "Word.Application")
```

```
wrd.Visible = True
Documents.Open "C:\My Documents\Macmillan\NEW LETTER.DOC"
End Sub
```

Change the `Documents.Open` statement to refer to the path to the file on your hard drive.

Working with ActiveX Controls

An ActiveX control is another object you can insert into a form, just like the built-in controls on the toolbox—text boxes, list boxes, combo boxes, images, and so on. To see a list of the ActiveX controls you have available, click the More Tools button on the toolbox. The list shows the built-in controls as well as ActiveX controls, such as the popular Calendar control (see Figure 17.25). You can also choose Insert|ActiveX Control to choose from the same list displayed in the Insert ActiveX Control dialog box.

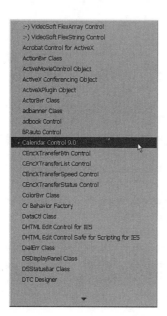

FIGURE 17.25
The More Controls list shows available ActiveX controls.

The subject of ActiveX controls is far too extensive to cover adequately here. A useful example is the Calendar control, which can be bound to a table that contains a list of events with their dates and other related information. To use this control, start a blank form based on the table named Calendar, which contains the event information, in the Elgin Enterprises database and then perform the following steps:

1. Choose More Controls on the toolbox or choose Insert|ActiveX Control and then choose Calendar Control 9.0 from the list.

2. Click the plus sign with the little hammer icon where you want the upper-left corner of the calendar.

3. In the Calendar Control property sheet, set the Control Source property to Date, the name of the date field in the table.

4. Resize and move the Calendar control as necessary.

5. Add two text boxes to display the name of the event and the list of attendees. Then add a title.

Figure 17.26 shows the completed Schedule form. The navigation buttons at the bottom of the form move you through the records in the Calendar table, highlighting the corresponding date on the control as you go.

FIGURE 17.26
The completed Schedule form.

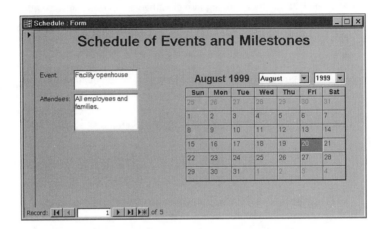

The Calendar control has many properties you can change within the property sheet, but it also has a custom properties dialog box (called Calendar Properties) in which you can set additional properties that change its appearance. To see this dialog box, click the Build button next to the Custom property in the property sheet. The dialog box has three tabs: General, Font, and Color (see Figure 17.27). Choosing Calendar Object|Properties also opens the Calendar Properties dialog box.

FIGURE 17.27
The Calendar Properties dialog box.

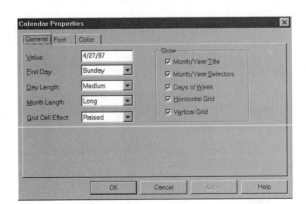

The General tab lets you set the length of text for the day and month names, the first day of the week, and what items to show in the calendar. The Font tab lets you choose different font settings for each section of the calendar, and the Color tab does the same with standard and custom colors.

Summary

Office 2000 offers many ways for its members to interact with one another. This chapter has investigated some of them, beginning with simple copy-and-paste operations from one to another and then moving into creating live connections through Office Links. Word becomes an important tool for Access as a publishing arm, and Access returns the favor by providing the data source for mail merge operations. Excel has many analytic capabilities to offer to Access, including the PivotTable Wizard.

The Automation environment makes it easy for all the members to share their objects for use in Visual Basic code. Properly written procedures can use the type libraries of other components of the Automation model to work with objects from other applications. The final topic in this chapter briefly addressed the subject of ActiveX controls.

Peter Norton

Part VI

Advanced Access Programming

Working in a Multiuser Environment

So far in these chapters, the Elgin Enterprises database has been described as if it's a straightforward, single-user database that exists on only one computer in the Elgin Enterprises offices. Nothing could be further from the truth. Consider for a moment the wide variety of data stored in this database: real-estate descriptions, income and expenses data, agents' names and phone numbers, and so on. This information is intended to be used by several different people at Elgin Enterprises as well as the company's customers and clients.

The Need for Multiuser Data Access

NETWORKING

Back when personal computers were first becoming popular in business environments, there was no easy way to share information among several users. Sharing data often meant having to copy files onto floppy disks and physically carry the disks from computer to computer, often referred to as "sneaker-ware." Each user then copied the files onto his or her own computer before beginning to work. Keeping the data coordinated under these conditions was a nightmare. Often, only one user could make updates to the data at a time. If more than one user added new records, deleted old records, or changed the data in existing records, someone had to be responsible for ensuring that the changes were collected and coordinated to keep the data synchronized on all computers in the office.

The situation is actually worse when the shared information resides in an Access MDB file. Most MDB files are quite large and would never fit on a single floppy disk, making it impossible to share data using this type of disk medium. Also, because all the database objects, including tables, forms, and reports, reside in the same file, any time changes are made to these objects, they must be imported or exported into the working database—a tedious, time-consuming process at best.

Over the last 10 years or so, computer networks have become a standard part of most offices. Now, more than 80 percent of the business computers in the United States are connected to a network of some kind. The network usually is a *local area network* (LAN) serving all the computers in an office or building. Often, a company's network extends beyond a single building to multiple buildings or even across the country as a *wide area network* (WAN).

When computers are connected via a network, making information available to multiple users is greatly simplified. The data can reside on a single place on the network and be made accessible to all users. Data files do not have to be copied onto floppy disks and carried from computer to computer. Other operations, such as backing up the data to protect it from catastrophic loss, are made much easier by keeping the data files in a single location in the business.

However, as soon as more than one user is working with the data at the same time, several new problems arise. For example, a method must be devised to make sure that only one user can make changes to a record at a time. If more than one user is able to edit the same record, important changes might accidentally be overwritten. Also, because data is so important, very often the data must be protected by limiting access to it with passwords and other protective mechanisms.

DEVELOPMENT

This chapter answers three very important questions about multiuser databases: how to set up Access databases so the data can be shared by all users, how to protect the data from being changed by more than one user at a time, and how to make sure that everyone is working with the same information. This chapter does not discuss networking or network architecture. Instead, it concentrates on the steps a developer must take to ensure that the data in an Access database is efficiently and accurately shared among several users. Chapter 19, "Adding Security to the Application," discusses how to secure a database by adding password protection to the tables and other database objects.

LOOKING AHEAD

The good news is that Microsoft Access was created with multiuser capabilities in mind. As you'll soon see, you have all the options and capabilities you could ever ask for at your disposal as you begin sharing your databases with other users. In fact, as you'll see near the end of this chapter, sharing more than just the data in Access databases is quite easy. Access 2000 makes it easy to share new forms and reports with other users regardless of the multiuser architecture you choose for your environment.

The first method discussed involves splitting a database for simultaneous access by users connected by a network, either local or wide area. The second method creates a set of independent copies of the database for use by multiple users. The set of replicas is carefully synchronized periodically so that users always have access to reasonably up-to-date data and design features.

Where to Put the Data

ARCHITECTURE

Obviously, the data in a multiuser environment must be put someplace on the network that's accessible to all users who need the information. Even though all the database objects, such as tables, forms, and reports, in an Access database live in a single MDB file, you'll soon see that you're not limited to this arrangement. As a developer, you have several options when it comes to determining your database's architecture. In this context, *architecture* simple means where on the network you put all the tables, forms, reports, and code in your application. Very often the best solution involves breaking the

MDB file into several pieces and distributing these pieces where they'll do the most good.

The Simple Approach

An easy solution is to simply put the Access MDB file on a *server* computer on the network. Depending on the network configuration, the server might be the network's file server (most often in a Novell-type LAN) or a computer that's designated as the database server (in the case of a Windows 95/98 or Windows NT network). Figure 18.1 illustrates this type of network arrangement.

FIGURE 18.1
One option for multiuser database access.

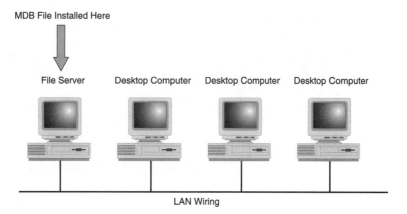

The arrangement you see in Figure 18.1 is easy to implement. In the case of the Elgin database, the single MDB file is moved or copied to the computer on the network that's working as the database file server. As mentioned earlier in this chapter, this computer might be the actual file server in a Novell LAN or a designated server on a Microsoft Windows Networking network. Each of the desktop computers in this figure has its own copy of Microsoft Access installed, but the database file exists only on the server.

| TROUBLESHOOTING | Unfortunately, there are several problems with this approach. Every time a user opens a form or report in the centrally located MDB file, a large amount of information must flow across the network from the MDB file to the local copy of Access. This information includes a lot more than the data behind the form or report. All the information necessary to display the form or report must also travel across the network. This information includes the form's or report's design details such as the size, position, and color of the controls, the text that appears in the labels on the form or report, and other details such as the size and position of the form or report on the screen. |

| PERFORMANCE | If very few users are working with the database at one time or if the network is otherwise very lightly loaded, the network traffic generated by the arrangement you see in Figure 18.1 probably is not much of an issue. In these cases, a user might notice a very slight delay as the form or report is opened on his or her computer. If, however, there's a large |

number of users trying to use the same database or if the network is being used for print-ing, Internet access, or file sharing with other applications, the delay can be uncomfort-ably long.

Many other factors enter into the network performance equation, including the speed of the database server, the type of LAN wiring used in the network, how many other appli-cations are moving data across the network at the same time, and so on. It's hard to gen-eralize the performance you can expect from this simple approach to sharing Access databases, but performance is bound to become an issue in this arrangement sooner or later.

A Better Solution

NETWORKING

ARCHITECTURE

Figure 18.2 illustrates an alternative approach to sharing Access databases. In this arrangement, a *back-end* database is installed on the server, and *front-end* databases exist on each desktop computer. The back-end database contains the data tables, and each front-end MDB contains the other database components—queries, forms, reports, macros, modules, and shortcuts to data access pages. The tables in the back-end database are linked to each front-end MDB on the users' desktops.

FIGURE 18.2
Splitting a data-base for multiuser access.

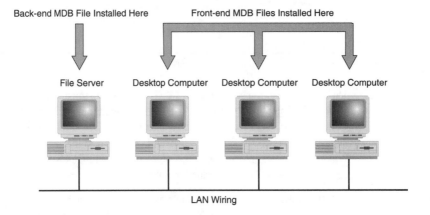

There are several major advantages to this arrangement. First, because the forms, reports, and other user interface components are kept in the local copy of the front-end database, they load very quickly. No information moves across the network as a form opens unless that form contains data. Therefore, loading unbound forms such as switchboards and dia-log boxes takes very little time because nothing must move over the network.

PERFORMANCE

Second, because the user interface components are kept separate from the tables, updating a form or report is as easy as replacing the front-end MDB on a user's desktop computer. In fact, the easiest way to keep users updated is to put a copy of the front-end database on the file server and instruct each user how to copy that MDB file to his or her own desktop computer.

A third big advantage of the database architecture you see in Figure 18.2 is that different users can have "custom" front-end databases. For example, the needs of the order-entry people in a company are quite different from the folks in the Sales department. Figure 18.3 shows how the database system might be set up so that each department has its own customized user interface, including the switchboards, data and dialog forms, reports, and data access pages that make the most sense for the department. Meanwhile, all these departments are sharing the same data reservoir in the back-end MDB file.

Figure 18.3

A custom front-end database for each department.

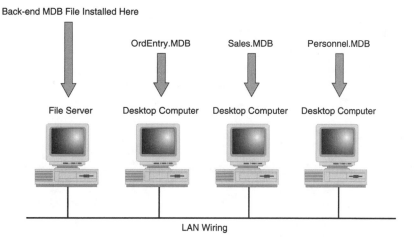

The arrangement you see in Figure 18.3 is incredibly powerful. Using this architecture, you can treat each department as a separate client or customer. With different front-end databases, it's easy to provide an individual department with a customized form or report or to update an existing form or report. Because each department has its own user interface, the people in the Sales department don't even need to know about the Human Resources department's information stored in the back-end database. A high level of security can be provided for sensitive tables in the back-end database by making the tables unavailable to departments that have no need for the information stored there.

Development

Obviously, there's more work involved in setting up the scheme illustrated in Figure 18.3. You must create a separate database for each department, doubling or tripling the work involved for creating the database system. One way to minimize the work involved is to create a "master" database that contains all the forms, reports, code, and other objects needed by all the departments. You (the developer) keep the master database on your computer, making it easy for you to make changes to any of the objects used by the users. The master "development" database also makes it easy for you to apply the same appearance attributes to all the forms and reports used by everyone.

After you have a reasonably complete master database, copy it once for each department, assigning an appropriate name to each copy. Then, make the final adjustments to each copy to suit the intended audience. As you complete each departmental database, copy it as a "department master" onto the server computer to make it available to its intended users. Later, as you update each individual departmental database, export the updated component to the department master and let your users make copies from the master.

ARCHITECTURE

Figure 18.4 illustrates the principle of maintaining a development master on one computer and the department masters and the department back-end databases on the server. It shouldn't be too hard to train users how to copy objects from the department master.

FIGURE 18.4
Keep the master database on the developer's computer.

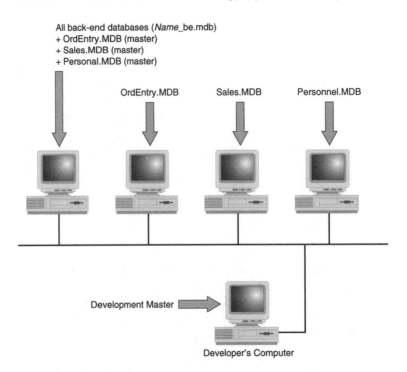

All back-end databases (*Name*_be.mdb)
+ OrdEntry.MDB (master)
+ Sales.MDB (master)
+ Personal.MDB (master)

OrdEntry.MDB   Sales.MDB   Personnel.MDB

Development Master

Developer's Computer

LOOKING AHEAD

You're probably wondering just how you're going to produce the separate front-end and back-end databases. Later in this chapter (in the section titled "Using the Database Splitter"), you'll learn all about a utility built into Access 2000 that makes splitting databases a fast and easy process.

Fine-Tuning for Performance

PERFORMANCE

So far, the process of splitting a database into separate front-end and back-end pieces seems relatively straightforward. All the tables go into the back end, and all the user interface and code goes into the front end to minimize network traffic and improve performance. There's one final step to take to optimize this arrangement.

Most databases contain a number of tables that contain largely static data. For example, a table of Zip codes and cities isn't likely to change very much. The table is there simply to make it easy to find the city corresponding to a particular Zip code. Such a table is often referred to as a *lookup table*. In contrast, the data stored in an orders or employees table is likely to be quite dynamic, constantly changing and being updated. There's no reason to keep static data in the back-end database on the server computer.

DEVELOPMENT
As you set up your databases as distinct front-end and back-end components, look for opportunities to keep lookup tables on the user's desktop computer in the front-end database. Each time an inquiry is made against a lookup table stored in the front-end database, you save a considerable amount of network traffic. In the rare event that a lookup table needs to be updated, you can put the updated table in the master front-end database on the server and let users copy the master to their own computers.

As a final consideration, if your application creates any temporary tables, the temporary tables should always be stored on the local computer. Not only will this arrangement help minimize network traffic, it will prevent the inevitable conflicts that arise if more than one user tries to create the same temporary table on the back-end copy of the database.

Using the Database Splitter

The "split database" design has become so common in many environments that Microsoft built a splitter utility into Access 2000. The Database Splitter simplifies the process of creating a back-end database, exporting files to the back end, and linking the tables between the two halves. In fact, the Database Splitter does not actually "split" an existing database. Instead, it creates an entirely new back-end database and exports all the tables to that database. After verifying that the tables have been exported without error, the Database Splitter then deletes the tables in the current database and creates links to each of the tables in the back-end portion. In this way, the Database Splitter preserves the original database architecture so that you can use it as a development master.

Peter's Principle

It's always better to be safe than sorry, and this applies strongly to database development. Before doing anything that's not easily reversible, such as splitting a database, always make a backup copy of the database in another folder or on another computer, if possible. This advice is even more relevant to replicating a database (discussed later in this chapter) because Access adds several new system tables and new fields to the database tables. It also adds some new properties to the database and its objects. You can restore the database from the replicated version to its original configuration, but it's a difficult and complicated process. Better to keep a copy in a safe place.

To start the splitter utility, choose Tools|Database Utilities|Database Splitter. The opening dialog box of the Database Splitter opens in response (see Figure 18.5).

FIGURE 18.5
The Database Splitter is a powerful tool for structuring multiuser databases.

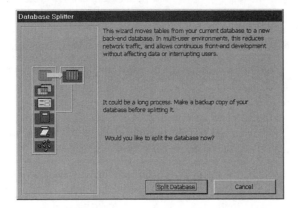

Be prepared for the Database Splitter to require a lot of time when it's splitting large databases. Creating the back-end database takes only a few seconds. What can take a long time is exporting the tables to the back-end database. Exporting the tables will also generate a tremendous amount of network traffic, assuming you're posting the back-end database on a server computer on the network. Click the Split Database button in the dialog box you see in Figure 18.5 to continue.

The next dialog box of the Database Splitter lets you specify where to drop the back-end part of the split database (see Figure 18.6). Notice that the Database Splitter suggests appending "_be" to the end of the database name. This convention makes it easy to recognize when a database is serving as the back end to another database.

FIGURE 18.6
Put the back-end database on the database server.

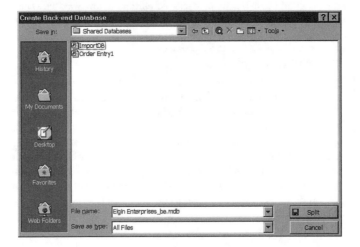

The Save In drop-down box at the top of the Create Back-End Database dialog box in Figure 18.6 is network-aware. There's a Network Neighborhood entry on the drop-down list that lets you locate any computer on the LAN to use as the database server. As soon as you click the Split button in the Create Back-End Database dialog box, Access begins the splitting process.

> **Warning:** You should not interrupt the splitting process unless it's absolutely necessary. Keep in mind that Access is actually deleting the tables in the current database, which could lead to a problem if Access is not allowed to complete the task.

Figure 18.7 shows the Tables tab of the Database window after the splitting process is complete. Notice that all the tables are actually links to another database. Figure 18.8 shows the Linked Table Manager dialog box (accessed through the Linked Table Manager command in the Tools|Database Utilities menu) showing that the tables in the Elgin Enterprises database are linked to `Elgin Enterprises_be` on the computer named Gandalf on the LAN.

FIGURE 18.7
The tables after the splitting process.

FIGURE 18.8
All tables are now links to the back-end database.

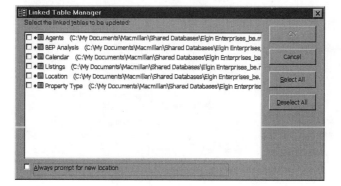

Figure 18.9 shows the Tables page in Elgin Enterprises_be database. This database actually contains all the data tables for the split database system. Any data changes will occur in this back-end database.

FIGURE 18.9
Elgin Enterprises_be contains the tables for the split database.

The next step in the splitting process is to import any lookup tables from the back-end database to the front-end component. Notice that the Database Splitter moved every table to the back-end file. This might not be what you prefer in your final application. Be sure to move the lookup tables to the front-end database before distributing it to users.

As a last check of your new multiuser database system, make sure the Shared option button is selected in the Default Open Mode area on the Advanced tab of the Options dialog box (see Figure 18.10). You open this dialog box with the Options command on the Tools menu. The Shared option means that Access will enable more than one person to use the data in a database at a time.

FIGURE 18.10
The Shared option button enables multiple users to open the same database at the same time.

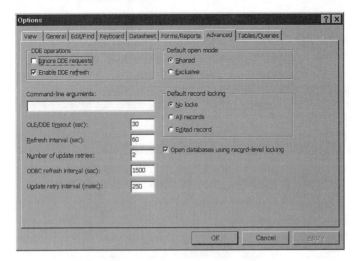

Record Locking: Controlling Access to Records

Now that you've installed the back-end database on the file server, the users each have their own copies of a front-end database, and databases are being opened in shared mode, look at how Access helps you protect the data in the tables.

One of the most serious problems that can occur in shared databases happens when more than one user makes changes to the same record at the same time. Consider the situation in which no control is maintained over multiple access to the records in database tables. Suppose two users (Shirley and Bob) are updating some records in the Elgin Enterprises database. Even though they each have a copy of the front-end database installed on their desktop PC, the data with which they're both working is stored on the same back-end database on the server. Therefore, if they both are working on a particular listing, they both actually are working on the same record in the Listings table.

Imagine the confusion that would occur if Bob gets a call from a client as he's working on the listings in the Elgin Enterprises database. The call is from a client who has decided that the new list price he arranged with Shirley the day before isn't quite what he thinks will best sell his property. During the phone call Bob opens the listing in question and continues his dialog with the client. Meanwhile, Shirley is in her office inputting the "old" list price she discussed with the client the day before. Bob completes his phone call, saves the record with the new list price, and moves on to another record in the database. Coincidentally, the second after Bob saves the record he's been working on, Shirley completes her changes and moves on to another record.

In this particular scenario, even though Shirley's data was incorrect, she "won" the changes in the database because she saved her changes after Bob completed his. Keep in mind that one of the preconditions of this scenario is that no control over access to database records is in place. This means that neither Bob nor Shirley was aware that the other was making changes to the client's record at the same time. When Shirley saved the record, she was not informed that she was overwriting changes made by another user while she had the record open.

The situation described in the preceding paragraphs would be disastrous in many environments. In the case of the Elgin Enterprises database, the worst that could happen is that a sale would be lost if the incorrect list price is too high to sell the property. Or, the client might be forced into an awkward situation if the incorrect list price is lower than the correct price and a buyer insisted that the client honor the too-low price. In either case, Elgin Enterprises is exposed to possible legal action as a result of mishandling the client's listing.

The very least that would happen is that the incorrect list price would show up on forms and reports for a few days until someone noticed the error. Eventually, someone would realize the incorrect price had been stored in the database and would correct the error.

Fortunately, the Access *locking mechanism* reduces the chance that errors such as this will damage the data in the tables. As soon as a user begins editing the data in a record (this includes adding new records to the database), Access notices the edit activity and imposes a *lock* on the record, thus preventing other users from making changes to the same record. Access provides several levels of record locking that you can fine-tune to suit how your users work with their data.

To set the default record-locking scheme for a database, use the Options dialog box. If you want to set record locking for an individual form, set the form's Record Locks property.

Pessimistic Locking

In many cases, simultaneous changes to the same record is an undesirable situation. In environments where it's important that the data in a record be completely updated before another user can begin making changes to the same record, *pessimistic locking* is required. Under this scheme, as soon as a user begins making changes to a record, Access clamps down on the edited record, preventing other users from making changes to it. The other users can view the record in a form or report, but they cannot make changes to it. Figure 18.11 illustrates pessimistic locking at work.

FIGURE 18.11
Pessimistic locking is needed in many situations.

In Figure 18.11, the List Price text box on the form on the left is being changed from $310,000 to $315,000. Notice that the icon in the form's record selector (the vertical gray bar along the left edge of the form) is a pencil, indicating the current record is being edited. The record selector on the form on the right (Pessimistic2) displays the international "Not" symbol, indicating that the record in Pessimistic2 is currently unavailable for editing.

The Not symbol tells you that Access has locked the recordset behind the Pessimistic2 form. This means that only the person using the Pessimistic1 form is able to make changes to the record at this time. The Pessimistic2 user will have to wait until the Pessimistic1 user is finished with his edits before proceeding.

The Not symbol does not appear instantly. In an effort to reduce processing overhead, Access checks the lock state of a form's recordset at intervals specified by the Refresh Interval setting in the Advanced tab of the Options dialog box. (The refresh interval appears in the lower-left group of options in Figure 18.10.) If, at the end of the refresh interval, Access determines the records in the form's recordset are locked, the Not symbol appears in the form's record selector area. By default, the refresh interval is set to 60 seconds, which might be too long in dynamic environments. Set it to a lower value if users complain that they can't tell when another user has locked records they're trying to use.

Access also checks the lock state as soon as a user tries to edit a record. Even if the refresh interval has not expired, Access will instantly display the Not symbol as the user begins changing data in a locked form.

Pessimistic locking must be specified; it's not the default setting for Access 2000 forms. You set pessimistic locking by specifying Edited Record as the value for a form's Record Locks property (see Figure 18.12). The next section describes *optimistic locking*, an alternative locking scheme that's the default for all new forms in Access databases.

FIGURE 18.12
You establish pessimistic locking by setting Record Locks to Edited Record.

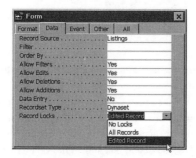

Optimistic Locking

The default lock setting in Access is *optimistic locking*. Optimistic locking assumes that record conflicts will be rare events. The assumption is that in most cases, a user will complete an edit on a record before another user tries to edit the same record. Therefore, there's minimal need to handle edit conflicts.

You set optimistic locking in the bound form by setting the Record Locks property to No Locks (see Figure 18.13). The edited records are locked only at the instant they're actually being saved in the database. Using optimistic locking, a true lock conflict is a rare event. A *write conflict*, however, occurs if two users try to edit and save the same record at the same time (more on write conflicts later in this section).

FIGURE 18.13
Optimistic locking is appropriate in many situations.

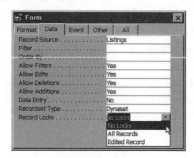

Figure 18.14 illustrates optimistic locking in action. In this figure, two forms are displaying the same data from a single record in the Elgin Enterprises database. Optimistic1 (the form on the left) is in the middle of an edit (the list price is being changed from $173,000 to $170,000). Notice that the icon in the form's record selector is a pencil, indicating the current record is being edited. The record selector on the Optimistic2 form on the right is also displaying the pencil icon, indicating the same record is being edited in the Pessimistic2 form (the Taxes field is being changed from $1,700 to $1,750).

FIGURE 18.14

More than one user can be editing the same record under optimistic locking.

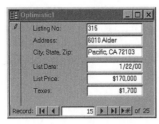

The Optimistic2 form remains available and editable forever. No matter how long the user on the left holds the edit state on the current record, the record selector in form Optimistic2 does not change to the Not symbol. The only time the Optimistic2 user will be aware that a problem exists is when he tries to commit his changes. If Optimistic1 completes her edits and commits the changes by moving on to another record, when Optimistic2 tries to save his changes, the dialog box shown in Figure 18.15 appears.

FIGURE 18.15

A write conflict occurs when two users make changes to the same record.

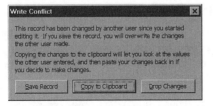

The Write Conflict dialog box informs the user that someone else on the network has also made changes to the record at the same time as his or her edits. Here are the options available to the user at this point:

- Go ahead and save the record, overwriting the changes made by the user on form Optimistic1. This means the change made to the list price by the Optimistic1 user will disappear from the database.
- Copy the new data to the Office Clipboard so that the changes made by the other user can be viewed on the form.
- Discard edits and allow the other user's edits to be displayed on the form. In this case, the Optimistic2 user will have to reenter his or her changes to the data.

If you choose to use optimistic locking, you'll have to train your users how to deal with the Write Conflict dialog box. Experiment with the three write conflict options to see which one is best suited for your users' data.

Locking Entire Tables

The last locking scheme you'll learn is obtained by setting a form's Record Locks property to All Records. In this case, Access locks all the records in the tables or queries providing information to a form. While the All Records lock is in place, of course, no other users can make changes to the data. In most environments, this is an unacceptable situation, but there are times when the All Records setting is needed. For example, if the form runs an update or delete query that's going to modify the data in several different records, you'll want the query to lock all records so that it's able to complete its work. If optimistic or pessimistic locking is used in these situations, some records might be held open by other users, and the update or delete query would either fail or incompletely modify the data in the table.

> **Note:** You might have noticed a file with the same name as an open database but with an .LDB filename extension in the Windows Explorer. This file contains the information that Access needs to manage locks on the open database. Do not delete this file while a database is open. In fact, there should almost never be a reason for you to manually delete this file. Under normal conditions, Access will automatically remove this file when the last user working with the data has closed the database.

Choosing a Locking Scheme

Here are several factors you should consider when selecting a locking scheme for your database:

- You should use pessimistic locking whenever it's important to prevent a user's changes from being overwritten by another user. Pessimistic locking forces only a single user to access a record at a time.

- Pessimistic locking almost always locks more than one record at a time.

- Generally speaking, you'll get fewer complaints from users with optimistic locking because more users can get to more records without encountering locks.

- You'll have to train your users how to deal with the Write Conflict dialog box if you choose optimistic locking.

The preceding discussions have described the Access locking schemes as if they affect individual records at a time. Unlike many other database systems, however, Access does not actually lock a single record at a time. Access uses a *page locking* mechanism that actually locks a 4KB (4096 bytes) buffer in the MDB file. This page size has doubled in Access 2000 in support of the new Unicode format used for storing characters.

This page locking used by Access means that more than one record will be affected by a lock imposed by a user as he or she edits data. The effect of page locking becomes especially important when working with very small records in tables. It's possible that 40 or 50 records will be locked if each record contains 100 or fewer bytes of data.

One way to prevent such large blocks of data from being locked is to apply the new record-level locking option available in Access 2000. *Record-level locking* locks only a single record instead of a whole page of records. When you check this option, it becomes the default locking behavior for working with data in a form, a datasheet, or any code that uses a recordset object in a loop structure. It does not apply to action queries or code that executes bulk operations with SQL statements. To choose record-level locking, check Open Databases Using Record-Level Locking in the Advanced tab of the Options dialog box.

If you've selected pessimistic locking and your users frequently complain that they can't edit records because some other user is making changes, try applying record-level locking. If they're still not pleased, you should consider changing to optimistic locking.

Setting the Default Locking Scheme

The Advanced tab of the Options dialog box contains several more settings that affect the locking implemented in your applications. You've already learned about the Default Open Mode setting in the upper-right corner of this dialog box and the Refresh Interval in the lower-left corner. Notice the Default Record Locking group of settings beneath Default Open Mode. When Access is first installed, Default Record Locking is set to No Locks (optimistic locking), as you saw in Figure 18.10. If you decide that pessimistic locking is more appropriate for your environment, select the Edited Record setting. This means that all new forms in the database will automatically be set to pessimistic locking at the time they're created. They do not apply to existing forms or dynasets.

Implementing Locking in Visual Basic Code

So far, this chapter has dealt with locking as if the only way locking is implemented in Access databases is by setting the database's default record-locking scheme or a form's Record Locks property. In Chapter 16, "Customizing Input and Output," and Chapter 17, " Linking with Other Office Applications," you saw code such as the following:

```
Dim dbsCurrent As Object
Dim rstList As Object
Set dbsCurrent = CurrentDb
Set rstList = dbsCurrent.OpenRecordset("Listings", dbOpenDynaset)
```

These statements, of course, set up and build a dynaset-type recordset object that contains data from the Listings table. By default, all Access recordsets implement pessimistic locking.

There are times, however, when the default setting is not appropriate for the recordset you've created. You might want to use optimistic locking in situations in which performance is critical and users complain that they can't get their work done.

All dynaset and table-type recordsets have a `LockEdits` property that enables you to specify optimistic or pessimistic locking. The following statements create a recordset named `rstList` and set its locking to optimistic:

```
Dim dbsCurrent As Object
Dim rstList As Object
Set dbsCurrent = CurrentDb
Set rstList = dbsCurrent.OpenRecordset("Listings", dbOpenDynaset)
rstList.LockEdits = False
```

Setting `LockEdits` to `False` is the same as setting a form's `Record Locks` property to `No Locks`. `LockEdits` is set to `True` by default (pessimistic locking).

> **Tip:** You can also set the `LockEdits` value when you open the `rstList` recordset by setting the *lockedits* argument of the `Open Recordset` method. If you set the argument to `dbPessimistic`, the `LockEdits` property is set to `True`. Any other value sets the property to `False`.

Snapshot-type recordsets have no `LockEdits` property. Because a snapshot cannot be updated, there's no need to provide a locking mechanism for these objects.

Keeping Data Views Up-to-Date

Consider for a moment a form that's designed mostly for data review. Perhaps the form is intended as part of an online orders support application. Customers call in to check on the status of their orders, and the clerk uses the form to confirm the items and quantities ordered as well as to see if the order has been packed or shipped. In this kind of application, it's critical to make sure that the data view the clerk sees is completely up-to-date. In dynamic environments such as large mail-order companies (LL Bean, Sears & Roebuck, and JC Whitney, for example), the data in the order-entry database changes by the second. Giving a customer incorrect information about an order could be very damaging.

Access provides several options that control the "timeliness" of the data displayed on forms. The most important of these are the refresh interval and the `Refresh` and `Requery` methods. A *refresh* updates the data displayed onscreen, whereas a *requery* completely rebuilds the recordset underlying the form. Either a refresh or requery will be called for, depending on the needs of your users.

In either case, the view the user sees will change before his eyes as the refresh or requery cycle is completed. As long as the data displayed onscreen is from a dynaset or table-type recordset, Access maintains live connections back to the tables underlying the form.

As soon as the data changes and the refresh or requery cycle ends, the data displayed on the form will be updated to reflect the changes.

Refresh

You've already visited the Refresh Interval setting in the Options dialog box. By default, this value is set to 60 seconds, much too long in truly dynamic environments. If it's critical that users see an up-to-date view of the data, set the refresh interval to something smaller, perhaps as low as 10 or 15 seconds. Be careful not to set it too low, of course, because each refresh cycle generates network traffic and consumes processing time on the computer. The increased overhead is a small price to pay when accurate views are essential. Keep in mind, however, that the Refresh Interval setting in the Options dialog box affects all recordsets in all forms in the application.

A user can also force a refresh by selecting the Refresh command from the Records menu. If you'd prefer that the user click a button on a form to refresh the data, use the following code in the Click event procedure for a command button:

```
Me.Refresh
```

All forms have a Refresh method that can be triggered at any time. Alternatively, you can use the form's timer interval (measured in milliseconds) to trigger the Timer event. Use the same Refresh method in the Timer event procedure and set the timer interval to the desired number of milliseconds between refresh intervals. Using the Timer event lets you set the refresh interval on a form-by-form basis rather than affecting the overall application with the Refresh Interval setting in the Options dialog box.

A refresh does not guarantee 100 percent accuracy in its view of the underlying data. For example, records that have been added to the database since the recordset was constructed for the form are not displayed. Also, if the sort order has changed for some reason, the records underlying the form are not resorted and records that no longer meet the specified criteria are not removed. However, deleted records are marked with #Delete in all fields.

Requery

A requery is a more drastic view update than a refresh. When the form's Requery method is invoked, Access completely rebuilds the recordset underlying the form. A requery guarantees that the data is completely accurate: New records are displayed, the data is sorted in the proper order, and deleted records are removed from the recordset. The only problem from the user's perspective is that the data in the form returns to the first record in the recordset. Therefore, if the user is working on a particular customer's order before the requery, he or she will have to return to that customer's record before continuing.

You trigger a requery by pressing the Shift+F9 key combination or by running the form's Requery method:

```
Me.Requery
```

Choosing Refresh or Requery

You should consider using either the Refresh or Requery method when it's important that your users see an up-to-date view of the data. A refresh provides a fast update to the form's data and is easily triggered in code with a button or Timer event, but it might not show a completely accurate view of the data. A requery provides a 100-percent accurate view of the data, but it takes more time, consumes more resources, and generates more network traffic than a refresh. A requery is also easily triggered in code but has the disconcerting effect of returning the user to the first record in the underlying recordset.

> **Note:** Although you can't update a snapshot-type recordset, the Requery method can be used with such a recordset if its Restartable property is not set to False.

Changing a Shared Database Design

If you need to make changes in the shared database design, you must make sure no one else is working with it. The safest way is to open the database in exclusive mode. If you're the only current user and try to change a form or other object (except for a table or query), Access promotes you temporarily to exclusive mode. After saving the changes you revert to shared mode.

Access distinguishes between major and minor changes. When you try to make a major change in shared mode, Access displays a message that you might not be able to save the changes. Minor changes do not cause an alert.

Some examples of major database changes include the following:

- Changing objects in design view
- Making a change in a form property sheet while in form view
- Renaming, deleting, or pasting an object
- Modifying or adding items on a command bar
- Creating, renaming, moving, or deleting a data access page

Some examples of changes Access considers minor include the following:

- Changing datasheet formatting properties such as lines and shading
- Freezing/unfreezing or hiding/showing columns in a datasheet
- Changing a filter or sort order of the data in a form or datasheet
- Expanding or collapsing a subdatasheet
- Modifying printer settings
- Docking, floating, or hiding a command bar

An exception is the data access page. You still need exclusive access to create, delete, rename, or move a data access page. You can, however, edit the page in shared mode because you're actually editing the HTML file that's stored outside the database.

The best strategy is to make sure you have exclusive access to the database before attempting to make any design changes.

Replicating a Database

When you replicate a database, you're making copies of it for use in different locations, but these copies can periodically be completely and accurately synchronized. Each user works with a separate copy of the database; the master file is centrally located, where it can be updated with data from the remote members of the replica set and, in turn, pass on the changes to the other members.

One advantage to creating replicas is that you can dedicate one member to a single activity, such as printing lengthy reports or large numbers of form letters, thus saving the others for less time-consuming activities. You can also create a replica for your laptop computer and take it elsewhere to work on. When you return, you can update the master with the changes.

The master is updated frequently with the changes made in the replicas. If you need nearly 100 percent currency between members, replication is not advised. Even if you synchronize the replica set frequently, it still may not meet the requirements for currency.

When you create a replica set, the first copy becomes the *design master*. Subsequent copies are called *replicas*. Each member of the replica set is assigned a specific degree of visibility that determines which other members it can synchronize with (be updated by) and whether it can become the design master.

A *global* replica has the flexibility to synchronize with almost any other member of the set as well as any replica it has created. A *local* replica can synchronize only with the global replica that created it. A global replica with several local replicas creates a star configuration in which synchronization always passes through the global replica at the hub to the other local replicas. A local replica can be reassigned as the design master.

An *anonymous* replica can also synchronize only with the global replica that created it, but the anonymous replica must be the one to initiate the synchronization. An anonymous replica cannot become the design master.

Creating a Replica Set

When you replicate a database, Access converts it to the design master, where you can make additional replicas. Before beginning to create a replicated database from the back-up copy, make sure you're the only one using the database. If the database is protected by a password, it must be removed before replicating. To create the design master, do the following:

1. With the database open in exclusive mode, choose Tools|Replication|Create Replica.

2. In the first dialog box, shown in Figure 18.16, Access asks whether you want to close this database and convert it to the design master. The message also warns you that replicating the database will increase its size. Choose Yes to continue. The database closes.

FIGURE 18.16

Access offers to close the database before creating the replica.

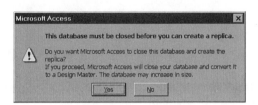

3. The next message box, shown in Figure 18.17, offers to create a backup of the database if you haven't already done so. If you choose Yes, the backup database is saved to the same folder as the original with a .bak file extension. If you've already created the backup, choose No to proceed. You can also cancel the operation or choose Help to see what kind of changes will be made to the database upon replication.

FIGURE 18.17

Access will make a backup copy of your database.

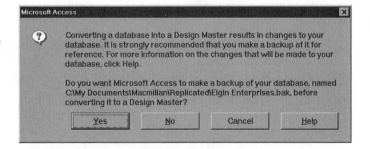

4. If you choose Yes, the Location of New Replica dialog box opens (see Figure 18.18). Here, you can choose the folder in which to save the replica. Choose OK to proceed creating the design master.

Other options are available in the Location of New Replica dialog box. When you create other replicas, you can specify the type of replica—global, local, or anonymous—by choosing from the Save as Type box. You can also set the replica's priority by clicking Priority and entering a percentage between 0 and 100 in the Priority dialog box. The default is 100 percent for the design master and 90 percent of the parent replica's priority for other replicas. The priority of a replica determines who wins in the case of a synchronization conflict. You'll learn more about conflict resolution in section titled "Dealing with Synchronization Conflicts."

FIGURE 18.18

The Location of New Replica dialog box.

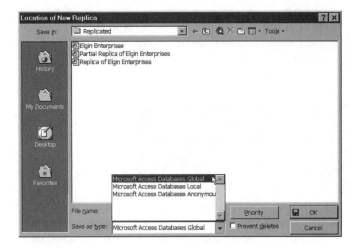

In previous versions of Access, the winning record in a conflict was the record that changed most often. In Access 2000, the replica with the highest priority prevails. If the priorities are the same, the replica with the lowest ReplicaID value (the senior member) wins, and the losing change is recorded as a conflict in a system table that's added to all replicas. Local and anonymous replicas automatically have 0 priority, so they never win in a conflict.

Another option in the Location of New Replica dialog box is Prevent Deletes. Check this option to keep users from deleting any records from the database. Applying this option can be important when remote users are tempted to remove information they feel is not relevant to their jobs, whereas to other users, the data may be essential and its deletion disastrous.

After the conversion is complete, Access displays an information message that the conversion was successful. Figure 18.19 shows the new Elgin Enterprises design master database. Notice the replicable icon that's attached to each table and other object in the design master. You can now create other replicas from this design master.

> **Note:** If you've set custom startup options for the database you're replicating, such as an opening switchboard, you'll have to reset the settings for the design master. Each replica you create from it will then include the startup options.

FIGURE 18.19

The new design master for the Elgin Enterprises database.

Replicating with VB Code

You can also create an additional replica from an existing design master using the `MakeReplica` method in a Visual Basic function. The function arguments enable you to create a full replica, a read-only replica, or a partial replica. You can even combine the arguments to create a read-only partial replica.

The following statements create a full read/write replica from the Elgin Enterprises design master:

```
Set dbsTemp = OpenDatabase ("Elgin Enterprises")
DbsTemp.MakeReplica stNewReplica, "Replicax of Elgin Enterprises"
```

Here, `stNewReplica` is the path and filename of the new replica. If you want to make the new replica read-only, add the argument `dbRepMakeReadOnly` to the `MakeReplica` method. The argument, `dbRepMakePartial`, creates a partial replica. Concatenate the two arguments to apply both restrictions to the new replica.

> **Note:** If you use the Partial Replica Wizard to create a partial replica, the data that passes the filter you entered is added to the replica. When you use the `MakeReplica` method to create a partial replica, you must also set the `Filter` property to set the filters and relationships to screen the data to replicate. Then you use the `PopulatePartial` method to transfer the records that meet the criteria from the full replica.

When you create a partial replica with `MakeReplica`, the new member contains no data. You must use the `PopulatePartial` method.

Preventing Replication

By default, all database objects are included in the replication along with the data. If you want to keep the forms, reports, macros, and modules private, change the database's

ReplicateProject property to No before creating the first replica. To do this, open the original database and choose File|Database Properties (see Figure 18.20). Then, do the following:

FIGURE 18.20

*Change the
ReplicateProject
property to keep
objects private.*

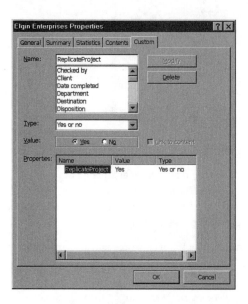

1. Select ReplicateProject in the Properties pane. You can drag the column dividers to see the whole name.

2. Click the No option button and then choose Modify. The Yes value changes to No, and the database objects remain local. Click OK to close the Database Properties dialog box.

When you keep objects local, they remain in the database where they were created or to which they're imported and are not shared with other members of the replica set. Replicable objects are dispersed to all other members of the set and any changes to them are also passed on.

In Access 2000, all database objects except tables and queries are designated as either all local or all replicable. They cannot be specified individually as replicable. Only tables and queries can be individually specified as replicable because they're the only objects that actually contain data. The Replicable property applies to databases as well as TableDef and QueryDef objects.

To change the Replicable property, select the table or query in the database window and click the Properties toolbar button or choose View|Properties. Figure 18.21 shows the General Properties dialog box for the Agents table with the Replicable property box checked. Clear the check box to prevent replication of the Agents table in subsequent replicas. The next time you synchronize the design master with the existing replicas, the Agents table is removed from the replicas. This also removes the Replicable icon from the table name in the design master database window.

FIGURE 18.21
*Clear the table's
Replicable prop-
erty to prevent
replication.*

Note: If the Replicable property appears checked but dimmed in the table's General Properties dialog box, the table may already be replicated. You may also be looking at it in one of the replicas instead of the design master.

To restore the Agents table as replicable, check the table's property in the design master and synchronize it with the other replicas.

You can also set the Replicable property with VB code. Before setting the property, you must create it and add it to the object's Properties collection. Setting the Replicable property to True for a database makes it replicable. Setting it to True for an object in the database actually replicates the object in all the members in the replica set. If the property is already checked in the object's property sheet, you can't use code.

After opening the dbsXYZ database in exclusive mode, the following code creates the Replicable property, adds it to the Properties collection, and sets it to True:

```
With dbsXYZ
  Set propNew = .CreateProperty ("Replicable", dbText, "T")
  .Properties.Append prpNew
  .Properties ("Replicable") = "T"
  .close
End With
```

The dbText argument indicates that the property value is a text data type.

Setting the `Replicable` property for a TableDef or a QueryDef uses the same syntax. For example, the following statements append the property to a QueryDef `Properties` collection and sets it to `True` to make the query replicable (the database that contains the query must also be replicable):

```
Set prpNew = qdfTemp.CreateProperty ("Replicable", dbText, "T")
qdf.Temp.Properties.Append prpNew
qdf.Temp.Properties("Replicable") = "T"
```

You can also apply the `KeepLocal` property to a table, query, form, report, macro, or module object to prevent replicating it when the database is replicated. If you want to apply this property to a TableDef or QueryDef object, you must first create it and append it to the object's `Properties` collection, the same as with the `Replicable` property. You can't apply the `KeepLocal` property to objects that have already been replicated.

The following code adds the `KeepLocal` property to the `Properties` collection of the `frmTemp` form and sets the property to `True`:

```
Set prpNew = frmTemp.CreateProperty ("KeepLocal",dbText, "T")
FrmTemp.Properties.Append prpNew
FrmTemp.Properties ("KeepLocal") = "T"
```

Creating a Partial Replica

The partial replica comes in handy when remote users require only certain information rather than the entire database. For example, the registrar's office at the university would be interested primarily in students and their expenses, whereas the curriculum office would be more focused on schedules and available instructors. You could create and distribute a partial replica for each of the diverse departments.

Partial replicas also reduce the load on the network, provide a greater measure of security, and result in smaller local databases.

To create a partial replica for the Elgin database that includes only information about apartments and industrial properties, limit the replica to Listing records that contain the value "1100" or "1200" in the Type Code field (the codes for those types of properties). To create this partial replica, do the following:

1. Open the design master or one of the full replicas and choose File|Replication|Partial Replica Wizard.

2. In the first dialog box, choose Create a New Partial Replica in the wizard dialog box and choose Next. You also have the choice of modifying an existing partial replica in this dialog box.

3. Enter a path and name for the new partial replica in the next dialog box or accept the default. Then click Next.

4. The third dialog box contains the means to create a filter for one of the tables in the database that will limit the records copied to the partial replica. Although you can choose only one table to filter, you can combine several fields into a filter expression.

5. Choose the Listings table in the Table to Filter box and Type Code in the Fields in the Table list. Click Paste to place the field name in the Filter Expression box. Type **"1100"** to replace the placeholder.

6. Click Or and then repeat step 5 to add **"1200"** to the criteria. Figure 18.22 shows the filter created for the Listings table that limits the records to those with 1100 or 1200 in the Type Code field.

FIGURE 18.22

Create a filter to limit the records in the partial replica.

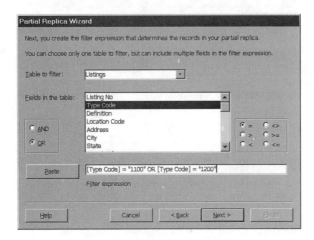

7. The next dialog box, as shown in Figure 18.23, displays a list of all the tables in the database that the filter does not apply to. Notice that the Listings table is not among those you can remove from the partial replica. Tables that are related with referential integrity enforced to the one you're filtering are automatically included in the partial replica. You may choose to keep all the tables or remove some individually from the replica.

FIGURE 18.23

Choose the other tables you want in the partial replica.

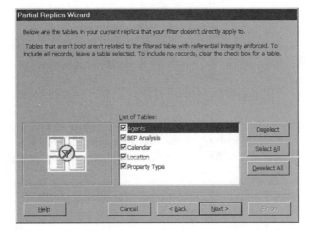

8. The final Partial Replica Wizard dialog box offers to create a temporary report of the changes made to the original replica in order to create the partial replica. Figure 18.24 shows the preview of the Beta Report. You may print this report to have a record of the specifications of the partial replica. Notice that the filter you created appears next to the Listings TableDef.

FIGURE 18.24

The Partial Replica Wizard displays a report of the changes to the original replica.

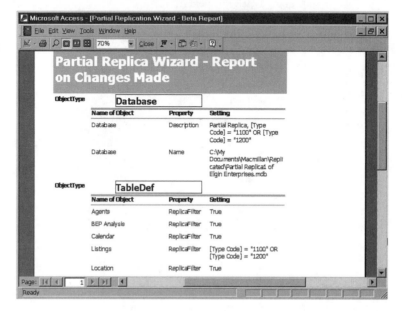

Creating a Briefcase Replica

Access has included the briefcase replica as a tool for those who take their database home or on the road on a laptop. Once the briefcase replica is created, it can be synchronized with the design master like any other replica.

> **Note:** The Briefcase Replication feature is not among those normally installed when you install Access. You may need to run Access Setup again to install it. You'll find Briefcase Replication in the Office 2000 feature tree.

To create a briefcase replica, locate the database file in the Windows Explorer window and drag the database file to the My Briefcase icon on the desktop. If you don't see the My Briefcase icon, refer to Window Help for information about installing this accessory.

After you drop the file icon on the briefcase, a series of message boxes appears that asks for confirmation of the process, offers to make a backup copy of the original database before replicating, and inquires which copy is to be the design master. You'll see numerous papers flying back and forth during the replication process as you respond to the messages. In the third such message box, shown in Figure 18.25, choose to specify the original copy as the design master and then choose OK.

FIGURE 18.25
Creating a brief-case replica.

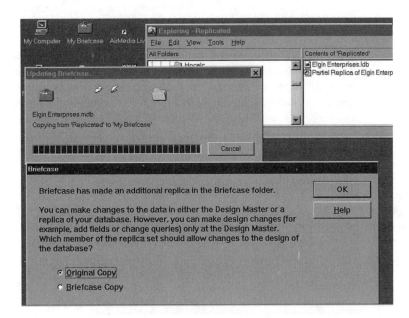

After the replication is complete, you can double-click the My Briefcase icon to open the window and view the contents. To open one of the databases in the briefcase, double-click the filename or select it and choose File|Open. The briefcase window also displays the current status of each of the files—Up-to-Date or Needs Updating.

Synchronizing Replica Set Members

Members of a replica set are not in direct, full-time connection with each other, which requires periodic updating to retain database integrity. The process of synchronization exchanges all updated records and objects between two members of the set. Access offers three types of synchronization:

- *Direct synchronization* is used when all members of the set are connected directly via a local area network and are available in shared folders. Direct synchronization is not appropriate for updating when some of the members are operating remotely. If the member isn't found when synchronization is requested, the member is removed from the set.

- *Indirect synchronization* is used when you require the database to be available to remote or transient users. You must call upon the Replication Manager in the Microsoft Office 2000 Developer (MOD) to carry out indirect synchronization.

- *Internet synchronization* is used to update remote replicas that have access to an Internet server. This type of synchronization must also be done with the Replication Manager.

This chapter discusses only direct synchronization. See the Office 2000 Help topic for information about using the Replication Manager.

To synchronize two members of the replica set, open the member you want to update and choose Tools|Replication|Synchronize Now. In the Synchronize Database *databasename* dialog box, choose the Directly with Replica option and select the member you want to synchronize with from the drop-down list of current members (see Figure 18.26). If you have the design master open, the list contains all the replicas in the set. Choose the one you want to update and click OK. All changes are exchanged between the two members of the replica set.

FIGURE 18.26

Choose the replica with which to synchronize.

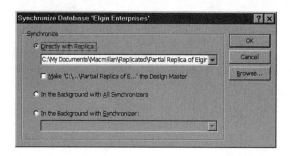

The other options in the dialog box include the following:

- A check box that assigns the replica currently selected in the list as the design master. If the selected replica is a partial replica, Access will not make it the design master but will continue with the synchronization.

- The In the Background with All Synchronizers option adds the selected member to the list of replicated databases managed by any synchronizer. Updating takes place in the background as resources permit.

- The In the Background with Synchronizer option enables you to name the synchronizer you want to run in the background. The drop-down list contains a list of available synchronizers.

After you click OK, a message box informs you that the database must be closed before synchronizing but that it can be automatically reopened if desired. After synchronizing is complete, a message lets you know that the process was successful.

> **Tip:** If the database has a switchboard that automatically opens at startup, you can hold down the Shift key when you close the final message box to suppress the startup options when the database reopens.

If you've created a briefcase replica, you can update it using the method just described or from the My Briefcase window. In the My Briefcase window, select the database file and choose Briefcase|Update Selection. If all the database files need updating, choose Update All instead. In the Update My Briefcase dialog box, choose the direction in which you want the change to take effect and click Update.

Synchronizing with VB Code

You can use the Synchronize method in VB code to synchronize two members of a replica set. This method is limited to Microsoft Jet databases. When you apply the Synchronize method, you specify the database that's the replica database, a string containing the path and filename of the target replica, and an optional argument that indicates the direction in which you want the synchronization to go between the two.

The following statements open the design master, synchronize it with one of its replicas, and send the changes from the design master to the new replica:

```
Set dbsTemp = OpenDatabase("My Design Master")
DbsTemp.Synchronize "NewReplica", dbRepExportChanges
DbsTemp.Close
```

If you want the changes to pass from the replica to the design master, use the dbRepImportChanges argument. To send changes in both directions, use the dbRepImpExpChanges argument. The dbRepSynchInternet argument exchanges data between files connected via an Internet path, which requires the Replication Manager.

Dealing with Synchronization Conflicts

In Access 2000, a synchronization conflict occurs when the change affects the same column in the same record. This is called *column-level resolution* and it's the default setting. If you want to retain row-level resolution as used in previous versions of Access, you must change the RowLevelTracking property of one or more tables before replicating the database.

When conflicts occur, the winning change is selected and applied to all the replicas. The losing change is logged in a system table as a conflict also in all replicas. Conflict tables are, by default, hidden from view, but if you check Show Hidden Objects in the View tab of the Options dialog box, they appear dimmed in the Tables page of the database window.

Several types of conflicts can occur when you try to synchronize two members of the set after changes have been made to both of them:

- Simultaneous update conflicts occur when two replicas update the same record.
- A unique key conflict can occur if two replicas enter a new record with the same primary key field value or a replica adds two or more records with the same key value as that created by the design master.

- Table-level validation conflicts occur when data violates the table-level validation rule. You may cause this type of conflict if you add such a validation rule without checking to see whether any of the existing records already violate it.

- Update referential integrity conflicts occur when the primary key is updated at one replica and new child records, referring to the original primary key, are added to a different replica.

- Delete referential integrity conflicts occur when a primary key record is deleted in one replica while new child records are added to a second replica.

- Locking conflicts occur when one user has locked the table to which records are to be applied during synchronization. After several unsuccessful tries, synchronization ends and the transaction returns to its original status.

- Foreign key conflicts occur when there's an invalid primary key record.

Resolving Conflicts

If conflicts have occurred during synchronization, the next time you open the replica, a message informs you of the conflicts and asks if you would like to resolve them now (see Figure 18.27). Choose Yes to start the Replication Conflict Viewer, where you can examine the conflicts and determine the resolution. If the replica is already open, you can start the Viewer by choosing Tools|Replication|Resolve Conflicts.

FIGURE 18.27
Synchronization conflicts exist in this replica.

The Replication Conflict Viewer displays a list of tables with conflicts with the number of conflicts in each table (see Figure 18.28).

To view and possibly resolve a conflict, select the table name in the dialog box and choose View. The next Replication Conflict Viewer dialog box shows the existing data and the conflicting data as shown in Figure 18.29. In this example, a new agent was added to two different replicas, resulting in a unique key violation, as described in the Reason for Conflict box. Both agents carry the F Agent Code primary key value, but the names and addresses are different. Agent Barbara Kelley was added to the design master, and Ed Taylor was added to one of the other replicas. The design master has a 100-percent priority, so that record is considered the winning change.

You can either accept the winning change, overwrite with the losing change, or revise either change as the resolution. In the Show Fields box, you have a choice of viewing only the fields in the records that are conflicting or all fields. After you've made a selection, click Resolve. If you prefer to wait until you have more complete information about the changes, you can postpone the resolution until later.

FIGURE 18.28

The Replication Conflict Viewer displays a list of tables that contain conflicts.

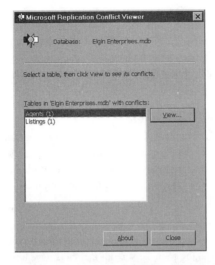

FIGURE 18.29.

The Replication Conflict Viewer displays the selected conflict.

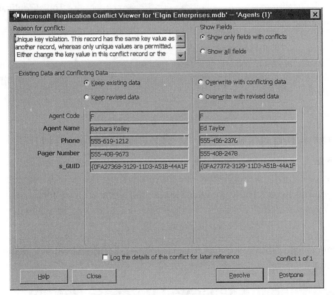

Warning: If you delete or move a replica that contains a conflict, you can lose the record of conflicts, and the replicas may no longer be accurate. Be sure to check the replica for conflicts before deleting or moving it.

Modifying the Replica Set

As work progresses, you may need to recover the design master, add replicas to or remove replicas from the set, or restore the replicated database to its previous status. There may also be some design changes in some of the database objects that need to be promulgated to the replicas.

Recovering the Design Master

You saw how to assign one of the replicas as the design master in the Synchronize Database dialog box. This causes the designated replica to change places with the design master, which now becomes a normal replica. If the design master file has been lost, renamed, moved, or damaged, you can assign one of the other replicas, but not a partial replica, as the design master.

Before trying to recover the design master, be sure that there's no design master in the set. Then select the replica you want to use as the design master and synchronize all other replicas with it. After checking to make sure all members have been synchronized with the design master–to-be and no conflicts exist, choose Tools|Replication|Recover Design Master and click Yes.

> **Tip:** If, by some chance, you find yourself with two design masters in the replica set, the only way you can solve the problem is by deleting one of them with Windows Explorer.

Removing a Member from the Replica Set

You must use Windows Explorer to delete members of the replica set. Be sure all conflicts have been resolved before deleting a member. The deleted member remains in the drop-down list of members in the Synchronize Database dialog box until you try to synchronize it with another replica set member. When the synchronization fails, the other members are informed of the deletion.

Avoid deleting the design master unless it's damaged. Without a design master, you can't change the design of the database.

Modifying the Replicated Database Design

As with most changes in a replicated database, be sure to synchronize all members before making the design changes so that you start with everyone equal. Some considerations must be addressed when changing the design in a replicated database. For example, if you're adding a new field or object, make sure the name isn't already in use as a local object. If it is, the local object will be renamed, which can cause problems.

When creating new relationships between tables, be sure that all the tables will be replicable or all local. Do not create relationships between a local table and a table you intend to replicate.

Restoring a Normal Database

Restoring a replicated database to its regular status is not an easy task. You cannot simply convert it back because of all the added system tables and fields. If you no longer have the need for the replicated database and want to reduce the storage requirements of the database, you can create a new, normal database that contains all the objects and data but none of the system tables and fields that were in the replicated database.

To restore a normal database from the replicated database, create a new empty database and import all the objects, except the tables, from the replicated database. Choose File|Get External Data|Import and then select all the objects on each tab except the Tables tab. Then click OK.

To add the table data, create a make-table query for each table in the replicated database that includes all the data fields but none of the system fields. After adding the tables, re-create the indexes for the tables and the relationships that existed in the replicated database.

Summary

This chapter has explored the challenges of preparing Access databases for use by multiple users. Turning a database into a multiuser environment involves much more than copying the MDB file to the file server. You must consider how the users will be working with their data, the importance of maintaining data integrity while providing adequate performance, and keeping data views in forms up-to-date.

Microsoft has done an outstanding job in providing the developer with a wide variety of options when setting up databases for multiuser access, including splitting the database for sharing or replicating the database into a set of multiple members. Your choices will be driven by the business requirements of the users and their data.

Adding Security to the Application

Chapter 18, "Working in a Multiuser Environment," described all the issues to consider when you're moving an Access application from the individual desktop to a multiuser environment. However, simply splitting a database and setting locking options or replicating the database and synchronizing all changes and then training users how to work in a shared environment is only part of the story. After you move a database from a controlled local environment to a public server on the network, you must consider the security implications of the database's increased exposure.

The Need for Security

Usually, when we think of database security, our major concern is unauthorized access to the information stored in a database's tables. The primary job of security in a database is to protect the data from being viewed or edited by unauthorized people. In this way, security ensures that the data can't be corrupted or stolen by a competitor or disgruntled employee.

Everyone has heard horror stories about the employee who steals a company's secrets just before quitting or being fired. With the proliferation and widespread use of laptop computers, a large portion of many companies' assets are vulnerable to theft or accidental loss. Access 2000 security can guarantee that unauthorized people are unable to view or use the data stored in its tables.

A second, equally important job is to protect the database design from modification by unqualified individuals. Let's face it—application development is time-consuming and costly. It's a mistake to expose your carefully designed and painfully implemented application to modification by summer interns or temporary help with a hankering to explore.

Access 2000 applications are particularly vulnerable to modification by unqualified people. Microsoft has distributed millions of copies of Access as part of the Microsoft Office package and as a standalone product. This means that there are millions of copies of Access available to do-it-yourself database engineers who'd like nothing more than to change the design of a form or report in your databases.

Although the majority of do-it-yourselfers are well-intentioned, unless they fully understand and appreciate the rationale behind a particular design element of an application, they can unknowingly damage the application's integrity or performance. Sometimes, relatively trivial details, such as a validation rule on a field or the name of a text box, can have profound impact on the operation of the database. Even seemingly benign changes, such as moving or changing the size of a control on a report, can cause unexpected results.

For all these reasons, you'll more than likely want to establish a reasonable and rational level of security in your Access 2000 applications. This is particularly true of the database back end residing on the server. This is where the majority of the valuable information is stored—information that's vulnerable to intentional or accidental loss or corruption. (In this context, *"corruption"* means inaccurate or incorrect data entry as well as data loss due to scrambled or unusable entry.)

The Database Password: The First Level of Security

You can quickly and easily protect your Access 2000 databases by using the database password feature. Using this security feature, you assign a single password that all users enter when they begin work with the database. You open the Set Database Password dialog box with the Tools|Security|Set Database Password command (see Figure 19.1).

FIGURE 19.1
The database password provides blanket protection for your databases.

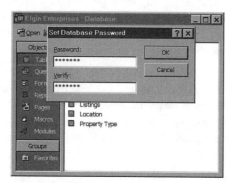

The database must be opened in exclusive mode before you set the database password. To open the database in exclusive mode, choose the File|Open command and select Open Exclusive, as shown in Figure 19.2. You won't be able to open the database in exclusive mode if another user is working with the database.

After you set a database password, all users are challenged by the Password Required dialog box you see in Figure 19.3. Notice that nothing but the password is required for entry to the database. When a user is admitted to the application, every object is available to him or her.

FIGURE 19.2
Open the database in exclusive mode before setting the database password.

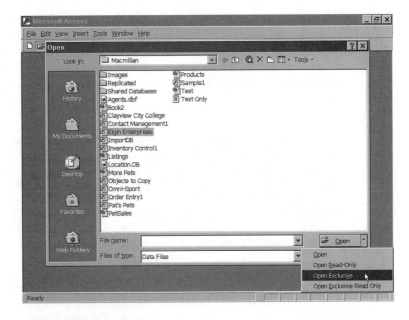

FIGURE 19.3
A single password services all users.

The database password provides a mediocre level of security to an Access database. Because a single password is shared by all the database users, it's impossible to control exactly who knows the password. It would be very easy for an unauthorized user to learn the password in most cases.

LOOKING AHEAD

The database password provides no way to identify an individual user. All users are logged into the database as Admin, a powerful and dangerous user (as you'll read later in this chapter). When the database password is used, Access has no way to differentiate between users. All users are the same "person" to Access.

LOOKING AHEAD

Also, because the database password provides no object-level protection, you have no way to secure individual components of the database. As you'll see later in this chapter, Access security is based on user and group accounts. The owner of a database object, such as a table or form, is the ultimate authority over the object. Only the owner is able to grant access permission to other users and groups in the database. When database password security is used, every user is a database administrator and has complete authority over all objects in the database. In other words, a database password provides virtually no security at all.

Finally, the database password represents a distinct danger to a database. Anyone who knows the database password can invoke the Tools|Security|Unset Database Password command (this command is seen only when a password is imposed on the database) to remove the current password. When the password has been disabled, this person can then maliciously assign a bogus password to the database, effectively locking every other person out of the database.

> **Warning:** Be careful about using a password to protect a database that provides linked tables to another database. When you supply the correct password to link the tables, Access stores the password in an unencrypted form with the link information. Then any user who can open the database the table is linked to can also open the linked table. Upon opening the linked table, Access uses the stored password to open the database. A better scheme is to use user-level security rather than a password to protect a database that provides linked table data to an unsecured database.

All things considered, the database password does not provide a significant level of security. In most environments where security is an issue, a stronger and more capable form of security is called for. Fortunately, Access has one of the best security features of any desktop database.

Understanding the Access Security Model

The Access security model is designed around the notion of *workgroups*. A workgroup can contain several other groups within it. Consider a large company with sales, marketing, and production departments. Each department might be considered a workgroup because the members share certain responsibilities within the company. Within the sales workgroup, you might have regional, international, and government sales groups, each having specific sales objectives.

Elgin Enterprises, however, is a very small company. Each employee has a different title, even though all employees share certain responsibilities among them. Therefore, we'll have a single workgroup with several groups within the workgroup. Each group parallels some business function, such as sales or marketing. Each of the Elgin employees will belong to one or more groups and will have certain security rights based on who they are and which groups they belong to.

LOOKING AHEAD

One interesting aspect of Access security is that it's always "on." You don't need to explicitly enable security in your databases. You don't really see any of the Access security measures until you assign a password to the Admin user, the default database administrator (more on this later in the section titled "Activating Security in Access 2000").

Understanding the Workgroup File

As you already know, Access is a general-purpose database system. You can use the Access installation on your computer to open and work with any number of databases. Needing to assign users, groups, and permissions in every database would be an administrative nightmare. Consider the amount of redundant work you'd have to do if you had to create a sales group, a marketing group, and a management group for every database. Furthermore, unless Access helps you set up security, you'd have to create user accounts for every employee in every database used in the company.

Fortunately, Microsoft considered these issues as it designed Microsoft Access. You must set up the group and user accounts only one time. The group and user information you enter is stored in a special database file with an .MDW filename extension. The "W" indicates that this file stores workgroup information. By default, the name of the workgroup information file is System.mdw. Figure 19.4 illustrates this concept.

FIGURE 19.4

Group and user information is stored in the workgroup information file (by default, System.mdw).

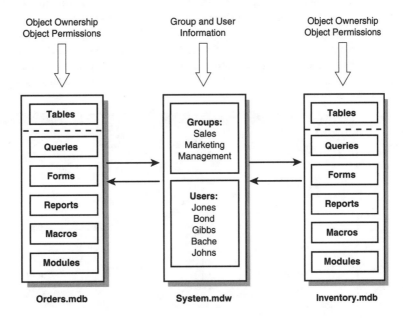

This arrangement enables the same group and user information to be shared among several different databases. Figure 19.4 shows how two databases (Orders and Inventory) at the Elgin Enterprises company both use the same System.mdw file. In this illustration, System.mdw contains information about three groups (Sales, Marketing, and Management) and five users (Jones, Bond, Gibbs, Bache, and Johns). Each of the five users belongs to one or more of the groups in the System.mdw file.

> **Tip:** The workgroup file does not have to be named System.mdw. In fact, in most cases, it's a good idea not to use the default System.mdw file, because anyone who has used Access in this system is a member of the default workgroup. Instead, you should create a custom workgroup file that's associated with the workgroup that will be using Access on its network.

Creating a Workgroup

Office 2000 includes a utility called the Workgroup Administrator that establishes a new workgroup file. In a secured environment, you usually do not want to use the default System.mdw in order to avoid "contamination" from users or groups that might have been installed in the past. A nice, new clean system file is the best start to a new security scheme.

To start the Workgroup Administrator, use the Windows Explorer to locate the MS Access Workgroup Administrator shortcut. The shortcut usually is found in the Program Files\Microsoft Office\Office folder (see Figure 19.5). You may have installed Office in a different folder. If so, look there for the shortcut. Double-click the shortcut to start the Administrator. You can also use the Run command on the Start menu to run Wrkgadm.exe. Use the Browse button on the Run dialog box to locate Wrkgadm.exe.

FIGURE 19.5

Double-click the MS Access Workgroup Administrator shortcut.

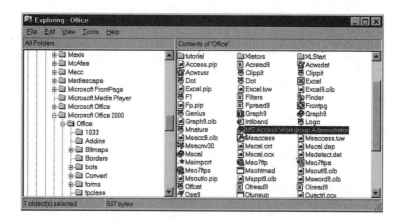

> **Note:** The Wrkgadm.exe program file is actually stored in the language subfolder of the Office folder. The language folder contains several translated files corresponding to the installation locale. In a U.S. English installation, the locale identification number (LCID) is 1033. If you look in the 1033 subfolder, you will find the Wrkgadm.exe and many other objects. Double-clicking the filename in the 1033 folder also starts the Workgroup Administrator.

The Workgroup Administrator is quite simple. The first dialog box (not shown here) explains that the Workgroup Administrator is intended to be used to create the workgroup information file for an Access installation. The first dialog box contains three buttons that let you create a new workgroup information file, join an existing workgroup, and exit the Workgroup Administrator, respectively. Because you're installing security for the first time on the computer, use the Create button to build an entirely new workgroup information file.

The second dialog box ("Workgroup Owner Information," shown in Figure 19.6) actually asks for the information needed to identify the owner and other information needed by the workgroup information file. Of these bits of information, the most interesting is the Workgroup ID (WID). The WID is a case-sensitive string of 4 to 20 characters. Be sure to record the WID you use and keep it in a safe place. Think of the WID as a "password" you need to reconstruct the workgroup information file in the unlikely event it's ever lost to accidental erasure or hardware failure.

FIGURE 19.6

This information is important when you're reconstructing a workgroup information file.

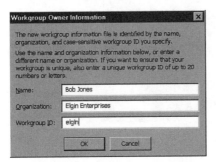

If you try to create a new workgroup information file and use the wrong owner information (including the WID), you won't be able to open any databases using the workgroup information file. Storing this information in a safe location is imperative. If you use an obvious, easily guessed owner, organization, and WID, an unauthorized user will be able to construct his own workgroup information file and use the built-in administrator account in the new workgroup information file to gain access to your databases. This is the primary reason you don't want to use the default workgroup information file (System.mdw) with a secured application.

When you click OK in this dialog box, you're asked where you want Access to create the new workgroup information file. Normally, you'll want the file placed in a shared folder on a file server on the network. In Figure 19.7, Elgin Enterprises is using the networking built into Microsoft Windows 95, and the developer's computer is the designated file server for the company. Therefore, the workgroup information file is being placed in the Shared Databases folder on the developer's computer.

FIGURE 19.7
*Put the work-
group information
file in a shared
folder on an
accessible
computer.*

The last dialog box of the Workgroup Administrator asks you to confirm the information you've provided to create the workgroup information file (see Figure 19.8). This is your last chance to verify and record this data for safekeeping. After you click OK, the Workgroup Administrator builds the workgroup information file and changes the computer's system Registry to point Access to the new file. Only one workgroup information file can be used on a computer at a time, although you can create and save more than one.

FIGURE 19.8
*Confirm and
record this infor-
mation before
proceeding!*

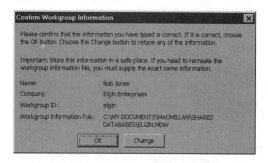

You can, however, switch to a different workgroup by specifying its location with the /wrkgrp command-line switch. Look for the "Command Line" topic in the Access 2000 online Help for instructions on setting command-line arguments under Windows 95/98.

Restoring a Workgroup Information File

If your WIF becomes damaged or is moved, you won't be able to open the database that relies on it for user information. There are ways to repair a damaged WIF, depending on how you created it and whether you have saved a backup copy of it. If you have a backup copy, use the Windows Explorer to copy the most recent copy to the folder where Access is installed or to the original path, if different.

If you created the WIF with the help of the Workgroup Administrator and did not keep a backup copy, you must re-create the file with the Workgroup Administrator. You must enter exactly the same case-sensitive information you used to create the original WIF. If you used the default WIF and did not save a copy, you have to reinstall Access and start over to re-create the WIF.

The security account information is stored in the WIF, so if you have to re-create the file, you'll have to build the security accounts with the same names and personal ID entries. The permissions and object ownership information is stored in the secure database, and you don't need to redefine them. However, they must be connected with the same accounts as in the original database.

If you create a new WIF and save it with a different name or in a different location, be sure to inform the other users and have them join the new WIF.

Working with Groups and Users

The security within an Access database is built around the groups, users, and objects in the database. There are several groups in most Access database security schemes, each with many users. In most cases, the security groups parallel functional groups within the company using the database. A user can belong to more than one group, particularly when a person's responsibilities overlap more than one functional group.

LOOKING AHEAD

Later in this chapter, you'll see how to assign permissions to the objects in a database. Permissions protect the data and objects in the database. A group or user might or might not have permission to look at the data in a table, run a query, or modify the design of a table, query, form, or some other database object. In this way, you can grant relatively comprehensive and specific permissions to skilled and responsible users while keeping things locked up and out of the reach of less privileged individuals.

Back in Figure 19.4, you saw how the security information in an Access database is divided between the workgroup information file and individual databases. This design permits multiple databases to share the group and user information stored in the workgroup information file while maintaining object permissions stored with the Access database file.

When you start Access 2000 in a secured environment, you're asked for your username and password (see Figure 19.9). Access checks this information against the group and user data stored in the workgroup information file to verify that you're a valid Access user on the system. If Access cannot match your username with any of the entries in workgroup information file or if the password you provide does not match your password, the logon fails and you're not permitted entry into Access.

FIGURE 19.9

The user is challenged to provide a valid username and corresponding password.

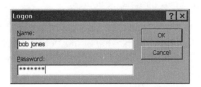

LOOKING AHEAD

This first barrier to unauthorized access is more than adequate to stop casual unauthorized browsers from trying to open any databases in Access 2000. Later in this chapter, in the section titled "Adding New Users," you'll see how a user is assigned a password.

Built-In Groups

Every copy of Access has many built-in groups and users. These groups and users become important when you're considering the implications of improperly setting up security in an Access database. As you'll see, one of the steps of securing an Access database is to disable a dangerous default user:

- *Admins*. All members of the Admins group are administrators of the Access database. An administrator is able to add new groups and users, change ownership of database objects, and change permissions on any database objects. Administrators, therefore, are powerful individuals in the database.
- *Users*. Every user is a member of the Users group. Normally, the Users group has no real authority in the database and is provided for "guests" who might not be part of a database's security scheme.

Neither the Admins nor the Users group can be deleted or renamed. They are permanent and immutable parts of the Access security scheme. You must take other measures to deprive them of their omnipotence.

Built-In Users

Looking Ahead

Access has one built-in user account. The Admin user, a member of the Admins group, is in every copy of System.mdw that's created when Access 2000 is installed. This means that millions of copies of System.mdw exist, each with a default user who is able to open, view, and modify all the data and database objects in every Access database ever created. Later, you'll see how to change the Admin user's group and permissions in your databases.

Understanding Object Ownership

All objects (tables, queries, forms, and so on) in an Access database must be owned by some user. By default, all objects are owned by the owner of the database itself. Also by default, the owner of all databases and all objects within all databases is Admin. When security is implemented in an Access installation, each user is able to create new databases and objects (with appropriate permissions, of course).

Looking Ahead

Groups can own objects just as users do. In fact, in many cases, it makes more sense to have group ownership than individual user ownership of most objects. As an administrator, your job is complicated whenever you have to change the ownership of database objects each time a person's job responsibilities change or a person leaves the company. Later, in the section titled "Assigning Object Ownership," you'll see how to set an object's ownership.

The owner of an object is the ultimate authority of that object. This means that an object's owner can modify the design of the object, view any data the object holds, and export or import the object to other Access databases. There are other permissions; for example, printing the object's design or outputting the object to various formats such as HTML (Hypertext Markup Language) or RTF (Rich Text Format). An object's owner is also able to grant permissions to other groups and users with respect to that object.

Activating Security in Access 2000

Earlier in this chapter you read that you don't have to explicitly install security or turn it on. Security is always in place in your databases and becomes visible only when you assign a password to the Admin user.

Because the default user is Admin, each time you open an Access database in an unsecured environment, you log on as Admin. This means that you are the database owner and administrator and own all the objects in the database.

Open the User and Group Accounts dialog box by selecting Tools|Security|User and Group Accounts. This dialog box contains three tabs when you log on as Admin. The first two tabs, Users and Groups, enable you to create new users and groups; the third tab, Change Logon Password, shown in Figure 19.10, has the text boxes required for you to assign a password to Admin.

FIGURE 19.10

Set the Admin user's password in the User and Group Accounts dialog box.

Because there is no password for the Admin user to start with, leave the Old Password box blank and tab to the New Password box. Enter the new password for Admin; then, tab to the Verify box and retype the password. When you've completed this simple operation, security is enabled, and anyone trying to use the database will encounter the dialog box shown in Figure 19.9. Nothing more is required to make security visible in an Access 2000 database.

You should shut down Access and restart it to test the new Admin password. Notice that you must provide the password before you open any databases. When you're in Access as the Admin user, you can open any database and set up the security within that database.

Designing an Access Security System

The first step in designing a security system for an Access database is to decide which users should belong to which group. Generally, this process is quite straightforward. Table 19.1 shows a reasonable security setup for the Elgin Enterprises database.

Table 19.1 User and Group Information for Elgin Enterprises

Username	Job Title	Group
Bob Jones	Owner	Management
Jane Bond	Vice President	Management, Marketing, Sales
Shirley Gibbs	Marketing Assistant	Marketing
Joe Bache	Sales Associate	Sales
Betty Johns	Office Manager	Management, Sales

Notice that Jane Bond and Betty Johns belong to more than one group. Jane Bond (the sales and marketing manager) often works as a salesperson in addition to her marketing tasks, whereas Betty Johns (the office manager) sometimes participates in sales activities.

The Elgin Enterprises database, therefore, requires three security groups (Management, Sales, and Marketing) and five user accounts (Bob Jones, Jane Bond, Shirley Gibbs, Joe Bache, and Betty Johns).

Adding New Groups

While you're logged on as Admin, open the Tools|Security|User and Group Accounts dialog box. Click the Groups tab to begin adding groups (see Figure 19.11).

FIGURE 19.11
Adding groups to an Access database is straightforward.

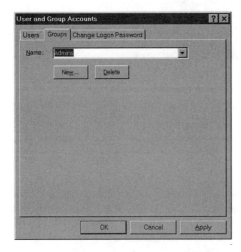

The drop-down list at the top of the User and Group Accounts dialog box contains the names of all the groups in the current workgroup information file (you'll recall that user and group information is stored in the workgroup information file and not in the database).

Click the New button to open the New User/Group dialog box (see Figure 19.12). Enter the name of the group and a *personal identifier* (PID) for the group. Be sure to record the PID you assign. It's a case-sensitive string between 4 and 20 alphanumeric characters in length, and you'll need it if you ever have to reconstruct the workgroup information file. The PID you see in Figure 19.12 is formed using a "one off" code. For each character in the alphabet, the next character in the alphabet is chosen for encoding purposes. Using this scheme, an *"a"* becomes *"b,"* a *"q"* becomes *"r,"* and so on. Given Management as the group name, the encoded group name is *nbobnfnfou* (all characters are coded in lowercase for simplicity).

FIGURE 19.12

Be sure to record the PID you assign to the new group.

The group name and PID you assign are combined by Access to create an *SID* (security ID). Access actually uses the SID to verify a group's identification. The SID is "tagged" onto all objects owned by the group and is used to look up a group's permission on objects in the database.

In this way, the database administrator actually controls security. Because a group (or user) is not able to assign its own PID, there's no chance an unauthorized user is able to create a group or user account and gain access to the database and its objects. Unless you make the PID something obvious and easily guessed, you needn't worry about unauthorized groups in your security environment.

Adding New Users

After the three Elgin Enterprises groups have been added, it's time to add the five users to the security system. Select the Users tab in the User and Group Accounts dialog box to enter the information needed to create group accounts (see Figure 19.13). The drop-down list at the top of the dialog box contains the names of all users in the workgroup information file.

FIGURE 19.13

You assign a user to the available groups as you create the user account.

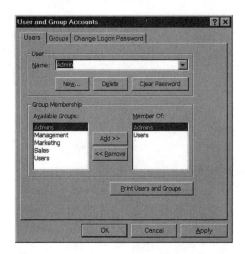

Clicking the New button in the top half of the Users tab opens the New User/Group dialog box you saw in Figure 19.12. Enter the username. The name can contain up to 20 alphabetic characters, numbers, and spaces. Do not use any of the special characters, a leading space, or control characters (ASCII 10 through 31). Again, you're required to assign a case-sensitive PID to the new user. As with the other IDs in the Access security scheme, be sure to record the PID and store it in a safe location. Click OK in the New User/Group dialog box after you've provided the required information.

Notice the selection lists at the bottom of the Users tab. The left list contains the names of all the groups in the workgroup information file, and the right list contains the names of the groups to which the current user has been assigned. In Figure 19.14, notice that Jane Bond has been assigned to the Management, Marketing, and Sales groups as well as the Users group. The Users group membership happens by default and cannot be removed from the membership list. The other groups are completely configurable and can be deleted or renamed.

As the database administrator, you should close Access and log on as each of the users you create. Once you've logged onto Access, use the Change Logon Password tab of the User and Group Accounts dialog box to assign the initial password to each user. It's a bad idea to leave this important step up to the individual users. Many people won't bother setting a password for themselves, thus creating a serious security breach. If nothing else, their accounts will be protected by the initial passwords you assign to them. Your users are able to establish new passwords at any time.

FIGURE 19.14
Jane Bond belongs to more than one group.

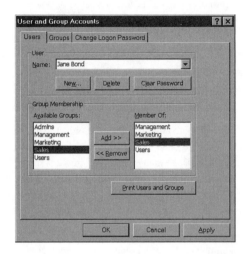

Assigning a New Administrator

Before moving on to permissions, you should create a new administrative user. This is an essential step in securing your database. As long as you leave an Admin user who's a member of the Admins group in your database, it's vulnerable to unauthorized snooping. Every workgroup information file contains an Admin user who's a member of the Admins group. Therefore, as long as this user exists in your databases, an unauthorized user is able to use *any* workgroup information file to open and access your database. Unfortunately, because Admin is a default user in all Access databases, you cannot actually remove this person. You can, however, reassign the group to take Admin out of the Admins group and remove permissions from the Admin user account.

Here are the steps required to disable the Admin user in your database:

1. Create a new user account and assign the user a password.
2. Add the new user to the Admins group.
3. Log off and log back on as the new administrator to test the new account.
4. Assign a completely bogus password to the (old) Admin user.
5. Remove the Admins group from the membership list for the Admin user.

LOOKING AHEAD

Later, in the section titled "Assigning Object Permissions," you'll learn how to revoke permissions to all objects from the Admin user. This multistep process effectively disables the Admin user by establishing an alternative administrator, removing the Admin account from the Admins group, and then assigning an unguessable password to the

Admin account. When this process is complete, even if an unauthorized user is able to finagle a bogus workgroup information file to try to open the secured database, he'll discover the Admin user is no longer an administrator in the secured database. As a member of the Users group, the Admin user has no special privileges or power over the data and objects in the database.

Assigning Object Ownership

By default, the owner of the database owns all the objects in the database. This means that, until security is activated, all objects are owned by the Admin user. In most situations, it's appropriate to assign ownership to other users or groups in the database.

The owner of an object is the ultimate authority over the object. An owner has all permissions on the object and is able to change its design, the data it contains, and grant permissions to other users or groups. In many cases, you might want an administrator to retain ownership of the database objects because there's no one within a group who is qualified to make changes to the objects. In other cases, however, it makes sense to let a group write its own queries and make changes to forms and reports (within reason, of course).

Access enables you to assign ownership of an object to a single user or group but not to multiple users or groups. To begin assigning ownership, open the User and Group Permissions dialog box. Open this dialog box by selecting Tools|Security|User and Group Permissions. Click the Change Owner tab to see the object ownership options (see Figure 19.15).

Figure 19.15
Assign object ownership where appropriate.

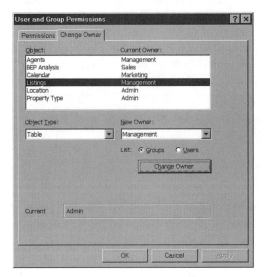

The list at the top of the Change Owner tab contains all the objects specified in the Object Type drop-down list in the lower-left side of the dialog box. The New Owner drop-down list to the right contains the names of all the groups or users in the workgroup information file, depending on which option button (Groups or Users) is selected. By default, the Users option button is selected, letting you assign ownership to individual users of the database.

Changing ownership is easy. Select the object type from the Object Type drop-down list and tell Access whether you want to assign ownership to a user or group. Then use the New Owner drop-down list to select the new owner. You must explicitly click the Change Owner button for the ownership assignment to take effect.

> **Tip:** You're generally better off assigning ownership to groups than you are assigning ownership to individuals. Groups such as Sales and Marketing are unlikely to disappear entirely from a company, even if the individual people in each of those groups change. If you assign ownership to individual users, you must go back into the security setup and change ownership as the people in the organization change jobs within the company or leave the company. There's no reason for Shirley Gibbs, a marketing assistant, to retain ownership of any of the marketing objects if she takes a job with the sales department.

Keep in mind that all members of a group share permissions and privileges equally. That means anyone from the Marketing group will have complete access to any object owned by the Marketing group, unless specific permissions are revoked. For this reason, you might find it necessary to create distinct MarketingManagement and Marketing groups. Only true managers would then have access to objects owned by the MarketingManagement group, even though the functions of the two groups are similar.

Understanding Access Permissions

At this point, you have many groups and users in the database. The Admin user has been assigned to a harmless account, and a new administrator is in place. It's now time to assign permissions to the objects in the secured database.

Permissions give users access to the data, forms, and reports in the database for specific activities. Both individual users and groups can have permissions assigned. In fact, the permissions granted to an individual user are the sum of all the permissions given to any groups the user belongs to plus the individual permissions assigned to the user.

Consider Jane Bond, the Elgin Enterprises Vice President. Bond is a member of both the Marketing and Sales groups in addition to the Management group. Therefore, Jane's permissions will be all those permissions granted to the Management, Sales, and Marketing groups as well as any permissions assigned specifically to her as a user.

Generally, you'll find it much less work to assign permissions to groups and let users have the permissions they enjoy by virtue of their membership in the various groups. Trying to set all the permissions on all the objects in several databases for the dozens of users in most environments is a daunting task, indeed!

All objects in an Access database have several permissions associated with them. For the most part, these permissions reflect how the objects are used in the database. For example, a table has Read Design, Modify Design, Read Data, and other permissions related to its role as a repository of data. A module, on the other hand, has only Read Design, Modify Design, and Administer permissions. Table 19.2 lists all the permissions possible for Access database objects.

Table 19.2 Object Permissions in Access 2000

Object	Open/ Run	Read Design	Modify Design	Administer	Read Data	Update Data	Insert Data	Delete Data
Tables		X	X	X	X	X	X	X
Queries		X	X	X	X	X	X	X
Forms	X	X	X	X				
Reports	X	X	X	X				
Macros	X	X	X	X				
Modules		X	X	X				

Here's a brief description of each of these types of permissions:

- *Open/Run*. The user can open a database, form, report, or macro. This permission is required for a user or group to be able to work with a form or report. If this permission is denied, the user or group cannot view the form or report and cannot run any macros associated with the form or report.
- *Read Design*. The user can open an object in design view. This permission is required by any users or groups who are responsible for changing the design of a table, query, form, report, macro, or module.
- *Modify Design*. The user can view and change the design of a database object. This permission is required before changing the design of any database object.
- *Administer*. The user has full access to all objects and the security system. This permission includes the right to assign permissions to other users.
- *Read Data*. The user can view the data in tables or queries.
- *Update Data*. The user can view or modify the data in a table or query but cannot add new records or delete existing records.
- *Insert Data*. The user can insert new data but cannot modify or delete existing data.
- *Delete Data*. The user can delete existing data but cannot modify or insert data.

You can assign virtually any or all of these permissions to users and groups in the workgroup information file. Certain permissions, such as Read Design, are required by other permissions—Modify Design, in this case. Therefore, you won't be able to assign Modify Design to a user or group without also assigning Read Design. When you select the Modify Design permission, you'll notice that Access automatically selects Read Design. If you notice this behavior, do not try to remove the Read Design permission, because Access will then remove the Modify Design permission. Don't worry if you notice Access removing or adding permissions as you change a group's or user's permissions. Rest assured that Access will only change the permissions required to satisfy the permissions you specify in the User and Group Permissions dialog box.

Planning Object Permissions

As a database administrator, you have a tremendous amount of flexibility in designing the security scheme for your database. At the same time, this flexibility means that assigning security is a complex process. You must plan which permissions to assign to which users and groups. Table 19.3 shows the permissions that might be given to the tables in the Elgin Enterprises database.

Table 19.3 The Table Security Scheme for Elgin Enterprises

Table	Management	Sales	Marketing
Agents	Yes	No	No
BEP Analysis	Yes	Yes	No
Calendar	Yes	Yes	Yes
Listings	Yes	Yes	No
Location	Yes	Yes	No
Property Type	Yes	Yes	No

It's easy to see how complicated designing database security can be. In this case, there are only three groups and six tables. In addition to these tables, there are queries, forms, and reports to consider as well as the macros and modules needed to support the forms and reports. All in all, it's quite a complex task.

Imagine how difficult security would be if you had to individually assign permissions to every user. The Elgin Enterprises database contains just five users, more than enough to keep the database administrator busy for an hour or more setting up security.

Assigning Object Permissions

Finally, you're ready to actually assign object permissions to the users or groups in the organization. Open the User and Group Permissions dialog box once again (select Tools|Security|User and Group Permissions). This time, click the Permissions tab to reveal the permissions assignments in the database (see Figure 19.16).

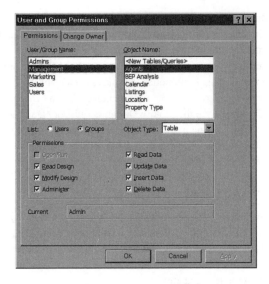

The Permissions dialog box operates much like the other security dialog boxes you've seen. The User/Group Name list in the upper-left corner of the dialog box contains the names of all the users or groups in the category indicated by the selected option buttons below the list. In Figure 19.16, the Groups option button has been selected, so you see all the groups in the Elgin Enterprises database in this list.

The Object Name list in the upper-right corner of this dialog box contains the names of all the objects of the type selected in the Object Type drop-down list, just below the Object Name list. In this case, the list shows you the names of the tables in the database.

At the bottom of the Permissions tab is a text box displaying the name of the current user. In this case, the current user is SuperUser, the system administrator who has replaced the Admin user in this database.

The Permissions area contains all the permissions possible for the objects in the database. Check or uncheck permissions as needed to give the groups (or users) in the database the appropriate permissions.

Keep in mind that an individual user's actual permissions are the sum of the permissions granted by group membership plus any individual ownership you assign the user. Carefully planning the security scheme goes a long way toward making the assignment process a less painful task.

Disabling the Users Account

Make sure you remove all permissions to all objects in the database from the default Users group. You can select multiple items in the Object Name list (hold down the Ctrl key and click objects or hold down the Shift key and scroll though the Object Names list). Use this feature to remove all permissions from the Users group. This will prevent unauthorized users from logging into Access with a dummy name and viewing or changing the objects in the database.

Testing the Security Scheme

As administrator, it's your responsibility to properly assign permissions to groups and users and to verify the operation of the security scheme you've implemented. The only way to fully test security is to log on to Access as some user and try opening a table or form the user is not supposed to be able to view. It's often surprising how many gaps exist in an otherwise well-designed security scheme because of some simple oversight during the setup process.

Using the User-Level Security Wizard

The new Access 2000 User-Level Security Wizard helps you apply a security scheme to your database without having to use the Workgroup Administrator or any of the security dialog boxes. The wizard creates an unsecured backup of your database and then secures the current copy. All the relationships and linked tables you've established in the database are exported to the secured copy. The backup copy is owned by the user who's authorized to run the wizard.

When the wizard is finished, you can print a report with details of all the groups, users, and permissions. Be sure to keep the report in a safe place because it contains sensitive information. You can use the report to re-create the workgroup file if it becomes damaged.

LOOKING AHEAD

If you've protected Visual Basic code in your database with a Visual Basic Environment password, you must unlock it before running the User-Level Security Wizard. See the section "Securing Visual Basic Code" for information about locking and unlocking modules in a database.

To start the User-Level Security Wizard, choose Tools|Security|User-Level Security Wizard. The first dialog box offers the choice of creating a new workgroup information file or modifying the current one. After choosing to create a new one, click Next to open the next dialog box, where you enter a unique workgroup ID (WID).

The WID is a 4-to-20-character string that's case sensitive. You can also enter your name and the name of your company, if desired. In this dialog box, you also have the choice of assigning this WIF as the default for this database or creating a shortcut that will open the new secured database. When you click Next, the next wizard dialog box contains seven tabs showing all the objects in the current database (see Figure 19.17). The Other tab includes items for securing all new objects of each type. By default, all existing and new objects are checked. If you want to keep an object's security as it's currently set, clear the check mark next to the object name.

FIGURE 19.17
Specifying the security of individual objects in the database.

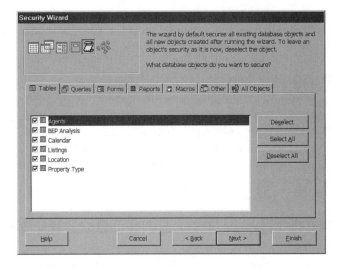

After setting individual object security, click Next. The wizard dialog box enables you to set up the security group accounts you want included in the WIF. Figure 19.18 shows the list of optional groups you can include in your WIF. You can assign individual users to these groups later.

FIGURE 19.18
Adding optional group accounts to the WIF.

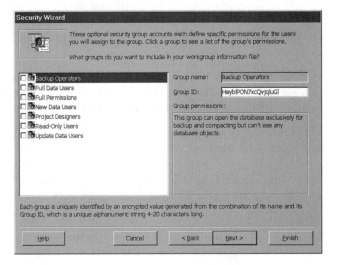

When you select a group, you can read the specific permissions that are automatically granted to each group. For example, the New Data Users group has permissions to read and insert data but it can't delete or update data. It also doesn't have permission to modify any object designs. In addition to a group name, each group also has a unique group ID.

In the next wizard dialog box, shown in Figure 19.19, you can assign some specific permissions to the Users group. By default, the wizard does not grant any permissions to the Users group because anyone who has a copy of Access is considered a member of the Users group and would be granted these permissions. If you do choose to grant permissions, the wizard displays a warning that granting permissions to the Users group invalidates any security measures.

FIGURE 19.19
Granting special permissions to the Users group.

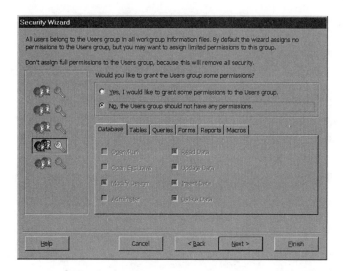

In the next wizard dialog box, you can add new users to the WIF. Type the username and password in the appropriate boxes and then click Add This User to the List. You can also delete a user who you've previously added to the WIF. Figure 19.20 shows Bob Jones added to the list of users. When you enter a username, the wizard creates a PID that you may change if you want. The PID combined and encrypted with the username creates a unique identifier for each user.

When you move to the next wizard dialog box, shown in Figure 19.21, you assign the users you added in the previous dialog box to a group. You have two ways to do this: Select a user and assign the user to a group, as shown in Figure 19.21, or select a group and assign users to it. The results will be the same. In the final wizard dialog box, you're prompted for a name for the unsecured backup copy of the database. The copy will include the .bak file extension.

After creating the new WIF and security scheme, the wizard displays a report of the settings used in the file. You have the option of saving the report in a file or printing the report. Keep this information in a safe place because you'll need it to re-create the WIF should it become damaged.

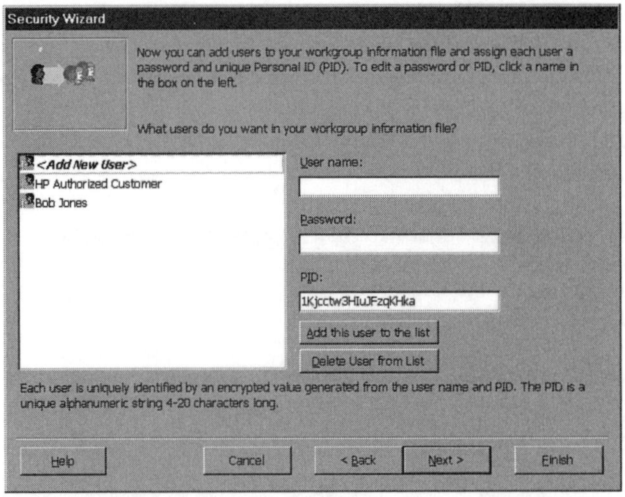

FIGURE 19.20

Adding users to groups in the workgroup.

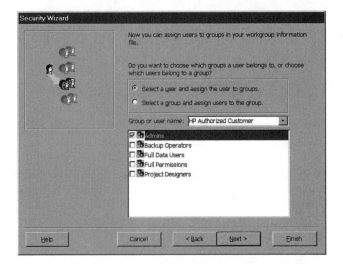

FIGURE 19.21

Assigning users to groups in the workgroup.

Protecting Data Access Pages

You have a few problems to deal with when securing a database that includes data access pages. Not only must you be able to protect the data access page shortcut stored in the Access database, you must also protect the corresponding HTML file located elsewhere in your computer's file system. A further complication arises from the need to protect the secured database from being accessed through the page.

One way to protect the data access page shortcut and HTML file is to make the database itself read-only for other users. Once you've published the page, you can specify read-only for the file and folder where the HTML file is located on the Web server.

Once you've published the page, you must also be concerned about protecting and controlling entry to the database from the page. You need to prevent unauthorized access to the database and, once users have logged on, control the level of their access. If you've applied user-level security to the database and you also want user-level security through the page, you must specify the correct WIF in the connection information for the page. The WIF must also be in a public network share that's available to all users. Use the Data Link Properties dialog box to change the connection to the page.

> **Note:** If the database requires a password, you'll be prompted for the password the first time you open the page.

LOOKING AHEAD Never save the username and password with the page. This would allow any user to log onto the database. Clear the Allow Saving of Password option in the Connection tab of the Data Link Properties dialog box. See Chapter 20, "Posting Your Database to the Web," for more information about creating and using data access pages.

Removing User-Level Security

To remove user-level security that has been created for a database, you must return ownership of the database and all its objects to the default Admin user. You must be able to log on as the workgroup administrator who's a member of the Admins group. After giving the default Users group full permissions for all objects, exit Access and restart it, logging on as Admin. Next, create a new, empty database and import all the objects from the original database.

This results in a completely unsecured database that any workgroup or user can open. The WIF that's in effect when you import the objects to the new database is the one that's used for the Admin group with the new database.

Implementing Other Security Measures

In addition to the rather rigorous security measures built into Access, there are several other measures you can take to truly ensure the protection of your databases and the data they contain.

Securing Visual Basic Code

Class modules behind forms and reports are no longer protected by user-level security, as in previous versions of Access. Although the forms and report designs are protected by user-level security, you must take other measures to secure the code behind them and other modules. In Access 2000, you protect all code with a password you set in the

Visual Basic Editor window. Once the password is set, you must enter it to be able to view, edit, cut, copy, paste, export, or delete any module in the database.

To set password protection for the code in the database, open the Visual Basic Editor window and do the following:

1. Choose Tools|<*databasename*> Project Properties to open the Project Properties dialog box, which has two tabs.
2. Click the Protection tab and check the Lock for Viewing check box.
3. Enter a password in the Password box and confirm the password by entering it again in the Confirm Password box.

When you reopen the database, the code will be protected by requiring you to enter the password before you can view or edit the code. If you've entered a password but haven't checked the Lock for Viewing option, you can view or edit the code but you can't open the Project Properties dialog box. To remove the password, open the Project Properties dialog box and clear all the entries on the Protection tab.

Warning: Don't forget your password. Without it, you won't be able to view or edit the code or change any of the project properties.

Another way to secure code in a database is to compile all the code and save the database as an MDE file. Compiling removes all editable source code and compacts the destination database. The code will run successfully, but it won't be available for viewing or editing. Compacting the database reduces the size because the source code is removed when it's compiled. It also saves processing time because the code does not need to be compiled before running.

As always, be sure to save a backup copy of the database before converting to an MDE file. If you need to make any changes to forms, reports, or modules, you'll need to open the original database, make the changes, and save it again as an MDE file.

After the database has been saved as an MDE file, you can no longer do any of the following:

- View, modify, or create forms, reports, or modules in design view.
- Add, delete, or change any references to object libraries or other databases.
- Change code using the VB or Access properties or methods, because the MDE file doesn't contain any source code you can edit.
- Import or export forms, reports, or modules. Tables, queries, data access pages, and macros can be imported to or exported from non-MDE databases. Tables, queries, data access pages, and macros can be imported from an MDE file into another database.

To save a database as an MDE file, first close the database and make sure no one else is using it; then choose Tools|Database Utilities|Make MDE File. In the Database To Save as MDE section, select the database you want to save and then click Make MDE. In the Save MDE As dialog box, choose the location where you want to save the MDE file and click Save. If the database is already open, you go directly to the Save MDE As dialog box.

If you've already secured the database with user-level security, there may be some criteria you must meet before you can save it as an MDE file. See the Access Help topic for more information about creating and using MDE files.

Securing a Replicated Database

Although you can't protect a replicated database with a password, you can set user permissions on replicated database objects. You can't replicate a password-protected database. Another way to protect a replica is to keep it in an unshared folder and use the Replication Manager to synchronize it indirectly. If you need direct synchronization, you can set permissions on the replica's share to give access to specific users. Do not specify the share as read-only, which prevents synchronization with other members of the replica set.

Encryption

Although the database file is stored on the hard disk in a binary format, there's nothing to prevent an experienced computer user from using a sector-editing tool such as the Norton Utilities to view the raw data on the disk. The text and numeric data in a database is there in the bits and bytes stored on the computer's disk, exposed to prying eyes.

Normally, this is not a problem. There's no way to use a sector editor to view the relationships between tables or to decipher OLE or the other binary data in the database file. However, if absolute security is important, Access provides an encryption tool for scrambling and unscrambling data as it's written to or read from disk. You must have enough disk space to store both the original and the encrypted database.

To encrypt an Access database, close the database and select Tools|Security|Encrypt/Decrypt. This command uses a secret algorithm to quickly convert the database contents to a totally random sequence of bits on the computer's disk. No password is required for encryption or decryption. Access simply encrypts the database contents and stores the encrypted format on the computer's disk. Encryption can take a few minutes or more, depending on the size of the database.

Note: If you've already secured the database with user-level security, you must be either the owner of the database or a member of the Admins group who has Open Exclusive permission for the database.

Reading an encrypted database requires no special steps. Simply open the database, and Access performs the decryption as the database is opened. You might notice a slight delay as the decryption process occurs, but the user is not challenged for an encryption password.

The biggest noticeable difference between an encrypted and unencrypted database is that an encrypted database cannot be compressed by utilities such as PKZip. Because the byte sequence on the disk is totally random, there are no repeating patterns for a compression utility to exploit. An encrypted database may take longer to transmit electronically for the same reason. Even modems that use efficient real-time compression routines to shorten transmission times will have trouble applying those routines to an encrypted Access database.

Disguising Database Objects

One popular security technique is to simply assign a misleading name to an object that must be kept covert. This can be as simple as naming a table that contains salary information something such as HireDates or some other misleading name. In a large database, even the most diligent snooper is discouraged from going to the trouble of poking through dozens of tables looking for something interesting.

Along similar lines, if keeping certain data secret is important, you can set up a dummy table with a very attractive name such as RegionalSales2000 and fill it with completely erroneous information. Then, if there's a security leak, you can be assured the correct information did not leak out of the company, and you also have the chance to locate the source of the leak.

Hiding Database Objects

A simple technique that's easy to implement in Access databases is to preface sensitive objects with *USys* (USysSalaries, for example). Anything with a USys (or MSys, for that matter) prefix is invisible in the Database window. You must use the System Objects check box in the View tab of the Options dialog box to see objects hidden with the USys prefix trick (see Figure 19.22).

All but the most diligent and motivated snoopers will be unable to find objects hidden with the USys prefix. In fact, many experienced Access developers are unaware of this feature.

Utilizing Network and Operating System Security

Most network operating systems provide some level of security. For example, the networking built into Windows 95/98 and Windows NT provides a password-verification mechanism that prevents unauthorized users from simply turning on a computer and having full access to the files on that system. In addition, each folder on a Windows 95/98 or Windows NT computer can have certain sharing privileges imposed that restrict admission to certain individuals.

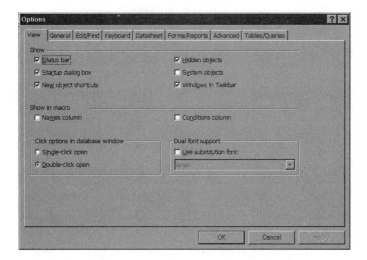

Although the network security in Windows 95/98 is fairly easy to circumvent (by booting the computer from a floppy disk), the security in Windows NT is much more stringent. If the simple password security in Windows 95/98 is inadequate for your users, you should investigate the more rigorous user Registry system built into Windows NT. Access 2000 runs equally well under both of these operating systems.

Summary

Implementing database security in an Access database can be a daunting exercise. You must first understand the Access security model, which includes user and group information stored in the workgroup information file. Next, you must master the hierarchy of object ownership and the permissions granted to groups and users within a database. Good planning is essential to implementing an effective security system in an Access database.

Security does not end with the password-based system in an Access database. There are other measures, such as hiding or disguising sensitive tables, forms, and queries, that go a long way toward keeping out all but the most experienced Access developers. The new User-Level Security Wizard can make the job much easier, and the VBE lockout feature can extend the security umbrella to Visual Basic modules.

Special consideration must be focused on security surrounding data access pages because of the two-way passage of information. Finally, encrypting a secured database will ensure total protection from unauthorized access to the stored data.

Posting Your Database to the Web

Now that you've created a database full of valuable information and written an application to maintain and use the data, wouldn't it be great to share it with the world? Or even your company or close friends? Microsoft Access 97 introduced some revolutionary features that make it almost trivial to convert database tables, queries, forms, and reports to formats usable by Web browsers such as Internet Explorer and Netscape Navigator. Now Access 2000 has arrived with the new data access page object, a special type of Web page that you and others can use to view and work with data stored in an Access database.

This chapter assumes that you're familiar with the Internet and know a little bit about HTML and how Web pages work. This doesn't mean that you have to know enough to create Web pages from scratch but rather that you've surfed the Web a bit. If you want to learn more, there are gazillions of books available at your local bookshop.

Two terms are used repeatedly in this chapter, and you should be familiar with them:

- *HTML (HyperText Markup Language)*. This is the set of codes and tags a Web browser uses to display a Web page. Sometimes, a scripting language such as VBScript or JavaScript is embedded within the page as well.
- *URL (Universal Resource Locator)*. A URL is the address of the document you want to open in a Web browser. Typically, it's the address of a Web page out on the Internet, but it can also be a Word document on your local machine or almost any type of file located anywhere.

This chapter continues to use the Elgin real estate listing database, introduced and used in earlier chapters, to create the HTML pages.

Types of Web Pages

In the prehistoric days of the Web, until early 1996 or so, Web pages were static, unchanging entities. Web developers laid out a Web page like a page in a book; when they saved the HTML file, it was set in stone. When users fired up browsers and connected to Web servers, they received the page exactly as designed by the developer, except that the users could elect to not download graphics. Every user got the exact same page, possibly with minor variations depending on the browser he or she used. These are called *static* Web pages.

Web pages have become far more responsive these days, which means you can log on to a site and get something completely different from the last user who logged on, depending on the time of day, the type of browser you're using, and almost any other condition that the Web page developer chooses. With these *server-generated* Web pages, the Web server is creating pages on-the-fly in response to specific requests the user makes. These *dynamic* Web pages function much like a custom application, responding to choices the user makes, the type of data requested, whether the user has logged on to this site before, and so on.

An example of a dynamic Web page is the result of a Web search using an engine such as AltaVista or Excite. When you first log on to the search site, you receive a static Web page, the same as any other user sees (except that the ad banner changes, but let's not quibble). After you set your search parameters, the search engine responds by sending you a dynamic Web page with hot links to the sites that meet your search criteria. It created this page by receiving your search definition, searching its database for the sites that meet your requirements, and creating an HTML page listing those sites.

The third type of Web page, the data access page, is also dynamic and is designed so that the user can view, edit, delete, filter, group, and sort live data stored in an Access database or a SQL server database. You must have Microsoft Internet Explorer 5.0 or later installed to make use of data access pages. This type of Web page can also contain controls that include data from other applications such as spreadsheets, PivotTables, and charts.

Using Access and the other tools in Microsoft Office, you can create either static or dynamic Web pages that display your data, or both. The type of page you decide to use to publish your data on the Internet or an intranet depends on how frequently the data changes, the need to allow users to perform custom searches, the amount of data you want to publish, and other factors specific to particular types of data.

For example, the sample Elgin Enterprises real estate database contains information about property for sale. Depending on the size of Elgin Enterprises and the volume of real estate it sells or leases, the data is unlikely to change daily. However, it could change weekly, so you'll want to build a Web page that uses the latest information. A user-friendly Web page would let a user customize a search by filtering and sorting the data instead of slogging through the entire fixed list of properties.

Technical Note: One other important difference between static and dynamic Web pages is the method you use to actually expose the page to the network. You can copy static pages via FTP to your Web server; then users open them in their browsers in the same way you open a text file in Notepad or FrontPage.

Dynamic pages, however, require a more sophisticated server that can receive requests from users, retrieve the recordset, and then create Web pages on-the-fly to send back to the users. The end result, from the users' perspective, is the exact same: an HTML page displayed in the browser showing your data. Microsoft's Internet Information Server, shipped with Windows NT, performs such functions, and it's easy to use with Access databases. However, Netscape and many other companies have servers that can perform the same functions. With such a page, the prospective buyer may look up a certain type of property or one in a specific price range.

Converting Access Data to HTML

In general, Microsoft Access provides four ways for you to save data from your database as HTML documents and publish these documents on the Internet:

- *Save data as static HTML documents.* You can create static HTML documents from tables, queries, form datasheets, and reports. When you save data as static HTML documents, the resulting pages reflect the state of the data at the time it was saved, like a snapshot. If your data changes, you must save the pages again to publish the new data.

- *Save data as server-generated HTML files.* You can save your tables, queries, and form datasheets as Internet Database Connector/HTML extension (IDC/HTX) or Active Server Pages (ASP) files that generate HTML documents by querying a copy of your database located on a Web server.

- *Create a data access page.* You can create a data access page object in Access that contains a shortcut to the location of the corresponding HTML file.

- *Automate the publishing of dynamic and static HTML documents.* You can use the Microsoft Office 2000 Web Publishing Wizard to automate the transfer of your Web pages to your service provider.

Which method you use depends primarily on the timeliness of the data and the server you have for making the HTML pages available.

A couple of limitations exist for using the built-in Access tools for publishing data this way. One is that there's no way to save OLE Object fields to the HTML page, so you can't include any images stored in the database and automatically include them in the HTML page. For example, if you export the Elgin Results report to HTML, you'll see that the photographs of the properties are not included in the Web page. You can always edit the HTML page by hand to include them, but that kind of defeats the purpose of automating the page generation.

DEVELOPMENT

You also can't control which fields are included in the HTML page when you create a page from an Access table. If you want to include only certain fields, sort the data, or otherwise massage it, you need to create a query and then create the HTML page from the query. With dynamic HTML pages, you can also manually edit the query's SQL statement in the resulting pages.

Exporting Access Data to Static HTML Documents

The simplest way to create static HTML pages with Microsoft Access 2000 is to save tables, queries, form datasheets, and reports using File|Export from the Access main menu. When you save a table, query, or form as an HTML document, the resulting HTML document is based on the table or query associated with the datasheet, including the current setting of the OrderBy or Filter property of the table or query. The HTML page created from a form shows the data in datasheet view. None of the form design features are exported with the data.

If you do not specify a different location for the new HTML file, Access will store it in the same folder as the source database.

Publishing Tables, Queries, and Form Datasheets

To output a table, query, or form to a static HTML file, do the following:

1. In the Database window, select the table, query, form, or report you want to save (for example, the Elgin Enterprises Listings table).

2. Choose File|Export.

3. In the Export Table "Listings" As dialog box, select HTML Documents in the Save As Type box.

4. If you want to preserve formatting, select the Save Formatted check box. If you've selected a form to export to HTML, the Save Formatted option is automatically checked and dimmed.

5. To automatically open the resulting HTML document in your Web browser, select the Autostart check box (this isn't required, but the new page will immediately load into your browser). Figure 20.1 shows the Export Table "Listings" As dialog box.

6. Enter the filename and directory location where you want to save the file and then click Save All.

7. In the HTML Output Options dialog box, if you want Microsoft Access to merge an HTML template with the resulting HTML document, specify that as well and then click OK. (See the "Customizing with HTML Templates" section for more information about this option.) If you don't want to use a template, just click OK without entering the name of a template file.

The end result of saving the Listings table from the Elgin database is shown in Figure 20.2. This will load into your browser automatically if you selected the Autostart option when you created the page. Otherwise, you must open the page yourself.

FIGURE 20.1

Exporting the Elgin Listings table as a static HTML page.

FIGURE 20.2

Elgin's Listings table as a static HTML page.

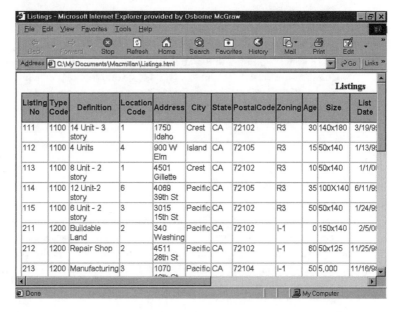

You can't save a regular Access form as an HTML document because a form, by nature, is not a static document. A typical form has navigation buttons, which require an underlying mechanism for navigating a recordset and refreshing the data in the bound controls on the form. This is outside the realm of capabilities of a static HTML page. Therefore, Access saves a form as the underlying datasheet.

If you select the Save Formatted check box, the HTML document contains an HTML table that reflects as closely as possible the appearance of the datasheet by using the appropriate HTML tags to specify color, font, and alignment. The HTML document also follows as closely as possible the page orientation and margins of the datasheet.

Whenever you want to use settings that are different from the default orientation and margins for a datasheet, you must first open the datasheet and then select File|Page Setup to change the settings before you save the datasheet as an HTML document. The HTML document will then reflect these new settings, more or less. Access does its best to maintain consistent formatting, but HTML has far less flexible formatting options.

Technical Note: With the Save Formatted check box selected, when a field has a `Format` or `InputMask` property setting, those settings are reflected in the data in the HTML document. For example, if a field's `Format` property is set to `Currency` and you have English (United States) selected in the Windows Regional settings in the Control Panel, the data in the HTML document is formatted with a dollar sign, a comma as the thousand separator, and two decimal places. The HTML page will reflect the regional settings in Windows.

Note: If you're using a particular international version of Windows, Access doesn't always pick up all the applicable regional settings. For example, in the United States version of Windows NT 4.0, setting the Regional Settings to German (Standard) causes currency to be displayed in the HTML page with a dollar sign ($) but with a decimal as the thousands separator. Be sure to test for all combinations of Windows versions and regional settings where your application will be used.

Publishing Access Reports

When saving table, query, and form datasheets, Microsoft Access saves each datasheet to a single HTML file, but it saves reports as multiple HTML documents, with one HTML file per printed page. To name each page, Microsoft Access uses the name of the object and appends Page*XX* to the end of each page's filename after the first page. Therefore, if you save the Listing report from the Elgin real estate database, the first page is `Listing.htm`, followed by `ListingPage2.htm`, `ListingPage3.htm`, and so on. Figure 20.3 shows a report in Access, and Figure 20.4 shows the HTML page generated. The hyperlinks in the lower-left corner of the HTML screen jump to other pages in the report.

FIGURE 20.3
Elgin's All Results report in Access.

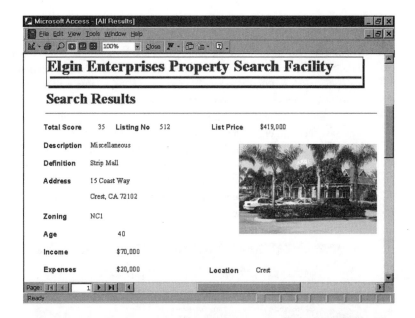

FIGURE 20.4
Elgin's All Results report as an HTML page.

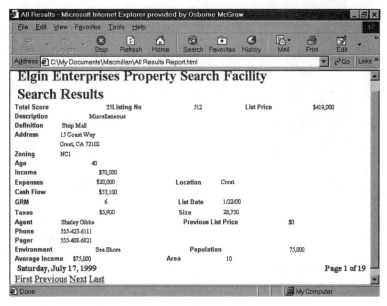

This series of HTML documents is based on the report's underlying table or query, including the current OrderBy or Filter property settings of the table or query. These documents also approximate the proportions and layout of the actual report and the page orientation and margins set for the report. To change the page orientation and margins, open the report in Print Preview and then use the Page Setup command to change settings before you save the report as HTML documents. These settings are saved from session to session for reports, so if you change them once, they will be used the next time you save the form or report as HTML documents. Figure 20.5 shows the Open dialog box displaying the series of HTML files that were created when the All Results Report was exported to HTML. As with the Listings report discussed earlier, each page of the report results in a separate HTML file. The All Results Report HTML file contains the first page of the report. The second page of the report is in a separate HTML file named All Results ReportPage2, and so on.

FIGURE 20.5
Elgin's All Results report HTML files.

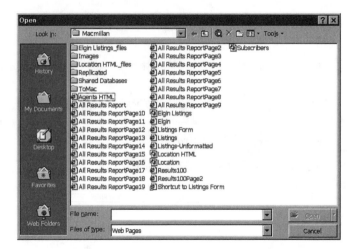

Creating Server-Generated HTML Files

Publishing static HTML data pages is fine for some applications, but in many cases you'll want to present the latest, up-to-date data at any given moment. For example, if Elgin Enterprises is a large real estate office with many properties being sold and listed every day, you'll want to get the data from the database at the time the user does a search. Otherwise, the data will be outdated. To do this, the Web server dynamically creates HTML pages in response to user requests.

It's important, however, to understand that the data presented is the latest at the time the HTML page is created, but it's not automatically updated to reflect changes. Therefore, the data is more like a snapshot-type recordset than a dynaset. If you connect to a Web site and request data, you'll get data current as of that moment. Only by refreshing the page will you get any updates to the data. You can also use HTML META tags to automatically refresh the data at some interval, but this is just the same as if the user clicked the Refresh or Reload buttons in the Web browser.

The alternative is to export the Access data to a server-generated HTML format. Access supports two types: Internet Database Connector and Active Server Pages. Both methods require that the pages be hosted on Microsoft's Internet Information Server (IIS).

Internet Database Connector

Access enables you to save a table, query, or form datasheet as Internet Database Connector/HTML extension that generate HTML documents by querying your database located on a Web server.

Here's how to save a table, query, or form datasheet as an IDC/HTX file:

1. In the database window, select the table, query, or form you want to save and then choose File|Export.

2. In the Export Table "Listings" As dialog box, select Microsoft IIS 1-2 in the Save As Type box. The Save Formatted option is checked and dimmed.

3. Enter the filename and directory location where you want to save the file and then click Save.

4. In the HTX/IDC Output Options dialog box, specify the following:

   - An HTML template, if you want Microsoft Access to merge one with the HTML extension (HTX) file. (See the "Customizing with HTML Templates" section for more information about using templates.)

   - The data source name that will be used for a copy of the current database.

   - A username and password, if required to open the database.

   - You can specify any of these items later, except the HTML template, by editing the resulting IDC file in a text editor such as Notepad or FrontPage.

5. Click OK.

When you save Internet Connector files, Access creates two files: an Internet Database Connector (IDC) file and an HTML extension (HTX) file. These files are used to generate a Web page that displays current data from your database.

Technical Note: Once you've saved the new files, you can view the results by opening them in Notepad or some other text editor. An IDC file contains the necessary information to connect to the Open Database Connectivity (ODBC) data source you entered in the HTML Output Options dialog box and to run a

continues

SQL statement that queries the database. When you save the Listings datasheet from the Elgin real estate database as IDC/HTX files, Access creates the following IDC file:

```
Datasource:Listings DSN
Template:Listings.htx
SQLStatement:SELECT * FROM [Listings]
Password:
Username:
```

Because this IDC file was created from a table, the SQLStatement entry is a simple SQL statement that selects all the records and fields in the table. Had this been created from an existing Access QueryDef, this entry would contain the full SQL statement underlying the query. Note, however, that because the SQL statement is specified in this file, any user who opens this Web page will receive the results of the same query, reflecting the current recordset that meets the query's specifications. The ODBC "Listings DSN" data source name must exist on the Web server running IIS, thus allowing an ODBC connection to the Listings data.

An IDC file also contains the name and location of an HTML extension (HTX) file. The HTX file is a template for the HTML document; it contains field merge codes that indicate where the values returned by the SQL statement should be inserted. For the Listings table, Access creates the following HTX file (to save space here, some repetitive lines have been deleted, indicated by an ellipsis):

```
<HTML>
<HEAD>
<META HTTP-EQUIV="Content-Type" CONTENT="text/html;charset=windows-1252">
<TITLE>Listings</TITLE>
</HEAD>
<BODY>
<TABLE BORDER=1 BGCOLOR=#ffffff CELLSPACING=0><FONT FACE="Arial"
COLOR=#000000><CAPTION><B>Listings</B></CAPTION></FONT>

<THEAD>
<TR>
<TH BGCOLOR=#c0c0c0 BORDERCOLOR=#000000 ><FONT SIZE=2 FACE="Arial"
COLOR=#000000>Listing No</FONT></TH>

<TH BGCOLOR=#c0c0c0 BORDERCOLOR=#000000 ><FONT SIZE=2 FACE="Arial"
COLOR=#000000>Type Code</FONT></TH>

<TH BGCOLOR=#c0c0c0 BORDERCOLOR=#000000 ><FONT SIZE=2 FACE="Arial"
COLOR=#000000>Definition</FONT></TH>

...(more background color specifications)

</TR>
</THEAD>
```

```
<TBODY>
<%BeginDetail%>
<TR VALIGN=TOP>
<TD BORDERCOLOR=#c0c0c0 ><FONT SIZE=2 FACE="Arial"
COLOR=#000000><%Listing No%><BR></FONT></TD>

<TD BORDERCOLOR=#c0c0c0 ><FONT SIZE=2 FACE="Arial"
COLOR=#000000><%Type Code%><BR></FONT></TD>

<TD BORDERCOLOR=#c0c0c0 ><FONT SIZE=2 FACE="Arial"
COLOR=#000000><%Definition%><BR></FONT></TD>

...(more border color specifications)

</TR>
<%EndDetail%>
</TBODY>
<TFOOT></TFOOT>
</TABLE>
</BODY>
</HTML>
```

The lines in the HTX file that use the <TH> and <TD> HTML tags format the data in the resulting HTML page sent to the user. The <TH> tag contains the field names for the column headings; you can edit the HTX file to customize these headings. The <TD> tag contains placeholders for the actual data in the resulting recordset, forming the body of the table in the HTML page. The field names appear between the percent signs (for example, <%Listing No%>).

Microsoft Access saves the HTX file to be used with an IDC file with the same name as the IDC file, except with .HTX and .IDC filename extensions. When a user requests the page from the server, IIS merges the database information into the HTML document and returns it to the user's Web browser. The appearance of the HTML page will be the same as a static page. See the section "Publishing Server-Generated HTML Files" for information about using these types of files on the Web.

Active Server Pages

The process of saving a table, query, or form as an ASP file is similar to saving as an IDC/HTX file. After you choose Active Server Pages in the Save As Type box, the main difference is that in the Microsoft Active Server Pages Output Options dialog box, you must specify two additional items:

- The URL for the server where the Active Server Page will reside.
- The Session Timeout setting, which determines how long a connection to the server is maintained after the user stops working with the Active Server Page.

The resulting ASP file contains HTML tags mixed in with one or more SQL queries, template directives, and Visual Basic Script code that references the ActiveX Server controls. Figure 20.6 shows part of the ASP file created for the Listings form. The Visual Basic Script opens the Listings recordset.

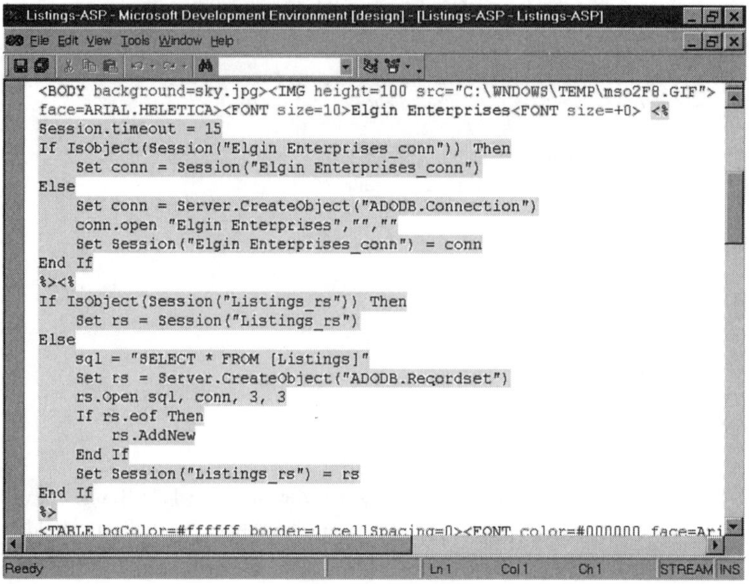

FIGURE 20.6

Visual Basic Script in the Listings ASP file.

```
Listings-ASP - Microsoft Development Environment [design] - [Listings-ASP - Listings-ASP]
File  Edit  View  Tools  Window  Help
<BODY background=sky.jpg><IMG height=100 src="C:\WNDOWS\TEMP\mso2F8.GIF">
face=ARIAL.HELETICA><FONT size=10>Elgin Enterprises<FONT size=+0> <%
Session.timeout = 15
If IsObject(Session("Elgin Enterprises_conn")) Then
    Set conn = Session("Elgin Enterprises_conn")
Else
    Set conn = Server.CreateObject("ADODB.Connection")
    conn.open "Elgin Enterprises","",""
    Set Session("Elgin Enterprises_conn") = conn
End If
%><%
If IsObject(Session("Listings_rs")) Then
    Set rs = Session("Listings_rs")
Else
    sql = "SELECT * FROM [Listings]"
    Set rs = Server.CreateObject("ADODB.Recordset")
    rs.Open sql, conn, 3, 3
    If rs.eof Then
        rs.AddNew
    End If
    Set Session("Listings_rs") = rs
End If
%>
<TABLE bgColor=#ffffff border=1 cellSpacing=0><FONT color=#000000 face=Ari
Ready                                          Ln 1       Col 1      Ch 1      STREAM INS
```

With Access, you can save a form as an Active Server Page that behaves much like your form, displaying controls and enabling the user to navigate through the recordset. Access saves most, but not all, controls on the form as ActiveX controls that perform the same or similar functions. A much better solution is to use data access pages to publish your data with custom controls.

Microsoft Access also doesn't save or run Visual Basic code behind the form or controls. If you need to duplicate the features of VB code, you'll need to edit the resulting ASP file using Visual Basic Script. Visual Basic Script is a subset of Visual Basic that lets you embed code in a Web page to control how the page is displayed and the data it shows. You can find more information about VBScript at http://msdn.microsoft.com/scripting.

To copy the layout of your form as closely as possible, Microsoft Access uses the Microsoft HTML Layout control to position the controls on Active Server Pages. (The HTML Layout control is typically installed with Microsoft Internet Explorer.) The resulting page uses a feature of Active Server called *server-side scripting* to connect to a copy of your database on an Internet server.

DEVELOPMENT

You can also use the OutputTo method to export Access objects to a Web site. This is especially helpful if you need to output multiple datasheets or output repeatedly to test a new Web site. The OutputTo method has six arguments, including the type and name of the object to output, the output format, the path of the output file, whether to start the destination software immediately after output, and the path and name of a template file, if desired. Acceptable output formats include HTML, ASP, Excel, IDC/HTX, text, RTF, report snapshot (SNP), and data access pages (HTML). For example, the following statement outputs the Elgin Listings form to an HTML file named "OutList" using the Elgin template and opens the Internet Explorer to display the file:

```
DoCmd.OutputTo acOutputForm, "Listings", acFormatHTML, _
    "C:\My Documents\Macmillan\OutList.htm", True, "Elgin.htm"
```

> **Peter's Principle:** Visual Basic Script
>
> A *script*, just like in the theater, is a special set of instructions and words that you can use to make a Web page dynamic and active. When you gain experience programming you can add action to your Web page. Scripting enables you to write special computer code and manipulate objects on the Web page. For example, you can include counters that will count the occurrences of events or count down to a target date. Other scripts can handle events that occur to objects on the Web page.
>
> You need some advanced programming knowledge to successfully use this Office feature. You can create and modify a script right on a Web page in Access or use the Microsoft Script Editor to view and edit the HTML code. A finished script is acted out by the Web browser when you open the page.
>
> Be careful when you copy or move a script. Many of the scripts are self-contained and can be correctly applied in any location but others depend on the structure of the Web page.

Creating Data Access Pages

The new data access page object is a very versatile tool for publishing dynamic data contained in an Access database to the Web. You can create three types of data access pages:

- Data access pages to be used to group information stored in the database and summarize it as necessary. When you group records, for example, by property type, you can view just the group header or expand the group to see the detailed records.

- Data access pages to be used for data entry, much the same as forms are used in a local computer setting.

- Data access pages to be used to interactively analyze the data in the database. For example, you can include a PivotTable list that can be manipulated to compare data and detect trends or patterns.

Designing a data access page is much the same as designing a form or report. You use a toolbox, field list, controls, property sheets, and the Sorting and Grouping dialog box to place all the controls in the data access page design. Many of the same controls are included in the toolbox, with quite a few added interactive controls such as scrolling text, movie, and a hot spot image used as a hyperlink.

You have four ways to create a data access page: using the AutoPage feature, adding controls directly in the design view, getting help from a wizard, and saving from an existing HTML file. Working in design view and using the Data Access Page Wizard are much the same as creating a form, but using an existing HTML file is a little different.

If you've exported the Location table to an HTML file, you can make a data access page out of it by doing the following:

1. Double-click the Edit Web Page That Already Exists item in the Pages page of the database window.

2. Select the Location HTML file and click Open. The HTML file opens in the Access window.

3. Choose File|Web Page Preview and click Yes when prompted to save the data access page. This places the shortcut icon in the Pages page. The new data access page appears in the Internet Explorer window (see Figure 20.7).

4. If you want to make changes to the data access page, choose File|Edit with Microsoft Access for Windows and then switch to design view.

FIGURE 20.7
Creating a data access page from an HTML file.

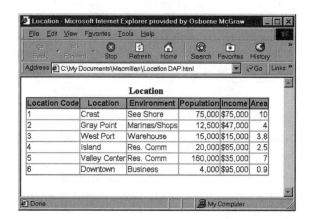

Grouping Data in a Data Access Page

Grouping records in a data access page enables you to see as much detail as you want at a time. You can group records with the help of the Data Access Page Wizard when you first create the page, or you can promote a Text Box control to a higher group level. Figure 20.8 shows a data access page that groups the Elgin Listings by the Type Code field. This page was begun using the wizard, but many design changes were made after the wizard was finished.

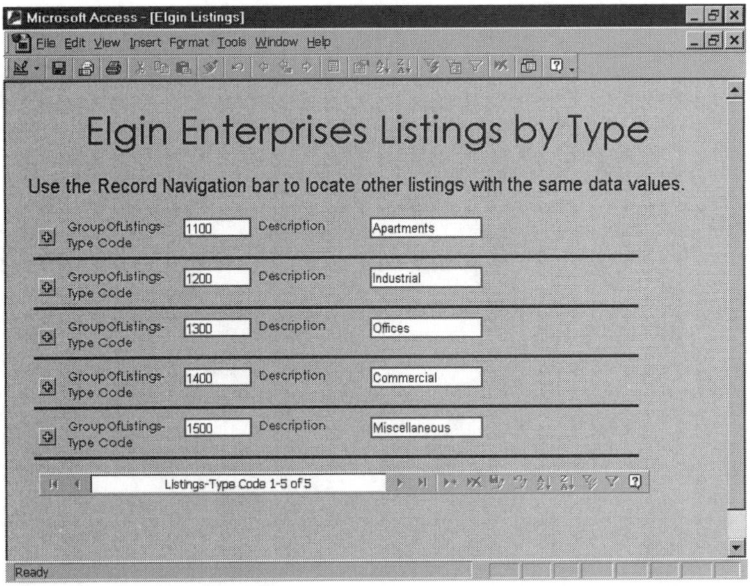

FIGURE 20.8

The Elgin Enterprises Listings by Type data access page.

Note: The Record Navigation bar enables you to move among the groups in the data access page. In this example, the Data Page Size property for the Listings-Type Code is set to 5, which is the total number of property types in the record-set (see Figure 20.9). Therefore, no other sets of group headers appear within the recordset. If there were 20 types, the Record Navigation bar could be used to move among them in groups of five.

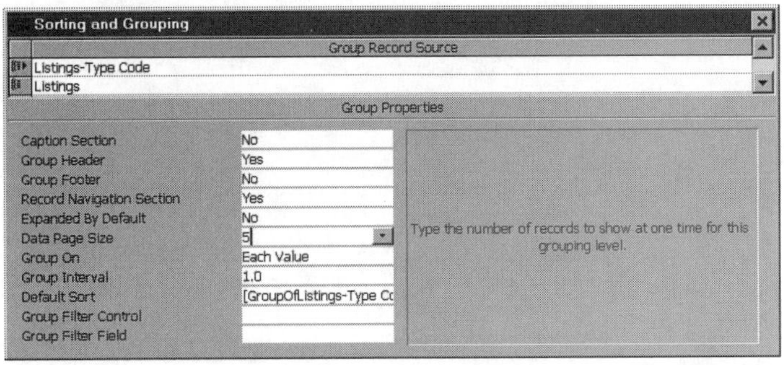

FIGURE 20.9

Setting the group properties.

When you click the Expand icon, the group expands to show individual listings within the group (see Figure 20.10). The viewer can use the Record Navigation bar to move among the records in the expanded group, sort records, or filter the group to view records with a specific value. Data in a grouped data access page is not editable.

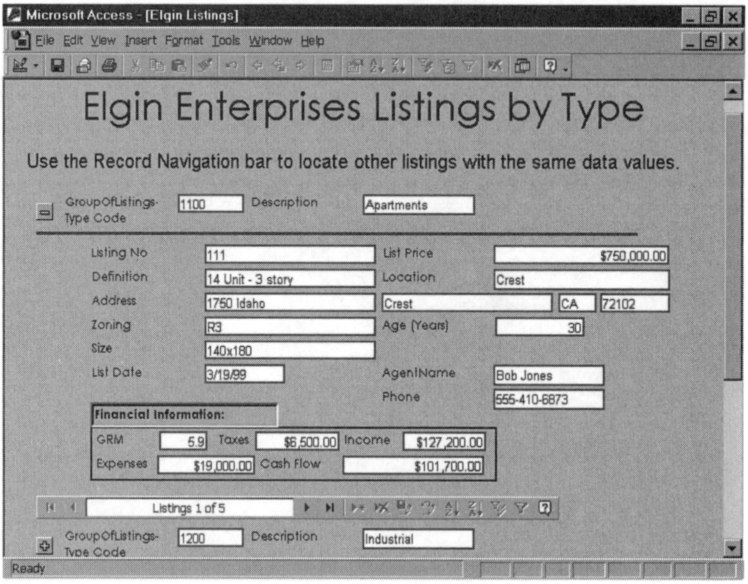

FIGURE 20.10
*Expanding the
Apartments
listing.*

Figure 20.11 shows the Elgin Listings data access page design. The page includes fields
from related tables, such as the location description from the Locations table in place of
the location code in the Listings table. The Agent information was also added from the
Agents table.

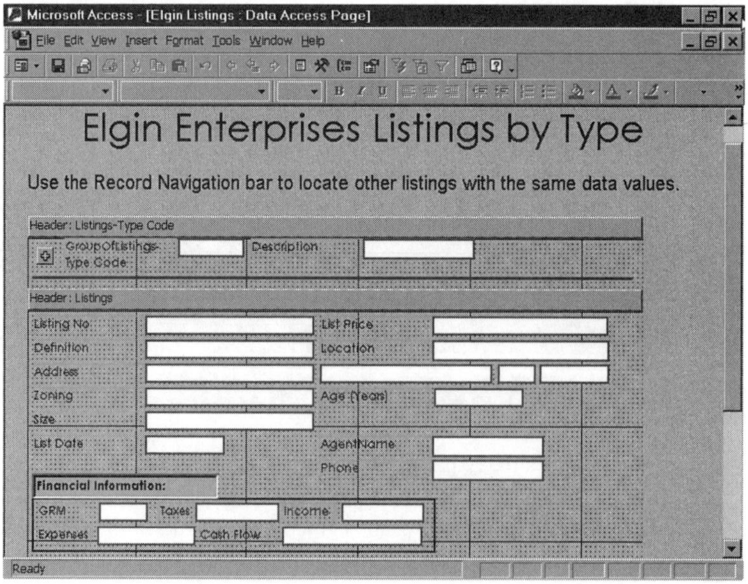

FIGURE 20.11
*The finished Elgin
Listings data
access page
design.*

Summarizing Data in a Data Access Page

Once data is grouped, you can summarize field values to increase the ease of interpreting the underlying information. Grouping and summarizing in a page is much like grouping and summarizing in a report. You can add controls that summarize the data within the group and overall groups. For example, you can add controls to the Elgin Listings data access page that count the number of listings of each type and calculate the average list price.

To add summaries to a grouped data access page, you add bound HTML controls to the group header and set their Control Source and Total Type properties. To add the property count and average list price, do the following:

1. Open the Elgin Listings page in design view and click the Bound HTML Control toolbox button. Place the control in the Header: Listings-Type Code section. You'll probably need to enlarge the header section to make room.

2. Open the property sheet, click the Control Source down arrow, and choose one of the fields in the Listings table that you know will have a unique value, such as Listing No or Address.

3. Set the Total Type property to Count.

4. Place another bound HTML control in the header and choose List Price as the Control Source and Avg as the Total Type.

5. Resize and move the new controls as necessary and add appropriate labels. Then switch to page view.

Figure 20.12 shows the Elgin Listings data access page with the new summaries in the group header.

FIGURE 20.12

Adding summaries to a grouped data access page.

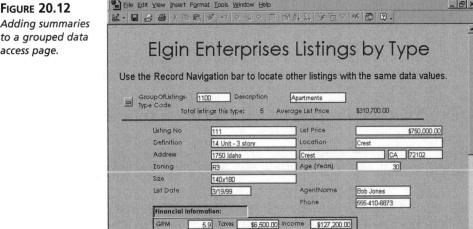

Customizing with Themes

A *theme* enables you to apply a special formatting scheme to a data access page that can reflect the type of data or the audience. For example, you can choose from a variety of preformatted themes that include background colors and patterns, fonts, horizontal lines, and bullet styles. When you create a data access page with the wizard, the final dialog box offers the option to choose a theme.

If you don't specify a theme, a default theme is automatically applied to a new data access page, which you can change in design view. To change the theme of the page, open it in design view and choose Format|Theme. In the Theme dialog box, shown in Figure 20.13, select from the list of themes and view the selected theme's appearance in the right pane. If the theme is not available, you can install it from the Office 2000 CD-ROM by clicking the Install button.

FIGURE 20.13
Choosing a theme for a data access page.

After selecting a theme, you can set the following options to apply to the current page before clicking OK:

- *Vivid Colors*. Displays the text link and button colors using a brighter color selection.
- *Active Graphics*. Refers to animated graphic files (GIFs). The animations appear static in Access but are animated when viewed in a Web browser.
- *Background Image*. Toggles the background image.
- *Set Default*. Changes the default theme to the currently selected theme.

Looking at HTML and Other Languages

Web pages are usually based on HTML, the standard markup language. HTML adds commands, called *tags*, that define the structure and format of the page when it's viewed in a Web browser. In the previous sections, the Access objects that were exported to HTML format were converted to standard HTML. These HTML files resulted in static Web pages.

When you create a data access page with Access 2000, other languages may be combined with HTML to create dynamic Web pages. Cascading Style Sheets and the Extensible Markup Language are often called upon to create specific elements of the Web page appearance and behavior.

Hypertext Markup Language

If you've ever, in the distant past, used one of the early word processing programs such as Wordstar, you may remember having to insert markers to specify blocks of bold or italicized text. HTML uses the same technique to create a language so simple it can be interpreted by many different Web browsers.

HTML is based on tags that precisely define the way the page is to be displayed. When you save a file as HTML format, the file is saved as a text file with the .HTM file extension, and you can view it with any text editor.

To see the code behind an HTML file while in Access, open the object in design view and choose View|HTML Source. (You may be prompted to install the feature from the Office Premium CD-ROM.) The Microsoft Development Environment window opens displaying the HTML code. Figure 20.14 shows a very small piece of the HTML file created when the Listings table was exported to HTML.

> **Note:** If you're viewing the HTML page in the Internet Explorer window, choose View|Source to see the HTML code. (This opens Notepad to display the code.)

The different elements of the language appear in different colors on the screen. In HTML, the tags are enclosed in angle brackets (< >). For example, in Figure 20.14, the <TITLE> tag indicates that the text that follows (Listings) is to be displayed as the page title. Many tags occur in pairs: one to start the action and one to stop it. The closing tag uses the same name but is preceded by a slash (/). The statement

<TITLE>Listings</TITLE>

creates the complete title. You can also see, at the end of the fifth line, the tag <HEAD>, which indicates the beginning of the code that defines the Web page header. The </HEAD>

tag near the bottom of the screen follows the header contents, and the <BODY> tag begins the body section of the page by setting the appearance and contents of the table and the captions.

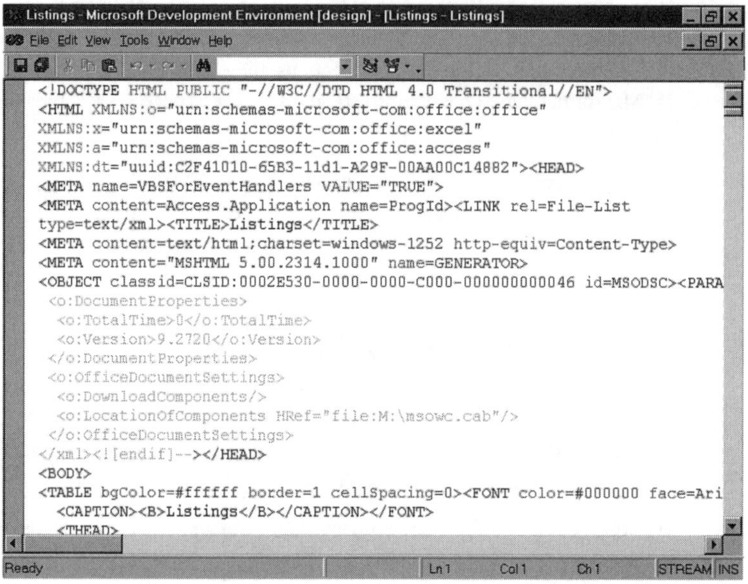

FIGURE 20.14

The Listings table HTML file.

```
<!DOCTYPE HTML PUBLIC "-//W3C//DTD HTML 4.0 Transitional//EN">
<HTML XMLNS:o="urn:schemas-microsoft-com:office:office"
XMLNS:x="urn:schemas-microsoft-com:office:excel"
XMLNS:a="urn:schemas-microsoft-com:office:access"
XMLNS:dt="uuid:C2F41010-65B3-11d1-A29F-00AA00C14882"><HEAD>
<META name=VBSForEventHandlers VALUE="TRUE">
<META content=Access.Application name=ProgId><LINK rel=File-List
type=text/xml><TITLE>Listings</TITLE>
<META content=text/html;charset=windows-1252 http-equiv=Content-Type>
<META content="MSHTML 5.00.2314.1000" name=GENERATOR>
<OBJECT classid=CLSID:0002E530-0000-0000-C000-000000000046 id=MSODSC><PARA
 <o:DocumentProperties>
  <o:TotalTime>0</o:TotalTime>
  <o:Version>9.2720</o:Version>
 </o:DocumentProperties>
 <o:OfficeDocumentSettings>
  <o:DownloadComponents/>
  <o:LocationOfComponents HRef="file:M:\msowc.cab"/>
 </o:OfficeDocumentSettings>
</xml><![endif]--></HEAD>
<BODY>
<TABLE bgColor=#ffffff border=1 cellSpacing=0><FONT color=#000000 face=Ari
 <CAPTION><B>Listings</B></CAPTION></FONT>
  <THEAD>
```

> **Note:** You can tell by the horizontal and vertical scrollbar buttons in the figure that what you're seeing is a very small piece of the large HTML file.

Many tags also include attributes. For example, the <TABLE> tag includes attributes such as background color, border style, and cell spacing.

You can use the Microsoft Development Environment window to edit an HTML file. You can also use any text editor, such as Notepad or FrontPage.

Cascading Style Sheets

Cascading Style Sheets (CSS) is part of Dynamic HTML 4.0. This feature enables you to specify the appearance of the data access page, such as borders and fonts, or layout features, such as margins and indents. If you open the Elgin Listings data access page in the Development Environment window, you'll see the following line:

```
<STYLE> id=MSODAPDEFAULTS type=text/CSS rel="stylesheet"></STYLE>
```

You can add your own styles by adding selectors and the styles to apply to the <STYLE> tag. A *selector* is the tag for the element whose style you want to specify. For example, to set the style for the text in the body of a page, you can insert the following between the <STYLE> and </STYLE> tags:

```
BODY {
    FONT-FAMILY: Arial; FONT-SIZE: 8 pt
}
```

The BODY selector refers to the HTML BODY tag. The styles are enclosed in curly braces and include a property and a value for this property, separated by a colon. If you include more than one style, separate them with semicolons.

An additional advantage to Cascading Style Sheets is the ability to create different classes of an HTML tag and apply a different style to each class.

For more information about Cascading Style Sheets, consult the style sheets page of the World Wide Web Consortium at http://www.w3.org/style/.

Extensible Markup Language

The Extensible Markup Language (XML) was invented for those Web publishers who were not satisfied with the standard markup language. Using XML, you can define custom formatting tags and specify which elements and attributes are to be included in the XML document by creating a Document Type Definition (DTD). Microsoft has created a sophisticated DTD that includes XML tags that can format Access documents. Unfortunately, Microsoft Internet Explorer 5.0 is the first browser to support XML tags created in Access. No doubt others will follow; but for now, you are limited.

Customizing with HTML Templates

Frankly, the HTML pages produced using any of the preceding methods are very ordinary or at least not customized to your specifications. However, you can use an HTML template to customize the appearance of the resulting pages and give them a consistent look. For example, you can include standard corporate information in a page's header, use a custom background, or add custom buttons to a report footer—in other words, anything that you can do with a regular HTML page.

You can use an HTML template when you save data as static or server-generated HTML files.

Technical Note: The HTML template is simply a text file saved with the .HTM extension that includes HTML tags and user-specified text and references, called *tokens*. The template should include placeholders that tell Microsoft Access where to insert certain pieces of data in the HTML documents. Then, when data is saved as HTML documents, the template merges with the HTML file and the placeholders are replaced with data. Table 20.1 describes each of the placeholders you can use in an HTML template.

Table 20.1   Placeholders for Access Data in an HTML Template

Placeholder	Location	Description
`<!--AccessTemplate_Title-->`	Between `<TITLE>` and `</TITLE>`	The object being saved
`<!--AccessTemplate_Body-->`	Between `<BODY>` and `</BODY>`	The data or object being saved
`<!--AccessTemplate_FirstPage-->`	Between `<BODY>` and `</BODY>` or after `</BODY>`	An anchor tag to the first page
`<!--AccessTemplate_PreviousPage-->`	Between `<BODY>` and `</BODY>` or after `</BODY>`	An anchor tag to the previous page
`<!--AccessTemplate_NextPage-->`	Between `<BODY>` and `</BODY>` or after `</BODY>`	An anchor tag to the next page
`<!--AccessTemplate_LastPage-->`	Between `<BODY>` and `</BODY>` or after `</BODY>`	An anchor tag to the last page
`<!--AccessTemplate_PageNumber-->`	Between `<BODY>` and `</BODY>` or after `</BODY>`	The current page number

Only the first two placeholders, `<!--AccessTemplate_Title-->` and `<!--AccessTemplate_Body-->`, are used with table, query, and form datasheets. The other placeholders are used with the multiple HTML pages created from multipage reports. If you specify an HTML template that contains placeholders for navigation controls when you save a report as multiple HTML documents, Microsoft Access creates hyperlinks that the user can use to navigate to the first, previous, next, and last pages in the publication. Where Access places the hyperlinks depends on where you locate the placeholders in the HTML template.

Figure 20.15 shows the same static HTML page as Figure 20.2, but it uses the HTML template Elgin.htm. The code in this template controls how the page appears, adding logos and a heading, so that all pages you create using the template will have a similar appearance:

```
<HTML>
<TITLE><!--AccessTemplate_TITLE--></TITLE>
<BODY background = "sky.jpg">
<IMG SRC = "C:\My Documents\Macmillan\INVENTRY.GIF" height=100>
<font FACE = "ARIAL.HELETICA"><font SIZE = 10>
Elgin Enterprises<font>
```

```
<HR><BR>

<!--AccessTemplate_BODY-->

</BODY>
<BR><BR>
<IMG SRC = "SERVICE.GIF">
</HTML>
```

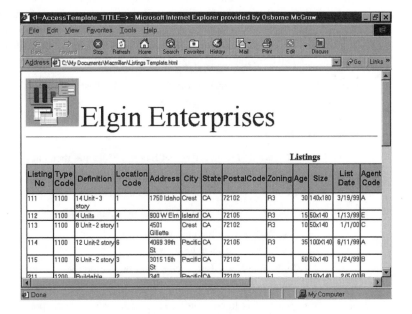

FIGURE 20.15
Elgin's Listings table as a static HTML page using the Elgin.htm *template.*

The <HR> tag inserts a horizontal line beneath the page title. The <BR> tags add line breaks. The <IMG> tag specifies the source (SRC) of the image. GIF and JPG files are compatible with most browsers.

> **Tip:** When you create or edit the HTML template with a text editor, be sure to save it with the .HTM file extension. If you save it as a text file, the changes won't be applied.

When you install Microsoft Access, sample HTML template files and graphics files are contained in four subfolders of the 1033 folder: CSS (Cascading Style Sheets), Frames, Pages, and Web. The 1033 folder is by default installed in

C:\Program Files\Microsoft Office\Templates\1033

Looking at these templates is a good way to get a feel for what you can do with templates. You'll also find several JPG and GIF image files you can insert.

Importing and Linking Data from HTML Files

You can import or link data formatted as an HTML table or list to a Microsoft Access database the same as you can from any database. Because of the nature of HTML files, there are a few differences from using other conventional databases. In order to use the data, Access copies it into the local cache—an area of memory where Windows and applications store data for intermediate use. Whenever you open a linked table, Microsoft Access makes a local copy from the original on the Internet or an intranet before opening it. The data in the table, therefore, is read-only, because there's no mechanism for moving changed data from the cache to the original HTML files.

Importing data stores the actual data in the Access database, whereas *linking* leaves the data where it is but saves information in Access where it can be found when needed. The steps used to import or link data from HTML tables are similar to those used for other database types:

1. In the Access File menu, select Get External Data and then click either Import or Link Tables.

2. In the Files of Type list, select HTML Documents.

3. Select the file to import or link from using one of the following methods:

   - Use the Look In box and the list of files below it to browse through the file system on your local hard drive or network.

   - In the File Name box, type a valid Internet `http://` or `ftp://` URL. (`http:` searches the Web and `ftp:` uses the Internet's File Transfer Protocol.)

   - In the Look In box, click FTP Locations and select a previously defined FTP site.

   - In the Look In box, click Add|Modify FTP Locations and then specify a new FTP site and browse its files. Any FTP site you define here will be available in the FTP Locations list the next time you use this method.

4. Click Import or Link.

5. Access launches the Import HTML Wizard, using the first table it finds in the HTML file. The rest of the steps in this wizard use the same techniques as importing text and other types of files, enabling you to specify whether the first row contains field names, to refine the data types of each column, and to add a primary key (or you can let Access do it). You can also opt to append the data to an existing table or create a new table.

Refer to Chapter 17, "Linking with Other Office Applications," for more information about importing and linking with other file types.

When you import or link data from an HTML table, Microsoft Access parses the information contained within the standard HTML tag pairs:

- `<TABLE>...</TABLE>`
- `<TH...>...</TH>` (table heading)
- `<TR...>...</TR>` (table row)
- `<TD...>...</TD>` (table data cell)
- `<CAPTION...>...</CAPTION>`

TROUBLESHOOTING
You might have a problem if a table's data cell contains anything other than text or an HTML hyperlink. An embedded graphic file uses an HTML `<IMG SRC...>` tag to identify the image file displayed. This tag may or may not have additional text that would be displayed, such as if the server can't find the file or the user clicks the browser's Stop button before the image is downloaded. If additional text is present, Microsoft Access imports it as the contents of the field but doesn't import the embedded graphic and the tag that defines it. Access imports anchor tags `<A HREF>` as hyperlink fields.

LOOKING AHEAD
See the section "Hyperlinks to Web Documents" for more information about using hyperlink anchor tags.

HTML tables can contain lists that are embedded within a table cell. Lists in an HTML table cell are formatted with the `<LI>` and `</LI>` tags. Microsoft Access inserts a carriage return and line feed (`<CR><LF>`) after each list item and imports each item in the list as a separate field for that record. HTML tables can also contain tables that are embedded within a table data cell. You can import these as separate tables.

Publishing to the Web

Once you've created the HTML files and data access pages, you need to know how to access the data through a Web browser. The browser downloads the file from the Web server you have running. Static, server-generated HTML files and Active Server Pages are supported by all Web browsers, but you must have Microsoft Internet Explorer 5 or later to publish data access pages that use dynamic HTML 4.0 or later.

Creating and Managing Web Folders

A Web folder in Access is a shortcut to your Web server where you can publish HTML files and data access pages. In order to be able to create and use Web folders, you must have access to a Web server that supports the Web folder feature. You can use the Microsoft Personal Web Server or Internet Information Server, both of which come with Office 2000. The Web server can be on your local network or on a server operated by your Internet Service Provider or a Web hosting service.

To create a new Web folder for an existing Web server location, choose File|Open and click the Web Folders button. In the Open dialog box, click the New Folder button and enter the Web address.

To add a data access page or other HTML file to an existing Web folder, click the Web Folders button in the Save As dialog box and enter the name for the page.

Publishing Static HTML Files

To publish a static HTML file, all you need to do is copy the file to a Web folder using Windows Explorer. If you want to copy the file to a Web server, copy it to a folder in the root directory of the server, again using the Windows Explorer. If you're using Microsoft Personal Web Server, the default root directory is \Webshare\Wwwroot. The root directory for Microsoft Internet Information Server is \Inetpub\Wwwroot.

After you copy the HTML file, be sure to copy all the related files, such as graphics, style sheets, and linked files, and any folder that may contain related files. If you don't want to copy them all, be sure the Web server can locate them when necessary.

Publishing Server-Generated HTML Files

Publishing ASP or IDC/HTX server-generated HTML files is similar to publishing static HTML files. The main difference is that the Web server must have access to the underlying database or ODBC data source.

After copying the HTML and related files to the Web folder, you must define the ODBC data source as a system DSN on the Web server. Be sure the name you enter is the same as the one you entered in the Output Options dialog box when you saved the Access object as the ASP or IDC/HTX file. You can define user-level security for the data source by creating a username and password. The username and password must match the ones you enter in the User to Connect As and Password for User boxes in the Output Options dialog box.

> **Warning:** Be sure to use a universal naming convention (UNC) path when sharing an ODBC data source. Using the drive letter of the network drive in the path is unreliable because it can vary from computer to computer or might not be defined at all. A UNC path is always consistent as a path to the data source.

COMPATIBILITY

To use IDC/HTX files, your database and the IDC/HTX files must reside on a Microsoft Windows NT server running Microsoft Internet Information Server or on a computer running Windows 95 or Windows NT Workstation and Personal Web Server. Microsoft Internet Information Server and Personal Web Server use a component called the *Internet Database Connector* (Httpodbc.dll) to generate Web pages from IDC/HTX files.

> **Technical Note:** Internet Database Connector requires ODBC drivers to access a database. To access an Access database, the Microsoft Access Desktop driver (`Odbcjt32.dll`) must be installed on your Web server. This driver is installed when you install Microsoft Internet Information Server if you select the ODBC Drivers and Administration check box during setup (but it isn't installed with Personal Web Server). If Access is installed on the computer you're using to run Personal Web Server and if you selected the driver when you installed Microsoft Access, the driver is already available.

After the Access Desktop driver is installed, you must create either a system DSN or a user DSN that specifies the name and connection information for each database you want to use on the server. You then specify that DSN when you generate the IDC/HTX files. See the Microsoft Office documentation for more information about ODBC.

To display and use an Active Server Page, a copy of your database and the Active Server Page must reside on a Microsoft Windows NT server running Microsoft Internet Information Server version 3.0 and Active Server. Active Server Pages require the Microsoft Access Desktop driver and a valid DSN to access a database.

Publishing Data Access Pages

You have the same two ways to publish data access pages: Save the page to a Web folder with the Windows Explorer or copy the underlying HTML file to a folder underneath the Web server's root directory.

When you save the page to a Web folder, Access automatically saves all the related files in a supporting folder, so you don't have to copy them separately. However, if you move or copy the page to another location, you'll have to move the supporting folder as well.

If you copy the page HTML file to the Web server, you must copy all the related files yourself. To copy a data access page to a Web server in Access, open the data access page and choose File|Save As. Then enter a name for the page. In the Save As Data Access Page dialog box, click Web Folders on the Places bar. Open the folder where you want to save the data access page and click Save.

Once you've copied the data access page to a Web server, you can open it from Access by double-clicking the shortcut "Edit Web Page That Already Exists" and then clicking Web Folders on the Places bar. Locate and open the folder that contains the page and double-click the desired page.

You can also save a data access page directly to an FTP server using Export from the Access File menu, saving the data as any file type. Note that this is similar to saving the data as HTML files (described earlier in this chapter), but you can put it anywhere on the network or Internet where you have write permission.

Here's how to export a data access page from Access to an Internet FTP server:

1. Open the data access page in page or design view and choose File|Save As.

2. In the Save As dialog box, type the name for the link to the page and click OK.

3. In the Save As Data Access Page dialog box, click FTP Locations in the Save In box and double-click the site you want and the location where you want to save the data access page.

4. Type a name for the HTM file in the File Name box and then click Save.

Using the Microsoft Web Publishing Wizard

Now that you've seen all the different ways you can use Access to create HTML pages to publish your data, let's look at a wizard that makes it easier to do the work. The Microsoft Web Publishing Wizard included with Microsoft Office 2000 helps you post your Web pages to an Internet or intranet site. The wizard connects to your service provider, determines the appropriate protocol, copies the files, and uploads them to the HTML document directory at your service provider.

You have three ways to start the Web Publishing Wizard:

- Choose it from the Start|Programs menu.

- In the Windows Explorer window, right-click the file or directory you want to post and choose Send To|Web Publishing Wizard from the shortcut menu.

- Place a shortcut to the wizard on your desktop and then drag and drop the files or directories to the icon.

> **Note:** You may have to look around in the Program menus to find the Web Publishing Wizard. It may be included in the Internet Explorer menu or among the list of accessories.

Before you can publish your Access pages, you need access to the Internet through a service provider or a proxy server. You Web browser must also be set up to work with the wizard.

If you want to publish several files at once (for example, your publishing images to accompany the HTML files), copy them all to a temporary directory and publish the directory.

To use the Web Publishing Wizard, do the following:

1. Choose Start|Programs|Accessories|Internet Tools|Web Publishing Wizard. (Your menu arrangement may be different.)

2. The first dialog box displays a description of the publishing process. After reading the information, click Next.

3. In the second dialog box, shown in Figure 20.16, enter the file or folder you want to publish. Use the Browse Folders or Browse Files button to select the name of the folder or file. If you select a folder, all the files in the folder are included. If you clear the Include Subfolders option, the files in the subfolders are not published. Click Next.

FIGURE 20.16

Enter the file or folder you want to publish.

4. The next dialog box prompts you to choose or enter a name for your Web server. In the Description Name box, enter the name you want to use to identify the Web server. Click the Advanced button to see a list of options, including FrontPage Extended Web, FTP Server, HTTP Post, and Microsoft Content Replication System. The default setting is Automatically Select Service Provider. Click Next.

5. In the next dialog box, shown in Figure 20.17, enter your URL in the URL or Internet Address box. Then enter the path to your Access files in the Local Directory box. Click Next.

6. The next dialog box prompts you for your username and password. Check the Save This Password in Your Password List option so the wizard will remember it and not ask for it again. Click Next.

7. Click Finish. After the files are transferred, a message indicates that the process was successful.

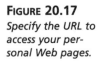

FIGURE 20.17
Specify the URL to access your personal Web pages.

Hyperlinks to Web Documents

Access 97 introduced the new Hyperlink data type you can include in any table. It lets the user of your application jump to other objects or locations on the network. Hyperlinks can jump to two kinds of objects: to a Web page or other content on the Internet or an intranet or to a Microsoft Office document, such as a Word document, an Excel worksheet, a PowerPoint slideshow, or an Access database stored on a local hard disk or the local network.

> **Tip:** You can create a field with the Hyperlink data type to store hyperlink addresses in a table and then bind that field to a text box on a form. This is useful when you have several different hyperlinks associated with different records in the database. As with other bound fields, as the user moves from record to record, the value in the text box changes to display the current record's hyperlink value. For example, you can use hyperlinks in this way to create an application in which users can jump to Web pages or to other content on the Internet or an intranet from a predefined list of addresses. You can also use hyperlinks in this way to create an application that displays and manages Microsoft Office documents.

If you need to simply provide a way for a user to jump to another location, you can create a label, Image control, or command button on a form that references a specified hyperlink address. In this case, the hyperlink doesn't change as you move from record to record. For example, you can use hyperlinks in this way to navigate to other database objects within the same database or to open a Web page on an intranet that contains updated information on how to use your application.

When you include hyperlinks in your applications, you can use the Web toolbar (available in all the Office applications to navigate between hyperlinks), just like when you're surfing the Web. Therefore, if the user follows a hyperlink from a Microsoft Access form to open a Microsoft Word document, he or she can click the Back button on the Web toolbar in Microsoft Word to return to the Access form.

Creating a Hyperlink Field

To create a Hyperlink field, add a field in the table's design view and set its DataType property to Hyperlink, just as you add any other new field to a table. Then you can follow a hyperlink stored in a table by clicking it in the table or when it appears in a control on a form.

A Hyperlink field stores up to three pieces of information: the *displaytext*, the *address*, and the *subaddress*. Each piece of information is separated by a pound sign (#), in the following format:

displaytext#address#subaddress

ANALYSIS

The *displaytext* portion of the hyperlink, which is optional, contains the text the user sees in the Hyperlink field in a table or in a text box bound to the Hyperlink field. This string is typically used as a descriptive name for the Web site or object specified by the address and subaddress. If you do not specify display text, Microsoft Access displays the value of *address* instead.

The *address* is a valid URL that points to a page or file on the Internet or an intranet or the path to a file on a local hard drive or network. If you enter a path on a network, you can omit a mapped drive letter and use the universal naming convention (UNC) format: \\server\path\filename. (See your network documentation for more information about UNC paths.) This item is required unless the subaddress points to an object in the current Access database file.

A *subaddress* specifies the location within a file or document, such as a form or report in a database. When you refer to a database object, the name of the object should be preceded by its type: Table, Query, Form, Report, Macro, or Module. You can also specify a bookmark in a Microsoft Word document, an anchor in an HTML document, a specific Microsoft PowerPoint slide, or a cell or range in a Microsoft Excel worksheet. This is an optional part of the hyperlink.

Each piece of the Hyperlink field's storage format can be up to 2,000 characters. The maximum length of the entire Hyperlink field value is 6,000 characters.

Table 20.2 gives a few examples of valid Hyperlink field values.

Table 20.2 Examples of Valid Hyperlink Values

Hyperlink Value	Action When Clicked
`#http://www.microsoft.com#`	Jumps to the Microsoft home page. Because the display text field isn't used, the address appears in the field or text box.
`Search Using Excite#http://www.excite.com/#`	Jumps to the Excite search engine. The text `Search Using Excite` appears in the field or text box.
`1999 Sales#\\BINKY\Reports\1999Sales.Doc#West`	Opens a Word document, `1999Sales.doc`, located on the local server BINKY, and jumps to the `West` bookmark in the document.
`#j:\Office\samples\northwind.mdb#Form Products`	Opens the Northwind database that ships with Access, located on the `J:` drive, and opens the Products form.
`Products Form##Form Products`	Opens the Products form.
`Mortgage Rates#d:\MyDocuments\Rates.xls#[Current Rates]!E15`	Opens the Rates Excel workbook located on the `D:` drive, opens the Current Rates worksheet, and makes E15 the current cell.

Protocols Supported by Access

Access supports an amazing number of protocols in hyperlinks, letting the user jump to almost any location on the local computer, network, or the Internet and opening any kind of file installed in the local Windows Registry. Most hyperlink URLs have to be in the following format:

Protocol://Serveraddress/Path

Protocol specifies the Internet protocol used to establish the connection to the server and is generally followed by a colon and two slash marks (such as `http://` for Web URLs). *Serveraddress* specifies the domain name of the Internet server or the name of the drive containing the desired file. *Path* specifies the location and name of the page or file. Table 20.2 shows several examples.

You can jump to Web pages using `http://`, FTP file sites with `ftp://`, and CompuServe with `cid://`. You also can start a Telnet connection with `telnet://`. Some of the protocols, such as `nntp://` for Internet news and the Telnet protocol, automatically start the client software needed for the particular task. For a current list of protocols, search Access Help under "Protocols for Hyperlinks." This list will no doubt expand over time.

Using Access Hyperlinks

Several of the Access custom controls have `HyperlinkAddress` and `HyperlinkSubAddress` properties you can use to specify where to jump or which document to open. These properties correspond to the address and subaddress elements discussed earlier. When you move the cursor over a command button, Image control, or Label control whose `HyperlinkAddress` property is set, the cursor changes to an upward-pointing hand. Clicking the control jumps to the object or Web page specified by the link. To open objects in the current database, leave the `HyperlinkAddress` property blank and specify the object type and object name you want to open in the `HyperlinkSubAddress` property.

Access also provides several other methods and properties for working with hyperlinks in your applications, as listed in Table 20.3.

Table 20.3   Hyperlink Methods and Properties

Item	Description
AddToFavorites method	When applied to the Application object, the AddToFavorites method adds a hyperlink address for the current database to the Favorites folder on the local machine. When applied to a Control object, the AddToFavorites method adds the hyperlink address contained in a control.
CreateNewDocument method	Creates a new document associated with the specified hyperlink contained in a control.
Follow method	Opens the document or Web page specified by a hyperlink address associated with a control on a form or report. It has the same effect as clicking a hyperlink. You don't have to specify the hyperlink as long as the control has the HyperlinkAddress or HyperlinkSubAddress property set.
FollowHyperlink method	Opens the document or Web page specified by a hyperlink address. This is a method of the Access Application object, which lets you specify a URL to open in code, that doesn't have to be set in a control.

continues

Table 20.3   Continued

Item	Description
`HyperlinkPart` method	Returns information about data stored as a Hyperlink data type. Depending on the value you set for the *part* argument, `HyperlinkPart` returns the displayed value, display text, address, or sub-address of the hyperlink.
`Hyperlink` property	Returns a reference to the Hyperlink object so that you can access the properties and methods of a control that contains a hyperlink.

Setting an Access Hyperlink Base

Rather than setting the path to the target of a hyperlink as an absolute link by specifying the full address, you can set a relative link. For example, if you want many hyperlinks in an application to jump to Web pages on an intranet server, you can create a hyperlink base for the database. Open the database and choose File|Database Properties. Then enter the path to the server in the Hyperlink Base box on the Summary tab of the Properties dialog box.

Then if you shift to a different server, you need to change only the `Hyperlink Base` property of the database to the new server. All the hyperlink relative links remain the same within the base.

Summary

This chapter has only scratched the surface of all the options you have for publishing your data to the World Wide Web. The good news is that Access 2000 provides many options and wizards, freeing you from the drudgery of writing HTML code by hand. At worst, you can fine-tune the HTML in the pages that Access generates.

Static Web pages are fine for data that rarely, if ever, changes and can be displayed on virtually any Web server. But you'll need to use more complex methods if the data changes frequently and the users need the most up-to-date data available. Publishing live data, however, means that you must use a Web server, such as Microsoft's Internet Information Server, to dynamically generate pages with your data.

Part VII

Appendixes

What's New in Programming Access 2000?

This appendix describes the changes Microsoft has made in the Access development and programming environment. Many improvements that were included in Access 97 are discussed as well as those new with Access 2000. Improvements made to the Access user environment are not specifically addressed in this appendix unless they markedly improve the development environment. It's assumed that readers of this book are already familiar with Access databases and how to create and use them.

What's New for the Developer?

Several new features of the database window can be of benefit to developers. The ability to view and edit related data in subdatasheets rather than creating a form with subforms is an important improvement. Subdatasheets can be manipulated with macros as well as VB code.

Microsoft has declared Office 2000 to be Y2K compliant. That is, it will not produce errors when processing date data related to the year changing from 1999 to 2000. The caveat is that you use accurate date data in accordance with the documentation and recommendations stated in the Microsoft Year 2000 Product Guide. Office 2000 treats two-digit year values by assuming any value of 29 or less belongs to the 21st century, whereas all values of 30 and over belong to the 20th century. The range is placed on a sliding scale, advancing one year each year. The new Use Four-Digit Year Formatting option can be found on the General tab of the Options dialog box. This requirement can be placed on the current database or all databases on your system.

Of course, the important new data access pages now enable you to place dynamic data on the Web, where users can access it as well as work with it. See Chapter 20, "Posting Your Database to the Web," for details of creating and using data access pages.

The new report snapshot is a file that contains a high-fidelity version of each page of an Access report. When a report is viewed with the Snapshot Viewer, you see a two-dimensional representation of the layout, including all the graphics and embedded objects in the report. The advantage of a snapshot report is that you can send the file to others who can view it and print only what they need. You don't have to copy and mail the entire printed report to every potential user. You can distribute report snapshots via email or publish them on the Web using macros or VB code.

The database window has a new feature that enables you to group shortcuts to objects in custom groups. You can add shortcuts to objects from other applications as well as Access objects.

The addition of conditional formatting improves the visual discernment of Access information. You can define conditional formatting rules for text boxes and other controls in a form to show different font color and size, background color, and other characteristics. The appearance of the data gives the user some visual feedback about the values, such as whether a value falls within a certain range or meets a specified criterion.

Name Autocorrect is an important new feature that helps prevent errors from occurring when you rename a field in a table or one of the Access objects. When you open a form or other object, Access checks to see if any of the referenced objects the form depends on have been renamed. If so, it corrects the discrepancies and continues. Name Autocorrect is automatically set for databases created in Access 2000, but when you convert databases from earlier versions, you must set the option on the General tab of the Options dialog box. This feature does not correct renaming errors in replicated databases, references in Visual Basic code, references to linked tables, and a few other instances.

What's New for the Programmer?

Access continues to make the development process easier and more foolproof. New macro actions have been added that you can use to open data access pages and the new objects in an Access project. Visual Basic 6.0 is included with Office 2000. This latest version of VBA is closer to the classic Visual Basic language. New language elements are introduced and others are more uniformly named.

New Macro Actions

Access 2000 has added four new macro actions for opening the new database objects associated with Access projects. These macro actions can also be carried out by using the equivalent new VB method with the DoCmd object. The new actions are as follows:

- OpenDataAccessPage—Opens a data access page in the current database in design or page view
- OpenDiagram—Opens a diagram in the current project
- OpenStoredProcedure—Opens a stored procedure in the current project in datasheet or design view or in print preview
- OpenView—Opens a view in the current project

New Visual Basic Language Elements

Most new language elements are a result of expanding Access to include projects that run in a client/server environment and the new data access page dynamic role on the Web. The following paragraphs describe the new and modified Visual Basic language elements.

New Objects

Several new objects and collections have been added to Visual Basic in Access 2000, as described in Table A.1.

Table A.1   New Visual Basic Objects and Collections

Objects	Description
AccessObject	Refers to a particular Access object and includes information about one instance of the object within the CodeData, CodeProject, CurrentData, or CurrentProject functionality
AccessObjectProperty, AccessObjectProperties	Represents a built-in or user-defined characteristic of an Access object within the CodeData, CodeProject, CurrentData or CurrentProject functionality
AllDataAccessPages, AllForms, AllMacros, AllModules, AllReports, AllDatabaseDiagrams, AllQueries, AllStoredProcedures, AllTables, AllViews	New collections that contain an Access object in the CurrentData or CurrentProject functionality for each object
CodeData, CodeProject	Refer to objects stored in the code database by the source application (Jet or SQL)
COMAddIns	A collection of COMAddIn objects that provides information about a Component Object Model add-in registered in the Windows Registry
CurrentData, CurrentProject	Refer to objects stored in the current database by the source application (Jet or SQL)
DataAccessPage, DataAccessPages	Refers to a data access page object or collection
DefaultWebOptions	Contains global attributes for the application that are used by Access when you save a data access page as a Web page or open a Web page

continues

Table A.1   Continued

Objects	Description
FileSearch	Represents the File Search functionality found in the Open command of the File menu.
FormatCondition, FormatConditions	Represents the new conditional formatting feature used with a combo box or a text box control
VBE	The root object that contains all other objects and collections represented in Visual Basic for Applications
WebOptions	Refers to a specific data access page's Web option properties

Six new objects have also been added to Visual Basic in Office 2000:

- AnswerWizard. Represents the Answer Wizard in the application.
- COMAddIn. Represents a Component Object Model in an Office host application.
- HTMLProject. Represents a top-level project branch in the Project Explorer or the Microsoft Script Editor.
- LanguageSettings. Returns information about the current language settings in an application.
- Script. Represents a block of HTML script in a Word document, an Excel spreadsheet, or a PowerPoint slide.
- WebPageFont. Represents the default font to be used when a document is saved as Web pages. This is specific to a particular character set.

New objects have also been added to the ActiveX Data Objects 2.0 library and the Office 9.0 Object library. See the respective Help topics for information about these new objects.

New and Hidden Properties

Many new properties have been added to Access 2000. Many new properties actually refer to new objects listed in Table A.1. Several others have been added to enhance data access page functionality as well as Web access. Table A.2 lists the new properties and the objects to which they apply.

Table A.2   New Access 2000 Properties

Objects	Properties
AccessObject	FullName
	IsLoaded
	PropertiesProperty (AccessObjectProperties collection)
	Type (AccessObject object)

Objects	Properties
Application	AnswerWizard
	CodeData
	CodeProject
	COMAddIns
	CurrentData
	CurrentProject
	DataAccessPages
	DefaultWebOptions
	FeatureInstall
	FileSearch
	LanguageSettings
	ProductCode
	Properties Property (Properties collection)
CodeData,	AllDatabaseDiagrams
CurrentData	AllQueries
	AllReports
	AllStoredProcedures
	AllTables
	AllViews
CodeProject,	AllDataAccessPages
CurrentProject	AllForms
	AllMacros
	AllModules
	AllReports
	BaseConnectionString
	Connection
	FullName
	IsConnected
	ProjectType
	PropertiesProperty (AccessObjectProperties collection)
DataAccessPage	ConnectionString
	Document
	WebOptions
DefaultWebOptions	AlwaysSaveInDefaultEncoding
	CheckIfOfficeHTMLEditor
	DownloadComponents
	Encoding
	FolderSuffix
	FollowHyperlinkColor
	HyperlinkColor

continues

Table A.2 Continued

Objects	Properties
	LocationOfComponents
	OrganizeInFolder
	UnderlineHyperlinks
	UseLongFileNames
Form	InputParameters
	MaxRecButton
	Recordset
	ResyncCommand
	ServerFilter
	ServerFilterByForm
	UniqueTable
FormatCondition	Enabled (FormatCondition object)
	Expression1
	Expression2
	Operator (FormatCondition object)
	Type (FormatCondition object)
Hyperlink	Address
	EmailSubject
	ScreenTip
	SubAddress
	TextToDisplay
Screen	ActiveDataAccessPage
WebOptions	DownloadComponents
	Encoding
	FolderSuffix
	LocationOfComponents
	OrganizeInFolder
	UserLongFileNames

COMPATIBILITY

A few properties have been hidden in Access 2000 Visual Basic because they've been replaced by new language elements. Although the properties are still accepted for backward compatibility, it's recommended that you use the current properties in your code. The hidden properties do not normally appear in the Object Browser window, but if you want to see them, you can right-click in the Object Browser window and choose Show Hidden Members from the shortcut menu.

Table A.3 lists the properties that have been hidden and suggests the replacement properties to be used in new code.

Table A.3 Hidden Properties

Affected Object	Hidden Property	Suggested Replacement
Form	AllowEditing	AllowAdditions, AllowDeletions
	DefaultEditing	AllowEdits, DataEntry
Form	AllowUpdating	RecordsetType
Form	Dynaset	RecordsetClone
Form	ShowGrid	DatasheetGridlinesBehavior
Form, report	MaxButton, Minbutton	MinMaxButtons (form only)
Bound object frame, check box, combo box, image, label, line, list box, option button, option group, rectangle, subform, and text box	BorderLineStyle	BorderStyle

New Methods

Several new methods have been added to existing objects in Access 2000 to enable working with the new Access projects and data access pages. Table A.4 lists the new methods and the objects they apply to, with a brief description of each method.

Table A.4 New Methods Added to Access 2000

Object	Method	Description
AccessObject-Properties	Add Remove	Adds a new property to the properties collection
Application	CreateAccessProject	Creates a new project (.adp) on disk
	CreateDataAccessPage	Creates a new data access page or opens an existing HTML file as a data access page
	GetHiddenAttribute	Returns the value of the hidden attribute of an object: True (hidden) or False (visible)
	NewAccessProject	Creates and opens a new project as the current project in the Access window

continues

Table A.4   Continued

Object	Method	Description
	OpenAccessProject	Opens an existing project as the current project in the Access window
	SetHiddenAttribute	Sets the hidden attribute of an object
CodeProject, CurrentProject	CloseConnection	Closes the current connection between the project and a specified database
	OpenConnection	Opens a connection between the project and a specified database
DataAccessPage	ApplyTheme	Specifies a theme for a data access page
DoCmd	AddMenu	Carries out the AddMenu macro action in VB to create custom menus and shortcut menus
	OpenDataAccessPage	Carries out the new macro action that opens a specified data access page in design or page view
	OpenDiagram	Carries out the new macro action that opens a database diagram in design view
	OpenStoredProcedure	Carries out the new macro action that opens a stored procedure in datasheet or design view or in print preview
	OpenView	Carries out the new macro action that opens a view in datasheet or design view or in print preview
FormatCondition	Delete	Removes a format condition from a text box or combo box
	Modify	Modifies an existing format condition

Object	Method	Description
FormatConditions	Add	Adds a conditional format to a text box or combo box
	Delete	Deletes a conditional format from a text box or combo box.
Hyperlink	CreateNewDocument	Creates a new document associated with an existing hyperlink
WebOptions	UseDefaultFolderSuffix	Sets the folder suffix for a data access page to the default suffix used by the current language

Language-Specific Properties and Methods

Access 2000 has many new language-specific properties and methods for use with Asian and other right-to-left languages. These properties and methods apply to controls that contain text-type data. If you've selected or installed such language support, the properties and methods listed in Table A.5 are available. See the Access Help topic for more detailed information about each property or method.

Table A.5   Language-Specific Properties and Methods

Property or Method	Objects
FELineBreak	Text box
FuriganaControl	Text box
IMEHold/HoldKanji-ConversionMode	Combo box, list box, and text box
IMEMode/Kanji-ConversionMode	Combo box, label, list box, and text box
IMESentenceMode	Combo box, label, list box, and text box
KeyboardLanguage	Combo box and text box
NumeralShapes	Combo box, label, list box, and text box
Orientation	Form
PostalAddress	Text box
ReadingOrder	Check box, combo box, command button, label, list box, option button, text box, and toggle button
ScrollBarAlign	Combo box, list box, and text box

New Events

One new event was added to Access 2000, and four others were included in Access 97.

The Dirty event is new in Access 2000 and applies to forms. This event occurs when the contents of a bound form or the text portion of a combo box changes but before the change is saved. It also occurs when you move from one page to another page in a Tab control in a form. Modifying a record within a form by using a macro or Visual Basic doesn't trigger this event. The Dirty event does not apply to an unbound form or a report.

Here are the events that were new in Access 97:

- The Initialize event applies to a class module and occurs when you create a new instance of that module directly by using the New keyword. It also occurs when you create a new instance of a class indirectly by setting or returning a property or by applying a method defined in a class module.
- The ItemAdded event applies to a References collection rather than to a form, control, or report. It occurs when a reference is added to the project by VBA, not when you check a reference in the References dialog box. The ItemAdded event can run only an event procedure, not a macro.
- The ItemRemoved event is similar to the ItemAdded event and occurs when a reference is deleted from the References collection by a VBA procedure, not by removing it from the list in the References dialog box.
- The Terminate event applies to a class module and occurs when all references to an instance of that class are removed from memory. Place the code you want to run when the event occurs in the Terminate event procedure for the class module.

Enumerated Constants

Many intrinsic constants have been changed and others have been added to create the lists of enumerated constants that display in the Auto List Members list in the Visual Basic Editor window. This list is very helpful for selecting arguments for Access methods, functions, and properties as you write code in the module window. You don't have to remember which ones are valid and how to spell them; instead, you can just select from the list.

Each method, function, or property argument has a set of enumerated constants. The name of the set is displayed in the syntax line for the method, function, or property when Auto Quick Info is activated. For example, if you're typing the OpenReport method of the DoCmd object, the syntax line shows

```
[View as AcReportView=acViewNormal]
```

for the View argument of the OpenReport method. acReportView is the name of the set of enumerated constants, and acViewNormal is the default setting for the argument.

The old constants still work. For example, if you used `acNormal` instead of `acViewNormal`, the result would be the same. However, it's good practice to use the most recent names and terminology.

COMPATIBILITY

In previous versions, you could leave many arguments blank and Access would insert the default argument. This is still true, but many of the default constants have changed. The exception to this is when you run code from a previous version by using Automation. Arguments left blank will cause an error if they have new default constants.

Table A.6 lists the new intrinsic constants that have been added to the enumerated constant lists for Access 2000. The name of the method that includes the argument is shown in the list as well as the name of the argument itself.

Table A.6 New and Changed Intrinsic Constants

Method	Argument	New Constant
Close	*objecttype*	acDataAccessPage
		acDiagram
		acServerView
		acStoredProcedure
CopyObject	*sourceobjecttype*	acDataAccessPage
		acDiagram
		acServerView
		acStoredProcedure
DeleteObject	*objecttype*	acDataAccessPage
		acDiagram
		acServerView
		acStoredProcedure
OpenDataAccessPage	*view*	acDataAccessPageBrowse
OutputTo	*objecttype*	acOutputDataAccessPage
		acOutputServerView
		acOutputStoredProcedure
Rename	*objecttype*	acDataAccessPage
		acDiagram
		acServerView
		acStoredProcedure
RepaintObject	*objecttype*	acDataAccessPage
		acDiagram
		acServerView
		acStoredProcedure

continues

Table A.6   Continued

Method	Argument	New Constant
RunCommand	*command*	acCmdDataAccessPageBrowse
		acCmdDataAccessPageDesignView
		acCmdDiagramAddRelatedPages
		acCmdDiagramAutosizeSelectedTables
		acCmdDiagramDeleteRelationship
		acCmdDiagramLayoutDiagram
		acCmdDiagramLayoutSelection
		acCmdDiagramModifyUserDefinedView
		acCmdDiagramNewLabel
		acCmdDiagramNewTable
		acCmdDiagramRecalculatePageBreaks
		acCmdDiagramRelationshipLabels
		acCmdDiagramViewPageBreaks
		acCmdEditTriggers
		acCmdHidePane
		acCmdMicrosoftScriptEditor
		acCmdNewObjectAutoDataAccessPage
		acCmdNewObjectDataAccessPage
		acCmdNewObjectDiagram
		acCmdNewObjectStoredProcedure
		acCmdNewObjectView
		acCmdQueryAddToOutput
		acCmdSelectDataAccessPage
		acCmdShowPaneDiagram
		acShowPaneGrid
		acCmdShowPaneView
		acCmdViewDataAccessPage
		acCmdViewDiagrams
		acCmdViewFieldList
		acCmdViewStoredProcedures
		acCmdViewTableColumnNames
		acCmdViewTableColumnProperties
		acCmdViewTableKeys
		acCmdViewTableNameOnly
		acCmdViewTableUserView
		acCmdViewViewVerifySQL
		acCmdViewViewViews
		acCmdZoomSelection

Method	Argument	New Constant
Save	objecttype	acDataAccessPage
		acDiagram
		acServerView
		acStoredProcedure
SelectObject	objecttype	acDataAccessPage
		acDiagram
		acServerView
		acStoredProcedure
SendObject	objecttype	acSendDataAccessPage
TransferDatabase	objecttype	acDataAccessPage
		acDiagram
		acServerView
		acStoredProcedure

Automation

What was formerly known as *OLE Automation* is now called simply *Automation* and is a feature of the Component Object Model (COM). Access is an *ActiveX component*, an application that can use objects supplied by other components and can make its own objects available to other components. These applications were previously called *OLE Automation servers and controllers*.

PERFORMANCE

In Access, you can set a reference to another component's type library to view the objects from that library in the Object Browser. You can also view the objects' methods and properties. This improves performance when working with objects in another application. Conversely, the other ActiveX component can also view the objects in the Access type library.

See Chapter 17, "Linking with Other Office Applications," for more information on working with Access objects through Automation and ActiveX controls.

Working in the Visual Basic Editor Window

Aside from some rearrangement of toolbar buttons and menu items, working in the Visual Basic Editor window has not changed much from Access 97. One significant difference is that all the Editor window options are now set from within the window itself instead of from the Access window. Figure A.1 shows the VBE Options dialog box with four tabs. The Editor tab contains the options that formerly appeared in the Module tab of the Access Options dialog box.

FIGURE A.1
*Setting Visual
Basic Editor
options.*

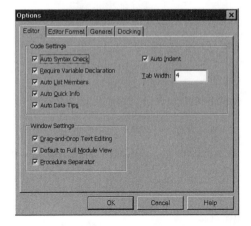

FIGURE A.1
*Setting Visual
Basic Editor
options.*

Figure A.2 shows the formatting options that were also part of the Access Module
Options dialog box. Figure A.3 shows the General tab of the Options dialog box, where
you can modify runtime behavior and set the grid feature in the Editor window. The
Error Trapping options were included in the Advanced tab of the Access 97 Options dialog box.

FIGURE A.2
*Changing the
Visual Basic Editor
appearance.*

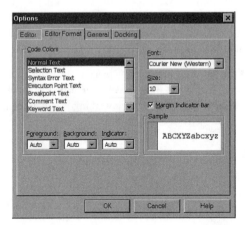

One other significant difference is that there's no longer a Debug window. The three
debug panes—Immediate, Locals, and Watch—are still available by themselves in addition to the Quick Watch pane. There are, however, additional toolbars available in the
VBE window. A Debug toolbar includes many of the commands that were included on
the Standard toolbar. The commands are also available from the Debug menu. The Edit
toolbar includes commands that set tools that help you write correct code, such as List
Properties/Methods and List Constants. The UserForm toolbar includes format commands for the object with code that appears in the Editor window. Figure A.4 shows the
Editor window with all four toolbars.

FIGURE A.3
Modifying Visual Basic's behavior.

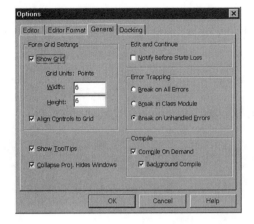

FIGURE A.4
Four toolbars are available in the VBE window.

Project Explorer

View MS Access   Design Mode | Properties

A few new buttons appear on the Standard toolbar:

- *View MS Access*. Returns to the Access window without closing the Editor window.

- *Design Mode*. Toggles design mode on and off for the current project. During design mode, no code from the project is running and events from the host or project will not execute.

- *Project Explorer*. Opens the Project Explorer window, which displays a hierarchical list of all objects contained in or referenced by the database or project (see Figure A.5). Notice that six of the forms in the Elgin database have class modules but only one report does.

- *Properties*. Lists the design-time properties for selected objects and their current settings. You can view the list either in alphabetic order or categorized by type of property (see Figure A.6).

FIGURE A.5
Displaying the Project Explorer window.

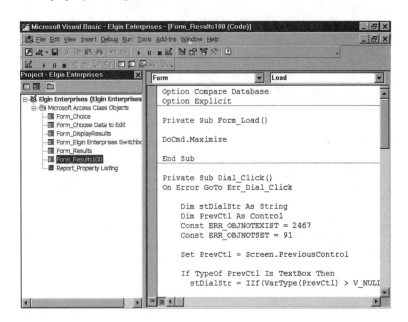

FIGURE A.5
Displaying the Project Explorer window.

FIGURE A.6
Displaying the Properties window.

> **Note:** Both the Project Explorer and Properties windows are dockable by default, but you can change this option in the Docking tab of the Options dialog box.

Office 2000 Developer Tools

The Microsoft Office 2000 Developer provides advanced tools for developing and distributing custom applications. Among the tools that are useful in developing an Access application are the Replication Manager, Visual SourceSafe 6.0, Make Add-In, HTML Help Workshop, and additional ActiveX controls that can duplicate Windows 95 functionality.

There are several more tools in the Office Developer kit. See the Help topic for a complete list.

The Replication Manager

The Office Replication Manager helps you manage a large number of replicas of your database. Not only does the Replication Manager support multiple users in the workplace, it also synchronizes data with laptop users who are not always connected to the network. After creating the replicas of the database, the Replication Manager schedules synchronization of the members and helps resolve conflicts and errors. See Chapter 18, "Working in a Multiuser Environment," for more information about replicating a database.

Source Code Control

NETWORKING

The source code control tool supports developing an application in a team environment. When several programmers are working on the same project, confusion can set in if the code is not strictly managed. The source code control program can keep track of and store changes to the programs during development.

The key feature of a source code control program is the checkout process. When a programmer wants to make a change to one of the application objects, he or she must check it out from the source code control project.

The source code control project is not the same as the development project. The source code control project is a collection of files and objects stored centrally in the source code control program. When you check an object out to work on it, it's not removed from the source code control project. The development project is a copy of the object in your local workstation that you can change. The object in the source code control project is locked and not available to others until you check it back in. When you do check it back in, the changes you've made are copied to the object stored in the source code control project.

The Microsoft Visual SourceSafe 6.0, which is included in the Office 2000 Developer CD, is an advanced tool that you can use to maintain code integrity during development.

The basic process of developing an application in a multideveloper atmosphere is as follows:

1. Create the new Access 2000 database.

2. Create the forms, reports, queries, modules, and other objects for the new database. As you save each one, the source code control provider asks if you want to add it to the source code control project.

3. After the objects are checked in to the source code control project, a programmer must check them in and out from within Access.

4. To change an object, check it out of the source code control, make the changes in Access, and then check it back in to copy the changes to the source code control project. While you have it in your local project, no one else can make any changes to it.

Improvements in Performance

PERFORMANCE

Many new features have been added to both Access 97 and 2000 that speed up loading, compiling, and running a database. Improvements have also been made in the Jet database engine version 4.0 and the DAO connection that optimize the performance of your Access projects.

Loading and Compilation

Forms and reports open much faster in Access 97 because they no longer load the associated class module, unless it contains event procedures for the form or report or the Has Module property is set to True. When you create a new form or report, it doesn't automatically have a module associated with it. The module is not created until you add code to it. As a result, your project may have fewer modules to compile, and each form or report without a module will load more quickly than those with modules.

In addition, Access doesn't load a form or report module until the code in the module is executed. This also improves project performance. In Access 95, when you ran a procedure in one module, all the modules that could be called by a procedure in the first module were loaded but not compiled until a procedure within them was called. Access 97 and Access 2000 load modules only when needed. For this reason, you can help improve your database performance by grouping procedures in modules with other procedures that they call instead of having them call procedures in unrelated modules.

Access 2000 does a better job of managing the compiled state of your database modules. All code is kept compiled unless you make a change in the module. Then, only the code you've changed and any code that depends on it is uncompiled—the rest remains compiled.

PERFORMANCE

The new Compile On Demand option, available in the General tab of the Visual Basic Editor Options dialog box, can improve performance. When this option is selected, Access doesn't compile a module until it's loaded for execution. If this option is not selected, an uncompiled module is compiled when a module that contains a procedure that calls one of the procedures in the uncompiled module is loaded, whether or not the call is ever made. You can improve performance by keeping the Compile On Demand option selected. Better yet, you can keep all your modules stored in a compiled state by using the new Compile <*databasename*> option in the Debug menu.

Also, Access no longer loads software components such as VB and DAO until the database needs them. As a result, your database loads more quickly and its overall performance is improved.

Processing Speed

PERFORMANCE

The performance of several controls has been improved in both Access 97 and Access 2000. Embedded ActiveX controls and combo boxes work even faster in Access 2000 than in earlier versions. You can now display unbound pictures in forms and reports much faster as Image controls instead of unbound object frames. Report previewing also goes faster because the Error, Focus, Print and Window events are triggered only the first time you page through the report.

The Performance Analyzer, first introduced in Access 95, is a wizard that looks over your database objects and makes suggestions as to how you can speed up your processing. You can select any or all the database objects you want to optimize. To use the Performance Analyzer, follow these steps:

1. Choose Tools|Analyze|Performance. The Performance Analyzer dialog box opens, showing eight tabs: one for each type of database object and one for all objects (see Figure A.7).

2. Click the tab of the type of object you want to optimize or click All.

3. Select the names of the objects you want the Performance Analyzer to examine and then click Select or Select All.

4. Open another tab to select from other object lists and click OK. After a few moments, the Performance Analyzer's results dialog box opens.

Figure A.8 shows the results of analyzing all objects in the Elgin Enterprises database. The Analyzer displays three categories of results: Recommendation, Suggestion, and Idea. When you select an item in the list of analysis results, information about it is displayed in the Analysis Notes box below the list. The Performance Analyzer can carry out a Recommendation or Suggestion optimization if you select it and click Optimize. After the optimization, the item is marked as Fixed. You want to carry out the Idea optimizations yourself. These optimization suggestions apply only to your database, not to Access itself or to your system.

Choose the objects you want analyzed in the Performance Analyzer dialog box.

FIGURE A.8
The Performance Analyzer offers optimization tips.

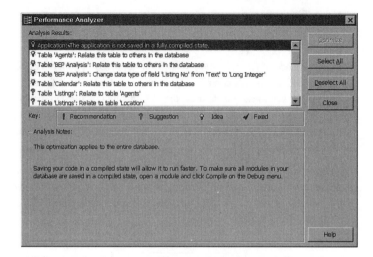

NETWORKING

Another improvement in processing speed is the ability to run action queries on more than one record at once. Now you can run bulk update and delete action queries against an Object Database Connectivity (ODBC) source such as the SQL Server, which processes all the appropriate records at once instead of one at a time. The new (in Access 97) FailOnError property specifies whether to stop processing if an error occurs.

DEVELOPMENT

With the FailOnError property set to Yes, the query will be sent to the server if it executes against a single table and doesn't contain any expression that the server can't evaluate. An error terminates the query, and the table is rolled back to its original state. If FailOnError is set to No, the query runs against local data and works the same as in earlier versions. Errors don't stop the query; when the query is completed, the reason for any error is displayed with the number of records that are affected. You can then accept the query results or roll back any changes.

Compacting and Repairing

Access 2000 offers an improved compacting utility that combines compacting and repairing databases and projects into a single process, which is safer and more effective than separate operations. If you want the database automatically compacted when you're through working with it, set the new Compact On Close option in the General tab of the Options dialog box. Compacting does not occur if another user is still using the database or project.

Database Replication

NETWORKING

Database replication was introduced in Access 95 and provides a method of enabling users in different physical locations to share a database. Each user works on his or her own copy of the database and shares or synchronizes the changes he or she makes with the other users. Several new features improve the reliability of the replica set members and help resolve any conflicts that result from synchronization.

The assignment of a replica priority is new to Access 2000. In previous versions, the winner of a conflict was decided by which record changed most often. In Access 2000, the replica with the highest priority prevails. If the priorities are equal, the member with the lower ReplicaID number (the senior member) wins. The Design Master is assigned a priority of 100 percent, and each subsequent replica is assigned 90 percent of the priority value of its parent.

Local and anonymous replicas are new to Access 2000. Each replica type may synchronize only with the global replica that created it. An anonymous replica, however, must be the member that initiates the synchronization. A local replica can be reassigned as the Design Master, but an anonymous replica cannot. Local and anonymous replicas have a priority of 0 by default.

Prevent Deletes is an option in the Location of New Replica dialog box. This new property is important to keep remote users from removing information they feel is not necessary to them but can be important to other users.

In Access 2000, conflicts are tracked to the column level. That is, conflicts occur only if the data in the same field of the same record is changed by two users at the same time. If you would rather track conflicts at the row (record) level, set the table's Row Level Tracking property to True in the Design Master. The property is not available for any member except the Design Master.

The new Conflict Viewer is the tool you use to examine and resolve conflicts that occur between replica members. You can choose to retain the winning change, override with the losing change, or make your own changes in the Conflict Viewer dialog box.

When conflicts occur, Access records them in a system table in all replicas. You can set the retention period property to control the number of days you want to retain the nonsynchronized records in the system table. The default retention period depends on the tool you use to replicate the database. The default for replicas created in Access or Briefcase is 1,000 days, but you can set it in the Design Master to a value from 5 to 32,000 days.

See Chapter 18, "Working in a Multiuser Environment," for more information about creating and using database replicas.

Database Security

Although you can still use the several dialog boxes available in the Tools|Security menu to enact user-level security, it's much easier to use the new User-Level Security Wizard. With this wizard, you create an elaborate security scheme that defines exactly who has access to what objects and for which activities. In Access 2000, you can also protect Visual Basic code with password control because code is no longer protected by user-level security.

Some virus-detecting tools are already incorporated into Office 2000. A developer of Access databases can incorporate additional virus checkers by using the Office programming interface.

When you download an application that includes macros, you're often warned about viruses and asked if you know the source of the macros. In Office 2000, you can digitally sign your VB macros so the receiving users will know where they originated. These users will also know the macros have not been altered by third parties.

Jet Database Engine Improvements

The new Jet 4.0 database engine enables Unicode interfaces in place of ANSI. Data stored in Unicode format is internationally enabled. If you have installed Jet 4.0, you'll need to install Borland's database engine to be able to interchange data with dBASE and Paradox. Jet 4.0 also does not provide a Visual FoxPro ISAM.

ARCHITECTURE

The Jet database engine version 3.5 contains many improvements over version 3.0, which was used with Access 95, and over the version used with Access 1.x and 2.0. Here are some of the enhancements over the 3.0 version that improve performance:

PERFORMANCE

- Large queries run faster because of new Registry settings and improvements in the SQL statements. The MaxLocksPerFile setting forces transactions to commit when the lock threshold is reached. Use the SetOption DAO method to override the setting at runtime and improve performance in NetWare and Windows NT–based server environments.

- Version 3.5 allows users to create partial replications of a table by placing row restrictions on the table. Partial replication uses two types of filters: Boolean and relationship. A Boolean filter selects only those rows that meet the criteria and is represented in DAO by the ReplicaFilter property of a table definition. The relationship filter applies to related tables and enforces a relationship between two partially replicated tables. Setting the PartialReplica property of a relation object allows that relation to be used in partial replication.

NETWORKING

- Indexed table field columns improve multiuser access to a table. More users can update indexed columns and avoid locking conflicts.

- The Jet database engine can now allocate up to 64KB of disk space at a time, which speeds up sequential read operations.
- Temporary queries and queries that contain an inequality operator (<>) in a criterion run faster.

Here are some improvements over the version 1.x and 2.0 environments:

PERFORMANCE

- The new index structure requires less storage space and lessens the time required to create indexes on two or more fields. When a database is compacted, the indexes are updated and optimized for better performance. Compact the database regularly to take advantage of this optimization.
- When you use a `Delete` operation, portions of the page are removed all at once instead of a row at a time.
- Improvements in the engine's page-allocation algorithm makes it more likely that data from the same table will be stored in adjacent pages.
- The engine is multithreaded so that one thread reads ahead while another writes behind. In addition, a dynamically configured cache is included that bases the size of the cache on the amount of memory available at startup.
- The Jet database engine has built-in implicit transactions that take the place of the explicit `BeginTrans` and `CommitTrans` methods. This can speed up transaction processing. Revert to the explicit methods when writing data to disk so that you have control over the write operation.
- A new sorting mechanism improves sorting performance.

DAO Connection and ODBCDirect

The only feature that has been changed in the new DAO 3.6 is that it has been updated to work with the Jet 4.0 database engine, which supports Unicode (internationally enabled) format rather than ANSI. Other features have been changed in DAO version 3.5

ARCHITECTURE

NETWORKING

The new DAO version 3.5 includes a new client/server connection mode that establishes a connection with an ODBC data source without using the Jet database engine. ODBCDirect is helpful when you need to use specific ODBC features.

ODBCDirect offers several advantages for ODBC operations:

PERFORMANCE

- The direct access to ODBC data sources makes your code run faster and more efficiently because it doesn't need to load the Jet database engine.
- You have improved access to server-specific features, such as cursor specification, as well as improved interaction with stored procedures at the server level.
- You can run asynchronous queries and also run other operations without waiting for the query to finish.
- With batch updating, changes are cached locally and then sent to the server in a single batch.

- You can create simple result sets or more complex cursors for running queries. You can create a query to return any number of result sets and limit the number of rows to be returned.

The Connection object is the connection to an ODBC database, and it contains information about the connection to an ODBC data source. It's similar to a database object on an ODBC data source; they represent different references to the same object. The new properties of both let you have a reference to the other object, which simplifies converting existing client applications from the Jet engine to the ODBCDirect server.

TROUBLESHOOTING

A new batch update cursor can be used by client applications. This allows them to store update information on many records in a batch and update them all at once instead of updating each record one at a time. Collisions can occur during the time lag between opening a recordset for updating and sending the updates back to the server. Other users can get in and change the original data before the changes are received by the server, so your changes collide with those of other users. Some new features help identify where collisions have occurred and help you resolve them.

The dbRunAsync option, which can be used with the Execute, MoveLast, OpenConnection, and OpenRecordset methods, allows the client to run the update in the background while carrying out other tasks.

Table A.7 describes the new methods and properties included in the new DAO 3.6 interface with ODBCDirect.

Table A.7   New Interfaces with ODBCDirect

Method or Property	Applies To	Description
Cancel method	Connection, QueryDef, and Recordset	Cancels execution of an asynchronous operation
NextRecordset method	Recordset	Retrieves the next set of records returned by a query that resulted in multiple sets of records and indicates whether it was successful
OpenConnection method	Workspace	Opens a connection object on an ODBC data source
BatchCollisionCount property	Recordset	Returns the number of records that were not completed during the last batch update
BatchCollisions property	Recordset	Returns an array of bookmarks showing the rows that caused collisions during last batch update

Method or Property	Applies To	Description
BatchSize property	Recordset	Sets or returns the number of statements sent back to the server in each batch
Connection property	Recordset	Returns the connection object that corresponds to the database or owns the recordset
Database property	Connection	Returns the name of the database object corresponding to the connection
DefaultCursorDriver property	Workspace	Sets or returns the type of cursor driver used for recordset objects
DefaultType property	DBEngine	Shows what type of workspace will be created by the next CreateWorkspace method call
Direction property	Parameter	Indicates whether a parameter object is input, output, or both, or if it's returned from a stored procedure
MaxRecords property	QueryDef	Sets or returns the maximum number of records to return from the query
OriginalValue property	Field	Returns the value of a field that existed when the last batch update began
Prepare property	QueryDef	Returns a value that indicates whether a query is to be prepared and stored or executed directly
RecordStatus property	Recordset	Returns the update status of the current record if it's part of the batch update
StillExecuting property	Connection	Returns a value that indicates whether the asynchronous operation is finished

continues

Table A.7   Continued

Method or Property	Applies To	Description
UpdateOptions property	Recordset	Returns a value that indicates how the WHERE clause is defined and how the update is to be executed
VisibleValue property	Recordset	Returns a value in the database that's newer than the OriginalValue, as compared by a batch update conflict

DAO 3.5 also supports a new recordset type, which behaves the same as a DAO 3.0 snapshot recordset opened with the dbForwardOnly option. The new type argument used with the OpenRecordset method is dbOpenFormardOnly.

DAO 3.5 also has some new interfaces with the Jet database engine, as described in Table A.8.

Table A.8   New Interfaces with the Jet Database Engine

Method or Property	Applies To	Description
PopulatePartial method	Database	Synchronizes changes in a partial replica with the full replica. Clears the partial replica and repopulates the partial replica based on the current replica filters.
SetOption method	DBEngine	Overrides Registry values for the duration of the current instance of DAO.
FieldSize property	Field	Replaces the FieldSize method.
MaxRecords property	QueryDef	Sets or returns the maximum number of records to return from query.
ReplicaFilter property	TableDef	Returns a value that indicates which subset of records is replicated in this partial replica from a full replica.
PartialReplica	Relation	Indicates which relation property object is to be used when populating a partial replica from a full replica.

The ODBCDirect–to–Jet engine interface is necessary for several reasons. It can provide different but complimentary functionality. To access .mdb files and ISAM data formats, you must use a Jet workspace. The Jet engine also has some unique capabilities that

ODBCDirect does not have. For example, if you have recordset objects based on multiple-table joins or joins from different data sources, you must update them in a Jet workspace. All DDL operations using DAO must also be performed in a Jet workspace. In addition, if any of your forms or controls are bound to data in an ODBC data source, you must use Jet to access them.

You can mix and match Jet and ODBCDirect workspaces in your application and use the capabilities of each as necessary.

DAO 3.6 Object Library Compatibility

Access 2000 has replaced many DAO objects, methods, and properties that were used in earlier versions. If you've used any of these older language elements, it's recommended that you modify the code and replace them with the newer DAO 3.6 elements. Table A.9 lists the elements that are not included in DAO 3.6 and suggests suitable replacements.

Table A.9   Elements No Longer Included in DAO 3.6

Element	Recommend Replacement
FreeLocks	Idle method of the DBEngine object (not necessary for Access 2000 databases)
SetDefaultWorkspace	DefaultUser/DefaultPassword properties of the DBEngine object
SetDataAccessOption	IniPath property of the DBEngine object
database.BeginTrans	workspace.BeginTrans
database.CommitTrans	workspace.CommitTrans
database.CreateDynaset	database.OpenRecordset of type dbOpenDynaset
database.CreateSnapshot	database.OpenRecordset of type dbOpenSnapshot
database.DeleteQueryDef	Delete method of the QueryDefs collection
database.ExecuteSQL	database.Execute method and database.RecordsAffected property
database.ListTables	database.TableDefs collection
database.OpenQueryDef	database.QueryDefs collection
database.OpenTable	database.OpenRecordset of type dbOpenTable
database.Rollback	workspace.Rollback
ListFields method of the Table, Dynaset, Snapshot objects	recordset.Fields collection
table.ListIndexes	tabledef.Indexes collection

continues

Table A.9 Continued

Element	Recommend Replacement
querydef.CreateDynaset	*querydef*.OpenRecordset
querydef.CreateSnapshop	*querydef*.OpenRecordset
querydef.ListParameters	*querydef*.Parameters collection
Dynaset object	Dynaset-type Recordset object
Snapshot object	Snapshot-type Recordset object
Table object	Table-type Recordset object
CreateDynaset method of the Dynaset and QueryDef objects	*recordset*.OpenRecordset with dbOpenDynaset parameter
CreateSnapshot method of the Dynaset and QueryDef objects	*recordset*.OpenRecordset with dbOpenSnapshot parameter

New Outside Connections

When you want to use objects from another application, set a reference to that application's type library. You can set references to a project in another Access database or to a type library in another Office application such as Excel or Word.

Many new features in Access give you an entry into the Internet, where you can publish your own Web page, import or link information from an HTML file, and export datasheets and forms to HTML format.

References to Type Libraries

You can set a reference to an application type library from the Visual Basic Editor window or with VB code. The VBE window must be in design view. To set a reference, choose Tools|References in the Editor window and set the reference in the References dialog box. To set a reference from VB code, you create a new Reference object by using the AddFromFile or AddFromGUID method of the References collection. If you want to remove a reference that's no longer useful, use the Remove method.

There are many advantages to setting references, including faster execution of your Automation code.

DEVELOPMENT

You can also set a reference to a VB project in another Access database. The VB project is the set of all the modules, both class and standard, in the project. When you set a reference from one project to a project in an Access database, a library database, or an add-in in an .mde file, you can run the procedures in the referenced project. You can also run any of the public procedures contained in a standard module. You cannot run procedures in a class module or any that are labeled Private.

If you want to set a reference to a project created with Access 95 or earlier, you must convert it to Access 2000 first.

Connect to Other Applications

PERFORMANCE

Although you can work with objects from another application without setting a reference to that application's type library, your code will run faster if you first set the reference. For example, you can simply declare an object variable that represents an Excel worksheet as a specific type, as in the following declaration statement:

```
Dim appExl As New Excel.Application
```

> **Tip:** Another advantage of using references to type libraries is that all the objects, along with their methods and properties, will appear in the Object Browser. This makes it easy to see what's available and how to spell them or even copy and paste them into the code.

With Access 2000, you can now create an Access database from data in another file format. All you need to do is open the file in Access and it automatically converts from the other format—such as text, dBASE, Paradox, or even a spreadsheet—to an Access format.

When you add a spreadsheet, PivotTable, chart or graph, or another object created in another application, you can edit the object from within Access. When you double-click the object, the source application launches in place without leaving the Access window.

See Chapter 17, "Linking with Other Office Applications," for more information on exchanging data and working with other products.

New Internet Features

NETWORKING

The most significant enhancement in Access 2000 is the new data access pages that enable you to post dynamic data to the Web. Once these pages are created, you can use them to add, edit, view, and manipulate current data in an Access database or a SQL Server database from the Web.

One of the new hyperlink features is that you can assign a hyperlink to a toolbar button or menu command that will jump to a location on your computer, a network, an intranet, or the Internet.

See Chapter 20, "Posting Your Database on the Web," for more information on hyperlinks and how to import and export information using the Internet.

Converting from Earlier Versions of Access

COMPATIBILITY

Although you can open a database created in an earlier version of Access to run in Access 2000 without converting it, most of the time you'll want to convert it. Most conversions take place with little or no user involvement. However, there are some programming considerations to be taken into account. New features are added and others removed. This appendix discusses some of the concerns relating to converting Access objects. It also points out some changes to your code that you need to know about and other changes you need to make so that your application runs successfully in Access 2000. After it's converted, the database can no longer be opened by the earlier version, but you can use Access 2000 to convert a database back to Access 97.

Visual Basic for Applications code that you've used in earlier versions of Access is automatically converted to VB with only a few details that need your attention. Some new keywords must be avoided in the converted code, and some data types have been changed. Some of the VB functions behave differently and may cause runtime errors. The main difference between Access Basic used in version 95 and earlier is that VB now operates in a 32-bit environment, whereas the Access Basic code runs in a 16-bit environment.

Enable or Convert?

In order to decide on an upgrade strategy for your Access database, you need to consider how it is used. You'll most likely choose to convert the previous-version database to Access 2000, but there are some situations in which it would make sense to enable the previous version without actually converting it.

For example, if your database is shared in a multiuser environment where not all users can upgrade at the same time, you can choose to upgrade parts of the database and leave the rest of the original database unchanged.

Once you've converted the database to Access 2000, you won't be able to open it in the earlier version. If you convert from Access 97, you can convert the 2000 version back to Access 97, if necessary.

Enabling a Previous-Version Database

You can enable a database created in Access version 2.0, 95, or 97 and use it in Access 2000. When you enable the database, you can view, edit, and delete data, but you're not permitted to make any object design changes or use any of the new Access 2000 features. If you want to modify the design of an object, you must open the database in the version used to create it.

To enable a previous-version database, choose File|Open or click the Open toolbar button. In the Open dialog box, locate and select the database and then click Open. In the Convert/Open Database dialog box, shown in Figure B.1, choose Open Database and click OK. The database opens in Access 2000. When you switch among the pages in the database window, you can see that the New and Design buttons are dimmed. In addition, the leading items on each object page that normally enable you to create new objects in design view or with the help of a wizard are missing.

FIGURE B.1

Enable an earlier version database in Access 2000.

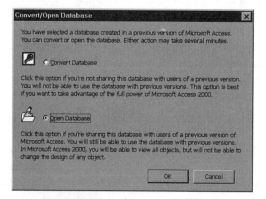

> **Note:** Each time you enable the database in a later version (for example, from Access 2.0 to 95 and then from 95 to 97), it increases in size. Before repeatedly enabling the database, consider converting as an alternative to improve database efficiency.

If you want to enable a secured database, you should re-create the workgroup information file in Access 2000 to retain the secured status. If this is not possible, use the Workgroup Administrator to join the previous-version Workgroup Information File (WIF). Try to convert the WIF to Access 2000 before you join it. If you use the enabled database with the original WIF, all the security is retained except the module permissions. Access 2000 protects modules with a password rather than user-level security.

As an alternative to enabling a database in a front-end/back-end shared environment, you can keep the back end (with the data) in the oldest version and upgrade the front ends to a mixture of versions 2.0, 95, 97, and 2000, as necessary for the variety of local user upgrades.

Converting a Database

Before converting a database to Access 2000, be sure to make a backup copy and keep the copy in a safe place until you're confident that the conversion was successful. Also make sure no one else is using the database before starting the conversion.

To convert a normal, single-user database from an earlier version of Access, perform the following steps:

1. In the blank Access 2000 window, choose Tools|Database Utilities|Convert Database.
2. Select the database you want to convert in the Database To Convert From dialog box and click Convert.
3. In the Convert Database Into dialog box, type a new name for the database if you want to convert it in place. If you want to put it in another location, choose the location and keep the same name or enter a new one. (You can't convert a database to the same name and location as the original.)
4. Click Save.

You can also use the same technique as described for enabling a database in Access 2000 to convert a database, except choose Convert Database in the Convert/Open dialog box.

While the conversion is going on, you may see some messages about compile errors because some of the VB commands used in your modules may no longer be valid. Don't worry, you can correct the code later.

DEVELOPMENT

Warning: If your database has linked tables, be sure that the external tables remain in the same folder they were in when the database was created. You won't be able to use the converted database if Access can't find the linked tables. After you convert the database, you can move the linked tables and relink them with the Linked Table Manager. The linked tables are not converted with the database.

Tip: If you don't want all the objects from the previous-version database in your new Access 2000 database, create a new blank database with Access 2000 and import just the objects you want. These objects are converted as they are imported.

Access 97 and Access 2000 use a new style of toolbars and menu bars. When you convert a version 2.0 or 95 database, the custom toolbars are automatically converted to the new style along with the built-in toolbars. Custom menu bars created with the Menu Builder in Access 95 or with a macro are treated as new style menu bars but are not actually converted. You cannot use the Customize dialog box to edit them. If you create a new style menu bar from a macro with the Tools|Create Menu (or Shortcut Menu) From Macro command, the result is a new style menu that can be edited with the Customize dialog box.

You must take special measures if the database is shared with other users who might not be converting to Access 2000 at the same time. Secured databases also present special problems. See the section titled "Converting a Secured Database" for more information.

Converting a Workgroup Information File

Access 2000 includes many advances in security and performance that you can take advantage of if you convert the workgroup information file for a multiuser database. The best way is to re-create the WIF using Access 2000 with the exact, case-sensitive name, company name, and workgroup ID that was used for the original file. Each entry must be exactly as it was entered in the original WIF; otherwise, the Admins group will be invalid.

Next, re-create all the group and user accounts, again entering exactly the case-sensitive names and Personal IDs (PIDs) for each group and user. After the new WIF is complete, inform all the users in the workgroup to use the Workgroup Administrator to join the new WIF.

Converting a Shared Database

NETWORKING

When not all the users who share a multiuser database can upgrade to Access 2000 at the same time, you can upgrade part of the database and leave the original database as is. Users of all versions then share the same data whether the database is one file or already split into a front-end/back-end application.

If your shared database is in one file, perform the following steps to convert it to Access 2000:

1. Convert the database and give it a new name.

2. Choose Tools|Add-Ins|Database Splitter and use the Database Splitter Wizard to split the newly converted database into a front-end/back-end application.

3. Use the original database as the back-end database so that all the users work with the same data. The back-end database should be the oldest version of the lot. To do this, delete the back-end database that was created by the wizard.

4. Choose Tools|Add-Ins and run the Linked Table Manager to link the new Access 2000 front-end database to the previous-version back-end database.

All the users still have access to the original data in the back-end database, and the Access 2000 users can enhance their front-end database objects to take advantage of the new features.

If the database was already split, convert the front end only and leave the back-end database alone. Then run the Linked Table Manager, as before, to link the new Access 2000 front-end database to the original back-end database.

Converting a Secured Database

Some additional steps are required when the database you want to convert is a secured database. First, you must join the workgroup information file in which the user accounts are defined or the one that was in use when the database was secured. To join an Access workgroup, you must exit Access and open the Workgroup Administrator. The process then depends on your operating system. Refer to Chapter 19, "Adding Security to the Application," for information on working with secured databases.

Your user account must have the following permissions:

- Open/Run and Open Exclusive at the database level.
- Modify Design or Administer for all the tables (or you must be the owner of all the tables).
- Read Design for all the database objects.

NETWORKING
If all the users are upgrading at once, convert the database and its workgroup information file to Access 2000. If not, the users can share the database and the workgroup information file across the various versions of Access.

How you convert a secured database depends on which version of Access it's upgrading from. If you're converting from a version 1.x or 2.0 secured database, you convert both the database and the workgroup information file, usually named System.mda by default. Then, tell the users to join the converted workgroup information file, now named System.mdw, before opening the converted database.

If you're converting from Access 95 or Access 97, convert only the database. The workgroup information file can be used without converting, but it should be compacted before it's used with the converted database. To convert an Access 95 or Access 97 secured database, perform the following steps:

1. Convert the database.
2. Compact the database and exit Access.
3. Temporarily join another workgroup information file and restart Access without opening any database.
4. Compact the workgroup information file that was used with the secured database.
5. Tell users to join the newly compacted workgroup information file before opening the converted database.

CAUTION
Access 2000 no longer protects VB code with user-level security, so additional steps are required when you convert a secured database to prevent others from viewing or changing code.

See Chapter 18, "Working in a Multiuser Environment," for more information about workgroups and shared databases. See Chapter 19, "Adding Security to the Application," for information about secured databases.

Converting a Replicated Database

Versions of Access prior to 97 were unable to replicate a database and therefore can't use replicated databases. You can convert a replica set created in Access 97 by creating a completely separate test set of replicas to verify that the set will synchronize properly after conversion. Then, when you're satisfied, you can convert the original set to Access 2000. Once converted, a member of the replica set can't be opened again in Access 97.

CAUTION

It's very important that you keep the test replica set completely isolated from the working set and that you do not synchronize the test Design Master with any of the working set members.

After you make sure all the users have upgraded to Access 2000, convert the replica set by doing the following:

1. Make a test copy of the working Design Master and isolate it completely from every member of the original 97 set. Store it on a different computer, if possible.
2. In Access 97, open the new test copy of the Design Master and specify it as the Design Master by choosing Tools|Replication|Recover Design Master.
3. Create three or four replicas from the test Design Master.
4. Convert the test Design Master and each of the replicas to Access 2000.
5. Synchronize the converted test Design Master with the new converted replicas.
6. Run the test replica set until you're satisfied that the conversion was successful for all members.
7. Delete the test Design Master and the converted test replicas.
8. Convert the original Access 97 Design Master and each of the replicas to Access 2000.

Converting Database Objects

If you don't want to convert all the objects in the previous-version database to Access 2000, you can convert them separately by importing them to an empty Access 2000 database.

Tables, Forms, and Reports

Database objects converted from Access 97 should function correctly, but there are several changes in Access 2000 that might affect how your version 1.x, 2.0 and 95 applications operate. Many of the important changes that influence the behavior of your tables, forms, reports, and workspaces are described in the following list:

TROUBLESHOOTING

- The Jet DBEngine 3.5 used in Access 2000 creates indexes for tables on both sides of a relationship. An Access table is limited to 32 indexes, so if you have complex tables with many relationships, you might exceed this limit and the conversion will fail. If this happens, delete some of the relationships and try again.

- In version 2.0, a combo box whose LimitToList property was set to True would not accept a Null value unless it was included in the list. In Access 2000, a combo box will accept a Null value when LimitToList is set to True, whether Null is in the list or not. Therefore, if you want to be sure the users do not enter a Null value, set the combo box's Required property to Yes.

- In Access 2000, you cannot use an expression to refer to a control on a read-only form that's bound to an empty record source. In earlier versions, the expression would return a Null value if the form was empty, but Access 2000 displays an error message. You can add code to test for an empty record source before opening the form.

- In earlier versions, a form or report had a class module assigned to it even if there was no code associated with the object. If you're not planning to add any code to the class module, set the HasModule property to False. A form or report without an associated class module takes up less disk space and loads faster.

- When you convert forms and reports that contain ActiveX controls, check carefully to make sure they've been converted correctly. Access 2.0 supported 16-bit OLE controls, whereas Access 2000 supports only the new 32-bit ActiveX controls. If you system does not have the 32-bit version of the control you want to convert, you'll get an error message. Then you must get the 32-bit version of the control and register it in the Windows Registry. After updating the OLE control to the ActiveX equivalent, close and reopen the database to complete the conversion.

- If reports you created in version 2.0 do not print properly, the margins might be the problem. If the report had some margins set to 0, they're no longer set to 0 when the report is converted. They're set instead to the minimum margin that's acceptable to the default printer.

- If you used the version 2.0 or 7.0 Command Button Wizard to generate code calls to another application, you should replace the buttons in Access 2000. Delete the buttons and use the Access 2000 Command Button Wizard to re-create them.

The SendKeys statement or action might require recoding. With so many changes to the menus and submenus, all SendKey key combinations must be reviewed. Many of the submenus have moved to different menus, so the key combinations will be different. For example, the Add-Ins submenu has moved to the Tools menu (key combination Alt+T+I) from the File menu (key combination Alt+F+I). Many other menu items have been reworded. For example, the Import submenu on the File menu has been changed to Get External Data.

It's better to avoid the very explicit SendKeys action and use some other method of carrying out commands or filling in dialog boxes. Here are some alternatives:

- Use an equivalent macro action or VB method.

- If no equivalent macro or method is available, use the RunCommand action, which has several arguments indicating the position of the item in the menu instead of the specific key letters.

- Use the GetOption and SetOption methods to set options in the Options dialog box, because the option text can change, which also changes the key combinations.

- If all else fails, define keystrokes as constants and then refer to them in the SendKeys statement. They're easier to update as constants defined in a single location than they are if scattered throughout your code.

Converting Macros

When you convert a version 1.x or 2.0 database to Access 2000, any DoCmd statements and the actions they execute in Access Basic code are converted to methods of the DoCmd object in VB simply by replacing the space with a dot (.). Some macro actions have changed from versions 1.x, 2.0 and 95.

If you created the database in Access 1.x or 2.0, you may encounter some of the following differences:

- Access 2000 cannot import Excel version 2.0 or Lotus 1-2-3 version 1.0 spreadsheets. If your converted database included a macro that used the TransferSpreadsheet action, converting to Access 2000 automatically changes the Spreadsheet Type argument to Excel 3.0 (if you specified version 2.0) or causes an error (if you specified Lotus 1-2-3 version 1.0). To solve this problem, convert the spreadsheets to later versions before converting the Access database that imports the spreadsheet.

- You can no longer use a SQL statement to specify the data to export when you use the TransferText or TransferSpreadsheet action. You must first create a query and refer to the query by name in the action.

- If you used a comparison operator to compare the values returned by two expressions and one of the expressions was Null, Access Basic returned True or False, depending on which comparison operator you used. Access 2000 returns Null for a comparison in which either one of the expressions is Null. Use the IsNull function to check for Null values before applying the comparison.

In Access 95, you could use the DoMenuItem action to carry out a menu command. While the macro action is retained for backward compatibility, you should use the replacement RunCommand action instead. When you convert a database from a previous version, the DoMenuItem actions in the macros are replaced by RunCommand actions the first time you save the macro after conversion. Any DoMenuItem methods that are used in VB procedures are left unchanged.

Converting Modules

ARCHITECTURE

The modules containing procedures not specific to any form or report module were called *global modules* in Access 1.*x* and 2.0. Now they're called *standard modules*. Access 2000 also includes *class modules* that can be used to create custom forms and reports. They can exist either in association with or independent of a specific form or report.

In Access 1.*x* and 2.0, you were limited to the procedures defined within a form or report and could not call routines from any other form or report module. In Access 2000, you can call a public procedure in a form or report module from anywhere in the current database. You must, however, refer to it by the full class name of its source. For example, if you want to call the ShowCategories procedure from the Transactions Log form, you would use the following syntax:

```
Form_Transaction_Log.ShowCategories
```

DEVELOPMENT

It's better practice to place all the procedures you may call from an external source in a standard module. This way, they're always available, even if you delete the form or report whose module contained the code.

Each form or report contains one module, and VB limits the number of modules to 1,082 per database. If you have more than that, you'll get an Out of memory error message when you try to convert the database to Access 2000. To solve this problem, eliminate some of the objects or split the database into two or more separate databases. Another solution might be to store very large modules in a library database that does not count against the current database. Procedures in a library database can be accessed by any application after establishing a reference from the current database to the library database.

Other Conversion Issues

When converting from Access 95 or earlier versions, you may encounter problems with changed data types, formatting differences, and using some properties.

Data Types

Data types in Access 97 databases will convert correctly to Access 2000, but you may have problems with earlier versions. Some properties now return string variables that in previous versions returned Variant values. You must be sure that the converted code produces no data type–related errors. Some of the optional arguments that were Variant are now also strictly typed. Among those affected are the following:

- The GoToPage method of a Form object
- The OpenCurrentDatabase, Echo, Quit, CreateForm, CreateReport, CreateControl, and CreateReportControl methods of the Application object
- The Column property of a combo box or list box
- Domain aggregate functions such as DAvg(), DCount, DMin, and DMax

If your application includes any of these, you should check to make sure no errors occur after the conversion: first by compiling all the modules and then by running the application to catch runtime errors. Errors such as Type mismatch and Invalid use of Null are the most common runtime errors that occur because of the new strict data typing.

Other errors might occur that are not found at runtime, for example, using a record source property for a control that previously referred to a Variant value, which is now converted to a string. You might have included code to check for Null values in the field. A string value cannot be Null, so your code will not do what you intended. If you use the IsNull() function to test the value, it will never return True. Instead, you should change the code to test for a zero-length string by comparing the value returned by the Len() function.

OLE objects and other binary data should be converted to an array of bytes in VB. In Access 1.x and 2.0, you assigned OLE objects and data returned by the GetChunk method to string variables when you needed to manipulate them in code. VB now has a Byte data type, which is stored as an unsigned 8-bit number. In Access 2000, you should store binary data in an array of bytes instead of a string variable and use byte functions to work with the data. For example, the byte version of the Len() function is LenB().

When you declared a variable in Access 1.x and 2.0 to store the channel number for a DDE channel, you used an integer number. In Access 2000, you can declare the channel number, which is a Long Integer value, as either Long Integer or Variant. Be sure to change the declaration statement to reflect the changed data type when you convert to Access 2000.

You'll have trouble if you try to convert a string containing a percent sign (%) to a variable or field of the number data type. For example, the first of the following statements will cause an error, whereas the second statement will convert properly:

```
Dim intNum1 As Double, intNum2 As Double
     intNum1 = "125%"      'Causes Runtime error #13, Type mismatch.
     IntNum2 = "125"      'Is correct.
```

The Time portion of Date/Time values has changed in Access 2000. If you have any query criteria that depend on Date/Time values, they might return different results than did previous versions. You might also have trouble with this when you try to link tables from an earlier database with databases created in Access 2000.

Formats

The Format() function works differently in Access 2000 than in Access 2.0. In Access 2.0, you could use the Format() function to return one value if the argument contained a Null value and a different value if it was a zero-length string. The following Access 2.0 statement formats the string passed to it and displays the string if it contains characters, as specified by the @ character. The words, "Zero Length" are displayed if it contains a zero-length string, and "Null" if it contains a Null value:

```
Dim varResult As Variant, strMsg As String
'Give the strMsg a value and pass to the Format() function.
varResult = Format(strMsg, "@;Zero Length;Null")
```

In Access 2000, the string format expression in the Format() function has only two sections: one for the characters in the string and the second to be used if the string is either empty or Null. You must test separately for a Null value. One way to accomplish this is to change your code to test first for a Null value and then use the Format function to decide on the appropriate value to return based on the results of the IIf() function. The following statement will return the same result as the previous statement:

```
varResult = IIf(IsNull(strMsg), "Null", Format(strMsg, "@;Zero Length"))
```

You no longer can use the Format property in a table datasheet view to distinguish between Null values and zero-length strings. If you have depended on either of these uses of formatting, change the code or property settings accordingly.

Properties

The hWnd property determines the handle that's assigned by Windows to the current window. The property applies to forms and reports and is used when making calls to Windows API functions or other external routines. In Access 1.*x* and 2.0, the hWnd property value is an Integer value, whereas in Access 2000 it's a Long Integer value. For this reason, you should change your code to accept the new data type or pass the hWnd property directly to the routine rather than assign it to a variable.

The Parent property of a control in VB code or in an expression usually returns the name of the form or report that contains the control. For example, in Access 2000 the code

```
Forms!Transaction_Log!Transaction_ID.Parent
```

would refer to the Transaction Log form. However, if the control is an attached label, it returns the name of the control to which it's attached. If the control is one of the options in an option group, the Parent property returns the name of the option group control.

The Category property is no longer supported for form, report, and control objects.

Command-line Switches

The /runtime command-line switch is no longer supported in the standalone and Office Professional editions of Access 2000. If you want to use /runtime, you must use the Office Developer edition of Access 2000.

Converting to Visual Basic Code

COMPATIBILITY

Access 95 and earlier versions used Access Basic, whereas Access 97 used Visual Basic for Applications, which is a programming language similar to Visual Basic that's shared by all Microsoft Office 2000 products. When you convert a database created by an earlier version of Access, your code is automatically converted to VB. VB is nearly identical to VBA and Access Basic, but there are a few things to watch out for. The conversion process changes some of the code automatically, and other changes you need to make yourself.

The main difference between Access Basic and Visual Basic is that VB is a 32-bit application that runs on the 32-bit version of Windows. Access Basic is a 16-bit application that runs on a 16-bit version of Windows.

Another significant difference is the upgrading of DAO code from the 2.5/3.5 version to 3.5 and, in some cases, 3.6. There are new DAO objects, methods, and properties that replace some of the earlier elements. Some functions also behave differently from their earlier versions, mostly because of the data type changes mentioned previously.

Converting DAO Code

COMPATIBILITY

DAO code is backward compatible now but might not be in the future. You should use the new DAO objects, methods, and properties with new applications and change to them when you modify current applications. If you need to keep using older DAO versions, establish a reference to the DAO 2.5/3.5 Compatibility Library (choose Tools|References). This enables you to use DAO elements from versions 1.x, 2.0, and 95 (7.0).

The DAO 3.5 library doesn't include the older elements and is automatically selected for all new applications. If you don't use any of the old DAO elements, you don't need to include the DAO 2.5/3.5 Compatibility Library when you distribute the application to the users, which saves disk space.

To check the dependency of an application on the DAO 2.5/3.5 Compatibility Library, clear it in the References dialog box and recompile the application. If no errors occur, your application doesn't need the Compatibility Library anymore.

To modify existing code and remove the need for the Compatibility Library, change the functionality that doesn't appear in DAO 3.5 to the recommended replacement. For example, if you're converting from Access 97 to Access 2000, you can no longer declare a variable as a database or a recordset. In Access 95 or 97, you may have used the following:

```
Dim dbs As Database, rst As Recordset
Set dbs = CurrentDB
Set rst = dbs.OpenRecordset("Customers",dbOpenTable)
```

In Access 2000, you would replace these statements with this:

```
Dim dbs A ADODB.Connection, rst As New ADODB.Recordset
Set dbs = CurrentProject.Connection
Set rst = dbs!Customers.OpenRecordset(dbOpenTable)
```

Refer to the Access 2000 Help topic "DAO Object Library Compatibility" for a list of items to change. The topic "Examples of Converting DAO Code" shows many helpful examples of converting code constructs from earlier versions to DAO 3.5.

Table B.1 lists the obsolete DAO features, the objects they apply to, and their recommended replacements.

Table B.1   Replacement Features for DAO 3.5

Obsolete Feature	Replacement Feature
CreateDynaset methods (all)	OpenRecordset method type dbOpenDynaset
CreateSnapshot methods (all)	OpenRecordset method type dbOpenSnapshot
ListFields methods (all)	Fields collection
ListIndexes methods (all)	Indexes collection
DBEngine.FreeLocks method	Idle method
DBEngine.SetDefaultWorkspace	DefaultUser and Password properties method
DBEngineSetDataAccessOption	IniPath property method
Database.BeginTrans method	Workspace.BeginTrans method
Database.CommitTrans method	Workspace.CommitTrans method
Database.Rollback method	Workspace.Rollback method
Database.DeleteQueryDef method	Delete method
Database.ExecuteSQL method	Execute method
Database.ListTables method	TableDefs collection
Database.OpenQueryDef method	QueryDefs collection
Database.OpenTable method	OpenRecordset method type OpenTable
QueryDef.ListParameters method	Parameters collection
Snapshot object	Recordset object type snapshot
Dynaset object	Recordset object type dynaset
Table object	Recordset object type table

Code That Calls a Dynamic Link Library

The Windows Application Programming Interface (API) is actually a group of dynamic link libraries (DLLs) that provide all the functions, data types, structures, messages, and statements you use to create an application to run on a Windows 95 or Windows NT platform. Before you can call these procedures from VB, you must declare them with a declaration statement.

You might need to make some changes in your code when you convert the version 1.*x* or 2.0 database to Access 2000. The following suggestions can help you find and fix problem areas:

- If a Declare statement calls a 16-bit Windows API, you must change the references to call the DLLs by their new 32-bit names:

    User.dll becomes User32.dll

    Kernel.dll becomes Kernel32.dll

    GUI.dll becomes GUI32.dll

- Check the names of the API functions your code calls. Some names have been changed, and all names are now case sensitive.

- Check for new parameter data types in function calls.

- Avoid having a 16-bit DLL with the same name as a 32-bit DLL. Access might try to call the wrong one.

- Some functions in 32-bit DLLs have two different versions to accommodate both ANSI and Unicode strings. A function name ending with an *A* is the ANSI version; a *W* indicates the Unicode version. If the function in your code takes string arguments, you should call the function with the trailing A.

If you get the message Specified DLL function not found when converting to a 32-bit version, add 32 to the end of the library name and A to the name of the routine you're calling. This will usually correct the error.

If your database calls procedures in DLLs other than the API, you must have the 32-bit versions and make the appropriate changes in your code when you convert. If you can't find the 32-bit versions, you might be able to convert the 16-bit DLL with the help of an intermediary DLL.

Microsoft provides several sources for more information about 32-bit API procedures, including the following:

- The Microsoft Office 2000 Developer Edition Windows API Viewer contains information about the syntax for all the 32-bit declarations, data types, and constants.

- Information about porting a 16-bit, Office-based application to a 32-bit platform is contained in the Microsoft Office Resource Kit.

- For complete information about 32-bit API procedures, consult the Microsoft Win32 Software Development Kit.

Function Procedure Behavior

To return a Database object variable that refers to the current database, use the CurrentDB function instead of DBengine(0)(0). The DBengine(0)(0) function refers only to the open copy of the current database, which limits your ability to use more than one variable to refer to the current database. The CurrentDB function creates another instance of the database, which enables you to refer to the database with more than one Database type variable. DBengine is still supported for backward compatibility, but using CurrentDB instead might prevent conflicts if you should open the database for multiuser access.

The behavior of the CurDir function has changed in Access 2000 because of the way applications interact in the Windows 95 environment. Each application has its own folder, and double-clicking a Windows 95 folder icon does not change the current folder in Access. CurDir always returns the current path.

Most functions can be used in expressions as well as in VB code. Six functions can no longer be used outside a user-defined procedure. They are EOF(), FileAttr(), FreeFile(), Loc(), LOF(), and Seek(). However, they can be indirectly used in an expression by calling the function from within a user-defined function procedure.

If any of the lines in your converted Access 1.x or 2.0 modules are assigned line numbers greater than 65,529, you must reassign them lower numbers.

Debugging and Error Handling

VB now lets ActiveX objects that support Automation return more specific error information. Automation was previously called *OLE Automation servers*. In Access 1.x and 2.0, only a single Automation error message was available. If your database includes error trapping based on that one error, you might want to expand the code to handle the more specific errors that are now reported.

The properties of the Err object in Access 2000 give you information about the Access error that has occurred. The Err.Number property returns the error code number, and Err.Description returns its description. If you want information about Access, VB, or DAO errors, you can use the AccessError method. An error need not occur before you can acquire information with the AccessError method.

TROUBLESHOOTING

ActiveX controls were formerly called *OLE controls* or *custom controls*. If your application contains any that were set up in Access 2.0, you might need to pass them to a procedure with the ByVal keyword. To find out if you need to add ByVal, choose Debug|Compile All Modules in the module design window. If you see the message Event procedure declaration doesn't match description of event having the same name, you need to insert the ByVal keyword in front of the argument. New procedures using ActiveX controls as arguments automatically include the ByVal keyword.

When you're testing new code, you must use full references to objects you want to see in the Watch window unless you've suspended execution. For example, to refer to the Type control in the Transaction Log form in form view, use the code Forms!Transaction_Log!Type. You may not use the Me keyword in the Watch window unless execution is suspended.

In Access 1.*x* and 2.0, the module toolbar included two buttons that are no longer available in Access 2000: Next Procedure and Previous Procedure. If you've created a custom toolbar that includes those buttons for your application and converted the application to Access 2000, the buttons will still appear in the toolbar but they will have no effect when clicked.

Using References

If you enable a large database created in Access 1.*x* or 2.0 without converting it to Access 2000, your default buffer size might be insufficient. To increase it, you need to open the Windows Registry. To do this, click Start and then Run. Next, type **regedit** in the Run dialog box and then click OK. In the Registry Editor dialog box, navigate to the following folder:

`\HKEY_LOCAL\MACHINE\SOFTWARE\Microsoft\Jet\3.0\Engines\Jet2.x`

Next, choose Edit|New|Key and add a new key named `ISAM`; then add a new `DWORD` value called `MaxBufferSize`. Enter **1024** (kilobytes) as the new value for `MaxBufferSize`. The buffer size can be set to a value between 9 and 4096, with the default value 512KB.

The new exclamation point (!) operator refers to user-named objects in Access 2000. If you used the dot (.) operator exclusively in Access 1.*x* and 2.0, you must change those references to use the ! operator. If you don't want to modify the operators, you can establish a reference to the Microsoft DAO 2.5/3.5 Compatibility Library in the References dialog box. To open this dialog box, choose Tools|References while in the module design window. Then, check the box next to the option in the Available References list and choose OK.

ARCHITECTURE

Access 2.0 made no distinction between wizards and libraries. All the public code contained in them was available to the current database. You could call procedures in a wizard just as easily as you could call one in a library. Access 2000 no longer treats wizards as libraries, so after you convert the application, you must establish a reference from it to the wizard database where the procedures you need are stored. Wizards also add more and more capability with each version of Access, so you might need to redo the code to accommodate these changes.

Some code, such as the AutoDialer code, is no longer available from a wizard but has been added to the special library database named `Utility.mda`. A reference to the `Utility.mda` add-ins file is automatically added when you convert to Access 2000. If not, you can add it yourself by opening the References Editor dialog box and choosing Browse. Next, use the Add Reference dialog box to search for the `Utility.mda` file. It's usually located in the `Office` subfolder of the `Microsoft Office` folder. After locating the file, click Add and it's added to the Available References list, where you can check to establish the reference.

You can rename a database, but when you do, all the code is decompiled and must be recompiled. You can wait until you want to run the application again, or you can recompile immediately by opening a module in design view and choosing Debug|Compile and Save All Modules.

You cannot set a reference within Access 2000 to a database from an earlier version without converting it first.

Scope and Object Name Compatibility

The naming rules in Access 2000 forbid beginning a module name with the name of an Access or DAO object. When you try to convert the database, you'll get a compilation error message and will be asked to rename a module with such a name before the conversion is completed. For example, a module named Report_NewProduct would trigger an error. Rename the module and move on with the conversion.

VB has added some new reserved keywords that also cannot be used as identifiers. If the database you want to convert uses any of the new keywords as identifiers, you'll get a compile error. Here's a list of the new keywords:

AddressOf	Event
Assert	Friend
Decimal	Implements
DefDec	RaiseEvent
Enum	WithEvents

Rename the identifiers to complete the conversion.

In prior Access versions, the project name was simply the name of the database. In Access 2000, you can specify a project name that's different from the database name as specified by the ProjectName property setting. The project name may not be the same as an object name. If your database has the same name as a class of objects, Access adds an underscore character to the project name to differentiate it from the corresponding object name.

Library Databases and Add-Ins

If you intend to use library databases and add-ins that you created in prior versions, you must first convert them to Access 2000. You might also need to make some changes in the objects, procedures, and macros to make sure they work the way you want.

DEVELOPMENT

To use a converted library database, you must establish a reference to it for each of the applications that need it. Choose Tools|References while in the module design window and check the desired library database. The referenced database must also be in Access 2000 format.

Access 2000 no longer allows circular references among libraries, which was possible in versions 1.x and 2.0. That is, if Library A includes a reference to Library B, you cannot establish a reference from Library B to Library A.

In Access 2000, you can see all the intrinsic constants in the type libraries in the Object Browser. Microsoft Access, Data Access Objects, ActiveX Data Objects (ADO), and Visual Basic libraries all include intrinsic constants. In the list of constants, some of the names are all uppercase and include the underscore character (for example, A_FORM). This is a constant held over from versions 1.*x* and 2.0. The new format is a combination of upper- and lowercase (for example, acForm). The old formats will still work and are not automatically converted to the new format.

Converting from Access 2000 to Access 97

If you find that you need to run the database you've converted to Access 2000 on version 97 after all, you can convert it back if it's not a member of a replica set. Many of the new features and functionality of Access 2000 will be lost in the conversion, including the following:

- The links to data access pages will be lost. Access 97 does not support data access pages.

- A database that contains a table with a number whose Field Size property is set to the new Decimal setting can't be converted. You must change the Field Size property to Single or Double or change the field data type to Currency.

- Any table data that relied on the new Unicode compression may not convert correctly. Some of the characters used in Access 2000 may not have equivalent characters in the shorter Access 97 256-character set.

If you've secured the Access 2000 database with user-level security, remove it before attempting to convert to Access 97. After converting, you can restore security. If the database is protected with a password, you can convert it without removing the password. However, if you have protected the VB code with a password, you must supply the password before you can convert to Access 97.

To convert an Access 2000 database to Access 97, do the following:

1. Make sure no one else is using the database; then open the database you want to convert and remove user-level security, if it has been imposed.

2. Choose Tools|Database Utilities|Convert Database and then click To Prior Access Database Version.

3. In the Convert Database Into dialog box, locate the folder where you want the database stored and type a name for the database in the File Name box. Click Save.

After you've converted the database to Access 97, you may need to correct any missing references. If the 2000 database used add-ins or library databases that were created in Access 2000, you'll have to convert them back as well.

Troubleshooting Conversion

It doesn't matter what the application is, whenever you try to convert from one version to another, some difficulties are bound to occur. In addition, every database is a little different, so some unique problems can also arise. In addition to those mentioned earlier in this appendix, here are some other common problems that can pop up when converting Access databases from earlier versions:

- Your Visual Basic code will not compile and you get error messages. When the version 2.0 database is converted, the conversion utility converts the Access Basic code to VBA, which is not always compatible with VB. To fix the problems, open a module in design mode and choose Debug|Compile All Modules. The Visual Basic Editor will step through the code and stop at each line that contains an error.

- One of your identifiers may be the same as one of the new reserved keywords. Change the identifier to a unique name.

- You may have named a module and a procedure with the same name. In version 2.0, this was permitted, but in 95 or later, they must have different names.

- One of the tables may include more than the limit of 32 indexes. Complex tables that involve many relationships may result in an excess of indexes because the Jet DBEngine 3.5 automatically generates indexes on both sides of a relationship. To correct this problem, remove the less important relationships before converting.

- The Access 97 and 2000 Y2K compliance may cause problems with queries created in earlier versions that return time or date values. Queries that contain dates between 1900 and 1929 may assume the dates fall between 2000 and 2029. If you need to work with dates in the early 1900s, be sure to use the full four-digit year value.

If you need more help converting databases from other versions of Access, the Help topics "Conversion and Compatibility Issues" and "Convert Access Basic Code to Visual Basic" have a lot of information.

Index

SYMBOLS

A

I

Q

Get FREE books and more...when you register this book online for our Personal Bookshelf Program

http://register.samspublishing.com/

SAMS

 Register online and you can sign up for our *FREE Personal Bookshelf Program...*unlimited access to the electronic version of more than 200 complete computer books—immediately! That means you'll have 100,000 pages of valuable information onscreen, at your fingertips!

 Plus, you can access product support, including complimentary downloads, technical support files, book-focused links, companion Web sites, author sites, and more!

 And you'll be automatically registered to receive a *FREE subscription to a weekly email newsletter* to help you stay current with news, announcements, sample book chapters, and special events, including sweepstakes, contests, and various product giveaways!

 We value your comments! Best of all, the entire registration process takes only a few minutes to complete, so go online and get the greatest value going—absolutely FREE!

Don't Miss Out On This Great Opportunity!

Sams is a brand of Macmillan Computer Publishing USA.

For more information, please visit *www.mcp.com*

What's on the CD-ROM

The companion CD-ROM contains all of the authors' source code and samples from the book.

Windows 95/98/NT 4 Installation Instructions

1. Insert the CD-ROM disc into your CD-ROM drive.
2. From the Windows 95 desktop, double-click on the My Computer icon.
3. Double-click on the icon representing your CD-ROM drive.
4. Double-click on the icon titled SETUP.EXE to run the installation program.
5. Installation creates a program group named "PN Access Programming" This group will contain icons to browse the CD-ROM.

Note: If you have the AutoPlay CD-ROM feature enabled, the SETUP.EXE program starts automatically when you insert the disc into your CD-ROM drive.